ROUTLEDGE HANDBOOK OF THE CHINESE COMMUNIST PARTY

Whilst the Chinese Communist Party is one of the most powerful political institutions in the world, it is also one of the least understood, due to the party's secrecy and tight control over the archives, the press and the Internet. Having governed the People's Republic of China for nearly 70 years though, much interest remains in how this quintessentially Leninist party governs one-fifth of the world and runs the world's second-largest economy.

The *Routledge Handbook of the Chinese Communist Party* gives a comprehensive and multi-faceted picture of the party's traditions and values – as well as its efforts to stay relevant in the twenty-first century. It uses a wealth of contemporary data and qualitative analysis to explore the intriguing relationship between the party on the one hand, and the government, the legal and judicial establishment and the armed forces, on the other. Tracing the influence of Marx, Engels, Lenin and Stalin, as well as Mao Zedong, on contemporary leaders ranging from Deng Xiaoping and Jiang Zemin to Hu Jintao and Xi Jinping, the sections cover:

- the party's history and traditions;
- how the party works and seeks to remain relevant;
- major policy arenas;
- the CCP in the twenty-first century.

The *Routledge Handbook of the Chinese Communist Party* will be of interest to students and scholars of Chinese Politics, Asian Politics, Political Parties and International Relations.

Willy Wo-Lap Lam is Adjunct Professor at the Centre for China Studies and the Department of History at the Chinese University of Hong Kong.

Up-to-date analyses, encyclopedic in scope, by some of the world's leading authorities.

Perry Link, *University of California Riverside*

The *Routledge Handbook of the Chinese Communist Party* is an invaluable resource for anyone who wants to understand how China is governed and how its political system has evolved over the past seven decades. Willy Wo-Lap Lam has assembled an unrivalled group of China scholars and produced one of the most illuminating volumes on contemporary China.

Minxin Pei, *Claremont McKenna College*

In this edited collection, veteran China specialist Willy Lam has assembled a diverse group of authors who dissect the various elements and instruments in CCP rule. The section on "how the party works" is particularly valuable. All China watchers will find value in this volume.

David Shambaugh, *George Washington University*

As usual, the deeply perceptive Willy Lam provides what is almost certainly the best guide to the current state of China, the problems with which her leaders must grapple most importantly.

Arthur Waldron, *University of Pennsylvania*

ROUTLEDGE HANDBOOK OF THE CHINESE COMMUNIST PARTY

Edited by Willy Wo-Lap Lam

Routledge
Taylor & Francis Group
LONDON AND NEW YORK

First published 2018
by Routledge
2 Park Square, Milton Park, Abingdon, Oxon OX14 4RN

and by Routledge
52 Vanderbilt Avenue, New York, NY 10017

First issued in paperback 2020

Routledge is an imprint of the Taylor & Francis Group, an informa business

British Library Cataloguing in Publication Data
A catalogue record for this book is available from the British Library

Library of Congress Cataloging in Publication Data
A catalog record for this book has been requested

ISBN 13: 978-0-367-58116-9 (pbk)
ISBN 13: 978-1-138-68443-0 (hbk)

Typeset in Bembo
by Wearset Ltd, Boldon, Tyne and Wear

For Grace, Ching-Wen and Wen-Chung

CONTENTS

List of illustrations *x*
Notes on contributors *xi*
Preface *xvii*
List of acronyms *xix*

PART I
Overview and introduction **1**

1 The agenda of Xi Jinping: is the Chinese Communist Party capable of thorough reforms? 3
Willy Wo-Lap Lam

PART II
History and traditions **29**

2 The legacy of Mao Zedong 31
Yiu-Chung Wong and Willy Wo-Lap Lam

3 The CCP's exploitation of Confucianism and Legalism 47
Delia Lin

4 The CCP's use and abuse of nationalism 59
Edward Friedman

PART III
How the Party works and stays relevant **73**

5 The Party runs the show: how the CCP controls the state and towers over the government, legislature and judiciary 75
Jean-Pierre Cabestan

6 The role of Party congresses 92
Guoguang Wu

7 The PLA as the lifeline of the Party 108
Ka Po Ng

8 Factional politics in the Party-state apparatus 122
Bo Zhiyue

9 Evolution of the Party since 1976: ideological and functional adoptions 135
Joseph Yu-shek Cheng

10 The CCP's meritocratic cadre system 153
Akio Takahara

11 "The new (old) normal": the CCP propaganda system under Jiang, Hu, and Xi 165
Anne-Marie Brady

PART IV
Major policy arenas **181**

12 How the party-state runs the economy: a model of elite decision-making in the financial market 183
Victor Shih

13 Implementing tax reform and rural reconstruction in China: a case study of the CCP's agrarian policy 205
Chiew-Siang Bryan Ho

14 The Party's policy toward labor 219
Bill Taylor

15 Reform, repression, co-optation: the CCP's policy toward intellectuals 232
Jean-Philippe Béja

16 The Party and the law 248
Eva Pils

17 Two steps forward, one backward: the CCP's policy toward women 266
Marina Thorborg

18 Public policy and LGBT people and activism in mainland China 283
Elaine Jeffreys

19 The CCP's Tibet policy: stability through coercion and development 297
Tsering Topgyal

20 The party-state's nationalist strategy to control the Uyghur: silenced voices 312
Dru C. Gladney

PART V
The CCP in the twenty-first century **333**

21 The future of the Chinese Communist Party 335
Kerry Brown and Konstantinos Tsimonis

22 Changing patterns of Chinese civil society: comparing the Hu-Wen and Xi Jinping eras 352
Chloé Froissart

23 Can the Internet and social media change the Party? 372
David Bandurski

24 China and the world: from the Chinese Dream to the Chinese World Order 391
Simon Shen

Index *406*

ILLUSTRATIONS

Figures

3.1 The number of articles containing *rujia, ruxue* or *guoxue* as the keyword in *People's Daily* (2000–2015) 51
3.2 The percentage of articles on Confucianism on the Chinese classics page in *Guangming Daily* (2013–2016) 51
3.3 The number of articles containing *wenhua zixin* as the keyword in *People's Daily* (2000–2015) 56
12.1 Financial policy process 196

Tables

6.1 Terms of the National Party Congress, from irregularity to regularity 95
6.2 The 18th National Party Congress (2012) at a glance 98
6.3 Instability of congressional-elected provincial party leaderships, 2011–2016 102
12.1 Main consumers of financial policies 188
12.2 Producer agencies 195
19.1 Tibetan cadres in TAR 299

CONTRIBUTORS

Editor

Willy Wo-Lap Lam is an Adjunct Professor at the History Department and the Center for China Studies, Chinese University of Hong Kong. He is a Senior Fellow at Jamestown Foundation, Washington, DC. Dr Lam specializes in elite politics, China's economic and political reforms, and Chinese diplomacy. He is the author of seven books on China, including *Chinese Politics in the Hu Jintao Era: New Leaders, New Challenges* (Routledge, 2006) and *Chinese Politics in the Era of Xi Jinping: Renaissance, Reform or Retrogression?* (Routledge, 2015). His books have been translated into Chinese and Japanese.

Chapter authors

David Bandurski is Editor of the China Media Project research website at the University of Hong Kong, where he is Honorary Lecturer at the Journalism and Media Studies Centre. A frequent commentator on Chinese media and current affairs, his writings have appeared in the *New York Times*, the *Wall Street Journal*, *ChinaFile*, *Index on Censorship*, the *Far Eastern Economic Review* and other publications. He is the author of *Dragons in Diamond Village* (Melville House, 2016), a work of non-fiction on urban villages in China, and co-author of *Investigative Journalism in China* (Hong Kong University Press, 2010).

Jean-Philippe Béja is Senior Research-Fellow Emeritus, Centre National de la Recherche Scientifique (CNRS), CERI-Sciences-Po, Paris. Dr. Béja's research areas cover ideological and political reforms in China, including the plight of intellectuals. He is the author of *A la recherche d'une ombre chinoise: Le mouvement pour la démocratie en Chine, 1919–2004* (Gallimard, 2004). He is also the editor, with Fu Hualing and Eva Pils, of *Liu Xiaobo, Charter 08 and the Challenges of Political Reform in China* (Hong Kong University Press, 2012).

Bo Zhiyue has written widely on China's elite politics and policy-making. He is the Founder and President of the Bo Zhiyue China Institute, a China-focused consulting firm. Dr. Bo has taught at Peking University, Roosevelt University, the University of Chicago, American University, St. John Fisher College, Tarleton State University, the Chinese

University of Hong Kong, National University of Singapore and Victoria University of Wellington. He obtained his Bachelor of Law and Master of Law in International Politics from Peking University and his Ph.D. in Political Science from the University of Chicago. His research interests include China's elite politics, Chinese provincial leaders, central-local relations, cross-strait relations, Sino-US relations and international relations. He is the author of nine books (published by World Scientific), including *Chinese Provincial Leaders: Economic Performance and Political Mobility since 1949* (2002), *China's Elite Politics: Political Transition and Power Balancing* (2007) and *China's Elite Politics: Governance and Democratization* (2010). His most recent books are *China–US Relations in a Global Perspective* (Victoria University Press, 2016) (edited) and *China's Political Dynamics under Xi Jinping* (World Scientific, 2017).

Anne-Marie Brady is Professor in Political Science at the University of Canterbury, a Global Fellow at the Woodrow Wilson Center in Washington, DC and a Senior Fellow at the China Policy Institute at the University of Nottingham. A highly regarded specialist on Chinese politics as well as polar politics, she is Editor-in-Chief of *The Polar Journal*, and the author of nine books including *Making the Foreign Serve China: Managing Foreigners in the People's Republic* (Rowman & Littlefield, 2003), *Marketing Dictatorship: Propaganda and Thought Work in Contemporary China* (Rowman & Littlefield, 2008) and her most recent book *China as a Polar Great Power* (Cambridge University Press, 2017).

Kerry Brown is Professor of Chinese Studies and Director of the Lau China Institute at King's College London, and an Associate Fellow on the Asia Programme at Chatham House. His main interests are the modern history of China, the politics and leadership of the Communist Party and China's political economy and international relations. He is the author of over 13 books on China, the most recent of which are *CEO China: The Rise of Xi Jinping* (I.B. Tauris, 2016), *China and the New Maoists* (Zed Books, 2016, with Simone Van Neuwenhuizen) and *China's World* (a study of China's international relations, forthcoming).

Jean-Pierre Cabestan is Professor and Head, Department of Government and International Studies at Hong Kong Baptist University. He is also an associate researcher at the Asia Centre, Paris and at the French Centre for Research on Contemporary China, Hong Kong. His main themes of research are Chinese politics and law, China's foreign and security policies, China–Taiwan relations and Taiwanese politics. His most recent publications include *Le système politique chinois. Un nouvel équilibre autoritaire* [*The Chinese Political System: A New Authoritarian Equilibrium*] (Presses de Sciences Po, 2014) and *Political Changes in Taiwan Under Ma Ying-jeou: Partisan Conflict, Policy Choices, External Constraints and Security Challenges* (Routledge, 2014, co-edited with Jacques deLisle).

Joseph Yu-shek Cheng is retired Professor of Political Science and former Coordinator of the Contemporary China Research Project, City University of Hong Kong. He is the founding editor of the *Hong Kong Journal of Social Sciences* and the *Journal of Comparative Asian Development*. He has published widely on the political development in China and Hong Kong, Chinese foreign policy and local government in southern China. Volumes on China he has recently completed include *China's Japan Policy: Adjusting to New Challenges* (World Scientific, 2015) and *China's Foreign Policy: Challenges and Prospects* (World Scientific, 2016). He served as the Convener of the Alliance for True Democracy in Hong Kong in 2013–14.

Edward Friedman is Professor Emeritus in the Political Science Department at the University of Wisconsin where he teaches about Chinese foreign policy. Since 1965, he has worked on and off for various branches of the US Government on PRC foreign policy. His books dealing with Chinese foreign policy include *America's Asia* (Pantheon, 1969), *Taiwan and American Policy* (Praeger, 1971), *The Politics of Democratization: Generalizing East Asian Experiences* (Westview, 1994), *National Identity and Democratic Prospects in Socialist China* (M.E. Sharpe, 1995), *What If China Doesn't Democratize? Implications for War and Peace* (M.E. Sharpe, 2000), *China's Rise, Taiwan's Dilemmas and International Peace* (Routledge, 2005), *Asia's Giants: Comparing China and India* (Palgrave, 2005), *Regional Cooperation and Its Enemies in Northeast Asia* (Routledge, 2006) and *Political Transitions in Dominant Party Systems* (Routledge, 2008).

Chloé Froissart is Director of Tsinghua University Sino-French Centre in Social Sciences in Beijing, Senior Researcher in Political Sociology at the French Centre for Research on Contemporary China (CEFC) in Hong Kong and Associate Professor at the University of Rennes 2 (France). She studied Chinese and Chinese Studies at the Institut National des Langues et Civilisations Etrangères (INALCO, Paris) as well as Political Science at Paris Institute of Political Sciences, where she received her Ph.D. in 2007. Dr. Froissart has taught at various institutions, such as INALCO, Paris Institute of Political Sciences and the School for Higher Studies in Social Sciences (Paris). Her research interests focus on the development of civil society in China, citizenship and political participation, especially in the fields of labor and environmental politics. She is the author of *La Chine et ses migrants: La conquête d'une citoyenneté* (Presses Universitaires de Rennes, 2013). She has written numerous articles on the development of civil society in authoritarian regimes, social protest movements and the rule of law. She sits on the editorial boards of *China Perspectives* and *Critique Internationale.* Aside from her scientific research, Dr. Froissart has been involved in advisory work for several governmental and non-governmental bodies and she has testified before the US Congressional Executive Commission on China.

Dru C. Gladney is Professor of Anthropology at Pomona College in Claremont, California. He is the author of *Muslim Chinese: Ethnic Nationalism in the People's Republic* (Harvard University Press, 1996), *Ethnic Identity in China: The Making of a Muslim Minority Nationality* (Cengage, 1998) and *Making Majorities: Constituting the Nation in Japan, China, Korea, Malaysia, Fiji, Turkey, and the U.S.* (editor, Stanford University Press, 1998). His most recent book is *Dislocating China: Muslims, Minorities, and Other Sub-Altern Subjects* (University of Chicago Press, 2004).

Chiew-Siang Bryan Ho teaches in the Government and Public Administration Department at the University of Macau. His research interests include electoral participation and the legitimation of power in rural China as well as issues relating to governance, political participation, democratization, public management and policy studies in Chinese states and societies. His publications (English and Chinese) include a book on *Policy Implementation in Rural China* (co-authored with Bolong Liu and Qianwei Zhu in Chinese, Fudan University Press, 2011) and book chapters as well as journal articles on electoral participation in rural China, political culture, social movement and governability in Macao, and governance and development in Singapore, Hong Kong and Macao. His papers have appeared in the *Journal of Chinese Political Science*, the *Journal of Comparative Asian Development*, *Asian Affairs: An American Review* and *Asian Education and Development Studies*. He is currently working on a research project on state collaboration and policy implementation in China and Singapore.

Elaine Jeffreys is Professor in the School of International Studies, Faculty of Arts and Social Sciences, University of Technology Sydney. She is the author of *China, Sex and Prostitution* (Routledge, 2004), *Prostitution Scandals in China: Policing, Media and Society* (Routledge, 2012) and *Sex in China*, with Haiqing Yu (Polity, 2015). She is the editor of *Sex and Sexuality in China* (Routledge, 2006), *China's Governmentalities: Governing Change, Changing Government* (Routledge, 2009), *Celebrity in China*, with Louise Edwards (Hong Kong University Press, 2010), *Celebrity Philanthropy*, with Paul Allatson (University of Chicago Press, 2015) and *New Mentalities of Government in China*, with David Bray (Routledge, 2016).

Delia Lin gained her Ph.D. in Humanities (Political Culture) from Griffith University, Australia. She lectures in the School of Social Sciences at the University of Adelaide. Her research interests include political thought, governance, ideology and discourse. Her monograph *Civilising Citizens in Post-Mao China: Understanding the Rhetoric of Suzhi* (Routledge, 2017) is the first book to provide an in-depth study of the dominant discourse of *suzhi* – a term that denotes the idea of cultivating a "quality" citizenship – and its relevance to governance and Chinese society.

Ka Po Ng has a Ph.D. from the University of Queensland and is a professor at the University of Niigata Prefecture, where he teaches both postgraduate and undergraduate courses on security studies, international relations theory and Chinese politics. He has published books and articles on relevant subjects. One of his latest publications is a book chapter on Chinese military politics under the Xi Jinping leadership. He is currently working on a project about the security dimensions of China's relations with Japan.

Eva Pils is Reader in Transnational Law at The Dickson Poon School of Law at King's College London. She studied law, philosophy and sinology in Heidelberg, London and Beijing and holds a Ph.D. in Law from University College London. Her scholarship focuses on human rights, authoritarianism and law in China. She has written on these topics in both academic publications and the popular press, and is author of *China's Human Rights Lawyers: Advocacy and Resistance* (Routledge, 2014) and of *Human Rights in China: A Social Practice in the Shadows of Authoritarianism* (forthcoming). Before joining King's, she was an associate professor at The Chinese University of Hong Kong Faculty of Law. She is a Non-resident Senior Research Fellow at the US–Asia Law Institute of New York University Law School, an external member of the Chinese University of Hong Kong Centre for Social Innovation Studies, an external fellow of the Bingham Centre for the Rule of Law, and a legal action committee member of the Global Legal Action Network. In April 2017, she became a Visiting Professor of Law at Columbia Law School.

Simon Shen is an Associate Professor of the Faculty of Social Science, Chinese University of Hong Kong, serving as its Director of Global Studies Programme, Director of Master of Global Political Economy Programme and Co-Director of International Affairs Research Institute. He is a prominent international relations commentator, serving as the Lead Writer (Glocal) of the *Hong Kong Economic Journal* and has contributed to media all over the world. In Hong Kong he has served in various government consultation committees and founded several think tanks that have close interaction with the government, academia and civil society. His research interests include China–US relations, Chinese nationalism, and regional security and external relations of Hong Kong, among others. He has worked as visiting fellows at Brookings Institution, Warwick University, East-West Center and Rikkyo University. His latest publications include *Deconstructing the Chinese Dream* (Chinese University of Hong Kong Press, 2015) and *Hong Kong in the World: Implications to Geopolitics and Competitiveness* (World Scientific, 2016).

Victor Shih is a political economist at the University of California at San Diego specializing in China. Dr. Shih received his doctorate in Government from Harvard University. He is the author of *Factions and Finance in China: Elite Conflict and Inflation* (Cambridge University Press, 2009), which is the first book to inquire about the linkages between elite politics and banking policies in China. He is also the author of numerous articles appearing in academic and business journals, including *The American Political Science Review*, *The China Quarterly*, *Comparative Political Studies*, *Journal of Politics*, *The Wall Street Journal* and *The China Business Review*, and frequent adviser to the financial community. Dr. Shih holds a BA from the George Washington University, where he studied on a University Presidential Fellowship and graduated summa cum laude in East Asian studies with a minor in Economics. His current research concerns coalition composition under Mao and Deng. Dr. Shih also has ongoing research projects on quantitative measurements of factions and the impact of factions on elite promotions, rent-seeking activities and the growth of the private sector.

Akio Takahara is Professor of Contemporary Chinese Politics at the Graduate School of Law and Politics and Vice-Dean of the Graduate School of Public Policy, the University of Tokyo. He received his D.Phil in 1988 from the University of Sussex, and later spent several years as Visiting Scholar at the Consulate-General of Japan in Hong Kong (1989–91), the Japanese Embassy in Beijing (1996–98), the Fairbank Center for East Asian Research, Harvard University (2005–06), the School of International Studies, Peking University (2014–15) and the Mercator Institute for China Studies, Berlin (January 2016). He also served as a Member of the Governing Body of the Institute of Development Studies, UK (1999–2003), and as the Secretary General of the New Japan-China Friendship 21st Century Committee (2009–14). He currently serves as a senior researcher of the Tokyo Foundation, senior adjunct fellow of the Japan Institute of International Affairs and a senior researcher of the Japan International Forum. His publications include: *The Politics of Wage Policy in Post-Revolutionary China* (Macmillan, 1992); *New Developments in East Asian Security* (Akashi Shoten, 2005, co-editor, in Japanese); *Beyond the Borders: Contemporary Asian Studies Volume One* (Keio University Press, 2008, co-editor, in Japanese); *The History of Japan–China Relations 1972–2012: Volume 1: Politics* (University of Tokyo Press, 2012, co-editor, in Japanese); *To the Era of Developmentalism, 1972–2014*, Series on China's Modern History, Volume 5 (Iwanami Shoten, 2014, co-author, in Japanese) and *Japan–China Relations in the Modern Era* (Routledge, 2017, co-author).

Bill Taylor is Associate Professor at the Department of Public Policy, City University of Hong Kong. His areas of research interest include labor and employment issues, mostly focused on China and covering the management of labor, collective organizations and, recently, CSR. Dr. Taylor is also active in the area of collective human rights. He is the author, with Bill Chang Kai and Li Qi, of *Industrial Relations in China* (Edward Elgar, 2003).

Marina Thorborg is Professor of Economic History at Södertörn University, Sweden, former China Research Associate at the Nordic Institute of Asian Studies, Copenhagen University, Dean and Director of The Gender Research Institute at Lund University and Associate Professor of Political Science at Aarhus University. Her areas of speciality include the Chinese labor market, employment, development, gender policies and international and East

European development. She is the author of numerous books and papers on the issue of labor market, development and gender policies in particularly China, East Asia and Eastern Europe. Her recent publications include "Where Have All the Young Girls Gone? Fatal Discrimination of Daughters – A Regional Comparison," *China Perspectives*, No. 57, 2005; "Chinese Workers and Labour Conditions from State Industry to Globalized Factories: How to Stop the Race to the Bottom?" in M. Mehlman, M. Soffritti, P. Landrigan and E. Bingham (eds.) *Living in a Chemical World: Framing the Future in the Light of the Past* (New York Academy of Sciences, 2006); *Kvinnor i Kina: pirater, järnflickor och finanslejon* [*Women in China: Pirates, Iron-girls, and Financial Wizards*] (Bokförlaget Atlantis, 2014); and "From White Elephants to Flying Geese: China in Africa, A New Model for Development or More of the Same," in Young-Chan Kim (ed.) *China and Africa: A New Paradigm of Global Business* (Palgrave Macmillan, 2017).

Tsering Topgyal is Lecturer in International Relations, Department of Political Science and International Studies, University of Birmingham. His research interests encompass Tibet, Chinese foreign and security policy, and the international politics of the Indo-Pacific region. A selection of Dr. Topgyal's most recent publications include: "The Tibetan Self-Immolations as Counter-Securitization: An Inter-Unit Theory of Securitization," *Asian Security*, 12:3, 2016: 166–187; *China and Tibet: The Perils of Insecurity* (Hurst, 2016); and "South Asian Responses to the Rise of China: Indian and Nepalese Handling of the Tibet Issue," in Michael Clarke and Doug Stokes (eds.) *China's Frontier Regions* (I.B. Tauris, 2016).

Konstantinos Tsimonis completed his Ph.D. at the School of Oriental and African Studies (SOAS), where he taught classes on Chinese politics for two years. He is Lecturer in Chinese Society, Lau China Institute, King's College London. His research, conference papers and publications concentrate on the adaptation of Chinese mass organizations and on the PRC's engagement with international and regional anti-corruption regimes. He is currently working on a manuscript on the Communist Youth League and China's youth.

Yiu-Chung Wong is Professor in the Department of Political Science at Lingnan University, Hong Kong. He graduated from the Chinese University of Hong Kong and gained his doctoral degree from the Department of Government, University of Queensland. His research areas include China's political reform, Hong Kong democratic transition, cross-strait relations and Greater China. He is author of *From Deng Xiaoping to Jiang Zemin: Two Decades of Political Reform in the People's Republic of China* (Rowman & Littlefield, 2005) and editor of *One Country, Two Systems in Crisis: Hong Kong's Transformation Since the Handover* (Rowman & Littlefield, 2004). He has also edited four volumes of articles on the politics and foreign policies of the People's Republic of China. His latest paper is "Civil Disobedience Movement in Hong Kong: A Civil Society Perspective" (co-author with Jason K.H. Chan), forthcoming in *Asian Education and Development Studies.*

Guoguang Wu is Professor of Political Science, Professor of History and Chair in China and Asia-Pacific Relations at the University of Victoria, Canada. His research interests follow two tracks: political institutions in China and the political economy of capitalism. He is author of four books, including *China's Party Congress: Power, Legitimacy, and Institutional Manipulation* (Cambridge University Press, 2015) and *Globalization Against Democracy: A Political Economy of Capitalism after its Global Triumph* (Cambridge University Press, 2017).

PREFACE

A Taiwan poet and fellow fan of T.S. Eliot has turned his famous "History is now and England" into "History is now and China." This comprehensive anthology, which analyzes and assesses different aspects of the Chinese Communist Party (CCP), is being published on the eve of its 19th National Congress, which is due to endorse Party General Secretary and State President Xi Jinping as China's supreme leader for the early twenty-first century. This timely book is written by 25 China experts who have delved into the CCP's history and traditions; the party's secretive organization and its strategy for monopolizing power; its policies in various political, economic, social and cultural sectors; and possible paths for the party's evolution in the coming one to two decades. Readers will be well equipped to make their own judgment on not only major events such as party congresses and Central Committee plenums but also the ideology, policies and decision-making processes of strongman Xi and his fast-developing Xi Jinping Faction.

While the *Routledge Handbook of the Chinese Communist Party* is primarily about domestic issues, it will also throw light on "core leader" Xi's overarching nationalistic ambitions, particularly his "Chinese dream" mantra of global power projection. Early interactions between Xi and United States President Donald Trump have demonstrated China's expanding role in setting global agendas and tackling flashpoints in regions ranging from the Middle East to the Asia-Pacific.

Yet as the Chinese saying goes, "a poor country can't do much in foreign affairs." As the world's second biggest economy and largest trading country, China is flaunting its wealth by offering economic aid to and forgiving the debts of dozens of developing countries. Yet the party-state apparatus suffers from what reformist intellectuals call a "poverty of philosophy," namely, failure to consider goals and objectives that could vitiate the CCP's hold on power. Chapters in this book that appraise the CCP's political and socio-economic policies – especially the party's refusal to pick up the threads of political and economic reforms – show up the increasingly obvious chinks in the armor of the vaunted "China model." The overriding obsession of Xi and his colleagues appears to be grabbing power for themselves – and ensuring the CCP's "perennial ruling party" status. Even as the party's multi-billion dollar quasi-police state apparatus seems capable of reining in muck-racking journalists, social-media bloggers, liberal intellectuals and NGO activists, China's capacity for innovation in economic and technological sectors as well as the art of governance is found wanting.

Xi's answer to the question of China's repeated failure to comply with international norms, including United Nations covenants on civil rights to which it has acceded, is that values such as universal-suffrage elections and freedom of expression are "Western" ideas that are alien to the Chinese tradition. "Whether a pair of shoes fits only the feet can tell," Xi likes to say. Chapters in this *Handbook* on the well-being of groups ranging from workers and peasants to ethnic minorities such as Tibetans and Uyghurs, however, show that at the very least, a) these disadvantaged classes are not given their rightful share of the economic pie and b) they have few channels to air their grievances let alone press for changes in the authoritarian political and economic system.

Even without getting into arguments about the relative merits of the "China model" versus globally recognized democratic development – which has been attained in numerous countries in Asia – we can reference Francis Fukuyama and Chris Patten's view that China suffers from the lack of simple "good governance." A party-state apparatus that values its own survival – and the perpetuation of the special privileges of the "red aristocracy" – above all else will continue to command the world's attention thanks to the country's quasi-superpower status. Yet the only way that China can get back on what former president Bill Clinton called "the right side of history" is to embrace universal-style economic and political reforms and to halt the alarming regression to Maoism that President Xi is championing. The last section of this book, which contains chapters mapping the future development of the party and country, offers scenarios for the CPP's trajectory into the 2020s and 2030s. They include possibilities that the party-state apparatus might be forced to adopt meaningful reforms owing to factors such as growing pressure put to bear on the authorities by disaffected classes within the country as well as China's enhanced interactions with the global community. The prospect also exists that the CCP might implode due to intensifying factional strife triggered by cataclysmic mishaps in domestic or foreign-policy arenas.

It is this editor's conviction that the insights and analytic tools provided by the veteran Sinologists who wrote this book's 24 chapters will enable readers to make well-informed assessment of the CCP's intriguing and fast-paced evolution. The China story will likely dominate the headlines for a long time to come.

Willy Wo-Lap Lam

ACRONYMS

ACFTU	All-China Federation of Trade Unions
ACWF	All-China Women's Federation
AIIB	Asia Infrastructure Investment Bank
APEC	Asia-Pacific Economic Cooperation
ASEAN	Association of Southeast Asian Nations
BNSC	Building a new socialist countryside
CAC	Cyberspace Administration of China
CAS	Chinese Academy of Sciences
CASS	Chinese Academy of Social Sciences
CAT	Convention against Torture and Other Cruel, Inhuman or Degrading Treatment or Punishment
CBRC	China Banking Regulatory Commission
CC	Central Committee
CCDI	Central Commission for Discipline Inspection
CCP	Chinese Communist Party
CCTV	China Central Television
CEDAW	Convention on the Elimination of All Forms of Discrimination against Women
CERD	Convention on the Elimination of All Forms of Racial Discrimination
CFWC	Central Finance Work Committee
CICA	Conference on Interaction and Confidence-Building Measures in Asia
CIRC	China Insurance Regulatory Commission
CLB	China Labor Bulletin
CLGCA	Central Leading Group for Cyberspace Affairs
CLGCDR	Central Leading Group for Comprehensively Deepening Reforms
CLGCI	Central Leading Group for Cybersecurity and Informatization
CLGFA	Central Leading Group for Foreign Affairs
CLGFE	Central Leading Group for Finance and Economics
CLGPIW	Central Leading Group for Propaganda and Ideology Work
CLGs	Central Leading Groups
CMC	Central Military Commission
CMR	Civil–Military Relations

CNSC	Central National Security Commission
COD	Central Organization Department
CPLC	Central Politics and Law Commission
CPPCC	Chinese People's Political Consultative Conference
CRC	Convention on the Rights of the Child
CRPD	Convention on the Rights of Persons with Disabilities
CSRC	China Securities Regulatory Commission
CYL	Communist Youth League
CYLF	Communist Youth League Faction
FTZ	Free Trade Zone
FYP	Five-Year Plan
GDP	Gross Domestic Product
ICCPR	International Covenant on Civil and Political Rights
ICESCR	International Covenant on Economic, Social and Cultural Rights
KMT	Kuomintang (Guomindang)
LGBT	Lesbian, gay, bisexual and transgender
LGFV	Local government financing vehicle
MOC	Ministry of Commerce
MOF	Ministry of Finance
MOFA	Ministry of Foreign Affairs
MPS	Ministry of Public Security
MSS	Ministry of State Security
NDRC	National Development and Reform Commission
NPC	National People's Congress
OBOR	One Belt One Road
PAP	People's Armed Police
PBOC	People's Bank of China
PBSC	Politburo Standing Committee
PLA	People's Liberation Army
PRC	People's Republic of China
QDII	Qualified Domestic Institutional Investor
QFII	Qualified Foreign Institutional Investor
RMB	Renminbi
RTFR	Rural Tax-for-fee Reform
SAPPRFT	State Administration of Press, Publication, Radio, Film and Television
SAR	Special Administration Region
SASAC	State Assets Supervision and Administration Commission
SC	State Council
SCO	Shanghai Cooperation Organization
SOE	State-owned Enterprise
TAR	Tibet Autonomous Region
VPN	Virtual Private Network
WHO	World Health Organization
WTO	World Trade Organization
XUAR	Xinjiang Uyghur Autonomous Region

PART I

Overview and introduction

1

THE AGENDA OF XI JINPING

Is the Chinese Communist Party capable of thorough reforms?

Willy Wo-Lap Lam

Introduction: China's authoritarianism goes global

Despite the virtual end of the "Chinese economic miracle," China's global footprint has increased by leaps and bounds since Fifth-Generation leader Xi Jinping took over the helm of the Chinese Communist Party (CCP) in 2012. The Chinese economy accounts for more than 25 percent of total global growth. The People's Republic of China (PRC) is the largest contributor of troops to United Nations-mandated peacekeeping missions. China is a major player in global forums such as the G20 and the Asia-Pacific Economic Cooperation (APEC). More significantly, Chinese outbound direct investment (ODI) has since 2015 exceeded inward capital flow – to the extent that "China buys the world" has become the rallying cry of PRC multinationals snapping up oilfields, farms and hi-tech firms around the world (*China Daily* 2016; Reuters 2016a). President Xi's "One Belt One Road" gameplan is a bold attempt to bond China with dozens of countries in Asia, Central Asia, Europe and Africa via infrastructure projects such as bridges, ports and high-speed railways, many of which are financed by Chinese banks and corporations. This is despite worries that with the country's shrinking foreign exchange reserves – and the CCP administration's fears about uncontrolled capital outflow – Beijing's ability to buy influence or project power through means such as ODI and bankrolling infrastructure projects could soon run into serious hiccups (CNBC.com 2017; Xinhua News Agency 2017a).[1]

While President Xi and his Politburo colleagues have emphasized that Beijing has no intention of challenging the international order laid down largely by the United States after WWII, it seems evident that the CCP leadership is exploiting weak links in the status quo so as to lay down its own rules. The protectionist and nationalistic posture of the Donald Trump administration has provided President Xi with an opening to boost China's rule-making potentials in the global arena. At an early 2017 speech at the World Economic Forum in Davos, Xi criticized unnamed world leaders for "locking oneself in a dark room." The supreme leader of one-fifth of mankind reassured WEF delegates that China "will keep its door wide open and not close it." In a veiled reference to Trump's decision to renege on America's commitment to fighting global problems such as climate change, Xi pledged to redouble China's efforts to cut carbon emissions, saying that this was "a responsibility we must assume for future generations" (Reuters 2017; Xinhua News Agency 2017b).

Apart from the OBOR, Beijing is behind the establishment of the Asian Infrastructure Investment Bank (AIIB) and the BRICs Bank, on which the Xi leadership hopes to anchor a Sinocentric global financial structure. The PRC displaced the U.S. as Africa's largest trading partner and investor several years ago. And in the wake of the Trump administration's abandonment of the Transpacific Pact (TPP), Beijing is putting extra efforts to persuade Asia-Pacific countries to join China-led free-trade arrangements such as the Regional Comprehensive Economic Partnership (RCEP).[2] A dozen-odd countries ranging from Laos and Cambodia in Asia to Angola, Zimbabwe and the Sudan in Africa have become virtual client states of Big Brother China. Sinologist Andrew Nathan cited a "growing worry among Western analysts about the extent to which China, as its power grows, will seek to remake the world in its authoritarian image" (Nathan 2016: 23; Brown and Huang 2016). China's Great Leap Outward prompted former president Barack Obama's famous line that "we can't let countries like China write the rules of the global economy" (The White House 2015). In a similar vein, British Prime Minister Theresa May zeroed in on the consequences of the Western alliance's failure to provide global leadership. While touring America in January 2017, she cautioned that the U.S. and the U.K. "have a joint responsibility to lead." In a thinly veiled reference to China, May warned of an "eclipse of the West" when rising Asian powers "step up and we step back" (*Financial Times* 2017). (See Chapter 24, "China and the World: From the Chinese Dream to the Chinese World Order.")

The leap forward in China's international clout has been made possible by the viability of the CCP, which is the brains and the brawn behind President Xi's "Chinese dream," namely, that the PRC will attain superpower status by the late 2040s. Despite stunning aberrations ranging from the Cultural Revolution (1966–1976) and the Tiananmen Square massacre (1989), the party seems to have morphed into a gritty and aggressive behemoth that is the envy of political institutions around the world. As Orville Schell and John Delury point out,

> in contemplating the future, it is always important to remember that, despite all its rigidities and infirmities, the CCP has repeatedly surprised the world with its ability to change course and prevail, including the most recent feat of steering China into the twenty-first century as a nascent superpower.
>
> *(Schell and Delury 2013: 384)*

Yet chinks in the armor of the mind-set and policies of the CCP leadership are also becoming obvious. Beijing has taken a cavalier attitude toward international law. This is demonstrated by the large-scale reclamation works undertaken by the People's Liberation Army (PLA) engineering corps on several islets in the South China Sea whose sovereignty is disputed by China's neighbors. These artificially enlarged islets have since been converted into air and naval bases. The Xi leadership simply ignored the July 2016 ruling by the Permanent Court of Arbitration in the Hague that its territorial claims to the South China Sea were without legal basis (*Foreign Policy* 2016; Rapp-Hooper 2016). Yet another example of Beijing violating international law is the kidnapping in October 2015 of Swedish national Gui Minhai – a Hong Kong-based publisher specializing in political-gossip books that Beijing finds embarrassing – in Thailand by Chinese state security agents[3] (Gui 2016).

Other notable transgressions of international diplomatic norms, which are observed by both Western and "non-Western" nations, include using economic weapons to punish countries which have allegedly challenged China's "core national interests." European leaders who had met the Dalai Lama were warned that they would suffer consequences such as a reduction of Chinese investment. In reaction against human rights icon Liu Xiaobo being awarded the Nobel

Peace Prize in 2010, Beijing froze relations with Norway for six years (Reuters 2016b). This was despite the fact that the Norwegian Nobel Committee is an NGO whose members are appointed by the Storting (Parliament), not the government. And in retaliation against Seoul's installation of America's THAAD missile defense system, Beijing has instigated a large-scale "boycott Korean products" campaign that could result in a trade war between the two neighbors (Huang 2016; Sun 2017).

The glaring self-righteousness in Beijing's global posture can be understood by looking at the mentality and governing philosophy of the CCP. This chapter examines the values and norms that have sustained this political party of close to 90 million members. What is the rationale behind the party's monopolization of political, and to a considerable extent, economic resources of this mammoth country? What undergirds the official dogma of "socialism with Chinese characteristics" – and is it incompatible with universal values? How potent and sustainable is the "China model" that the party has licked into shape since late patriarch Deng Xiaoping unleased the reform and open-door policy 40 years ago? Are ordinary Chinese enjoying the fruits of the party's apparent success? Above all, is the CCP under current supreme leader Xi capable of thorough-going political and economic reforms? This chapter also serves as an introduction to the 23 other chapters in this *Routledge Handbook of the Chinese Communist Party*.

What the party stands for

At the heart of the quasi-superpower's global projection of hard and soft power is the CCP, the most powerful political organization on earth. What does the CCP stand for? For a party whose devastatingly erroneous policies accounted for the death of at least 40 million Chinese, what are the reasons behind its stunning longevity? Is the party capable of far-reaching reforms which could enable it to tackle the challenges of the twenty-first century?

The priorities of the CCP, as laid down by President Xi, who is expected to run the country at least until 2027, are preservationist rather than forward-looking.[4] The foremost task of Xi (born 1953), who gained the penultimate title of "core of the leadership" in late 2016, is holding down the fort of party predominance and not venturing into the unknown and potentially dangerous terrain of reform. Xi's oft-repeated mantra is that officials and people alike must have "self-confidence in the path, the beliefs, the institutions and the culture of socialism with Chinese characteristics" (Xi 2013a, 2016c). Xi further cautioned on the 95th birthday of the CCP on July 1, 2016 that "the decline of political parties begins with a deficit in the beliefs in the ideals [of the party]." "Vacillations about our ideals and beliefs are the most dangerous vacillations," he said, adding that "the downhill trajectory of ideals and beliefs" could not be tolerated. Earlier, the General Secretary had warned party members against "a deficiency of calcium" in their conviction about the CCP's auspicious future (China News Service 2016; Wang, X. 2013).

That Xi's philosophy is retrogressive – rather than progressive – is also evidenced by his paranoia about the party losing power. Way back in 2008, when Xi was vice-president and president of the CCP Central Party School, he underscored the imperative of the party's preserving its quasi-omnipotence: "Whatever [powers] we possessed in the past we may not possess now; whatever [powers] we possess now doesn't mean we can possess them forever," Xi said in 2008 (Xi 2008b).

This sense of insecurity is due to the fact that party leaders of Xi's generation are obsessed with the pitfalls of the Communist Party of the Soviet Union (CPSU), which collapsed suddenly after having been in power for 74 years. This monomaniacal streak was revealed by Xi on an inspection tour to Shenzhen in December 2012, one month after taking power. Xi warned in an unpublicized speech that the party could disintegrate if it failed to heed the lessons from the demise of the CPSU. According to Xi, the Soviet party collapsed because "their ideals and convictions wavered." The Fifth-Generation titan indicated that first, the CCP must never denigrate its founding fathers, particularly Mao. Second, the party must weed out dangerous Western ideas. Third, it must be in control of the military and the police (Buckley 2013). Xi's psychology is very typical of members of his generation. As the *People's Daily* noted in early 2013: "Today, the Soviet Union, with his 74-year history, has been dissolved for 22 years. For more than two decades, socialist China has never stopped reflecting on how the Soviet Communists lost their party and country" (Ren 2013).

Given this background, it is not surprising that Xi has presided over the large-scale resuscitation of Maoist norms (see Chapter 2: "The Legacy of Mao Zedong"). In a 2013 speech marking the 120th birthday of Mao, Xi praised the Great Helmsman for "establishing the fundamental socialist order, obtaining the fundamental achievements of socialist construction, as well as accumulating the experience and providing the conditions for our exploration of the path of building socialism with Chinese characteristics." Xi added that party members would "sink into the quagmire of historical nihilism" if they were to denounce Mao because of his mistakes[5] (Xi 2013f). At the same time, Xi – and his predecessors such as ex-president Hu Jintao – have argued that the so-called "Western democracy system" is not suitable for China. Both Xi and Hu waxed eloquent on the fact that the CCP "will not go down the *xielu* [alien and treacherous path] that will lead to the changing of the flags and standards [of the party]" (Xi 2016d). The CCP's propaganda machinery has stepped up ideological movements to warn citizens about "anti-Chinese forces" in the West trying to subvert the socialist order through infiltration and espionage. In April 2016, Chinese authorities ran a so-called "dangerous love" campaign warning female civil servants to beware of "honey traps": "foreign spies" who want to ferret state secrets out of them under the guise of romance (*The Guardian* 2016).

The Xi administration's preoccupation with preserving the status quo has inevitably affected its capacity for political and economic reforms (see following sections). Policies are designed to uphold stability rather than initiate fundamental changes. "We must seek progress and accomplishments in the midst of stability," the president said one year after taking office. What most concerned Xi is that "erroneous and overly hasty" measures might jeopardize the "socialist road." "Our direction must be correct, the navigation must be stable, and in particular we must avoid errors that would subvert [the socialist system]," he instructed (Xi 2013c). Li Zhanshu, a Politburo member and close adviser to Xi, argued in a *People's Daily* article that "incremental reforms" were needed to avoid "subversive errors" – meaning mistakes that will result in a collapse of the socialist system and the party's authority (Li, Z. 2013).

Xi and his colleagues have, of course, reiterated that the CCP is a learning-oriented, innovation-driven party. In a 2009 speech, Xi urged party cadres to seek "innovation in concepts of development, innovation in approaches to development, innovation in development policies, and innovation in leadership methodology" (Xi 2009). Yet the initiatives laid out by Xi do not seem to match the people's expectations about either liberalizing the decision-making processes of the party or boosting the market elements of the economy. Instead of seeking to integrate China with international values, the "core leader" has gone the opposite direction by asking his countrymen to go after the illusive realm of Communism. "We cannot reach Communism in one go," he said in 2015. "But we cannot regard Communism as a mirage simply because it requires a protracted process." Xi called on CCP affiliates "to become honest and dedicated Communists." "Revolutionary ideals are as high as the sky," he said. "Realizing Communism is the highest ideal of every Communist Party member" (Tian 2015).

Since the demise of Chairman Mao Zedong, few cadres and members have retained any faith in socialism, let alone Communism, which even Karl Marx deemed a Utopian ideal. After all,

Deng Xiaoping sought to demystify socialism by inventing the concept of *shehui zhuyi chuji jieduan* ("the primary state of socialism"), which is a euphemism for Chinese-style capitalism. The Great Architect of Reform famously said that the preliminary stage of socialism could last up to 200 years, meaning that China's particular form of "capitalism within a cage" would last for generations.[6] Xi's singing the praises of a Communist order being ushered into China in the not-too-distant future seems symptomatic of a particularly befuddled form of "historical nihilism."

The CCP and the "China model"?

The "China model" explained

As we trace the ideology and statecraft of leaders from Deng Xiaoping and Jiang Zemin to Hu Jintao and Xi Jinping, new ideas about reform are in increasing short supply. Nonetheless, officials and scholars in both Western and Asian nations have credited the CCP with having come up with a novel approach of governance called the "China model." Admirers of the China model ranging from Daniel Bell to Martin Jacques have claimed that the Chinese way of doing things might be significantly better than the so-called "Western model" of laissez-faire economics, universal-suffrange elections and the rule of law. What exactly is the China model and will it enable the party to attain a sustainable development plan that will defuse entrenched contradictions in Chinese society?

Bell wrote in his 2015 book *The China Model: Political Meritocracy and the Limits of Democracy* that "the China model is a combination of economic freedom and political oppression." Bell, however, noted that the CCP's authoritarianism was tempered with "democracy at the bottom, experimentation in the middle, and meritocracy at the top," qualities which are responsible for the regime's ability to make economic progress and uphold social stability (Bell 2015: 179–180). In a similar vein, Suizheng Zhao characterizes the China model as an effort to "strike a balance between economic growth and political stability and between a market-oriented economy and an authoritarian state to sustain its continued economic growth in its modernization efforts." While Bell seems to have a positive appraisal of institutional reforms undertaken by the party, Zhao has expressed qualms about inadequacies such as corruption as well as socio-economic inequality and injustice. "China's economic performance improvement came mostly when China became less brutal and allowed greater personal and economic freedoms," he wrote[7] (Zhao 2010).

As most of the chapters in this anthology suggest, the China model reduced to its basics consists of an amalgamation of Leninism (the CCP monopolizing economic and political resources – and controlling the hearts and minds of party members and citizens alike); nationalism; a generous helping of ancient Chinese tradition, particularly Confucianism and Legalism; and a supposedly super-efficient top-down policymaking mechanism sometimes known as "neo-authoritarianism."

Scholars who have studied the academic sources of the Great Helmsman's works have pointed out that 18 percent of the references and citations were from Stalin, 24 percent from Lenin and 22 percent from Confucianist and other classical Chinese writings. Only 4 percent were from Marx and Engels (Holubnychy 1964). (See Chapter 3, "The CCP's Exploitation of Confucianism and Legalism.") Party leaders ranging from Mao to Xi have used a crypto-Leninist police-state apparatus to tackle destabilizing elements in society. Oxford political scientist Stein Ringen's *The Perfect Dictatorship* is but one of many treatises which have exposed the fact that much of the China model consists of a "controlocracy": a Leninist – or Orwellian – machinery of control "of a size and complexity unprecedented in world history." "The threat of terror is omnipresent," writes Ringen. "And that threat is backed up by a physical use of violence that is sufficient for citizens to know very well that the threat is not an idle one" (Ringen 2016: 139–140). Similarly, Andrew Nathan refers to how the CCP has used its "large fiscal resources, technological sophistication, a well-trained and loyal security apparatus, and sufficient political discipline" to keep destabilizing forces at bay (Nathan 2016: 27). In 2013, the last year in which comparable figures were available, China's budget for maintaining social stability was 769.1 billion yuan, or 28.5 billion yuan more than the publicized military spending for that year (Reuters 2013a).

Not unlike his good friend President Vladimir Putin, whose ambition is to bring back the "imperial glory" of the Soviet Empire, Xi aspires to re-create the Middle Kingdom of the Tang and Song Dynasties. This is inherent in his Chinese dream mantra, which is destined to be one of Xi's most important initiatives. The "Chinese dream" is geared toward the realization of the "great renaissance of the Chinese nation." A key goal of the Chinese dream is that by the year 2049, the centenary of the establishment of the PRC, China will have closed the gap with the U.S. in most measures of national comprehensive strength. This, however, is much more an appeal to raw emotions than substantial policy[8] (Xi 2013d).

Post-Tiananmen, the regime is essentially left with two pillars of legitimacy: one is economic growth and improvement in ordinary people's livelihood; the other is nationalism. Given that high-speed GDP expansion is a thing of the past, nationalism has become an indispensable cornerstone of party legitimacy. As Joseph Fewsmith pointed out, "there is no denying the widespread patriotic feelings of the Chinese people." Yet as Fewsmith notes, "patriotism in China is a two-edged sword, providing support for the government but also holding up a standard that is perhaps impossible for the government to attain"[9] (Fewsmith 2016: 105–107). (See Chapter 4, "The CCP's Use and Abuse of Nationalism.")

It is somewhat ironic that while Xi has based the party's legitimacy on a Sinicized version of socialism, he has at the same time used age-old Chinese wisdom to buttress Chinese patriotism. It is no accident that Xi favors Confucianism, one of whose tenets is respect for authority and conformism with orthodoxy. "CCP members are the faithful successors and developers of superior traditional Chinese culture," Xi said. The supreme leader noted that Chinese culture could be of great benefit in helping party members and citizens to "establish the correct world view, philosophy of life and values." "Traditional Chinese culture is deeply etched onto the DNA of the Chinese people," Xi argued. "Our superior culture has provided nutrient for the renaissance of the Chinese nation. It can be considered the 'calcium of the spirit' " (Cui 2014; *People's Daily* 2014a).

Another aspect of the "China model" consists of the claim that authoritarian, top-down decision-making makes for efficiency. Believers in so-called *xin quanwei zhuyi*, or "neo-authoritarianism" – which surprisingly includes Deng Xiaoping and even liberal icon, the ousted general secretary Zhao Ziyang – argue that in such a complex and divided country as China, a leader needs to have overriding powers to push through reforms.[10] It can be argued that since major policies are made by the CCP Politburo Standing Committee (PBSC), which does not need to worry about either the "opposition" or, to a considerable extent, public opinion, efficiency of implementation can be guaranteed. Examples that apparently illustrate the merits of Chinese-style management include the way in which Jiang Zemin and Zhu Rongji managed to fast-track China's accession process to the WTO despite substantial opposition from numerous ministries as well as local administrations. Others have praised Premier Wen's resolute decision to inject 4 trillion yuan into the economy in late 2008, which supposedly spared China from the adverse impact of the global financial crisis that broke out that year. As the following sections illustrate, however, this non-democratic approach to governance not only militates against Deng Xiaoping-style reform but could result in ill-considered decisions as well as bureaucratic paralysis.

Are "universal values" incompatible with Chinese modernization?

To justify the CCP's socialism with Chinese characteristics, President Xi has claimed that no any single set of values in the world, including what is usually known as "universal values" in global intellectual discourse, is valid for all countries. Demonstrating Mao's unique gift of using earthy language to express abstract concepts, he said in 2013 that "whether a pair of shoes fits only the feet can tell; whether a country's developmental path [is suitable] only people in that country will know" (China News Service 2013).

It is ironical, therefore, that the long list of "core socialist values" cited by the party contains norms and goals that seem to have a universal resonance. These values comprise "prosperity and strength, democracy, civilization, harmony, freedom, equality, justice, rule of law, patriotism, respect for work, honesty and trust, benevolence" (*People's Daily* 2013). Many Chinese observers have become cynical about the apparent ease with which Chinese propagandists have twisted – and Sinicized – their interpretations of words and phrases such as "rule of law" and "democracy." (The trick seems to be to add the qualifier "with Chinese characteristics" after these terms.)

Quite a few liberal intellectuals, however, have argued that values such as democracy as understood in the Western world should be adopted by China. Yu Keping, a Peking University professor and one-time senior cadre at the Central Compilation and Translation Bureau, attracted a lot of attention when he published the article "Democracy is a good thing" in 2006. The one-time adviser to ex-president Hu seemed to be talking about the universal version of "democracy" rather than the Chinese one. It is no accident that when the political climate changed upon Xi's ascendency, Yu has pretty much kept his mouth shut. He resigned from his government post in 2015 (Mai 2015; Yu 2006). Similarly, notable sociologist Yu Jianrong highly recommended "Western-style" norms such as civil liberties, rule of law and mass elections in his "open letter" to central party authorities in early 2016 (Yu 2016).

And to the extent that the Chinese government and legislature have signed several United Nations instruments on human rights, Beijing has at least indicated that it is willing to be held to account regarding whether it has abided by clear-cut sets of global norms (Sceats and Breslin 2012). This is despite the fact that while China signed the International Covenant on Civil and Political Rights in 1998, it has yet to ratify it. And while Beijing signed and ratified the International Covenant on Economic, Social and Cultural Rights in 2000, it indicated that it would only implement Article 8, Clause 1 within the parameters of the Chinese Constitution. (The clause in question stipulates that workers have the right to form trade unions, a key right that is not honored in the PRC) (China Labor Bulletin 2001; Human Rights Watch 2013).

Among forward-looking senior cadres, ex-premier Wen Jiabao stood out as perhaps the only one who has explicitly endorsed *pushijiazhi*, or universal values or norms. The former aide to ousted liberal icons Hu Yaobang and Zhao Ziyang argued in an early 2007 article that China should unhesitatingly embrace *pushijiazhi*. "Democracy, a [fair] legal system, freedom, human rights, egalitarianism … are not unique to capitalism," Wen noted. "They are values that all humankind is jointly pursuing" (Wen 2007).

Liberal intellectuals who have been barred from the official media can only reminisce over how large numbers of First- and Second-Generation revolutionaries seemed unabashed advocates of "Western" political ideals before the CCP seized power in 1949. Testimonies by an older generation of intellectuals pointed to the fact that they joined the revolution in the 1920s and 1930s precisely to fight for "Western values." Dai Huang (1928–2016), one of Xinhua News Agency's earliest journalists, had this to say about why he joined the New Fourth Army at the age of 16: "We wanted to sacrifice our lives to achieve 'liberty, democracy, equality and fraternity' for China." "However, after the party had conquered heaven and earth [in 1949], these [ideals] vanished like ghosts" (Dai 2016).

The Harbingers of History: The Promises Once Made by the CCP, which was edited by dissident writer Xiao Shu, contains many pledges that Mao Zedong and other early revolutionaries made before 1949. Mao said in 1947, two years before taking power, that "we support the abolition of one-party dictatorship." He added that the CCP would not "imitate the social and political order of the Soviet Union." Liu Shaoqi, who would become China's first president, said before Liberation that "one-party rule is against democracy; and the CCP will not institute one-party dictatorship." Deng Xiaoping went on the record in 1941 as saying that "we are against the concept of 'the party running the country'." Then there were innumerable editorials of CCP newspapers proclaiming progressive ideas such as "Democracy is possible only after ending one-party rule" and "One party dictatorship will bring forth disasters all over China" (Xiao 2013: 340–360).

As Lord Patten, the "last governor of Hong Kong," indicated during a tour of the Special Administrative Region in 2016, "there are not separate and distinct Western, African or Asian models. Just as human rights are universal, so too is good governance." The question of whether "culture is destiny," or whether it is possible for Asian countries to develop democracy, was long ago answered by South Korean president Kim Dae-jung (1924–2009). The Nobel Laureate indicated that historical development has shown that "countries practicing democratic capitalism or democratic socialism, despite temporary setbacks, have prospered." Kim persuasively punctured the myth, raised by "Asia's authoritarian leaders," that "cultural differences make the 'Western concept' of democracy and human rights inapplicable to East Asia" (Kim 1994).

The primacy of the party and whether the CCP is capable of far-reaching reforms

The party not only made possible the triumph of Chinese-style socialism in 1949; it has provided both the ideological and organizational underpinning for the continuation of the special powers and privileges of China's new ruling class. Above all, the party has facilitated the apparent triumph of Chinese exceptionalism, the fact that China has emerged in record time as a quasi-superpower despite not following the bulk of "universal values" such as rule of law and freedom of expression and religion.[11] Even the most zealous defenders of the CCP, however, may recognize that it is also the extremely rigid party orthodoxy that has ensured that Chinese both as individuals and as a whole cannot attain the lofty goal raised in Marxist teachings, here summarized by the eminent social scientist Erich Fromm: "the spiritual emancipation of man, of his liberation from the chains of economic determination, of restituting him in his human wholeness, of enabling him to find unity and harmony with his fellow man and with nature" (Fromm 1961).

Following the Leninist tradition to the hilt, Mao – and Xi – has used the party and the "dictatorship of the proletariat" to maintain tight control over not only party members but all Chinese. Xi has revived Mao's dictums issued at the Yan'an Talks on Literature and Art (1942), whereby the Great Helmsman ordained that *dangxing* (党性 or "party nature") overrides *renxing* (人性 or "human nature") or renminxing (人民性 or "the nature of the people"). Each party member must subsume his individual aspirations under *dangxing* and become the proverbial "cog in the machinery" of the regime. Mao and Xi have also insisted that all knowledge has its *dangxing* and knowledge that is anti-party must be banished[12] (Mao 1942; *Study Times* 2013).

To boost the power of the party, or more accurately, the power of himself and his coterie of advisers and cronies, Xi has abandoned yet another institutional reform, *dangzheng fenkai* (the separation of party and government). In his *Political Report to the 13th Party Congress* of 1987, then party general secretary Zhao Ziyang said that the CCP must resolve the "fundamental question of the non-separation of party and government as well as the party doing the work of the government." Zhao, who enjoyed the backing of Deng, argued that the party should focus on weighty and long-term issues such as "political principles, political directions and major decision-making." Government units, Zhao added, should have full responsibility over the execution of policy and the day-to-day administration of the country[13] (Zhao 1987).

While the process of refocusing powers in the party began with ex-president Jiang, Xi will go down in history as having stood the *dangzheng fenkai* principle on its head. As discussed in Chapter 5, "The Party Runs the Show: How the CCP Controls the State and Towers over the Government, Legislature and Judiciary," decision-making powers in areas ranging from military and foreign policies to the economy have been arrogated by a dozen-odd Central Leading Groups or Central Commissions. Most of these top-level units are headed by Xi; and they report only to the PBSC. They are totally non-transparent, and are beyond the scrutiny of the legislature, the Chinese People's Political Consultative Conference, the judiciary and, of course, the media and public opinion (McGregor 2010: 1–33; Lam 2015a: 99–103).

The most striking example is that the economic decision-making powers of the premier, who is head of the State Council or central government, have been drastically truncated. Up to the Xi era, the premier headed the Central Leading Group for Finance and Economics (CLGFE), which is the most authoritative decision-making body on the economy. Not only did Xi take over the chairmanship of the CLGFE on day one of his administration, he created in 2013 another powerful policy-setting body called the Central Leading Group for Comprehensively Deepening Reforms, which he heads. Moreover, while the CLGFE was set up in the early 1980s, its members largely stayed in the background. From 2013 onwards, however, senior members of the CLGFE such as the Director and Deputy Director of its General Office, respectively Liu He and Shu Guozeng, began regularly talking to the media on specific policy issues. The Harvard-educated Liu, who first got to know Xi when they were studying at the same high school in Beijing in the 1960s, regularly contradicted Premier Li on a whole range of economic and financial policies (*The Economist* 2015; T. Mitchell 2016; Xu 2015).

For Xi Jinping, preservation of the party's near-omnipotence is so paramount a consideration that he once told officials to steer clear of policies and goals which might be worthy and salutary – but which could detract from the party's powers and longevity. "If the party collapses, all achievements will be meaningless," he said. "If our party becomes weak, attenuated, broken down, what meaning will any achievements [in governance] have?" (Xi 2014a). In other words, the criteria for measuring the success of administration is neither GDP growth, nor improving the environment, nor boosting the happiness of the people. "Party construction," a code word for boosting the authority and viability of the CCP, has become the be-all and end-all of governance.

Equally significant is the fact that Xi seems to have equated the interests of the CCP to those of the "red aristocracy," of which he and fellow princelings such as the ousted Politburo member and Chongqing party secretary Bo Xilai are prime representatives. The princelings are using the Maoist crusade to lobby for more clout in the polity by highlighting their illustrious lineage and political correctness. As the famous Chinese proverb goes: "After the father has won heaven and earth, the son has the right to rule over them." This was the basis of the "revolutionary legitimacy" of the First- and Second-Generation leadership under Mao and Deng, respectively. As the sons and daughters of Long March veterans, princelings regard their "revolutionary bloodline" as a prime political resource (Chen 2007). Thus, while visiting the "revolutionary mecca" of Jinggangshan in Jiangxi Province in 2008, Xi paid homage to the "countless martyrs of the revolution who gave their blood and lives to win over this country." "They laid a strong foundation for the good livelihood [that we now enjoy]," he said. "Under no circumstances can we forsake this tradition" (Xi 2008a). While Bo was a bitter political foe of Xi's, the former expressed similar sentiments about the empowerment of the princelings. While marking National Day on October 1, 2008, Bo urged Chongqing's cadres "to forever bear in mind the ideals and hot-blooded [devotion] of our elders." "Forsaking [their revolutionary tradition] is tantamount to betrayal," Bo stated (Bo 2008).

According to the *China Daily*, the top 1 percent of Chinese families control 41.4 percent of the country's wealth. Other official media reported in the late 2000s that 91 percent of Chinese citizens who owned more than RMB 100 million came from "high-cadre families." Apart from ideological opposition to political and economic liberalization, the Xi-led administration seems to be resisting reforms out of their desire to protect the vested interests of the "red aristocracy" (Chen 2010; Han *et al.* 2013; Rajagopalan 2013).

A retrogression on reform?

In a discussion on the relationship between national strength and reform, Tsinghua University Professor Yan Xuetong noted in 2016 that "national strength is to a large extent based on the country's capacity for reform." Yan cited ancient legalist philosopher Guan Zi (723–645 BC) on the fact that "if the country is big and the political leadership is weak, the country will become weak; a country may be small but if the leadership is strong, the country will become massively strong" (Yan 2016). The basic factor behind the "Chinese economic miracle" was the pro-market reforms of Deng and his comrades. Xi, however, seems destined to preside over not only the stagnation but possibly the retrogression of both economic and political liberalization (Blumenthal and Scissors 2016).

Stagnation in political liberalization

Given that China's one-party rule system lacks institutional checks and balances as well as supervision from the media and the civil society, the most important political reforms pertain to ways and means to promote "intra-party democracy" and to render decision-making "democratic and scientific." It is significant that while the First Generation of reformist leaders under Deng Xiaoping, for example, then General Secretary Hu Yaobang and then NPC Chairman Wan Li, were noted patrons of what they called the *ruan kexue* ("soft science") of democratic decision-making, this concern for the modernization of public administration or government management has not been shared by Fourth- and Fifth-Generation leaders (Wan 2015; Zhu 2013).

Sinologists have used the term authoritarian resilience to denote how the CCP leadership has maintained power and upheld stability through institutional changes that stop short of democratization. In a much-noted 2003 article, Andrew Nathan cited "institutionalization of orderly succession processes, meritocratic promotions, bureaucratic differentiation and channels of mass participation and appeal" as modus operandi that the party-and-state apparatus could employ to prolong its mandate of heaven without introducing real democracy (Nathan 2003: 6–7). Similarly, Minxin Pei has pinpointed ways that the CCP leadership had tried to introduce "resilient" methods to prevent the CCP going the way of the CPSU. These included "ending international isolation; placating the intelligentsia; and boosting the confidence of the business community." Both Nathan and Pei have serious doubts as to whether the party is committed to these measures, however circumscribed they are. Pei argued that owing to its refusal to entertain real political changes, the CCP was "fragile rather than resilient"[14] (Pei 2013: 110–111).

Two of Xi's immediate predecessors, Jiang Zemin and Hu Jintao, deserve some credit for at least tinkering with the system. (See Chapter 9, "Evolution of the Party since 1976: Ideological and Functional Adoptions.") Through his "Theory of the Three Represents," Jiang Zemin attempted to improve the meritocratic system by allowing private entrepreneurs, professors as well as "returnees" (Chinese with degrees from Western universities) not only to enter the party but to be appointed to ministerial-level positions (Fewsmith 2003; Lam 2006: 65–68). Both Jiang and Hu introduced elements of the "Western" civil service into CCP administration. They included public examination to select officials as well as transparent criteria for promotion. For Daniel Bell, a meritocratic personnel system is key to the success of the "China model." "Cadres are put through a grueling process of talent selection, and only those with an excellent record of past performance are likely to make it to the highest levels of government," he wrote (Bell 2015: 172).

However, as Chapter 10, "The CCP's Meritocratic Cadre System" illustrates, there are grave misgivings as to whether meritocratic norms can truly be established within the framework of a one-party dictatorship. The large number of corruption cases exposed by Xi's five-year-old anti-graft campaign shows up serious flaws in procedures for cadre selection and supervision. The buying and selling of plum jobs has become routine. Both Xi and his PBSC colleague in charge of graft-busting, Wang Qishan, admitted that corruption had become "systematic." Within four years of Xi's so-called "tiger hunting campaign," more than 1 million party members were prosecuted with receiving bribes and related economic crimes (BBC News 2016a; News.sohu.com 2016).

Moreover, a prerequisite of a meritocratic cadre system is that it must be rule-based; criteria for promotion must not be subject to the whims of the top leaders. The Hu era developed a fairly "scientific" model for assessment of cadres who are up for elevation. Criteria include strict retirement ages; the GDP growth rate of areas under their jurisdiction; assessment by "examiners" (senior officials); and in many cases "open evaluation," whereby the suitability of candidates for promotion must be appraised by respectable members of society who can cast "votes" in sessions of public appraisal. Yet in a statement issued in late 2014, the Central Organization Department pointed out that

> we must deepen the reform of the institution of selecting cadres for promotion and assessment criteria so as to solve the problem of [selection] based on "paying sole attention to *piao* [number of votes from public assessors], marks [assessment grades given by examiners], GDP growth, and age.
>
> *(Xinhua News Agency 2014a)*

What the COD's oblique instruction actually meant was that criteria such as retirement age should not be rigidly adhered to if there were countervailing circumstances. This was widely interpreted as an indication that Xi's right-hand man Wang Qishan (born 1948) need not retire from the PBSC at the 19th CCP Congress. Indeed, Deng Maosheng, a drafter of top-level documents attached to the Central Committee Secretariat, noted in late 2016 that the well-known convention "*qishang baxia*" (roughly, a 68-year-old cadre is too old for consideration for induction to the PBSC) was just "hearsay" and not party policy. This further boosted the possibility that Wang, who would be 69 at the time of the 19th Congress, could remain in the PBSC for five more years (Lam 2016b; *Singtao Daily* 2016).

More importantly, the ideal of meritocracy could be dealt a severe blow by factionalism, or the tendency for top-level cadres to establish their own cliques and camarillas – and to appoint their protégés to choice slots in the party-state apparatus. Often, these personnel movements are based on loyalty rather than merit. Recent examples have included the Shanghai Faction under Jiang Zemin, the Communist Youth League Faction under Hu Jintao, and the inchoate but fast-expanding Xi Jinping Faction under the "leadership core" Xi. Since 2015, possession of *hexin yishi* ("core consciousness"), meaning willingness to pledge full allegiance to "core leader Xi," has become a prerequisite for promotion to top posts (Agence France Presse 2016; Chang 2015). (See Chapter 8, "Factional Politics in the Party-State Apparatus.")

And how about the prospects for "intra-party democracy"? In the second half of the Hu administration (2007–2012), the Fourth-Generation leader made much about promoting *dangnei minzhu* ("democracy within the party" or "intra-party democracy"). In guinea-pig counties nationwide, the party secretaries of county-level party committees were selected on a one-person one-vote basis by all party members resident in the areas concerned. One of Hu's seminal initiatives was to reempower the party congresses at both the national and local levels. For example, local-level congresses in selected jurisdictions met once a year so as to have executive supervisory powers over the ruling party committees that they had earlier selected (Lam 2011). As Guoguang Wu notes in Chapter 6, "The Role of Party Congresses," however, the reform of the party congress system remains a case of too little, too late.

Given that in his first five-year term, Xi seemed to have focused his energy on recentralization powers to the topmost echelons of the party – and to have himself declared the undisputed supremo – it is unlikely that the Fifth-Generation princeling will attempt any genuine political reform, including promoting democracy within the party. According to Singapore-based Sinologists Zheng Yongnian and Yang Lijun, "democracy within the party has yet to be established." "An unwholesome intra-party democratic system often leads to internal crises within governing parties," they warned. Pointing to obvious signs of recentralization under President Xi, they raised the disturbing issue of "how recentralized powers can be transformed into institutionalized power." Equally significant was the question of how "a model of intra-party democracy" can be instituted without rule of law (Zheng and Yang 2016: 33–43).

Indeed, an important yardstick for administrative reform is the promotion of some form of rule of law, or in the Chinese case, rule by law. Reformers from Deng Xiaoping onwards have stressed that policies and other government actions must be anchored on the Constitution and the law. Both ex-president Hu and President Xi have given strong rhetorical support for *yifa zhiguo* or "running the country according to law," a concept that is sometimes described as "rule by law with Chinese characteristics." There is a big chasm between universal-style rule of law and rule by law, which essentially means the CCP running the country according to laws that it has formulated (Lam 2009). The party has never recognized the principle of the independence of the judiciary. For example, in a national meeting of the *zhengfa* (political and legal) system in 2008, Hu called upon "judicial workers" to follow three *zhishang* ("foremost priorities"): "the party's enterprise; the people's interest; and the Constitution and the laws" (Xinhua News Agency 2008). It is very clear that the party's interests come before the law.

Xi's rhetorical commitments to "rule of law with Chinese characteristics" notwithstanding, it is clear that the party continues to ride roughshod over legislative and judicial organs (see Chapter 16, "The Party and the Law"). For example, Xi indicated more than once that "party organizations of all levels should insist on acting within the parameters of the Constitution and the laws." Cadres, he added, should "maintain sentiments of respect and awe in the face of the Constitution and the law" (Xi 2014b). At the same time, the CCP General Secretary has upheld the party's leadership over *zhengfa* (political-legal) organs such as the police, the courts and procuratorates. Xi noted at a meeting of *zhengfa* cadres in early 2014 that cadres must "unswervingly uphold the party's leadership over *zhengfa* work ... [and] strengthen and improve the party's leadership over *zhengfa* work" (*People's Daily* 2014b).[15] The large-scale detention and incarceration of human rights lawyers in mid-2015 testified to the Xi administration's problematic attitudes to rule of law and due process (Jacobs and Buckley 2015).

The uncertain future of economic reform

Through-going economic reform – in the sense of the substitution of state fiats by market forces – was evident only for some six months after Li Keqiang was confirmed premier at the NPC in 2013. A pro-market cadre, Li famously compared the bold reformer to "a brave person who [was so committed to achieving his goal] that he wouldn't mind cutting off his arm." "Let the market do what it does best," said Li, who also wanted to drastically cut stupendous levels of loans that had underwritten the Chinese economic growth. Most Western economists estimate that China's total social debt is around 280 percent of GDP, a level which is unsustainable. However, Li's approach, sometimes known as "Likonomics," was mentioned in the media for only six months (Bloomberg 2013; Lam 2015a: 157–161; Li, K. 2013).

In line with Xi's broad governance philosophy, emphasis was placed on *dingchen shezhi* or ("top-level design") and the rolling out of reform measures under tight centralized supervision. This was evidenced from the *Decision on Some Major Issues Concerning Comprehensively Deepening Reforms*, which was promulgated at a Central Committee Plenum in late 2013. "The comprehensive deepening of reforms necessarily requires strengthening and improving party leadership," the *Decision* said. "We must fully develop the core functions of the party taking charge of the whole situation and coordinating various [sectors]" (China.org.cn 2014). The document also repeated Xi's ingrained belief in the "organic unification of the [principles of] leadership of the Party, the people mastering their own affairs and governing the country according to law" (*Study and Research* 2013; Xi 2013e). In his interview with Russian television while attending the Sochi Olympics in January 2014, Xi characterized reform as "10 percent design and 90 percent implementation." "Tasks regarding major issues must be uniformly designed, planned and coordinated," he said. The idea of "90 percent implementation" reflects his insistence that reform be calibrated and executed under the tight supervision of an elaborate party-state apparatus (Xinhua News Agency 2014b).

That an economy as complicated as China cannot be run with a top-down command-and-control system seems evident. Tsinghua University's Yuan Gangming noted that "the risk is that a regime with highly concentrated power is prone to make policy choices which are incorrect" (Cai 2016). Chapter 12 in this book, "How the Party-State Runs the Economy: A Model of Elite Decision-Making in the Financial Market," and Chapter 13, "Implementing Tax Reform and Rural Reconstruction in China: A Case Study of the CCP's Agrarian Policy," have cogently demonstrated the problematic nature of Chinese decision-making in the area of finance and agriculture.

The most obvious example that the CCP administration may have missed the boat of reform is the age-old problem of restructuring the economy, that is, excessive reliance on government investments to prop up GDP growth. While Xi himself has also come out with liberal-sounding slogans such as "supply-side reforms," the party-state apparatus is still resorting to trusted measures such as government injections in infrastructure projects (*The Economist* 2016a; National Public Radio 2015). In 2017, 23 provinces planned to splash out a total of 45 trillion yuan in fixed-assets investment; this is despite the fact that many local-level administrations were already heavily in debt (Leng and Tang 2017). That the Xi leadership has tremendous difficulties weaning itself off old-style state diktats was evidenced by the inept and hamfisted way in which the party-state apparatus handled the stock market crash of July 2015 (Xu 2016). Instead of laying out a credible blueprint for market liberalization, the authorities dusted off executive fiats that were reminiscent of the command economy in pre-reform days. Moreover, actions taken by the government to "save the market" were not based on laws and regulations. Top executives of large securities firms were summoned to Beijing, where they got ironclad directives to avoid selling stocks at all costs. The leadership even sent police officers to intimidate brokers accused of short-selling (Riley and Chang 2015; Wong *et al.* 2015).

Equally problematic for the future of reform is Xi's determination to ensure that state-owned enterprise (SOE) conglomerates, which account for 40 percent of Chinese industry, should be solidly controlled by the party-state apparatus. The supreme leader pointed out at a 2016 conference on the development of SOEs that "party leadership and strengthening the role of the party are the root and soul for state-owned enterprises." "The party's leadership in state-owned enterprises is a major political principle, and that principle must be upheld," he said, adding that "weakening, fading, blurring or marginalisation" of party leadership in state firms would not be tolerated (Bloomberg 2016; Feng 2016). Noted China economist Nicholas Lardy pointed out that "the signals sent by Xi [on SOEs] are confusing and inconsistent." He added that the sluggish pace of state-sector reform was "the biggest risk to China's economy" (Wu 2016).

Similarly, Sinologist Barry Naughton argued that in the sensitive arena of economic reform, Xi could at best consolidate changes, not initiate them. Yet Naughton also cast doubt on the president's ability to merely persevere with existing liberalization measures. "Xi's multiple policy objectives, and particularly his stress on leadership, on the Communist Party, and on the revival of ideological mobilization and control clearly conflict with the needs of reform consolidation," argued Naughton (Naughton 2016: 86).

Is the party serving the interests of the people?

While multi-lingual channels of the CCTV and *China Daily* are singing the praises of global prestige-building schemes such as the One Belt One Road, the most relevant question as to whether the party is doing its job is whether 1.3 billion Chinese are happy with the system. Jin Kai, a former PLA officer who teaches at Yonsei University in South Korea, asks a significant question about not just Xi's Chinese Dream mantra but the entire system of a party-driven authoritarian state: "How is China's rise benefiting China's people?" In an article entitled "The rise of China vs. the rise of the Chinese," Jin argued that "whether the 'Chinese' have equally 'risen' remains uncertain" (Jin 2016). According to Ringen, "in spite of economic growth, there has been no improvement in happiness in the Chinese population" (Ringen 2016: 150).

Based on fairly exhaustive opinion polls conducted in China, Wenfang Tang indicated in his book *Populist Authoritarianism* (2016) that there is "strong political support" in areas including "key political institutions, national identity, satisfaction with government performance, support for one's own political system, or support for incumbent leaders." Tang contended that this was based on "mass line ideology, strong community solidarity, widespread public involvement and political participation, and a paranoidly responsive government" (Tang 2016: 159).

It is, however, difficult to conceive how "widespread public involvement and political participation" is possible when the leadership is adopting draconian measures to censor the media and to constrict the public's freedom of expression. (See Chapter 11, "The New (Old) Normal": the CCP Propaganda System under Jiang, Hu, and Xi"; Chapter 23, "Can the Internet and Social Media Change the Party?") The Xi leadership has significantly tightened restrictions on news reporting. While the Hu administration allowed isolated media such as the Guangdong-based

Nanfang group of papers to occasionally report politically controversial stories, Xi is adamant that all media be "surnamed CCP" – meaning that they must be the tongue and throat of the party (Xi 2016b). Moreover, Xi, who heads the CCP Central Leading Group on Cyberspace Affairs, is using IT innovations such as "big data" files to establish a "digital dictatorship" in order to keep track of the "social credit" and political loyalty of citizens (*The Economist* 2016b).

It is also difficult to imagine how widespread political participation – and government responsiveness – can be possible when the great majority of Chinese live in the shadow of the party's jealously guarded monopoly of power. A look at the background of the 370-odd full and alternative members of the policy-setting CCP Central Committee shows the abysmal level of representation of workers, peasants, intellectuals, private businesspeople, professionals, not to mention members of minority peoples such as Uyghurs and Tibetans. By contrast, generals of the PLA and the People's Armed Police, who play a pivotal role in upholding the party's "perennial rule," are guaranteed 20 percent of the seats of this top-level ruling council. (See Chapter 7, "The PLA as the Lifeline of the Party.")

The Xi leadership's policy toward two sectors that are best placed to speed up modernization of the country – intellectuals and civil-society groups – has become progressively harsher than those of former presidents Jiang and Hu. (See Chapter 15, "Reform, Repression, Co-Optation: The CCP's Policy Toward Intellectuals" and Chapter 22, "Changing Patterns of Chinese Civil Society: Comparing the Hu-Wen and Xi Jinping Eras.") A record number of influential professors in China's top universities have been forbidden to give public speeches or forced into exile. Until the end of the Hu Jintao administration, liberal bloggers who happened to be billionaires were often treated with kid gloves by the authorities. Xi, however, has penalized several billionaire IT-based opinion leaders (Philips 2016; Schell 2016). While the Hu administration has to some extent tolerated loosely defined NGOs, Xi has sought to replace NGOs with so-called "People's Organizations." The dramatic tightening of public space has put a damper on organizations that advocate women's rights and those of LGBT groups. (See Chapter 17, "Two Steps Forward, One Backward: The CCP's Policy toward Women" and Chapter 18, "Public Policy and LGBT People and Activism in Mainland China.")

As Chapter 14, "The Party's Policy toward Labor," shows, the CCP is not prepared to allow the "vanguard of the proletariat" to have a say in improving their political and economic standing. Workers are not allowed to form independent trade unions. Farmers, who find themselves in the bottom of the barrel in the new social hierarchy, are still subjected to exploitations both by the state, and since the early 2000s, by unscrupulous cadres and developers. Some 60 percent of China's riots and disturbances have to do with the phenomenon of "land grab," in which greedy local officials illegally sell off peasants' private plots to developers, during which process farmers receive merely 10 percent of what their land could fetch on the open market (Reuters 2013b; Roberts 2013).

And how about the ethnic minorities, particularly visible ethnic minorities such as the Uyghurs and the Tibetans? Take the situation in the Xinjiang Uyghur Autonomous Region (XUAR). Even admirers of the "China model" cannot close their eyes to the fact that the moral equivalent of a cultural genocide is going on in China's Far West. Uyghurs are told not to observe religious festivals as important as the Ramadan. In late 2016, Beijing suddenly decided to confiscate the passports of all Uyghurs. Moreover, the Xi leadership is said to be reducing the number of mosques in the region. This is despite the fact that almost all the mosques are already under the tight control of police (BBC News 2016b; Lam 2017). As for Tibet, self-immolation by monks and nuns as a protest against Chinese misrule has continued unabated. In the wake of Beijing's arrests of even moderate Tibetan intellectuals, dialogues between Tibetans and Han Chinese have closed down (Tibet-net 2016). (See Chapter 19, "The CCP's Tibet Policy:

Stability through Coercion and Development" and Chapter 20, "The Party-State's Nationalist Strategy to Control the Uyghur: Silenced Voices.")

Actually, one of the best indications of whether the CCP's "populist authoritarianism" is really working is the disturbing phenomenon of elite emigration: tens of thousands of members of the business, middle and professional classes leaving mostly for the West but also for Hong Kong, Singapore and other destinations (Cendrowski 2014; Lam 2015a: 291–294; Zhelyazkov 2015). This development, alarming as it is, tends to be underestimated due to two reasons. Given the country's huge size, emigrants still form a tiny proportion of the populace. Second, many of the "returnees" who are working in the most productive sectors of the economy actually hold foreign passports. They are ready to leave with their families if things go sour in China.

Conclusion: change versus no change

Chinese exceptionalism – or how the CCP has been able to defy the odds of social science textbooks by not only staying in power but reaching new heights of global influence – has produced a large body of works predicting the future development of the world's most powerful political party as well as most populous nation (see Chapter 21 "The Future of the Chinese Communist Party").

Despite exciting developments in China's high-tech area, which seem to defy another conventional wisdom – that it would be difficult for countries with no freedom of expression to excel in IT and related fields – the CCP is perilously mired in the past. Xi has styled himself the "Mao Zedong of the 21st Century." Yet he obviously lacks Mao's ability (at least before 1949) to, to use a Chinese proverb, "fashion new heavens, new earths." One is reminded of a conversation in 1945 between Mao and famous pro-democracy scholar Huang Yanpei. Huang told Mao a version of the theory of the "dynastic cycle," saying, "While dynasties of the past might have prospered to great heights, they collapsed all of a sudden." Huang said he hoped the Communist Party could jump out of this cycle. Mao's reply: "We have found a new path. We can break out of this law. This new path is called democracy" (*Twenty-First Century History* 2012).

In his essay titled "Chinese communism and the 70-year itch," veteran theorist on democracy Larry Diamond cited the irony inherent in the fact that "in his obsession with avoiding becoming another Gorbachev, he [Xi] is governing in a way that will bring about Gorbachev's fate – the collapse of the party and the regime under his rule." "For Xi and his colleagues, there is a way out," Diamond wrote. "They could buy significant time by launching a gradual process of democratization – something like what their old rival, the Kuomintang (KMT), did in Taiwan after losing the Chinese civil war" (Diamond 2013). Unfortunately, Xi, like Mao before him, lacks the guts and the vision to try out alternative models that could prove "subversive" to one-party dictatorship. Similarly, James Palmer contended in a 2016 *Foreign Policy* article entitled "What China didn't learn from the collapse of the Soviet Union," that the CCP made a big mistake by thinking they could perpetuate party rule by halting political liberalization and banning Western influence. "Today, the lessons Beijing is drawing seem likely to keep sending it backward," wrote Palmer (Palmer 2016).

Indeed, Xi is pushing a policy of inertia and procrastination similar to those ultra-conservative leaders before Gorbachev. In his famous critique of the government mentality of the U.S.S.R., George Kennan wrote that "the whole Soviet governmental machine … moves inexorably along the prescribed path, like a persistent toy automobile wound up and headed in a given direction, stopping only when it meets with some unanswerable force" (Kennan 1947). People's University professor Yang Guangbin used some of Kennan's logic and vocabulary to lambast the American capitalist system. In an article entitled "A 'chariot system' driven by vested interests,"

Yang claimed that Kennan's argument was more applicable to America. "In the U.S.," Yang contended, "a 'monster' made up of the power of capital is driving a forever-charging 'chariot system' that renders its expansionist actions unstoppable" (Yang 2016). At least for this author, however, Kennan's 1940s argument is in many ways an apt description of what is happening in the PRC in the twenty-first century. A regime that is fearful of change – and hell-bent on guarding the prerogatives of the "red aristocracy" – is charging on regardless of factors such as opposition from the intelligentsia, stagnation in most aspects of reform, and the sizable wave of emigration to Western countries by its elite. It is difficult to predict when an "unanswerable force," perhaps a combination of domestic revolt and repercussions from a failed foreign adventure, may strike. But it is almost certain that perpetual procrastination regarding genuine reform is no magic bullet for prolonging the party's Mandate of Heaven.

For communist leaders from Jiang Zemin to Xi Jinping who have tried to borrow legitimacy from the classics, it is amazing that they have failed to appreciate the dialectics of "change versus no change" embodied in ancient fountainheads of wisdom such as *I Ching* or *The Book of Changes*. Two of the most-quoted aphorisms from this mother lode of wisdom said: *qiong ze bian, bian ze tong* ("When there seems to be no path, make changes; make changes and you will break through"); and *buke wei dianyao, weibian suoshi* ("do not [blindly] stick to texts; make changes according to what is suitable") (Wang 2015). While Xi in 2014 made a pro forma reference to the *qiong ze bian* message out of the *I Ching*, he has repeatedly emphasized that "subversive changes," or those that could weaken the CCP's grip on power, are to be avoided at all cost (Cao 2015).

As Sinologist David Shambaugh sees it, "hard authoritarianism is a recipe for economic stagnation, social instability and the political decline of the CCP." Shambaugh thinks that at the very least, the CCP has to make changes such as "empowering all citizens with the right to vote … making the judiciary and the NPC autonomous branches of government from the CCP" and abolishing party cells in government units and enterprises. "Would the CCP be willing to undertake these changes and subject itself to such constraints on its current complete monopoly of power?" asked Shambaugh, who thinks the chances for this happening are "close to zero" (Shambaugh 2016: 135–136). Similarly, veteran China watcher Jonathan Fenby noted that ingrained problems "are now piling up in a dangerous fashion and there may not be much time to deal with the combination of pressures." "Decision-making will be difficult for a leadership which has long avoided hard choices and is hemmed in by the cocoon of embedded Party rule," he wrote (Fenby 2014: 125–126).

Peking University economist Zhang Weiying agrees that the CCP is suffering from a "paucity of bold ideas." "In the first two decades of China's transition, such ideas trumped vested interests, which is why reform overcame interest groups' opposition," wrote Zhang. "However, in the past decade, it is the vested interests that have dominated the ideas. Various anti-reform policies have been implemented for protecting and strengthening interest groups" (Zhang 2012). Zhang has proposed a "marketplace for ideas," where a "debate of different opinions, beliefs, theories, and ideologies … [can] produce new and right ideas." The respected public intellectual cautioned, however, that "the idea market in China is underdeveloped and heavily restricted because of the monopoly of the Communist ideologies" (Zhang, W. 2015). Given President Xi's anxiety to preserve the status quo and to quash China's already much-depleted public sphere, it is difficult to foresee when a new era of "thought liberation" might again take place.

Notes

1 The "One Belt One Road" is a reference to the New Silkroad Economic Belt, which stretches from Central Asia to Eastern Europe, and the 21st Century Maritime Silkroad, which links up Southeast

Asia, the Indian Subcontinent and East Africa. For a discussion of the viability of China's ambitious gameplan, see Cendrowski (2016) and Kynge (2016). President Xi Jinping indicated in late 2016 that progress of the OBOR had "exceeded anticipation" (Xi 2016a). However, Zhang Yunling, an international relations expert at the Chinese Academy of Social Sciences, said that the One Belt One Road project "could take 20, 50, and even 100 years to complete." "We can't be in a hurry," he indicated. "We should pick as priority projects whose effectiveness is obvious. We do it one at a time" (Zhang, Y. 2015). Financier and National People's Congress delegate Lai Xiaomin noted in early 2016 that the anticipated cost for the OBOR project is US$8 trillion. This compared with a relatively meager total assets of US$240 billion of the Asian Infrastructure Construction Bank, the BRICS Bank and the Silk Road Fund (*Financial News* 2016).

2 The TPP, a mammoth free-trade area that does not cover China, is deemed a weapon by the United States to exclude the PRC. It was key to former president Obama's "pivot to Asia" strategy. After Trump decided to drop the TPP, Beijing has been pushing the establishment of the RCEP, which will rope in the ten ASEAN members plus China, Japan, South Korea, Australia and New Zealand. See Harding and Smyth (2017) and Wong (2017).

3 Human Rights Watch and other international watchdogs have also condemned both Beijing and Bangkok for the forced repatriation of Uyghur political refugees from Thailand back to the PRC (Human Rights Watch 2014; Radio Free Asia 2015). There are reports about Chinese state security agents becoming more active in North America. For example, in mid-2015, such agents reportedly tried to kidnap California-based Chinese-American businessman Ling Wancheng – the brother of Ling Jihua, a former right-hand man of ex-president Hu Jintao – who was supposed to be in possession of state secrets passed to him by his brother (Forsythe and Mazzetti 2015).

4 For a discussion that Xi Jinping will break with tradition and rule for more than two terms of five years each, see, for example, Callick (2016) and C. Mitchell (2016). At the Sixth Plenum of the 18th Central Committee in October 2016, Xi was conferred with the title "leadership core." Given that the concept of the "core" carries no age or term limits, there are suggestions that Xi might be aiming for "life tenure" (Lam 2016a).

5 Xi laid down the now-famous dictum of the *liangge buneng fouding* (the theory of "the two forbidden negotiations"): the Party should "not differentiate [post-1949 CCP] history into the pre-reform period and the post-reform period." "These two periods should not be [arbitrarily] cut off from each other – and one period should not be used to negate the other," Xi said in a January 2013 speech (Xi 2013b).

6 Deng Xiaoping first raised the concept of the primary stage of socialism in the seminal document summing up the lessons of the Cultural Revolution, the "Resolution on Certain Questions in Our Party's History since the Founding of the PRC" (1981). For a discussion of the primary (sometimes called "preliminary" or "initial") stage of socialism, see for example, Li (2004) and Wilson (1989).

7 For a discussion of the definition and connotation of the "China model," also see Ding (2014), Ferchen (2013), Freeman and Yuan (2010), Naughton (2010) and Zhang (2006). It is significant that the term "China model" does not appear often in state media. For an explication of how semi-official scholars interpret the "China model," see, for example, Peng and Yang (2010).

8 Many liberal intellectuals have argued that the "Chinese dream" should not be monopolized by the party-state apparatus. For example, Bao Tong, former secretary of late leader Zhao Ziyang, called upon Xi Jinping "to return the dream to the people." "The country should allow us common people to each dream his own dream," he said. Similarly, Peking University law professor and public intellectual He Weifang noted that "the most important goal of a modernized nation is to allow the people to have dignity, freedom and [civil] rights so that each person can work hard to fulfill his own dream" (Bao 2013; He 2013).

9 For a discussion of the peculiar nature of Chinese nationalism, see Gries (2004), Xiao (2011) and Zhao (2005).

10 Noted Shanghai historian Xiao Gongqin argues that the ideology and statecraft of Xi Jinping has amounted to "a strengthened version of neo-authoritarianism" (Xiao 2015). For samples of Western scholars' views of "neo-authoritarianism" in China, see, for example, Petracca and Xiong (1990) and Sautman (1992).

11 For a discussion of "Chinese exceptionalism," see, for example, Ho (2013), Walt (2012) and Zhang (2011).

12 Xi Jinping said in a 2013 conference on ideology and propaganda that "*Dangxing* [nature of the Party] and *renminxing* [nature of the people] have always tallied with each other and are unified." See Lam (2015a: 94–95). For a compilation of Xi's views on *dangxing*, see Dangjian Net (2016).

13 Zhao Ziyang pointed out in his *Political Report to the 13th Party Congress* that "the non-separation of party and government has resulted in the party occupying the front line of administrative work, which results in the party becoming ... the focal point of contradictions." The liberal party chief warned that "the non-separation of party and government results in the party assuming the role of the direct executor [of policy]." "Only with separation of party and government will party organizations be in a position to exercise supervision and to effectively prevent and overcome bureaucratic tendencies," he said. Zhao also laid out his views on the separation of party and government at the Seventh Plenum of the 12th Central Committee in October 1987. See Zhao (2011).

14 For a discussion of "authoritarian resilience" and its limits, see, for example, Cheng (2012), Gilley (2003) and Su *et al.* (2013).

15 Zhou Qiang, the President of the Supreme People's Court, shocked the judicial and legal community when he noted in early 2017 that "we should resolutely resist erroneous influence from the West [such as] 'constitutional democracy,' 'separation of powers' and 'independence of the judiciary.'" "We must make clear our stand and dare to show the sword," he told the nation's legal officials (*New York Times* 2017).

References

Agence France Presse (2016) "Xi move on faction suggests China elite struggle: Experts," April 29, www.straitstimes.com/asia/east-asia/xi-move-on-faction-suggests-china-elite-struggle-experts.

Bao, T. (2013) Xi Jinping de zhongguomeng shi "renmin de meng" ("Bao Tong: Xi Jinping's Chinese dream is 'the people's dream'"), DWNews.com, March 21, http://china.dwnews.com/big5/news/2013-03-21/59157761.html.

BBC News (2016a) "'One million' Chinese officials punished for corruption," October 24, www.bbc.com/news/world-asia-china-37748241.

BBC News (2016b) "China confiscates passports of Xinjiang people," November 24, www.bbc.com/news/world-asia-china-38093370.

Bell, D. (2015) *The China Model: Political Meritocracy and the Limits of Democracy*, Princeton, N.J.: Princeton University Press.

Bloomberg (2013) "China vows bigger role for markets as party closes summit," November 12, www.bloomberg.com/news/articles/2013-11-12/china-pledges-decisive-role-for-markets-after-policy-summit.

Bloomberg (2016) "Why China's $1 trillion merger makeover could fail," July 7, Bloomberg, www.bloomberg.com/news/articles/2016-09-07/china-s-1-trillion-makeover-of-bloated-soes-attracts-skeptics.

Blumenthal, D. and Scissors, D.M. (2016) "China's great stagnation," *The National Interest*, October 17, http://nationalinterest.org/feature/chinas-great-stagnation-18073.

Bo, X. (2008) Yao yongyuan jizhu qianbei de lixiang he rexue ("We must forever bear in mind the ideals and passion of our forebears"), *Chongqing Daily*, October 2, http://cpc.people.com.cn/GB/64093/64094/8126279.html.

Brown, K. and Huang, S. (2016) "China: New steps forward in Africa," www.e-ir.info, November 15, www.e-ir.info/2016/11/15/china-new-steps-forward-in-africa/.

Buckley, C. (2013) "Vows of change belie private warning," *New York Times*, February 14, www.nytimes.com/2013/02/15/world/asia/vowing-reform-chinas-leader-xi-jinping-airs-other-message-in-private.html.

Cai, J. (2016) "Will China's 'core' leader Xi Jinping now turn attention to economic reform?" *South China Morning Post*, November 1, www.scmp.com/news/china/policies-politics/article/2041896/will-chinas-core-leader-xi-jinping-now-turn-attention.

Callick, R. (2016) "China's unstable house of cards," *The Australian*, October 3, www.theaustralian.com.au/news/inquirer/chinas-unstable-house-of-cards/news-story/5c332780f297d0eb282105b8a771494f.

Cao, Y. (2015) Xi jiping yinyong Zhou Yi tan yushi jujin: Qiong ze bian, bian ze tong ("Xi Jinping invokes the I Ching to talk about changing with the times: When you see no way out, make changes"), *Guangming Net*, September 24, http://rufodao.qq.com/a/20150924/026160.htm.

Cendrowski, S. (2014) "Why China's rich are leaving," *Fortune*, June 6, http://fortune.com/2014/06/05/china-rich-immigration/.

Cendrowski, S. (2016) "Inside China's global spending spree," *Fortune*, December 12, http://fortune.com/china-belt-road-investment/.

Chang, G.G. (2015) "The Xi Jinping faction in China," *World Affairs*, April 1, www.worldaffairsjournal.org/blog/gordon-g-chang/xi-jinping-faction-china.
Chen, P. (2007) "The CCP has elevated a large number of princelings," www.Chinesepen.org, December 9, www.chinesepen.org/Article/hyxz/200712/Article_20071209210450.shtml.
Chen, W. (2010) "Income gap, a woe for China and U.S.," *China Daily*, October 12, http://usa.chinadaily.com.cn/2010-10/12/content_11399998.htm.
Cheng, L. (2012) "The end of the CCP's resilient authoritarianism? A tripartite assessment of shifting power in China authoritarian resilience," *The China Quarterly*, 211, September, 595–623.
China Daily (2016) "China's WTO entry benefits world," December 10, www.chinadaily.com.cn/business/2016-12/10/content_27631565.htm.
China Labor Bulletin (2001) "China ratifies ICESCR: A change in sight or more of the same?" January 3, www.clb.org.hk/en/content/china-ratifies-icescr-change-sight-or-more-same.
China News Service (2013) Xi Jinping tan fazhan daolu: Xiezi hebuhe jiaochuanzhe cai zhidao ("Xi Jinping on the path of development: Whether a pair of shoes fits only the feet can tell"), March 23, www.chinanews.com/gn/2013/03-23/4670131.shtml.
China News Service (2016) Xi Jinping zai qingzhu zhongguo gongchan dang chengli 95 zhounian dahui shang de jianghua ("Xi Jinping's speech on the occasion of the 95th anniversary of the establishment of the Chinese Communist Party"), July 1, www.chinanews.com/gn/2016/07-01/7924310.shtml.
China.org.cn (2014) "Decision of the Central Committee of the Communist Party of China on some major issues concerning comprehensively deepening the reform," January 16, www.china.org.cn/china/third_plenary_session/2014-01/16/content_31212602.htm.
Chu, Anping (1957) Xiang Mao Zhuxi Zhou Zongli tixue yijian ("Some suggestions for Chairman Mao and Premier Zhou"), *Guangming Daily*, June 1, http://blog.sina.com.cn/s/blog_5bbbd9ff01011vow.html.
CNBC.com (2017) "China Jan FX reserves fall more than expected to $2.998 trillion, near 6-year low," February 7, www.cnbc.com/2017/02/07/china-jan-fx-reserves-fall-more-than-expected-to-2998-trillion-near-6-year-low.html.
CNTV (2014) "Xi gives an interview to a Russian TV channel in Sochi," CNTV, February 8, http://english.cntv.cn/program/newsupdate/20140208/101983.shtml.
Cui, X. (2014) Yinian sanci qinjin rujia: Xi jinping weihe ruci qiangdiao zhongxi chuantong wenhua? ("Xi has touched upon Confucianism three times in one year: Why has Xi Jinping given so much stress to taking up traditional culture?"), *People's Daily*, September 25, http://cpc.people.com.cn/n/2014/0925/c164113-25731729.html.
Dai, H. (2016) Dai Huang: Zuo yige jiang zhenhua de ren ("Dai Huang: Be a person who speaks the truth"), Chinesepen.org, February 20, www.chinesepen.org/blog/archives/46936.
Dangjian Net (2016) Xi Jinping lun dangxing ("Xi Jinping's discourse on party nature"), www.wenming.cn, March 24, www.wenming.cn/djw/sy/jjq/zxdjxx/201603/t20160324_3234080.shtml.
Diamond, L. (2013) "Chinese communism and the 70-year itch," *The Atlantic*, October 29, www.theatlantic.com/china/archive/2013/10/chinese-communism-and-the-70-year-itch/280960/.
Ding, X. (2014) *The China Model: For or Against*, Hong Kong: Oxford University Press.
The Economist (2015) "A very Chinese coup: Li Keqiang is the weakest Chinese prime minister in decades," October 15, www.economist.com/news/china/21674793-li-keqiang-weakest-chinese-prime-minister-decades-very-chinese-coup.
The Economist (2016a) "The worries about China's slowing growth," January 20, http://discover.economist.com/?a=21688673&cid1=d/dsp/Outbrain/dyn/21688673/20160120-00:00am/paid/display-LA/BR-FT/BRPII/n/subs/HK/BR-LIT&cid3=UM.
The Economist (2016b), "China's digital dictatorship," December 17, www.economist.com/news/leaders/21711904-worrying-experiments-new-form-social-control-chinas-digital-dictatorship.
Fallows, J. (2016) "China's great leap backward," *The Atlantic*, www.theatlantic.com/magazine/archive/2016/12/chinas-great-leap-backward/505817/.
Fenby, J. (2014) *Will China Dominate the 21st Century?* Cambridge, U.K.: Polity Press.
Feng, E. (2016) "Xi Jinping reminds China's state companies of who's the boss," *New York Times*, October 13, www.nytimes.com/2016/10/14/world/asia/china-soe-state-owned-enterprises.html?_r=0.
Ferchen, M. (2013) "Whose China model is it anyway? The contentious search for consensus," *Review of International Political Economy*, 20:2, 390–420, DOI:10.1080/09692290.2012.660184.
Fewsmith, J. (2003) "Studying the three represents," *China Leadership Monitor*, No. 8, http://media.hoover.org/sites/default/files/documents/clm8_jf.pdf.

Fewsmith, J. (2016) "The challenges of stability and legitimacy," in Ross, R.S. and Bekkevold J.I. (eds.), *China in the Era of Xi Jinping*, Washington, D.C.: Georgetown University Press.
Financial News (2016) Quanguo Renda daibiao Lai Xiaomin: Goujian yidai yilu zhanlue jinrong zhichi xitong ("NPC member Lai Xiaomin: Build up a strategic financial support system for 'One Belt One Road'"), *Financial News*, March 17, www.financialnews.com.cn/zt/2016lh/taya/201603/t20160317_94102.html.
Financial Times (2017) "Theresa May urges UK and US to resist 'eclipse of the west'," January 27, www.ft.com/content/61003ea0-e3ee-11e6-8405-9e5580d6e5fb.
Foreign Policy (2016) "What is the future of the South China Sea," *Foreign Policy*, July 12, http://foreignpolicy.com/2016/07/12/what-is-the-future-of-the-south-china-sea/.
Forsythe, M. and Mazzetti, M. (2015) "China seeks businessman said to have fled to the U.S., further straining ties," August 3, *New York Times*, www.nytimes.com/2015/08/04/world/asia/china-seeks-ling-wancheng-businessman-said-to-have-fled-to-us.html.
Freeman, C. and Yuan, W. (2010) "China's new left and the China model debate after the financial crisis," Center for Strategic and International Analysis, https://csis-prod.s3.amazonaws.com/s3fs-public/legacy_files/files/publication/110728_Freeman_ChinaNewLeftists_Web.pdf.
Fromm, E. (1961) *Marx's Concept of Man*, New York: Frederick Ungar Publishing, www.marxists.org/archive/fromm/works/1961/man/ch04.htm.
Gilley, B. (2003) "The limits of authoritarian resilience," *Journal of Democracy*, 14.1, 18–26.
Gries, P.H. (2004) *China's New Nationalism: Pride, Politics, and Diplomacy*, Berkeley: University of California Press, pp. 116–150.
The Guardian (2016) "Beware of 'dangerous love' with foreign spies, China tells its women," *The Guardian*, April 20, www.theguardian.com/world/2016/apr/20/beware-of-dangerous-love-with-foreign-spies-china-tells-its-women.
Gui, A. (2016) "Who will remember my father, Gui Minhai?" *Washington Post*, October 17, www.washingtonpost.com/news/global-opinions/wp/2016/10/17/who-will-remember-my-father-gui-minhai/?utm_term=.aac03372862a.
Han, M., Guo, X. and Cui, Y. (2013), "China's new reforms must breach vested interests," Xinhua News Agency, November 4, http://news.xinhuanet.com/english/indepth/2013-11/04/c_132857921.htm.
Harding, R. and Smyth, J. (2017) "Asia looks to Beijing for new trade deals after Trump quits TPP," *Financial Times*, January 24, www.ft.com/content/eeaa19f0-e1fb-11e6-8405-9e5580d6e5fb.
He, W. (2013) Zhongguo meng shi yige zenyang de meng ("What kind of dream should the Chinese Dream be?") He Weifang blog, March 29, http://blog.caijing.com.cn/expert_article-151302-49719.shtml.
Ho, B. (2013) "The rising chorus of Chinese exceptionalism," RSIS Working Paper, No. 256, Singapore: Nanyang Technological University, http://hdl.handle.net/10220/20050.
Holubnychy, V. (1964) "Mao Tse-tung's materialistic dialectics," *The China Quarterly*, 19, 3–37.
Huang, E. (2016) "South Korea says China is retaliating against its missile-defense system by taking aim at Korean dramas," *Quartz*, November 29, http://qz.com/847900/chinas-retaliating-against-south-koreas-missile-defense-system-by-taking-aim-at-korean-dramas/.
Human Rights Watch (2013) "China: Ratify key international human rights treaty," October 8, www.hrw.org/news/2013/10/08/china-ratify-key-international-human-rights-treaty.
Human Rights Watch (2014) "Thailand: Don't forcibly return Uighurs to China," March 14, www.hrw.org/news/2014/03/14/thailand-dont-forcibly-return-uighurs-china.
Jacobs, A. and Buckley, C. (2015) "China targeting rights lawyers in a crackdown," *New York Times*, July 22, www.nytimes.com/2015/07/23/world/asia/china-crackdown-human-rights-lawyers.html?_r=0.
Jin, K. (2016) "The rise of China vs. the rise of the Chinese," *The Diplomat*, May 13, http://thediplomat.com/2016/05/the-rise-of-china-vs-the-rise-of-the-chinese/.
Kennan, G.F. (1947) "The sources of Soviet conduct," *Foreign Affairs*, July, www.foreignaffairs.com/articles/russian-federation/1947-07-01/sources-soviet-conduct.
Kim, D.J. (1994) "Is culture destiny: The myth of Asia's anti-democratic values," *Foreign Affairs*, 73:6 (Nov/Dec), www.foreignaffairs.com/articles/southeast-asia/1994-11-01/culture-destiny-myth-asias-anti-democratic-values.
Kynge, J. (2016) "How the Silk Road plans will be financed," *Financial Times*, May 10, www.ft.com/content/e83ced94-0bd8-11e6-9456-444ab5211a2f.
Lam, W. (2006) *Chinese Politics in the Hu Jintao Era: New Leaders, New Challenges*, Armonk, NY: M.E. Sharpe, pp. 65–68.

Lam, W. (2009) "The politicization of China's law-enforcement and judicial apparatus," *China Perspectives*, 2, 42–51, http://search.proquest.com/openview/42a7863f0503642230f049f8431668ae/1?pq-origsite=gscholar.

Lam, W. (2011) "Intra-party democracy with Chinese characteristics," in Cheng, J. (ed.), *Whither China's Democracy: Democratization in China since the Tiananmen Incident*, Hong Kong: Hong Kong City University Press, pp. 33–64.

Lam, W. (2015a) *Chinese Politics in the Era of Xi Jinping: Renaissance, Reform or Retrogression*, London and New York: Routledge.

Lam, W. (2015b) "Xi Jinping forever," *Foreign Policy*, April 1, http://foreignpolicy.com/2015/04/01/xi-jinping-forever-china-president-term-limits/.

Lam, W. (2016a) "Xi Jinping uses new 'leadership core' status to boost his faction," *China Brief*, Jamestown Foundation, November 11, https://jamestown.org/program/xi-jinping-uses-new-leadership-core-status-boost-faction/#sthash.9HVJkb3S.dpuf.

Lam, W. (2016b) "The emergence of the Wang Qishan faction," *China Brief*, Jamestown Foundation, December 21, https://jamestown.org/program/emergence-wang-qishan-faction/.

Lam, W. (2017) "Beijing's new scorched-earth policy against the Uighurs," *China Brief*, Jamestown Foundation, February 6, https://jamestown.org/program/beijings-new-scorched-earth-policy-uighurs/.

Leng, S. and Tang F. (2017) "China 'must prepare to face the unexpected'," *South China Morning Post*, March 4, p. A3.

Li, K. (2013) Li Keqiang: Yong zhuangshi duanwan juexin tuidong gaige ("Li Keqiang: Use the determination of a brave fighter cutting off his wrist to push forward reform"), China News Service, http://news.sohu.com/20130910/n386313722.shtml.

Li, Z. (2004) Deng Xiaoping yu shehui zhuyi chuji jieduan de jiben luxian ("Deng Xiaoping and the basic line of the primary stage of socialism"), *Zhonggong dangshi yanjiu* (*Research on History of the Chinese Communist Party*), 5, 10–18.

Li, Z. (2013) Zunxun sige jianchi de gaige jingyan ("Follow the reform experience under the 'Four Cardinal Principles' "), *People's Daily*, November 26, http://opinion.people.com.cn/n/2013/1126/c1003-23658969.html.

McGregor, R. (2010) *The Party: The Secret World of China's Communist Rulers*, New York: HarperCollins, pp. 1–33.

Mai, J. (2015) "Chinese author of 'Democracy is a Good Thing' resigns from Communist Party bureau," *South China Morning Post*, October 28, www.scmp.com/news/china/policies-politics/article/1873493/chinese-author-democracy-good-thing-resigns-communist.

Mitchell, C. (2016) "Speculation grows Xi Jinping will defy China rule on leadership retirement," *Financial Times*, October 11, www.ft.com/content/09cc1044-8f77-11e6-a72e-b428cb934b78.

Mao, Z. (1942) "Talks at the Yan'an forum on literature and art," in *Selected Works of Mao Tse-tung*, www.marxists.org/reference/archive/mao/selected-works/volume-3/mswv3_08.html.

Mitchell, T. (2016) "Xi's China: The rise of party politics. Part one: The president is wresting control of economic policy away from other parts of government," *Financial Times*, July 25, www.ft.com/content/57371736-4b69-11e6-88c5-db83e98a590a.

Nathan, A.J. (2003) "Authoritarian resilience," *Journal of Democracy*, 14.1, 6–17.

Nathan, A.J. (2016) "China's challenge," in Diamond, L., Plaattner, M.F. and Walker, C. (eds.), *Authoritarianism Goes Global: The Challenge to Democracy*, Baltimore, M.D.: Johns Hopkins University Press.

National Public Radio (2015) "China is weak and bloated by government investment, experts say," www.npr.org, August 21, www.npr.org/2015/08/21/433402287/china-is-weak-and-bloated-by-government-investment-experts-say.

Naughton, B. (2010) "China's distinctive system: Can it be a model for others?" *Journal of Contemporary China*, 19:65, 437–460.

Naughton, B. (2016) "The challenges of economic growth and reform," in Ross, R.S. and J.I. Bekkevold (eds.), *China in the Era of Xi Jinping: Domestic and Foreign Policy Challenges*, Washington, D.C.: Georgetown University Press, pp. 66–91.

New York Times (2017) "China's Chief Justice rejects an independent judiciary, and reformers wince," January 18, www.nytimes.com/2017/01/18/world/asia/china-chief-justice-courts-zhou-qiang.html?_r=0.

News.sohu.com (2016) Wang Qishan qunian tichu de zhe qida renwu, xianzai du ruhe le? ("Wang Qishan last year raised seven major tasks: What have become of them now?"), January 12, http://news.sohu.com/20160112/n434315608.shtml.

Palmer, J. (2016) "What China didn't learn from the collapse of the Soviet Union," *Foreign Policy*, December 24, http://foreignpolicy.com/2016/12/24/what-china-didnt-learn-from-the-collapse-of-the-soviet-union/.

Pei, M. (2013) "Is CCP rule fragile or resilient?" in Nathan, A.J. *et al.* (eds.), *Will China Democratize?* Baltimore, M.D.: Johns Hopkins University Press.

Peng, G. and Yang, X. (2010) Ruhe lijie "zhongguo moshi" ("How to interpret the 'China model'"?), *People's Daily*, September 15, http://news.xinhuanet.com/politics/2010-09/15/c_12552989.htm.

People's Daily (2013) Shenke lijie shehui zhuyi hexin jiazhiguan de naihan he yiyi ("Deeply understand the contents and significance of core socialist values"), May 22, http://theory.people.com.cn/n/2013/0522/c40531-21565926.html.

People's Daily (2014a) Xin shejishi xi jinping: Wenhua bian ("New architect Xi Jinping's discourse on culture"), November 14, http://politics.people.com.cn/n/2014/1115/c1001-26032453.html.

People's Daily (2014b) Xijinping chuxi zhongyang zhengfa gongzuo huiyi bing fabiao zhongyao jianghua ("Xi Jinping appears in Central Political-Legal Work Meeting and makes important speech"), January 9, http://cpc.people.com.cn/n/2014/0109/c64094-24065903.html.

Petracca, M.P. and Xiong, M. (1990) "The concept of Chinese neo-authoritarianism: An exploration and democratic critique," *Asian Survey*, 30:11 (Nov), 1099–1117.

Philips, T. (2016) "No country for academics: Chinese crackdown forces intellectuals abroad," *The Guardian*, May 24, www.theguardian.com/world/2016/may/24/academics-china-crackdown-forces-intellectuals-abroad.

Radio Free Asia (2015) "Thailand forcibly repatriating more than 90 Uyghurs to China: Exile group," July 8, www.rfa.org/english/news/uyghur/repatriation-07082015175513.html.

Rajagopalan, M. (2013) "Vested interests won't block China's reforms: Party official," Reuters, November 22, www.reuters.com/article/2013/11/22/us-china-reforms-idUSBRE9AL0G120131122/.

Rapp-Hooper, R. (2016) "Parting the South China Sea: How to uphold the law," *Foreign Affairs*, July 22, www.foreignaffairs.com/articles/china/2016-07-22/parting-south-china-sea.

Ren, Z. (2013) Shouhe renmin zhengdang de shengmingxian ("Safeguard the lifeline of the people's party"), *People's Daily*, October 14, http://opinion.people.com.cn/n/2013/1014/c1003-23187114.html.

Reuters (2013a) "China hikes defense budget, to spend more on domestic security," March 5, www.reuters.com/article/us-china-parliament-defence-idUSBRE92403620130305.

Reuters (2013b) "China's top farm official reins in land reform expectations," December 5, www.reuters.com/article/2013/12/05/china-agriculture-land-idUSL4N0J51GF20131205/.

Reuters (2016a) "China financial outbound direct investment surges 26 percent in 2015," September 22, www.reuters.com/article/us-china-economy-odi-idUSKCN11S06X.

Reuters (2016b) "Norway, China normalize ties after Nobel Peace Prize row," December 19, www.reuters.com/article/us-norway-china-idUSKBN1480R4.

Reuters (2017) "As Trump stresses 'America First,' China plays the world leader," January 15, www.reuters.com/article/us-usa-trump-china-analysis-idUSKBN1590KJ.

Riley, C. and Chang, W. (2015) "China is blaming short sellers for its stock market crash," CNN, August 4, http://money.cnn.com/2015/08/04/investing/china-stock-market-short-selling/.

Ringen, S. (2016) *The Perfect Dictatorship: China in the 21st Century*, Hong Kong: Hong Kong University Press.

Roberts, D. (2013) "Is land reform finally coming to China?" *Businessweek*, November 20, www.bloomberg.com/news/articles/2013-11-20/is-land-reform-finally-coming-to-china.

Sautman, B. (1992) "Sirens of the strongman: Neo-authoritarianism in recent Chinese political theory," *The China Quarterly*, 129 (March), 72–102.

Sceats, S. and Breslin, S. (2012) "China and the international human rights system," London, Chatham House, October, www.chathamhouse.org/sites/files/chathamhouse/public/Research/International%20Law/r1012_sceatsbreslin.pdf.

Schell, O. (2016) "Crackdown in China: Worse and worse," *New York Review of Books*/China File, April 6, www.chinafile.com/nyrb-china-archive/crackdown-china-worse-and-worse.

Schell, O. and Delury, J. (2013) *Wealth and Power: China's Long March to the Twenty-First Century*, London: Abacus.

Shambaugh, D. (2016) *China's Future*, Malden, M.A.: Polity Press.

Singtao Daily (2016) "Xi hexin" jian quanwei, "qishangbaxia" buzu xin ("Core leader Xi has built up his authority, the retire at 68 rule is not trustworthy"), November 1, www.singpao.com.hk/index.php?fi=news1&id=8518.

Smith, J. (2016) "The challenges of stability and legitimacy," in Ross, R.S. and Bekkevold, J.I. (eds.), *China in the Era of Xi Jinping: Domestic and Foreign Policy Challenges*, Washington, D.C.: Georgetown University Press.
Study and Research (2013) Chujin dangde lingdao renmin dangjia zuozhu yifa zhiguo youji tongyi ("Foster the organic unification of party leadership, the people mastering their own affairs, and governing the country according to law"), February 25, http://theory.people.com.cn/n/2013/0225/c49150-20593862.html.
Study Times (2013) Dangxing shi renxing de youhua, shenghua he jiejing ("Party nature is the improvement, sublimation, and crystallization of human nature"), August 19, http://news.china.com/domestic/945/20130819/18003473.html.
Su, Z., Zhao, H. and He, J. (2013) "Authoritarianism and contestation," in Nathan, A.J., Diamond, L. and Plattner, M.F. (eds.), *Will China Democratize?* Baltimore, M.D.: Johns Hopkins University Press, pp. 137–152.
Sun, M. (2017) "China protests South Korea's antimissile system – with consumer boycotts," *Christian Science Monitor*, March 4, www.csmonitor.com/World/2017/0304/China-protests-South-Korea-s-antimissile-system-with-consumer-boycotts.
Tang, W. (2016) *Populist Authoritarianism: Chinese Political Culture and Regime Sustainability*, New York: Oxford University Press.
Tao, W. (2013) *Ruhe lijie buzou xielou* ("How to understand not going down a 'devious path'"), *Beijing Daily*, May 30, http://theory.people.com.cn/n/2013/0520/c49150-21537604.html.
Tian, X. (2015) Jingti "gongchan zhuyi xuwu piaomiao" lun ("Beware of the theory that 'Communism is ethereal and hard to touch'"), Xinhua News Agency, October 12, http://news.xinhuanet.com/politics/2015-10/12/c_128308807.htm.
Tibet.net (2016) "A Tibetan self-immolates in Tibet," December 8, http://tibet.net/2016/12/a-tibetan-self-immolates-in-tibet/.
Twenty-First Century History (2012) "Dialogue between Chairman Mao and Huang Yanpei on the law of cycles in history," December 27, http://news.21cn.com/history/lishijiaodian/2012/12/27/14187388.shtml.
Walt, M.W. (2012) "The myth of Chinese exceptionalism," *Foreign Policy*, March 6, http://foreignpolicy.com/2012/03/06/the-myth-of-chinese-exceptionalism/.
Wan, L. (2015) "Wan Li: Rendering decision-making democratic and scientific is an important issue for reform of the political structure," *Caixin Net*, July 16, http://opinion.caixin.com/2015-07-16/100829416.html.
Wang, C. (2015) Shengsheng zhiwei yi: Zhouyi de sanchong aoyi ("Change consists in infinite creativity: The three mysterious meanings of *Zhou Yi*"), *Guangming Daily*, September 28, http://xueshu.baidu.com/s?wd=paperuri%3A%28c08575f97e3b47e4a2b2e0a8dd4dda62%29&filter=sc_long_sign&tn=SE_xueshusource_2kduw22v&sc_vurl=http%3A%2F%2Fwww.qstheory.cn%2Fculture%2F2015-09%2F28%2Fm_1116698336.htm&ie=utf-8&sc_us=11577259795973866797.
Wang, X. (2013) Lixang xinnian shi gongchan dangren jingshenshang de "gai" ("Ideals and beliefs are the spiritual 'calcium' of Communists"), *People's Daily*, December 5, http://theory.people.com.cn/n/2013/1205/c40537-23757123.html.
Wen, J. (2007) "Wen Jiabao: On several questions about the historical tasks of the preliminary stage of socialism and China's policy toward other countries," Xinhua News Agency, February 26, http://news.xinhuanet.com/politics/2007-02/26/content_5775212.htm.
The White House (2015) "Statement by the President on the Trans-Pacific Partnership," The White House Press Office, October 5, www.whitehouse.gov/the-press-office/2015/10/05/statement-president-trans-pacific-partnership.
Wilson, I. (1989) "Socialism with Chinese characteristics: China and the theory of the initial stage of socialism," *Australian Journal of Political Science*, 24:1, 77–84.
Wong, C. (2017) "China to push forward own trade vision after Trump withdraws from Pacific deal," *South China Morning Post*, January 24, www.scmp.com/news/china/diplomacy-defence/article/2064956/chinese-analysts-cautious-over-whether-us-withdrawal.
Wong, E., Gough, N. and Stevenson, A. (2015) "China's response to stock plunge rattles traders," *New York Times*, September 10, www.nytimes.com/2015/09/10/world/asia/in-china-a-forceful-crackdown-in-response-to-stock-market-crisis.html?_r=0.
Wu, W. (2016) "China's leaders sending 'confusing, inconsistent' messages over economic reform," *South China Morning Post*, November 16, www.scmp.com/news/china/economy/article/2046500/chinese-leadership-sending-confusing-messages-over-reform-state.

Xi, J. (2008a) Xi Jinping qiangdiao jianchi gaige chuangxin tuidong nongcun fazhan, hongyang youliang chuangtong jiaqiang dang de jiangshe ("Xi Jinping emphasizes the need to develop the villages through reform and innovation, and to strengthen party construction by developing our superior tradition"), CCTV, October 5, http://tv.people.com.cn/GB/61600/8179126.html.

Xi, J. (2008b) Dangde zhizheng diwei bushi yilao yongyi ("The Party's ruling status cannot always be taken for granted"), September 9, www.southcn.com/nfdaily/china/shizheng/content/2008-09/09/content_4589087.htm.

Xi, J. (2009) Xi Jinping: Quan shehui yao hongyang chuangxin jingshen tigao chuangxin nengli ("Xi Jinping: The entire society should develop the spirit of innovation and raise its ability in innovation"), Xinhua News Agency, September 20, http://news.xinhuanet.com/politics/2009-09/20/content_12081594.htm.

Xi, J. (2013a) Xi Jinping: Bixu jianding zhongguo tese shehui zhuyi zixin ("Xi Jinping: We must uphold self-confidence in socialism with Chinese characteristics"), *Dongfang Zaobao*, June 7, http://news.sina.com.cn/c/2013-06-27/100027511991.shtml.

Xi, J. (2013b) Xi Jinping: Buneng yong gaigekaifang qianhou lishi xianghe fouding ("Xi Jinping: We cannot use the pre-reform period of history to negate the post-reform period of history, or vice versa"), Xinhua News Agency, January 5, www.zj.xinhuanet.com/newscenter/InAndAbroad/2013-01/05/c_114258858.htm.

Xi, J. (2013c) Xi jinping, genben wentishang buneng chuxian dianfuxing cuowu ("Xi Jinping: Subversive mistakes must not be made over fundamental issues"), China News Service, October 8, www.china-news.com/gn/2013/10-08/5347578.shtml.

Xi, J. (2013d) Xi Jinping guanyu shixian zhonghua minzu weida fuxing de zhongguomeng lunshu ("Xi Jinping's discourse on the Chinese dream of the great renaissance of the Chinese people"), *People's Daily*, December 5, http://theory.people.com.cn/n/2013/1205/c40555-23756883.html.

Xi, J. (2013e) Xi Jinping: Yao jianchi dangde lingdao, renmin dangjia zuozhu, yifazhiguo youji tongyi ("Xi Jinping: We must uphold the organic unification of party leadership, the people mastering their own affairs, and governing the country according to law"), Xinhua News Agency, March 17, http://gb.cri.cn/42071/2013/03/17/4865s4055118.htm.

Xi, J. (2013f) The maozedong tongzhi danchen 120 zhounian zuotanhui shang de jianghua ("Talk at the seminar marking the 120th birthday of Comrade Mao Zedong"), December 26, http://news.xinhuanet.com/politics/2013-12/26/c_118723453.htm.

Xi, J. (2014a) Xi Jinping: Ruguo dang kuale, zhengji haiyou he yiyi? ("Xi Jinping: If the party were to collapse, what meaning will policy achievements have?"), *Jinghua Times*, October 9, http://news.sohu.com/20141009/n404926662.shtml.

Xi, J. (2014b) Xi Jinping youguan yifa zhiguo lunshu ("Xi Jinping's discourse on administering the country according to law"), *People's Daily* Overseas Edition, October 17, http://news.sina.com.cn/c/2014-10-17/075731003162.shtml.

Xi, J. (2016a) Xi Jinping tan "yidai yilu": Zhe sannian chaochu yuqi ("Xi Jinping on 'One Belt One Road': Expectations have been exceeded in these three years"), *Global Times*, September 12, http://china.huanqiu.com/article/2016-09/9430904.html.

Xi, J. (2016b) Xi Jinping: Dang he zhengfu zhuban meiti buxu xingdang ("Xi Jinping: Media run by the party and government must have the party as their surnames"), *New Beijing Post*, February 20, http://news.china.com/domesticgd/10000159/20160220/21558094.html.

Xi, J. (2016c) Xi Jinping tan wenhua zixin ("Xi Jinping on cultural self-confidence"), *People's Daily*, July 13, http://cpc.people.com.cn/n1/2016/0713/c64094-28548844.html.

Xi, J. (2016d) Xi Jinping: Ji buzou fengbi jianghua de lulao, ye buzou gaiqi yizhi de xielu ("Xi Jinping: We will not pursue closed and stultified paths, nor will we go down evil roads that [will result in] the changing of our flags and standards"), Xinhua News Agency, July 1, http://news.youth.cn/sz/201607/t20160701_ 8216014.htm.

Xiao, G. (2011) Minzhu zhuyi de "qujijin hua" qushi ("The 'deradicalizing' trend of nationalism"), *Renmin luntan* (People's Tribune), 1, 26–27.

Xiao, G. (2015) Xi Jinping xinzheng shi xin quanwei zhuyi qianghua ban ("The new governance of Xi Jinping is a strengthened version of neo-authoritarianism"), News.ifeng.com, January 8, http://news.ifeng.com:8080/exclusive/lecture/special/xiaogongqin3/.

Xiao, S. (2013) *The Harbingers of History*, Hong Kong: Media Studies Center, University of Hong Kong.

Xinhua News Agency (2008) Renmin fayuan yao jianchi "sange zhishang" zhidao sixiang ("The people's courts must uphold the guiding thought of 'the three top priorities' "), August 4, www.qh.xinhuanet.com/qhpeace/2008-08/04/content_14020362.htm.

Xinhua News Agency (2014a) Zhongzubu: Xuan ganbu buzai weipiao weifen weiGDP ("Central Organization Department: Selection of cadres should not be based solely on votes, marks and GDP"), September 2, http://news.wenweipo.com/2014/09/02/IN1409020051.htm.

Xinhua News Agency (2014b) "Xi Jinping gives interview to Russian TV," February 9, http://news.xinhuanet.com/world/2014-02/09/c_119248735.htm.

Xinhua News Agency (2015) "China champions legal protection of human rights," July 24, http://news.xinhuanet.com/english/2015-07/24/c_134444752.htm.

Xinhua News Agency (2017a) "China's ODI down 35.7 pct in January," February 16, www.ecns.cn/business/2017/02-16/245674.shtml.

Xinhua News Agency (2017b) "Spotlight: Growing foreign cooperation attests China's commitment to opening-up," March 2, http://news.xinhuanet.com/english/2017-03/02/c_136096338.htm.

Xu, C. (2016) Guanli yaoyong fazhi erfei xingzheng mingling ("Management must be based on rule of law and not executive fiats"), *First Financial Daily*, December 4, http://money.163.com/16/1204/14/C7ET4NB6002581PP.html.

Xu, Z. (2015) "Shu Guozeng introduces the three important substantial results of China-U.S. economic cooperation," *People's Daily*, September 18, http://politics.people.com.cn/n/2015/0918/c1001-27601375.html.

Yan, X. (2016) Gaige nengli yingxiang guojia de shili ("The capacity for reform affects the nation's strength"), Chinareform.org.cn, November 10, www.chinareform.org.cn/Explore/perspectives/201611/t20161110_257260.htm.

Yang, G. (2016) "A 'chariot system' driven by vested interests," Chinareform.org.cn, September 18, www.chinareform.org.cn/open/governance/201609/t20160918_255513.htm.

Yu, J. (2016) Yu Jianrong gei zhongyang lingdao ti shige "buyao" (Yu jianrong raises 'ten don'ts' in open letter to central leadership"), Weibo.com, February 26, www.weibo.com/ttarticle/p/show?id=2309403946812338757529.

Yu, K. (2006) Minzhu shige hao dongxi ("Democracy is a good thing"), *People's Daily*, December 28, http://theory.people.com.cn/GB/49150/49152/5224247.html.

Zhang, F. (2011) "The rise of Chinese exceptionalism in international relations," *European Journal of International Relations*, October 27, http://journals.sagepub.com/doi/abs/10.1177/1354066111421038.

Zhang, W. (2006) "The allure of the Chinese model," *International Herald Tribune*, November 2, www.sinoptic.ch/textes/articles/2006/20061102_zhang.weiwei_chinese.model-en.pdf.

Zhang, W. (2012) "Ideas will determine China's future," *Wall Street Journal*, August 1, www.wsj.com/articles/SB10000872396390444320704577562463319136168.

Zhang, W. (2015) "The power of ideas and leadership in China's transition to a liberal society," *Cato Journal*, 35:1 (Winter), https://object.cato.org/sites/cato.org/files/serials/files/cato-journal/2015/2/cj-v35n1-full.pdf.

Zhang, Y. (2015) Yidai yilu you fengxian, keneng yibai nian cai jiancheng (" 'One Belt One Road' carries risks; it could take 100 years"), Gb.cri.cn, March 6, http://gb.cri.cn/42071/2015/03/06/8011s4892016.htm.

Zhao, S. (2005) "Nationalism's double edge," *The Wilson Quarterly*, 29:4, 76–82.

Zhao, S. (2010) "The China model: Can it replace the Western model of modernization?" *Journal of Contemporary China*, 19:65, 419–436, DOI:10.1080/10670561003666061.

Zhao, Z. (1987) Zhao Ziyang zai zhongguo gongchan dang di shisanci quanguo daibiao dahui shang de baogao ("Zhao Ziyang's report on the 13th National Congress of the Chinese Communist Party"), October 25, http://cpc.people.com.cn/GB/64162/64168/64566/65447/4526370.html.

Zhao, Z. (2011) Guanyu dangzheng fengkai ("On the separation of party and government"), China.com.cn, April 12, www.china.com.cn/info/txt/2011-04/12/content_22343328.htm.

Zhelyazkov, I. (2015) "Most popular emigration destinations for China's elite," Internchina.com, February 10, https://internchina.com/most-popular-emigration-destinations-for-chinas-elite/.

Zheng, Y. and Yang, L. (2016) *The Mistakes that China Cannot Afford to Make during its Rise*, Beijing: China Citic Press.

Zhu, H. (2013) Wan, Li: Shixing juece de minzhuhua kexuehua ("Wan Li: Implementing democratic and scientific decision-making"), *People's Daily*, May 21, http://dangshi.people.com.cn/n/2013/0521/c364217-21561993.html.

PART II

History and traditions

2

THE LEGACY OF MAO ZEDONG

Yiu-Chung Wong and Willy Wo-Lap Lam

Introduction: "we are all students of the Great Helmsman"

Despite accusations that the Great Proletarian Cultural Revolution (GPCR) and other horrendous policies of Mao Zedong led to the deaths of some 40 million Chinese, the image of the charismatic Great Helmsman looms large not only in the country's history but also its future. As Cui Jian, China's talented rock singer, pointed out a few years ago, as long as the giant portrait of the Chairman is still hanging over the rostrum of Tiananmen Square, the Cultural Revolution – and the Maoist phase of Chinese history – has not really ended (Cui 2014).

The year 2016 being the 50th anniversary of the start of the GPCR (1966–76), there is much speculation among intellectuals and liberal cadres whether the Ten Years of Chaos might make a comeback. Retired cadre Yu Youjun spoke for many when he noted during a lecture at Sun Yat-Sen University in Guangdong Province that "the soil for the Cultural Revolution is still fertile." Yu, a former governor of Shanxi Province and party secretary of the Ministry of Culture, indicated that "especially when the people have no reasonable and profound knowledge of Mao's mistakes, the GPCR may partially recur, under certain historical conditions" (*Global Times* 2015).

Yet Mao is of much more importance than historical interest. Chinese Communist Party (CCP) General Secretary Xi Jinping, who is deemed a "closet Maoist," is restituting many of Mao's norms and ambitions with gusto. It was perhaps not coincidental that two of the most influential Western publications ran in the spring of 2016 similar cover stories comparing Xi to Mao. "Chairman Xi: China's President makes like Mao," said *Time* magazine. "Beware the cult of Xi," intoned *The Economist*. (Both issues were banned in China.) A popular YouTube paean to Xi, entitled "The East is red again; the sun is once more on the rise," asserted that "Xi Jinping is the successor of Mao Zedong," and that he is "the people's Lucky Star" and "the Nation's Guide" (V.qq.com 2016).

This chapter looks at Mao's successful adaptation of Marxism and Leninism to Chinese soil. This is despite the fact that by most definitions of Marxism, China of the 1920s and 1930s was not "ripe" for a revolution with workers as the vanguard. The Chairman's genius lay in his applying Lenin's idea of the revolutionary party as well as "dictatorship of the proletariat" to establish the CCP and to enable the party to assume near-absolutist powers over all sectors of society. Deng Xiaoping's deMaoification campaign, including economic and political liberalization policies, will be examined. However, the Chief Architect of Reform's repressive measures, which culminated in the Tiananmen Square massacre, showed that the so-called Maoist credo of zero tolerance for dissent was alive and well. How former general secretaries Jiang Zemin and Hu Jintao handled the remnants of Maoism will be discussed in detail. This chapter ends by examining President Xi's restitution of important Maoist norms such as ideological campaigns and suppression of freedom of expression – and how this will impact the development of the party-state apparatus in the coming decade or so.

Mao's debt to Marx, Engels, Lenin and Stalin

To elucidate the massive influence which Mao and Maoism have had on the development of China until today, it is important to note that Mao's knowledge of the teachings of Karl Marx and Friedrich Engels was limited. By contrast, the Great Helmsman inherited Lenin's utilitarian – some might say Machiavellian – ways of ensuring the supremacy of the party by subjugating all forces of opposition, including the well-educated intelligentsia, under the "dictatorship of the proletariat."

Historically, socialism emerged as a reaction to the seamy sides of the capitalist order: it was an indictment of the greed and exploitation that went hand in hand with private enterprises. Socialist movements are geared toward creating a fair and just society that would eliminate the evils brought about by capitalism. The organization of production through the market is replaced by production based on plans formulated by a supposedly benign state machinery. The driving force of capitalist accumulation will be replaced by the conscious striving to reach generous social goals such as egalitarianism and a welfare state (Sweezy 1949: 7; Huberman and Sweezy 1968: 39–52).

Marx's historical materialism asserts that one stage of social development will inevitably be replaced by a more advanced stage. In *Socialism: Utopian and Scientific*, Engels describes vividly how the capitalist mode of production will pave the way for the rise of proletariats, which will in turn lead to the awakening of class consciousness and the revolutionary overthrow of exploiting classes (Tucker 1978: 605–639). In *Critique of the Gotha Program*, Marx envisages an advanced stage of society in which workers will not be enslaved by division of labor ordained by the owners of the factors of production. Labor will cease to be a demeaning way to make ends meet – and will become a fountainhead of satisfaction and achievement. The ideal state characterized by Marx's famous adage – "From each according to his ability, to each according to his needs!" – will be reached (Tucker 1978: 531).

For Marx, communism or socialism is an ideal state of society, where phenomena of human self-estrangement and the strong preying on the weak will be consigned to the dustbin of history. Production is not for profit but the social good. Even nature will be brought into control by human rationality (Marx 1976: 365). However, Marxist notions of socialism or the higher stage of communism are vague; Marx, Engels and their colleagues never elaborated on the concept of a Communist Party and its ruling methods (Tucker 1978: 483). Both Marxists and non-Marxists recognize that Marx and Engels never clearly formulated comprehensive notions of socialism. For example, noted American Marxist scholar Bertell Ollman pointed out that Marx never offered a systematic account of communism aside from some general guidelines. For Marx, communism or socialism was an ideal society, where human estrangement or alienation was superseded. Communism was the "negation of negation" and the realm of freedom

> cannot consist of anything but the fact that socialized mankind, the associated producers, regulate their interchange with nature rationally instead of being ruled by it as by some

> blind power, and accomplish their task ... under such conditions as are proper and worthy for human beings.
>
> *(Marx 1909: 954; Tucker 1975: 365)*

Alec Nove also pointed out that "Marx had little to say about the economics of socialism" (Nove 1983: 10).

While Marx and Engels were theorists, Lenin was a pragmatic revolutionary activist. The central goal of Lenin's political activities was to overthrow Tsarist despotism and establish a socialist country. Marxism was subsumed under this goal; indeed Lenin and the Bolsheviks played fast and loose with Marxist concepts to suit political realities of the day and to justify draconian dictatorship to be imposed by the top echelon of the Communist Party of the Soviet Union (CPSU). A seminal theme of Lenin's writings was the imperative of theoretical struggles. His work was always polemical. He seemed to be constantly waging verbal wars against ideological foes such as Marxist theorists George Plekhanov (1856–1918) and Karl Kautsky (1854–1938). As Lenin put it, "Without revolutionary theory there can be no revolutionary movement" (Tucker 1975: 20).

The second contribution of Lenin is the concept of the dictatorship of the proletariat – a means to focus the "special coercive force" of the state for the purpose of destroying class enemies such as the bourgeoisie. The phenomenon of millions of working people being exploited by a handful of the rich must be stopped. Moreover, proletarian dictatorship must be exercised by a party that assumes near-omnipotent power (Tucker 1975: 274). As historian Hal Draper pointed out, Marx and Engels' definition of the "dictatorship of the proletariat" was simply "rule of the proletariat" – the conquest of political power by the working class and the establishment of a fairly vague "workers' state in the immediate post-revolutionary period" (Draper 1987: 26). For Lenin, however, dictatorship of the proletariat meant "a special organized dictatorial regime, dictatorial in the sense that had become increasingly dominant and increasingly counter-posed to abstract democracy" (Draper 1987: 104–105).

For Marx the revolutionary dictatorship of the proletariat was only a brief interim period between capitalism and socialism or communism. It was Lenin who extended the notion to cover the entire transition phase (Sik 1976: 376). Lenin's mobilization activities centered on the notion of a "revolutionary vanguard party" which was only hinted at by Marx but never fully elaborated (Tucker 1978: 527–539). Lenin's aim was to set up a purpose-made revolutionary party organization for Russia's specific conditions. To meet the needs of clandestine activities, the party would consist of professional revolutionaries for whom seizing – and holding – power was the be-all and end-all of their calling. As Lenin put it with characteristic verve: "Give us an organization of revolutionaries, and we shall overturn the whole of Russia!" Lenin also put forward the idea of "democratic centralism" to centralize powers at the very top echelon of the revolutionary party (Tucker 1975: xl).

It seemed obvious that the Leninist approach to power and governance could succumb to the totalitarian temptation. Marxist scholar Rosa Luxemburg, who was a contemporary of Lenin, saw very early on the danger of a ruling party, whatever its ideological inclination, riding herd over the masses. She wrote:

> In reality only a dozen outstanding heads do the leading and an elite of the working class is invited from time to time to meeting where they are to applaud the speeches of the leaders and to approve proposed resolutions unanimously, a dictatorship to be sure, not the dictatorship of the proletariat but only the dictatorship of a handful of politicians,
>
> *(Looker 1974: 245–247)*

The notion that socialism and communism constituted successive phases of social development began to play a larger role in Lenin's writings after the Bolshevik Revolution. By 1919, he made the distinction quite clearly. Lenin admitted that Russia had not even attained the lower stage of socialism. The revolution had created the trappings of a socialist state and proclaimed the nationalization of the means of production; yet the proletarian state as represented by the vanguard party should carry on the task of "building socialism." Lenin's successor Joseph Stalin pushed through collectivization drives to nationalize or socialize all means of production. Individual or private farms and work units were nationalized in what was known as a "revolution from above." In the late 1920s, some 25 million individual farms were forcefully collectivized, many of which were converted to *kolkhozy* or collective farms, which were run by coercive administrative units.

The collectivization campaign, in fact, was a bloody war against the peasantry. "Collectivization degenerated into military operation, a cruel civil war. Rebellious villages were surrounded by machine guns and forced to surrender" (Deutscher 1990: 324–325). The "Stalin Model" emphasized the importance of centralized planning, priority investment in heavy industries, neglect of consumer industries, brutal and forced transformation of individual farming into collective and state farms. In tandem with Leninist "democratic centralism," Stalin also began the building of a personality cult unrivalled in the annals of European history. Under the rule of Stalin, in fact, a mono-organizational and largely monolithic society was formed. Soviet historian Roy Medvedev noted that Stalin's "pseudo-socialism was the gross violation of human principles, under cover of lying, talking about love for the people and socialist ideals … [there was] nothing socialist in mass arrests and the murder of innocent people" (Medvedev 1989: 856).

Mao's idea of socialism, dictatorship of the proletariat and the uninterrupted revolution

Marx and Engels very seldom mentioned China in their works – for the very simple reason that they did not think China, which remained a predominantly feudal country until the early twentieth century, was ripe for a Marxist-style revolution. After all, Marxist historical materialism outlines a five-stage development, from "primitive communal," through slavery, feudalism, capitalism and finally socialism/communism (Tucker 1978: 701–717). Mao also understood well that national conditions were not ready for the usual type of Marxist revolution. In his landmark "Analysis of the Classes in Chinese Society," the young revolutionary wrote that Chinese society was made up of five strata: "the big bourgeoisie, the middle bourgeoisie, the petite bourgeoisie, semi-proletariats and proletariats." Mao admitted that in China, "the modern industrial proletariat numbers about two million." "Though not very numerous, the industrial proletariat represents China's new productive forces, is the most progressive class in modern China and has become the leading force in the revolutionary movement," Mao claimed (Mao 1926). It was very clear, however, that Mao differed from early leaders of the CCP who followed the Russian line by trying to start insurrection in the cities. For the tactical genius, the path to victory was through converting millions of peasants to the cause of the revolution.

Mao's notion of socialism and socialist rule came mainly via Lenin and Stalin rather than Marx or Engels. In launching a successful revolution in an underdeveloped country like China, Mao attributed his success to three weapons, namely first, building up and strengthening a Leninist-style party; second, implementing the policies of United Front; and third, establishing military power and encircling cities by the guerrilla warfare waged from the countryside. The tactics resulted in overthrowing the Kuomintang (KMT) regime which ruled the Republic of

China (ROC) from 1927 to 1949 in mainland China (Mao 1975, Vol. II: 285–296). Among the three weapons, Mao, who founded the Red Army, no doubt relied mostly on military power. This was summed up in one of Mao's most renowned dictums: "Power grows out of the barrel of a gun." Mao remained chairman of the CCP's Central Military Commission from 1935 to 1976. Because of the vast hinterland in Chinese rural areas and strong fortification build-up in the big cities by the KMT, Mao invented the revolutionary strategies of developing "red bases" in the countryside and gradually encircling big cities until power was seized nationwide.

Mao was a faithful follower of the Leninist doctrine that the socialist cause must be embraced by a dedicated cadre of revolutionaries at the apex of the party – and that opponents must be crushed in the name of the "dictatorship of the proletariat," the nature of which will be determined by the revolutionary leaders. Following the Leninist tradition, Dictatorship of the Proletariat simply means the dictatorship of the party so as to ensure the CCP's status as China's "perennial ruling party." Tactical modifications occurred due to political situations. Over the past six-plus decades, the notion of the Dictatorship of the Proletariat was changed to People's Democratic Dictatorship at the beginning of the 1950s and changed back to Dictatorship of the Proletariat during the Cultural Revolution but changed back to People's Democratic Dictatorship again in the Reform and Open era.[1]

Mao put together a so-called "theory of perpetual revolution" or "continuous revolution under the dictatorship of the proletariat," which culminated in the Ten Years of Chaos. While Stalin had in the 1930s declared an end to class struggles, Mao proclaimed the continuation of such struggles despite the apparent disappearance of foreign imperialist powers as well as exploiting classes. "Our revolutions follow each other, one after another," the Great Helmsman announced.

> Our revolution is like fighting a war. After winning one battle, we must immediately put forward new tasks. In this way, we can maintain the revolutionary enthusiasm of the cadres and the masses, and diminish their self-satisfaction ... new tasks keep pressing in, and everyone devotes his mind to the question of how to fulfill the new tasks.
>
> *(Schram 1971: 227)*

Through the 1950s and 1960s, Mao was still looking for internal anti-socialist forces, which manifested themselves in alternative – and for Mao, treacherous – political lines advocated by his contemporaries. Mao had continuously warned of corrupt traitors restoring capitalism after the classes were supposedly abolished. At the Tenth Plenum of the Eighth CCP Central Committee in 1962, Mao declared that the socialist society covers a considerably long historical period and in this historical period of socialism, there are still classes, class contradictions and class struggles. There are class struggles between the socialist road and capitalist road, and there is the danger of capitalist restoration. "We must recognize the protracted and complex nature of this struggle ... Whether a socialist society will advance to communism or revert to capitalism depends upon the culture of this protracted struggle" (Selden 1979: 503–505).

In the course of revolutionary struggles, Mao divided contradictions into "primary" or "main" contradictions and "secondary" contradictions. The main contradictions denoted primary enemies whom he aimed to destroy; and the secondary contradictions involved so-called sympathizers and potential friends to the communist cause who could be won over. However, once the main enemies had been eliminated the secondary contradictions might become primary ones; this means that previous sympathizers and fellow travelers might become main enemies who must be exterminated. Political expediency is the only criterion for defining the nature of the contradictions. The same logic lies behind Mao's famous theory distinguishing "contradictions between ourselves and the enemy" and "contradictions among the people." The first type, which are "antagonistic contradictions," could only end in the destruction of the enemy; whereas there were possibilities of resolving "contradictions among the people" through united front work and other modes of reconciliation (Mao 1957). Given Mao's dictatorial nature and his penchant for settling personal scores by appealing to lofty revolutionary principles, it soon became apparent to all that the criteria for defining the different types of contradictions were based on Mao's self-serving desire to dominate his comrades.

Coupled with Mao's penchant for *zhengren* (rectifying and penalizing people) is his theory – again borrowed from Lenin – that participants in revolution are not allowed to preserve their distinctive personality or personal aspirations. In his famous *Talk on Art and Literature in Yan'an*, Mao said, à la Lenin, that cadres and comrades were but "cogs in the machinery" of the revolution. *Renxing* (human nature) must be subsumed under *dangxing* ("party nature") or the requirements of the party (Mao 1942). Owing to his humble origins and lack of formal education, Mao was snubbed by full-time professors while he occupied the lowly position of a library assistant in Peking University. His hatred of intellectuals partly explained the large numbers of well-educated – and patriotic – writers, artists and men of letters who suffered long jail terms or who committed suicide during the Anti-Rightist Movement and the Cultural Revolution (Fang and Liu 2007).

Liu Shaoqi, then State President, on the other hand, argued that class struggles had basically disappeared after the collectivization and nationalization drives in the late 1950s. According to the moderate leader, the main contradiction in China was only between the country's "backward production forces" and "the advanced socialist system" to which the party and people aspired. Therefore, the principal task of the party was to raise the production force as soon as possible and meet the people's demands for a better livelihood. Liu had the support of Deng Xiaoping as well as a plethora of civilian and military leaders. But they could not prevail over the demigod Mao, whose charisma and Machiavellian machinations carried the day (Liu 1956).

After the death of Mao and the arrest of the "Gang of Four," Mao's political line was completely overhauled and his conception of the rapid transition to socialism/communism was severely criticized as "ultra-leftist errors." The views of pragmatists led by Deng Xiaoping on the Cultural Revolution were expressed in the seminal document *Resolution on certain questions in the history of our party since the founding of the People's Republic of China* (hereafter "Resolution") that was published in mid-1981. Deng and his comrades labeled this Cultural Revolution period as "the greatest catastrophe" since 1949. It was "responsible for the most severe setback and the heaviest losses suffered by the Party, the state and the people since the founding of the People's Republic" (Resolution 1981; Deng 1984: 47–51). Mao was criticized for misjudging the political situation by insisting that workers, farmers and students must still be mobilized to overthrow capitalist roaders inside the party (Shao 1989: 32–55).

The Deng Xiaoping era: redressing most – but not all – of Mao's mistakes

What Mark Selden termed as the mass-mobilization collectivism era (Selden 1988: 11) ended when the party convened the Third Plenum of the Eleventh CCP Central Committee in December 1978. The Congress formally abandoned Mao's "Theory of the continued revolution under the dictatorship of the proletariat." The slogan "class struggle as the key link" was abandoned and the party made the strategic decision of shifting the focus of party work to socialist modernization. The *Resolution* asserted that the new leadership would rectify "conscientiously and comprehensively the 'leftist' errors of the Cultural Revolution" (Resolution 1981: 49). It condemned the cult of personality created by Mao and urged party members and ordinary people to emancipate their minds, to "seek truth from facts" and to focus on economic construction for future generations. While praising Mao's contribution to the revolutionary triumph of the CCP in 1949, the new leadership tried to reinterpret Mao Zedong Thought in such a way as to render it compatible with the new reformist credo. Mao Zedong Thought was reduced to three basic points: to "seek truth from facts," to always take the mass line and to achieve an independent foreign policy (*Resolution* 1981: 67). Mao Zedong Thought was de-ideologized.

Deng lost no time in committing the country to a path of national reconstruction. During his visit to Tokyo one month before the Third Plenum, Deng soaked in Japan's advanced industrialization and told his colleagues, "only now do I realize what modernization meant" (Xinhua News Agency 2008). Deng, who had never had much patience for political dogma, abandoned the "politics in command" or "ideology in command" of Mao's days. The New Helmsman posited economic work as the "core" of the party's work. His "two cats" theory as well as the theory of *bu zhenglun* ("no controversies" or "no hair-splitting") showcased the Second-Generation leader as a man who disdained theory (Deng 2012). One of Deng's greatest contributions to Chinese modernization is that he said goodbye to Mao's penchant for periodically launching *qunzhong yundong* (mass movements) and other political campaigns to rectify and purify the thinking of cadres and intellectuals. At least until 1989, Deng opposed several waves of "anti-bourgeois liberalization campaigns" launched by leftist party elders because they were seen as disrupting China's economic growth (Lam 2015b: xiii).

For Deng as well as his two hand-picked successors, party general secretaries Hu Yaobang and Zhao Ziyang, "practice is the sole criteria of truth." Whether a policy should be picked by the party should solely be determined by results – not whether the policy is "surnamed" socialist or capitalist (Wu 2008). At times of uncertainty about the best way forward, Deng said, the party and state apparatus would "cross the river while feeling out for the boulders." In economics, Deng was a liberal experimenter. He revived private capital both in rural and urban areas. Most significantly, Deng threw out the autarkist tradition of the Maoists and began the large-scale introduction of the special economic zones, where foreign capital would play a significant role (Naughton 1993).

As discussed above, Mao expounded the "theory of uninterrupted revolution" or "perpetual revolution" the better to indulge in his never-ending ideological wars with enemies in the party. By contrast, Deng Xiaoping and Zhao Ziyang proposed the "theory of the primary stage of socialism." Zhao's *Political Report to the Thirteenth CCP Congress* in 1987 pointed out that China's socialist development was still in the primary stage of development which might last for a hundred years, during which period the main contradiction in the country is the "contradiction between the primary material and cultural needs of the people and [the country's] backward production [capacity]" (*Documents of the Thirteenth National Congress of the CCP* 1987: 10–11). Deng's extension of the socialist enterprise to a hundred years or more was based on an entirely different premise to Mao's "theory of perpetual revolution." The Chief Architect of Reform realized that Mao had taken an erroneous great leap forward from peasant society to socialism. In other words, China had to take "remedial lessons" in capitalism. Concepts such as the "commodity economy" and the "primary stage of socialism" could be construed as Chinese-style capitalism; after all, the capitalist phase was an important stage in the Marxist idea of dialectical historical progression.[2]

At least up to the mid-1980s – when the CCP began to get worried about the coming demise of communist parties in Poland and other Eastern European countries – Deng threw his support behind a significant degree of political and institutional reform. First, Deng banned personality cults and indicated that Cultural Revolution-style political movements should be avoided. In a 1980 *People's Daily* article entitled "On the Reform of the Leadership Institutions of the Party and State," the Chief Architect of Reform underscored the importance of building some form of checks and balances in the party-state system. Moreover, Deng spoke in favor of having fixed tenures and retirement ages for top officials (Deng 1980).

Yet perhaps Deng's boldest experiment – which was worked out together with Zhao Ziyang – was the separation of party and government. This meant that while the party should concern itself with long-term goals and directions of the country, day-to-day running of the administration, businesses and colleges should be left in the hands of professional managers. This new idea amounted to an assault of the Leninist concept of the party as the progenitor – as well as executor – of all initiatives. The theory of separation of party and government was enshrined in the *Political Report to the 13th Party Congress* delivered by Zhao Ziyang. And even after the June 4 crackdown, Deng said "not one word of the 13th Party Congress Political Report should be changed."[3]

Deng turned conservative after the December 1986 student protests in several cities, which were seen as a precursor of the 1989 "turmoil." He reinstated two of Mao's ingrained ethos when he ordered the troops to use force to clear out Tiananmen Square: "dictatorship of the proletariat" and "power grows out of the barrel of the gun." It should be noted, however, that like many CCP leaders, Deng was a two-faced man who harbored conservative as well as forward-looking worldviews in accordance with political expediency. Deng was a principal executor of Mao's Anti-Rightist Movement (1958–61). And while the revered reformer put forward his "reform and open door" policies, he indicated that they must go hand in hand with the Four Cardinal Principles (Marxism, Leninism and Mao Zedong Thought; CCP leadership; the socialist road; and dictatorship of the proletariat) (Deng 1979; Baum 1994: 66–93).

Moreover, Deng himself violated some of the institution-building exercises which were meant to prevent a return of Mao-style despotic rule. The Second-Generation titan broke his own regulations about fixed tenure of office by remaining the power behind the throne of successors ranging from Hu Yaobang to Jiang Zemin. Hu was fired in an "enlarged Politburo meeting" in January 1987, in contravention to the stipulation in the CCP Charter that a general secretary can only be sacked by a full seating of the Central Committee. Moreover, Zhao Ziyang was imprisoned, and given a de facto house detention for life, without going through legal procedures (Zhao 2009). While Deng still enjoys a high prestige in and out of China, the reputation of the person who was credited with China's modernization would forever be dented by his resumption of Maoist tactics when the CCP's survival was at stake (Yahuda 1993).

Jiang Zemin and Hu Jintao's handling of the Maoist tradition

Given that Jiang Zemin took over the party leadership immediately after the Tiananmen Square crackdown, the putative head of the "Shanghai Faction" cleaved to Mao's "dictatorship of the proletariat" credo. Thousands of party members, intellectuals and students were incarcerated for participation in the "revolutionary turmoil." Mao's notorious *yiyantang* ("one voice chamber") was reinstated as the Jiang administration clamped down on the media and other channels of communication. Jiang even put an end to some of the economic reforms begun by Deng. For example, owing to the fact that individual non-state enterprises had given financial and other kinds of support to the demonstrators, Jiang vowed that he would "bankrupt all private companies" (Radio Free Asia 2002). And in contradistinction to predecessor Zhao's advocacy of "separation between party and government," Jiang reinstated the tradition of party organs – not State Council units – making decisions on the nitty-gritty of governance. For example, the Central Leading Group of Finance and Economics (CLGFE), the country's highest decision-making unit on economic policy, was expanded under Jiang's watch. However, Jiang followed tradition by allowing Premier Zhu Rongji, whose expertise on economics was unchallenged in the Politburo, to head the CLGFE (Lam 1999).

Deng's much-noted *nanxun* ("imperial tour of the south"), however, tipped the balance in favor of more economic – and even some significant political – reforms. The late patriarch's talks in Shenzhen and Zhuhai revived the legitimacy of private enterprise. Deng's admonition about no-holds-barred marketization of the economy would form the foundation of China's speeded-up application to join the World Trade Organization (WTO) (Fewsmith 2001; Zweig 2001). Owing to their perceived capitulation to the tariff-lowering demands of the United States and other capitalist countries, Jiang and Zhu were in 1999 and 2000 lambasted by members of the Maoist old guard as "pro-U.S." and even "traitors."

Yet Jiang's signature policy that did the most in deconstructing Maoism was the "Theory of the Three Represents." The "core" of the Third-Generation leadership indicated in the late 1990s that if the CCP were to remain relevant in the new century, it must represent "the development trend of advanced productive forces, the orientation of advanced culture, and the fundamental interests of the overwhelming majority of the people in China" (Xinhua News Agency 2001). In a now-famous speech made on July 1, 2001, the 80th birthday of the CCP, Jiang surprised everybody by allowing private entrepreneurs, professionals and returnees (Chinese educated in the West) to become CCP members. According to Jiang's understanding, only well-educated Chinese – and Chinese knowledgeable about advanced technology – could be said to represent "advanced productive forces and advanced culture." By contrast, the proletariats, including farmers and factory workers, many of whom have not even finished high school, can no longer be called the "vanguard of the party." In the new social, economic and political hierarchy, traditional proletariats, including peasants, would be relegated to the bottom of the barrel.

Equally shocking to mainstream party members was the last of the "three represents," namely, that the party represents "the fundamental interests of the overwhelming majority of the people in China." If the party were to serve pretty much all Chinese, the CCP needs to become a *quanmindang* (party for all the people) – and "class struggle" will be a thing of the past (Lam 2006: 154–155). Mao's strict delineations of various forms and shades of contradictions among the different classes will become meaningless. The "Theory of the Three Represents" was so unorthodox that at least a few tens of thousands of CCP members resigned from the party in protest.

Given that Jiang had retained his control over the PLA during the bulk of Hu Jintao's ten-year tenure (2002–12), the Fourth-Generation leader and colleagues such as Premier Wen Jiabao did not deviate much from the policies of the chief of the Shanghai Faction. President Hu, who spent his formative years during the Cultural Revolution, reinstated some Maoist values which fortunately did not result in a major lurch to the left. Foremost was the major mantra of the Fourth-Generation leadership: that it would pursue "the scientific outlook on development." Not only was Hu paying tribute to Marx's dialectical view on historical development; he was also making a covert criticism that Deng's policies such as "crossing the river while feeling out for the boulders" were "not scientific enough." In fact, while neither Hu nor Wen criticized Deng on the record, they were clearly opposed to the master reformers' axiom of "letting one part of the population get rich first" or "letting one part of the country get rich first." Hu's *yiren weiben* ("taking people first") credo echoed Mao's famous "serve the people" mantra. "Taking people first" was also an expression of his dissatisfaction with the elitist bent of the "Three Represents" dictum. It was in the 2000s that the Hu–Wen team abolished all agrarian taxes and extended social-security benefits including health insurance to the bulk of the countryside (Lam 2006: 40–44; Zheng and Tok 2007).

The one politician in the Hu era who successfully exploited Maoist social values for his own political purposes is former Politburo member Bo Xilai, who was party secretary of China's fourth directly administered city of Chongqing from 2007 to 2012. Bo, who personally led a "Westernized," corrupt lifestyle, sought to burnish his chances of making the PBSC at the 18th Party Congress by reviving Maoist norms in Chongqing. All residents were urged to learn by heart 36 Maoist-era "revolutionary songs." Radio and TV stations in the city broadcast songs, operas and videos that lauded the larger than-life exploits of national heroes and "proletariat paragons." Bo often asked his assistants to text-message sayings by Mao to the city's Netizens. Bo's favorite Mao quotations included: "The world is ours; we must all take part in running [public] affairs"; "Human beings need to have [a revolutionary] spirit"; and "Once the political line has been settled, [the quality of] cadres is the deciding factor" (Bo 2011). Bo's fame spread throughout the country because of his ability to exploit two popular Maoist values: egalitarianism and nationalism. Bo promoted social welfare such as subsidized housing for the poor. Moreover, in a daring move to partially abolish the hated *hukou* system, rural residents in the outskirts of the metropolis were allowed to work in urban areas. Bo also equated Maoism with nationalistic fervor. As Bo put it, *changhong* ("singing red songs") was equivalent to "a theoretical foundation for finding one's roots in history, the return of ideals, the revival of [the Chinese] race, and the rise of the nation" (Lam 2015a: 70).

Conclusion: Xi's restitution of Maoist norms and the future of the party

Owing to the fact that his father, the late party elder Xi Zhongxun, was a right-hand man of Hu Yaobang and a liberal icon of the party, there were expectations among the CCP's moderate wing that General Secretary Xi Jinping would commit the country to a path of liberalization (Wong and Ansfield 2012). Yet it did not take long for observers to conclude that Xi is a closet Maoist who is reviving many of the Great Helmsmen's norms with gusto.

First of all, Xi is opposed to any critique of the CCP's founding fathers, particularly Mao. The Fifth-Generation titan attributed the collapse of the CPSU to the de-Stalinization campaign. "The wholesale negation of the history of the Soviet Union and the CPSU, the negation of Lenin and Stalin … spawned historical nihilism and confusion of thoughts," Xi said in an internal speech in late 2012. "Various levels of Party organizations [in the Soviet Union] almost lost all their functions" (Li, H. 2013). In January 2013, Xi put forward his now-famous theory that the party should "not differentiate [post-1949 CCP] history into the pre-reform period and the post-reform period." "While socialism with Chinese characteristics was initiated during the period of the reform and open door, this [creed] was established on the basis of more than twenty years of [socialist] construction [after 1949]," he said, "These two periods should not be [arbitrarily] cut off from each other – and one period should not be used to negate the other" (Xi 2013e).

Xi's instructions, which have come to be known as "the theory of the two forbidden negotiations" (*liangge bunengfouding*), amounted to an unreserved defense of the contributions of Chairman Mao despite the horrific catastrophes he inflicted on his people. In a mid-2013 commentary in the official *Guangming Daily*, party theorist Qi Biao lauded Xi for "correctly upholding and defending party history and consolidating the foundation of party rule." Qi, who is a senior staffer in the Party History Research Office, contended that the Great Leap Forward and the Cultural Revolution were "minor tributaries in the river of time" that did not detract from "the CCP's great attainments" during that epoch (Qi 2013).

Xi's embrace of Mao's ideals has gone beyond the current leader's use of Maoist tactics to erect a larger-than-life personality cult. His insistence that senior cadres must follow "political rules" – particularly the stipulation that officials must not *wangyi zhongyang* ("make groundless criticisms of the central authorities") – demonstrates a lack of tolerance of dissent that has gone beyond Deng, Jiang or Hu (*People's Daily* 2015). Not unlike Mao, Xi has used the anti-corruption campaigns to nail political opponents that included former Chongqing party secretary Bo Xilai, former member of the Politburo Standing Committee in charge of security Zhou Yongkang, and two vice-chairmen of the Central Military Commission, Politburo members General Guo Boxiong and General Xu Caihou (*Global Times* 2016). On a more general level, Xi has revived the "*dangxing* theory" of the Great Helmsman, saying that all citizens, and intellectuals in particular, should subordinate their individual aspirations under the dictates of the party leadership.

Yet perhaps the most pronounced Maoist trait in Xi's governing philosophy is the priority that the latter has given to ideology. Almost without an exception, Deng and his followers were convinced that indulgence in ideological hair-splitting will not only sow dissension among cadres and party members but obstruct economic construction. In a much-noted speech in August 2013, however, Xi elevated "ideological work" to the same level as building up the economy. In a conference on *yishixingtai* (ideology and thoughts), the General Secretary said: "Economic construction is the central task of the party; ideological and thought work are an extremely important work of the party" (Xi 2013c).

Apart from personal inclinations, there were many reasons why Xi should have reinstated the ideological imperative. Xi took over China at a time when most members of the educated, professional and business classes have fallen to the siren songs of capitalistic culture and lifestyle. So-called elite emigration by the moneyed and educated sectors of society has reached dangerous levels (*Wall Street Journal* 2014). Xi's antidote to these centrifugal propensities is to emphasize the so-called "threefold self-confidences": "self-confidence in the path, the theories and the institutions of socialism." Xi also began launching a Maoist-style rectification campaign geared toward "thoroughly cleaning up the work style" of the CCP's 90 million members. For a one-year period beginning mid-2013, officials in civilian and military departments who failed to rid themselves of the undesirable traits of "formalism, bureaucratism, hedonism, and extravagance" would be penalized or kicked out of the Party (Xi 2013d).

The year-long *zhengfeng* (rectification) exercise, formally called the "Campaign on Mass-Line Education and Practice," was the largest-scale purge launched by party authorities since the end of the Cultural Revolution. In language that was reminiscent of Chairman Mao's masterly blend of the metaphysical and the vernacular, Xi urged cadres and party members to "purify themselves and to perfect themselves." "We must closely rely on the people and fully mobilize the enthusiasm, initiative and creativity of the broad masses," he said in the June 18 nationally televised speech. "We must look in the mirror, tidy our attire, take a bath, and cure our sickness," added Xi (Xi 2013b). In a commentary on the *zhengfeng* crusade, Xinhua pointed out that the Mao-style purge would serve the purpose of "bolstering the cohesiveness of the hearts of the Party and people – and consolidating the blood-and-flesh ties between the Party and the people" (Xinhua News Agency 2013). Shaanxi party secretary Zhao Yongzheng compared Xi's ideological exercise to Mao Zedong's famous rectification movement in Yan'an in 1942, in which the Great Helmsman first tried to impose his uniquely authoritarian view of Marxism on the CCP's first batches of cadres (Zhao 2013).

Xi also reintroduced the Maoist practice of "criticism and self-criticism" (*piping yu ziwopiping*), which was used extensively in the infamous "struggle sections" during the Cultural Revolution. "Criticism and self-criticism" were banned by Deng Xiaoping and used sparingly during ideological movements undertaken by Jiang Zemin and Hu Jintao. Yet Xi was so keen on reviving this Maoist institution that he performed a day-long "master class" in "struggle sessions" with members of the Hebei Provincial Party Committee in September 2013. He told the Hebei leadership team that "criticism and self-criticism are a forceful weapon for resolving contradictions within the Party." This practice, Xi instructed, would "promote democratic centralism, bolster stringent rules for life within the Party … and earnestly raise the ability of leadership teams to discover and solve problems" (Xi 2013a). Moreover, Xi revised one of the key reforms of Deng Xiaoping: separation of party and government. Power relating to all areas of policy-making has been concentrated in central leading groups and commissions directly under the PBSC. Three such major units – the Central National Security Commission, the Central Leading Group for Comprehensively Deepening Reforms and the Central Leading Group for Cyberspace Affairs – were created by Xi, who also appointed himself their directors (Zhai and Ruan 2014; Lam 2016).

Yet the most lasting influence of Maoism on the tenure of Xi – and probably beyond – is the untrammeled glorification of nationalism. After the demise of the CPSU and its satellite communist states in the early 1990s, the CCP has been left with only two viable pillars of legitimacy: economic growth and nationalism. Premier Li Keqiang has gone on the record saying that a 7.2 percent GDP growth rate is the "minimum" to ensure socio-political stability (*South China Morning Post* 2013). Now that, as the authorities pointed out, the economic growth might follow an L-shaped trajectory, the Xi administration is exploiting patriotic pride to justify the CCP's "perennial ruling-party status."

On October 1, 1949, Mao Zedong signified an end to one-and-a-half centuries of colonial humiliation of China by pronouncing on the rostrum of Tiananmen Square that "Chinese have stood up." Xi, the putative Mao Zedong of the twenty-first century, announces through his "Chinese dream," that by 2049, the centenary of the establishment of the PRC, China will have overtaken the United States as the world's foremost superpower. Xi's ambitious One Belt One Road (OBOR) strategy consists of a series of infrastructure and related projects that will bond China with countries ranging from Central Asia to Eastern Europe (the Silk Road Economic Belt) and the ten ASEAN members through the Indian Subcontinent to East Africa (the 21st Century Maritime Silk Road). The OBOR has been compared to Chairman Mao's bold plans in the 1950s to become the proud leader of the Third World. The game plan can be interpreted as an updated version of Mao's theory of "Three Worlds" in which the U.S. and Soviet Union were seen as main enemies, Western European countries as friends and African and Latin American countries as allies. While the "Three Worlds" theory seemed to have been buried upon Mao's death, the success of Xi's grand strategy remains to be seen.[4]

While 2049 is still several decades away, it is worthwhile heeding the opinion of Li Rui, Mao's personal secretary before the Cultural Revolution, on the Chairman's residual influence on the development of the party and state. In 2013, the 96-year-old liberal cadre said there would be no hope for Chinese modernization unless "China were to emerge from Mao's shadow." The nonagenarian government critic pointed out that Mao stood out in world history as a vicious dictator because "he knew how to brainwash people." "Mao inherited the manipulative techniques of the emperors of yore," Li said. "He also absorbed the dictatorship mechanisms of recent [Communist] regimes" (Li, R. 2013). While it is most unlikely that such a diehard Mao fan as Xi would change his course during this tenure, possibilities do exist that whoever runs China after Xi might opt for a course that would satisfy the demands of the people even as it nudges China more in line with global norms.

Notes

1 For a discussion of Mao's original conception of the people's dictatorship, see Mao (1949).
2 For a discussion of the concept of "taking remedial lessons in capitalism," see, for example, Ning (1991). Also see Wu (1988).
3 For a discussion of Deng's views on the separation of party and government, see, for example, Oksenberg (2001).
4 For a comparison of the One Belt One Road strategy to the foreign policy game plans of Mao Zedong, see, for example, Casarini (2016). Also see Van de Ven (2016).

References

Baum, R. (1994) *Burying Mao: Chinese Politics in the Age of Deng Xiaoping*. Princeton, N.J.: Princeton University Press, 66–93.

Bettelheim, Charles (1976 and 1978) *Class Struggles in the U.S.S.R.* Vol. 1 and Vol 2. New York: Monthly Review Press.

Bo (2011) Bo Xilai: chang hongge bushi jizuo yundong ("Bo Xilai: singing red songs is not an ultra-leftist campaign"), *China Daily*, May 1, http://news.163.com/11/0501/16/7300JN4Q0001124J.html.

Casarini, N. (2016) "When all roads lead to Beijing: Assessing China's New Silk Road and its implications for Europe," *The International Spectator: Italian Journal of International Affairs*, 51:4 (October 10), 95–108.

Chen, L. (1988) *Zhongguo shehuizhuyi shehui shijieduanlum* (*The Four Stages of Chinese Socialist Society*). Chengdu: Sichuan Sheng Shehui Kexue Yuan Publishing House.

Cheng, J. (2015) "The Chongqing model: what it means to China today," in Cheng, J. (ed.), *The Use of Mao and the Chongqing Model*. Hong Kong: City University of Hong Kong Press, 181–212.

Cui, J. (2014) "The times have not changed as long as Mao's portrait hangs on Tiananmen Square," *Apple Daily* (Hong Kong), February 10, www.appledaily.com.tw/appledaily/article/international/20140210/35630463/.

Deng, X. (1979) Deng Xiaoping: jianchi sixiang jiben yuanze ("Deng Xiaoping: upholding the four cardinal principles"), *People's Daily*, March 30, www.people.com.cn/GB/channel1/10/20000529/80791.html.

Deng, X. (1980) Dang he guojia lingdao zhidu de gaige ("On reforming the leadership institutions of the party and government"), *People's Daily*, August 18, http://cpc.people.com.cn/GB/64162/64165/68640/68658/4709791.html.

Deng, X. (1984) *Selected Works*. Beijing: Foreign Languages Press.

Deng, X. (2012) Deng Xiaoping 1992nian nanxun jianghua ("Deng Xiaoping's talks during his tour of the south in 1992"), Sohu.com, January 13, http://business.sohu.com/20120113/n332115956.shtml.

Deutscher, I. (1990) *Stalin*. London: Penguin Books.

Documents of the Thirteenth National Congress of the Communist Party of China (1987) Beijing: Foreign Languages Press.

Draper, H. (1987) *The Dictatorship of the Proletariat from Marx to Lenin*. New York: Monthly Review Press.

The Economist (2016) "Beware the cult of Xi," April 2, www.economist.com/news/leaders/21695881-xi-jinping-stronger-his-predecessors-his-power-damaging-country-beware-cult.

Fang, Y. and Liu, D. (2007) Mao Zedong yu beida tushuguan de jige wenti kaoxi ("Explanation of several questions regarding Mao Zedong and the Peking University Library"), *Dangshi Wenyuan* (*Articles on Party History*), 8, http://history.sina.com.cn/bk/ds/2013-12-21/105777602.shtml.

Fewsmith, J. (2001) "The political and social implications of China's accession to the WTO," *The China Quarterly*, 167 (September), 573–591.

Global Times (2015) "Fallen political star gives uni lectures on Cultural Revolution," December 10, www.globaltimes.cn/content/957602.shtml.

Global Times (2016) Xi Jinping dui zhongyang "wuhu" zai fanghua ("Xi Jinping talks again on the 'Five Tigers' among the central leadership"), China.com.cn, January 4, www.china.com.cn/guoqing/2016-01/04/content_37448466.htm.

Huberman, L. and Sweezy, P. (1968) *Introduction to Socialism*. New York: Monthly Review Press.

Lam, W. (1999) *The Era of Jiang Zemin*. Singapore: Simon and Schuster, 86–88.

Lam, W. (2006) *Chinese Politics in the Hu Jintao Era*. London and New York: Routledge.

Lam, W. (2012) "The Maoist revival and the conservative turn in Chinese politics," *Chinese Perspectives*, 2, 5–16.
Lam, W. (2015a) "The Maoist revival and the conservative turn in Chinese politics," in Cheng, J. (ed.), *The Use of Mao and the Chongqing Model*. Hong Kong: City University of Hong Kong Press, 65–104.
Lam, W. (2015b) *Chinese Politics in the Era of Xi Jinping*. New York and London: Routledge.
Lam, W. (2016) "Xi Jinping's ideology and statecraft," *Chinese Law and Government*, 48:6, 409–417.
Lane, D. (1985) *Politics and Society in the Soviet Union*. London: Allan & Unwin.
Lenin, V. (1975) *Selected Works*. Moscow: Progress Publishers.
Li, H. (2013) Xi jinping zongshuji zongjie sugong wangdang jiaoxun qiaoxiang shenme jingzhong? ("What kind of alarm bells has General Secretary Xi Jinping sounded from drawing lessons from the collapse of the Soviet party?"), *People's Daily*, September 26, http://news.ifeng.com/history/zhongguoxiandaishi/detail_2013_09/26/29895368_0.shtml.
Li, R. (2013) Zhongguo minzhuhua de guanjian zaiyu zouchu Mao Zedong ("The key to China's democratization is to go out of [the shadow of] Mao Zedong"), *Gongxi Net*, March 15, http://bbs.tianya.cn/post-207-46847-1.shtml.
Liu, S. (1956) "Political report to the Eighth National Congress of Deputies of the Chinese Communist Party," *People's Daily*, September 17, www.doc88.com/p-5078781382020.html.
Looker, R., ed. (1974) *Selected Writings: Rosa Luxemburg*. New York: Grove Press Inc.
Ma, Ji (1988) Shehui chuji jieduan ji ma jesi zhuyi de fazhan ("Primary stage of socialism and the development of Marxism"), *China Social Science Quarterly*, 1, 3–9.
Mao, Z. (1926) "Analysis of the classes in Chinese society," *Selected Works of Mao Tse-tung*, March, www.marxists.org/reference/archive/mao/selected-works/volume-1/mswv1_1.htm.
Mao, Z. (1942) "Talks at the Yenan Forum on Literature and Art," *Selected Works of Mao Tse-tung*, May 2, www.marxists.org/reference/archive/mao/selected-works/volume-3/mswv3_08.htm.
Mao, Z. (1949) "On the People's Democratic Dictatorship," *Selected Works of Mao Tse-tung*, June 30, www.marxists.org/reference/archive/mao/selected-works/volume-4/mswv4_65.htm.
Mao, Z. (1957) "On the correct handling of the contradictions among the people," *People's Daily*, February 27, www.marxists.org/reference/archive/mao/selected-works/volume-5/mswv5_58.htm.
Mao, Z. (1975) *Selected Works*, 4 volumes. Peking: Foreign Languages Press.
Marx, K. (1909) *Capital, Vol. III*, translated by Ernest Untermann. Chicago: Charles H. Kerr & Co.
Marx, K. (1976) *Capital, Vol. 1*. London: Penguin Books Ltd.
Medvedev, R. (1989) *Let History Judge*. New York: Columbia University Press.
Naughton, B. (1993) "Deng Xiaoping: the economist," *The China Quarterly*, 135 (September), 491–514.
Ning, J. (1991) Ziben zhuyi buke lun ("A critique on 'taking remedial lessons in capitalism'"), *Hunan Shehui Kexue (Hunan Social Science)*, 3, 60–64.
Nove, A. (1983) *The Economics of Feasible Socialism*. London: George Allen and Unwin Ltd.
Oksenberg, M. (2001) "China's political system: Challenges of the twenty-first century," *The China Journal*, 45 (January), 21–35.
People's Daily (2015) Zhong jiwei jiexi "wangyi zhongyang" ("Central Commission for Discipline Inspection explains 'making groundless criticism of the party leadership'"), November 2, http://politics.people.com.cn/n/2015/1102/c70731-27766237.html.
Qi, B. (2013) "Liangge buneng fouding" de zhongda zhengzhi yiyi ("The important political significance behind the 'two forbidden negotiations'"), *Guangming Daily* (Beijing), May 7, http://politics.gmw.cn/2013-05/07/content_7538912.htm.
Radio Free Asia (2002) Jiang Zemin de xingyun yu zhongguo de buxing ("Jiang Zemin's luck and China's running out of luck"), September 3, www.rfa.org/cantonese/commentaries/88741-20020903.html.
Resolution on Certain Questions in the History of our Party since the Founding of the People's Republic of China. (1981) Beijing: Foreign Languages Press, www.marxists.org/subject/china/documents/cpc/history/01.htm.
Schram, S.R. (1971) "Mao Tse-tung and the theory of the permanent revolution, 1958–69," *The China Quarterly*, 46, 221–244.
Selden, M. (1979) *People's Republic of China*. New York: Monthly Review Press.
Selden, M. (1988) *The Political Economy of Chinese Socialism*. New York: M.E. Sharpe, Inc.
Shao, Y. (1989) *Wannian Mao Zedong (The Old Mao Zedong)*. Beijing: Chun Qiu Publishing House.
Sik, O. (1976) *The Third Way*. New York: International Arts and Sciences Press, Inc.

South China Morning Post (2013) "China needs 7.2pc economic growth, Premier Li Keqiang says," November 5, www.scmp.com/business/economy/article/1348151/china-needs-72-cent-economic-growth-premier-li-keqiang-says.

Sweezy, P. (1949) *Socialism*. New York: McGraw-Hill Book Co.

Sweezy, P. (1987) Interview with P. Sweezy, *Monthly Review*, 38:11, 1–28.

Time (2016) "China's chairman builds a cult of personality," March 31, http://time.com/4277504/chinas-chairman/.

Tucker, R. (1975) *The Lenin Anthology*. New York: W.W. Norton and Company, Inc.

Tucker, R. (1978) *The Marx-Engels Reader*. New York: W.W. Norton and Company, Inc.

V.qq.com (2016) "The East is red again," V.qq.com (Tencent Videos), September 3, www.youtube.com/watch?v=uAHWOnByDdU&feature=youtu.be.

Van de Ven, J. (2016) "One belt one road: something old, something new," China-Cooperative.com, April 17, www.china-cooperative.com/single-post/2016/04/17/One-belt-one-road-something-old-something-new.

Wall Street Journal (2014) "The great Chinese exodus," August 15, www.wsj.com/articles/the-great-chinese-exodus-1408120906.

Wen, J. (2007) Guanyu shehui zhuyi chuji jieduan de lishi renwu he woguo duiwai zhengce de jige wenti ("On several questions about the historical tasks of the primary stage of socialism and China's policy toward other countries"), Xinhua News Agency, February 26, http://news.xinhuanet.com/politics/2007-02/26/content_5775212.htm.

Wen Wei Po (2012) Deng Xiaoping weihe fangan zhengzhi yundong ("Why was Deng Xiaoping against political campaigns?"), *Wen Wei Po* (Hong Kong), April 3, http://info.wenweipo.com/index.php/?action-viewnews-itemid-53745/.

Wong, E. and Ansfield, J. (2012) "Many urge next leader of China to liberalize," *New York Times*, October 21, www.nytimes.com/2012/10/22/world/asia/many-urge-chinas-next-leader-to-enact-reform.html?_r=0.

Wong, Y. (2005) *From Deng Xiaoping to Jiang Zemin – Two Decades of Political Reform in the People's Republic of China*. New York: University of America Press.

Wu, G. (1988) Chuji jieduan yu "bukelun" de genben qubie zai nali? ("What is the fundamental difference between the primary stage and 'taking remedial lessons'?"), *Xueshi yu Shijian (Study and Practice)*, 1, 62–63.

Wu, G. (2008) "Democracy and rule of law in Zhao Ziyang's reform," in Wu G. and Lansdowne H. (eds.), *Zhao Ziyang and China's Political Reform*. New York: Routledge, 32–57.

Xi, J. (2013a) Jianchi yonghao piping yu ziwo piping de wuqi, tigao lingdao banzi jiejue zishen wenti nengli ("Insist on using well the weapon of criticism and self-criticism; raise the ability of leadership corps in solving their problems"), *People's Daily*, September 25, http://politics.people.com.cn/n/2013/0925/c1024-23034947.html.

Xi, J. (2013b) Xi Jinping zai dangde qunzhong luxian jiaoyu shijian huodong gongzuo huiyi shang de jianghua ("Xi Jinping's talk on the work conference on activities regarding the mass line education and practice"), *People's Daily*, July 29, www.mofcom.gov.cn/article/zt_swbqzlx/lanmuone/201307/20130700218344.shtml.

Xi, J. (2013c) Yishixingtai gongzuo shi dangde yixiang jiduan zhongyan gongzuo ("Work on ideology and thoughts is a very important work of the party"), Xinhua News Agency, August 20, http://news.xinhuanet.com/politics/2013-08/20/c_117021464.htm.

Xi, J. (2013d) Dangde qunzhong luxian jiaoyu shijian huodong gongzuo huiyi zhaokai, Xi Jinping fabiao zhongyao jianghua ("Xi Jinping makes major speech during conference on the Campaign on Mass-Line Education and Practice"), Xinhua News Agency, June 18, http://news.xinhuanet.com/politics/2013-06/18/c_116194026.htm.

Xi, J. (2013e) Buneng gelie gange kaifang qianhou lishi bing xianghu fouding ("We cannot arbitrarily separate history into the pre-Cultural Revolution period and the post-Cultural Revolution period and then use one to negate the other"), China News Service, January 5, 2013, www.chinanews.com/gn/2013/01-05/4460409.shtml.

Xi, J. (2014) *Tan zhiquo lizheng* (*On Governance*). Beijing: Foreign Languages Publisher Ltd.

Xinhua News Agency (2001) "The 'Three Represents' theory," June 25, http://news.xinhuanet.com/english/20010625/422678.htm.

Xinhua News Agency (2008) 1978nian Deng Xiaoping fangwen riben xuedaole shenme ("What did Deng Xiaoping learn during his 1978 visit to Japan?"), Xinhua News Agency, December 3, http://news.xinhuanet.com/world/2008-12/03/content_10447411.htm.

Xinhua News Agency (2013) Duanzheng xingwei zheng yiguan – sanping kaizhan dangde qunzhong luxian jiaoyu shijian yundong ("Render your behavior and attire proper: Third commentary on the Campaign on Mass-Line Education and Practice"), Xinhua News Agency, June 20, http://news.xinhuanet.com/politics/2013-06/20/c_116229156.htm.

Yahuda, M. (1993) "Deng Xiaoping: The statesman," *The China Quarterly*, 135 (September), 551–572.

Zhai, K. and Ruan, V. (2014) "Xinhua reveals Xi Jinping is leading finance and economic affairs group," *South China Morning Post*, April 14, www.scmp.com/news/china/article/1532177/xinhua-reveals-xi-jinping-leading-finance-and-economic-affairs-group.

Zhao, Y. (2013) Yong Yanan chengfeng jingshen kaizhan qunzhong luxian jiaoyu shijian huodong ("Use the spirit of the Yan'an Rectification movement to implement the Campaign on Mass-Line Education and Practice"), *People's Daily*, August 19, http://news.xinhuanet.com/politics/2013-08/19/c_125194350.htm.

Zhao, Z. (2009) *Prisoner of the State: The Secret Journal of Premier Zhao Ziyang*. New York: Simon & Schuster, 51–72.

Zheng, Y. and Tok, S.K. (2007) "'Harmonious society' and 'harmonious world': China's policy discourse under Hu Jintao," Nottingham University China Policy Institute, Briefing Series (26).

Zweig, D. (2001) "China's stalled 'Five Wave': Zhu Rongji's reform package of 1998–2000," *Asian Survey*, 41:2, 231–247.

3

THE CCP'S EXPLOITATION OF CONFUCIANISM AND LEGALISM

Delia Lin

Introduction

Early Chinese Communist Party (CCP) founders once deemed traditional political philosophies such as Confucianism and Legalism as inappropriate for building a modern, democratic China. Under Mao Zedong, Confucianism was first extolled and then it gradually became an object of condemnation to be purged from society. Since the 1980s Confucian studies and ceremonies began to revive, and today's CCP has taken one step further to seek to implant Confucianism into its official ideology, Marxism. How and why are traditional philosophies such as Confucianism and Legalism playing an unprecedentedly significant role in shaping the ideological landscape of China today? This chapter analyses from a political philosophical perspective the need and tactics of the CCP's exploitation of Confucianism and Legalism. It argues that in Mao's era traditional political philosophies were used as ammunition in the ideological battlefield, and that this pattern is being repeated by President Xi Jinping today. Under the Xi regime, Confucianism and Legalism have become particularly important for two reasons. First, these traditional philosophies are capable of offering a shared fund of political ideas and principles that could justify not only highly centralized authoritarian rule but also Xi's dual rhetoric of "rule by virtue" and "governing the nation in accordance with law." Second, by tapping into these cultural and philosophical roots, the CCP is not only able to legitimize its leadership and governing principles but also claim "cultural self-confidence" in formulating ideologies that are separate from the kind of political liberalism that has dominated Western society. The revival of Confucianism under Xi therefore should be seen as a top-down, conscious and purposeful process of Sinicizing Marxism so as to buttress the party's cultural and ideological legitimacy.

Confucius: Saint or Satan?

The relationship between the CCP and Confucius has been a complex one. Confucian studies (*ruxue* 儒学) had been the state dogma for over two millennia since the reign of Emperor Wu of the Han dynasty (156 BC–87 BC), hence the central role Confucianism plays in Chinese culture and politics. It is highly likely that as a person of wisdom and discipline, Confucius himself was already proclaimed "saint" by people of his time (Zhou 2010). Han Fei Zi, founder of Legalist political philosophy, who was born around 270 years later than Confucius, referred to Confucius as a "Saint" (Han Fei Zi, Chapter 49). The "sainthood" of Confucius and his ideas had continued throughout the dynasties, but for the first time was challenged by activists and scholars through the early Republican Era including the initial founders of the CCP. *New Youth*, the magazine established in 1915 by Chen Duxiu, an early CCP leader, became a prime platform where traditional ideas especially Confucianism were critiqued. In 1916 Chen Duxiu published his well-known article "Our Last Awareness" in which he argued that Confucian ethics based on three cardinal ethos (*san gang* 三纲) was geared toward creating a hierarchical system and that it was incompatible with the principles of freedom, equality and independence required for a constitutional republic (Chen 1916). The same issue of *New Youth* published the first half of the two-part "Critique of Confucius" by Yi Baisha, arguably the very first article in modern China devoted to a critique of Confucianism. In the article Yi (1916) argues that while Confucius has been exploited as a puppet by politicians and emperors over dynasties, such exploitation can be attributed to four inherent weaknesses within Confucianism itself. First, the Confucian reverence for those in power creates political dictatorship that fails to pose limits on how power is exercised. Second, Confucian teaching easily leads to dictatorship of ideas as questioning the status quo is not permitted. Third, unlike Mo Zi or Han Fei Zi, Confucius did not have consistent moral or philosophical principles. Confucian teaching, much of which emphasized the suitability to the current situation (*shi* 时), was saturated with contradictory ideas and beliefs. That is why Confucianism can be used and reinterpreted to suit various purposes. Fourth, the Confucian focus on nurturing officials who are capable and loyal servants of the emperor while neglecting the concerns and aspirations of ordinary folks makes people despise the poor and lower classes. These early revolutionaries were well versed in the Confucian canon. Their negative appraisal of Confucianism should be seen from two perspectives. One is that in their quest to build a new, democratic, constitutional republic of China they saw the limitations of Confucianism regarding the cultivation of freedom, equality and independence, which they believed to be prerequisites for a modern republic. They faulted Confucianism for its advocacy of obedience and hierarchy as well as its tendency to nurture political and intellectual dictatorship. Second, the critique was necessary to resist the revival of monarchy promoted by warlord Yuan Shikai (1859–1916) and conservative thinker Kang Youwei (1858–1927), who had used Confucianism as an ideological rationale for reviving the monarchy after Dr. Sun Yat-sen's 1911 Republican Revolution.

It can be argued that early critiques of Confucianism by revolutionaries who had fallen under the sway of Western ideas about democracy, civil liberties and science were motivated by an active, genuine dialogue with their own cultural and philosophical heritage. These unorthodox reassessments were generally balanced and analytical; they also included acknowledgment of the merits of Confucianism and its contribution to Chinese culture and history.

Mao Zedong, however, seemed to have gone down a different trajectory of relationship with Confucius and Confucianism. He is known to be an ardent reader of Chinese classics especially Confucianism and yet his readings in Marxist classics were not very extensive (Holubnychy 1964; Xing 2011). Holubnychy (1964) has made a study of references and quotations in all four volumes of Mao's published works and the resulting approximate classification shows that the top three sources of references come from Stalin (24 percent), Confucian and Neo-Confucian writings (22 percent) and Lenin (18 percent). References from Marx and Engels are the least, only 4 percent. Young Mao Zedong worshipped Confucius. In his article published in *New Youth* on the importance of sports and physical education, Mao (1917) placed Confucius in parallel with Śākyamuni, founder of Buddhism, and Jesus Christ, and acclaimed them "saints" and "great thinkers." As Mao accepted Marxism and communism as his dominant ideology, his vision was to create a Chinese version of Marxism that was deeply rooted in age-old Confucian ideas. In his speech at the Sixth Plenary Session of the Sixth Central Committee of the CCP in 1938, the conference that established Mao's unrivalled preeminence within the leadership, Mao stated that the CCP members must study China's "historical heritage" and "preserve the precious legacy from Confucius to San Yat-sen" (Mao 1938) in order to adapt Marxism and Leninism to the specific conditions of China. Mao was also a vehement opponent of "liberalism" (*ziyou zhuyi* 自由主义), claiming it was originated from the selfishness of the petite bourgeoisie who placed their personal interest first (Mao 1937). In his article "Against liberalism" (1937) Mao calls on CCP members to place revolutionary goals as their life's first priority and to subsume their personal interests and aspirations under the demands of the revolution. As I shall discuss later, this belittling of self-interest and glorification of the public interest echo both Confucian and Legalist theories.

Mao's positive attitudes toward Confucius and Confucianism, however, undertook an about-turn in his ideological construction after the People's Republic was founded. In his praise for socialist communes established in Confucius' hometown Qufu, Mao (1955) made a point that socialism is much more superior to the teaching of Confucius who neglected agricultural productivity. He advised those who intended to visit the Confucian temples in Qufu to visit the Qufu communes instead. Then prior to the launch of the Cultural Revolution, Mao had classified traditional political philosophers into opposing ideological camps. He was fond of Emperor Qin and his Legalist advisors whereas Confucianism represented by Confucius and Mencius was placed in the enemy's camp. "Confucius and Mencius were idealism (*weixin zhuyi* 唯心主义)," said Mao to then president of the democratic republic of Vietnam Hồ Chí Minh on his visit to China on June 13, 1965 (Xu 1995: 171). "Xun Zi was materialism (*weihu zhuyi* 唯物主义) and was the left wing of Confucianism. Confucius represented slave owners and aristocrats while Xun Zi represented the landlord class," Mao added. Xun Zi was the teacher of the two Legalist founders, Li Si and Han Fei Zi. Under Chinese socialism, materialism was and still is considered as absolute truth whereas idealism is fallacious and anti-revolutionary. Through this statement, therefore, not only was Confucius defined as a philosophical bugbear but also ideologically dangerous owing to the fact that the Sage was deemed a right-wing defender of the interests of aristocrats and slave owners, the worst enemies of the people.

Based on this ideological categorization of Confucius in the 1960s, the "Criticize Lin, Criticize Confucius" campaign (*pilin pikong yundong* 批林批孔运动) from 1973 to 1976, initiated by Mao and his wife Jiang Qing, came as little surprise. In her analysis of this political and ideological campaign, Xing Beinan (2016) has revealed an interesting detail of why Lin Biao and Confucius became objects of condemnation together. Unable to find evidence through Lin Biao's history that would prove that he had long held anti-party beliefs, the CCP used handwritten notes containing quotes from Confucius and Mencius found in Lin Biao's home as important proof of the ideological roots of Lin Biao's alleged anti-party actions. In Mao's era, be it a friend or enemy, Confucianism had been used as ammunition in the ideological battlefield.

The revival of Confucianism and Chinese classics in post-Mao China

History seems to be uncannily repeating itself. Mao's early ambition of localizing Marxism through injecting elements of Chinese classics into the Western creed is being realized at full throttle under the party and government led by President Xi Jinping. Once again Confucianism is used to do battle with the Western ideology of liberalism.

It must be noted that the revival of Confucianism under the current government is not a new, sudden phenomenon. Confucius and Confucianism have been enjoying increasing government-endorsed acknowledgment in the cultural, educational and political arenas in the Post-Mao era. Annual activities commemorating Confucius' birth have been held since 1984 and were attended by government officials with ever more seniority (Yuan 2014). In 1989, Wu Xueqian, then member of the CCP Politburo, attended the 2540th anniversary of Confucius' birth. Between 1995 and 2009, the commemorating openings were attended twice by Li Ruihuan and Jia Qinglin, the 6th and 7th Chairmen of the Chinese People's Political Consultative Conference. Confucius has been presented to the outside world as a cultural symbol of China. Starting in 2004, over 500 Confucius Institutes have been built across the world to promote Chinese language and culture, admittedly a means of delivering Chinese soft power (Xinhua Wang 2016). Despite the increasing concerns in Western countries over academic freedom due to the establishment of Confucius Institutes at education institutions (see, for example, Cohen 2016), the Hanban (the abbreviated Chinese word for the Office of Chinese Language Council International, which oversees all Confucius Institutes) has the ambition to establish 1,000 Confucius Institutes outside of China by 2020 (Xinhua Wang 2016). In 2004, then President Hu Jintao launched the "Harmonious Society" national development strategy. Couched in Confucian language, the concept and strategies of the "Harmonious Society" represented a more serious move toward a Confucianist approach to politics and governance.

Accompanied with the official launching of the "Harmonious Society" discourse was the government-backed "Chinese classics fever" (*guoxue re* 国学热), that is, a fervor for studying classical Chinese books such as the *Analects of Confucius*. Since January 10, 2005, *Guangming Ribao*, or *Guangming Daily*, one of the key national newspapers, has added a new page called *guoxue ban* (Chinese classics page) specially devoted to articles on traditional learning.

Confucian revival reached new heights after Xi Jinping's speech at an international conference commemorating the 2565th anniversary of Confucius' birth on September 24, 2014. It marked the first time that a Chinese president formally attended celebrations marking the birth of Confucius. In the same year the CCP publicly ordered its officials nationwide to attend lectures on Confucius and other classical Chinese thinkers (Page 2015). Xi himself has been such an ardent user of classics quotes that in 2015, *People's Daily* Press compiled a volume containing a collection of 274 classics quotes used by the president taken from 70 of his speeches since 2012 (*People's Daily* Editorial Department 2015). *People's Daily* reports that of the nearly 300 quotes by President Xi, Confucianism is the most quoted philosophy, followed by Legalism (*People's Daily* 2015).

A search on the number of articles on *People's Daily* from 2000 to 2015 containing the keyword *rujia* (Confucianism, the Confucian School), *ruxue* (Confucianism, Confucian studies) or *guoxue* (Chinese classics), shows that the use of the three keywords has been increasing over time, but surged in 2004 and 2014, especially 2014 (see Figure 3.1). This shows that 2004 and 2014, especially 2014, marked a dramatic increase in the promotion of Confucianism and the learning of Chinese classics.

Confucianism is increasingly becoming central among the learning of Chinese classics endorsed by the CCP. A further search on the Chinese classics page of *Guangming Daily* from 2013 to 2016 shows that the percentage of articles on Confucianism is on the rise annually, reaching 54 percent in the second half of 2015 and 51 percent in the first half of 2016 (see Figure 3.2).

Two significant and far-reaching official projects to promote Confucianism and Chinese classics learning were accomplished in 2016. The first was the National Chinese Classics Centre, one of the three major cultural projects under the 12th Five-Year Plan (2011–2015). The Centre was established at the Beijing Olympic Park on August 30, 2016, with a total building area of 81,362 square metres and a height of 68 metres (*Xunjie Jiaoyu* 2016). The second was that the Ministry of Education launched after seven years of preparation a series of textbooks for

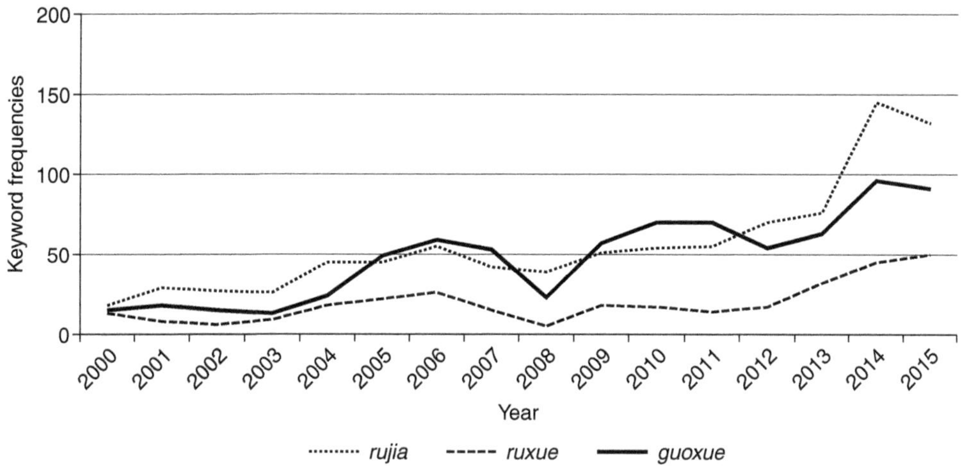

Figure 3.1 The number of articles containing *rujia*, *ruxue* or *guoxue* as the keyword in *People's Daily* (2000–2015).

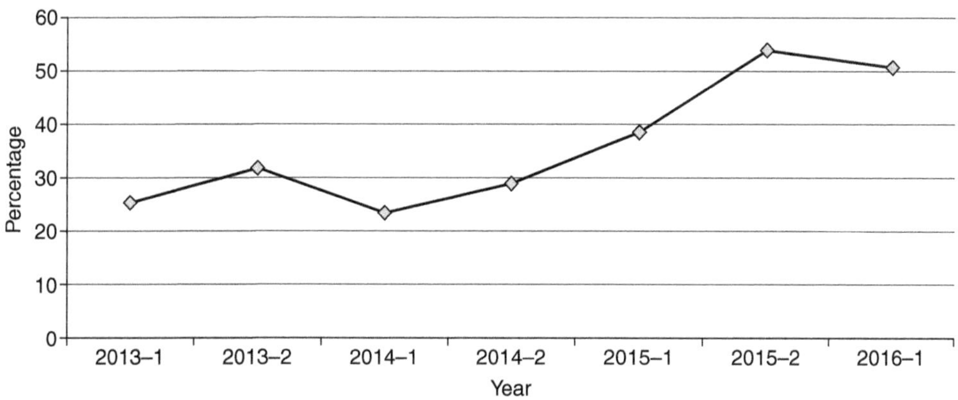

Figure 3.2 The percentage of articles on Confucianism on the Chinese classics page in *Guangming Daily* (2013–2016).

teaching Chinese traditions. Originally a project under the 11th Five-Year Plan (2006–2010), this set of textbooks are to be used from kindergarten through high school aiming at cultivating "perfect character" (*wanmei renge* 完美人格) among young Chinese (*Xunjie Jiaoyu* 2016). Canonical Confucian texts comprise the majority of the book list.

How to interpret this wholesale and unprecedented return to cultural roots under President Xi? Guo Yingjie (2016) has offered an illuminating interpretation from the perspective of nationalism. Guo postulates that Chinese nationalism can be split into cultural nationalism and political nationalism. Whereas cultural nationalism is aimed at maintaining cultural autonomy, unity and identity by defending a distinctive and historically rooted way of life, political nationalism seeks to reconstruct political authority of the state by placing China's cultural heritage within a new culture that is congenial to state building. Guo argues that from the early twentieth century to the late 1980s these two types of nationalism contended with one another with the former being dominated by the latter. This, however, has changed under President Xi. What we are witnessing is an attempt by the authorities to reanchor political norms and institutions on cultural roots – and to derive sustenance and legitimacy from them. The CCP is not only justifying China's political system, values and development model on the basis of "national conditions"; it is also doing so on the back of age-old Chinese traditions.

While agreeing with Guo Yingjie's observation of the CCP putting together a potent cultural underpinning for its political superstructure, I argue that this phenomenon should be understood as an attempt by the Xi-led party to project a novel ideological universe of discourse that can rival Western political liberalism. Before I elaborate on this point, I would like to outline, from a political-philosophical perspective, how and why Confucianism and Legalism are capable of offering a shared fund of political ideas and principles congenial to a highly centralized regime – as well as Xi's dual rhetoric of "rule by virtue" and "governing the nation in accordance with law."

What can Confucianism and Legalism offer?

Confucius has a dream. He calls it *da tong* (大同), literally meaning the Grand Unity. It is also known as "One World" in English. It is a vision of global unification oriented to civic equality and self-government. For Confucius, it is the kind of governance that is guided by the *Grand Path* (*da dao* 大道), the way of Heaven, that he believes is the bequest of the ancient god-kings. *Da tong*, for Confucius, is a world of ultimate harmony, peace, happiness and equality, but the world Confucius actually faced then was one that was sinking into endless wars and violence.

The Confucian approach to realizing the utopian vision of *da tong* can be best summarized by what political philosopher Yang Yang (1995) first called in the early 1990s: integration of politics and religion/education (*zhengjiao heyi* 政教合一). *Zhengjiao heyi* is the Chinese term used to refer to the political system in Europe prior to separation between church and state. While admitting that Confucianism may not be a religion per se, Yang uses the *zhengjiao heyi* concept to argue that the moral, ethical, sociological and spiritual space that Confucian political philosophy occupies has elevated it to the realm of a religion, so much so that those in political power assume the kind of absolute moral authority that is typically exercised by religious leaders. Yang Yang's thesis of *zhengjiao heyi* has been widely used by scholars in China to describe Confucianist political theory.

The Confucian paradigm of *zhengjiao heyi* is consistent with the Confucian definition of human nature as a summation of virtuous traits bestowed by Heaven. The Confucian thesis of human nature being good, however, does not lead to a confidence in the benignity of character attributes bequeathed by the "state of nature." On the contrary, Confucianism insists on the elimination of "animal instincts" within human nature. Confucius and his disciples teach that progress for humanity is only possible through abandoning the animal essence of the human make-up – and to embark on a ceaseless cultivation, refinement and transformation of the self from inside out so as to realize the maximum moral potentials of human nature. It is therefore the primary political responsibility of virtuous emperors to guide their subjects to exercise *li* (礼 decorum and ritual propriety) so as to nurture a perfect moral character. The Confucian utopian vision places perfect morality and the practice of decorum and ritual propriety (*li*) on the same metaphysical level as Heaven and the Way (*dao*). Any transgression of the prescribed decorum and ritual propriety will not be tolerated and a person who does so will be judged and treated as a "sub-human."

The ruler, who is construed as internally a saint, naturally becomes the nation's moral teacher under the so-called *junshi heyi* (君师合一) principle. The Confucian ethos of internally a saint and outwardly a king (*neisheng waiwang* 内圣外王) creates a model of authority recognition: it establishes the Chinese political-cultural norm whereby a regime's mandate to rule relies on its moral authority. In other words, political legitimacy is established through establishing moral authority. Pan-moralism (*fan daodehua* 泛道德化), that is, a tendency to justify political agendas through a moral purpose, and pan-politicization (*fan zhengzhihua* 泛政治化), that is, a tendency to treat moral choices, however trivial or personal, as a political issue, are the twin processes within a state governed by Confucian principles. The dual pan-moralism and pan-politicization processes underpin a public culture marked by suspicion and intolerance of doctrines other than state orthodoxy, which must be embraced by the masses.

Legalism, on the other hand, holds that human actions are driven by self-interest and this cannot be changed by education and other remedial measures. A sovereign, therefore, should not lead through moral aspirations but through balancing subjects' and the ruler's interests using standardized rules that equally apply to everyone. The legalist founder Han Fei Zi has no trust in "smart" government officials who would always use their resources to satisfy their personal and family's interests before serving the public interest. Therefore he calls for absolute power and authority to be bestowed on the ruler, so that he is equipped to tackle fraud and deception of canny officials who appear to be prudent (*zhi*智) (see Han Fei Zi, Chapter 47). Han repudiates the kind of pedagogy and rites Confucius deemed necessary to maintain personal relationships or to serve family interests; instead, he advocates the concept of *gongyi* (公义), which places the ruler's and the nation's public interest over different types of personal interest (Han Fei Zi, Chapter 19).

As political philosophies, Confucianism and Legalism both center on the problem of order but they propose very different architectures for maintaining order. The former relies on orderly social relationships enforced by doctrines of moral codes and modes of behavior (*li*) to be affirmed by the masses who are led by supposedly morally superior leaders in the hierarchy (i.e., the king, the magistrate, the father, the husband, the teacher and the older brother). The latter, however, is skeptical of any form of self-claimed altruism or morality and instead advocates uniformity of law (*fa* 法) enforcement. Law and society in imperial China was characterized by what Tung-Tsu Ch'ü (2011) aptly terms the Confucianization of law, defined by Bodde and Morris (1967: 29) as "the incorporation of the spirit and sometimes of the actual provisions of Confucian *li* into the legal codes."

I have argued that the political theory behind President Xi's governing strategy of "governing the country according to law" (*yifa zhiguo* 依法治国) can be coined "Confucianized Legalism" (Lin in press), that is, incorporation of the spirit and sometimes of the actual provisions of prescribed moral rules into law enforcement. At the Fourth Plenum of the Eighteenth CCP Central Committee, party authorities for the first time made "governing the country according to law" (*yifa zhiguo*) the leitmotif at a plenary session. The Fourth Plenum Decision – CCP Central Committee Decision Regarding Some Major Questions in Comprehensively Promoting Governance According to the Law – marked a new CCP governing strategy of relying on law enforcement to maintain order and stability, coupled with absolute authority and leadership of the party. As Trevaskes (2016) rightly observes, President Xi's "governing the country according to law" is not a new idea of rule of law rather a greater accentuation of the dialectical unity of party leadership and the rule of law. The *Decision* declares that the party's leadership is the most essential characteristic of and the most fundamental prerequisite for socialist rule of law. The narrative is that only if the party leads every aspect of governance through law-making, law reform and law enforcement can the people become the masters of the nation and can social order be maintained. This would have been of little surprise to Han Fei Zi, who advocates the organic synthesis of tough laws and absolute power of the ruler so as to minimize obstruction from local officials who are prone to corruption.

The dual emphasis on moral influence expressed in the *Decision* shows a strong Confucian orientation. The *Decision* states that rule of law and rule by virtue (*yide zhiguo* 以德治国) must be integrated with one another and that dual emphasis must be placed on the normative role of law and the educational function of morality. Morality includes "socialist core values, Chinese traditional virtues and morals, social morals, professional ethics, family virtues and morals, and personal character" (Zhonggong zhongyang guanyu quanmian tuijin yifazhiguo ruogan zhongda wenti de jueding 2014). The *Decision* explains the dialectical relationship between rule of law and rule by virtue as follows: rule of law is to reflect moral concepts, therefore the propelling role of law must be strengthened through moral construction; morality is to nurture the spirit of rule of law, and therefore the supporting role of morality must be strengthened through constructing the culture of rule of law. All this, as the *Decision* states, is to realize the complementary relationship between law and morality, and between rule of law and rule by virtue. Demonstrated here is the supremacy of morality and the use of law to reinforce moral values prescribed by the ruling party. At its core are pan-moralism and pan-politicization and the belief that order and stability can only be brought about through banishing alien creeds and ideologies.

Unifying beliefs and thoughts are of particular importance to a rationale of "rule by virtue" that echoes a Confucian way of integrating politics and religion/education into one (*zhengjiao heyi*). On February 28, 2016 the CCP Central Committee issued the Education Scheme for All Party Members. The latter are asked to pursue "studies of the Party Constitution and Party Regulations, [and] of the series of [Xi Jinping] speeches [so as] to become bona fide party members." This is the so-called "two studies and one become" (*liangxue yizuo* 两学一做) campaign that is being implemented on a regular basis across the board. The content of the first series of "studies" includes: clarifying basic criteria of party members; establishing behavioral regulations; studying the party Constitution line by line; studying the history of the party as well as exemplary revolutionary figures; studying party laws and regulations; learning lessons from corrupt officials who have broken the law and party rules, such as Zhou Yongkang, Bo Xilai, Xu Caihou, Guo Boxiong and Ling Jihua; and living by principle (Tu jie 2016). The second series of "studies" means studying Xi Jinping's speeches on reform, development and stability; on domestic politics and foreign affairs; on defense and governing the party, the nation and the military; and on the new concepts, thoughts and strategies of governance. "Becoming a bona fide party member" means to possess "four emphases and four haves" (*sijiang siyou* 四讲四有) in their spirit and character – "emphasizing politics, having faith; emphasizing regulations, having discipline; emphasizing morality, having good conduct; emphasizing selfless dedication, having [politically correct] action" (Tu jie 2016). This dual strategy of using law to harness political power – a legalist stance – and imposing moral principles through education – a Confucian method – underpins the governing philosophy of Xi Jinping.

Establishing cultural and ideological legitimacy of the CCP: Sinicizing Marxism

It has become evident that Xi Jinping's highest priority is to maintain and enhance the legitimacy of the CCP so as to ensure its "perennial" rule. The unprecedented revival of Confucianism and Chinese classics should not be seen as motivated by mere nostalgia for a lost tradition though it may be couched as such by propagandists. The turn toward Confucianism is a carefully crafted project to establish cultural and ideological legitimacy of the CCP; the key approach, in Xi's own words, is to "Sinicize Marxism" through Confucianism (Xi 2014a).

What is important to bear in mind is that Xi Jinping's political dream goes beyond establishing legitimacy of the CCP. His ultimate goal is to create a discourse and reality of the "China model," one that is opposed to the Western model of liberal democracy. This China model consists of a highly centralized, authoritarian socialist regime led by the CCP. Xi Jinping's argument is based on traditional and cultural determinism. He argues that liberal democracy of the West stems from ancient Greek concepts of democracy and is therefore suitable for Western society. A different ruling blood line runs through China's body politic and governs its people; China therefore must choose a different path, that is, a socialist regime based on a socialist core value system (*shehui zhuyi hexi jiazhi tixi* 社会主义核心价值体系) that is administered by the CCP. As Xi Jinping said to Greek Prime Minister Antonis Samaras, "Your democracy is ancient Greek and Roman democracy. That is your tradition. We have our own tradition" (Xi 2014b). Xi Jinping cited the example of the death penalty. Many Western countries have abolished the death penalty from the perspective of human rights, Xi argued, but if a "referendum" were carried out in China, many Chinese people would reject abolishing the death penalty as the view that murderers are the most evil and must pay back with their lives is deeply rooted in Chinese tradition (Xi 2014b).

In his address to the Confucius Research Institute in Qufu in 2013, President Xi emphasized that four aspects must be stated clearly in promoting Confucius and Confucianism across the world. First, every country and nation differs in their historical tradition, cultural heritage and national conditions and therefore must choose their unique path of development. Second, Chinese traditional culture contains the deepest spiritual pursuit of the Chinese people and has nurtured the nation from generation to generation. Third, Chinese traditional culture is the extraordinary strength of the Chinese nation and its most profound cultural soft power. Fourth, socialism with Chinese characteristics has profound historical origins and broad realistic foundation: it is deeply rooted in Chinese culture, it reflects the will of the Chinese people and it is therefore suitable for China and for the advancement of society (Xi 2014b). Xi emphasizes that one must hold a Marxian historical materialist (*lishi weiwu zhuyi* 历史唯物主义) stance toward Confucian theories (Xi 2014b), which shows his conviction in tailoring the past for today's political purposes.

Calling for political pluralism (*zhengzhi de duoyuan xing* 政治的多元性), Xi is asking the world to accept the set of ideas and governing principles of Chinese socialism. His political ambition is to create a Sino-centric discourse and Chinese civilization in parallel with the Euro-centric Western civilization. Once accomplished, all the criticisms on and suspicions of one-party rule from the standpoint of liberty, human rights, individualism will be resolved once and for all. "Western" concepts are deemed irrelevant as China, which will be run based on its own deeply rooted governing principles.

There are still two issues to be resolved. One is the issue of ideology. The official ideology of the CCP still is Marxism, which is a Western idea. If tradition determines a nation's future, how can one justify a borrowed guiding ideology? The second is the issue of consistency of the CCP. If Xi were to create a discourse and reality called the "Chinese model," this has to be a consistent story told by all CCP leaders. For example, how to tell the story of Mao Zedong, whose ideas conflicted with those of later CCP leaders? Xi Jinping's solution is to play up the Sinicization of Marxism (*zhongguo hua de makesi zhuyi* 马克思主义中国化). In his 2013 speech marking the 120th anniversary of the birth of Mao Zedong, Xi praised Mao as being "the great pioneer in Sinicizing Marxism" (Wang 2014) while at the same time referring to his attachment to Confucianism as a young Communist. This way, the succeeding state ideologies, such as the Deng Xiaoping Theory, Jiang Zemin's "Theory of the Three Represents" and Hu Jintao's "Scientific Outlook on Development," became an extension of Mao Zedong's contribution to the Sinicization of Marxism. In 2014 Xi officially added cultural confidence to the three "confidences," namely, confidence in the [socialist] road, confidence in the [socialist] theory and

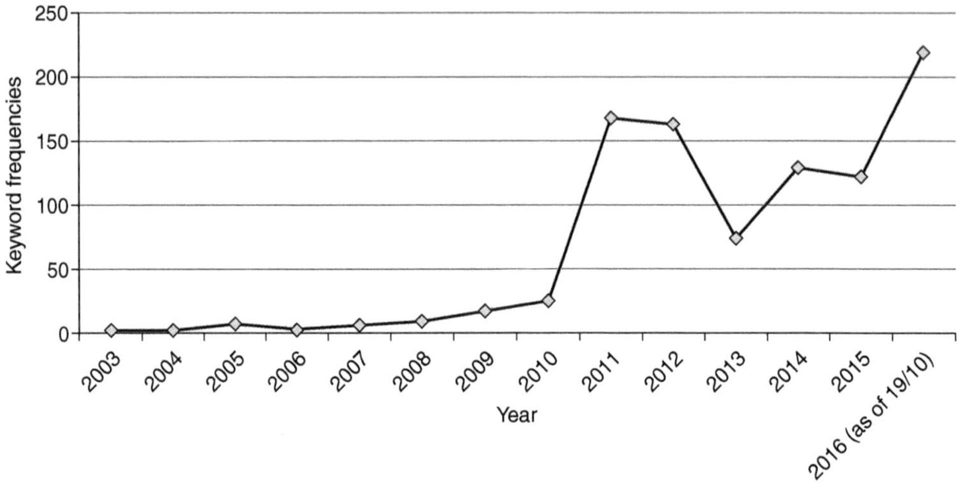

Figure 3.3 The number of articles containing *wenhua zixin* as the keyword in *People's Daily* (2000–2015).

confidence in [socialist] systems. Figure 3.3 shows the trajectory that the phrase "cultural confidence" has traveled on *People's Daily* from 2003, when the term first appeared, to 2016. A surge in the use of the term occurred in 2011, from 25 articles to 168, and the term became a catchphrase again last year, already appearing 219 times as of October 19, 2016, as opposed to 122 in 2015.

Conclusion

As political philosophies Confucianism and Legalism are capable of supporting a highly centralized authoritarian regime and they have provided ideas and governing principles that underpin the socialist rule in China, past and present. On the other hand, they have been used as ammunition in the ideological battlefield to reject political liberalism that has dominated Western society. Today's unprecedented revival of Confucianism and Chinese classics should be seen as part of a systematic effort by the current government to gain discursive authority of legitimacy for the CCP and the Chinese socialist regime. This will only result in an increasingly dogmatic insistence on the moral high ground based on a rigid claim of excellence for the Chinese way of governing – and an outright rejection of universal liberal principles. It remains to be seen how this will affect China's relations with countries – both in the West and in Asia – that are practicing political liberalism and democracy. It also remains to be seen how an increasingly authoritarian rule can co-exist with increasing economic freedom of the people, who would demand civil liberties that are outside the parameters of Confucianism and Legalism.

References

Bodde, D. and Morris, C. (1967) *Law in Imperial China: Exemplified by 190 Ch'ing Dynasty Cases Translated from the Hsing-an Hui-lan with Historical, Social and Juridical Commentaries*. University of Pennsylvania Press, Philadelphia.

Chen, Duxiu. (1916) Wuren zhi zuihou zhi juewu (Our last awareness). *Qingnian Zazhi* (New Youth), 1(6).

Ch'ü, Tung-Tsu. (2011) *Law and Society in Traditional China.* The Commercial Press, Beijing.

Cohen, Hagar. (2016) Australian universities the latest battleground in Chinese soft power offensive. Available at: www.abc.net.au/news/2016-10-14/universities-latest-battleground-in-chinese-soft-power-offensive/7931958 [October 15, 2016].

Guo, Yingjie. (2016) The CCP returns to Chinese cultural roots. *East Asia Forum*, October 3. Available at: www.eastasiaforum.org/2016/10/03/the-ccp-returns-to-chinese-cultural-roots/ [October 10, 2016].

Han Fei Zi, *Gushiwen wang*. Available at: http://so.gushiwen.org/guwen/book.aspx?b=%E9%9F%A9%E9%9D%9E%E5%AD%90 [July 12, 2016].

Holubnychy, Vsevolod. (1964) Mao Tse-tung's materialistic dialectics. *The China Quarterly*, 19, pp. 3–37.

Lin, Delia. (in press) High justice versus low justice: the legacy of Confucian and Legalist notions of justice. In Flora Sapio *et al.* (eds.), *Justice, the China Experience*. Cambridge University Press, Cambridge.

Mao, Zedong. (1917) Tiyu zhi yanjiu (Research on physical education). *Xin Qingnian* (New Youth), 3(2).

Mao, Zedong. (1937) Fandui ziyou zhuyi (Against liberalism). Available at: www.people.com.cn/GB/channel1/10/20000529/80819.html [July 8, 2016].

Mao, Zedong. (1938) Zhongguo gongchandang zai minzu zhanzheng zhong de diwei (The status of the CCP in the national war). Available at: www.marxists.org/chinese/maozedong/marxist.org-chinese-mao-19381014.htm [July 8, 2016].

Mao, Zedong. (1955) Zhongguo nongcun de shehuihuyi gaochao (The socialist climax in Chinese villages). Available at: www.people.com.cn/GB/shizheng/8198/30446/30452/2196125.html [July 8, 2016].

Page, Jeremy. (2015) Why China is turning back to Confucius. *The Wall Street Journal*, September 20. Available at: www.wsj.com/articles/why-china-is-turning-back-to-confucius-1442754000 [September 22, 2015].

People's Daily. (2015) Dashuju fenxi: Xi Jinping yongdian 300 ju, zuichang yinyong najia napai? (Big data analysis: what are the most quoted philosophies and schools of the 300 quotes by Xi Jinping?). Available at: http://china.huanqiu.com/article/2015-02/5779831.html [November 8, 2016].

People's Daily Editorial Department. (2015) *Xi Jinping Yongdian* (Classics Quotes Used by Xi Jinping). Renmin Ribao Chubanshe, Beijing.

Trevaskes, Susan. (2016) "Rule of law" narrative building in the Xi Jinping period. Griffith University seminar.

Tu jie: mianxiang quanti dangyuan kaizhan de "liang xue yi zuo" jiujing shi shenme (Graph explanation: what does "two studies and one become" that is to be carried out amongst all party members mean exactly?" (2016). Available at http://cpc.people.com.cn/xuexi/n1/2016/0301/c385474-28162054.html [November 18, 2016].

Wang, Ren. (2014) Xi Jinping ping "Mao" shifang de xinhao (Messages behind Xi Jinping's comments on Mao). Available at: http://club.china.com/data/thread/1011/2767/45/90/7_1.html [October 10, 2016].

Xi, Jinping. (2014a) Xi Jinping: zai jinian Kongzi danchen 2576 zhounian guoji xueshu yantaohui shang de jianghua (Speech by President Xi Jinping at the international conference commemorating the 2565th anniversary of Confucius' birth). *Xinhua wang*. Available at: http://news.xinhuanet.com/politics/2014-09/24/c_1112612018.htm [October 10, 2016].

Xi, Jinping. (2014b) Xi Jinping zhuxi Qufu jianghua: shijie ruxue chuanbo, zhongguo yao baochi chongfen huayuquan (Speech by President Xi Jinping in Qufu: In promoting Confucianism around the world, China must maintain sufficient discursive power). *Guancha zhe*. Available at: www.guancha.cn/XiJin-Ping/2014_09_29_271934.shtml [October 10, 2016].

Xing, Beinan. (2016) "Pi Lin Pi Kong" yundong zhong "Pi Kong" de jiben tezheng cong zhongguo gongchan dang yu rujia wenhua guanxi de shijiao lai jiexi (An analysis of the relationship between the CCP and Confucian culture: the characteristics of criticising Confucius during the Movement of Criticising Li Biao and Confucius). In Wu Chengmo (ed.), *Hong Huo – Wenge Wushi Zhounian Xueshu Lunwen Ji (1966–2016)* (Red Disaster: A Collection of Academic Papers on the 50th Anniversary of the Cultural Revolution). New York: World Chinese Publishing, pp. 274–290.

Xing, Meiling. (2011) Mao Zedong yu rujia sixiang (Mao Zedong and Confucian ideas). *Yanbian Daxue Xuebao (Shehui Kexue Ban)* (Journal of Yanbian University: Social Sciences), 44 (1), pp. 69–73.

Xinhua Wang. (2016) Confucius Institute: promoting language, culture and friendliness. Available at: http://news.xinhuanet.com/english/2006-10/02/content_5521722.htm [October 3, 2016].

Xu, Jin. (1995) *Mao Zedong Zhi Hun* (The Spirit of Mao Zedong). Zhongyang wenxian chuban she, Beijing.

Xunjie Jiaoyu (2016) Zhongguo guoxue zhongxin zai Beijing jiancheng, Zhongyang jueding zai quanguo zhongxiaoxue tuiguang guoxue fanli jiaoyu (Chinese classics center established in Beijing and the central government to implement learning selected Chinese classics in primary and secondary schools). Available at: www.jtxlszx.com/a/xydt/jyxw/2016/1006/150402.html [October 15, 2016].

Yang Yang. (1995) Zhongguo chuantong zhengjiao heyi guannian poxi (Study of the Chinese traditional idea of politics and religion/education in one). *Tianjin Social Sciences*, 6, pp. 51–57.

Yi, Baisha. (1916) Kongzi pingyi shang (A critique of Confucius I). *Qingnian Zazhi* (New Youth), 1(6).

Yuan, Gangong. (2014) Xi Jinping chaogao guige jinian Kongzi de zhenshi yitu (Real motivations behind Xi Jinping's high-profile effort in commemorating Confucius). Available at: www.szhgh.com/Article/opinion/zatan/2014-09-25/63613.html [October 10, 2016].

Zhonggong zhongyang guanyu quanmian tuijin yifazhiguo ruogan zhongda wenti de jueding (CCP Central Committee Decision Regarding Some Major Questions in Comprehensively Promoting Governance According to the Law). (2014) *Xinhua wang*, October 28. Available from: http://news.xinhuanet.com/politics/2014-10/28/c_1113015330.htm [January 10, 2015].

Zhou, Zhicheng. (2010) Lun Kongzi chengwei shengren zhi guocheng ji qita (On the process through which Confucius became a Saint and other matters). *Kong Zi Yanjiu* (Studies of Confucius), 4, pp. 30–39.

4
THE CCP'S USE AND ABUSE OF NATIONALISM

Edward Friedman

Introduction

The politics of Chinese nationalism, that is, what narrative of China's past and what future it augurs or demands, and how that narrative of the nation motivates and mobilizes foreign policy decision-making in the PRC can be the difference between peace and war. There are many ways to tell a story. It is not the case that only one narrative is true and all others are false, although all make factual claims in promising a glorious future for the nation. How each nation understands events depends on time and place and goals and interests and values and how future possibility is imagined. Of course, this complexity produces multiple explanatory narratives of a nation's past and promise. What is of great consequence is that different national narratives facilitate and rationalize different political and policy futures. Inside the history of the Chinese nation, including the PRC era led by the Chinese Communist Party, there naturally are multiple perspectives on China's past, present and future. Some are more war-prone than others. It is the dangerous nationalism which is the focus of this chapter. Its prevalence diminishes hopes to maximize the possibility of peace persisting.

Being multi-stranded in its possibilities, nationalism is contested and mutable. One way to highlight the contrasts between peaceful and war-prone orientations within the CCP is to starkly compare the foreign policy orientations of Supreme Leader Deng Xiaoping, who reigned from August 1977 to sometime before his death two decades later, with the orientation of CCP supreme leaders, Hu Jintao and Xi Jinping. Starting at the end of 2008, after China had successfully staged an awesome Summer Olympics, and after Chinese students abroad had passionately challenged human rights demonstrators, from France to South Korea, who protested the cruel mistreatment of Tibetans in the PRC, with the student patriots wrongly asserting that non-Chinese media told negative lies about China's policy toward Tibetans, a large change occurred.

As a result of these 2008 events, the CCP leadership was increasingly confident that, backed by a patriotic Chinese people, the CCP was returning China to the glory of civilized centrality, as in the Tang dynasty more than a millennia ago. Except that, in contrast to the Tang's focus on continental Asia, the PRC, after 2008, was more focused on maritime Asia. Since 1993, CCP ruling groups have facilitated the international quest for energy by the PRC's petro-SOEs. Looking at ocean sources of energy and vulnerable sea lanes to the oil rich Middle East, CCP ruling groups concluded that for China again to be a central civilization, the PRC had to incorporate maritime Asia. The PRC needed a global blue water navy.

This feeling that China was winning and would establish its superiority was reinforced by major economic ruptures. Since China had entered the World Trade Organization (WTO) at the end of 2001, barriers to Chinese exports had fallen all around the world. With China applying the policies of the East Asian variety of capitalism borrowed from neo-mercantilist Japan and others to win globally in industrial exports, PRC exports soared. Eventually US$4 trillion in foreign exchange would be amassed, earning China the capacity for enormous international influence founded on loans, aid, investments, bribes, scholarships, building infrastructure and creating multi-billion dollar multilateral international organizations. These CCP initiatives would make China central to the world economy. In addition, the 2007–2008 financial crash in the USA persuaded many Chinese leaders that, in contrast to a rapidly rising China, America's best days were behind it, while China's best days lay just ahead. The USA was in a terminal decline. The future belonged to China. This Chinese nation was imagined in the CCP both as a great power on its way to becoming the world's largest economy and as the world's most successful post-colonial nation, the natural leader of post-colonial states, a moral force in international politics.

Exacerbation of nationalism after the 2008 financial crisis

In response to a sudden decline in Chinese exports caused by the deep American 2008 recession, the CCP enacted a huge stimulus package which got the Chinese economy swiftly back to high and, hopefully, steady growth. This produced confidence in China's leadership that the CCP could keep the PRC economy roaring ahead at 8 percent or higher a year, as related by Chinese analyst Hu Angang. As a result of imagining China's continuous rapid rise and American decline, Chinese ruling groups persuaded themselves that they could abandon former Supreme Leader Deng's policy, followed by Deng's successor, Jiang Zemin, of prioritizing economic cooperation with America and pursuing a charm policy with Asia-Pacific neighbors (Jiang excluded Japan from his charm policy) and instead, after 2008, act on their own recent territorially expansionist view of China's sovereign rights in maritime Asia and their own notion of building a China-centered international order. China's national narrative was reimagined. The dominant nationalism among CCP ruling groups mutated from Deng's notion of growing by avoiding the errors of the late Ming and of the Mao era self-isolation to instead benefit from the most advanced forces of the world market in a USA-centered set of international organizations. Since the nationalist rupture of 2008, CCP ruling groups embraced a more war-prone notion of China imposing its will in maritime Asia and luring and leading the world into building a China-centered global order. This confident and assertive post-Deng nationalism took the CCP state into war-prone clashes with others in the Indo-Pacific region. Which nationalism prevails and which national narrative is embraced by the CCP supreme leader and his supporters is crucial for war or peace.

Some students of international relations described the switch from Deng's nationalism to the nationalism of Supreme Leader Xi Jinping as similar to the rise of a racist, militarist nationalism in Kaiser Wilhelm's Germany after the fall of Otto Bismarck, who had chosen to cooperate with Britain to facilitate Germany's rise. In this analogy, China's Deng is Bismarck and America is Britain. Both Deng and Bismarck cooperated with the leading economic power, America for Deng and Britain for Bismarck, so that their nation rose toward becoming number one, yet made sure to avoid clashes with the then leading power. Before the late 2008 CCP switch to a policy of chauvinistic assertiveness – a move away from Deng's policy of cooperating with

America – China Central TV produced in 2006 a series entitled "The Rise of Great Powers." The TV series includes a particularly instructive episode on Germany. Worshipful filmmakers credited Bismarck with securing 20 years of peace for newly united Germany. The television series showers praise on the Iron Chancellor for muting envy and fear in European capitals, and keeping a vengeful France in check. In contrast, the succeeding German regime of Kaiser Wilhelm II promoted a racist chauvinism and arms races with France and Britain, unleashing dynamics which facilitated the First World War (Holmes 2010).

Henry Kissinger, who has known all of China's leaders since Mao, looking at China's post-2008 assertiveness, saw China as moving in this dangerous Wilhelmite direction. These leaders "could generate a growing adversarial relationship, much as Germany and Britain drifted from friendship [in the Bismarck era] to confrontation," as occurred under Wilhelm II (Beenhold 2010). The struggle for power and primacy within the CCP is therefore key to whether or not China will act on a war-prone nationalism. The politics of nationalist contestation within CCP ruling groups is decisive. It matters whether China's national narrative emphasizes as a negative example, as did Deng, China's decline after the death of Ming dynasty emperor Yong Le, Ming Zhu Di and again turns away from oceanic trade, as did Mao, a narrative in which joining the world market meant opening China to imperialist exploitation and enslavement, as supposedly occurred after the British-initiated Opium War around 1840. The new nationalist narrative shaped to serve the policy preferences of Supreme Leader Xi imagined a global order in which, in contrast to Deng's nationalism, others accepted subordination in a China-centered order because China, uniquely, supposedly offered win-win magnanimity.

Some analysts see the comparison between Deng and post-Deng foreign and security policy in China and Bismarck and post-Bismarck policy in Imperial Germany as misleadingly Eurocentric. They see more similarity in a comparison of post-Deng China with Imperial Japan after the Taisho era. In both East Asian instances, an ever more influential, autonomous and hawkish military, finding itself contained by global liberal forces, became ever more powerful at home and assertive abroad.

Sufficient persuasive data for this conclusion is not readily available from a secretive CCP regime which tries to hide the role of the military. Some see this military as trying to block forces of peace and instead promoting provocative initiatives. These analysts note how the Chinese military more than once has sparked border incidents when civilian leaders from Beijing and New Delhi met to further peaceful cooperation. In like manner, American leaders promoting cooperation have been greeted by provocative Chinese military acts. In contrast, analysts who imagine the CCP as a unitary actor not riven by internal divisions in which military hardliners are ever more influential point out that the purported Chinese military provocateurs were not publicly punished, not noticing that getting away with military provocations could be evidence of the entrenched strength of the military.

As all serious observers of CCP politics understand, the CCP strives mightily to obscure crucial internal divisions and misleadingly present CCP ruling groups as united and single-minded, something that would be a unique global occurrence. The struggle over the nature of Chinese nationalism and PRC foreign policy manifestly reflect a politics of struggle over the narrative of Chinese nationalism.

Nationalism as a pillar of regime legitimacy

After the death of Mao Zedong in September 1976, senior Chinese Communist Party officials and other leaders from state and military, along with their intellectual advisers, met to discuss future policy. Led by Deng Xiaoping, after his ascension to Supreme Leader in mid-1977, the consensus within ruling groups was that the loss of Mao's charismatic authority could threaten the CCP's very legitimacy. The ruling group in the CCP therefore needed new sources of legitimacy, including a new nationalist narrative for an age where China would prosper from openness to the world market.

The CCP then committed itself to Asian development state growth policies that could raise standards of living and deliver performance legitimacy for the CCP. In addition, the CCP facilitated demonstrations in 1981–1982 against Japanese who supposedly tried to cover up the atrocious behavior in China of Hirohito's military from 1931 to 1945. A new nationalism began to be crafted by the CCP that would allow the ruling Leninist dictatorship to claim that the CCP had saved China from General Tojo's cruel invaders in the past and that only this authoritarian CCP could protect China from national humiliation in the future. A new national history was needed to make this narrative persuasive. In short, if one were a Chinese patriot who loved the country, one should love and support the CCP. In the post-Mao era, to avoid humiliations similar to what happened to Chinese in the militaristic Showa era of Emperor Hirohito, a new nationalism – which built in a Hobbesian legitimacy based on the notion that, without the CCP in power, the Chinese people would face chaos and disorder, even civil war – was then constructed in the PRC, a political instrument meant to perpetuate an unaccountable monopoly of power for the CCP.

But Supreme Leader Deng was not anti-Japan. He actually encouraged other leaders to visit Japan in the 1980s to learn from a rapidly rising Japan how to build a strong economy that would be the envy of the world. Even after ordering the spring 1989 crushing of a nationwide Chinese democracy movement, Deng sought a visit by the Emperor of Japan in 1993 to show to the world that China was a legitimate member of the world community which should not be treated as a pariah and a target of economic sanctions because of the slaughter ordered by Supreme Leader Deng of peaceful pro-democracy Chinese citizens on June 4, 1989.

What Deng feared most for the CCP in 1989 and after was not a supposed revanchist threat from an actually peaceful, even pacifistic-tending Japan, but the economic stagnation of Leninist state command economics that had de-legitimated and helped bring down the Communist Party of the Soviet Union in August 1991. While Supreme Leader Deng, as his predecessors (Sun Yat-sen, Chiang Kai-shek and Mao Zedong) and successors (Jiang Zemin, Hu Jintao and Xi Jinping), also wanted China to become the leading state in the world, Deng's understanding of why China had lost the civilizational centrality of the early Tang began with the Ming dynasty's end of support for oceanic commerce after the death of Emperor Ming Zhu Di in the fifteenth century. For Deng, imperial China's abandoning of the benefits of openness to global best practices had allowed a rising Europe to overtake a once-powerful China. Deng understood Mao's policies of economic autarky as producing similar economic stagnation in the era of the PRC. Deng wanted China to grow to global centrality by opening to the world market and maximizing industrial exports as had Japan and South Korea. Deng's successor, Supreme Leader Jiang Zemin (1992–2002), built on Deng's economic openness orientation by welcoming IT-related FDI from IT software leader Taiwan so China would not be locked into low wage assembly and light industry labor. Deng dismissed neo-Maoist claims that opening to the world market would make China a slave to America. Jiang compromised with the US, EU and India to gain PRC entrance to the WTO. That policy facilitated a huge surge in Chinese exports as import barriers limiting Chinese exports fell all over the world. As with Deng, so with Jiang, China's global rise in wealth and power required cooperative relations with the USA and defeating, at the highest levels of CCP politics, the chauvinists whose nationalism supported economic autarky.

There were – and still are – many people within CCP leadership circles who did not agree with Deng's and Jiang's nationalism. National identity and the construction of a useful nationalist narrative were contested. More chauvinistic and totalitarian minded CCP leaders opposed opening to the world. They saw Deng's economic reform ventures as a dangerous opening to so-called bourgeois democratic forces that somehow might de-legitimate and undermine the supposedly socialist CCP's monopoly of arbitrary power. The fearful nationalism of these secret police (Stalinist KGB) nativists was very different from the more open nationalism of Deng and Jiang. The nationalist narrative was contested. Indeed, some analysts find Xi Jinping, who became supreme leader in 2012, as leaning toward these ever stronger conservative chauvinists, even praising the Stalinist Sultanate in North Korea.

The rise of racist and hawkish nationalism

What has been making CCP nationalism far more dangerous than a nationalism understood as a natural love of country is the growing power of ever-more racist and hawkish forces within CCP ruling groups. These anxious leaders reject Deng's more cooperative nationalism, as Wilhelm II rejected Bismarck era cooperation with Britain. This more dangerous nationalism has roots within the institutional make-up of the PRC's Leninist, single-party dictatorship. Most critical of the opening to the world in the inner party struggle over post-Mao nationalism were people within the apparatuses of the security forces, the propaganda apparatus and state-owned enterprises (SOE), such as the Petroleum Faction, which feared competitive market forces. In their nativist nationalism, China (actually the Buddhist Manchu conquerors of the Sinicized Ming people who created the Manchu Qing Empire) was doing just fine during the Ming and Qing dynasties until Western imperialists ignited an Opium War in 1839.

Western imperialism then supposedly turned Chinese into opium addicts, de-vitalizing the nation, and draining China of its silver, thereby destroying the silver-based economy, making a strong China (actually a declining Manchu empire) weak. Given the purported enslaving nature of the so-called imperialist world market, Mao's anti-imperialist policies were imagined inside the nationalism of the Mao era CCP as having protected China from exploitative forces which would otherwise have kept China down, blocking its supposedly independent path to global centrality, actually economically irrational policies which kept the China of high Maoism (1957–1977) poor, weak and stagnant. The Deng/Jiang policies of openness to the world market (e.g., cooperation with the IMF and World Bank and WTO membership) and of market cooperation with the USA were said by the racialist chauvinists to expose China to a return to enslavement by capitalist imperialism. Clashing nationalisms infuse the CCP. Given the attractiveness of their chauvinistic narratives, the economic disasters brought by chauvinistic autarky do not dissuade Maoist true believers.

It is of course quite easy to demonstrate that the anti-Western imperialism nationalist narrative of the conservative chauvinist bears little or no resemblance to actual historical events. The Qing dynasty, after all, had already banned opium in the 1720s because, more than a century before the Opium War, the Manchu rulers of the Qing found Chinese to already be addicted to opium. The silver drain which engendered a financial crisis actually occurred before the Opium War. It happened when Bolivarian revolutions in South America blocked the export of silver to China from the Petosi mines in Peru whose silver had hitherto been shipped to China through the port of Acapulco in Mexico.

But while Mao's Opium War story was not true, that is not decisive. Actually most nationalist narratives tend to be largely mythic. Mao's constructed national narrative was not scholarly history. It was, as is regularly the case with nationalist narratives, a useful political instrument in legitimizing Mao's anti-market, anti-money, anti-mobility policies. The policies however were economically irrational and therefore self-wounding for China. The policies backfired and brought economic stagnation to the people of the PRC at a very low standard of living.

Embracing Mao and his national narrative was, however, politically useful to post-Mao chauvinistic Stalinists whose highest priority was to entrench their power and fend off forces which would open China to liberalization. Hence, they claimed that openness was a threat to the CCP and China. These nationalists found that Mikhail Gorbachev's openness in the Soviet Union led to the loss of power for the CPSU and to the implosion of the USSR into 16 states. The nationalism of the Chinese leftist nativists therefore opposed compromise with the USA to get the PRC into the WTO and insisted instead on the repression of religion and ethnic communities and promoters of legal due process or space for civil society in order to save the CCP a fall from power, as happened to the CPSU, and from a Soviet-style implosion. The "PRC will follow the Soviet Union in ethno-national collapse" if it does not pursue a policy of "fusion," forced assimilation of non-Han communities, which can be seen as a racist policy of "cultured genocide" (Carrico and Gries 2016: 427). This is a huge shift from the original CCP nationalities policy taken from the CPSU in which Han people were expected to respect ethnic customs including veiling (Leibold and Grose 2016: 83). Internally, the new chauvinism pushes the Chinese party-state toward policies of cultural genocide. The national narrative is a tool for and a legitimator of an ever crueler set of policies.

The centrality of "othering" non-Han in and out of China to the new chauvinist national identity is clearly manifested in Han CCP policy to minority (non-Han) communities, whether Lama Buddhist Tibetans, Mongols or Uyghur Turkic Muslims. After Mao died and the more open and humane Hu Yaobang became party secretary and the 1982 constitution created a right "to preserve … their own … customs" (Leibold and Grose 2016: 88), the CCP "shifted … to more accommodating approaches" (Leibold and Grose 2016: 89). When the nativist chauvinists, who had originally opposed Deng's policies of openness and also opposed economic cooperation with Japan and America, helped topple the more pluralist and tolerant Hu Yaobang in late 1986, they were able to impose policies of coerced assimilation on minority communities. Their new nationalist myth is a facilitator of great suffering for over 100 million non-Han people and their cultures in the PRC.

Han nationalism vs. borderland minority communities

This new CCP nationalism also has large foreign policy implications. These can be highlighted by an approach known as fourth-world studies and borderland studies (Friedman 2014). This perspective calls attention to how new states tend to claim the maximum territory of the former empire, in China's case, the militarily expansionist Manchu whose Qing dynasty came to rule more than twice the territory of the Sinicized Ming. Minority communities who previously moved freely on both sides of the new border in the nation-state, an old frontier region, are suddenly at risk. Cross-border communities are suspected of disloyalty. The new state center imagines these fourth-world communities as traitors backed by neighboring states which supposedly seek to split the new state and thereby make China weak. To defend China's sovereignty, the CCP imagines that it must destroy the traitors and their ill-willed foreign supporters. Self-aggrandizing centers demand purity and loyalty.

The chauvinist CCP imagines India as working to split Tibet from China. Similar anxieties about Chinese of Korean descent exist toward both North Korea and South Korea, toward Buddhist countries of Asia vis-à-vis Tibetans and Mongols, toward Central Asian Muslim republics and Russia with regard to Uyghurs, toward America and Japan with regard to the Taiwanese, etc. All of these Qing Empire communities are reimagined as potential traitors to a new nation-state dominated by Han people.

While China actually is ever more militarily powerful and able to bully neighbors, it nonetheless imagines itself as ever more threatened by those neighbors. The new nationalism structures a discourse which demands strong Chinese action against neighbors seen as interfering in sensitive domestic politics. This makes more likely victory for the initiatives of war-prone Chinese ruling groups which imagine anxious neighbors as actual threats to China.

How the state center responds to the imagined threat of border communities informs and reflects the nationalist policies at the state center. A human rights discourse which criticizes CCP repression of border communities tends to be seen as ill-willed and anti-China, a hypocritical attempt to undermine Chinese unity and greatness. Border people and their international friends are imagined as anti-Chinese elements which should be targeted. War may be imagined in Beijing as the price of survival for a glorious China. The Chinese state, as other late-emerging states, tends to have a good conscience about its nasty cultural parochialism, racism and aggression because post-colonial ruling groups, remembering their nation as a victim of imperialism, cannot entertain the possibility that they are now acting in an imperial manner.

The Han CCP cannot easily ask itself why it tested nuclear weapons on Uyghur lands and did so only when the wind was blowing away from Beijing. The CCP cannot find anything to criticize in stationing Han soldiers in Xinjiang, turning demobilized Han into permanent settlers situated antagonistically against Uyghurs. Why wouldn't the Han CCP wish to marginalize disloyal Uyghur and overwhelm them in numbers with loyal Han who, in contrast to Uyghurs (or Mongols), would resist the blandishments of expansionistic Russians? Policies flowing from the new nationalism turn the border communities into peripherialized and endangered minorities on what once was their land. The kind of nationalism which patriots embrace is a matter of life and death for many.

In short, there are many Chinese nationalisms. They are instruments for contending political coalitions and political purposes. It was very easy to construct an anti-Russian nationalist narrative. It was done in the late Mao era. In this narrative, an expansionist Tsarist Russia stole the most territory from China. It was imperialist enemy number one. It courted Uyghurs and Mongols to turn against the Han CCP. It considered invading and bombing Mao era China. It armed and prodded India to march north toward Tibet in 1961–1962.

It was persuasive yet, after Mao died, new supreme leader Deng normalized relations with Moscow and settled disputed borders. There was hardly any fuss about reconciliation with Russia raised by Chinese people who had just been passionately imagining Russia as threat number one.

Many different nationalisms are possible and persuasive. Were there a real pro-American ruling group in Beijing, it could easily imagine a nationalist narrative to legitimate that policy perspective. After all, it was the USA which led the armed forces coalition that defeated Hirohito's Imperial military and liberated Chinese from a cruel occupation by Tojo's military. It was America, opposed by Britain, France and Russia, which insisted on China as one of the five permanent members of the UN Security Council with veto power. It was America, when China was militarily threatened by CPSU leader Brezhnev's doctrine legitimating Soviet invasions to topple unfriendly Communist Party states, which made an entente with the PRC, the Nixon-Mao axis, to deter Russian aggressors. And, it was America, when Supreme Leader Deng initiated economic reforms, which awarded China the largest quotas for apparel exports under the Multi Fiber Agreement and agreed to award China Most Favored Nation treatment for its exports to the USA even though China was not a market economy. That is, American policies which were uniquely favorable to Chinese exports facilitated China becoming the factory of the world, thereby greatly aiding China's stunning economic rise. In this narrative, cooperation with America is a prerequisite of China's awesome global preeminence.

That actual expansionist and chauvinist narrative that the CCP constructed in the post-Mao era is far more incredible than a nationalism of cooperation with the USA. Throughout Chinese history, a dominant discourse has been about resisting invaders from the north and west. National heroes were Han defenders against invasion by Xiongnu, Liao, Jin, Mongols and Manchus. These resisters to northern invaders are celebrated in history and poetry. Sun Yat-sen's patriots experienced the Manchu's Qing dynasty, established by non-Confucian northern invaders, as 267 years of humiliation. The patriots of the 1911 revolution who toppled the Manchu imperium in 1911–1912 carried out racist pogroms against the Manchus. Some nationalists celebrated Confucian Han patriots who courageously resisted Ming despots. These Chinese Confucians saw the anti-Confucian practices of the Ming despots as a continuation of the alien tyranny of the Mongols who overthrew the historic Confucian balance of state forces and concentrated all power in the hands of the Zhu lineage. In addition, those Han who helped the Mongols defeat the Sinicized Song were denounced as traitors. Before 1911, there were long-accepted narratives describing Han heroes who resisted invaders.

And then, suddenly, after the 1911 republican revolution and again after Mao died and the CCP lost the legitimation of Mao's charisma, Han rulers, living in a global racist order, invented a blood, racist nationalism, a narrative in which all who lived in the Manchu Qing Empire, at the height of its military expansionism, were one shared blood people supposedly going back to the times, millennia past, of rule by the emperors Yan and Huang. Mongols and Manchus were not alien invaders, as the prior consensus held. Now, amazingly, it was those who resisted Mongol, Manchu and other invaders from the north and west who were redefined as splittists opposing the reunification of China. A somewhat persuasive rightist, racialist chauvinist myth was constructed (and contested) in the era of neo-fascism associated with Chiang Kai-shek's Republic of China (ROC).

China's nationalist narrative has been constructed and reconstructed and challenged. It has greatly changed since Mao's death. As the founders of Israel initially would not embrace a national identity rooted in being victims of European anti-Semitism but instead celebrated the heroes of the war for independence, so Mao rejected a national identity discourse in which the Chinese nation were mere victims humiliated by Britain in the 1839–1842 Opium War and by cruel Japanese invaders from 1931 to 1945. Mao instead promoted a nationalism predicated on a unique history of heroic peasant rebels. In Mao's nationalism, the people united – under Mao's leadership – could never be defeated. By 1955 Mao was telling Japanese visitors to stop apologizing for their crimes against Chinese humanity and get on with life. Chinese patriots were heroes, not victims.

Chinese nationalism morphs into chauvinistic xenophobia

But, after Mao's death in 1976, and the loss for the ruling CCP Leninist single-party dictatorship of Mao's legitimating charisma, imagining China as the victim of barbaric invaders from Japan against whom the CCP fought to successfully protect China from humiliation was a narrative promoted as a better instrument for legitimating the CCP's unaccountable monopoly of arbitrary state power. That is, Chinese nationalism, as other nationalisms, is an instrument to serve the changing interests of changing ruling groups. It is not a historical or cultural primordial essence. It surely has little to do with the facts of history. It almost never does.

But ruling groups and their chosen nationalism can change in large and unexpected ways. The pro-Deng Xiaoping economic reformers who came to power after Mao died and who copied the Japanese economic model, nonetheless, launched a new anti-Japan nationalism at the start of the 1990s, thereby unleashing a neo-fascist racism that augurs cultural genocide and settler colonialism for Mongols, Uyghurs and Tibetans and a Han chauvinism that imagines a glorious Chinese past and future that is arrogantly demeaning of smaller neighbors. (See Chapter

19, "The CCP's Tibet Policy: Stability through Coercion and Development," and Chapter 20, "The Party-State's Nationalist Strategy to Control the Uyghur: Silenced Voices.") The new chauvinist discourse imagines subordinating neighboring peoples as a Chinese blessing for those supposedly less advanced nations that, to the CCP, only anti-China racists could reject. Therefore, Americans or Indians or Vietnamese or any people which resisted or balanced against China's imperial and expansionist post-Deng nationalist project were imagined among CCP ruling groups as an enemy which had to be resisted or destroyed. The unintended consequences of purposeful action, the long-term impacts of the new racial chauvinism on reform and reformers could be devastating for China and the world. The new racialist patriotism promoted a war-prone set of policies that could win power for a war party and treat the Deng era project of China growing wealthy and powerful from world market participation as a treasonous sell-out of the nation to ill-willed, less civilized world powers. As a racialized Israeli nationalism undermined progressive leaders and legitimated a turn toward hard-right xenophobes, so it could be with China.

Because of how Han people, especially those in the CCP, have come to imagine their destiny, the narrative of the nativistic neo-totalitarians is compelling and attractive. The prior Deng/Jiang narrative seeking cooperation to promote wealth and power seemed weak. Han Chinese, believing in the superior ethical quality of Chinese families, embraced a nationalist narrative in which they were duty bound to civilize non-Han. Even in the late Qing era, when defeat of the Qing Empire by the Meiji Empire of Japan in an 1894–1895 war fought largely about hegemony in Korea led to a Han nationalist backlash against being ruled, humiliated and made vulnerable to more foreign domination because of the policies of useless alien Manchu conquerors, the Han insisted on restoring Han centrality premised on Han superiority. Patriots welcomed narratives which made the Han superior.

> When Whites were seen as a conquering "race," Chinese … asserted that the Chinese were of Middle Eastern Origin and that "Caucasian blood" predominated among ancient Chinese sages; that Moses was the ancient philosopher Mo Zi, and Christianity succeeded because Jesus translated Confucius into Latin … Liang Qichao … claimed that because of its supposed founding by [Asian] Huns …, Hungary was "established by the yellow race on the territory of the whites." Hungary's Golden Bull … showed that it was the "yellow race" that "first established a civilized polity in the world."
>
> *(Sautman 2001: 111)*

> Both Sun [Yat-Sen] and Mao share the "China Dream" … to revive the ancient civilizational glory of China … making China the wealthiest, strongest, and most advanced country in the world.
>
> *(Yang 2016: 78)*

> China possesses a superior cultural gene needed to become the world's leader.
>
> *(Yu 2014)*

But, of course, Han Chinese are not the only people in the world who embrace a national narrative of unique civilizational superiority. What makes the Han chauvinist nationalism dangerous in the post-Mao era is how it is combined with China's awesome, rapid rise in wealth, power and ambition. Consider the matter of contested territory in what Chinese call the East Sea and the South Sea. CCP ruling groups had to decide on their goals. Since nationalism functions "as a frame of reference to order priorities and claims of different actors" (Duara 2016: 422),

CCP leaders who embraced the Deng nationalism of economic openness and political cooperation would pursue policies that were very different from the policies of the reactionary Stalinist chauvinists who feared openness. National identity impacts "how China … operates on the world stage" (Leibold 2016a: 424). At home in the CCP, Han practices, in contrast to supposedly "backward" minority communities, became equated with the "modern" (Leibold and Grose 2016: 89–92). The nativist Stalinists joined, after the implosion of the USSR in 1991, by many former moderate Dengists, sought to socialize Chinese to fear minority cultures as a vehicle of hostile foreign forces trying to split China and weaken the CCP state by creating civil war and chaos. Cultural genocide of the non-Han was presented by nativists in the Han CCP as a life and death issue for Han Chinese (Lin 2016). Various ethnic communities were endangered (Baranovitch 2016). Hardest line nationalists along with coercive assimilationists became ever more influential in an "increasing nationalist and xenophobic body politic in China" (Leibold 2016b). Clearly, which nationalism dominates in the CCP is extraordinarily consequential.

The nationalistic roots of Chinese hegemony

So too on the issue of Chinese territorial expansion in the South Sea. The moderates have been marginalized by ever more influential left chauvinists (Zhang 2016). The patriots whose narrative had China rising when it was open economically and cooperative politically long had argued that China should put aside territorial disputes in the South Sea. After bracketing the territorial disputes, the PRC should then cooperate with neighboring governments to share energy, resources and fisheries. China would thereby diminish its imagined Malacca Strait Dilemma of supposedly having needed energy from the Middle East pass through narrow waters controlled by the US Navy. No neighbor would feel a need for the US Navy. A China cooperating with its neighbors abutting the South China Sea would be secure from the US military and also enjoy food and energy security. Seen by neighbors as a partner, not a threat, neighbors, responding to the cooperative nationalism of CCP moderates, would have little reason to invite the US military into the region. Therefore, in the region, China would be more influential, more secure and more prosperous if it rejected the assertive nationalism of the left chauvinists. Why this moderate nationalist narrative is rejected is because the CCP does not seek security. Its goal is centrality and dominance, precisely as offensive realists would expect.

This power goal helps clarify why the nativist chauvinists have increasingly prevailed in the policy debate in China. Their nationalism is attractive to ruling groups. In their constructed nationalist narrative, China, for millennia, was the center and leader of Asia. China's global glory was interrupted by Western imperialism. China now is returning to its historical and natural global glory. For such Chinese centrality to be realized, China must dominate maritime Asia. In a world of Chinese hegemony, as supposedly proven by a long history of Chinese magnanimity, in eras of Chinese centrality, a uniquely beneficent China will welcome its neighbors to prosper from Chinese reciprocity and fair-mindedness, uniquely Chinese virtues supposedly produced by Confucian civilization and family socialization to superior ethics. It is not easy for Han Chinese to reject this happy depiction of a uniquely ethical Han people with an especially glorious past, and well-deserved future. Neighboring countries which refuse such a seemingly generous Chinese offer of win-win economics as a reward for international subordination are imagined by Han patriots as ungrateful and trouble-making. Such supposedly irrationally anti-China forces, from the perspective of a war-prone Chinese nationalism, deserve to be punished.

In sum, Chinese leadership, in this nationalism, is good for everyone, whereas in this attractive Chinese constructed discourse, American hegemony, in contrast to Chinese leadership, is greedy and exploitative and war-prone, bad for the people of the world. What neighboring governments find to be an immoral expansionist Chinese project, the neo-Chinese nationalism imagines as uniquely ethical.

Needless to say, there is no truth in this imagined Chinese history of unique magnanimity. But it seems rather a pervasive narrative within Chinese leadership circles. CCP leaders are not persuaded by a Vietnamese national history in which the enemy of Vietnamese independence, for millennia, has been China. As Vietnamese say, after suffering millennia of Chinese invasion or occupation, aggression runs in Chinese blood, while resistance runs in Vietnamese blood. Obviously, neighbors who experienced the supposed glories of Chinese imperial expansion are not persuaded by historical narratives which are promoted in Supreme Leader Xi Jinping's preferred construction. Given their patriotic narrative of unique beneficence to the point of softness, Chinese are even offended by the realist claim that China is just another nation-state and acts as do other nation-states. For example, China's history of invading Vietnam and treating Vietnamese cruelly does not in fact make China uniquely aggressive. Vietnam's history of invading Cambodia and treating Khmer people cruelly is similar. China's offensive realism is not an embodiment of a unique Chinese quest for ever more power.

Nationalism makes the CCP believe that China has a special and magnanimous mission in the world. Many Chinese patriots believe that because Chinese are so good, even naïve, others take advantage of China. Mearsheimer's notion that China is just a realist polity ignores the Chinese sense of mission. Mearsheimer obscures the consequences of the new national identity constructed by conservative Chinese chauvinists who find the notion that Chinese are just another nation absurd and insulting. In fact, Xi era CCP foreign policy ambitions flow from a very particular Chinese nationalism, one which legitimates Chinese centrality as the natural and ethical outcome of superior Chinese virtues.

However, this particular version of Chinese nationalism which serves the interests and values of a leading faction within the CCP is also war-prone. Peace in the region may rest on other versions of Chinese nationalism not being wiped out by the recently more powerful expansionist chauvinists. An alternate version of Chinese nationalism, one which counts on continuing cooperation with the USA, Japan, India, the EU, etc. actually remains alive. It continues to dwell within the commanding heights of state power. These leaders are more concerned about avoiding war with America. They know that China cannot become richer and more powerful if it loses the benefits of economic cooperation with the democracies, from South Korea and Taiwan to the European Union. But there is no guarantee that mutually beneficial cooperation will continue if the hard-line nativists succeed in portraying the nationalism of openness and cooperation as national betrayal, as compromise with purportedly anti-Chinese forces which dangerously resist supposedly magnanimous Chinese policies legitimated by the conservative's hawkish and chauvinist national narrative of a uniquely benign and generous China which must, at long last, stand up for justice.

Nationalism: China's past and China's future

Given the centrality and uncertainty of this contestation in the CCP over nationalism, international analysts naturally forecast very different Chinese futures. The political future of China is unknowable. But clearly the rise of the chauvinist narrative does not strengthen the forces of peace and cooperation. None of us can know the future because, among other reasons, politics is a contingent arena. There is no methodology to apply which will accurately forecast the political future of the PRC, none to guarantee which nationalism prevails in the CCP. But the politics of nationalism within the CCP has great consequences for the CCP choice for war or peace.

What the history of Han nationalism demonstrates is that the empire-like, racist, expansionist nationalism of the CCP in the post-Mao, post-Deng, post-Jiang era is not a pure invention of some idiosyncratic subsequent Chinese Leninist supreme leaders. This nasty nationalism was born in the late nineteenth century, an era of racism, an era in which profoundly patriotic opponents of the Ottoman Empire, the Tsarist Russian Empire, the Germanic Hohenzollern Empire as well as the Manchu Qing Empire imagined their national future in terms of a unique racial/cultural superiority. Post-1911 revolution Han pogroms against Manchus did not make Chinese uniquely racist. Such racism pervaded the globe.

Sun Yat-sen's Han Chinese successor, Chiang Kai-shek, leader of the Kuomintang or Chinese Nationalist Party (KMT), sought to incorporate, as part of the new Republic of China, the territorial conquests of the prior gunpowder empire of the hated alien Manchu. This imperial mission was, naturally for the racist era, imagined in racially charged notions of superior blood.

What is seldom noted is how different was the patriotism of Mao Zedong, who was conscious of and opposed Great Han Chauvinism, seeing it as the fascist ideology of Mao's civil war adversary, the Nazi-like (to Mao) KMT of Chiang. Whereas Chiang executed as many Japanese war criminals as possible for their savagery against Chinese during the occupation of the Republic of China by Hirohito's imperial military, Mao courted post-war Japan not to join the USA in a military alliance. By 1955, Mao was telling Japanese visitors, "There is no point in calling you guys to account for past debts." "You have already apologized. You can't apologize everyday now, can you? It isn't good for a nation to keep whining all the time. This is something we [Chinese] understand quite well" (Jacobs 2011: 152).

Seeking good relations with Japan to balance against Brezhnev's militarist threat to China, Mao, by 1972, banned any negative portrayals of Japan in the Chinese media. Mao never commemorated the 1937–1938 massacre in Nanjing by murderous Japanese occupiers. Nanjing, after all, was the pro-Chiang capital of the reactionary KMT. Mao did not mourn the deaths of counter-revolutionaries. In addition, Sun Yat-sen, the titular leader of the revolution which overthrew the Manchu monarchy in 1911–1912, thought of Japan as an ally in Sun's anti-Manchu revolutionary mobilization, with Japanese thought of as people who were of the same blood and the same race and civilization as the Han Chinese.

Obviously, there is nothing natural in Chinese hating Japanese, a policy promoted in so-called patriotic education since 1991. That nationalist narrative is a construction of the post-Mao CCP. The racist anti-Japan narrative of the twenty-first century CCP was even opposed by Supreme Leader Hu Jintao who, from 2006 to 2010, bravely sought conciliation and cooperation with Japan until defeated by anti-Japan forces in the CCP led by former Supreme Leader Jiang Zemin. Nationalism and foreign policy choices are intertwined.

Conclusion

In sum, it is not deep Chinese history that constructs Chinese nationalisms. Many competing national narratives have been constructed and used instrumentally by different Chinese political forces. What is decisive for which nationalism informs CCP policy decision-making combines deeply institutionalized history (the entrenched institutional power of the military which brought the CCP to power in 1949 and kept it in power in 1989) with quite mutable forces inside the CCP (e.g., coalition-building) and larger global tendencies.

To many analysts, today's Chinese nationalism, in which a recently risen economic superpower presents itself as a victim of the USA or the West, seems odd. "Perceived as aggressors, they see themselves as victims, condemned as intolerant, they complain about intolerance of their views" (Ruthven 2016: 142). That sentence was written to describe Islamists. The Chinese nationalist discourse is not uniquely Chinese. It is not only the majority Han who have imagined a discourse where the dominant community imagines itself a victim of minorities, such as non-Han Chinese. In Donald Trump's America, "the average white person now feels that anti-white bias is a bigger problem than other forms of racial discrimination" (Vance 2016: 25). While Tibetans and Uyghurs face cultural genocide, Han Chinese tend to see these victimized communities as lazy ingrates who have been unfairly privileged on everything from child-bearing to college entrance. The bullying Han feel unfairly bullied. In sum, in China, as elsewhere, there are nasty surging rightist, populist nationalisms. What makes the recent chauvinistic CCP nationalism different is that it is able to mobilize the wealth of an economic superpower whose growing world-class military power can serve imperial ambitions inherent in the new nationalism and thereby threaten the peace of the Indo-Pacific. In the Xi Jinping era, the CCP's use and abuse of nationalism strengthens war-prone forces.

References

Baranovitch, Nimrod (2016), "Ecological Degradation and Endangered Ethnicities," *Journal of Asian Studies*, 75.1 (February): 181–205.

Beenhold, K. (2010), "Mutual Trust Called Crucial to U.S.–China Relations," *New York Times*, September 12, www.nytimes.com/2010/09/13/world/europe/13geneva.html.

Carrico, Kevin and Peter Gries (2016), "Race, Knowledge Production and Chinese Nationalism," *Nations and Nationalism*, 22.3: 428–432.

Duara, Prasenjit (2016), "The Temporal Analytics of Nationalism," *Nations and Nationalism*, 22.3: 419–423.

Friedman, Edward (2014), "China's Fourth World Borderlands," *China Review International*, 21.2: 97–104.

Holmes, James (2010), "History Rhymes: The German Precedent for Chinese Seapower," *Orbis*, January, 54.1: 14.

Holmes, James (2011), "Is Bismarck China's Man?" *The Diplomat*, February 19, http://thediplomat.com/2011/02/is-bismarck-chinas-man/.

Hu Angang (2011), *China in 2020*, Washington, D.C., Brookings.

Jacobs, Justin (2011), "Preparing the People for Mass Clemency," *The China Quarterly*: 152–172.

Leibold, James (2016a), "The Minzu Net," *Nations and Nationalism*, 22.3: 423–428.

Leibold, James (2016b), "Creeping Islamophobia," *China Brief*, 16.10.

Leibold, James and Timothy Grose (2016), "Islamic Veiling in Xinjiang," *The China Journal*, 76: 78–102.

Lin Le (2016), "China's Perception of External Threats and Its Current Tibet Policy," *The China Journal*, 76: 103–123.

Paramore, Kiri (2015), "Civil Religion and Confucianism," *Journal of Asian Studies*, 74.2 (May): 269–282.

Ruthven, Malise (2016), "Mosque and State," *Foreign Affairs* (September/October): 142–148.

Sautman, Barry (2001), "Peking Man and the Politics of Paleoanthropological Nationalism in China," *Journal of Asian Studies*, 60.1 (February): 95–124.

Vance, J.D. (2016), "Two Underclasses," *National Review* (August 29): 23–26.

Wang, Zheng (2012), *Never Forget National Humiliation*, New York, Columbia University Press.

Yang, Kuisong (2016), "Studying the Chinese Communist Party in Historical Context," *Journal of Modern Chinese History*, 10.1: 67–86.

Yu, Haiyang (2014), "Glorious Memories of Imperial China and the Rise of Chinese Populist Nationalism," *Journal of Contemporary China*, 23.90: 1174–1187.

Yu, Miles Maochun (2016), "Understanding China's Strategic Culture Through Its South China Sea Gambit," *Military History in the News*, May 8.

Zhang, Feng (2016), "The Fight Inside China Over the South China Sea," *Foreign Policy*, June 23.

Zheng, Feng (2015), *Chinese Hegemony*, Stanford, Stanford University Press.

PART III

How the Party works and stays relevant

5

THE PARTY RUNS THE SHOW

How the CCP controls the state and towers over the government, legislature and judiciary

Jean-Pierre Cabestan

Introduction: factors underlying the Party's omnipotence

It is almost a truism to say that the Chinese Communist Party (CCP) plays a leading role not only in the People's Republic of China (PRC)'s political system but also in the whole economy and society. The CCP is the cornerstone of the Chinese political system and, in many ways, *is* the political system, since all decisions are made in the Party and carried out by Party cadres, whether they work in the CCP apparatus, the government, the legislature, the judiciary or the People's Liberation Army (PLA). As a result, many analysts, including myself, refer to CCP not so much as a ruling Party – what the PRC authorities claim to be – but rather as a Party-state (Cabestan 2014; Wright 2015).

The CCP constitution has constantly underscored this leading role:

> The Communist Party of China is the vanguard both of the Chinese working class and of the Chinese people and the Chinese nation. It is the core of leadership (*lingdao hexin*) for the cause of socialism with Chinese characteristics and represents (*daibiao*) the development trend of China's advanced productive forces, the orientation of China's advanced culture and the fundamental interests of the overwhelming majority of the Chinese people.
>
> (*Constitution of the Communist Party of China 2012)*

Imagined by Marx and instituted by Lenin, the Communist Party's leading role cannot be questioned: in China as in other defunct or remaining socialist countries, it is rooted in the revolutionary process and the Party's victory over other political forces. As a result, the CCP's ability to represent the interests of the Chinese society is quasi immanent to its existence and constitutes the main ideological justification of the monopolistic and durable political power that it exerts over the society.

However, how the Party runs the show is more complex than it appears at a first glance. Its role is much larger than its official mission. Its organization principles look democratic but, rooted in Soviet Russia's "war communism," are mainly top-down, as in the military. Its formal structure and leading organs give a good idea of the role of the CCP's supremo, the Secretary General, today Xi Jinping, and the distribution of major government, legislative, judicial and military powers among his colleagues as well as among the various branches of the local bureaucracy; but it does not inform us much about the relationships among these major levers of power, between the center and the periphery or among the various levels of the periphery. More importantly, while the Party constitution draws a clear line between its leading cadres, its non-leading cadres and its simple members, it does not specify the relationship among these three major groups. In other words, while the Party leads, it does not tell us how it leads. Keen to protect the "Party secrets," it is particularly opaque about its internal operation, its decision-making processes as well as its control mechanisms. Consequently, it can be argued that, as other ruling communist parties, the CCP operates as a secret society, the largest secret society on earth (89 million members in 2016), but a secret society that acts as a political organization that runs the country from behind and mainly through its "state facade" – the government, the legislature and the judiciary in particular – as well as the military.

The mission of the Party: leadership and control

The main mission of the Party is clearly to lead. However, its other key official missions are to control the state and remain the guarantor of the people's interests. "Leadership by the Party means mainly political, ideological and organizational leadership," says the CCP constitution, adding that "it must concentrate on leading economic development" (Constitution of the Communist Party of China 2012). In the Party's jargon, political leadership includes deciding the country's "political line" (*luxian*), its general policies (*fangzhen*) and its specific public policies (*zhengce*). The state apparatus and the military can only implement these decisions. Ideological leadership means that the CCP, through its propaganda departments and PLA's General Political Department, disseminates its official discourse and makes sure that all Party, state and military units stick to and themselves propagate this discourse. Organizational leadership includes a structural control of both the government and the PLA as well as all state organizations: the legislature, the judiciary but also state-owned enterprises and public institutions (*shiye danwei*), such as universities or hospitals, and a monopoly on the choice and promotion of cadres within all these organizations, the well-known *Nomenklatura* system (see Chapter 10, "The CCP's Meritocratic Cadre System"). Although the reform and open-door policy of 1979 – and the emergence of the private sector – has loosened its ability to manage the economy, the Party is keen to keep its control of the so-called "commanding heights" of the industry and the service sector (e.g., energy, heavy industry, telecommunications).

The second mission of the CCP – control – has always been harder to achieve since its leading cadres both lead and manage all state organizations or the military which they dominate by their sheer numbers (see below): under such conditions, how can the Party control the state or the military's actions? One answer has been to empower the Party's discipline inspection commissions (DICs) and make them more autonomous from the Party's leading organs. That is precisely what Xi has encouraged since the launching of an unprecedented anti-corruption campaign in 2013. However, most observers doubt that this will be enough to overcome the long-existing tension between management and control. Moreover, based on the "mass line" (*qunzhong luxian*), according to which the Party must remain close to and inspired by the people, its role of guarantor of the people's interests is difficult to evaluate without genuine open and democratic elections of its leaders (although central and local Party leaders do regularly organize opinion surveys for their own consumption).

In any event, the Party's main problem has always been its structural difficulty to establish a distinction between leadership, management and control, even if, as we will see, a better division of labor has taken shape between the Party apparatus, state organizations and the military.

The organization principles and structure of the Party

On paper, the main organization principles of the Party look very democratic: democratic centralism, collective leadership and election of leaders (Constitution of the Communist Party of China 2012). In reality, the CCP is very hierarchical: ultimate responsibility is personally exerted by the Party committee secretary at each level as well as in every state organization (*yibashou*), and leaders are coopted, the election being relegated to a formalistic final step in the process, usually with very little competition or uncertainty. In addition the CCP is a huge and diverse organization that can be divided into three major groups: the roughly 60 million Party simple members (out of a total of 89 million at the end of 2015) who are not cadres and are distributed among some 4.4 million grass-root Party cells or branches (*China Daily* 2016); the approximately 19 million CCP ordinary cadres who hold responsibilities in but mainly outside of the Party (including the quasi-totality of the 7 million public servants working in the government structure) (Ang 2012; Wang 2012); and the 10 million CCP leading cadres (*lingdao ganbu*) who in their large majority run Party, state and military structures at various levels (Cabestan 2014: 420). It is this latter group that guarantees the Party control over the country. While the exact contours of the *Nomenklatura* system remain unknown, it is assumed that 95 percent of the leading cadres are Party members and that all leading cadres are managed and promoted by the powerful CCP organization departments, including the ones who do not belong to the CCP or are members of one of the eight "democratic parties," small groupings that operate under the leadership of the CCP. Among them, 5,000 national and provincial-level leading cadres are directly appointed by the Central Organization Department (COD) and another 39,000 have their nomination reported to the COD (Burns 1994, 2006; Chan 2004). In any event, the *Nomenklatura* system can only turn elections both within and outside of the CCP, with a few exceptions, into a highly perfunctory procedure, the results of which are known in advance (see below).

In its constitution, the CCP establishes a distinction between its national, local and grass-root organizations. While the latter play an important role in social control, only the first two types of Party organizations can lead state and military organizations. In addition, the CCP exerts its control of what it calls "organizations outside of the Party" in establishing inside each of them "Party leading groups" (*dangzu*) which make the final decisions on every matter. Such leading groups are in particular set up in government bodies, the legislature and the judiciary at and above the county level (*xian*) (around 86,440 in 2008) (Gore 2010: 36). Similarly, Party committees are established in the PLA and in security forces at the company level (*lian*) and above (around 90,000 in 2012) (McGregor 2010: 117).

But it is first and foremost through its own leading organs that the Party runs the show and controls state and military organizations.

How the Party controls the state at the national level

At the national level, the best way to comprehend the articulation between the Party, the state and the military is first to present the respective positions occupied by the seven members of the CCP Politburo Standing Committee (PBSC), the Party's top decision-making body. Unpacking the CCP Politburo and Secretariat membership also gives a good idea of how power is distributed at the center. Because of the Cultural Revolution (1966–76) and the partial and temporary destruction of the Party apparatus, a division of labor different from other socialist countries (as for instance the defunct Soviet Union) has taken shape in China between the CCP Secretariat and the State Council, the official name of the central government: while the former is nearly exclusively responsible for Party affairs, the latter is mainly in charge of economic and social reforms. However, Party-based decision-making bodies, in particular central leading groups (CLGs) (also called leading small groups [*lingdao xiaozu*, LSGs]), have continued to play a key (and arguably are playing a growing) role in steering and coordinating the action in both CCP and state institutions in all key sectors of activity (Miller 2008, 2014): each of them is in charge of what has been called since the foundation of the PRC a distinct "functional network," known in Chinese as *xitong*. The major *xitong* are the following: Party affairs, organization, propaganda, security and justice, finance and economy, agriculture, united front, foreign affairs and military affairs (Barnett 1967: 456–457; Lieberthal 2004: 218–233). These networks all cross the boundaries between formal institutions and constitute the best assurance of Party control of the state and the military.

The Politburo Standing Committee and the state

The PBSC is made up of the seven most powerful leaders of the Party and the country since 2012, against nine members between 2002 and 2012.

The CCP Secretary General, Xi Jinping since 2012, is the only leader to have a foot in the three major sets of institutions that together form the PRC political system: the Party (*dang*), the state or the government (*zheng*) and the military (*jun*). While he chairs and drafts the agenda of the PBSC meetings, he is also President of the Republic and Chairman of both the Party and the state Central Military Commission (CMC), the two bodies being identical. No other PBSC member sits in the CMC, except after a successor to the Party Supremo has been chosen (who becomes its first Vice-Chair). The fusion of these three positions (*sanheyi*) was introduced by Deng Xiaoping in 1992–93, when Jiang Zemin was confirmed as the Party Secretary General, and has been upheld since then with the exception of the 2002–04 awkward transition between Jiang and Hu Jintao, when the former, after retiring from both his Party and state positions, kept for two years the CMC chairmanship. Since the early 1990s, the Party Secretary General also chairs the CLGs in charge of foreign affairs, security and Taiwan. What Xi has done after he succeeded Hu has been to consolidate even further his role, in taking over the control of a key CLG (finance and economics) as well as in creating additional CLGs, such as the ones in charge of maritime security, that appeared in mid-2012 and were already then headed by Xi (Jacobson 2014), to "deepen overall reforms" (*quanmian shenhua gaige*, November 2013) and on cybersecurity and informatization (December 2013). These CLGs and other new CCP structures, such as the Central National Security Commission (*zhongyang guojia anquan weiyuanhui*, CNSC, November 2013) which has since then replaced the security CLG, are all chaired by Xi ("Decision..." 2013). This means that the Party Secretary General is now directly in charge of four *xitong*: military affairs, foreign affairs, law and justice as well as finance and economy.

While Xi has moved back more power within the Party, he has also continued to rely on state institutions to draft, implement and, when need be, turn into laws the decisions endorsed by the PBSC and, for the most important of them, formally approved by the CCP Central Committee at its annual plenum.

Since 2012–13, the second most important member of the PBSC is attributed *ex officio* to the Premier of the State Council (today Li Keqiang). Before, for 20 years, this second position was occupied by the National People's Congress (NPC)'s Chairperson. Leading the central government, the Premier supervises all the ministries, commissions and other central state bureaus, as well as, indirectly, their local branches. For a long time, the Premier was more specifically in charge of the economy but Xi questioned this institutional tradition in taking over in 2013 the chairmanship of the CCP Central Leading Group for Finance and Economics (*Zhongyang caijing lingdao xiaozu*, Li is its first Vice-Chairman).[1]

The third most important PBSC (and national) member is the NPC Chairperson (today Zhang Dejiang). We will see below how the CCP leads the local people's congresses at various levels. Suffice it to indicate here that this "pattern" is often followed at the local level but not always. In order to strengthen its control over the local people's congress, the CCP committee secretary of the locality often arrogates to himself or herself the chairmanship of this officially elected body.

The fourth PBSC member in the official lineup is the Chairperson of the China People's Political Consultative Conference (CPPCC, today Yu Zhengsheng), a rather weak institution made in its majority of non-CCP members and that symbolizes the united front. Consequently, the CPPCC Chairperson is the top national leader in charge of united front work, aimed at rallying around the CCP and under its leadership all other political forces or elites.

The fifth PBSC member is usually in charge of the Party Secretariat as well as, since 2012 (after the reduction from nine to seven of the PBSC membership), the propaganda apparatus (Liu Yunshan). The Secretariat is quasi exclusively in charge of Party affairs. However, it leads and coordinates powerful administrative organs of the Central Committee (such as the General Office or the Organization, the Propaganda and the United Front Departments) that play a key role in guaranteeing the Party leadership on the government, the NPC, the CPPCC and all other state institutions. Today, Liu Yunshan chairs two important CCP leading groups responsible respectively for Party edification, and ideology and propaganda.

The sixth PPSC member is since 2012 in charge of Party discipline (Wang Qishan, his predecessor was No. 8 out of 9). Since the reactivation of the CCP Central Commission for Discipline Inspection (CCDI) in 1978, its Secretary has always sat in the PBSC. However, the CCDI is not only responsible for investigating Party members whether they work in the CCP apparatus, the state structures or the military (one of the deputy CCDI secretaries is in charge of Party discipline in the PLA), but also for any public servant suspected of corruption or political deviation. Another CCDI deputy secretary (today Yang Xiaodu), who doubles as the Minister of Supervision, is especially dedicated to the task of tackling corruption within government departments of all levels and particularly among non-CCP government officials.

The seventh BPSC member is the Executive Vice-Premier (today Zhang Gaoli). Introduced when Zhu Rongji occupied this position to assist (and check) Prime Minister Li Peng (1993–98), this arrangement reflects the crucial role played by the State Council in implementing economic and social reforms, of course under the supervision of Xi and the CLG for Finance and Economics, of which Zhang is the second vice-chairman.

We don't know much about the way the PBSC operates since its sessions are far from being always publicly reported (Miller 2011, 2013). It is said that it meets every week on Thursday morning and reaches decisions by consensus rather than by vote. In any event, since Xi took over, the role of the Secretary General has been strengthened, limiting the autonomy of the other leaders sitting in this supreme body as well as the five institutions that they represent (State Council, NPC, CPPCC, CCP Secretariat and CCDI), three of them belonging to the state structure. Xi's dominance over his PBSC colleagues was further consolidated after he secured the all-important title of "core of the leadership" at the Sixth Plenum of the Central Committee called in October 2016 (*Wall Street Journal* 2016).

The Politburo and the state

Formal CCP Politburo sessions (25 members) also contribute to strengthening the Party's leadership of the state since 5 out of its 18 other members work in the state structure: one is Vice-President of the Republic (Li Yuanchao), who assists Xi in his diplomatic tasks; three are Vice-Premiers (Ms. Liu Yandong, Ma Kai, Wang Yang) in charge of key areas of the State Council's mission; and one (Li Jianguo) is General Secretary of the NPC and responsible for the day-to-day operation of the Chinese legislature. Other Politburo members lead key CCP central departments or provincial-level CCP committees. Nevertheless, meeting on a monthly basis, the Politburo is a secondary power locus: usually, it formally endorses decisions that have already been approved by the PBSC, and, on occasions, it also convenes to discuss important domestic or international issues with experts (Miller 2004).

The CCP Secretariat and the state

We know even less about the manner in which the CCP Central Secretariat works. Made up of seven members since 2012, it is officially the PBSC's "working body" (*banshi jigou*) (Constitution of the Communist Party of China 2012). As indicated above, this powerful body is mainly in charge of Party affairs. But controlling the CCP central departments responsible for the circulation of documents and information (General Office, headed by Politburo and Secretariat member Li Zhanshu), cadres' careers (the Organization Department, headed by Politburo and Secretariat member Zhao Leji) and the official discourse (the Propaganda Department headed by Politburo and Secretariat member Liu Qibao), it holds a large sway on governmental affairs. For instance, the Organization Department exerts direct leadership on all the state administrations in charge of personnel, such as the Ministry of Human Resources and Social Security. Similarly, the Propaganda Department regularly dispatches instructions to all departments in its area of competence, but also directly supervises the Ministries of Education and Culture.

The Secretariat also plays a role in strengthening the Party's control over the CPPCC since one of its members, Du Qinglin, a former CCP United Front Department Director, is also Vice-Chairman of this consultative assembly. In addition, the Secretariat coordinates with the CCDI since its sixth member, Zhao Hongzhu, is Wang Qishan's right-hand man (and No. 2 of the CCDI).

Finally, since 2012, one of the Secretariat's members (Yang Jing) has also been the General Secretary of the State Council, a key associate of the Prime Minister and member of the State Council Standing Committee (incorporating only the vice-premiers and the state councilors), a powerful body that meets weekly and de facto leads the central government (State Organs no date). This is the first time since 1997 that a member of the Secretariat is responsible for governmental affairs and the first time since the 1980s that he has occupied a concurrent position in the State Council. Aimed at better coordinating the work of both institutions, this appointment also constitutes an additional method for Xi, to whom Yang is close, to better control Li Keqiang and his team's day-to-day activities.

The CCP Central Leading Groups (CLGs), the *xitong* and the state

Already mentioned, the CCP CLGs as well as the newly created CNSC play an important role in guaranteeing Party control of state affairs, a role that Xi has obviously strengthened both as a way to consolidate his own power to the detriment of Premier Li Keqiang but also to boost the Party's overall leading and coordinating role (see above).

The oldest CLGs were created by Mao Zedong in the late 1950s (as the ones in charge of foreign affairs and politics and law turned into a commission in 1980) but most of them appeared in the reform era (Miller 2008). Since they are seldom mentioned in the PRC official media, it is hard to define with precision their role and fully identify their membership. Some of them are temporary but the most important of them are permanent and include representatives of both the Party and the government and sometimes the military. It should be added that the government and even the military also set up CLGs, particularly when they need to prioritize and better coordinate a particular task. However, the CCP CLGs, especially those chaired by a PBSC member, are not only the most powerful ones but also the CLGs that can best strengthen Party control over the state's major agencies.

On the whole, these CLGs help the CCP make sure that its decisions are carried out by all the bureaucracies that are part of the same *xitong*. But in associating representatives of related *xitong* they also facilitate coordination among Party and state agencies that usually do not have (or are not allowed to entertain) horizontal relations among themselves.

Let's take the example of the Central Leading Group for Foreign Affairs (*Zhongyang waishi gongzuo lingdao xiaozu*): chaired by Xi since the end of 2012, it includes the Vice-President of the Republic (Li Yuanchao, as its Vice-Chairman), the State Councilor in charge of this area (Yang Jiechi), who is also the director of this CLG's powerful office (*bangongshi*), the Foreign Minister (Wang Yi), the Director of the CCP International Liaison Department (Song Tao since 2015) as well as the ministers of Trade (Gao Hucheng), Defense (Chang Wanquan), Public Security (Guo Shengkun) and State Security (Chen Wenqing). Also siting on the CLG are the deputy-chief of the PLA general staff in charge of intelligence (Sun Jianguo), the directors of the State Bureau for Taiwan Affairs (Zhang Zhijun), the Hong Kong and Macau Affairs Bureau (Wang Guangya), the Overseas Chinese Affairs Bureau (Qiu Yuanping) and the State Council Information Office (Wang Chen) (Lam 2013b). The large majority of these officials work in the State Council. At the same time, they are all CCP cadres, most of whom are Central Committee members. More importantly perhaps, some of them also hold a concurrent Party position: apart from General Chang who belongs to the CMC, it is worth mentioning that Yang Yiechi is also director of the CC Foreign Affairs Bureau, a body that Xi relies on heavily, according to some sources (Glaser 2015), and that the Bureau in charge of Taiwan as well as the Information Office are both a Party and a state administration, according to the well-known Chinese expression: "one organ, two signs" (*yi ge jigou, liang ge paizi*). (The CCP facet of the Information Office is the International Propaganda Bureau.) It shows that for important matters, the Party manages state affairs directly: for example, the same principle applies to sensitive bureaucracies such as the State Archives Bureau and the State Bureau for Secrecy Protection (*Zhongguo Zhengyao* no date).

Having said that, much remains unknown regarding the actual role of this LSG, its modus operandi as well as its full membership.

The Taiwan Affairs CLG membership partly overlaps with the CLG on Foreign Affairs. Also chaired by Xi, it includes however the Chairman of the CPPCC as its Vice-Chair (Yu Zhengsheng), because of the crucial role he plays in united front work (see above). The somewhat less important Hong Kong and Macau CLG manifests some similarities with the two previous ones, although it is now chaired by the NPC Chairman (Zhang Dejiang), the Vice-President of the Republic (Li Yuanchao) being only its Vice-Chair (before 2012 it was chaired by Vice-President Xi Jinping).

Apart from the two CLGs headed by Liu Yunshan, in charge of Party Edification and Propaganda, the other important CLG that needs to be mentioned is the one in charge of agriculture. Created in 1994 and chaired since 2013 by a Politburo member, Wang Yang who is also one of the State Council Vice-Premiers, this CLG is not as prominent as the others. But agricultural development has always been at the top of the CCP agenda, the Party traditionally devoting every year its first official red-headed Central Committee document to this issue.

Let's turn now to the structures created by Xi after 2012, the CNSC, the Central Leading Group for Comprehensively Deepening Reforms and the Central Leading Group for Cyberspace Affairs (also known as the Central Leading Group for Cybersecurity and Informatization): all of them directly contribute to consolidating Xi's as well as the Party's leadership on law and order as well as economic reforms.

As soon as he became Secretary General, Xi took over the political-legal apparatus from Zhou Yongkang, the ex-ninth member of the PBSC in charge of this area (Zhou was sentenced to life imprisonment for corruption and abuse of power in 2015) (Lam 2013a). This move was aimed at reducing the autonomy of the powerful CCP Central Politics and Law Commission (CPLC) (*zhongyang zhengfa weiyuanhui*), whose secretary (or boss) was also Zhou before. Headed since November 2012 by Politburo member Meng Jianzhu, the CPLC continues to lead and coordinate all the institutions responsible for law enforcement and justice, including the Ministries of Public Security (which Meng was in charge of before), State Security and Justice, as well as the Supreme People's Court and the Supreme People's Procuratorate. However, its status has been downgraded and it is today more tightly supervised by the Party Supremo to whom it now directly reports (Lam 2013a). There have been speculations that the decision made at the CCP Third Plenum in November 2013 to empower the court system and make it more autonomous would weaken the CPLC and its local branches. However, the same decision has also clearly promised to keep the politics and law commissions in place and their leading role over the state bodies mentioned above intact ("Decision…" 2013). In other words, the Chinese judiciary, particularly the Supreme Court, have become more professional and are likely to expand their autonomy in non-sensitive (or non-political) cases. But under Xi, the CCP oversight on the judiciary, especially for every human rights or corruption case, has intensified rather than weakened.

The establishment of the CNSC, also chaired by Xi, has contributed to integrating the law and order *xitong* into a larger network and link up domestic and international security of China as well as the PRC regime. Although much remains unknown about the CNSC and its full membership, it is important to underscore that it is a Party and not a state body, its two Vice-Chairmen are Li Keqiang and Zhang Dejiang, the No. 2 and 3 of the CCP (and the PBSC). Equally significantly, the head of its general office is Li Zhanshu, Xi's right-hand man and the director of the powerful General Office of the Central Committee (Lampton 2015). Although the CNSC is mainly devoted to the domestic security of the PRC (Meng sits on it), it does not exclude international affairs from its realm of action (General Fan Changlong, the No. 2 of the CMC, and General Chang Wanquan are also members of the CNSC), creating potential overlaps and perhaps frictions with the CLG on Foreign Affairs (Saunders and Scobell 2015: 75, 146).

Having convened for the first time in February 2014, the Central Leading Group for Cyberspace Affairs (also known as the Central Leading Group on Cybersecurity and Informatization) is organized on a similar pattern although it is of a slightly lower status: its two Vice-Chairmen are Li Keqiang and Liu Yunshan and the Director of its General Office (a key member) is Xu Lin, who is Director of the State Council's Cyberspace Administration of China, and deputy-head of the CCP Propaganda Department. This CLG includes top Party apparatus leaders (such as Propaganda Chief Liu Qibao and Security Czar Meng Jianzhu), ministers of various portfolios (Public Security and State Security but also Foreign Affairs, Finance, Industry and Information Technology) and two CMC members: Generals Fan Changlong and Fang Fenghui, the chief of the general staff of the PLA (*Xinhua* 2014).

In the economic realm as well, Xi has asserted both his power and Party control. He has not only decided, as indicated above, to chair himself the CLG for Finance and Economics, but to appoint as the director of its office Liu He, a close personal ally and economic adviser. Although Liu is just one of the vice-chairmen of the National Development and Reform Commission (NDRC), he has helped Xi in sidelining Premier Li Keqiang and moving the management of the economy away from the State Council (Naughton 2016: 4). Liu is also suspected to be the "authoritative figure" who publicly contradicted Li in an article published in the *People's Daily* on May 9, 2016. In addition, this CLG, of which Vice-Premier Ma Kai is also Vice-Chairman, directly supervises the State-Owned Assets Supervision and Administration Commission (SASAC), the bureaucracy in charge of the state-owned enterprises, the state banks and the China Investment Corporation.

The establishment of the CCP CLG for Comprehensively Deepening Reforms (CLGCDR) in November 2013 participates in the same logic. However, on purpose mixing government and party responsibilities, this new CLG is also aimed at breaking *xitong* boundaries and compelling major systems to work together. Its three vice-chairmen are Li Keqiang, Liu Yunshan and Zhang Gaoli, and 18 other members, many of whom sit on the Politburo, represent key CCP departments (such as organization and propaganda), security and judicial institutions (Meng Jianzhu), financial and economic bureaucracies and even the military (General Xu Qiliang, second Vice-Chairman of the CMC). The CLGCDR is composed of six "project groups" (*zhuanxiang xiaozu*): economy and environment, democracy and law, culture, social structures, Party edification, and discipline inspection and structural reforms. While the reform of the economy remains important, meeting every month, the CLGCDR clearly has the ambition to pilot and coordinate other reforms whose objectives clearly include consolidating the one-Party system as well as Xi's supremacy at the top of the hierarchy.

The creation of this CLG also highlights the systemic difficulties for bureaucracies belonging to different *xitong* to cooperate and move in the same direction. Finally, the CLGCDR provides a vivid illustration of the way the Party runs the show under Xi, less and less from behind and more and more on the forefront of the political system. The same conclusions can be drawn from the other structures created by Xi, particularly the CNSC and the CLG on Cyberspace Affairs.

All in all, the CCP CLGs play a crucial role in enhancing the Party's control of state affairs. But they operate with the support of Central Committee Departments that also largely contribute to this task.

The CCP Central Committee Departments, the xitong *and the state*

Operating under the CCP Secretariat, the CCP Central Committee Departments do not constitute a very large bureaucracy: their number has varied and is around 20 today (against 16 in 1988 after an important streamlining) and their staff force is rather small and roughly estimated at 30,000 cadres. The major departments have already been cited and continue to lead their *xitong* across the Party-state divide as before: organization, propaganda, united front and international liaison, the latter being responsible in particular for the CCP's relations with foreign political parties. The Central Politics and Law Commission as well as the Central Party School, headed by Liu Yunshan and in charge of training senior cadres, are also part of this set of administrations. But the CCP central bureaucracy does not include any service dealing with financial, economic or social affairs: supervised and piloted by the above-mentioned CLGs, these *xitong* are managed by the State Council's ministries and commissions (50,000 public servants). Concurring with these estimations, the total number of CCP cadres working at the central level was around 70,000 in 2002 (Yang 2002: 299).

This division of labor has not weakened the Party's control of the government: over 90 percent of public servants are CCP members and nearly all ministers sit in the Central Committee (as full or alternate members); and the few top officials who don't belong to the CCP, such as Wang Gang, Minister of Science and Technology since 2008 or Chen Zhu, Minister of Health between 2007 and 2013 (and since then Chairman of the Peasants and Workers' Democratic Party, one of the eight "democratic parties"), must share power with the Ministry's Party Secretary and Party group that make the key decisions from behind.[2]

The Party's control over the NPC and the CPPCC

At the national level, the CCP tightly controls the membership, organization and operation of these two assemblies that convene for their plenary session every March for one week to ten days in the Great Hall of the People in Beijing. As we have seen, the chairman of these two prestigious state institutions both sit in the Party's PBSC as number three and four respectively of this powerful body. And the NPC General Secretary (and de facto number 2), Li Jianguo, belongs to the Politburo while his de facto alter ego in the CPPCC, Vice-Chairman Du Qinglin, is part of the CCP Central Secretariat.

The reactivation of these two institutions after the end of the Cultural Revolution has directly contributed to empowering them, especially the NPC, with some meaningful though limited competences. However, some observers have been over-optimistic about both the magnitude and the implications of the NPC empowerment (O'Brien 1990; Almén 2005). The vivid debates that they hold every year as well as the rather negative votes that they sometimes cast reflect in general differences of views and interests within the CCP itself rather than between the leading Party and independent political forces, which are illegal and therefore nonexistent in the PRC (Cabestan 2003, 2006).

Let's look first at who are the NPC delegates? They represent 35 constituencies: the 31 provincial-level administrative divisions (22 provinces, five autonomous regions and four municipalities), the Hong Kong and Macau Special Administrative Regions, Taiwan as well as the PLA. Delegates are in principle chosen by the CCP leadership of each constituency. Actually, the CCP Organization Department has a say in their selection which must also abide by a number of rules in terms of gender, educational and professional background, age and ethnicity. In each of the 31 main geographical constituencies, the NPC delegates are elected by the provincial-level people's congress and as a rule the number of candidates must be 20–50 percent higher than the number of seats. However, the process has remained opaque and, in any case, each provincial-level delegation to the NPC is led by the CCP top leaders of the constituency. While Hong Kong and Macau delegates are chosen by the CCP in consultation with the local pro-Beijing elites, Taiwan and PLA delegates are selected in a very secretive way. All in all, 72 percent of the 2,987 NPC delegates elected in 2013 are CCP members (Mo 2015).

The NPC delegates don't have much power. They can and do make their views public and they sometimes criticize the government; they can also in principle veto a bill, a report or even an appointment but they have never done so. While some performance reports issued by officials are better endorsed than other (the Supreme People's Procuratorate Report is often badly supported with nearly 30 percent of the delegates voting "no" in 2013), most state and government leaders are elected with more than 90 percent of the vote. The fact that there is always only one candidate for each position explains these results (Choi 2013b). Moreover, before each vote, CCP members are instructed to follow Party discipline. In this context, Zeng Qinghong's election to the post of vice-president of the Republic in 2003 with only 87.5 percent of the vote was considered exceptional and due to his close connection to the outgoing president Jiang Zemin (Cabestan 2003).

But the Chinese NPC is different from other parliaments in a sense that it is a two-level organization in which the higher level, the 174-member NPC Standing Committee (NPCSC), is in charge of the Assembly's day-to-day operation and exerts most of the competences of the NPC. Elected with a modest level of competitiveness (173 candidates for 160 seats) by the NPC delegates, the NPCSC also includes a Chairmen's Council which is constituted of the NPC Chairperson and 13 Vice-Chairpersons who are elected separately, with a very tiny dose of uncertainty since 2013. The NPCSC meets every two months and adopts the majority of the bills and decisions submitted to the NPC. It is the NPCSC that has sometimes turned down a draft law prepared by the State Council, such as the Bankruptcy Law in 1986 or the Highway Law in 2000. Most of the NPCSC members are active in one or several of the eight NPC commissions (such as law, financial and economic affairs, foreign affairs, etc.). In this respect the NPCSC has become a more influential power locus. But dominated by CCP semi-retired leaders, it is only formally located outside of the Party's domain (Cabestan 2006; Cabestan 2014: 317–322).

In any event, the most meaningful structures of the NPC are not elected but appointed by the NPC leadership, probably with the approval of the CCP Organization Department: these are the Law Working Committee and, since 2000, the Budget Working Committee of the NPCSC. Working closely with the State Council Legislative Affairs Office and headed by a well-known jurist (Li Shishi), the former plays an important role in the drafting of the bills that are later submitted to the NPCSC or the NPC plenary session for adoption. The latter has tried with a much more limited success to expand the NPC's oversight on the government budget though it has contributed to better informing the delegates about the government's fiscal revenues and expenditures.

In this CCP-led political system, the CPPCC is probably slightly more autonomous but much less influential than the NPC. As its name indicates, it is a consultative body. By tradition, CCP members constitute only a minority: around 30 percent of the delegates. But the other members are all selected by the CCP United Front Department along rules that are aimed at representing the diversity of the Chinese society and particularly its recognized elites. The CPPCC National Committee (2,237 delegates today) is made up of 34 functional constituencies including representatives of formal organizations such as the CCP, the Communist Youth League, the All-China Women Federation, the All-China Federation of Trade Unions and the eight "democratic parties" as well as of each of the 55 national minorities and various professions (teachers, artists, sport champions and private entrepreneurs). Every year, the plenary session debates about many national issues and submits a large number of motions to the government. Nevertheless, the role of the CPPCC is very marginal. And the institution itself has been more often criticized as a "famous people temple" (*mingrentang*) or even a "rich persons' club" (*furen julebu*) (Cabestan 2015). As a matter of fact, since the early 2000s, both the NPC and the CPPCC have been used to better integrate the country's new elites into the CCP-led political system and make sure that they do not venture into attempting to create their own political organizations.

The distribution of responsibilities among Party leaders at the central level therefore gives a good idea of the tools that the CCP can rely on to control the state; actually, this "power geography" underscores how meaningless the formal separation between the Party and the state can be: the latter is clearly a "façade" of the former. True, each institution has developed its own *modus operandi* and to some extent its autonomy but this autonomy should not be understood as the result of a dichotomy, let alone a tension between the Party and the state: it should be comprehended as the quasi-natural manifestation of bureaucratic interests in a political system that remains ruled more by men (and a few women) than law and by Party leading cadres, wherever they work, more than anyone else.

Relationship between the Party, the PLA and the state

In that context, the Party's control of the military constitutes a distinct and probably trickier issue. This control is very strong and is exerted through a number of institutions and mechanisms, such as the PLA General Political Department, the political commissar system and the CCP discipline inspection commissions' network inside the military. Moreover, practically all officers are CCP members. However, the PLA's integration into the Party-state structure has remained specific and somewhat problematic. Since the early 1990s, the CMC has become a purely military body, expanded to include the commanders of the Navy, the Air Force and the Second Artillery in 2004: its Chair is its only civilian (similarly for its first Vice-Chair who is often a successor to the General Secretary and CMC Chairman). Its two military Vice-Chairmen sit in the CCP Politburo (Fan Changlong and Xu Qiliang since 2012) but not in the PBSC; the other eight military members belong to the CCP Central Committee. Its only member who is formally part of the state structure is the Minister of National Defense (today Chang Wanquan). However, it is doubtful that Li Keqiang has any say on the way this ministry operates: in charge of the PLA personnel and administration, it directly reports to the CMC. In addition, in case of natural disaster, the Premier needs to receive from the CMC Chairman special and temporary delegation of authority over PLA troops deployed to the disaster zone. And this is a recent arrangement that was worked out after the Wenchuan earthquake in 2008 in order to overcome the lack of coordination between the military and the government (Mulvenon 2010; Li 2013; China Military Online 2014).

Moreover, PLA leaders tend to sit more often in Party than in state bodies: they are for example represented in the CLGs in charge of foreign affairs, Taiwan and even "comprehensively deepening reforms," cybersecurity and informatization as well as in the CNSC. The National Defense Law enacted in 1997 clearly states in its article 19 that the military is under the leadership of the CCP not the government ("Law..." 1997). In other words, the PLA remains a Party-led military and any danger of "nationalization" (*guojiahua*), although sometimes mentioned as a terrible *bête noire* in the official media, seems very remote.

This conclusion can be extended to the People's Armed Police (PAP), the part of the PLA that has been responsible since the Tiananmen Square Incident (1989) for maintaining order and security within society and the boundaries of the PRC. Placed under the Minister of Public Security who is its First Political Commissar, the PAP also directly reports to the CMC. This dual affiliation allows the Party supremo to decide or prevent any deployment of the PAP in case of social unrest and coordinate this deployment with a PLA involvement if the PAP is not strong enough to restore order. Officially numbering 660–800,000 officers and soldiers, it is nonetheless spread over a huge territory (20–25,000 per province on average) (Choi 2013a).

The reform of the military introduced by Xi in late 2015 has empowered the CMC to the detriment of the four major departments of the PLA (political, general staff, logistics and armament). And it has also empowered the CMC Chair, since April 2016 "commander-in-chief" of the PLA's "joint battle command" at the top of the system (see Chapter 7, "The PLA as the Lifeline of the Party").

How the Party controls the state at the local level

In China, there are four levels of local government: (1) the provincial level, which has already been mentioned; (2) the prefectural level (*diqu*) which includes because of urbanization an increasing number of large or prefectural-level municipalities (*dijishi*); the county (*xian*) level which for the same reason is more and more made up of smaller municipalities (*xianjishi*) or urban districts (*qu*) of big cities; and the rural township (*xiang*) level which also counts a growing number of towns (*zhen*). Under these four levels of government, there are what the state constitution calls "mass organizations of self-management at the grassroots level," namely villagers' committees in the countryside and urban residents' committees in the cities (Constitution 1982: art. 111).

Since 1949, the CCP has constantly and fully espoused the administrative geographical organization that it has put in place. Today, it includes over 3,000 local Party committees that lead all the governments established at each level (2012 figure). Similarly it has set up a grassroots committee in nearly every of the 600,000 villages and 87,000 urban citizens' committees (Gore 2010: 36).

As far as local governments are concerned, the Party committee always appoints its second most important member (the first deputy-secretary) as governor or mayor of the locality while the CCP secretary leads from behind all key political and governmental matters. While at the provincial level or the municipal level, the division of labor between the CCP apparatus and the government departments is quite clear, at the lower levels, the fusion, and the confusion, increase. The physical geography of power is a good indication of this de facto fusion: at these lower levels, the CCP committee and the government are often located in the same building, a red-character placard indicating the presence of the former on the left-hand side of the gate, and a black-character placard indicating the presence of the latter on the right-hand side of the gate.

In many respects, the local bureaucracy imitates the division of labor that the center has adopted. Typically, the local CCP committees are in charge of organization and propaganda, law and order as well as united front work (which includes the organization of people's congress elections and the selection of CPPCC members). The local government organs, on their side, are responsible for economic development, social, health, culture and education. Similarly, the government includes a public security bureau and a justice bureau (managing the lawyers and the notaries). However, these latter bureaucracies, as well as the local people's court and people's procuratorate, all report to the local-level CCP politics and law commission (PLC) that is usually led by one of the key deputy-secretaries of the Party committee. The establishment after the Third Central Committee Plenum in 2013 of circuit courts and cross-administrative boundaries courts has probably weakened the powers of the PLCs at the lower, particularly the prefectural and county, levels (there are no courts and procuratorates at the township level). However, this reform has also contributed to strengthening the role of the PLCs at the provincial level ("Decision…" 2013).

Similarly, the anti-corruption campaign launched by Xi in 2013 has led to a centralization of the CCP commission for discipline inspection (CDI) system: although still under the dual leadership of the Party committee at the same level and the CDI at the higher level, CDIs have been empowered to send investigation teams to local Party and state organs that only report to the CCDI or the provincial CDI (Yeo 2016). However, this reform has also strengthened rather than weakened the Party's control of the government and the state institutions in general.

In any case, the described division of labor should be taken with caution since, at the local level as well, the Party secretary can set up local-level leading groups if he or she wants to prioritize a particular task, as for instance the establishment of an industrial park or a special development zone.

The local Party committee's degree of control of the locality's people's congress may vary but it is never too loose. At the provincial level, around two thirds of the people's congresses are chaired by the Party secretary himself or herself to make sure that its activities would not deviate too much from the Party committee's priorities. A similar model has probably been adopted below. In any case, the direct election every five years of county and township levels' people's congresses has remained tightly managed by the local Party committees. The election committees that they set up strictly vet candidates in order both to exclude *ex ante* potential "trouble makers" (although ten citizens can in principle nominate a candidate), respect the national rules in terms of representation (gender, professional background, etc.; see above) and make sure that the local Party leading cadres are elected. Since 1979, a certain degree of uncertainty has been introduced: the number of candidates must be 33–100 percent higher than the number of seats; this is what the CCP calls *cha'e xuanju* (sometimes translated as "competitive elections"). However, in order to guarantee that the latter group of candidates is elected, a complex system has been introduced according to which electoral constituencies lose their additional seats, subject to competition, if these candidates are not elected (Shi 1999; Manion 2000; Chen and Zhong 2002; Li 2008). In any event, most candidatures are not spontaneous but rather proposed by the Party or the local organizations (He 2010). The delegates' profile has gradually changed: while many members of traditional elites, such as government and SOE cadres, still sit in the people's congresses, since the early 2000s more members of the new elites, particularly private entrepreneurs, sometimes using their economic influence or even their money, have been elected to them.

People's congresses at the prefectural and provincial levels are elected by the people's congresses at the lower level (counties for the former). These indirect elections are competitive (20–50 percent more candidates than seats) and can sometimes be hotly contested. However, their proceedings are more opaque and they are closely monitored by the outgoing standing committee of the congress that is to be elected.

The leaders of every people's congress are recommended by the CCP organization department of the higher level. The election of the chairperson is guaranteed since as a rule the principle of *dang'e xuanju* (one candidate, one seat) is applied. True, for deputy chairpersons and standing committee members (at the county level and above), elections are competitive and the CCP's choice can be questioned. And some studies have shown that this has been the case in quite a number of localities, particularly at the township and the county levels. But these cases have involved at most 5 percent of the candidates (Manion 2008).

According to the state constitution, people's congresses are empowered to elect governors and deputy governors (or mayors and deputy mayors) as well as top judges and procurators of the locality (Constitution 1982). While they usually follow the recommendation of the Party, they have on occasion elected their own candidate. This was the case of Guizhou governor Chen Sineng in 1993. However, since then such cases have become rarer and competition has concentrated on (and de facto been limited to) deputy's positions. This does not mean that a lot of bargaining is not taking place before every election, forcing the Party to introduce some flexibility in the *Nomenklatura* system, and to better take into account the elected elites' view, and beyond, the local public opinion. Similarly, in cases such as adopting the local budget and approving development plans and regulations (at the provincial and prefectural levels), people's congresses have more say in local governmental affairs. For instance, for the first time in 2001, Shenyang municipality's people's congress vetoed the local court's performance report (Cabestan 2006: 57).

While disseminating power away from the Party apparatus and favoring what is called in China "consultative democracy," this evolution is not without limits: many people's congresses are chaired by the CCP secretary of the locality; most delegates belong to the Party; and finally, many voters don't know the name of their delegate(s), let alone rely on them as an intermediary to ease their relation with the government (Yuan 2012: 73–101; Fewsmith 2013: 142–169).

Local CPPCCs are constituted by the Party's United Front Departments at the same level in a rather opaque manner: as a rule, potential members are approached by the CCP. Some rich people have tried and sometimes succeeded to buy their way into these assemblies. And far from being excluded, foreign nationals residing in China can be invited to sit in them as well (Callick 2013: 53). As is the case of people's congresses, the local CPPCCs are presented as vivid examples of "consultative democracy." However, they are controlled by the Party, usually chaired by retired Party leaders and, in any case, their role is marginal.

Conclusion: a Party obsessed with power and control

The Chinese Communist Party tightly controls the state institutions, particularly the government, the legislative and the judiciary. As indicated in the introduction, it is a Party-state. The division of labor that has emerged since the end of the Cultural Revolution and through the reform era is more rational, more adapted to the economic liberalization and easier to manage than in the now defunct Soviet Union. The Party apparatus is in charge of key political and security affairs; the government runs the economy; the legislature debates, votes the bills and consults the public; and the judiciary, more professional now, adjudicates with a bit more room for maneuver at least for cases deemed politically non-sensitive.

That is the objective and ideal that the Party leadership is trying to follow. In reality, things are more complex and the need to increase the number of Party CLGs and enhance their role clearly demonstrates that leading and coordinating remain the best way for the CCP leadership to drive the country, its economic and social reforms as well as its institutional and legal restructuring. Moreover, political differences and personal rivalries among leaders complicate the picture and also contribute to explaining why Xi has been so keen to move back power to the Party. Finally, Xi's obsession with political power and control can be understood as an attempt to stop the devolvement of economic and social power not only away from the Party but also from the state and its main institutions. In other words, it is a strategy to nip in the bud any dissenting political views and to rein in the burgeoning civil society that is taking shape in China. Will he succeed? In the short term, yes, in the longer term, it is more doubtful.

Notes

1 There are however exceptions to this unwritten rule: between 1992 and 1998, Jiang Zemin chaired the CLG for Finance and Economics in order to weaken Premier Li Peng's powers. But later both Premier Zhu Rongji and Wen Jiabao chaired this CLG.

2 All ministries now have a website in Chinese and sometimes in English which clearly indicates the leadership lineup and the Party group members. As a result, it is easy to check if the Minister is the number one of the ministry.

References

Almén, Oscar (2005) *Authoritarianism Constrained: The Role of Local People's Congress in China*, Ph.D. Dissertation, Department of Peace and Development Research, Göteborg University.

Ang, Yuen Yuen (2012) "Counting Cadres: A Comparative View of China's Public Employment," *The China Quarterly*, 211, September, 676–696.

Barnett, A. Doak (1967) *Cadres, Bureaucracy, and Political Power in Communist China*, New York: Columbia University Press.

Burns, John (1994) "Strengthening Central CCP Control of Leadership Selection: The 1990 *Nomenklatura*," *The China Quarterly*, 138, June, 458–491.

Burns, John (2006) "The Chinese Communist Party *Nomenklatura* System as a Leadership Selection Mechanism. An Evaluation," in Brodsgaard, Kjeld Erik and Zheng, Yongnian, eds., *The Chinese Communist Party in Reform*, London and New York: Routledge, 33–58.

Cabestan, Jean-Pierre (2003) "The 10th National People's Congress and After: Moving Towards a New Authoritarianism, Both Elitist and Consultative?" *China Perspectives*, 47, May–June, 4–20.
Cabestan, Jean-Pierre (2006) "More Power to the People's Congresses? Parliaments and Parliamentarianism in the People's Republic of China," *Asien*, 99, April, 42–69.
Cabestan, Jean-Pierre (2014) *Le système politique chinois. Un Nouvel équilibre authoritaire* (China's Political System. A New Authoritarian Equilibrium), Paris: Les Presses de Sciences Po.
Cabestan, Jean-Pierre (2015) "The Chinese People's Political Consultative Conference (CPPCC): Its Role and its Future," in Brown, Kerry, ed., *The EU–China Relationship: European Perspectives. A Manual for Policy Makers*, Hackensack, NJ and London, UK: Imperial College Press, 51–62.
Callick, Rowan (2013) *Inside China's Modern Communist Elite: The Party Forever*, New York: Palgrave Macmillan.
Chan, Hon S. (2004) "Cadre Personnel Management in China: The *Nomenklatura* System, 1990–1998," *The China Quarterly*, 179, September, 703–734.
Chen, Jie and Zhong, Yang (2002) "Why Do People Vote in Semicompetitive Elections in China?" *The Journal of Politics*, 64:3, 178–197.
China Daily (2016) "CPC Has More Than 88 Million Members," June 30, www.chinadailyasia.com/nation/2016-06/30/content_15456347.html (accessed on August 24, 2016).
China Military Online (2014) "Frequent Disaster Relief Operations Temper PLA's Combat Capability," August 11, http://english.chinamil.com.cn/news-channels/china-military-news/2014-08/11/content_6089285.htm.
Choi, Chi-Yuk (2013a) "Communist Party Leader Makes First Visit to People's Armed Police," *South China Morning Post*, January 30, www.scmp.com/news/china/article/1138959/communist-party-leader-makes-first-visit-peoples-armed-police.
Choi, Chi-Yuk (2013b) "Deputies Give Lowest Marks in Six Years to Budget and Court," *South China Morning Post*, March 18, www.scmp.com/news/china/article/1193218/deputies-give-lowest-marks-six-years-budget-and-court.
Constitution of the Communist Party of China (2012), revised and adopted at the 18th CPC National Congress on November 14, 2012, http://english.cpc.people.com.cn/206972/206981/8188065.html (accessed on August 15, 2016).
Constitution of the People's Republic of China (1982), adopted on December 4, 1982, full text after amendment on March 14, 2004, www.npc.gov.cn/englishnpc/Constitution/node_2825.htm.
"Decision of the Central Committee of the Communist Party of China on Some Major Issues Concerning Comprehensively Deepening Reform," adopted at the Third Plenary Session of the 18th Central Committee of the Communist Party of China on November 12, 2013, www.china.org.cn/china/third_plenary_session/2014-01/16/content_31212602.htm.
Fewsmith, Joseph (2013) *The Logic and Limits of Political Reform*, Cambridge: Cambridge University Press.
Glaser, Bonnie (2015) "China's Maritime Rights Protection Leading Small Group – Shrouded in Secrecy," Washington, DC: CSIS, Asia Maritime Transparency Initiative, September 11, http://amti.csis.org/chinas-maritime-rights-protection-leading-small-group-shrouded-in-secrecy/.
Gore, Lance (2010) *The Chinese Communist Party and China's Capitalist Revolution: The Political Impact of the Market*, New York: Routledge.
He, Junzhi (2010) "Independent Candidates in China's Local People's Congresses: A Typology," *Journal of Contemporary China*, 19:64, March, 311–333.
Jacobson, Linda (2014) "China's Unpredictable Maritime Security Actors," Sydney: Lowry Institute for International Policy, December, p. 13, www.lowryinstitute.org/sites/default/files/chinas-unpredictable-maritime-security-actors_3_0.pdf.
Lam, Willy (2013a) "All the General Secretary's Men: Xi Jinping's Inner Circle Revealed," *China Brief*, 13:4, February 15, www.jamestown.org/programs/chinabrief/single/?tx_ttnews%5Btt_news%5D=40461#.V72K_umD40o.
Lam, Willy (2013b) "Meet China's New Foreign Policy Team," *Foreign Policy*, March 8, http://foreignpolicy.com/2013/03/08/meet-chinas-new-foreign-policy-team/.
Lampton, David M. (2015) "Xi Jinping and the National Security Commission: Policy Coordination and Political Power," *Journal of Contemporary China*, 24:95, September, 759–777, DOI: 10.1080/10670564.2015.1013366.
"Law of the People's Republic of China on National Defense," adopted on March 14, 1997, Beijing: National People's Congress, Database on Laws and Regulations, www.npc.gov.cn/englishnpc/Law/2007-12/11/content_1383547.htm.

Li, Fan, ed. (2008) *2006–2007 Zhongguo jiceng renda daibiao xuanju shilu* (On China's Grassroots People's Congresses Delegates Elections), Beijing: Shijie yu Zhongguo yanjiusuo.
Li, Liguo (2013) "China's Progress in Coping with Major Natural Disasters," *Qiushi*, 5:4, October 1, http://english.qstheory.cn/magazine/201304/201311/t20131107_288111.htm.
Lieberthal, Kenneth (2004) *Governing China: From Revolution Through Reform*, New York: W.W. Norton.
Manion, Melanie (2000) "Chinese Democratization in Perspective: Electorates and Selectorates at the Township Level," *The China Quarterly*, 163, September, 764–782.
Manion, Melanie (2008) "When Communist Party Candidates Can Lose, Who Wins? Assessing the Role of Local People's Congresses in the Selection of Leaders in China," *The China Quarterly*, September, 607–630.
McGregor, James (2010) *The Party: The Secret World of China's Communist Rulers*, New York: Harper.
Miller, Alice (2008) "The CCP Central Committee Leading Small Groups," *China Leadership Monitor*, 26, September 2, www.hoover.org/sites/default/files/uploads/documents/CLM26AM.pdf.
Miller, Alice (2011) "The Politburo Standing Committee under Hu Jintao," *China Leadership Monitor*, 35, September 21, http://media.hoover.org/sites/default/files/documents/CLM35AM.pdf.
Miller, Alice (2013) "The New Party Politburo Leadership," *China Leadership Monitor*, 40, January 14, www.hoover.org/sites/default/files/uploads/documents/CLM40AM.pdf.
Miller, Alice (2014) "More Already on the Central Committee's Leading Small Groups," *China Leadership Monitor*, 44, July 28, www.hoover.org/sites/default/files/research/docs/clm44am.pdf.
Miller, H. Lyman (2004) "Hu Jintao and the Politburo," *China Leadership Monitor*, 9, January 30, www.hoover.org/sites/default/files/uploads/documents/clm9_lm.pdf.
Mo, Ganna (2015) "Qiantan dangyuan renda daibiao de shuangchong shenfen wenti" (Short Discussion on Party Members' Double Identity Issue), *Xueshumao* (Study Cat), July 5, www.scimao.com/read/2474918.
Mulvenon, James (2010) "Party-Military Coordination of the Yushu Earthquake Response," *China Leadership Monitor*, 33, June 28, www.hoover.org/sites/default/files/uploads/documents/CLM33JM.pdf.
Naughton, Barry (2016) "Two Trains Running: Supply-Side Reform, SOE Reform and the Authoritative Personage," *China Leadership Monitor*, 50, July 19, www.hoover.org/sites/default/files/research/docs/clm50bn.pdf#overlay-context=publications/china-leadership-monitor.
O'Brien, Kevin J. (1990) *Reform without Liberalization: China's National People's Congress and the Politics of Institutional Change*, New York: Cambridge University Press.
Saunders, Phillip and Scobell, Andrew, eds. (2015) *The PLA's Influence on China's National Security Policy-Making*, Stanford, CA: Stanford University Press.
Shi, Tianjian (1999) "Voting and Nonvoting in China: Voting Behavior in Plebiscitary and Limited-choice Elections," *The Journal of Politics*, 61:4, 1115–1139.
State Organs (no date) "The Composition, Power and Function of the State Council," http://english.moj.gov.cn/State-Organs/content/2009-02/03/content_1028259.htm (accessed on August 24, 2016).
Wall Street Journal (2016) "China's Xi Jinping Tightens His Hold on Communist Party," October 27, www.wsj.com/articles/chinas-xi-jinping-tightens-his-hold-on-communist-party-1477579202.
Wang, Xiaoqi (2012) *China's Civil Service Reform*, London and New York: Routledge.
Wright, Teresa (2015) *Party and State in Post-Mao China*, Cambridge, UK and Malden, MA: Polity Press.
Xinhua (2014) "Zhongyang Wangluo Anquan he Xinxihua Lingdao Xiaozu Chengli" (The Central Cybersecurity and Informatization Leading Small Group is Established), February 27, http://news.xinhuanet.com/info/2014-02/28/c_133148759.htm.
Yang, Chungui (2002) *Dangxiao jiaoxuelun* (On Party School Teaching), Beijing: Zhonggong zhongyang dangxiao chubanshe.
Yeo, Yukyung (2016) "Complementing the Local Discipline Inspection Commissions of the CCP: Empowerment of the Central Inspection Groups," *Journal of Contemporary China*, 25:97, January, 59–74, http://dx.doi.org/10.1080/10670564.2015.1062620.
Yuan, Zaijun (2012) *The Failure of China's Democratic Reforms*, Plymouth: Lexington Books.
Zhongguo Zhengyao (Summary of Chinese Politics) (no date) Zhonggong Zhongyang (The CCP Central Committee), http://cpc.people.com.cn/GB/64162/394696/index.html (accessed on August 24, 2016).

6
THE ROLE OF PARTY CONGRESSES

Guoguang Wu

Introduction

This chapter looks at the evolution and functions of one of the key components of the Chinese Communist Party (CCP) – Party congresses – which are claimed in the Party Charter as the highest decision-making bodies of the national and local Party structures. In reality, however, Party congresses have become rubber-stamp institutions that, rather than making decisions, merely endorse personnel and policy decisions of the top elite. This gap between its constitutional significance and practical impotency, which I have termed "institutional inconsistency" elsewhere (Wu 2015: 4–9), and, indeed, the existence of such congressional organizations that claim representation of members within the CCP, epitomizes the Party's Leninist authoritarian essence in the institutional sense;[1] through its structural expression of the Party's constitutional principle of so-called "democratic dictatorship," it has created a unique combination of mass members' nominal authority through congressional representation within the Party and a top-down organizational hierarchy of political power within the same Party. It sounds self-contradictory, but, to this author, without sufficient acknowledgment of and attention to such self-contradiction and inherent intension, it is impossible to comprehend the key issues around the CCP. Such issues include: as a now massive party of nearly 90 million members, how does the CCP organize, mobilize, and discipline its members nationwide; as the single ruling party of the People's Republic of China (PRC) for almost 70 years, how and why can the CCP leadership claim its political legitimacy in maintaining power and giving orders to the mass members of the Party itself and all residents of the PRC?

There are, of course, many complicated institutional arrangements and operational measures in place that allow the CCP to organize, mobilize, maintain power, and govern; among them, however, the significance of the system of Party congresses has for a long time been overlooked and underestimated in accordance with the Party's own practical downplay of their role. Historically speaking, in CCP politics there is a changing curve of the increasing significance of Party congresses, especially the National Party Congress, as chiefly reflected in the normalized frequency of congressional meetings and, accordingly, the regular exercise of the nominal roles of Party congresses through these meetings, primarily in the post-Mao period since the late 1970s. While this change further justifies the topic of the chapter, it also, more importantly, raises questions such as: Why such a change? What are the implications of the change for the CCP in particular and for Chinese politics in general?

This chapter will first introduce readers to the system of Party congresses, primarily the National Party Congress, with particular focus on its structure, position, functions, and problems, through which a dilemma of nominal superiority versus political impotency will be pointed out for the purpose of locating our discussion of Party congresses in the theoretical context of "institutional inconsistency," while simultaneously attempting an exploration of the dilemma through the theoretical lens of "institutional manipulation for authoritarian legitimization." Then the chapter will focus on the latest developments in institutions, operations, and the role of the National Party Congress for supplying an updated picture in which one can find how the decreasing curve of Party leaderships' legitimacy makes the National Party Congress work in its contemporary roles. In the third section, the chapter will turn to an examination of local Party congresses at various levels, which make up huge parts of the organizational structure of the Party congress system, and argue that this is a set of institutions much different from the National Party Congress in terms of functions and roles. Their connections with the National Party Congress will also be considered. In conclusion, the chapter will extend its investigations to a discussion of the nature of the CCP as an authoritarian political organization and its possibility of democratization via a transformation of the roles and operations of the Party congress system.

Party congresses: a dilemma between nominal authority and political impotency

In introducing the readers to the basics of Party congresses, three points should be highlighted to explain their features and roles. First, it is about the distinction between the system of Party congress and the system of people's congresses, which concerns the parallel structure within the Party-state regime of the PRC; second, the National Congress of the CCP, or the National Party Congress, stands out in this distinction, as the organization enjoys an extremely prestigious position in the CCP's Party Charter, though some obvious contradictions do exist in political practice to modify, constrain, empty, and even nullify its de facto functions; third, there are local Party congresses at various levels, and their relationship with the National Party Congress is organizationally complicated and politically subtle. Below this section will briefly discuss each of them.

The political system in the PRC is correctly termed the Party-state, in which the Communist Party is interwoven with and superior to the state for organizing and directing the regime.[2] There is a parallel structure, therefore, between the Communist Party and the state, as both have its system of congresses, including the National Congress and local congresses. For the state of the PRC, the National People's Congress (NPC) operates like a parliament, and local people's congresses are also set up at three levels of jurisdiction to work as local assemblies of, nominally, citizens' representatives. These three levels are: the provincial level, at which there are twenty-two provinces, four metropolises, and five autonomous regions;[3] the county level, now roughly divided into more than two thousand units nationwide; and the level between, which in China is referred to as the city-and-prefecture level (*di shi ji*), while more and more prefectures (*diqu*, or *zhuanshu*) in rural areas are reformatted into cities through the progress of urbanization. Each unit at these three levels, be it a province, a county, or a city, has its people's congress, collectively making a system that has recently received profound attention in China studies due to its increasing importance in national and local legislations and in many other state affairs.[4]

The Chinese Communist Party, the single ruling party of the nation since 1949, on the other hand, also has its own system of congresses, including the National Party Congress, local Party congresses at the subnational and lower levels exactly parallel to those of the people's congresses.

Moreover, within the Party congress system there are subnational congresses/assemblies not attached to given geographic administrative units; they also exist in non-territory units of the CCP, as exemplified by those within the PLA, the military police forces, the central CCP organs, the central state organs, and, in recent years, the central state-owned enterprises. With them as the third component in addition to the National Party Congress and local Party congresses, the Party congress system is a bit more complicated than the people's congress system, in which it is only for the National People's Congress that there is a PLA delegation in addition to all other delegations based on territorial administrative units. Party congresses in this form established along such non-territorial divisions, which perhaps can be referred to as "sectional Party congresses," are often different from what we call "local Party congresses" in organizational, operational, and functional details, as their major uniqueness, to this author's knowledge, lies in their lesser degree of institutionalization in all organizational aspects. For convenience of discussion, however, in the following pages we will use "local Party congresses" to cover all Party congresses except the National Party Congress. Also, the relevant investigation of them will focus on territorial local Party congresses.

This system of Party congresses, which is the subject of this chapter, possesses a political significance no lesser than the people's congress system, simply because for the Party-state regime it is the Party that dominates the state rather than vice versa. The role and power of the NPC has been growing but it is still far from altering the supremacy of the Party over the state in authority and power under such a political system, let alone the local people's congresses which are much less powerful than the NPC. Despite all the reforms and changes that China has experienced since the late 1970s, nobody would doubt the CCP's overriding dominance of Chinese politics,[5] thus the importance of the Party congress system seems a logical extension beyond dispute. In fact, in the case of the National Party Congress with its alleged constitutional functions in platform making, constitutional amendment, and leadership appointment, since the CCP became the ruling party of China, the PRC's state constitution has always followed the CCP's political platform in spirit and principle; any remaking or amendment of the Party Charter has always been later incorporated into the PRC state constitution wherever the clauses are applicable in state affairs; and, needless to say, the Party leadership appointment gained at the National Party Congress is always concurrently the highest leadership of China as a nation and a state. A sentence published decades ago to describe the Soviet Communist Party Congress, therefore, still applies perfectly to its Chinese counterpart: "According to party rules, the [Party] congress is the ultimate authority within the party, and given the relationship between the party and governmental institutions, it is, therefore, the ultimate authority in the entire political system" (Hough and Fainsod 1979: 449).

Within the Party, it is the Party Congress, more specifically the National Party Congress, that is constitutionally claimed to be the "highest decision-making body" of the entire CCP. Yes, the political history of the CCP is notorious for intensive intra-Party power struggles and the restless change of so-called "practical ideologies," in Franz Schurmann's famous term (1968); however, various editions of the Party Charter, against changing circumstances, have never failed to stipulate or reconfirm this prestigious position of the National Party Congress as the "supreme authority" in the Party's life (Xuanbianzu 2007). This is a shallow stipulation, however, as the organization never plays this role of "super authority" in real politics of the CCP. Over a long period of history until very recently, the National Party Congress was not even able to hold its meetings regularly as per the pertinent constitutional stipulation, though meetings of the Party Congress, as a leading American scholar on Chinese politics has observed, are always "major events" (Lieberthal 1995: 159). As Table 6.1 helps to show, it has been a very recent development that the National Party Congress follows the charter regulation to regularly meet every five years.

Table 6.1 Terms of the National Party Congress, from irregularity to regularity

Term	*Time of meeting held*	*Charter-stipulated duration of term*	*Number of delegates*★	*Interval leadership change*
1st	July 23–31, 1921	1 year	13	No change
2nd	July 16–23, 1922	1 year	12	No change
3rd	June 12–20, 1923	1 year	30	No change
4th	Jan. 11–22, 1925	1 year	20	No change
5th	Apr. 27–May 9, 1927	1 year	82	Major change
6th	June 18–July 11, 1928	1 year	142	Major change
7th	Apr. 23–June 11, 1945	3 years	547	Minor change
8th	Sept. 15–27, 1956★★	5 years	1,026	Major change
9th	Apr. 1–24, 1969	5 years	1,512	Major change
10th	Aug. 24–28, 1973	5 years	1,249	Major change
11th	Aug. 12–18, 1978	5 years	1,510	Major change
12th	Sept. 1–11, 1982	5 years	1,545	Major change
13th	Oct. 25–Nov. 1, 1987	5 years	1,936	Major change
14th	Oct. 12–18, 1992	5 years	1,989	Minor change
15th	Sept. 12–18, 1997	5 years	2,048	No change
16th	Nov. 8–14, 2002	5 years	2,114	No change
17th	Oct. 15–21, 2007	5 years	2,213	No change
18th	Nov. 8–14, 2012	5 years	2,268	No change

Sources: The author's research based on data found in Li Junru (2007), Li Ying (2008), Chen Feng and Gao Min (2008), and *Renmin Ribao*, November 7, 2012, p. 1.

Notes

★ Here only the number of formal delegates is listed, but one should be aware of the complicities regarding both numbers and categories of CCP's congressional delegates. In terms of numbers, early CCP National Congresses until the 6th often had no clear records available; in terms of categories, there were various delegates of other kinds than formal ones for different terms of the CCP National Congress, as such delegates could be categorized as "alternative delegates (*houbu daibiao*)," "attending delegates (*liexi daibiao*)," and, for those terms since the 13th, "specially invited delegates (*teyao daibiao*)," and some of them enjoyed the same rights as the formal delegates, including voting rights in leadership elections. A brief discussion of the 18th National Party Congress in this regard can be found later in this chapter; for more details, see Wu (2015: 68–71).

★★ The 8th Party Congress held its second "annual" session in May 1958, thus the interval period to the 9th Party Congress spanned from 1958 to 1969.

Meeting frequency is perhaps a superficial indicator of the National Party Congress' functioning, but it is also fundamental: different from the representatives to the people's congresses, delegates to Party congresses, including those to the National Party Congress, do not hold their position as delegates when the Party Congress does not meet.[6] That means, when the Party Congress does not meet, it does not exist; as delegates finish their meeting, they are no longer working as delegates. Also as indicated in Table 6.1, the meeting duration of the National Party Congress is usually very short, which in recent terms is about a week. The people's congresses, in addition, hold annual sessions; by contrast, Party congresses, including the National Party Congress, only hold a single meeting when they start their term.[7]

The above facts do not mean that the decisions made by the National Party Congress may be in effect for a period of time that is longer than its constitutional term. The reality is truly opposite: the congressional decisions in all facets, from political platform to leadership appointments, can be ignored, sidelined, changed, or overthrown by the Party leadership without any consultation with the Congress. For convenience of statement, Table 6.1 only tries to summarize leadership changes against congressional decisions, as changes in other aspects are not easy to state in brief.[8] In any case, the de jure authority and constitutional functions of the National Party Congress are obviously shallow in the sense that it is not able to maintain them substantially.

This gap between nominal authority/constitutional prestige and political impotency/practical powerlessness widely exists in many self-claimed democratic and legal organizations under authoritarian regimes; in China, this discrepancy also applies to varying degrees to the state constitution, the people's congress system, courts, and many other institutions. The National Party Congress, however, suffers most from such an "institutional inconsistency," simply because its nominal authority is "super," thus it is that much more distant from its real exercise which is itself extremely weak. I have elsewhere argued that this institutional inconsistency contains the secret of authoritarian politics (Wu 2015); we will come back to explain the dilemma in a later discussion.

When the National Party Congress claims its representation of the entire Party, the precondition is obviously the delegates having been elected by Party members nationwide. In this sense, one may talk about the "system" of Party congresses, which, as stated earlier, not only includes the National Party Congress but also local (including sectional) Party congresses. According to the current Party Charter, "The Party Congress of a province, autonomous region, municipality directly under the central government, city divided into districts, autonomous prefecture, county (banner), autonomous county, city not divided into districts, or municipal district is held once every five years."[9] It should be noted that in previous historical periods their terms were stipulated in different ways: first, those Party congresses below the provincial level usually had a term of three years; second, accordingly, there was a difference concerning the duration of a term between these lower-level Party congresses and those at the provincial level, as the latter's term was usually five years. To this author, the regularization of the term of Party congresses at all levels to five years helps to reduce some difficulties of operation of the Party congresses as a system, which will be discussed in the section concerning local Party congresses.

Local Party congresses are also stipulated in the Party Charter as "leadership organs" of localities.[10] There is a chapter of the Party Charter devoted to "local organizations" of the Party, in which, according to recent editions, four items of "functions and powers" (*zhiquan*) of local Party congresses are explicitly stipulated (Article 25) as quoted below:

> The functions and powers of the local Party congresses at all levels are as follows: 1) To hear and examine the reports of the Party committees at the corresponding levels; 2) To hear and examine the reports of the commissions for discipline inspection at the corresponding levels; 3) To discuss and adopt resolutions on major issues in the given areas; and 4) To elect the Party committees and commissions for discipline inspection at the corresponding levels.[11]

These four roles can be essentially summarized in two parts: the first is about matters on significant policy issues; the second concerns elections of the local Party leaderships. They parallel, though on local levels, two of three roles played by the National Party Congress, namely, deciding the Party's platform and electing the central leaderships; the responsibility in making or amending the Party Charter, obviously, is solely that of the National Party Congress, thus nothing to do with local congresses. As will be investigated later in some detail, local Party congresses are in fact not able to exercise these two fundamental functions as the Party Charter stipulates. They encounter even greater difficulties than the National Party Congress does in playing their constitutional role; therefore, the gap between nominal authority and political power also exists for local Party congresses.

A political show under institutional manipulation: the National Party Congress in perspective

Why has such a gap occurred for the Party congresses? What explains the institutional inconsistency between de jure prestigious authority and de facto ineffective power of the Party congress system in general, and the National Party Congress in particular? These are the questions I have attempted to answer in the above-mentioned monograph focusing on the case of the National Party Congress (Wu 2015); the current chapter can be regarded as a follow-up to that monograph by expanding the research scope to cover the entire system of Party congresses, especially in its inclusion of local Party congresses and their connections with the National Party Congress in the analysis. This section will take the 18th National Party Congress, held in November 2012, the most recent to date, as a case study for demonstrating the latest organizational conduct of the National Party Congress on how institutional manipulation is operated by the CCP around this institution for the purpose of legitimizing the leadership and its political program through consensus-building among Party elite, while the next section will extend such answers to understanding the role of local Party congresses.

As always, the world is not made aware of when the CCP has its meeting of the National Party Congress a long time before the Party Congress opens its session; for the 18th Party Congress, it was on November 5, 2012 when the 17th Central Committee closed its 7th, also the last, plenary session that it was announced that the Party Congress was scheduled to meet on November 8.[12] It still had to wait for two more days, however; then the public was told at a press conference that the Congressional meeting would last to November 14.[13] Such short notice was already an improvement in the increasing political transparency of the CCP, as the Party Congress in Mao Zedong's era usually held its meetings in secrecy, with the public learning about the event only after the Congress had closed. Interestingly, it seemingly never prevents the event from receiving wide attention and coverage from national and international media,[14] which helps to highlight the glory of the National Party Congress.

A spokesman at the press conference also declared that the 18th Party Congress would have five agendas, as decided at the congressional preparatory meeting on November 7. The agendas were: to hear and discuss the 17th Central Committee's report; to hear and discuss the report of the Central Commission for Discipline Inspection; to discuss and adopt the amendments of the Party Charter; to elect the 18th Central Committee; and to elect the 18th Central Commission for Discipline Inspection.[15] These were almost standard for the Party Congress in recent terms; one should not expect any major change in this regard for the future Party Congress meetings, provided no major political change or structural adjustment of the central leadership organizations takes place. Nothing like a motion proposed by a delegate or a delegation to revise the agenda has been reported over the history of the Party Congress, at least since the 1940s. In fact, for the procedure of the Party Congress, there is no such thing as a motion made by a delegate. The incumbent leadership, in other words, is always able to successfully decide upon the congressional agenda at will.

As Table 6.2 indicates, 2,268 formal delegates to the 18th Party Congress were elected by 40 electoral units; they were accordingly organized into 40 delegations. There were, however, an additional 57 persons sitting with them together, being empowered with all the same rights of formal delegates, including equal voting rights in all elections. As "specially invited delegates,"

Table 6.2 The 18th National Party Congress (2012) at a glance

Meeting time:	November 8–14, 2012 (7 days)
Number of total party members:	82,600,000
Number of delegates:	2,268 (formal delegates) + 57 (specially invited delegates) + 314 (attending delegates)
Number of delegations:	40
Number of delegates of the largest delegation:	251 (PLA)
Number of delegates of the smallest delegation:[1]	26 (Hainan)
Percentage of leading cadres among delegates:	69.5[2]
Number of assembly meetings:	2
Number of reports:	1
Number of delegates' assembly speeches:	0
Differences between candidates and seats of the Central Committee in preview elections:[3]	
For full members:	224/205 (9.3 percent)
For alternate members:	190/171 (11.1 percent)
Differences between candidates and seats of the Central Commission for Discipline Inspection in preview elections:[4]	141/130 (8.5 percent)

Sources: The author's research database, and the resources listed in relevant notes.

Notes

1 As numbers of delegates of three delegations (Hong Kong, Macao, Taiwan) are not available.
2 Zhongguo gongchandang xinwen wang, http://cpc.people.com.cn/n/2012/0817/c64387-18762767-4.html, accessed August 17, 2012.
3 Renmin wang, http://politics.people.com.cn/n/2012/1115/c1001-19584526.html, accessed November 15, 2012.
4 Ibid.

they were appointed by the incumbent central leadership, explicitly based on their seniority in Party membership and ranks-and-files of their Party careers (Wu 2015: 75–76). Moreover, 314 high-level Party officials were added under a category of "attending delegates"; they had no voting rights, but participated in all other activities of the Party Congress (Wu 2015: 76).

The congressional preparatory meeting also elected the Congressional Presidium; "the Congress," according to the spokesman, "will run under the leadership of the Presidium."[16] Being consisted of major incumbent and former leaders, the Presidium roughly reflected the image of the incumbent and next Central Committees, sitting at the top of the Party Congress's inner political hierarchy. Under it, the Party's central functionaries, with the Central Secretariat as their core, were working during the Party Congress in the name of the Congress Secretariat (*dahui mishu chu*), running all administrative matters of the Party Congress. Delegates are divided into delegations and, further, into small groups; for recent terms of the Party Congress, the 18th Party Congress being no exception, all delegation heads were incumbent Party leaders of the provinces and other electoral units (Wu 2015: 98–106). This organizational structure with the Presidium, the Secretariat, delegations with delegation heads, small groups with group coordinators, and, at the bottom, ordinary delegates, can be perhaps termed "the congressional regime" of the CCP, which simply mirrors the conventional regime of the Party but works only during the meeting time of the Party Congress.

It is a well-established norm that the first thing the delegates always do at their first formal meeting is to hear the report delivered by the Party chief on behalf of the incumbent Central

Committee, often referred to as the political report to differentiate it from other reports to the Party Congress (Wu 2015: 124). In the post-Mao eras, however, it has become the sole report orally delivered to the Party Congress,[17] which has helped to trim the congressional agenda to minimum simplicity, thus technically favoring the incumbent leadership in terms of avoiding any unexpected troubles arising during the congressional meeting beyond its well-tailored plans. The 18th Party Congress also received another report, which, circulated in print, was from the incumbent Central Commission for Discipline Inspection, and delegates spent half a day discussing it. The discussion of the political report, by contrast, occupied most of delegates' time, though such discussions were unfolding mainly as study (in the sense of learning, or *xuexi*) and digestion (*linghui*) rather than debate and deliberation. Constitutionally the delegates have the right to disapprove the report, but this has never happened so far over the CCP's history of 96 years. Instead, delegates are always in high praise of the report; at the 18th Party Congress, following the historical track, they unanimously approved the political platform elaborated in the report.

Obviously, the meeting duration of seven days is technically far from sufficient for 2,300 delegates to articulate their opinions concerning the most significant issues of the Party and of the country the Party rules. In fact, these more than 2,000 delegates had only two opportunities to see each other all at the same meeting venue, which were the opening session while listening to the political report and the closing session while adopting congressional resolutions. On the latter occasion, they also voted to elect the central leadership bodies. Between these two congressional assembly meetings, they were only attending group meetings and, in lesser frequency, the meetings of their delegation. They spoke only on such occasions, as no average delegate was allowed to speak in front of all other delegates at a congressional assembly meeting.[18] The Congress Secretariat sent out staff to hear all group and delegation meetings; it had the discretion to decide which delegate's speech and which point or paragraph of the speech could be circulated through printed briefings (*huiyi jianbao*) among all delegates. That is to say, in case a delegate dares to utter some dissident opinions to criticize the political report or other proposals made by the incumbent leadership, including the candidate slates of the central leadership elections, such opinions could be easily contained within a small circle of a delegate group, and the possible effect of arousing wide-spread opposition could be avoided (Wu 2015: 109–110).

This method, which we may term "meeting in dividing," is especially vital for the incumbent leadership to manage elections for actualizing its tailored plan of the composition of the next Central Committee. Election has been adopted from the very beginning of the history of the CCP as the mechanism of leadership appointment, but the CCP has since been able to develop its own norms, procedures, and methods to govern elections for the purpose of gaining the voters' confirmation of the incumbent leadership's nomination of the next leadership, rather than letting the majority of voters decide upon who would be elected. Especially since the 7th Party Congress in 1945, when Mao was inaugurated as the indisputable leader, this system of elections has become complicated with many delicate measures and subtle details, mature in both a political and institutional sense, and powerfully functional in actualizing its purpose of legitimizing the authoritarian leadership (Wu 2015: ch. 6). It has also experienced adjustments, changes, and, as during the 1980s when the 12th and 13th Party Congresses met, even reforms, but the Maoist nature of the electoral system has fundamentally remained and, in recent decades, been enriched (Wu 2015). It is a unique combination of the democratic appearance such as voting and the non-democratic spirit that is carried on through the leadership's skillful manipulation of various rules of elections.

The 18th Party Congress continued to adopt this electoral system, with which elections at the congressional meeting were roughly conducted at two stages. The first stage was the preview elections (*yuxuan*), at which the nomination slates made by the incumbent leadership were circulated among delegates for their discussions or, in the CCP lexicon, *yunniang*, literally meaning fermentation, a critical phase in winemaking to chemically transform grape juice into liquid with a proper percentage of alcohol and a desired taste, or, in the CCP electoral system, leading voters to accept the nominations, thus institutionally transforming the leadership's preferences into delegates' acquiescence. This process will be completed with the preview elections, in which delegates at their delegation's meeting vote over the slates; then the Presidium, in consulting the voting results, makes the decision on who the formal candidates are (Wu 2015). The second stage, namely, the formal elections, is much simpler, at which all voters are assembled together to cast ballots to choose Central Committee members among the formal candidates. A critical note must be made: here the number of candidates is equal to the number of elected posts. At the 18th Party Congress, delegates were allowed to "choose" 205 full members of the 18th Central Committee among 205 candidates (Wu 2015).

The electoral mechanism with more candidates than posts (*cha'e xuanju*) has already been practiced at the National Party Congress since 1987, when the 13th Party Congress introduced it for allowing limited competition among candidates and some autonomous participation of delegates in choosing their favorite candidates (Wu 2015). The mechanism, however, has only been applied to the preview elections, not the formal elections. As the preview election is held at a delegation meeting, it is convenient for the national leadership to figure out from which delegation disapproval ballots appear, and, accordingly, targeted persuasion can immediately follow for eliminating such trouble before the formal election, thus increasing the sureness of the final electoral outcome being fit to the incumbent leadership's personnel plan in organizing the next leadership.

In concluding, the Party Congress never fails to endorse all the plans made by the incumbent Party leadership, be it a plan concerning the Party's platform or the next leadership's composition; it is in this sense that the Party Congress enjoys its prestigious constitutional role only nominally, not substantially. Moreover, the leadership may sideline, change, and even overthrow any congressional decisions without consultation with the Party Congress, such as what frequently happened before the most recent decade and which has taken place to a lesser degree in recent years (Wu 2015). Two questions, as mentioned earlier, arise: First, how can the Party Congress be managed to always meet the incumbent leadership's expectations? Second, why does the CCP still pay extremely close attention to the Party Congress despite the shameful record of the Party Congress in fulfilling its constitutional role? To make the complicated answers short, my explanation is: through delicate institutional manipulation, upon which we have briefly touched above, the CCP national leadership is able to tame delegates to the degree that the delegates nearly "autonomously" follow the leadership's willingness in running the National Party Congress, thus making the Party Congress, in Mao's words, "a meeting of unity, a meeting of victory." Unity and victory, on the other hand, are of course important for the Party and its leadership; or, more exactly, it is unquestionably important for the Party and its leadership to show the members, cadres, the masses, and the wider public of the world the achievement of such unity of all Party elite and the victory of the Party leadership, as this achievement and its public performance powerfully confirm the authority, power, and legitimacy of the Party leadership. In other words, the National Party Congress works as a collective enactment of the Party leadership's wills through its ceremonial confirmation of the leadership-dominated consensus building among the CCP elite; only through institutional manipulation, however, is it possible to achieve such a perfect confirmation of all plans the leadership has premade. It is in this sense that I have, borrowing the concept of the theater state from Clifford Geertz (1980), argued that the Party Congress is a theater of power, which transforms naked power into legitimate authority via a pompous show. The real role of the National Party Congress, therefore, is nothing to do with those stipulated in the CCP's Party Charter; rather, it is authoritarian legitimization.

Local Party congresses: political awkwardness and institutional embarrassment

In the authoritarian hierarchy of power and coercion, legitimacy of local leaders is rooted in their appointment by the higher-level leaderships, ultimately by the central leaderships. There is no such question of legitimization, therefore, in the role of local Party congresses. What do they do, therefore, and how do they perform their tasks? This section will conduct a brief investigation in attempting to answer these questions. Our focus here, as corresponding to the above sections, will be on the latest historical period that covers the early twenty-first century, while, as a necessity emerges, considering some historical changes.

The difference between national and local Party congresses, however, is much more substantial than the above superficial comparison. First, as no legitimization is involved in local leadership elections, elections of local Party delegates to the Party congresses of the next higher level, eventually to the National Party Congress, are critical for the National Party Congress to claim and perform its legitimate role of "representing" the entire Party. To send delegates to the higher-level Party congresses, therefore, must be regarded as the most significant role the local Party congresses play in the constitutional sense. But, curiously enough, this role is not mentioned in the Party Charter at all. Why? In historical practice, rarely were local Party congresses able to do so, as even formalistic elections of delegates to the higher-level Party congresses were not held in the long history of the CCP at least prior to the 8th National Party Congress in 1956 (Wu 2015). After this followed the period of the Cultural Revolution, during which delegates to the 9th and 10th National Party Congresses were not, for the most part, produced through local Party congressional elections; and, notoriously enough, some of them were not even members of the CCP when they were attending the meetings of the CCP's "supreme decision-making body" (Wu 2015: 84). In post-Mao politics, various political norms have been restored or established, including the restoration of the role of local Party congresses in electing delegates to higher-level Party congresses. This process of institutionalization, however, has obviously not reached the point of being constitutionalized; the Party Charter still leaves discretion over how to produce the delegates to Party congresses of various levels, including to the National Party Congress, to the Party leadership's decision on a case-by-case basis.

The contradiction between the claimed, formalistic delegation of power from the bottom up through the chains of local Party congresses at various levels up to the National Party Congress, on one hand, and the real hierarchy of power from the top down, on the other hand, emerges to particularly trouble local Party congresses. To perform the nominal role of power delegation from ordinary Party members up to the National Party Congress, local Party congresses must hold their meetings prior to the session of the National Congress, for the purpose of electing delegates to the national organization. This has been the practice in recent decades, as exemplified, by the drafting of this chapter in the second half of 2016, in the latest series of provincial-level Party congresses being held in the months from October 2011 to July 2012, prior to the 18th National Party Congress meeting in November 2012. During this period, the Liaoning Province started the wave by calling its provincial Party congress in mid-October 2011, and the round was completed in early July 2012 when the Beijing Metropolis closed its Party congress meeting. All these provincial-level Party congresses elected their delegates to the 18th National Party Congress.[19]

They also elected their own provincial Party leaderships. As Table 6.3 attempts to show, Party congresses in the 31 provincial level administrative units elected their local Party committees, which then elected the Standing Committees as the highest political authority in their jurisdictions with the total members of 405 in the round.[20] By June 2016, as this chapter is drafted, however, only 146 of them still remain as members of these committees to which they were elected about four years earlier. That means, 259 members elected in 2011–2012, or 64 percent of the total, were transferred to other posts, dismissed due to various reasons (mainly because of corruption charges), or retired due to reaching the age ceiling for their posts, all

Table 6.3 Instability of congressional-elected provincial party leaderships, 2011–2016

Province	*Time of election*	*Number of elected standing committee members*	*Number of those who remained on committee by June 2016*	*Secretaries elected vs. those who remained on committee by June 2016*
Beijing	July 2012	13	4	3 vs. 2
Tianjin	May 2012	13	5	3 vs. 1
Hebei	Nov. 2011	13	4	3 vs. 2
Shanxi	Nov. 2011	13	4	3 vs. 0
Nengmenggu	Nov. 2011	13	6	3 vs. 1
Liaoning	Oct. 2011	13	3	3 vs. 0
Jilin	May 2012	13	5	3 vs. 0
Heilongjiang	Apr. 2012	13	4	3 vs. 1
Shanghai	May 2012	13	4	3 vs. 1
Jiangsu	Nov. 2011	13	7	3 vs. 2
Zhejiang	June 2012	13	6	3 vs. 1
Anhui	Oct. 2011	13	5	3 vs. 0
Fujian	Nov. 2011	13	2	3 vs. 0
Jiangxi	Oct. 2011	13	3	3 vs. 1
Shandong	May 2012	13	5	3 vs. 1
Henan	Oct. 2011	13	5	3 vs. 1
Hebei	June 2012	13	5	3 vs. 1
Hunan	Nov. 2011	13	4	3 vs. 1
Guangdong	May 2012	13	6	3 vs. 1
Guangxi	Nov. 2011	13	3	3 vs. 0
Hainan	Apr. 2012	12	5	3 vs. 1
Chongqing	June 2012	13	4	3 vs. 1
Sichuan	May 2012	12	2	3 vs. 0
Guizhou	Apr. 2012	13	6	3 vs. 1
Yunnan	Nov. 2011	13	6	3 vs. 1
Xizang	Nov. 2011	15	8	5 vs. 3
Shaanxi	May 2012	12	5	3 vs. 0
Gansu	Apr. 2012	13	8	3 vs. 2
Qinghai	May 2012	14	3	3 vs. 1
Ningxia	June 2012	13	3	3 vs. 1
Xinjiang	Oct. 2011	15	6	4 vs. 1
		Total: 405	Total: 146	Total: 96 vs. 29

Sources: The author's research and composition based on his own database of China's local leaderships.

taking place without consultation with the Party congresses which initially elected them to the committees. In some provinces, the percentage of personnel change regarding the standing committee members elected by the local Party congress was as high as 85, as exemplified in the Fujian Province, where, by June 2016, only 2 of the 13 members of the provincial Party standing committee elected in November 2011 remained in the elected positions; Sichuan Province is in a similar situation, where 2 of the 12 members of the provincial Party Standing Committee elected in May 2012 remained on the committee by June 2016. Moreover, those who have so far remained on the committee and were elected a few years ago are often not holding the exact positions for which they were initially elected onto the committee.

New members were appointed solely by the central leadership (the Politburo and its Standing Committee) without any consultation with the pertinent local Party congress. In practice, new local leaders are often appointed to local Party committees exactly prior to the scheduled meeting of local Party congresses, thus making the meeting simply a ceremony of local congress delegates accepting and endorsing the appointments, in recent years usually via formalistic elections. As provincial Party congresses of the new round are scheduled to meet in late 2016 and early 2017, in order to produce delegates to the forthcoming 19th National Party Congress while also having to elect the new provincial Party Committees,[21] it is expected that the central leadership will conduct a profound reshuffle of provincial Party leaders before the provincial Party congresses open their sessions. When provincial Party congresses meet, they just need to confirm these appointments of provincial leaders through congressional elections. And, more intricately, after the National Party Congress, which, in reorganizing the central leaderships, inevitably promotes some provincial leaders into the new central leaderships, those provincial Party leaderships newly elected by the latest local Party congresses immediately encounter another huge reshuffle. These provincial leaders have thus to move from their provincial posts to Beijing, and a series of significant personnel changes has to follow accordingly.

Local Party congresses, therefore, are even shallower than the National Party Congress in their organizational operation and political practice. Their significance in local politics is even less than local people's congresses, as the latter, especially those at the provincial level in the territorial units, are in post-Mao eras empowered to make local legislation and endorse the appointment of local governmental leaders, but local Party congresses are not able to perform either of these two major functions in both Party and government affairs. Generally speaking, all lower-level Party congresses, including both territorial/local and sectional/non-territorial ones at various levels, are much less important in multiple senses: they are not able to legitimize local leaderships because such resources of power and authority of local leaderships are not rooted in local representation but in their power delegation functions of higher-level authorities; there are basically no such things that may be called local platforms of politics and governance, as following the central leadership is always a political priority in CCP politics; their role in local governance is even less required than that of local people's congresses, as the latter have in recent years been more and more involved in local legislative actions. In terms of their position, function, and operation, local Party congresses are nearly useless, mainly due to the fundamental incompatibility between the authoritarian essence of the CCP in Leninist centralization of power and authority, on one hand, and local Party congresses as an organizational arrangement of nominal bottom-up representation, on the other hand. The former always overwhelms the latter.

Conclusion

The CCP has an inner system of Party congresses, which roughly consists of the National Party Congress and local congresses at various levels nationwide. This system enjoys a supreme constitutional position in the nominal sense, but its political functions are greatly limited and handicapped in practice. Party congresses of the CCP, therefore, are an awkward combination of the formal institution of representation of mass members and the institutional manipulation of such representation to endorse the incumbent leadership's political, policy, and personnel preferences. Along with the former line that is the formalistic representation, the existence of Party congresses helps the CCP to boost its Leninist "democracy" for claiming the leadership's legitimacy; with the latter as the essence of Party congress operations, the representation, participation, delegate deliberation, and elections in particular and the entire congressional decision-making processes in general are channeled and maneuvered by the leadership, thus being tamed and emptied for the purpose of becoming a huge show of "democracy" with the very spirit of authoritarianism. Together they make Party congresses a theater of power, where congressional meetings are performed as glorious shows in which delegates feel themselves to be honored but the episodes, role-distributions, and actions are designed, directed, and well-tailored by the incumbent leadership. Through such a show, the leadership gains endorsement from Party elite on its policy proposals and political authorities; its existing power is legitimized.

The essential role of the system of Party congresses, therefore, is authoritarian legitimization. In the system, the National Party Congress occupies the niche of operation, as it is the sole institution that is given the constitutional function to legitimize the national leadership of the CCP. The only meaningful role of local Party congresses is to elect delegates to the National Party Congress via a chain of representation, but this role is not recognized by the Party Charter due to the fact that in reality delegates to the National Party Congress were for a long time not elected by local Party congresses, and, as they are elected on the occasion, elections are only formalistically conducted, which means the absence of voters' autonomous participation and any mechanism of competition. Such an absence is even more obvious in local Party congresses' elections of local Party leaders.

Though the system of Party congresses, including the National Party Congress, has generally been impotent in performing its constitutional functions in political practice, this conclusion cannot be understood statically; in fact, the system has been constantly in institutional change over the long history of the CCP. Due to space limits, the chapter has not been able to investigate such changes systematically; a trend of change, however, is clear in indicating an increasing significance of the National Party Congress in CCP politics, especially in the post-Mao eras of political development. The new features of Party congresses as a system in the contemporary period, in a historically comparative perspective, primarily include the regularity and frequency of Party congress meetings, while some rules of congressional operation, especially in preparation for a meeting, delegate selection, mechanism of consensus building, and leadership elections, have been adjusted in order to adapt to the changing sociopolitical circumstances. Such a regularity of the Party Congress meetings, to this author, is required mainly by the demand of the post-Mao leaders in seeking elite legitimization, as these leaders possess weak resources of legitimacy, such as charisma or ideology, thus causing them to turn to the institutional one. In other words, it more indicates Party leadership's demand rather than the Party Congress's autonomy. In a similar vein, the increasing stability of the congressional elected national leaderships in the post-Mao eras does not imply that the authority of the Party Congress has been strengthened; rather, it signifies a decrease of power struggles within the leaderships due to various reasons. As with any important change that occurs in this so-called normalization of CCP political life, it is very possible that a leader elected by the National Party Congress can be purged without any congressional action.

All the changes, that is to say, have not reached the degree at which the essence of the system is affected, nor the substantial role of the system is institutionally changed or politically reinforced.

Instead, the changes have so far taken place toward more skillful institutional manipulation than otherwise for further preventing the system from any possibility of increasing its autonomy in decision-making against the background of growing socioeconomic diversity in Chinese society and its inevitable reflections in the CCP's political life. As some proto-democracy measures have been introduced in the operation of the National Party Congress, measures including public opinion surveys in delegate selection and candidate nomination for central leadership elections, the spirit of the Party congress system, that is, to hollow out democratic essence but build up elite consensus in a top-down well-managed way, continues to work. Such changes, therefore, help to ensure the incumbent leadership's gaining of support from the elite to smooth the congressional process of accepting and endorsing all of the leadership's plans in platform making and personnel arrangements. In this way, the system of Party congresses will not be able to increase its autonomous power in fulfilling its constitutional functions, let alone make any progress toward imagined "democracy within the Party."

Notes

1 This chapter understands the concept of "institutions" in the way of combining the definitions contributed by Douglass North and Stephen Krasner, respectively. According to North, "Institutions are the rules of the game in a society or, more formally, are the human devised constraints that shape human interaction" (North 1990: 3). In a similar vein but with the interchangeable use between "institutions" and "regimes" in studies of international politics, Krasner defines the concept as "sets of implicit or explicit principles, norms, rules, and decision-making procedures around which actors' expectations converge in a given area of international relations" (Krasner 1983: 2).

2 For the ruling party's supremacy over the state as a feature of such politics, see Friedrich and Brzezinski (1956); for its complicated expression in the People's Republic of China, see, for example, Zheng (1997) and Prybyla (2000).

3 Hong Kong and Macao as the Special Administrative Regions under the sovereignty of the PRC, however, don't have the local people's congresses.

4 For the increase of the NPC's power and its limits, see O'Brien (1990), Tanner (1999), Dowdle (2002), Xia (2011).

5 Even though its omnipresence has been shrinking with the marketization reform of the recent 30-plus years, as analyzed, for example, in Goldman and MacFarquhar (1999).

6 The 8th National Party Congress is an exception, as it adopted a system of so-called "permanent delegate" (*daibiao changren zhi*) (Shi Zhongquan *et al.* 1998).

7 The exception is the 8th National Party Congress, which, according to the Party Charter, should hold an annual meeting during its five-year term, though in practice it met only twice in 1956 and 1958 (Shi Zhongquan *et al.* 1998).

8 For an attempt to summarize such changes, see Wu (2015: 126).

9 Zhongguo gongchandang xinwen wang [News web of the CCP], "Full text of Constitution of Communist Party of China," http://english.cpc.people.com.cn/206972/206981/8188094.html, accessed June 30, 2016. "Banner" (*qi*) is a special title equal to county for some territorial administrative units in the regions with the Manchu tradition.

10 Item 3, Clause 10, Chapter 2 of the Party Charter in the recent editions since 1997. For such statements, see Xuanbianzu (2007: 151, 173).

11 See ft 9. These stipulations have remained the same since the 12th Party Congress adopted a new Party Charter in 1982, while other articles and clauses may have experienced revisions during the same historical period.

12 Renmin wang [People's web], http://cpc.people.com.cn/18/n/2012/1105/c350821-19493512.html, accessed June 30, 2016.

13 Renmin wang, http://cpc.people.com.cn/18/n/2012/1107/c351261-19521857.html, accessed June 30, 2016.

14 According to a delegate to the CCP's 16th Party Congress in 2002, 201 TV stations from all over the world live broadcasted the opening ceremony of that Congress, and on the first two days after the opening the Congress received 2,956 congratulatory telegrams from within China and overseas (Leng

Rong 2002: 6). As the world has been watching the rise of China, there is no reason to assume that such concern and attention to the CCP's Party Congress has since declined, if not increased.

15 Renmin wang, http://cpc.people.com.cn/18/n/2012/1107/c351261-19521957.html, accessed June 30, 2016.

16 Renmin wang, http://cpc.people.com.cn/18/n/2012/1107/c351261-19521957.html, accessed August 15, 2016.

17 Other reports, especially the report from the incumbent Central Disciplinary Inspection Committee in recent years, were circulated as printed documents to delegates.

18 This applies to most of the post-Mao Party Congress sessions, as earlier Party congresses had such delegates' speeches to the congressional assembly meetings.

19 "地方党委换届结束, 奠定十八大地方组织人事基础," 中国网, http://news.china.com.cn/2012-07/07/content_25845660.htm, posted July 7, 2012, accessed June 21, 2016.

20 According to relevant procedures, the Party Committee elects its Standing Committee in its full session. But this always takes place at the first full session that follows the Party Committee just elected by the Party Congress. Thus the election of the Standing Committee is regarded as a vital part of the Party Congress, rather than an election independently held in a different circumstance. Moreover, at the local levels there is usually no pertinent constitutional document claiming the CPC's Party leadership's supreme authority in local governance, but the PRC national constitution does stipulate the CPC's leadership authority in the country. The Party Committee, after all, does take the supreme authority in political practice in local affairs.

21 See a special page on this issue at Gongchan dangyuan wang [Web of the Communist Party members], www.12371.cn/special/ssxxldbzhj/, accessed August 2, 2016.

References

Chen Feng and Gao Min (2008), *Zhongguo gongchandang lici quanguo daibiao dahui* [The previous National Congresses of the Chinese Communist Party], Beijing: Zhonggong dangshi chubanshe.

Dowdle, Michael William (2002), "Constructing Citizenship: The NPC as Catalyst for Political Participation," in Merle Goldman and Elizabeth J. Perry eds., *Changing Meanings of Citizenship in Modern China*, Cambridge, MA: Harvard University Press, pp. 330–349.

Geertz, Clifford (1980), *Negara: The Theatre State in Nineteenth-Century Bali*, Princeton, NJ: Princeton University Press.

Goldman, Merle and Roderick MacFarquhar (1999), "Introduction," in Merle Goldman and Roderick MacFarquhar eds., *The Paradox of China's Post-Mao Reforms*, Cambridge, MA: Harvard University Press.

Friedrich, Carl J. and Zbigniew K. Brzezinski (1956), *Totalitarian Dictatorship and Autocracy*, Cambridge, MA: Harvard University Press.

Hough, Jerry F. and Merle Fainsod (1979), *How the Soviet Union Is Governed*, Cambridge, MA: Harvard University Press.

Krasner, Stephen D. (1983), "Structural Causes and Regime Consequences: Regime as Intervening Variable," in Stephen D. Krasner ed., *International Regimes*, Ithaca, NY: Cornell University Press, pp. 1–21.

Leng Rong (2002), "Xin shiji juyou zhongda er shenyuan yiyi de shenghui: canjia Zhonggong shiliuda de ganshou" [A magnificent meeting in the new century with significant and far-reaching implications: Impressions from participating in the CCP's 16th Party Congress], *Dang de wenxian*, No. 6: 6–10.

Li Junru (2007), *Zhongguo gongchandang lici quanguo daibiao dahui yanjiu* [A study of previous National Congresses of the Chinese Communist Party], Shanghai: Dongfang chuban zhongxin.

Li Ying (2008), *Cong yida dao shiqida, 1921–2007* [From the 1st to 17th National Party Congress, 1921–2007], Beijing: Renmin chubanshe.

Lieberthal, Kenneth (1995), *Governing China: From Revolution Through Reform*, New York: W.W. Norton.

North, Douglass C. (1990), *Institutions, Institutional Change and Economic Performance*, New York: Cambridge University Press.

O'Brien, Kevin J. (1990), *Reform Without Liberalization: China's National People's Congress and the Politics of Institutional Change*, New York: Cambridge University Press.

Prybyla, Jan (2000), "The Chinese Communist Economic State in Comparative Perspective," in David Shambaugh ed., *The Modern Chinese State*, New York: Cambridge University Press, pp. 188–215.

Schurmann, Franz (1968), *Ideology and Organization of the Chinese Communist Party*, Berkeley: University of California Press, 2nd ed.

Shi Zhongquan, Shen Zhengle, Yang Xiancun, and Han Gang (1998), *Zhonggong bada shi* [A history of the 8th Party Congress], Beijing: Renmin chubanshe.

Tanner, Murray Scot (1999), *The Politics of Lawmaking in Post-Mao China: Institutions, Processes and Democratic Prospects*, Oxford: Clarendon Press.

Wu, Guoguang (2015), *China's Party Congress: Power, Legitimacy, and Institutional Manipulation*, Cambridge: Cambridge University Press.

Xia, Ming (2011), *The People's Congresses and Governance in China: Toward a Network Mode of Governance*, New York: Routledge.

Xuanbianzu (2007), *Zhongguo gongchandang zhagcheng huibian: cong yida dao shiqida* [The compilation of the CCP Party Charters: from the 1st to the 17th Party Congress], Beijing: Zhonggong zhongyang dangxiao chubanshe.

Zheng, Shiping (1997), *Party vs. State in Post-1949 China: The Institutional Dilemma*, New York: Cambridge University Press.

7
THE PLA AS THE LIFELINE OF THE PARTY

Ka Po Ng

Introduction

Shortly after Xi Jinping ascended to the post of General Secretary of the Chinese Communist Party (CCP) in November 2012, it was widely reported that, during a trip to southern China, he lamented over the fragility of the Communist Party of the Soviet Union (CPSU) and its collapse in a snap of a finger more than 20 years ago. This trip was easily contrasted with Deng Xiaoping's in 1992. While Deng found the preservation of the communist regime in its capacity to deliver economic well-being through resuscitating economic reform, Xi looked to the importance of ideological purity and the party's control over the means of coercion and repression. A key lesson from the CPSU downfall, as he noted, was its failure to command the unwavering loyalty of the army (Buckley 2013).

Xi Jinping is obviously a good student of Mao Zedong's timeless teachings for all CCP members: "political power grows out of the gun barrel" (Mao 1938/1993). Although Mao continued in the same essay, "our principle is, the party commands the gun but the gun is absolutely not allowed to command the party," this betrays the fear that the powerful military may one day threaten its party masters. In this way, Mao provides an important lead for all students of Chinese civil–military relations (CMR).

As the CCP rose from the opposition to become *the* ruling party, the importance of the military in Chinese politics, from the Red Army to the People's Liberation Army (PLA),[1] has evolved to a level beyond what Mao had realized. The gun does not simply make the CCP the ruling party (Mao 1938/1993). It has served as the power broker and even the king maker at critical junctures of power struggle, the custodian of party interests, and an essential policy instrument. Not content with delving into empirical details alone, we have to tap the wisdom of CMR literature to put all this into perspective.

What has given the PLA such political prominence? Woo (2011: 11) rightly identifies security threats as a major factor which he calls a "structural cause" that shapes "political opportunities, incentives, and relative power positions of major domestic actors – namely, civilian leadership, the military, and civil society." He goes on to suggest that interactions among these actors are "structural modifiers" that "determine a more specific and nuanced aspect of civil-military dynamics." Threats, however, are not self-evident but subject to manipulation by civilian and military leaders to serve their political agendas (2011: 11). The leaderships' continuous emphasis on security threats has created their own dependence on the PLA.

This echoes Samuel E. Finer's views about the military's opportunity to intervene. He observes in *The Man on Horseback* that civilian leaders under certain circumstances are "abnormally dependent," especially in times of domestic political crisis and power vacuum (2002: 72). Finer also analyzes the political strengths and weaknesses of the military, its dispositions to intervene, as well as the mode and level of intervention. These concepts help organize findings in the Chinese case. Eric A. Nordlinger offers to study CMR from an alternative angle, i.e., civilian control. In his *Soldiers in Politics: Military Coups and Governments*, Nordlinger focuses on what he calls, "praetorianism," which refers to "a situation in which military officers are major or predominant political actors by virtue of their actual or threatened use of force" (1977: 2). To ensure civilian authority over the military, there are three major models of control and the communist system is one of penetration. It is through personnel appointments and political indoctrination that the party leaders exercise their control (Nordlinger 1977: 16–17). Of course, these theoretical insights do not mean their uncritical application to the study of China. The peculiarities of the Chinese experiences and political system, especially its symbiotic civil-military relationship and overlapping and inter-penetrating civil-military authorities, demands caution and attention to nuances. The ambiguous boundary between the civilian and military has characterized Chinese CMR until the installation of Jiang Zemin in 1989 as the first civilian Central Military Commission (CMC) chairman (Scobell 2003: 51–54; Miller 2006: 138–139).

This chapter employs the analytical tools offered by the literature on CMR to elucidate the historical experiences of the interaction between the CCP and its military with emphasis on policy relevance. It observes that the PLA has been largely subservient to its political master but, paradoxically, it is the party that provides space and creates the opportunities for military intervention, which, in Finer's lexicon, ranges from exercising political influence to supplanting the civilian government (2002: 168). While the PLA has mostly stayed on the political sideline, it has also been called upon by the party faction in power to take the center stage, be it for politically or militarily combating opposing political forces or for flexing muscles (Nathan and Scobell 2012: 57–58). The CCP's revolutionary and nation-building experiences, its ways to produce leadership, and its preferred use of coercive means in governance make it heavily dependent on the military from its quest for to its preservation of political power.

Through a historical survey, the following sections will examine how the PLA since the Red Army days has built up its capacity to intervene in politics, the party's dependence on the military, as well as its attempts to use it as a political tool while keeping it under control. Although CMR, as a field of study, generally covers the military's civilian interactions at both elitist and social levels, this chapter pays particular attention to the political leadership to reflect the highly centralized power structure.

Soldiers on the political stage

According to Finer (2002), the military has both political weaknesses and strengths. The general rejection of military rule or an intervening military and the lack of political skills put the soldiers on the disadvantageous side. In contrast, its characteristic centralized command and coherent organization give it clear superiority over civil groups. The PLA's Red Army precursor obviously falls short of this ideal model. However, even with its minimal capability as an instrument of violence and its relative organizational strength, the Red Army was strong enough to play a key role in CCP power struggles in an era of political chaos.

Quite different from its self-given name, "Chinese Workers' and Peasants' Red Army,"[2] the PLA started in August 1927 mainly with defected Chinese Nationalist or Kuomintang (KMT) troops. The previous failed struggles of worker strikes simply demonstrated how much the CCP needed an organized and specialized means of violence if its revolution was to succeed. The short-lived participation of CCP members in the running of China's first military educational institution, Whampao Military Academy, in 1924 had also raised the awareness of the value of the military (Zhi 1989: 50). A sense of urgency became prominent after the purge of CCP members by both Nationalist governments in 1927. It was at the "August 7 Conference" of 1927 that Mao Zedong and the leadership realized how indispensable the military was for seizing political power (Mao 1927/1993: 2; Gao and Xue 2011: 191).

To control the armed forces, various agencies have been formed at different times. They have ranged from the Military Department (*junshi bu*), a "military group," and Central Revolutionary Military Commission and finally to the CMC under the party's Politburo. The principle of party leadership over the military, according to official party discourse, was asserted at the Gutian Conference of 1929 (Kawashima 1988: 195–198; Kang 1990: 12–13; Yuan 2016: 104–105). However, these measures had not created a coherent military force. The diverse backgrounds of the Red Army and the geographically scattered forces inevitably caused factionalism (Luo 2016). Of course, this only reflected the CCP's own plight which was manifested in intense power struggles among disparate factions. Although Mao Zedong successfully established his new leadership after seizing military power at the Zunyi Conference in January 1935 and his eventual assumption of the chairmanship of the unified CMC in the following year, it was the virtual annihilation of Mao's arch rival Zhang Guotao's forces by the Nationalists that contributed to Mao's undisputed leadership (Zhi 1989: 51; Fei 2016). The role of military power in the party's internal strife featured prominently. As Xu Xiangqian, one of the PLA's ten marshals, recalled, without the support of Zhu De, the then Red Army's commander-in-chief, neither Zhang Guotao's CCP Central Committee nor the CMC under Zhou Enlai's control could have become a decisive force in politics (Wang 2016).

But why was the Red Army so important? The official CCP history depicts the Red Army's evasion from the pursuit and encirclement campaigns of the Nationalist troops in 1934–1935 as a victorious Long March but one indisputable fact is that it came out much weaker than what it had been. It had started with a strength of 190,000 troops but ended up with 50,000. The worst happened to the Central Red Army which lost 7,000 of its 86,000 troops (Xia 2016). So, it is not the army's combat capabilities that matters. The lack of centralized command, unity, and organizational coherence that characterize modern professional armies was already evident in the failed Nanchang Uprising (Kawashima 1988: 29). Zhang Guotao's split with Mao in 1935 accentuated such inadequacies. Nevertheless, the military made its debut as a political force and asserted its political importance because the CCP recognized that it was in dire struggle for survival and violence was the only way to achieve its immediate goal of seizing and consolidating power. Even with minimal military prowess and relative organizational strength, the Red Army found favor among the competing civilian leaders.

Such inadequacies were dramatically turned around during China's war with Japan. Having crushed the opposing KMT army in three major civil war campaigns between 1946 and 1949, the PLA marched victoriously into Beijing, where Mao would declare the establishment of the People's Republic in October 1949. At this stage, the utility and importance of organized violence are no more evident. Instead of going back to the barracks, the army's political influence was brought to new heights.

The military in politics and economics

Even with Mao's declaration on Tiananmen, the CCP's control over China was far from complete and secure. Remnant KMT forces in the mainland peripheries and, of course, in Taiwan, as well as armed resistance to communist rule posed serious threats to the new government. In the northeast of China, as the UN forces led by the US quickly overran Kim Il-sung's troops and, in defiance of warning from Beijing, crossed the 38th parallel, the Chinese army traversed the Yalu River to fight the world's superpower and its allies exactly one year after the declaration of the founding of the PRC. In the eyes of the Chinese leaders, the Korean War was a revolutionary struggle. At stake was the survival of the new Chinese regime and the communist struggle against imperialism (Mao 1953/1993: 341). In Woo's logic, the presence of such existential threats determined the continued dominant political influence of the military (2011). These domestic and external security challenges were as much military as political. The future of the revolution and that of the state were intricately linked to the army.

After 1949, the PLA's missions were changed from "seizing political power with military means and war to consolidating the people's democratic dictatorship, safeguarding the socialist revolution and construction, defending external aggression, and safeguarding national security and territorial integrity" (Gao and Xue 2011: 193). This official narrative, while highlighting the key role changes, does not clearly explain such development and misses its significance.

Perhaps "role changes" is an understatement. In accordance with Nordlinger's two principles of a political army, the "birth-right principle" and the "competence principle," the PLA was qualified for both (1977: 23). Not only because of its indispensable role in making the PRC possible but also its strength as the most organized and disciplined force available, it, in the face of imminent security threats, was naturally the preferred coercive policy instrument. In the early years of the republic, the military was given the task of governance.

As the PLA was advancing, the party leadership issued in 1948 decrees for establishing military control in all "liberated areas" under local military leaders to suppress oppositions and to cultivate local civilian support. Military Control Commissions (*junshi guanzhi weiyuanhui*) were formed in such major cities as Beiping (now Beijing), Shanghai, Wuhan, and Guangzhou. But the power of the military was tremendously expanded after 1949. According to the Common Program (*gongtong gangling*), the PRC's interim constitution, military control was to be implemented in newly liberated areas as a temporary measure and the duration would be determined by local military and political conditions. The country was divided into six large administrative regions; except for the North China and the Northeast China regions, the other four – the Northwest, Southwest, the Central-South, and East China – were run by the Military Administrative Commissions (*junzheng weiyuanhui*). These powerful organs, headed by prestigious military leaders, including Lin Biao, Liu Bocheng, and Peng Dehuai (who were in 1955 conferred the title of marshal), were to perform government functions (Wang 2010: 49–50; Teiwes 2011: 29–30).

This outright takeover of civilian governance phased out gradually and was ended with the abolition of the last Commission in 1954. Because of the interpenetration of civil-military authorities and the dual civil-military background of many senior leaders, the withdrawal of the military regimes was smooth (Wang 2010: 52; Teiwes 2011: 30). Perhaps a no less important factor was the improved security environment in light of the relative stability of the CCP regime and the end of the Korean War.

Parallel to the task of governing, the PLA, once described by Mao as "a combat team, a [mass] work team, a production team" (*zhandoudui, gongzuodui, shengchandui*), was officially called in December 1949 to engage in socio-economic construction (Yu *et al.* 1994: volume 1:

112; Xinhua 2008). Given the size of the troops to be demobilized first after the civil war and, later, after the Korean War, the leaders were hard-pressed to accommodate such tremendous redundant manpower. On top of 1.5 million troops demobilized in 1950, some 600,000 troops were converted into engineering teams to support infrastructure construction as well as to garrison and farm the frontiers a year later (Yu *et al.* 1994: volume 1: 110–116).

While the armistice brought a temporary end to the war on the Korean Peninsula, the struggle to build socialism continued worldwide. The military factor was also found in overall national construction. The fervent development of heavy industry that marked the First Five-Year Plan and socioeconomic development in the 1950s was attributable to the need for strengthening national defense (Li 1955). A survey of the geographical distribution of the industries showed that security calculations trumped the economic logic of building industries in locations with sound infrastructure and easy access to energy resources (Xia 2008). Entering the 1960s, this trend of military influence in state planning intensified and will be discussed in a later section.

The professionalization interlude

Being released from the pressure of dealing with existential threats and having experienced fighting conventional battles with one of the world's most advanced armies in Korea, the PLA brought home the urgency of building itself into a regular army. It was decided at a major meeting in December 1953 that the time allocated to military work, political work, and cultural work should be in the ratio of 6:2:2 (Yu *et al.* 1994: volume 1: 149–152). This was only an example of how the focus of army building had shifted.

Until its abrupt end in 1958 with the purge of Peng Dehuai and other senior military leaders, the significance of the professionalization drive of the 1950s cannot be overstated. It marked a decisive break of the Chinese military from the guerrilla tradition to take the path of a modern army. In terms of command and control, today's CMC was established in 1954 under the CCP Politburo with Mao Zedong as chairman, the "general departments" and military regions were reorganized, and the institution of the three service arms was confirmed. The research and development of military hardware were promoted at full throttle. No less important, as the PLA was streamlined to 2.4 million troops, its force structure was rationalized by reducing the size of the ground forces, especially the infantry, while increasing that of the air force and of the navy. More important, many institutions were put in place. The military service regulations, the officer service regulations, and the officers' ranks regulations were issued (Yu *et al.* 1994: volume 1: 154–164). In Finer's terms, all this considerably enhanced the PLA's political strength with a much more coherent organization and centralized command structure. These qualities made the army a valuable political asset and proved to be essential for it to reach an unprecedented level of political influence in the mid-1960s.

Return to the political center stage

The Chinese plan of military modernization had been modelled on the Soviet Red Army. Ideological rift between two countries became an easy excuse for Mao and his henchman in uniform, Lin Biao, to kill the project at an enlarged CMC meeting of 1958. But if politics had cost the PLA its professionalization, it would soon compensate it for bringing it back to power.

This attack on the army turned out to be a prelude to radical politics. The disastrous Great Leap Forward from 1958 to 1962 failed to deliver economic results but served well to demonstrate the potency of mass mobilization. The Cultural Revolution launched by Mao and his allies three years later brought this fearsome power to a zenith. As there is a wealth of studies on this subject, it does not need much ink here to describe the resulting chaos across China. Suffice it to say that the slogan of "putting politics in command" best captures how the nation was politicized.

The nationwide frenzy soon spilled onto the PLA. Military leaders as senior as Marshals Zhu De, Peng Dehuai, He Long, and Chen Yi, and many other generals were publicly humiliated and physically abused. Even the Ministry of Defense was stormed by the revolutionary Red Guards (Li and Hau 1989: 63–106 and 372–374; Scobell 2003: 96). Professionalization was rolled back as evidenced by the abolition of military ranks as a symbol of egalitarianism and challenging established authority, putting political education above military training, and the closure of many military academies. One of the most impactful developments was Mao's order of "three supports, two militaries" (*sanzhi liangjun*) in 1967 as the movement had got even out of the Chairman's hand. By supporting the leftists, the workers, the peasants, and implementing military control and military training, the PLA was practically asked to take over not only local governments but socioeconomic operations as institutions ranging from factories to schools lapsed into a state of virtual paralysis. Military Control Commissions returned to suppress the "rebels" and restore order (Li and Hau 1989: 226–248; Yu *et al.* 1994: volume 1: 241, 250). When the policy was abolished in 1972, over 2.8 million servicemen had been involved in various capacities (MacFarquhar and Schoenhals 2006: 177–183). Rarely is military intervention so pervasive in a country. The PLA penetrated deep into every civilian sector. In return, it was rewarded with tremendous political influence. At the Ninth CCP Central Committee of 1969, 45 percent of the members came from the PLA (Li and Hau 1989: 111).

Apart from being called to counter this domestic security threat, the PLA had to face an increasingly hostile international security environment. Following US escalation of intervention in Vietnam during the Kennedy administration and the 1962 border war with India, aggravated Sino-Soviet relations finally culminated in border skirmishes in 1969. Paradoxically, while professionalization had come to a halt and Mao's decree for the army to support particular factions caused internal divisions, it was the preparation for fighting an "imminent, all-out, nuclear war" that allowed the PLA to maintain its organizational cohesiveness and its minimal combat capabilities (Li and Hau 1989: 267; Yu *et al.* 1994: volume 1: 573; Scobell 2003: 110). That partly explains why the Chinese development program for strategic weapons – atomic bombs, ballistic missiles, and satellite – could continue to proceed. Defense industrial plants also continued to churn out conventional weapons though their quality and design were quite often in question (Li and Hau 1989: 279–311; Zheng *et al.* 1992: volume 1: 82–123).

The Cultural Revolution saw the peak of military intervention, invited and uninvited. Although details have remained shrouded in mystery,[3] the alleged coup attempt by Lin Biao, codenamed Project 571, concluded with a reported plane crash that killed the Marshal and his family in September 1971.

When Nordlinger (1977: 17) argues that civilian attempts at penetrating the army with appointments of political officers and with political indoctrination engender power interventionist motives among army officers, he refers to backfiring and resistance from the professional army. However, in the Chinese case, this strategy of civilian control involved the army so deeply in politics that the generals have become a political player – and a competitor with its civilian masters for political power. If Mao's invitation to the military to restore order vindicated the PLA's role as guardian of national welfare, the alleged coup represented attempts by ambitious military leaders emboldened to take up the role of ruling the country themselves (Nordlinger 1977: 20–22).

Mao's strongman leadership had helped ensure civilian control even in times of chaos. But once the Great Helmsman was gone in 1976, the political vacuum provided the environment for bold military intervention. Again, the PLA played the role of guardian of the national interest. Marshal Ye Jianying staged a classic palace coup, arresting the so-called Gang of Four, who were accused of causing the disorder and crimes in the bloody Cultural Revolution (Li and Hau 1989: 182–183). The support of Hua Guofeng, the then party's First Vice-Chairman, was no more than a civilian façade to cover the military intervention. After a transition of merely one year, Deng Xiaoping reemerged from political eclipse as the new paramount leader. The new patriarch not only had all his former posts as CCP Vice-Chairman, CMC Vice-Chairman, and PLA Chief of Staff restored but assumed in 1981 the CMC chairmanship, a position he held until 1989. In fact, as soon as he was in control, Deng lost no time to launch in 1978 his own development blueprint for his country, the "Four Modernizations" of agriculture, industry, science and technology, and national defense.

The difficult march of professionalization

Putting national defense as the last of the four modernizations reflected Deng Xiaoping's dual identity as civilian and military leader. Military affairs constitute only a component of his national development strategy. His decisions are based on an appraisal of political, socioeconomic, and military conditions. Therefore, in February 1979, shortly after announcing his modernization plan, Deng did not hesitate to "teach Vietnam a lesson" through a one-month border war. Though doubts have been cast about China's claim for victory, Deng was able to take this opportunity to assert his status as paramount leader and his control over the gun (Scobell 2003: 143). Such authority enabled him to overcome the odds to realize his strategic visions.

Already in 1975, Deng Xiaoping had been determined to rectify the negative impacts of the Cultural Revolution on the PLA – "bloating, laxity, conceit, extravagance and inertia" – a series of problems that he reiterated at a full CMC session in 1977 after his reinstatement (Deng 1975/1994: 15; 1977/1994: 75; Joffe 1987: 121). With the US withdrawing from Asia, Vietnam tamed, and the Soviet Union preoccupied by its Afghanistan adventure, Deng was apt to announce the overall easing of international security tensions. At the same time, internal security challenges did not worry the patriarch any longer. All this justified his overhaul of the PLA, disengaging the army from politics, and restarting the professionalization process (Joffe 1987: 27).

The landmark decision came in 1985 when Deng Xiaoping declared his plan to demobilize one million troops on the observation that "peace and development" would be the dominant theme of international affairs. This cleared the way for him to build what he called a "modernized and regularized revolutionary army" (*xiandaihua zhengguihua de geming jundui*). Unlike the expensive military modernization of most countries, the Chinese army had to proceed in a frugal way. It was asked to "persevere" (*rennai*) and subsume its interests under the "general situation" (*daju*) of national economic development (Deng 1985/1993: 126–129). It had to improve its manpower and equipment quality with funds released from force downsizing. This gave Deng the necessary maneuver room to reshuffle the senior military leadership and to restructure the army. Most notably, after Zhao Ziyang had been picked by Deng to replace Hu Yaobang as the CCP General Secretary in January 1987, he was appointed the CMC's First Vice-Chairman in November the same year with Deng himself as Chairman and Yang Shangkun, another former Red Army political commissar, as the Standing Vice-Chairman and Secretary-General. Other CMC members were also Deng's allies who played the double role of supporting and watching a civilian leader who had no military experience at all (Wang and Peng 1994: volume 1: 76; Yu *et al.* 1994: volume 1: 348).

Given the resource constraints, reforms in national defense were mainly about the software, such as doctrine, training, force structure, and institution building.[4] Particularly by restoring the officer ranks and the military service regulations, the army regained its organizational cohesiveness and esprit de corps.

If economic reforms inadvertently put the PLA in the doldrums of political influence, the missteps of these reforms gave it opportunity to return with a big bang. The runaway inflation, official corruption, and increasing socio-economic inequality spurred social unrest which culminated in the democracy movement of 1989. When the people defied the martial law and law enforcement forces, including the People's Armed Police (PAP) which had been reconstituted in 1982 for internal security purposes, were unable to contain revolts in the state capital and other major cities, Deng and other leaders found all this intolerable and sent in the PLA to violently clear Tiananmen Square, the headquarters and symbol of the movement (Baum 2011: 341).

Again, the army was summoned to rescue the party by forcefully suppressing the opposition. But this exacted a heavy toll not only on the lives of the people in Beijing[5] but also on Chinese CMR. On the one hand, the decision to use deadly force against civilians had caused internal divisions among both party and military leaders and even cases of insubordination; on the other, PLA and PAP casualties and destruction of army equipment by resisting crowds showed animosity between civilians and the military (Chi 1990: 3; Scobell 2003: 149–156). But the CCP's immediate response was to intensify ideological education, asserting its leadership over the baffled PLA, combating the "peaceful evolution" plots from the West, and emphasizing discipline. Moreover, the army was told that it served dual functions (*shuangchong zhineng*) – national defense and internal security. In 1990, the army was told to allocate 70 percent of its time to ideological education, hence reversing the emphasis on professional military training (Guo 1989: 8; Xu and Liu 1990: 16–27; Gregor 1991: 9; Miller 2006: 135–136). Obviously, these measures failed to address this CMR question: if the party must control the gun, why was it someone other than the party general secretary who actually commanded the PLA? While such supposedly anomalous events are not exactly rare in CCP history, the military intervention in 1989 practically undid all the institution building that Deng himself had painstakingly promoted. At the end, it is a matter of *who* really controls the gun.

The Jiang-Hu era

It is exactly this issue that continues to haunt post-Deng leaders. Although both Jiang Zemin and Hu Jintao, who were CCP general secretaries without any combat experience, scarcely ever departed from the Dengist army building trajectory, they had to traverse dangerous trails in civil–military relations.

Following the hasty installation of Jiang to the post of party general secretary in June 1989, Deng also turned over his CMC chairmanship to the latter in a few months, making him nominally China's political and military leader. But, Jiang knew well he was not yet the real leader in a CMC filled with generals picked by his predecessor. Finally, in 1992, Jiang, with the support of Deng and other PLA elders, purged from the CMC Yang Shangkun and his half-brother, Yang Baibing, who had served as Deng's trusted lieutenants, for their dominant influence in military affairs (Scobell 2003: 166). Jiang Zemin did not have the CMC in complete control until the retirement in 1997 of Liu Huaqing and Zhang Zheng, who represented the Deng legacy. This practice of a retired paramount leader trying to preserve his influence by stacking the CMC with senior members loyal to himself was continued by Jiang Zemin himself. Despite having retired from the Politburo – and the position of general secretary and state president after the 16th Party Congress of 2002, Jiang remained CMC chairman until 2004. And even after vacating the CMC, Jiang tried to preserve his influence by installing two protégés,

Guo Boxiong and Xu Caihou, as CMC vice-chairmen. Guo and Xu would later become principal protagonists in the CMR drama in the Xi Jinping era.

The fight for controlling the gun is not surprising. If the PLA has amply proven its value in power struggles and domestic political crisis, it got a further boost from a series of international security challenges entering the 1990s. The Gulf War of 1991, the Chinese decision to assert its claims in the South China Sea,[6] the US show of force in the 1996 Taiwan Strait Crisis,[7] the NATO armed intervention in the genocide in former Yugoslavia, and the "mistaken" bombing of the Chinese embassy in Belgrade by US forces in 1999 all reminded China of its capability gap with the world's advanced military powers – and of the advent of the "revolution in military affairs" (Yan *et al.* 1993: 67–77; Shambaugh 2002: 74–76; Cole 2010: 151–156). Still, domestically, the CCP under both Jiang and Hu, facing a legitimacy crisis, began to promote the national humiliation discourse to fill the ideological vacuum by contrasting present day achievements with the "100 years of humiliation" (Wang 2012: 91–93). This political mobilization strategy exposed the civilian leadership to even greater dependence on the military.

To secure PLA support, money was Jiang Zemin's preferred instrument. According to a study, military spending from 1979 to 1994 registered an average increase of 6.22 percent but, having discounted the inflation factor, it actually reported a negative growth rate of 1.08 percent (Gu and Quan 1999: 270). The financial interests and socio-political status of the army sank to the bottom and caused great anxiety among servicemen (Liu 1994: 36). This was reversed in Jiang's time when military spending began to pick up speed. And, this policy was continued by Hu Jintao. From 1998 till 2015, the defense budget has grown in double digits annually except for 2010. The spending boosts were regarded as "compensation" for the lean period under Deng (Huang and Zhang 2008; Buckley and Perlez 2016). Moreover, trying to make up the shortfalls, Jiang acquiesced on PLA units engaging in businesses, which once accounted for 25 percent of extra-budgetary income. When these entangled the PLA in endless scandals, Jiang ordered a stop of all commercial activities in 1998 (Cao 1998; Brömmelhörster and Ng 2000: 158–175).

Xi Jinping's new wine in old bottles

The avalanche-like collapse of the Soviet Union served Xi Jinping a harsh reminder of Mao Zedong's teaching on controlling the gun (Buckley 2013). But what Jiang Zemin had tried to achieve with money and inducement, Xi Jinping does with crude power. He decided that it was time to redress the CMR balance as the military was getting politically dominant. Starting with calls for rectifying working style, he systematically raised the stakes to a wholesale purge through organizational reforms and the anti-corruption drive (Ng 2017).

By the end of 2016, at least 53 generals and senior colonels had been brought under investigation ("At least 53 'Army Tigers'" 2016). The prosecution of Xu Caihou and Guo Boxiong simply epitomized how ruthless and determined Xi was to assert his control. It is noteworthy that they were accused of not only corruption but, more importantly, power abuse, bad political discipline, and factionalism as reflected in the polemics of the ensuing political education campaigns that called for ridding the army of the "pernicious vestiges" of both Xu and Guo (Jia *et al.* 2016; Liberation Army Daily Commentator 2016). The disgraced Xu's gravest sin was probably his attempts to "sideline" (*jiakong*) his civilian master, Hu Jintao (Phoenix News 2015). Xi Jinping is obviously a good disciple of Mao, who commented "it is our principle that the party commands the gun but it never allows the gun to control the party" (Mao 1938/1993: 421). Since the anti-corruption drive would achieve only limited results, more radical measures were needed.

For the sake of building his power base in the army, Xi Jinping was ready to break with convention. He was also eager to cultivate personal ties. Two days after assuming CMC chairmanship in 2012, Xi appointed a full general. Within barely one month of taking office, he inspected the then Guangzhou Theater; and in a little more than a year, he had inspected all seven Military Regions. His visit in army fatigues to the newly established CMC Joint Operations Command Center in 2016 sent an unambiguous message that he was both the leader and true commander of the armed forces. But, most importantly, he created a CMC Leading Group on Deepening Military Reforms in 2014 to promote his military reforms instead of following the precedent of convening enlarged CMC meetings. All these demonstrated his firm control over military affairs.

Xi Jinping's reforms were described by an army analyst as the biggest change to the PLA's command and leadership system since the PRC's establishment and a move that touched the vested interests at an "unprecedented depth" (Jin 2016). This is no exaggeration at all. By downgrading the four general departments (the General Staff Department, General Political Department, General Logistics Department, and General Armaments Department) to functional agencies under the CMC as part of an overhaul of the command-and-control apparatus, by replacing the seven military regions with five theater commands which are no longer given any army building authority, and by redeploying the troops, Xi practically dismantled the old power networks and made room for installing his own men. The demobilization of 300,000 troops announced in 2015 gave him further space for filling important positions with his men. As of late 2016, reforms above the provincial military district level were said to have been basically implemented (Zhang and Ma 2016). Already the personnel reshuffle is so extensive that the names of new leaders of different divisions are appearing in the media with unusual frequency. For example, since the 18th Party Congress, Xi Jinping has promoted 23 full generals. By January 2017, the top leaders of the PLA Navy and its three fleets had all been changed.

By reinventing the old tricks of purges, patronage, and political penetration which were repackaged into reform of the force structure as well as disciplinary and management reforms, Xi Jinping managed to tame the military, in the process putting the genie back into the bottle. However, his military reforms have already produced great anxiety inside the military, not only professionally but individually. The Office for Handling the Aftermath of Reform (*shanhou bangongshi*) has few resources to placate affected officers and soldiers. Moreover, without sufficient material incentives, the efficacy of political work and pampering officers and soldiers with honor has become dubious (Xiao 2016).

By contrast, Xi's heavy-handed imposition of political control domestically and his ambition to claim Chinese international leadership all require PLA support. Particularly when the civilian CMC chairman seriously contemplates the use of force to attain foreign-policy goals, the military's role in decision-making will inevitably be enhanced. In case of setbacks in a foreign-policy or military adventure, Xi would definitely be accused of inexperience by the top brass. Xi's overarching political ambition could also pave the way for generals to return to the political stage. It remains to be seen whether he is going to break another convention set by his predecessors – serving only two terms as party general secretary. If Xi aspires to rule beyond 2022, the ensuing power struggle and political uncertainty would set the stage for the PLA's return to prominence in the civilian sector.

Conclusion

The CCP, advancing toward its 100th anniversary, has learnt well the hard truth of controlling the gun. Constant power struggles, a legitimacy crisis, and governing by coercion on the one hand and international ideological threats and traditional military threats on the other have put the CCP regime in perpetual security challenges from within and without. All this makes sure that the PLA remains politically important. It has taken sides to make paramount leaders, has taken over government, has staged coups, and has influenced politics as an institution. The only questions are the opportunity and the form taken.

Party leaders want to harness the political strengths of the military to their own advantages but are apprehensive of what would follow once the power is unleashed. Mao used manipulation, Deng rebuilt the rules and institutions, Jiang pampered the military with money with Hu following suit, and Xi is trying to combine the methods of Mao and Deng. It should be noted, however, that even strongman leaders, like Mao and Deng, must count on the support of the gun during their reigns. As Finer observes, "abnormal" dependence of the civil power on the military will only increase the latter's opportunity to intervene (Finer 2002: 72).

Notes

1 For the sake of convenience in discussion, "PLA" hereafter refers to the Chinese army in general, including the Red Army period, although, according to Yue (2010), the name, People's Liberation Army, was not made official until 1947.
2 It was first called the "Chinese Workers' and Peasants' Revolutionary Army" after the so-called "Nanchang Uprising" on August 1, 1927 and was later renamed as "Red Army" in May 1928.
3 Very limited information about the alleged coup was made public by the Chinese government in 1972. Given the gaps in the story, there have been challenges to the official version. For example, see Qiu (1999); MacFarquhar and Schoenhals (2006: 333–336).
4 Due to limited space, for discussions about the reform content, see Wang and Peng (1994, volume 2, chapters 14–27); Shambaugh (2002); Ng (2005).
5 Official accounts of the suppression and casualty figures were disputed by many sources. However, our concern here is the impact on Chinese CMR.
6 Complaining about what was perceived to be a scramble for territories in the South China Sea in the 1980s, China passed in 1992 the Law of the Territorial Sea and Contiguous Zones.
7 A PLA official homepage, *Zhongguo Jun Wang* (Chinamil), published an article under the pen name "jinji de xiongbaba" (attacking father bear) on January 13, 2017, claiming the US moves had reinforced China's resolve to build its own aircraft carrier, viewed January 14, 2017. www.81.cn/jwgz/2017-01/13/content_7451287.htm.

References

"At Least 53 'Army Tigers' Have Been Dragged Down Since the Eighteenth Party Congress" 2016, *Wen Wei Po*, December 30, viewed February 1, 2017. http://news.wenweipo.com/2016/12/30/IN1612300005.htm.

Baum, R. 2011, "The Road to Tiananmen: Chinese Politics in the 1980s," in R. MacFarquhar (ed.), *The Politics of China: Sixty Years of the People's Republic of China*, 337–467, Cambridge University Press, Cambridge.

Brömmelhörster, J. and Ng, K.P. 2000, "Changed Priorities in China's Military Expenditures," in J. Brömmelhörster (ed.), *Demystifying the Peace Dividend*, 153–185, Nomos Verlagsgesellschaft, Baden-Baden.

Buckley, C. 2013, "Vows of Change in China Belie Private Warning," *New York Times*, February 14, viewed October 7, 2013. www.nytimes.com/2013/02/15/world/asia/vowing-reform-chinas-leader-xi-jinping-airs-other-message-in-private.html?pagewanted=all&_r=0.

Buckley, C. and Perlez, J. 2016, "China Military Budget to Rise Less Than 8%, Slower Than Usual," *New York Times*, March 4, viewed February 1, 2017. www.nytimes.com/2016/03/05/world/asia/china-military-spending.html?_r=0.

Cao, Z. 1998, "The Army and People's Armed Forces Seriously Study Chairman Jiang's Speech, Resolutely Combat Smuggling and Stop All Commercial Activities," *Renmin Ribao* (People's Daily), August 4.

Chi, H.T. 1990, "Preface," *Lun Jinxin Ningju* (On Unifying the Military Mind), 1–7, Jiefangjun Chubanshe, Beijing.
Cole, B. 2010, *The Great Wall at Sea: China's Navy in the Twenty-First Century*, second edition, Naval Institute Press, Annapolis.
Deng, X.P. 1975/1994, "The Army's Tasks of Rectification," in *Deng Xiaoping Wenxuan* (Selected Works of Deng Xiaoping), volume 2, 15–24, Renmin Chubanshe, Beijing.
Deng, X.P. 1977/1994, "Speech at the Full CMC Session," in *Deng Xiaoping Wenxuan* (Selected Works of Deng Xiaoping), volume 2, 72–84, Renmin Chubanshe, Beijing.
Deng, X.P. 1985/1993, "Speech at an Enlarged CMC Meeting," in *Deng Xiaoping Wenxuan* (Selected Works of Deng Xiaoping), volume 3, 126–129, Renmin Chubanshe, Beijing.
Fei, H.R. 2016, "Stories Behind the Zunyi Conference," *Renmin Wan* (People's Daily Web), April 11, viewed April 11, 2016. http://history.people.com.cn/n/2015/0421/c372327-26880825.html.
Finer, S.E. 2002, *The Man on Horseback: The Role of the Military in Politics*, with a new introduction by Jay Stanley, Transaction Publishers, New Brunswick, NJ.
Gao, M.Z. and Xue, X.R. 2011, *Zhongguo Junshi Zhengzhixue Lilun – Gongchandangren de Junzheng Guanxi Sixiang* (China's Theory of Military Politics – Communist Thoughts on Military-Civilian Relations), Shishi Publishing House, Beijing.
Gregor, A.J. 1991, "The People's Liberation Army and China's Crisis," *Armed Forces & Society* 18(1): 7–28.
Gu, G.S. and Quan, X.L. 1999, *Junfei Lun* (On Military Expenditure), Guofang Daxue Chubanshe, Beijing.
Guo, S.H. 1989, "National Security and Our Army's Functions," *Nanjing Zhengzhi Xueyuan Xuebao* (Journal of PLA Nanjing Institute of Politics) (5): 6–9.
Huang, R.X. and Zhang, X.B. 2008, "A Re-examination of the Nature of China's Military Budget Increase," *Jiefangjun Bao*, February 26.
Jia, C.W., Cao, X.J., and Cai, Z.B. 2016, "Overview of How Each Echelon of the Army Takes the 'Two Responsibilities' Seriously and Promotes Clean Governance," *Jiefangjun Bao*, October 23, viewed October 23, 2016. www.81.cn/jfjbmap/content/2016-10/23/content_159647.htm.
Jin, H. 2016, "After Military Reform, Why Did the 'Two Swords' on the Arm Badges of the Original 'Four General Departments' Disappear?" *Jun Zhengping Office Microblog*, China Military Online, November 27, viewed November 27, 2016. www.81.cn/jwgz/2016-11/27/content_7378332_4.htm.
Joffe, E. 1987, *The Chinese Army after Mao*, Harvard University Press, Cambridge, MA.
Kang, S.J. 1990, "The Establishment and Perfection of the PLA's Party Committee System," *Junshi Lishi* (Military History), 5: 12–17.
Kawashima, K. 1988, *Chugoku Tōgunkankei no Kenkyū* (A Study on Chinese Party-Army Relations), volume 1, Keiō Tsushin, Tokyo.
Li, F.C. 1955, "Report on the First Five-Year Plan on National Economic Development," *Renmin Ribao* (People's Daily), July 8, viewed October 18, 2013. http://news.xinhuanet.com/ziliao/2004-10/12/content_2080225.htm.
Li, K. and Hau, S.Z. 1989, *"Wenhua Degeming" zhong de Renmin Jiefangjun* (The PLA in the "Cultural Revolution"), Zhonggong Dangshi Ziliao Chubanshe, Beijing.
Liberation Army Daily Commentator 2016, "What Are the Criteria of Personnel Appointment?" *Jiefangjun Bao*, December 30, viewed December 30, 2016. www.81.cn/jfjbmap/content/2016-12/30/content_165537.htm.
Liu, M.F. 1994, "Reflecting on the Army's Status and Functions in the New Era," *Nanjing Zhengzhi Xueyuan Xuebao* (1): 35–36.
Luo, Y.C. 2016, "The Lifeline that Must Never Be Forgotten," *Liberation Army Daily*, July 1, viewed July 1, 2016. www.81.cn/jfjbmap/content/2016-07/01/content_149125.htm.
MacFarquhar, R. and Schoenhals, M. 2006, *Mao's Last Revolution*, Harvard University Press, Cambridge, MA.
Mao, Z.D. 1927/1993, "Speech at an Emergency Meeting of the CCP Central Committee," in *Mao Zedong Jushi Wenxuan* (Selected Military Works of Mao Zedong), volume 1, 1–3, Junshi Kexue Chubanshe and Zhongyang Wenxian Chubanshe, Beijing.
Mao, Z.D. 1938/1993, "Problems of War and Strategy," in *Mao Zedong Jushi Wenxuan* (Selected Military Works of Mao Zedong), volume 2, 416–433, Junshi Kexue Chubanshe and Zhongyang Wenxian Chubanshe, Beijing.

Mao, Z.D. 1953/1993, "The Struggle of Resisting America and Aiding Korea Must Continue to Intensify," in *Mao Zedong Junshi Wenxuan* (Selected Military Works of Mao Zedong), volume 6, 341–342, Junshi Kexue Chubanshe and Zhongyang Wenxian Chubanshe, Beijing.
Miller, L. 2006, "The Political Implications of PLA Professionalism," in D.M. Finkelstein and K. Gunness (eds.), *Civil-Military Relations in Today's China: Swimming in a New Sea*, M.E. Sharpe, New York.
Nathan, A.J. and Scobell, A. 2012, *China's Search for Security*, Columbia University Press, New York.
Ng, K.P. 2005, *Interpreting China's Military Power: Doctrine Makes Readiness*, Routledge, London.
Ng, K.P. 2017, "The Xi Jinping Imprint on the Chinese Military," in Tiang Boon Hoo (ed.), *Chinese Foreign Policy under Xi*, Routledge, London (forthcoming).
Nordlinger, E.A. 1977, *Soldiers in Politics: Military Coups and Governments*, Prentice-Hall, New Jersey.
Phoenix News 2015, "A Major-General Reveals Xu Caihou Selling Officer Appointments," March 6, viewed March 12, 2015. http://v.ifeng.com/mil/mainland/201503/01c3534e-301d-4e8c-aa20-69d9f7bb8977.shtml.
Qiu, J. 1999, *The Culture of Power: The Lin Biao Incident in the Cultural Revolution*, Stanford University Press, Stanford, CA.
Scobell, A. 2003, *China's Use of Military Force: Beyond the Great Wall and the Long March*, Cambridge University Press, Cambridge.
Shambaugh, D. 2002, *Modernizing China's Military: Progress, Problems, and Prospects*, University of California Press, Berkeley.
Teiwes, F.C. 2011, "The Establishment and Consolidation of the New Regime," in R. MacFarquhar (ed.), *The Politics of China: Sixty Years of the People's Republic of China*, Third Edition, 6–86, Cambridge University Press, Cambridge.
Wang, S.L. 2010, "Origin and Development of the Military and Administrative Commissions of the Greater Administrative Areas in the Early Years of New China [sic]," *Zhonggong Dangshi Yanjiu* (Chinese Communist Party History Study) (6): 46–53.
Wang, W.X. and Peng, Z.S. (chief eds.) 1994, *Dangdai Zhongguo Jundui de Junshi Gongzuo* (Contemporary Chinese Army's Military Work), 2 volumes, Zhongguo Shehui Kexue Chubanshe, Beijing.
Wang, Y.M. 2016, "How Zhu De Opposed Zhang Guotao's Plot for Splitting the Party during the Long March," *Liberation Army Daily*, December 14, viewed December 14, 2016. www.81.cn/jfjbmap/content/2016-12/14/content_164177.htm.
Wang, Z. 2012, *Never Forget National Humiliation: Historical Memory in Chinese Politics and Foreign Relations*, Columbia University Press, New York.
Woo, J. 2011, *Security Challenges and Military Politics in East Asia: From State-Building to Post-Democratization*, Continuum, New York.
Xia, F. 2008, "Third Line Construction: An Important Strategic Decision by Mao Zedon," *Dangshi Zhongheng* (Perspectives on Party History) (1), viewed October 18, 2013. http://dangshi.people.com.cn/GB/8627645.html.
Xia Hongping 2016, "The Red Landmarks on the Long March Track," *Liberation Army Daily*, October 21, viewed October 21, 2016. www.81.cn/jfjbmap/content/2016-10/21/content_159548.htm.
Xia, Y.S. 2016, "How to Dispel 'Reform Anxiety'," *Jiefangjun Bao*, November 9, viewed November 9, 2016. www.81.cn/jfjbmap/content/2016-11/09/content_161200.htm.
Xiao, Y.S. 2016, "How to Get Rid of the 'Reform Anxiety' in the Heart," *Jiefangjun Bao*, November 9, viewed November 9, 2016. www.81.cn/jfjbmap/content/2016-11/09/content_161200.htm.
Xinhua 2008, "Combat Team, Work Team, Production Team," Xinhuanet, February 29, viewed January 24, 2017. http://news.xinhuanet.com/mil/2008-02/29/content_7693506.htm.
Xu, A. and Liu, S.G. 1990, "Characteristics of Strategies of International Hostile Forces to Promote 'Peaceful Evolution'," in J. Wang *et al.* (eds.), *Wuxing de Zhanzheng* (Invisible War), 16–27, Gufang Daxue Chubanshe, Beijing.
Yan, H.S., Han, Z.J., and Bai, G. 1993, "China Plans to Build Aircraft Carrier to Protect Its Maritime Territory," *Dangdai* (Contemporary), May 15: 67–77.
Yu, H., Na, Q.X., and Lan, S.C. 1994, *Zhongguo Renmin Jiefangjun* (The Chinese People's Liberation Army), 2 volumes, Dangdai Zhongguo Chubanshe, Beijing.
Yuan, X.T. 2016, "The Formation and Development of the Party's Absolute Leadership over the Military and the Central Military Commission Chairman Responsibility System," *Dangde Wenxian* (Literature of CPC) 4: 104–113.
Yue, S.P. 2010, "Tracing the Title of the People's Liberation Army," *Liberation Army Daily*, September 6, viewed September 6, 2010. www.chinamil.com.cn/jfjbmap/content/2010-09/06/content_37799.htm.

Zhang, X.M. and Ma, J.L. 2016, "Submit Wonderful Answers to the Reform Tests," *Jiefangjun Bao*, September 15, viewed September 15, 2016. www.81.cn/jfjbmap/content/2016-09/15/content_156758.htm.
Zheng, Z.Y., Shen, S.Y., and Shen, W.K. *et al.* 1992, *Dangdai Zhongguo de Guofang Keji Shiye* (National Defence Science and Technology Undertakings of Contemporary China), volume 1, Dangdai Zhongguo Chubanshe, Beijing.
Zhi, S.Z. 1989, "An Overview of the Evolution of the Central Military Commission," *Junshi Lishi* (Military History) 6: 50–54.

8

FACTIONAL POLITICS IN THE PARTY-STATE APPARATUS

Bo Zhiyue

Introduction

Xi Jinping, the General Secretary of the Chinese Communist Party (CCP), has been vigorously combatting "factionalism" within the Party since he rose to power at the 18th Party Congress in November 2012. Like Mao Zedong, the most powerful leader in the histories of the CCP and the People's Republic of China (PRC), Xi seems to be doing the right thing in terms of official CCP ideology. While the Party has been riven with cliques and camarillas since its inception in 1921, factionalism has theoretically been condemned as pernicious to Party unity even as most CCP leaders go to great lengths to build up their own factions. Xi has in the past five years successfully put together a formidable Xi Jinping Faction which is based on the following sources: his protégés/underlings from Fujian, Zhejiang, and Shanghai (where he served as a senior administrator); associates with relations to his home province of Shaanxi; and loyal generals (including several who had served in the erstwhile Nanjing Military Region).

This chapter deals with the study of factional politics in the CCP in terms of four aspects. First, it introduces "factionalism" as a political label in CCP politics. Second, it presents "factionalism" as an analytic tool in the studies of CCP politics. Third, it provides a critical assessment of the state of the art in the subfield and reflects on its practical implications. Fourth, it points to promising ways forward for future study and highlights the relevance of the study of factionalism to our understanding of the Xi Jinping Faction.

"Factionalism" in CCP politics

The critical term, "factionalism," has unique connotations and implications when being applied to the study of CCP politics. For Chinese politicians, "factionalism" is a political label for illicit activities within the CCP. Whoever is involved in factional activities should be punished.

Mao Zedong, CCP chairman from June 19, 1945 to September 9, 1976, was a master user of various terms of factionalism against his political opponents. On February 1, 1942, Mao delivered a speech on the rectification of the Party's style at the opening ceremony of the Central Party School. In this speech, he pointed out that one of the purposes of the rectification campaign was to oppose factionalism (*zongpai zhuyi*) (Mao 1942). Mao used the rectification campaign to undermine his opponents such as Wang Ming (the leader of the international faction – a group of "twenty eight and a half Bolsheviks") and to consolidate his own power. As a result of the rectification campaign, Mao emerged as the undisputed leader of the Chinese Communist Party in 1945. Mao was elected chairman of the CCP at the Seventh Party Congress, and Mao Zedong Thought was written into the Party's charter as the guideline for all the work of the Party. His opponents were completely discredited ideologically and marginalized politically.

In the era of Mao Zedong from 1949 to 1976, several Politburo members fell victim to the political label of "factionalism." Gao Gang, a member of the Seventh Politburo and vice president of the People's Republic of China as well as the head of the Party, the government, and the military in the Northeast Region in the late 1940s and early 1950s, was the first major victim of "factionalism." In October 1952, he was transferred from the Northeast Region to Beijing to take up a very important position as chairman of the National Planning Commission of the Central People's Government of the PRC, which was independent from but much more powerful than the Government Administration Council of the Central People's Government under the leadership of Premier Zhou Enlai. He was used by Mao Zedong to undermine the power of Zhou Enlai and Liu Shaoqi (Mao's potential successor as President of the PRC and Party chairman). As a result of the strong resistance from Zhou and Liu, Mao changed his attitude and made Gao a scapegoat of his power struggle with Zhou and Liu (Teiwes and Sun 1990; Radchenko 2014; Shiraev and Yang 2014). Gao committed suicide on August 17, 1954 and was purged from the Party in March 1955. He was accused of having been involved in anti-Party factional activities since 1949 and of having plotted to become general secretary or vice chairman of the CCP as well as premier of the State Council.

Peng Dehuai, vice chairman of the Central Military Commission, defense minister, and vice premier in the 1950s as well as a member of the Seventh and Eighth Politburo, was the second major victim of factionalism. Because of his criticisms of Mao's Great Leap Forward policies at a Politburo meeting in July 1959, he was labeled the chief of an "anti-Party faction" by Mao Zedong and was subsequently dismissed as defense minister (but was allowed to retain his Politburo membership). Because of Peng's tremendous influence with the People's Liberation Army, 1,848 officers were branded "rightists" by the end of 1959 as a result of his downfall. In the meantime, due to Mao's anti-rightist campaign, millions of Chinese perished as a result of the Great Leap Forward policies (Yang 2008).

In the early 1970s, seven Politburo members including two standing members were lumped together as members of the Lin Biao Anti-Revolutionary Faction. Chen Boda, a Politburo Standing Committee member since 1966 and No. 3 ranking member of the 9th Politburo Standing Committee (after Mao Zedong and Lin Biao), was arrested in October 1970 after he had earlier echoed Lin Biao's call for promoting Mao as a genius at Mao's displeasure. Lin Biao and his wife, Ye Qun, both died in a plane crash in Outer Mongolia after their son, Lin Liguo, had failed to assassinate Mao. Huang Yongsheng (general chief of staff), Wu Faxian (deputy chief of staff and commander of the PLA Air Force), Li Zuopeng (deputy chief of staff and first political commissar of the PLA Navy), and Qiu Huizuo (deputy chief of staff and director of the General Logistics Department) were all subsequently arrested because of their connections with Lin Biao.

A few things are noteworthy in these cases of "factionalism" in the era of Mao. First, these victims of "factionalism" were not all necessarily Mao's political opponents. Gao Gang, for instance, was one of Mao's confidants in the late 1940s and 1950s. He shared Mao's views of the faster pace of moving toward socialism in China, which was at odds with the views of Liu Shaoqi and Zhou Enlai, who believed in a much longer transitional period from "new democracy" to "socialism." It was Mao who promoted Gao to Beijing to undermine the power of

Liu Shaoqi and Zhou Enlai. Unfortunately, because of Chen Yun's betrayal, Mao decided to sacrifice Gao Gang to compromise with Liu Shaoqi and Zhou Enlai.

Second, "factionalism" is a political label with negative connotations. It was only applicable to losers of a power struggle. Winners were exempt from this label. Gao Gang and his associates were labeled factionalists, for instance, because they were losers. Liu Shaoqi and Zhou Enlai were not factionalists because they were winners. Third, not all losers were labeled "factionalists" in the era of Mao. Liu Shaoqi, for instance, was not labeled a "factionalist." He was expelled from the CCP because he was "a traitor, enemy agent, and scab in the service of the criminal imperialists, modern revisionists and the Kuomintang reactionaries."

Fourth, it is most ironic that in less than one month after Mao's death, his wife (Jiang Qing, a Politburo member) and three other followers (Wang Hongwen, a Politburo Standing Committee member; Zhang Chunqiao, a Politburo Standing Committee member; and Yao Wenyuan, a Politburo member) were arrested as a "Gang of Four" with references to his own remarks about their factional activities by his chosen successor, Hua Guofeng. Mao had chosen Hua because of Hua's absolute personal loyalty to Mao, yet Hua arrested his wife shortly after his death.

Finally, in the post-Mao era, "factionalism" has rarely been used to denigrate political losers. Deng Xiaoping, for instance, maneuvered to dismiss the followers of Hua Guofeng but did not make them "factionalists." Wang Dongxing (alternate member of the 9th Politburo, member of the 10th Politburo, standing member of the 11th Politburo, and vice chairman of the Party), Ji Dengkui (alternate member of the 9th Politburo, member of the 10th and 11th Politburo, and vice premier), Wu De (member of the 10th and 11th Politburo and the first Party secretary of Beijing), and Chen Xilian (member of the 9th, 10th and 11th Politburo, vice premier, and commander of the Beijing Military Region) were all dismissed from all of their positions in early 1980 because they had followed the "whateverist policies" ("We will resolutely uphold whatever policy decisions Chairman Mao made, and unswervingly follow whatever instructions Chairman Mao gave") of Hua Guofeng (*People's Daily* 1977).

Theoretical debates on "factionalism" in the studies of CCP politics

For China scholars, "factionalism" is an analytic tool for the studies of CCP politics. "Factionalism" in the studies of CCP politics usually refers to activities of political groups within the CCP that are formed on various bases for power contestation. In other words, "factions" are not necessarily a negative political label for political losers but an "objective" description of political divisions within the CCP. Factions therefore could be used to describe not only losers but also winners.

In the literature of the CCP elite politics, however, there are theoretical debates on the definitions of "factions" in CCP politics, power bases of factions, and characteristics of factional politics in the CCP.

Definitions of "factions" in the studies of CCP politics

First, there are debates over the definitions of "factions" in the studies of CCP politics. For Jürgen Domes, factions are coherent groupings that "are based on alternative platforms and exclusive claims for political power and overall control" (Domes 1984: 29). Different from opinion groups that "are formed in clearly defined conflicts on practical issues and based on individual decisions during such conflicts, which concern on the very issue at stake" and that are latent and short-term, factions are intermediate-range to long-term (Domes 1984: 28–29).

The factions, according to Domes, could be developed from either structural or functional groups. Structural groups are based on common demographic characteristics or shared experiences such as "*tongxiang*" (common regional origin), "*tongxue*" (common educational background), or "*tonghang*" (common organizational experiences over many years) (Domes 1984: 27). Functional groups are formed on the basis of interests of functional subsystems such as the central and regional civilian party machines as well as the central military machine and the regional military commanders (Domes 1984: 28).

For Andrew Nathan, Domes' definition is too broad. In his efforts to build a "factionalism model" of CCP elite politics, Nathan provided a more refined definition of "factions" in terms of clientelist ties. In his view, a faction is a structure that is "mobilized on the basis of clientelist ties to engage in politics and consisting of a few, rather than a great many, layers of personnel" (Nathan 1973: 40). A clientelist tie, according to Nathan, is "a non-ascriptive two-person relationship founded on exchange, in which well-understood rights and obligations are established between the two parties" (Nathan 1973: 37). The clientelist ties are different from corporate ties "such as lineage relations, co-membership in an association, or co-membership in a group of blood brothers exceeding two in number" (Nathan 1973: 38).

Based on these clientelist ties, Nathan constructed two types of factions: simple factions and complex factions. In a simple faction, there is one leader and a number of followers. In a complex faction, there could be a few layers of these leader-follower relationships (Nathan 1973: 41). In other words, some of the followers of the primary leader could be the secondary leaders of their own followers, who in turn could be the tertiary leaders of their own followers. These factions, as Nathan saw them, could have one or more power bases or "support structures" (Nathan 1973: 40).

Factions, according to Nathan, have four structural characteristics. First, factions do not become corporatized after recruitment but remain structured along the lines of the original ties that formed the bases of recruitment (Nathan 1973: 42). This characteristic makes factions flexible because the leader could recruit members based on opportunities for political gain but the ability of a faction to deliver depends on the loyalty of factional members to the leader.

Second, whether a faction could continue or grow depends on the ability of the leader to secure and distribute rewards to his followers. If the leader is able to deliver, the faction will expand. Otherwise, the faction could contract or even be dissolved if the leader is removed from power. Since factions heavily depend on their leaders, they cannot survive their leaders. After the leader of a faction has retired or passed away, the faction will dissolve. Because of its unique configuration centered on the original leader, "the faction can never be taken over as a whole by a successor" (Nathan 1973: 43).

Third, complex factions tend to break down because the secondary leaders of simple factions within a complex faction are more likely to be responsible to their own followers for political spoils than to be loyal to the primary leader. Although this tendency increases along with the size and complexity of a complex faction, the vertical cleavages usually result in two major segments, which in turn would become two rival complex factions after the retirement or death of the primary leader.

Fourth, factions are generally limited in the amount and kinds of power they can wield and generate due to the nature of factional bases. Since members of a faction are recruited individually on the basis of exchange relationship, the faction is limited in its size and membership.

As will be discussed in detail below, Domes's "functional groups" are generally not considered "factions" in the literature of Chinese politics; his "structural groups" constitute the bases of factions but not factions by themselves. Nathan's definition is more precise in conceptual terms but not particularly applicable to CCP politics.

Power bases of factions in CCP politics

Second, there are debates about the power bases of factions in CCP politics. Domes believes, as mentioned above, that "functional groups" could also be considered as factions in Chinese politics because they share the same interests in the system. He is not alone in this view. Parris H. Chang (1978) and Susan L. Shirk (1993) have also made similar arguments implicitly. Both of them believe that provincial leaders constitute the most powerful bloc in the Central Committee of the Chinese Communist Party, so much so that Mao Zedong and Deng Xiaoping had to gain the support of provincial leaders for their own policies during their respective periods. But provincial leaders in China hardly function as a faction because they do not have "alternative platforms and exclusive claims for power and overall control."

According to David S.G. Goodman, provincial leaders are simply a categoric group (Goodman 1984: 68–82). They belong to the same category of Chinese political leaders but do not necessarily function as a political faction. Of course, individual provincial leaders might play some role in factional politics in two different ways (Bo 2015). On the one hand, they could be recruited by a central leader to strengthen his position vis-à-vis other central leaders. Mao Zedong, for instance, transferred five regional leaders (Gao Gang, Rao Shushi, Deng Zihui, Deng Xiaoping, and Xi Zhongxun) in the early 1950s to Beijing partly to undermine the power of other central leaders such as Liu Shaoqi and Zhou Enlai. Similarly, Deng Xiaoping recruited three provincial leaders (Peng Chong, Wan Li, and Xi Zhongxun) to the Secretariat of the CCP Central Committee in the 1980s in order to undermine the power of the Politburo under the leadership of Hua Guofeng. On the other hand, some provincial leaders could be mobilized to implement a certain central policy in their localities. But these functions of individual leaders do not make the category of provincial leaders a political faction.

In fact, there are two types of categoric groups in CCP politics: institutional and non-institutional. Institutional categoric groups include provincial leaders, military leaders, central bureaucrats, and corporate leaders (Bo 2010: 91–130). Non-institutional categoric groups include princelings (Bo 2006; 2007: 151–174; 2010: 139–147) and *mishu* (personal secretaries of high officials) clique (Li and Pye 1992; Mulvenon and Chase 2003).

By the same token, Domes's "structural groups" are not factions by themselves. Common demographic characteristics or shared experiences such as "*tongxiang*" (common regional origin), "*tongxue*" (common educational background), or "*tonghang*" (common organizational experiences over many years) are foundations on which factions may be developed.

In this regard, one may want to make a clear distinction between corporate groups and factional groups. A corporate group is a group of individuals who share the same organizational experiences. Those who have worked in the Central Committee of the Chinese Communist Youth League (CCYL) could be regarded as a corporate group, while those who have worked in the Secretariat during the same period of time may constitute a factional group.

For instance, I have identified 82 people in the Seventeenth Central Committee of the Chinese Communist Party with background in the Chinese Communist Youth League work at both local and central levels (Bo 2010: 147–165). These 82 people could be considered a categoric group, because they may or may have worked with each other in the same organization during the same period of time. Among those, there would be some who have worked in the Central Committee of the CCYL Central Committee during the same period of time. This subgroup would constitute a corporate group. Some of the subgroup who have developed personal ties with one another over the years could be considered a factional group. The factional groups are not factions, though the former is the basis of the latter (Bo 2007: 140–141; Li 2003: 31–40).

Similar distinctions can be applied to the Qinghua Clique and the Shanghai Gang. Graduates of the Qinghua University form a categoric group, those who attended the University in the same period constitute a corporate group, and only those who have developed personal ties can be considered a factional group. Again, those who worked in the Shanghai government and party apparatuses form a distinctive categoric group from those who worked in other localities, those who share working experiences in the Shanghai municipal government or Party Committee belong to the same corporate group, and only those who developed personal ties while working in Shanghai are members of the same factional group.

In conceptual terms, Nathan's definition of a faction makes more sense. For him, a faction is based on personal ties and these personal ties are founded on exchange. The fact that both Hu Jintao and Xi Jinping graduated from the same university does not necessarily make them members of the same faction. When Hu was enrolled at Qinghua University in 1959, Xi was only six years old. While Xi was studying at Qinghua from 1975 to 1979, Hu was working in Gansu. They share the same alma mater and belong to the same category but do not necessarily have shared educational experiences let alone forming personal ties at the University. The problem with Nathan is that he could not find any concrete examples of factions in Chinese politics according to his definition (Nathan 1973: 53).

Among four groups commonly identified as factions in the literature, according to my research, princelings are the closest to the definition of a categoric group, the Youth League Clique and the Qinghua Clique are examples of corporate groups, and the Shanghai Gang is the closest to the definition of a faction in Nathan's terms. With Jiang Zemin as its leader, members of the Shanghai Gang worked more or less like a faction in the eras of Jiang and Hu Jintao.

Characteristics of factional politics in China

Third, there are also debates about characteristics of factional politics in China. Andrew Nathan proposed 15 characteristics of factional politics in an ideal-typical political system of factions in three sets. The first set of his propositions is based on the power limitations of factions. Because of their limitations in power, factions manage their conduct according to a code of civility (character 1), adopt primarily defensive political strategies (character 2), and prepare their initiatives in secret for effective surprise offensive (character 3). In the face of an aggressive faction, other factions tend to form alliances against the aggressive faction (character 4), but these alliances are constantly shifting (character 5), making ideological agreement a primary condition impossible (character 6). The decisions of the factional system are based on consensus but the consensus is not enforceable (character 7). Therefore, there will be a cycle of consensus formation and decline (character 8) (Nathan 1973: 45–48).

His second set of propositions is based on "the fact that factions consist of a series of clientelist ties" (Nathan 1973: 48). In order to weaken their rivals, factions try to use various means such as rumor, character assassination, bribery, and deception to discredit members of their rival factions, dislodge them from their posts, and buy away their allies (character 9). They also tend to make small differences with their rival factions major issues of debates in terms of "doctrinalism" to discredit these factions as a whole (character 10) (Nathan 1973: 48–49).

His third set of propositions is based on the size and shape of the factional system as a whole. In a factional system, there is a limited number of factions. Ideally, there should be no more than two major factions (character 11). These factions could unite against external threats (character 12), and they usually do not challenge the legitimacy of the factional system (character 13). The factional system is immobile (character 14) yet stable (character 15) (Nathan 1973: 50–52).

Nathan's problem is his inability to apply his theoretical model to the analysis of real-life Chinese politics. In his analyses of the Cultural Revolution, he dismissed two characteristics of factional politics of immobilism and stability as "too early to reach a judgement," cast aside a third characteristic of a relatively small number of factions in the system as lacking adequate information, and found contradictions with a fourth characteristic of the principle of legitimacy (Nathan 1973: 55). Apparently, he did not have sufficient information to argue for the presence of other characteristics in Chinese politics (Nathan 1973: 58–66).

Tang Tsou, who debated with Andrew Nathan over the merits and demerits of Nathan's factionalism model (Tsou 1976), was not fully convinced of the utility of this model in understanding CCP politics. In Tsou's view, by designating Mao Zedong as the leader of a faction, Nathan "missed the key feature of Party politics" in China (Tsou 2002: 115). This is because Mao was not just an ordinary leader of one faction of the CCP. He was the core of the Party who occupied a special role in the CCP politics in his time (Tsou 2002: 114).

Tsou put Nathan's 15 characteristics of factional politics to the test by the history of elite CCP politics and found very little evidence to support these characteristics in "reality." For Tsou, for instance, there is no evidence to support the existence of "a code of civility" (characteristic 1) during the Cultural Revolution. Nor is there any evidence for "immobilism" (characteristic 14) and "doctrinalism" (characteristic 10).

According to Tsou, the "reason why many of Nathan's assertions about the 'characteristics' of 'factional politics' fail to pass the test" is because of the problem of his central thesis. Nathan's central thesis is that there is a relative balance of power among factions and no faction will be able to decisively and finally eliminate its rivals. But the events of the Cultural Revolution showed just the opposite. Liu Shaoqi's faction was destroyed; Peng Zhen and his colleagues and friends in Beijing were dispersed and disgraced; and Tao Zhu and his group in Guangdong and Central South China as well as Luo Ruiqing and his followers also suffered persecution and deprivations of their positions (Tsou 2002: 125).

For Tsou, Nathan basically missed the whole point about CCP elite politics or possibly Chinese politics throughout the twentieth century. Tsou's central thesis is that at irregular intervals the struggles for power among the Chinese elite, involving either supreme political power or power one level below that, always involves one side winning all and/or the other side losing all. This is a feature not only of elite CCP politics but of Chinese politics throughout the twentieth century (Tsou 2002: 100).

In other words, for Tsou, factional politics or elite CCP politics or Chinese politics in general are essentially a zero-sum game. The nature of the zero-sum game is especially true during the decade-long Cultural Revolution from 1966 to 1976, when Mao's political enemies were eliminated physically in many cases. But the same cannot be said of the era of Deng Xiaoping when a former Party chairman (Hua Guofeng) was allowed to stay on as a full member of the CCP Central Committee for another four terms after his purge, a former General Secretary (Hu Yaobang) died a Politburo member, and another former General Secretary (Zhao Ziyang) spent the rest of his life as a free man "technically."

Based on the observation of a relatively peaceful power transition from Jiang Zemin to Hu Jintao in 2002, this author has proposed a power-balancing model. Due to the political institutionalization of power structure in CCP politics, as I suggested, there would be a power balance among different holders of the key positions of General Secretary of the Party, President of the People's Republic of China, and Chairman of the Central Military Commission (Bo 2005; 2007: 1–8). That means, the game of CCP elite politics does not have to be zero-sum all the time. The winner of the game does not have to be a winner of all, and the loser of the game does not have to be a loser of all.

Yet the events that have unfolded since February 2012 seem to suggest a return toward the zero-sum end of the game. The winner of the game, Xi Jinping, for instance, has become a very powerful leader of China, while the loser of the game, Bo Xilai, is likely to spend the rest of his life in jail.

Research methods, theoretical gaps, and practical implications

Generally speaking, there are three groups of China watchers in the field of CCP factional politics. They adopt different research methods in their studies of CCP elite politics. One group of China watchers is interested more in theoretical model building than in empirical studies. Their efforts help clarify many conceptual issues, yet leaving many more empirical questions unanswered. Andrew Nathan, as mentioned above, managed to produce a conceptually consistent definition of factions but could not find its reflection in the political reality of CCP politics, even during the Cultural Revolution when factional activities were particularly conspicuous. Similarly, Li Cheng has produced a clear category of factions based on the background information of politicians in China but has erroneously included Wen Jiabao, China's premier from 2003 to 2013 who has had no official affiliation with the Chinese Communist Youth League in his entire political career, as a member of the Youth League Clique (*Tuan Pai* in his terms) (Li 2009).

Another group of China watchers follows closely what is happening in Beijing and tries to generalize based on limited and often unverified information. They tend to be more sensitive to signs of changes in elite interactions and tend to over-interpret small changes as signals of sweeping tendencies. Their methodology is akin to Kremlinology, a method developed to study the inner workings of a small circle of the top elites in the Soviet Union by paying close attentions to any sign of changes from the Kremlin – the seat of the government of the Soviet Union. In other words, their methodology can be called "Pekingology," a series of techniques to read and decipher signs from the Zhongnanhai, the seat of the government and Party apparatuses of China. Their discoveries can be very insightful, but their generalizations may not necessarily be correct all the time. Willy Wo-Lap Lam and myself, for instance, are very quick in spotting small changes in personnel alignments or interactions at Zhongnanhai that are seen as harbingers of major new trajectories (Lam 2015; Bo 2017). But their generalizations need to be tested against the new realities of later development.

A third group attempts to bridge theoretical models and empirical studies. They develop theoretical models based on their observations of elite interactions at the Zhongnanhai during certain periods and then try to update their models with fresh information. They have adopted various methods to understand factional dynamics but remain alert to new developments. Adopting a method of case studies, some scholars have tried to understand the nature of Chinese elite politics through careful analyses of various cases in the history of the People's Republic of China such as the Gao Gang Affair (Teiwes and Sun 1990), the Lin Biao Affair (Teiwes and Sun 1996; Jin 1999), the Gang of Four (Dittmer 1978), and the power transition from Jiang Zemin to Hu Jintao (Fewsmith 2003). Some cover much longer periods (Goldstein 1991; Kou 2010).

In my research on provincial leaders, I initially dismissed the applicability of the factionalism model to the study of Chinese provincial leaders (Bo 2002). In my view, the factionalism model suffers from two major problems: the model cannot explain "why people with similar backgrounds are involved in different factions"; nor can it account for factions whose members have diverse backgrounds (Bo 2002: 6). In my later works, I carefully compiled information on the background of political elites and grouped them as "factional groups" instead of "factions" (Bo 2007: 139–199; 2010: 131–173). Instead of exclusive factions, my research has revealed "factional overlaps" (Bo 2007: 194–197). In other words, some politicians have multiple identities which can be classified into several different factional groups. Liu Yandong, for instance, simultaneously belongs to the Qinghua Clique, the Princelings, and the Youth League Group. She is a graduate of Qinghua University, is the daughter of a veteran communist leader, and worked for the Youth League for almost a decade.

I have also tried to measure the group cohesion of four factional groups – the Shanghai Gang, the Youth League Group, the Princelings, and the Qinghua Clique – by aggregating the personal ties of the members of these groups and to compare their differences in terms of group cohesion indexes. My findings are that the group cohesion index for the Princelings is very low, making it more like a categoric group; and the Youth League Group has the highest score on the group cohesion index, making it the most cohesive group. The Shanghai Gang and the Qinghua Clique fall in between in terms of group cohesion indexes (Bo 2007: 198; 2010: 167).

China watchers of diverse research methods have generated a large body of knowledge on CCP factional politics, yet there are still a number of significant theoretical gaps. First, there is still no consensus on the definition of factions in the literature. The term "factions" is being used very loosely in the discussions of factional politics. The Princelings have been discussed as a faction in Chinese politics, especially after Xi Jinping took over as the most powerful man in China. But there is no analysis of why Xi Jinping is regarded as the head of this faction and how he has recruited other princelings as members of his faction. The Shanghai Gang and the Jiang Zemin Faction have been used interchangeably, but their membership should be different.

Second, there is confusion between corporate identities and factional identities. For instance, in the aftermath of Zhou Yongkang's downfall, the Chinese media discussed three factions related to Zhou. One is the "Petroleum Clique" ("Shiyoubang"), one is "Sichuan Clique," and one is the "Personal Secretary Gang" ("Mishubang") (Bo 2017: 53–54). In fact, these are not mutually exclusive and separate factions. They could be considered components of the same faction under the leadership of Zhou Yongkang. Likewise, Xi Jinping is also reportedly building his own faction from various sources: from his hometown of Shaanxi, from his past places of work such as Fujian, Zhejiang, and Shanghai, and from the Nanjing Military Region (Bo 2017: 121–122, 133–135, 141–148, 155–156, 161–163). Again, these are not separate factions but components of a Xi Jinping Faction.

Third, the literature as a whole has treated factions as if they were fixed in terms of membership but in reality factional identities are far more dynamic. It is very well-known that Yang Shangkun was a long-time follower of Deng Xiaoping. The two are from the same province, Sichuan, and they worked closely for more than 40 years. During Deng's famous "southern tour" in early 1992, Yang, president of the People's Republic of China and the executive vice chairman of the Central Military Commission, accompanied him throughout the tour. Yang Baibing, Yang Shangkun's half-brother and secretary-general of the Central Military Commission and director of the General Political Department of the People's Liberation Army, also pledged his support for Deng on behalf of the military. Yet in October of the same year, both Yangs were purged from the Central Military Commission.

Studies of CCP factional politics have strong practical implications. First, until factional politics is completely legitimized as suggested by Lucian W. Pye (2002: 55–57), factions will continue to be regarded as illegitimate associations of politicians in China. The CCP leadership under Xi Jinping, for instance, issued stern warnings against factionalism within the Party after a Politburo meeting on December 29, 2014. According to a Xinhua News Agency report, the Party leadership decided that the CCP would strengthen the enforcement of political disciplines and political rules – and factions or factionalist activities (*tuantuan huohuo, jiedang yingsi, labang jipai*) within the Party would not be tolerated. In other words, for the CCP, factions will continue to be a negative political label for losers instead of an objective analytical tool for both losers and winners. There will continue to be asymmetrical information for losers and winners. There will continue to be much more information available on factions whose leaders have lost out in power struggles than factions whose leaders are winners.

Second, a real faction is usually built around a certain high-ranking political leader. Common backgrounds and shared experiences are bases of factional groups, but they are far from sufficient conditions for the formation of a real faction. It is therefore useful to look at each individual leader (especially the preeminent leader such as the General Secretary of the Party, President of the PRC, and Chairman of the CMC) and see whether there is a faction with this leader as its head.

Third, a clear distinction should be made between loyalty and reliability. Ling Jihua, for instance, tried to demonstrate his loyalty to Xi Jinping by mentioning the name of the new Party boss 19 times in his article published in a CCP journal on December 15, 2014, but he was placed under investigation one week later (Bo 2017: 3–4). Cai Yingting was one of the most enthusiastic supporters of Xi's military leadership during the loyalty campaign of 2014 and the Nanjing Military Region has been a major source of high-ranking officers in various new posts, yet Cai has been skipped for promotion in the largest military reshuffle since the 1950s. In other words, the political loyalty from the point of view of followers or potential followers does not always automatically translate well into the political reliability from the point of view of the leader.

Fourth, it is useful to look at factions and factional politics from a dynamic perspective instead of a static perspective. No relations or patron-client ties last forever the same way. Today's allies could be tomorrow's enemies. Liu Shaoqi was the strongest ally of Mao Zedong from 1937 to 1962 (Gao 2011: 220–225) but he became Mao's enemy after 1962. Hu Yaobang and Zhao Ziyang were both Deng's trusted lieutenants, yet they were later dismissed by Deng himself.

Conclusion: future studies of CCP factional politics

In the future, scholars of CCP factional politics will continue to face both theoretical and empirical challenges of today. Theoretically, future scholars will have to come to a consensus on the definition of factions, the structure of factions, and the characteristics of factional politics. Empirically, they will have to find clear evidence for the existence and evolution of political factions in Chinese politics. They will have to be able to tell the difference between a factional group and a faction.

It will be very useful if future scholars are able to develop Pekingology as a full set of analytical tools to process information from the Zhongnanhai. In addition to the analysis of photos in official publications (MacFarquhar 1971), scholars in the future should also pay attention to videos of elite interactions as well as documents readily available online for major official functions. They should take advantage of the abundant information available and generate meaningful interpretations of factional dynamics among CCP top elite.

Future scholars should also take advantage of new analytic tools such as network analysis and statistical packages to test hypotheses related to faction formation and development. Moreover, they should also try to examine CCP factional politics in comparative terms. They should look at factionalism models in Japanese politics and see if there is anything that is comparable to CCP factional politics. They should also try to follow the political development in Vietnam and see whether Vietnamese politics offers any clues for the future development of Chinese politics.

It is also critically important for future scholars to place their studies of CCP factional politics in the context of political, economic, and social development of China. They should pay attention to the extent of political institutionalization and the balance between personal loyalty and institutional loyalty (Bo 2007: 8). They should make a clear distinction between political loyalty and political reliability and look at factional politics from both static and dynamic perspectives.

Finally, the studies of factional politics of the CCP should shed light on factional politics in action. As alluded to in the beginning of this chapter, while voicing his determination to fight against factionalism within the Party, Xi Jinping in fact has been attempting to form a political faction around himself by political necessity. A relatively mediocre politician who spent the majority of his career in provinces (Hebei, Fujian, Zhejiang, and Shanghai) until 2007 when he was inducted as a member of the Politburo Standing Committee, Xi had much weaker power bases than those of his immediate predecessors such as Jiang Zemin (who had the Shanghai Gang as his main power base) and Hu Jintao (who had the Youth League Clique as his main power base).

Essentially, the Xi Jinping faction is no different from other political factions in the CCP. First, it is based on clientelist ties between Xi and his associates in various sectors of the CCP system. His followers are mostly from those provincial units where he worked as a local leader previously (i.e., Fujian, Zhejiang, and Shanghai), his home province of Shaanxi, and the military units of the erstwhile Nanjing Military Region. Second, the Xi Jinping faction is a complex faction with a few layers. Some of Xi's followers such as Chen Xi, the Executive Deputy Director of the Central Organization Department of the 18th Central Committee of the CCP, for instance, have their own followers as secondary leaders. Third, it is a faction filled with politicians with rather shallow experiences at the national level. They are mostly newcomers in national politics. Most of Xi's followers are non-members of the 18th Central Committee of the CCP. Due to Xi's powerful position, these people are likely be inducted to the 19th Central Committee either as full members or as alternates at the 19th CCP Congress scheduled for late 2017. Also at the 19th Party Congress, a few of Xi's associates could make it to the Politburo, and a very small number of the members of the 18th Politburo who are closely associated with Xi could possibly be elevated to the Politburo Standing Committee.

Nevertheless, Xi's power bases would continue to be weak in spite of his strong political ambitions. In other words, a Xi Jinping era would feature a strong leader with a weak political power base. It will be fascinating to watch how this peculiar twist in factional politics could affect policy-making, political stability, and the capacity of the largely conservative Xi administration to pick up on the threads of reform.

References

Bo, Zhiyue (2002) *Chinese Provincial Leaders: Economic Performance and Political Mobility since 1949*, Armonk, NY: M.E. Sharpe.

Bo, Zhiyue (2005) "Political Succession and Elite Politics in Twenty-First Century China: Towards a Power-Balancing Perspective," *Issues & Studies*, vol. 41, no. 1 (March), 162–189.

Bo, Zhiyue (2006) "Princeling Generals in China: Breaking the Two Career Barriers?" *Issues & Studies*, vol. 42, no. 1 (March), 195–232.

Bo, Zhiyue (2007) *China's Elite Politics: Political Transition and Power Balancing*, Singapore: World Scientific.

Bo, Zhiyue (2008) "Balance of Factional Power in China: The Seventeenth Central Committee of the Chinese Communist Party," *East Asia: An International Quarterly*, vol. 25, no. 4 (December), 333–364.

Bo, Zhiyue (2010) *China's Elite Politics: Governance and Democratization*, Singapore: World Scientific.

Bo, Zhiyue (2015) "Provincial Politics," in David S.G. Goodman, ed., *Handbook of the Politics of China*, Cheltenham, UK: Edward Elgar Publishing, pp. 95–103.

Bo, Zhiyue (2017) *China's Political Dynamics under Xi Jinping*, Singapore: World Scientific.
Chang, Jung and Jon Halliday (2007) *Mao: The Unknown Story*, London: Vintage Books.
Chang, Parris H. (1978) *Power and Policy in China*, University Park: The Pennsylvania State University Press.
Dittmer, Lowell (1978) "Bases of Power in Chinese Politics: A Theory and Analysis of the Fall of the 'Gang of Four'," *World Politics*, vol. 31, no. 1 (October), 26–60.
Domes, Jürgen (1984) "Intra-Elite Group Formation and Conflict in the PRC," in David S.G. Goodman, ed., *Groups and Politics in the People's Republic of China*, Cardiff, UK: University College Cardiff Press, pp. 26–39.
Fewsmith, Joseph (2003) "The Sixteenth National Party Congress: The Succession That Didn't Happen," *The China Quarterly*, vol. 173 (March), 1–16.
Gao, Hua (2011) *Hongtaiyang Shi Zenyang Shengqi de – Yanan Zhengfeng de Lailong Qumai (How Did the Sun Rise over Yan'an? A History of the Rectification Movement)*, Hong Kong: Hong Kong Chinese University Press.
Goldstein, Avery (1991) *From Bandwagon to Balance-of-Power Politics: Structural Constraints and Politics in China, 1949–1978*, Stanford, CA: Stanford University Press.
Goodman, David S.G. (1984) "Provincial Party First Secretaries in National Politics: A Categoric or a Political Group?" in David S.G. Goodman, ed., *Groups and Politics in the People's Republic of China*, Cardiff, UK: University College Cardiff Press, pp. 68–82.
Jin, Qiu (1999) *The Culture of Power: The Lin Biao Incident in the Cultural Revolution*, Stanford, CA: Stanford University Press.
Kou, Chien-wen (2010) *Zhonggong jingying zhengzhi de yanbian: Zhiduhua yu quanli zhuanyi, 1978–2010 (The Transformation of Elite Politics of the Chinese Communist Party: Institutionalization and Power Transfer, 1978–2010)*, Taipei: Wunan tushu gongsi.
Lam, Willy Wo-Lap (2015) *Chinese Politics in the Era of Xi Jinping: Renaissance, Reform, or Retrogression?* New York and London: Routledge.
Li, Cheng (2003) "Poised to Take the Helm: Rising Stars and the Transition to the Fourth Generation," in David M. Finkelstein and Maryanne Kivlehan, eds., *China's Leadership in the 21st Century: The Rise of the Fourth Generation*, Armonk, NY: M.E. Sharpe, pp. 21–44.
Li, Cheng (2009) "China's Team of Rivals," *Foreign Policy*, no. 171 (March/April), 88–93.
Li, Wei and Lucian W. Pye (1992) "The Ubiquitous Role of the *Mishu* in Chinese Politics," *The China Quarterly*, vol. 132 (December), 913–936.
MacFarquhar, Roderick (1971) "On Photographs," *The China Quarterly*, vol. 46 (April/June), 289–307.
Mao Zedong (1942) "Guanyu Zhengdun Dangde Zuofeng" (February 1) ("On the rectification of the Party's style"), *Mao Zedong Xuanji* (Selected Works of Mao Zedong) (Vol. 3), http://cpc.people.com.cn/GB/64184/64185/66617/4488967.html.
Mulvenon, James C. and Michael S. Chase (2003) "The Role of *Mishu* in the Chinese Political System: Chang and Continuity," in David M. Finkelstein and Maryanne Kivlehan, eds., *China's Leadership in the 21st Century: The Rise of the Fourth Generation*, Armonk, NY: M.E. Sharpe, pp. 140–151.
Nathan, Andrew (1973) "A Factionalism Model of CCP Politics," *The China Quarterly*, vol. 53 (January/March), 34–66.
People's Daily (1977) "Xuehao Wenjian Zhazhu Gang" ("Understanding the Central Directives by Studying Two Important Documents"), February 7.
Pye, Lucian W. (2002) "Factions and the Politics of Guanxi: Paradoxes in Chinese Administrative and Political Behavior," in Jonathan Unger, ed., *The Nature of Chinese Politics: From Mao to Jiang*, Armonk, NY: M.E. Sharpe, pp. 38–57.
Radchenko, Sergey (2014) "China's First Great Tiger Hunt," *Foreign Policy*, December 15, http://foreignpolicy.com/2014/12/15/chinas-zhou-beria-corruption/.
Shiraev, Eric and Zi Yang (2014) "The Gao-Rao Affair: A Case of Character Assassination in Chinese Politics in the 1950s," in Martijn Icks and Eric Shiraev, eds., *Character Assassination Throughout the Ages*, New York: Palgrave Macmillan, pp. 237–252.
Shirk, Susan L. (1993) *The Political Logic of Economic Reform in China*, Berkeley, CA: University of California Press.
Teiwes, Frederick C. and Warren Sun (1990) *Politics at Mao's Court: Gao Gang and Party Factionalism in the Early 1950s*, Armonk, NY: M.E. Sharpe.
Teiwes, Frederick C. and Warren Sun (1996) *The Tragedy of Lin Biao*, Honolulu: University of Hawaii Press.

Tsou, Tang (1976) "Prolegomenon to the Study of Informal Groups in CCP Politics," *The China Quarterly*, vol. 65 (March), 98–117.

Tsou, Tang (2002) "Chinese Politics at the Top: Factionalism or Informal Politics? Balance-of-Power Politics or a Game to Win All?" in Jonathan Unger, ed., *The Nature of Chinese Politics: From Mao to Jiang*, Armonk, NY: M.E. Sharpe, pp. 98–159.

Yang, Jishen (2008) *Mubei – Zhongguo Liushiniandian Dajihuang Jishi (Gavestone: The Record of the Great Famine of the 1960s in China)*, Hong Kong: Tiandi Tongshu Youxian Gongsi (Cosmos Books).

9

EVOLUTION OF THE PARTY SINCE 1976

Ideological and functional adoptions

Joseph Yu-shek Cheng

Introduction

This chapter examines the Chinese Communist Party (CCP) from a historical approach, with an emphasis on the period since 1976, the beginning of the era of economic reforms and opening to the external world. There are two main themes in this historical survey: the ideological redefinitions and adjustments as well as the evolving functions of the Party in the modernization process. The Party needs to embrace "socialism with Chinese characteristics" in order to justify and legitimize its monopoly of political power, and it therefore has to develop a discourse on the stages of development of socialism to defend its acceptance of a market economy in China's economic reforms. These redefinitions and adjustments have been unavoidably controversial, and the general tendency of Chinese leaders has been to suppress debates.

At the beginning of the era of economic reforms and opening to the external world, the CCP leaders abandoned totalitarianism and the Maoist dictatorial style. Increasingly the totalitarian regime has been transformed into an authoritarian regime or even a soft authoritarian one in some aspects. The challenge of the Party has been to hold on to power through satisfying the demands of the people and maintaining its legitimacy. At the same time, it has to engage in reforms of its organization, recruitment and modes of operation in terms of its relations with the state, the economy and the society. It also has to enhance its attraction to the elites and loyalty among its members. These are formidable challenges.

This chapter studies how the Party regime has been attempting to overcome these challenges, admittedly with relative success. It has been able to deliver impressive economic growth as well as political and social stability. China's international status and influence have been improving and in turn have become a source of the Party regime's legitimacy. However, the absence of political reforms means that no effective checks and balances mechanisms have been developed because they have not been accepted by the regime. The development of civil society and the demand for democratization thus can only be suppressed.

Some indicators or benchmarks may be considered in the evaluations of the ideological redefinitions and adjustments as well as the evolution of the Party's functions in the modernization process. In the first place, the banner of socialism must not be abandoned so as to justify the continuation of the Party regime. Mild rectification and ideological education campaigns have been introduced from time to time to strengthen the ideological commitment of the cadre corps, though the impact has been limited.

Legitimacy has largely been maintained through economic development and improvement of the people's living standards. Nationalism has been exploited, especially in official claims of China's rising international status. There has been an awareness on the part of the leadership that there exists an official version of nationalism and many versions of nationalism among the intelligentsia; hence nationalism may become a "double-edged sword."

While there have been no serious political reforms since the Tiananmen Incident in 1989, efforts have been made to promote administrative reforms to improve the efficiency of the bureaucracy and its responsiveness to people's needs and complaints. Progress has been substantial in creating an attractive investment environment.

The Party regime's basic attitude toward the development of civil society has been hostile. But in recent years, there have been attempts to co-opt non-governmental organizations (NGOs) into the system for the delivery of social services. NGOs which are willing to toe the official line are thus given a constructive role within the regime; they may become the Party's mass organizations in a modern form in the future.

The costs of rapid economic development have been exposed, and its sustainability becomes doubtful. The highly inefficient use of resources and the neglect of environmental protection are now acknowledged by the Chinese authorities. Overdependence on exports and infrastructural development has to give way to domestic consumption, which has been handicapped by the concentration of resources in the hands of the Party regime and the widening of the gap between the rich and poor. The Party at this stage probably faces no fewer challenges than in 1979.

The Party before 1978

When the CCP seized power in 1949 and established the People's Republic of China, it was rather different from the Russian Bolsheviks in 1917; the former had considerable experience in governance already (Teiwes 2000). In the late 1920s and early 1930s, there were quasi-governments in Jinggangshan and other places; and during the war against Japan, the CCP governed territories in north and east China with a population of more than 100 million (Hartford 1989). The "Yan'an syndrome" or mass line and the "three magic weapons," i.e., Party leadership, armed struggle and a united front probably represented the gist of this legacy (Shum 1988). As the relative weakness of the Party, the need for allies and decentralized operations demanded pragmatism and adapting policy flexibly to suit local conditions, these features of policy-making and policy implementation emerged whenever the CCP leadership was prepared to be pragmatic, especially in the era of economic reforms and opening to the external world after 1978.

According to Frederick C. Teiwes (2000), the CCP rule in China from 1949 to 1976 may be divided into six sub-periods: (a) the consolidation of power, 1949–54; (b) the predominance of the Soviet model, 1954–57; (c) the Great Leap Forward, 1958–60; (d) the post-Leap adjustments and recovery, 1960–66; (e) the peak of the Cultural Revolution followed by years of military dominance 1966–71; and (f) the twilight of Maoism, 1972–76. In the period, Mao was the unchallenged leader most of the time, and Party rule functioned basically as a result of the interactions of no more than two dozen leaders (Teiwes 2000: 129 and 105).

Pragmatism managed to prevail in 1949–54 as the Party leadership had a sober understanding of the magnitude of the challenges it faced. There was, however, also a number of campaigns aimed at specific groups including the "Three-Anti and Five-Anti" campaign targeted at the bourgeoisie and cadres in economic work, thought reform aimed at intellectuals, and the suppression of counter-revolutionaries. As a result of these movements and the land reform programs, the CCP exposed the entire nation to its totalitarian objectives. Conflicts among cadres with different backgrounds became apparent though (Teiwes 1997: 15–40).

By 1954, both the achievement of economic recovery and the Party-state's increasing reach served to fulfill the Party leadership's determination to secure socio-economic change and the control of society necessary for the establishment of the Soviet model. The First Five-Year Plan period of 1953–57 was probably the most centralized period in the history of the PRC.

The apparent success of collectivization and the socialist transformation of industry and commerce in 1956, in the eyes of the CCP leadership, represented the fundamental triumph of socialism over capitalism in China and offered the foundation for a new stage of economic and social development. In this context Mao Zedong initiated the Hundred Flowers Campaign to invite people outside the Party, mainly intellectuals, to articulate their grievances which were anticipated to be legitimate and "non-antagonistic." But Mao was shocked subsequently by the criticisms and responded with a crackdown in the form of the Anti-Rightist Campaign. It was perceived as Mao's first major misjudgment after 1949, and the next phase of political relaxation had to wait till after his death.

The imitation of the Soviet model generated its problems, and its re-examination began in 1956–57. In the January 1958 Nanning conference, Mao declared that the earlier "opposing rash advance" program was a mistake which had encouraged the "bourgeois rightists" to attack the Party. He also severely criticized other leaders like Zhou Enlai and Chen Yun; and launched the Great Leap Forward campaign which was not only an act of revolutionary idealism, but sheer fantasy. Failure of the Leap demonstrated the staying power of the Party regime though, as well as the dictatorial authority of Mao in the absence of checks and balances, honest feedback and scientific policy research.

The crisis due to the failure of the Leap forced Mao to "retreat to the second front" and allow Liu Shaoqi to run the Party regime on the "first front" (MacFarquhar 1974: 152–156). The general trend of this period of adjustments and recovery was to reestablish bureaucratic regularity and greater central co-ordination. But by the summer of 1962, Mao considered that the policy retreat had gone far enough, and he sought to enhance the collective economy and guide ideological direction by proclaiming the slogan "never forget class struggle." In these processes, Mao became suspicious of the Party leaders on the "first front," and he accorded a more prominent political role for the People's Liberation Army (PLA) which was then guided by Lin Biao to promote the "Thought of Mao Zedong."

In this context, the Cultural Revolution emerged as a surprise in mid-1966. Liu Shaoqi was replaced by Lin Biao as the successor in the Central Committee meeting in August. Mao's motivations in launching the Cultural Revolution most probably included his concern about the fading of revolutionary idealism within the Party and the worry of the future prevalence of Soviet revisionism in China, as well as his attempt to regain power. The Cultural Revolution itself represented an attack on hitherto sacred Leninist norms and principles regarding Party leadership (Harding 1997).

When ordinary workers and students were called upon to "make revolution" by the Supreme Leader Mao, the legitimacy and authority of the Party regime were weakened. The new Revolutionary Committees established amalgamated the functions of Party and government, but could not maintain the discipline of the previous Party organization. Finally, the fall of Lin Biao revealed the serious factionalism loosened by the Cultural Revolution, which spread from the highest leadership level to the "rebel" organizations at the grassroots. With the benefit of hindsight, the political turmoil twisted human nature and left scars lasting for decades.

The demise of Lin Biao who was described as Mao's "best student" – and the military threat from the Soviet Union – probably helped to persuade Mao to allow Premier Zhou Enlai to introduce a series of policy measures to restrict the impact of the "ultra-left" practices now ascribed to Lin Biao. The ideological and political confusion, however, was likely exacerbated when at the end of 1972, Mao redefined Lin Biao's political crimes as "ultra-rightist" (MacFarquhar, 1997: 275–278 and 281–283).

In the final years of Mao, there was a fairly clear confrontation at the leadership level between a group led by Zhou Enlai and Deng Xiaoping favoring order and the pre-Cultural Revolution way on the one hand, and another group supporting Cultural Revolution values and fighting "revisionism" on the other. The struggle ended in the autumn of 1976 when Jiang Qing and her group were arrested shortly after the death of Mao. Hua Guofeng emerged as the new CCP Chairman, and the process of reversing the Cultural Revolution gradually began.

The Party and its modernization programs in the 1980s

After the fall of the "Gang of Four," the Party leadership with Deng Xiaoping as its head realized that the legitimacy of the Party regime had to from henceforward depend on its ability to raise the living standards of the people. To this end, the CCP leaders were willing to borrow from the West, not only capital and technology, but also management techniques and the market mechanism. Yet Deng would still insist on upholding the four cardinal principles which really amounted to leadership of the Party. On the other hand, in addition to the "Four Modernizations" of agriculture, industry, science and technology, and national defense, Chinese intellectuals since the late 1970s had also been demanding for the fifth modernization, i.e., democracy.

The remarkable change came in December 1978 when Deng and his supporters gained power in the Third Plenum of the Eleventh Central Committee of the Party. The post-Mao leaders were aware that the Cultural Revolution had much eroded the people's support for the regime. Instead there existed a crisis because of the prevalent lack of confidence in China's future, the absence of trust for the Party and the government, and the loss of conviction in the superiority of Communism. The new leadership accepted that regime legitimacy would henceforward have to depend on its ability to deliver the goods to improve people's living standards. It also promised that there would be no more political campaigns like the Cultural Revolution; and attempts were made to strengthen socialist legalism. In fact, the first criminal law and criminal procedural law only appeared in 1979 (Cheng 1989: ix–xix).

Major economic reforms in a Marxist-Leninist state certainly call for justifications in the ideological sphere (Schram 1984). In spring 1978, the reformers put forward the slogan "practice is the sole criterion for testing truth," which represented an offensive against the Maoists who still advocated: "Whatever policies Chairman Mao devised we will resolutely support, whatever directives Chairman Mao laid down we will forever observe" (Deng 1984a: 51–52). This offensive inevitably led to a reassessment of Mao's achievements and the Cultural Revolution, which was embodied in the "Resolution on certain questions in the history of our Party since the founding of the People's Republic of China" adopted in June 1981.[1] By then, however, Deng and his supporters were firmly in power and they did not want to create an ideological vacuum by completely negating Mao. The formula adopted was that Mao had made mistakes in his old age, but Mao Zedong Thought as the collective wisdom of the first generation of CCP leaders should still be upheld.

The emphasis on practice was accompanied by a campaign calling for liberation of thought and seeking truth from facts which together helped Deng to gain power at the end of 1978. At the same time, literary works on the tragedies of the Cultural Revolution blossomed in the late 1970s, and they were known as "scar literature." Demands for democracy and human rights also emerged among dissident groups who were encouraged by the reforms of the regime and its open-door policy which, among other things, paved the way for the introduction of Western ideas of democracy and democratic political institutions.

The conservatives within China's collective leadership responded with a crackdown on these groups in 1979, an anti-spiritual pollution campaign in 1983–84 and an anti-bourgeois liberalization campaign both in 1981 and 1986–87. As a staunch Marxist-Leninist, Deng could not tolerate the Party leadership being challenged. While trying to maintain the momentum of economic reforms, he was often willing to concede to the conservatives on the ideological, propaganda and literary fronts.

The seminal trend in the ideological arena was a search for a theoretical foundation to support the economic reforms (Delfs 1987: 50–52). In the late 1970s, theoreticians began to venture the idea that China had not gone through the complete state of capitalism which had only a brief history in the coastal areas while vast areas of China simply jumped from the feudalist stage to the socialist one. These theoreticians were ready to admit that capitalism has a contribution to make through raising productivity and laying the material foundation for advancing to socialism. They therefore considered that China was still in the initial stage of socialism with backward productive forces, and as such it would be justifiable to import Western capital, technology and management as well as allow private and mixed ownership of the means of production (including joint ventures with foreigners). This formulation also helped to defend the superiority of socialism which was widely doubted in China. The above trends logically led to a reassessment of Marxism. On December 7, 1984, the *People's Daily* carried a commentator's article entitled "Theory and the Reality" which stated:

> Marx passed away 101 years ago, his works are more than a century old, some were his visions at that time, after which the situation has changed greatly and some of this ideas are not necessarily appropriate. There are many things that Marx, Engels and Lenin never experienced or had any contact with. We cannot ask the works of Marx and Lenin to provide solutions to our current questions.

The next day, the *People's Daily* made an unprecedented correction of the article revising the last sentence of the above quotation to read: "We cannot ask the works of Marx and Lenin to provide all the solutions to our current questions."

In time, Deng and the reformers also appreciated the need for political reforms as a necessary condition for economic development and economic reforms. The destruction of the Party organs by the Red Guards during the Cultural Revolution had taught the post-Mao leadership the importance of maintaining socialist legalism. It further accepted that some form of division of labor between the Party and the state, between the National People's Congress and the State Council, between government organs and economic enterprises, etc. was necessary to improve efficiency and establish a clear system of accountability. The opening to the West was also accompanied by the introduction of Western ideas of democracy and human rights among Chinese intellectuals. For a while, Deng himself talked about democratization. In a speech to an enlarged session of Party Politburo on August 18, 1980 entitled "Reform of the Leadership Systems of the Party and the State," Deng called for "the democratization of the political life of the Party and the state, the democratization of the economic management, and the democratization of the life of society as well." He also discussed the need

> to develop in full measure people's democracy, and to ensure that the people as a whole truly enjoy the power to supervise the state in variety of effective ways, and

> especially to supervise political power at the basic level, as well as all enterprises and undertakings.

He then criticized the over-centralization of power, the excessive powers enjoyed by individual leaders (like Mao) and the confusion of functions between the Party and the state (Deng 1984b).

Meanwhile, the disillusionment of the people did not seem to have been dispelled by the modernization programs. Political apathy remained widespread, the confidence crisis continued and there was much confusion of values, especially among the young. At the same time, corruption and privileges became so rampant that China in the latter half of the 1980s was not much different from Indonesia or the Philippines. The heavy reliance on personal networks (*guanxi*) also eroded the impact of various incentive systems introduced. All these in turn reinforced the ideological vacuum and the individual pursuits of material gains.

Deng's response was that of a typical Leninist. As early as March 1979, he laid down the "Four Cardinal Principles" of upholding the leadership of the CCP, the guidance of Marxism-Leninism and Mao Zedong Thought, the people's democratic dictatorship and the socialist road (Deng 1984c). As the latter three were subject to various interpretations, Deng's response implied that the control of the Party could not be challenged. He too indicated that he would never be prepared to countenance disorder in society, lack of discipline in the Party and the spread of subversive ideas. It was therefore not surprising that he endorsed the anti-bourgeois liberalization campaigns.

By 1986, both economic and political reforms appeared to be running out of steam. The stalemate in the leadership meant that sufficient force could not be mobilized among the middle and lower level cadres to overcome the resistance. As the conservatives were complaining about the risks of "all-out Westernization," the reformers realized that a major push would be required to maintain the momentum of the reforms. The crucial plenary meeting of the CCP Central Committee held in September 1986 disappointed the reformers; it also failed to provide clear indicators to resolve the leadership succession problem. The difficulties described above as well as the severe drainage of China's foreign exchange reserves to pay for the massive imports in late 1984 and 1985 probably strengthened the hands of the conservatives.

The student demonstrations at the end of the year were in part an attempt to break the stalemate in favor of the reformers.[2] Contrary to the students' expectations, their demonstrations triggered the purge of Hu Yaobang and weakened the reformers. Deng endorsed the clampdown, and in fact he had earlier told the visiting Polish leader Wojciech Jaruzelski that the Polish Communist Party's failure to suppress the Solidarity in 1979–80 was a mistake.

The purge of Hu Yaobang did not mean the end of political reform efforts though. In the Thirteenth Party Congress in 1987, Zhao Ziyang's report formally put forward concrete political reform proposals in a comprehensive manner based on Deng's August 1980 speech.[3] Zhao Ziyang's political reforms attempted to separate the Party from the state. The Party should concentrate on broad policy guidelines, ideological and propaganda work, etc., and let state organs be responsible for daily administrative affairs. Further, Party personnel holding functional posts should not concurrently occupy administrative positions in the state hierarchy. Within the latter, some separation between the legislative and executive branches should be enforced through avoidance of leaders holding concurrent positions in both branches.

The idea was to achieve a clear-cut division of labor and establish mechanisms for checks and balances. Further, in 1988 Zhao Ziyang wanted to abolish Party core groups (*dangzu*) in most government departments; and he transferred the management of leading non-Party positions in universities, economic enterprises and service units, as well as many of the bureaus and offices directly subordinated to the State Council from the Party Central Organization Department to the State Council's Ministry of Personnel (Burns 1994). These measures were in part designed to set up a modem civil service system based on open recruitment.

In the wake of the Tiananmen Incident, Zhao's proposals and measures were dropped because they were seen to have weakened Party control. Political reforms as depicted in Jiang Zemin's report to the Fourteenth Party Congress were limited to administrative reforms such as streamlining the organizations of the Party and the state.[4] Separation of the Party and the state has not been mentioned since there is some speculation that the reversal of the verdict on the Tiananmen Incident would probably be the first signal of serious political reforms.

Setbacks of the Tiananmen Incident and subsequent adjustments

In June 1989 leading dissidents like Liu Binyan predicted that the Party regime would not last more than three months. The tragic event generated much skepticism about many of China's achievements in the recent past and a deep pessimism about its future. Deng Xiaoping's southern tour in early 1992 turned the tide, however. The leftism that emerged in the wake of the Tiananmen Incident, perhaps symbolized by Jiang Zemin's stated aim "to bankrupt the household entrepreneurs," was arrested. Chinese leaders had also identified the most threatening challenge – dissatisfaction in the countryside.

The Fourteenth Party Congress in 1992 was significant in that people were too busy improving their own livelihoods and paid scant attention to the Party Congress. The removal of the Yang Shangkun and Yang Baibing brothers from the leadership of the PLA surprised many China watchers, but it had limited impact on the economy and people's political attitudes. The Fourteenth Party Congress will go down in Chinese history as the first Party Congress after 1949 which ordinary people could afford to ignore.

About three years after the Tiananmen Incident, most intellectuals in China were willing to accept the military crackdown, though they still condemned the deployment of tanks and machine-guns. They saw what had happened in the former Soviet Union and Eastern Europe, and came to the conclusion that there was no alternative to the leadership of the CCP. There was nothing like the Catholic Church or the Polish Solidarity movement in China and it will remain so in the short term future (Hicks 1990).

Mao Zedong failed to arrange his successors, and Deng Xiaoping too failed twice. Economic stagnation plus maladministration by corrupt cadres can easily create an explosive situation because the status quo would then be no longer "acceptable" nor would the leadership of the Party be tolerable. The leadership succession process, however, could be, to borrow an economic term, a soft-landing if it coincided with a period of respectable growth and low inflation. A painful hard-landing would likely occur if succession took place in a difficult era of economic stagnation and intolerable inflation.

In late September 1994, the CCP held its Fourth Plenum of the Fourteenth Party Congress. Instead of discussing the serious economic problems, the Plenum surprised the outside world by focusing on only one theme: the construction of the Party. Chinese leaders probably shared the consensus that major problems always originated from the Party. They too hoped to prepare the Party for the coming leadership succession process. Deng Xiaoping was shown publicly in a wheelchair.

The communique of the Fourth Plenum acknowledged many obvious problems: "the Party not in control of the Party," lax discipline, weak organization, various phenomena of corruption, etc.[5] Official documents and media reports also indicated that a considerable proportion of basic-level Party organizations existed in name only, those which were functioning healthily were definitely a minority. Many Party members affiliated to town and township enterprises had lost contact with their Party organizations because they were constantly traveling and engaging in unreported business activities. Despite the honest recognition of the problems, the solution offered, i.e., to uphold and strengthen democratic centralism, was certainly disappointing. As the Party had been avoiding the issue of political reforms since the Tiananmen Incident, the strengthening of democratic centralism could only mean strengthening centralism.

Chinese leaders then, however, considered that the Party had to be strengthened. Basic-level Party groups, branches and committees were to be established in all economic enterprises, including joint ventures with foreign investors and those that were wholly owned by the latter. In the early 1990s, the streamlining of administration at the county level and below often led to the amalgamation of Party and state organs such as their general offices, the Organization Department of the former and the Personnel Bureau of the latter, etc. (Cheng 1995). There was a reluctance to join the Party immediately after the Tiananmen Incident, especially among the intellectuals. In the latter half of the 1990s, university students and individual entrepreneurs had been eager to join as they perceived that the Party provided a useful *guanxi* network.

The Party had lost its ideological appeal. Its authority to enforce discipline and launch rectification campaigns became limited. But it controlled appointments to all important Party, state and public sector positions. Its membership was the power elite, and it attracted talents who were eager to join and be recognized as part of the power elite.

The challenge of the Party therefore was the fulfillment of its political recruitment function so that its membership would be an all-embracing power elite providing leadership in all sectors. Success in this area would prevent alternative organizations such as independent trade unions from developing and winning the hearts of the workers. Similarly, absorption of the critical dissidents was important too. A Party of this nature may find it difficult to exercise iron discipline and to lead as the vanguard of the proletariat. But it would serve to aggregate interests and resolve contradictions within the Party. It would also accommodate a collective leadership more easily.

The reformers in China were often criticized for lack of a theory which could help to legitimize their reform programs. Deng's approach was aptly depicted by his statement "groping for the rocks while crossing the river." This experimental approach conformed to Deng's characteristic pragmatism and was also in line with the CCP tradition. China is too large a country for a uniformly implemented blueprint, and the Chinese Communist leadership normally allows and even encourages different approaches and models to emerge while following the spirit of the guidelines from the Party Centre. However, to uphold the leadership of the Party meant that the regime's policy programs had to be justified in terms of a socialist framework, if not a strictly Marxist-Leninist one. Furthermore, economic reforms were inter-connected and priorities had to be set. The absence of a comprehensive theory for reforms obviously handicapped the co-ordination of reform measures and the establishment priorities. It also facilitated the leftists to maintain their strongholds on the theoretical and propaganda fronts.

A major contribution of Deng Xiaoping's southern tour in early 1992 and Fourteenth Party Congress was the affirmation of the theme of a socialist market economy. In the absence of the development of a market economy, without confirmation that the socialist economy also had to adopt a market economic structure, economic reforms could not make such headway in the early 1990s in China. Deng's personal charisma and authority naturally assumed an important role in securing the acceptance of the theme. In fact, since 1979, Deng himself had used the concept of market economy a few times as the equivalent of a commodity economy, although the concept had not yet been adopted in formal Party documents. In Deng's speeches during this southern tour, he severely criticized the controversies regarding the distinction between capitalism and socialism. He instead presented the following three pragmatic criteria: beneficial for the development of productivity, beneficial for the raising of the people's living standards and beneficial for the growth of comprehensive national power.

The official recognition of the concept of socialist market economy concluded a fluctuating development process for more than a decade. At the end of 1978, the Third Plenum of the Eleventh Central Committee (CC) of the CCP advocated "the shifting of the emphasis of Party work to socialist modernizing construction"; it also appealed for the observance of economic laws and respect for the laws of value. At the Twelfth Party Congress in 1982, the policy line had been redefined as "economic planning as the mainstay, market as supplement." The Third Plenum of the Twelfth CC of the CCP adopted the "Decision on Economic Structure Reform" which raised the concept of "planned commodity economy on the basis of public ownership." At the Thirteenth Party Congress in 1987, the planned commodity economy was depicted as "a structure in which planning and market are unified internally." Since the Fourth Plenum of the Thirteenth CC, the term "economy structure integrating economic planning and market" had been commonly used; and it was at the Fourteenth Party Congress in 1992 that the concept of a "socialist market economy" finally secured official recognition.

Since 1978, Chinese leaders have increasingly accepted law as an instrument for social regulation and effective administration. Law has been recognized as essential for economic modernization and the basic means to resolve conflict (Lo 1995: 327–328). The momentum for further economic reforms since the Fourteenth Party Congress in 1992 brought renewed emphasis on providing legal infrastructure, reinforcing judicial independence, improving the quality of legal personnel, training lawyers and promoting popular legal awareness (*Beijing Review* 1993: 4). Both the Chinese leadership and the people have come to accept that the "rule of law" should replace the present "rule of persons (*renzhi*)." Certainly their conception of the "rule of law" differs from that in a Western liberal democracy; the former probably means rule by law or rule according to law. In the mid-1990s, this rule by law or rule according to law was still subordinated to Party leadership, but there was a distinct awareness that political arbitrariness had to be avoided, and there should be no return to the Maoist style of lawlessness.

Deng and his liberal followers deserved credit for introducing serious political reforms such as the separation of Party and government as well as elections at the grassroots level. A regular leadership succession system and a retirement system were established. However, the imperative of party dominance militated against the establishment of real checks and balances, without which the negative fallouts of economic reforms – corruption and the abuse of power – could not be effectively tackled. Moreover, while economic growth guaranteed the legitimacy of the Party, maintenance of political stability implied that crackdown on dissent was necessary.

The post-Deng leadership and the challenges of the twenty-first century

Chinese leaders in the post-Deng period were deeply engaged in a consensus-building process in policy formulation and policy implementation. The important interest groups concerned had to be fully consulted and their support secured through a bargaining process. Lack of consensus would usually imply the abandonment of the initiative, at least for the time being. As reforms became more complicated, and the benefits of each set of reforms would often be unevenly distributed, Chinese leaders found it increasingly difficult to forge a broad-based consensus in support of their reform programs. China's diversity had also been much exacerbated by the expanding gaps among regions in almost two decades of rapid economic growth.

The Jiang Zemin era (1987–2002) witnessed the co-existence of both reformist and conservative tendencies. China's accession to the World Trade Organization in November 2001 unleashed further initiatives in market-oriented reforms as well as efforts to link the country's economy with the global marketplace. In July the same year, Jiang presented his "Theory of the Three Represents," which paved the way for entrepreneurs, professionals and "returnees" (Chinese educated overseas) to be allowed to join the Party.[6] Jiang's "Three Represents" represented a significant redefinition of the role of the CCP at the beginning of the new century. To broaden the base of the Party, Jiang suggested that as long as these elements were willing "to struggle consciously to realize the Party line and platform and conform to the demands of Party members," then they should be absorbed into the Party.[7]

At the same time, the CCP leadership was worried that further opening up the country to the influences of the Western world would affect political stability and the Party's monopoly of political power. President Jiang openly called for "a reinforcement of legislation against information on the Internet," on the pretext that such information would contribute to the rise of "superstition, pornography, violence and pernicious information." This was despite the fact that Jiang also suggested that the Chinese government should make full use of the Internet to enhance transparency and facilitate greater public participation in politics.

A research report of the Central Propaganda Department of the Party in early 2001 indicated that two important lessons were to be drawn from the heavy loss of the Socialist Party in the presidential election in Yugoslavia in the previous year. The subsequent arrest of former President Slobodan Milosevic, an ardent ally of Beijing, caused considerable worry among Chinese leaders. They believed that control over the armed forces and the media had to be strengthened. Suggestions of "nationalization of the military" would only weaken the Party's control over the gun; as a result, such suggestions were severely criticized by the PLA as a conspiracy to subvert China by Western countries. Freedom of information and liberalization of the mass media were also perceived to have placed the governing party's propaganda work at a disadvantage.

The Chinese leadership understood that the base of the Party had to be expanded beyond the proletariat, as the Party had been transformed from a revolutionary party into a governing party. Furthermore, the leadership realized that the legitimacy of the CCP regime would depend on its ability to improve living standards. To claim that the Party represented the demand for the development of advanced productivity was certainly in line with the nation's central task of economic construction, though the emphasis then was on an intensive mode of development, with increasing reliance on scientific and technological inputs.

The Chinese leadership did not offer a concrete definition on the direction of progress of China's advanced culture. From Chiang Kai-shek's "*Xin Shenghuo Yundong* (New Life Movement)" to Mao Zedong's "socialist new man" and then to Jiang's advanced culture, Chinese leaders had been trying to shape the values and culture of the Chinese nation. Jiang and other Chinese leaders were aware of the ideological vacuum in Chinese society, and they to some extent were exploiting nationalism to fill this vacuum. Undeniably, nationalism has been a powerful trend of thought and political force in contemporary China (Whiting 1995). In the 1990s, unofficial, voluntary nationalism in China rose to a new peak, and the Chinese authorities consciously exploited this to maintain domestic solidarity and stability. The wave of nationalism in China following the NATO bombing of the Chinese embassy in Belgrade in May 1999 was a good example of the split of Chinese nationalism into official nationalism and unofficial, voluntary nationalism, as well as the interaction between the two. On the one hand the incident triggered massive waves of unofficial, voluntary nationalism; on the other hand it posed a severe test for official nationalism. Under the banner of patriotism, the latter allowed unofficial, voluntary nationalism considerable space and channels for expression. At the same time, it attempted to limit unofficial, voluntary nationalism within specified legal boundaries so that it would not get out of control and evolve into extreme nationalism engaging in confrontation with the West, especially the US (Cheng and Ngok 2004).

At the beginning of this century, Jiang began to preach "rule by virtue" as well, a principle that was perceived to be complementary to the rule of law. In view of the appeal of Christianity to the educated and the spread of superstitious practices in the rural areas (not to speak of the spread of the Falun Gong), the revival of traditional Confucian virtues was probably seen as a lesser evil. In this context, it was not surprising to see a vice-president of the Central Party School defining the fundamental task of developing socialist culture as "cultivating generations of citizens with ideals, a sense of morality, high cultural standards and discipline" (*Henan Ribao* 2001).

Jiang was attacked by both the conservatives and the reformers for his bold initiative. The conservatives opposed the proposal for ideological reasons; they were subsequently sanctioned for their open criticisms. The reformers supported the proposal, but were dissatisfied with Jiang's dictatorial, high-handed manner in presenting the proposal before securing the Party's endorsement. Yet, many local Party organs were quick to implement Jiang's proposal, indicating that this would be an inevitable trend.

Chinese leaders meanwhile continued to make efforts to improve the recruitment and strengthen the accountability of cadres. Open recruitment through civil service examinations and interviews was increasingly common. Concerning internal assessment and promotion exercises, greater weight was attached to "democratic assessment," in other words views from colleagues and clients on a cadre's performance. More choices were being provided to ensure responsiveness to public opinion. For example, when the Sixteenth Party Congress elected the new Central Committee in 2002, delegates were given a slate of 10 percent more candidates than the seats to be filled; at the town/township level, the Party committee concerned might nominate two or more candidates for "democratic assessment." This was not full democracy, but public opinion had a certain role to play while guaranteeing the principle that "the Party controls cadres."

Cadres at all levels were under greater pressure to perform. A manager whose incompetence was perceived to be the main cause for the losses of his state-owned enterprise (SOE) would find it difficult to retain his position, as workers and their families who were suffering a decline in income were bound to make complaints. To indicate the priority attached to implementation of an important policy, higher-level governments often demanded lower-level cadres' resignations if specific targets had not been fulfilled. Again, the emphasis was on performance and competence, whilst transparency and democratic accountability were relatively neglected.

In the first decade of the new century, Chinese leaders might well undergo a shift in paradigms concerning the nation's problems and their solutions. Economic development provided the Communist regime with a reasonable base of legitimacy in the era of economic reform and opening to the outside world. Yet the quantitative changes in the past two decades and more had brought about qualitative changes which posed new challenges. The issues of unemployment, social security and environmental protection were good examples. Entry into the WTO was a significant symbol of such qualitative changes and an important factor pushing for these qualitative changes (Harwit 2001).

Jiang's "Theory of the Three Represents" was a significant response to the changing socio-economic stratification in society as well as the demand for a modern cadre corps and Party membership to meet the challenges of modernization. Jiang's administration also began to exploit traditional Confucianism and "rule by virtue" to fill the ideological vacuum and restore the declining moral standards. These measures coincided with a higher degree of tolerance for dissent. Intellectuals and activists associated with inchoate NGOs were allowed to put forward proposals of reforms as long as the supremacy of the party would not be jeopardized.

New generation of Party leaders and new formula for political stability

The Sixteenth Party Congress in November 2002 was a congress of leadership succession and personnel arrangement. It was not a congress of policy changes and theoretical innovation. In terms of leadership succession, this was an orderly process in which political stability and economic growth were not adversely affected. But there was still very little institutionalization even when power was supposed to be handed over by the Third-Generation to the Fourth-Generation leaders.

The Hu Jintao-Wen Jiabao leadership realized that economic growth alone would not be enough to maintain the legitimacy of the Party regime. It began studying ways to set up a pension scheme for the country's 900 million rural residents; and a report was prepared for the central government's consideration in spring 2003. The new scheme initially would be built on a rural social endowment insurance program introduced in 1992 in provinces like Guangdong, Fujian and Zhejiang. More than 21 billion *yuan* had been collected for that program, although it was largely shelved in the late 1990s. This new scheme would not demand funding from the government, as individuals would contribute every month until they reached the retirement age of 60. The scheme expected to be voluntary though, with only contributors enjoying the benefits (*South China Morning Post* 2002).

While presenting the Proposal on the Eleventh Five-Year Program at the Fifth Session of the Central Committee of the CCP in October 2005, Premier Wen called for the stepping up of national efforts to build a harmonious society, indicating that employment, social security, poverty reduction, education, medical care, environmental protection and safety would be given priority. Wen emphasized the improvement of the insurance systems of pension, basic medical care, unemployment, industrial injuries and child birth, the tackling of the social security issue for migrant workers in cities, as well as the setting up of a social security system supporting minimum living standards in rural areas (GOV.cn 2005).

These measures were aimed at reducing the polarization of society. According to the National Development and Reform Commission, the income of the richest 20 percent of the urban population accounted for 59.7 percent of the overall income of urban residents, while that of the poorest fifth accounted for only 2.7 percent (*South China Morning Post* 2006). Further, fewer than 0.5 percent of the families owned over 60 percent of the nation's wealth in private hands, and 70 percent of this private wealth was in the hands of those families with financial assets exceeding US$0.5 million. This concentration was ten times as much as that in the US (Mainland Affairs Council, Republic of China [Taiwan] 2006: 2).

Apparently the ideal of the Hu-Wen team was to return to the good old days of the 1950s when the Party was in full control, and the vast majority of Party cadres were incorrupt, dedicated and selfless. Two major political projects initiated by President Hu were in line with achieving this ideal scenario. On December 26, 2005 (the 112th birthday anniversary of Mao Zedong), the Institute of Marxism-Leninism-Mao Zedong Thought of the Chinese Academy of Social Sciences was raised in status to a Marxism academy; its establishment was expanded from 75 professorial-rank researchers to 200. The Party Central Committee also launched a ten-year project in early 2004 for Marxist theoretical research.

In 2005 and 2006, a mild rectification campaign in the form of a self-improvement education drive was implemented to improve the vanguard character of Party members. In January 2005, the 69.6 million Party members were asked to study the Deng Xiaoping theory, the "Three Represents" thesis of Jiang Zemin, and the Scientific Outlook on Development of Hu Jintao. An important objective of the campaign was to tackle the problems of the weakening Party organizations at the grassroots level and the wavering ideological conviction of Party members.

In the absence of major political reforms, some administrative innovations were introduced by the Hu-Wen administration. The CCP leadership proposed at its Sixteenth Party Congress in 2002 systems of fixed terms, resignation and responsibility for leading cadres in the Party and government. In 2004, the "Temporary Regulations on the Resignation of Leading Cadres in the Party and Government" were promulgated, stipulating that the principal responsible officials have to resign to assume responsibility for serious neglect and mistakes in the management and supervision work in market regulation, environmental protection and social management leading to major damages. In April 2005, the "Civil Service Law" was adopted which provided the legal basis for cadres having to resign in the wake of major mishaps or policy failures within their jurisdictions.

To improve the quality of cadres, there was a general emphasis on academic qualifications and overseas experiences. The younger generation of cadres who were eager to seek promotions certainly responded. Many of them had postgraduate degrees and considerable exposure to the international scene. This not only applied to central government officials, but also to provincial and city officials.

Hu and the other Chinese leaders were aware of the sharpening social contradictions that went hand in hand with fast economic growth. This was the rationale behind the concept of a "harmonious society," meaning that more assistance would be given to underprivileged groups mainly through the establishment of a social security net. Efforts were made to maintain a better balance while avoiding undue emphasis on economic growth rates alone, including higher priority accorded to environmental protection, higher efficiency achieved in the utilization of natural resources, more encouragement of internal consumption and greater dependence placed on the domestic market. While the CCP leadership encouraged debate on ways and means to promote social stability, discussions about political reform were largely banned.

In general, the political atmosphere tightened since 2008 due to the riots in Tibet and the preparations for the Beijing Games. Some initiatives for the strengthening of intra-Party democracy were attempted, but the implementation was ineffective. The weaknesses of Party leadership from the top allowed the exacerbation of corruption and factionalism. While the Chinese economy rebounded strongly in the immediate aftermath of the 2008–09 global financial crisis, the Hu-Wen administration realized the deterioration in the domestic and international environment since then, and the official media no longer talked about "a glorious era" to come. The administration was worried about the impact of the "color revolutions" in the former Soviet republics and later that of the Arab Spring.

Challenges for the Xi Jinping administration: consolidating the "Beijing consensus" model

The Hu-Wen leadership quietly achieved much. The Chinese economy became the second largest in the world in 2010; China exports more than any other country and is the number one trader in the global economy. Beijing held the Olympics in 2008 and the Shanghai Expo in 2010. Chinese people really feel that they have stood up, as claimed by Mao on October 1, 1949 when the PRC was founded. Chinese people are proud of the country's impact on international affairs. This national pride has become an important source of the Party regime's legitimacy too.

The Party still has no intention of giving up its monopoly of political power; and in fact there have been no significant political reforms since 1989. Parallel to this rejection of democratization, the Hu-Wen leadership was very sensitive to potential unrest. There was a crackdown on dissidents, independent NGOs, human rights groups and freedom of information flow on the Internet in the two years or so before the Beijing Olympics. Even more than Jiang Zemin, ex-president Hu tapped Confucianist themes such as the creation of a "harmonious society" in the service of ensuring stability. Further, ethical norms upheld by Hu, such as the "eight honors" and "eight shames," had a distinctive Confucianist flavor.

Since the Sixteenth Party Congress in 2002, the selection and cultivation of young cadres has revealed several orientations which are known as the "five insistences": (1) insistence on talents and high ethical standards with priority given to the latter including high political standards, strong conviction in the Communist ideals, firm adherence to the Party line and a good record in observing Party discipline; (2) insistence on outstanding service record in difficult and complicated localities as a test of young cadres' political qualities and problem-solving capabilities; (3) insistence on experiences in grassroots frontline work, in this connection, fresh university graduates have been encouraged to serve in administrative villages and rural communities; (4) insistence on cultivation and training of young cadres, especially those selected for further promotions; and (5) insistence on the strict management of cadres (Sun 2014).

These orientations demonstrate a subtle yet significant difference in the era of the Hu-Wen administration and that of Xi Jinping. They actually reflect an awareness on the part of the Party leadership of the need to provide attractive incentives for talented young cadres to accept hardship posts; otherwise the most talented would concentrate on administrative positions in big cities and rich SOEs. In this way, governance at the grassroots level and in the rural areas would suffer, and stability would be adversely affected. The decision in early 2010 to equalize the representation rights of rural and urban residents in people's congresses at various levels was aimed to produce the same effect too; the increase in the number of deputies from the rural sector in people's congresses at various levels would mean more opportunities to reward rural cadres who would then have better prospects for promotion.

Within the Leninist framework, maintaining the Party's monopoly of power and political stability demands the accord of a high priority to Party-building work which in turn means the cultivation of a reliable cadre corps. In preparation for the Eighteenth Party Congress, in 2009 the Chinese leadership asked for lists of about 1,000 reserve cadres at the provincial/ministerial level, over 6,000 reserve cadres at the prefectural/bureau level and about 40,000 reserve cadres at the county/section(*chu*) level. These selection processes were designed to ensure the availability of talents to strengthen Party and state organizations on a long-term basis, including the appointment of younger cadres at all levels. The Central Organization Department also seriously warned against lobbying activities in these selection processes.

One focus regarding the Chinese leadership's concern for the survival of the Chinese Communist regime is the "color revolutions" in the former constituent republics of the Soviet Union in the early years of this century, i.e., the "rose revolution" in Georgia in 2003, the "orange revolution" in Ukraine in 2004 and the "(yellow) tulip revolution" in Kyrgyzstan in 2005. David Shambaugh believes that the Chinese leadership is very worried about the causes and implications of the "color revolutions" for the Chinese Communist regime. He identifies six major aspects of the Chinese analyses of the "color revolutions" in his survey: the nature of the "revolutions"; the role of the US; the role of international NGOs; the potential for more "color revolutions" in Central Asia; the implications for Russia; and those for China (Shambaugh 2006: 88). It was also said that President Vladimir Putin warned Hu Jintao at a 2005 Shanghai Co-operation Organization meeting about the subversive potential of the international

NGOs; and partly as a result of this warning, the Chinese authorities began to scrutinize NGOs operating in China (Shambaugh 2006: 91).

Compared to ex-presidents Jiang and Hu, Xi has demonstrated much less willingness to tinker with the Party's authoritarian ideology or structure so as to accommodate at least some of the demands of an increasingly well-educated and sophisticated people. One of the most frequently repeated mantras of the Fifth-Generation leader was that cadres and the people alike must have "self-confidence in the path, theory, institutions and culture" of socialism with Chinese characteristics. As discussed in Chapter 2, "The Legacy of Mao Zeding," Xi has breathed new life into Maoist institutions and exploited the legacy of Mao Zedong to enhance the legitimacy of his administration and fill the ideological vacuum. The entire Politburo Standing Committee (PBSC) visited the Mao Mausoleum on the 120th anniversary of Mao's birthday in late 2011, on which occasion Xi emphasized that "we shall forever hold aloft the flag of Mao Zedong Thought."

Not unlike Mao, Xi has tried to concentrate all powers at the topmost echelons of the party – and in the hands of the party chief. Xi has himself appointed the heads of at least ten of the high-level decision-making central leading groups and commissions that are directly under the Politburo Standing Committee (see Chapter 5, "The Party Runs the Show"). At the end of April 2013, the Party Central Office released a notice on ideological issues which, among other things, severely attacked "historical nihilism." The latter referred to the denials and criticisms of the Party's established positions on various historical questions, especially the attacks on Mao and Mao Zedong Thought. These criticisms were seen as attempts to erode the legitimacy of Party leadership (Yen 2013).

Xi began to severely constrict intellectual freedom and freedom of expression with the publication of Central Document No. 9 in 2013, which set limits to discussions among university teachers and the official media. Topics including universal values, freedom of the media, civil society, civil rights, independence of the judiciary, the Party's historical mistakes and the power-elite bourgeois class became taboos (BBC in Chinese 2013). The level of control exercised by the Xi regime on academia, the media, cyber societies and NGOs is significantly tighter than at any time since the Tiananmen Square incident.

The formula applied by the Hu-Wen administration to maintain political stability was economic growth plus a basic social security net covering the entire population plus good governance in the absence of democracy (Cheng 2012). Maintaining an economic growth rate of about 6–7 percent per annum in the coming five years or so should not be too difficult because the central government has ample resources to spend on infrastructural projects and the economic takeoff has been spreading from the coastal to the interior provinces. Much of the new spending, however, has been bankrolled by loans: total social debt reached at least 280 percent of GDP in 2015, a level that is not considered sustainable. Moreover, while the central coffers seem to remain well-endowed, the bulk of grassroots-level administrations are facing solvency problems. As economic growth slows down, the Party regime requires compensatory measures to maintain its legitimacy.

The Xi administration realizes that corruption is a serious threat, and will continue to try to make the cadre corps clean and responsive to the people's needs and grievances. It is, however, a question mark as to whether cracking down on corruption alone can solve all the problems associated with the absence of democratic institutions. This is particularly given the fact that Xi and his close associates such as Wang Qishan, the director of the top graft-busting organ, the Central Commission for Discipline Inspection, seem to be using the "anti-corruption" card to take out or marginalize Xi's political foes. Xi's apparent failure to apply strict codes of clean governance to top cadres was evidenced by the failure of the Sixth Plenum of the Eighteenth

Central Committee in late 2016 in passing an assets-disclosure rule that will oblige all senior officials and their close kin to publicize their wealth.

Xi and his quasi-police state apparatus have also pulled out all the stops to constrict civil society, which is seen as a benevolent agent of change by liberal social scientists such as Yu Keping, a one-time adviser to ex-president Hu on political reform. In times of numbers, it can be argued that civil society has continued to grow. Li Fan's perhaps overly optimistic and exaggerated estimates are that China had in the early 2010s about 7–8 million social organizations (including house churches and all kinds of grassroots groups) involving about 300 million people, i.e., about one fifth of China's total population; he considers this a "progressive civil society population" (Kellogg 2012: 53). (See Chapter 22, "Changing Patterns of Chinese Civil Society: Comparing the Hu-Wen and the Xi Jinping Eras.") Yet it must be noted that the police has employed a scorched-earth policy to quash NGOs that are perceived to pose a threat to the Party regime. The Chinese authorities are particularly sensitive to the emergence of cross-provincial or even nationwide autonomous civic organizations. While in theory nationwide campaigns can be organized via the Internet, the newly established Central Leading Group for Cyberspace Affairs – also headed by Xi – has significantly tightened control over social media and other Internet vehicles. The window of opportunity for political reforms and accommodation with civil society seems to have become much narrower during his administration.

Conclusion

The CCP remains a quintessentially Leninist party as it stubbornly refuses to give up its monopoly of political power. It has been relying on economic growth and the improvement of people's living standards as its basis of legitimacy. Since the Hu-Wen administration, the Party regime has realized that economic growth alone is inadequate, and it has been trying to provide a basic social security net covering the entire population and the improvement of governance in the absence of democracy. The Xi administration has been exploiting the popularity of the combat of corruption.

These policies are probably sufficient for the time being because the bulk of the Chinese population has been enjoying substantial improvements in living standards in the past three decades and more and still expects further improvements in the years to come. More significant still, it perceives no credible alternative to the Party regime and fears chaos and uncertainties; this is why Chinese people are critical of corrupt officials but seldom protest against the Party regime itself. There is also a fundamental cost-benefit analysis: confronting the regime is very costly and the chance of success is extremely low up till today. Chinese leaders believe that regarding sources of unrest, they have to adopt prompt and decisive action to nip them in the bud.

Under such circumstances, expectations of gradual reforms from the above have faded, and grievances among the people accumulate even as civil society develops by fits and starts. Chinese leaders understand that they have to adjust their population policy well in advance so as to avoid severe consequences in the intermediate and long-term future; but they reveal no such wisdom concerning political reforms which have been conspicuously absent since the Tiananmen Incident. The suppression of human rights lawyers is especially significant because they have been trying to work within the legal framework promulgated by the Party regime. The spread of underground churches demonstrates the ideological vacuum and the emergence of autonomous labor groups seeking not only better pay, but better working conditions and career prospects for young workers reveal the impotence of the official trade union. Both groups have encountered crackdowns in recent years.

To fill the values and ideological vacuum, Chinese leaders have been trying to exploit nationalism which is a double-edged sword. They have turned to traditional religious beliefs, Confucianism and, to a lesser extent, Taoism, etc. which are not considered to pose a threat to the Party regime. These measures all have their limitations and they also have the undesirable effect of adding confusion and weakening the appeal of socialism.

As shown by the research efforts of the official think-tanks, Chinese leaders have been eager to learn the lessons of the fall of the Berlin Wall, the breakup of the Soviet Union, the "color revolutions" and the Arab Spring, but the obvious lessons learnt seem to be further strengthening of the Party's control over the military, the media and civil society. The sense of insecurity revealed does not correspond to the existing state of economic growth and political stability.

Since political stability is not expected to be seriously threatened in the short-term future, there is still a window of opportunity for important political reforms. Reforms have their own risks and may generate instability, but the long-term risks of avoiding reforms may be greater. The tendency of path-dependence, however, remains strong, and Xi Jinping's efforts to concentrate power in his own hands do not bode well for political reforms. This window of opportunity may gradually fade away as economic growth slows down and civil society goes on strengthening despite repeated clampdowns.

Notes

1 For the English text of the resolution, see *Resolution on CCP History (1949–81)*, Beijing: Foreign Languages Press, 1981, pp. 1–86.
2 For an analysis of the student demonstrations in December 1986, see the author's "Following the Traditions of Half a Century," *Sunday Morning Post* (Hong Kong), December 28, 1986.
3 For the text of Zhao Ziyang's report entitled "Advance Along the Road of Socialism with Chinese Characteristics," see *Zhongguo Gongchandang Dishisan Jie Quanguo Daibiao Dahui Wenjian Huibian (A Compendium of the Documents of the Thirteenth National Congress of the Chinese Communist Party)*, Beijing: Renmin Chubanshe, 1987, pp. 41–59. See also Willy Wo-lap Lam, *The Era of Zhao Ziyang*, Hong Kong: A.B. Books & Stationery (International) Ltd., 1989, pp. 203–206.
4 Jiang Zemin delivered his report to the Party Congress on October 12, 1992. In Section Seven of Chapter Two of his report, he elaborated his ideas on administrative reforms. See *Wen Wei Po* (a pro-Beijing Chinese newspaper in Hong Kong), October 13, 1992, pp. 19–20.
5 For the text of the communique, see *Renmin Ribao* (*People's Daily*), September 29, 1994.
6 For the text of Jiang Zemin's speech on the eightieth anniversary of the establishment of the CCP, see *Renmin Ribao*, July 2, 2001.
7 See Jiang Zemin's speech on the eightieth anniversary of the establishment of the Chinese Communist Party, *Renmin Ribao*, July 2, 2001.

References

BBC in Chinese (2013) "Xi Jinping xinzheng: qibujiang hou youyou shiliutiao" (Xi Jinping's New Policy on "Seven Unmentionables"), May 28. Available at: www.bbc.com/zhongwen/trad/china/2013/05/130528_china_thought_control_youth (accessed on October 25, 2016).

Beijing Review (1993) "Political Reforms, Next Target," 36 (51), December 21–27, p. 4.

Burns, J. (1994) "Strengthening Central CCP Control of Leadership Selection: The 1990 Nomenclatura," *The China Quarterly*, 138, pp. 461–463.

Cheng, J. (1989) "Introduction: China's Modernization Programme in the 1980s," in Cheng, J. (ed.) *China: Modernization in the 1980s*. Hong Kong: The Chinese University Press.

Cheng, J. (1995) "Organizational Reforms in Local Government in Guangdong," in Cheng, J. and MacPherson, S. (eds.) *Development in Southern China*. Hong Kong: Longman, pp. 38–63.

Cheng, J. (2012) "Challenges for Hu-Wen and Their Successors: Consolidating the 'Beijing Consensus' Model," in Cheng, J. (ed.) *China – A New Stage Development for an Emerging Superpower*. Hong Kong: City University of Hong Kong Press, pp. 1–53.

Cheng, J. and Ngok, K. (2004) "Nationalism and Sino-US Relations: The NATO Bombing of the Chinese Embassy in Belgrade," in Liew, L. and Wang, S. (eds.) *Nationalism, Democracy and National Integration in China*. London: Routledge-Curzon, pp. 85–104.
Delfs, R. (1987) "Ideological Inconsistencies and in Search of Socialist Theory," *Far Eastern Economic Review*, 138 (41), October 8, pp. 50–52.
Deng, X. (1984a) "The 'Two Whatevers' Are Not in Accord with Marxism," in Deng, X. (ed.) *Selected Works of Deng Xiaoping, 1975–82*. Beijing: Foreign Languages Press, pp. 51–52.
Deng, X. (1984b) "On the Reform of the Leadership Systems of the Party and the State," in Deng, X. (ed.) *Selected Works of Deng Xiaoping, 1975–82*. Beijing: Foreign Languages Press, pp. 302–325.
Deng, X. (1984c) "Uphold the Four Basic Principles," in Deng, X. (ed.) *Selected Works of Deng Xiaoping, 1975–82*. Beijing: Foreign Languages Press, pp. 166–191.
GOV.cn (2005) "Wen: Explains Proposal on 11th 5-year Plan." Available at: www.gov.cn/english/2005-10/20/content_80097.htm (accessed on October 25, 2016).
Harding, H. (1997) "The Chinese State in Crisis, 1966–9," in MacFarquhar, R (ed.) *The Politics of China: The Eras of Mao and Deng*. 2nd edn. New York: Cambridge University Press, pp. 148–247.
Hartford, K. (1989) "Repression and Communist Success: The Case of Jin-Cha-Ji, 1938–1943," in Hartford, K. and Goldstein, S. (eds.) *Single Sparks: China's Rural Revolutions*. Armonk, NY: M.E. Sharpe, pp. 97–112.
Harwit, E. (2001) "The Impact of WTO Membership on the Automobile Industry in China," *The China Quarterly*, 67, pp. 573–670.
Henan Ribao (Zhengzhou) (2001) "Zhongguo Gongchandang Xinshiji de Zhengzhi Xuanyan-Xuexi Jiang Zemin Tongzhi 'Qiyi' Jianghua Fang" (The Political Declaration of the Communist Party of China for the New Century – Interview – on Studying Comrade Jiang Zemin's Talk on July 1), August 25.
Hicks, G. (ed.) (1990) *The Broken Mirror: China After Tiananmen*. Harlow: Longman.
Kellogg, T. (2012) "Western Funding for Rule of Law Initiatives in China: The Importance of a Civil Society Based Approach," *China Perspectives*, 92 (3), pp. 53–59.
Lo, C. (1995) *China's Legal Awakening: Legal Theory and Criminal Justice in Deng's Era*. Hong Kong: Hong Kong University Press.
MacFarquhar, R. (1974) *The Origins of the Cultural Revolution 1: Contradictions among the People 1956–1957*. New York: Columbia University Press.
MacFarquhar, R. (1997) "The Succession to Mao and the End of Maoism, 1969–82," in MacFarquhar, R. (ed.) *The Politics of China: The Eras of Mao and Deng*. 2nd edn. New York: Cambridge University Press, pp. 248–340.
Mainland Affairs Council, Republic of China (Taiwan) (2006) *Dalu Qingshi Guibao (Mainland China Situation)*. January issue. Available at: www.mac.gov.tw/ct.asp?xItem=51291&ctNode=5603&mp=1&xq_xCat=2006 (accessed on October 25, 2016).
Schram, S. (1984) "'Economics in Command?' Ideology and Policy since the Third Plenum, 1978–84," *The China Quarterly*, 99, pp. 417–461.
Shambaugh, D. (2006) *China's Communist Party – Atrophy and Adaptation*. Washington, DC: Woodrow Wilson Centre Press, and Berkeley, CA: University of California Press.
Shum, K. (1988) *The Chinese Communists' Road to Power: The Anti-Japanese United Front (1935–45)*. Hong Kong: Oxford University Press.
South China Morning Post (2002) "Farmers' Pension Scheme Studied," October 16.
South China Morning Post (2006) "Social Unrest Just a Phase, Police Say," February 8.
Sun, Q. (2014) "Dang ban ganbu yao yi 'Wuge Jianchi' lizhi luji" ("Party Cadres Should Use the 'Five Insistances' to Encourage Their Spirit and Discipline Themselves"), *People's Daily*, December 18. Available at: http://cpc.people.com.cn/n/2014/1218/c225450-26233508.html.
Teiwes, F. (1997) "The Establishment and Consolidation of the New Regime, 1949–57," in MacFarquhar, R. (ed.) *The Politics of China: The Eras of Mao and Deng*. 2nd edn. New York: Cambridge University Press, pp. 5–86.
Teiwes, F. (2000) "The Chinese State during the Maoist Era," in Shambaugh, D. (ed.) *The Modern Chinese State*. Cambridge and New York: Cambridge University Press, pp. 105–160.
Whiting, A. (1995) "Chinese Nationalism and Foreign Policy after Deng," *The China Quarterly*, pp. 295–316.
Yen, H. (2013) "Xi Jinping Zuo 'Diwang Mang'" (Xi Jinjing Making His 'Emperor Dream'), open.com.hk, June 6. Available at: www.open.com.hk/content.php?id=1339#.UteoPdlW3To (accessed on October 25, 2016).

10
THE CCP'S MERITOCRATIC CADRE SYSTEM

Akio Takahara

Introduction

A key to understanding China is to understand its bureaucracy. On top of the world's oldest bureaucratic tradition, the Chinese Communist Party (CCP) that came to power in 1949 has developed an extensive network of party organizations and cadres that reaches almost every nook and corner of the country. To this day, party and government cadres enjoy outstanding power and authority in society. In addition, under the planning system, all the non-political organizations and their staff, including for example universities and their professors or enterprises and their clerks, were stratified in parallel with the bureaucratic hierarchy. Compared to other societies, a prominent characteristic of Chinese society is the high degree to which it is bureaucratized.

Under the hyper-bureaucratized system, the question of cadre selection and appointment is of utmost importance. It constitutes the core of what the CCP calls the "organizational policy line" (*zuzhi luxian*), and relates to its ideology and policy direction. Thus, what kind of people should be selected and appointed, and how they should be selected and appointed, have been the focus of intense contention within the CCP. This chapter will discuss the development of the CCP's meritocratic cadre system in the post-Cultural Revolution era, with a view to analyzing its political factors.

Developments under Deng Xiaoping's leadership in the wake of the Cultural Revolution

When the Chinese leadership changed course in the wake of the Cultural Revolution and decided that economic development should be its primary task, one point of contention among the leaders was the cadre selection and appointment system. As was the case with other contentious issues such as the choice between marketization or planning, there was disagreement between Deng Xiaoping on one side and Chen Yun on the other. The disagreement between the two reflected the difference in their ideologies or policy tendencies. As regards the standards for cadres' selection and appointment, they agreed that cadres must be equipped with both "*de*" – virtue, and "*cai*" – talent, but differed over which should take priority.

According to Deng Xiaoping, the CCP needed to transform itself into a troop of cadres who were younger (*nianqing hua*), more intellectual (*zhishi hua*), and more professional (*zhuanye hua*).

Later, he added another requirement, to be more revolutionary (*geming hua*), and placed it on the top of the list, but it was clear to all that Deng attached more importance to merit than politics. Under this principle, what was dubbed the productive forces standard (*shengchan li biaozhun*) was introduced in selecting and appointing the cadres.

On the other hand, Chen Yun consistently argued that priority must be given to virtue. As early as 1940, when Chen was in charge of party cadre management as Director of the Central Organization Department, he stipulated that the standard for selecting cadres must be, "virtue and talent are both important, but virtue is primary" (*de cai bing zhong, yi de wei zhu*). He repeated this position in 1987, using the phrase that, "[a cadre should be] equipped with both virtue and talent, but still virtue should come first" (*de cai jianbei, de haishi diyi*).

This difference in the point of emphasis was reflected in their understanding of what virtue meant. Deng stated that the mainstay of virtue was to uphold the socialist road and party leadership, two of the four basic political principles that he advocated as the foundation of CCP rule (the other two were the democratic dictatorship of the people and Marxism-Leninism and Mao Zedong Thought). Upholding these principles was supposedly not so difficult for any party cadre. For Chen Yun, however, virtue implied a more rigorous political integrity as a party member (*dang xing*).

Such difference was to some extent reminiscent of the argument over the "professional" (*zhuan*) and the "red" (*hong*) in Mao Zedong's days. Although Mao said cadres must be both red and professional, he later downgraded the professionals and persecuted them in the Cultural Revolution. In the 1980s, however, the leaders that were inclined to increasing productivity, such as Deng and Premier Zhao Ziyang, promoted the role of professionals and placed them in positions with responsibility. In contrast, those cadres engaged in political work were gradually marginalized. After all, economic construction had been defined as the primary task of the CCP.

Besides the primacy of talent, there was another important development in the 1980s, which was the institutionalization of cadre promotion advocated by Deng Xiaoping. In January 1986, the party center issued the Circular on Selecting and Appointing Cadres Strictly According to Party Principles. This Circular pointed out that there were many problems in the selection and appointment of cadres at that time, such as favoritism, nepotism, bribery, and corruption (Zhonggong Zhongyang Zuzhi Bu 1995: 19–24). It set the procedure for the selection and appointment of leading cadres as follows: first, democratic recommendations, that is to collect opinions widely and nominate the candidates for the selection; second, after an investigation by the organization and personnel department, the party committee will make a decision after a collective discussion, and report to the upper level; third, the organization department of the upper level party committee will investigate further, and then send the case to the party committee on that level for discussion and approval.

It is intriguing that in the first stage of democratic recommendations, the Circular stated that a secret voting system should be adopted, and that those who do not get the support of the majority of the people in the workplace or the district should not be promoted. At the same time, it said they should avoid simply choosing people by the number of votes they get. As regards the standards for the investigation in the second and the third stages, the Circular said that virtue (*de*), ability (*neng*), diligence (*qin*), and achievement (*ji*) should be enquired historically and in an overall manner. It called on to pay attention to the performance (*biaoxian*) during the Cultural Revolution and since the Third Plenum of the 11th Central Committee in December 1978, and to investigate carefully the achievements in work in the past few years. In evaluating work achievements, the Circular stated that they should carefully discover and appoint those who could creatively execute the policies of the party and effectively initiate a new phase in their work.

The Circular stated that skipping a rank in promotion was only allowed in cases in which the cadres were excellent and the works were especially necessary. In order to strengthen supervision, the Circular stipulated a special procedure for the "princelings," that is children of the main leading cadres of the party center, the National People's Congress, the State Council, the Central Military Commission, the Central Advisory Commission, the Central Commission for Discipline and Inspection, and the Chinese People's Political Consultative Conference. If they were to be promoted to the position of county level or above by skipping a rank, all of the cases had to be reported to and be inspected by the Central Organization Department, and be approved by the Central Secretariat. The children of the provincial (ministerial) level cadres who were to be promoted by skipping a rank had to be reported to and be approved by the Central Organization Department (or the provincial/ministerial party committees if their parents were deputies). Nepotism and "princelings" were already an issue in the mid-1980s.

From the contents of the January 1986 Circular we can judge that this policy of cadre appointment reflected the needs of the early phase of systemic reform in the post-Cultural Revolution era. However, many problems arose in the implementation process. Half a year later, the July 1986 document issued by the Central Organization Department on the implementation of the Circular reprimanded those cadres that failed to digest the spirit of the document and did not seriously implement it (Zhonggong Zhongyang Zuzhi Bu ... 1995: 26–31).

The June 4th Incident (or the Second Tiananmen Incident) in 1989 brought about new policies. First, the Central Organization Department announced that cadres who fell into the following categories were resolutely disqualified from promotion: those with "bourgeois liberalization thought," weak party integrity, and lacking in the idea of party leadership; and those who committed serious mistakes during the "struggle to prevent turmoil and anti-revolutionary rebellion," i.e., the June 4th Incident in official terms (Zhonggong Zhongyang Zuzhi Bu 1995: 54).

As regards the standards for promotion and appointment, the conservative Premier Li Peng stated in August 1989 at the National Conference of Organization Department Directors that the "four more" standards introduced by Deng Xiaoping has aspects worth reconsidering (Liao *et al.* 1991: 998–999). The Party Central Circular on Strengthening Party Construction, which was published six days after this National Conference, stated the following: in selecting and appointing cadres, we must emphasize the political stance, ideological character, leadership abilities, and work achievements of the cadres, and prevent and check the erroneous tendency of stressing age and diploma; we cannot use "the productive forces standard" as a substitute to the principle of having both virtue and talent, and we must prevent paying more attention to talent and less to virtue (Zhonggong Zhongyang Wenxian Yanjiushi 1991: 591). In the surge of conservatism, Regulations on Workers' Evaluation were adopted by the State Council in July 1990, in which "thought and political expression" (*sixiang zhengzhi biaoxian*) was reinstated as the top standard for evaluation. Against this tide, one of the famous Huangfu Ping articles published in the Shanghai-based *Liberation Daily* in the spring of 1991 argued, "Be bold and let into the new leading organizations those who are acknowledged by the people as cadres that have upheld the line of reform and opening and made achievements at work" (Huangfu Ping 1991). This line in the original article was in quotation marks and was most likely a direct quote of Deng Xiaoping. However, Huangfu Ping articles were criticized in Beijing, and in December 1991, then Director of the Central Organization Department Lü Feng stated that "priority should be given to virtue over talent."[1] This statement was most significant since the crucially important 14th Party Congress was approaching, in which there were to be major changes in personnel at the high levels of party leadership. It likely constituted an important factor in urging Deng Xiaoping to take the "southern tour" and restore the policies of reform and opening in early 1992.

Developments under Jiang Zemin's leadership after the 1992 14th Party Congress

After the Southern Tour by Deng Xiaoping and the revival of economic reform and opening policies in 1992, the first significant development in the cadre system was the introduction of the civil service system that took place in 1993. The "Temporary Regulations on State Civil Servants" stated that its purpose was to realize the scientific management of civil servants, to guarantee their quality and incorruptibility, and to increase administrative efficiency (Zhonggong Zhongyang Zuzhi Bu 1995: 124). In the original blueprint presented by Zhao Ziyang at the 13th Party Congress in 1987, there was to be a distinction between the political civil servants and the administrative civil servants. This could have led to the development of a politically neutral civil service. However, no distinction was made this time. Civil servants were to be evaluated comprehensively according to their virtue (*de*), ability (*neng*), diligence (*qin*), and achievement (*ji*), with an emphasis on their achievements at work. When the Temporary Regulations were made into the Civil Servants Law and took effect in 2006, incorruptibility (*lian*) was added to the items for evaluation. Also, "to guarantee the legal rights and interests of the civil servants" was added as a purpose of the legislation.

It was an intriguing compromise of the two driving forces of cadre system reforms that occasioned the introduction of the civil service system four years after the June 4th Incident. First, there was the modernization drive to institutionalize the cadre system for more efficiency, predictability, protection of cadres' rights, and their cleanness. The surge of reforms in the wake of Deng Xiaoping's Southern Tour must have promoted this current. Second, there was the conservative drive to tighten the control of the CCP leadership over the cadres. The new civil service system was to cater to these two requirements at the same time. In other policy areas as well, discord over the balance between reform and continuity proved to be a central theme in Chinese politics while Jiang Zemin held the reins of power.

The communique of the Fourth Plenum of the 14th Party Central Committee in September 1994 announced that the transfer of power from the second generation of the party leadership to the third generation was completed. Now, Jiang Zemin was at the helm on his own. In the following month, the Central Organization Department issued a circular on checking the unhealthy tendencies in the selection and appointment of cadres. The listed malpractices included: favoritism by the leading cadres, including the practice of taking cadres from the original districts and workplaces to where he/she was newly appointed, and taking the opportunity and promoting his/her spouse or children; allowing subordinates craving for positions to establish underhand connections; and not following the rules on democratic recommendation and arbitrarily making decisions by oneself or among a small number of people (Zhonggong Zhongyang Zuzhi Bu 1995: 148–151). This circular looked as if it was a conservative critique against Jiang, who had promoted so many cadres from Shanghai, his previous place of work, to important positions in the central government.

Then in February 1995 the Temporary Regulations on Selecting and Appointing Leading Cadres in Party and Government was issued as a measure to establish a scientific and standardized system for cadre selection and appointment (Zhonggong Zhongyang Zuzhi Bu 1995: 152–165). It stipulated the principles and procedures for democratic recommendation (*minzhu tuijian*), investigation (*kaocha*), preliminary discussion (*yunniang*), and discussion and decision (*taolun jueding*). In selecting the leading cadres, certain qualifications were required. For example: for county (division) class leading positions, over five years of service and over two years of work at the basic level (*jiceng*); for leading positions of county (division) level or above, having served two or more positions at one level below; generally an educational background of and above the junior college level (*daxue zhuanke*), and for provincial (ministerial) level leading cadres, an educational background of and above university undergraduate level (*daxue benke*); having gone through training at party schools, administrative schools, or other training organizations for three months or longer.

One point worth mentioning in this period was the debate over who should nominate and appoint cadres in the enterprises. The 1992 14th Party Congress officially adopted the policy to establish a socialist market economy, and the 1994 Corporation Law stipulated that the top executives would be appointed at the general meeting of shareholders and provided the management with power over personnel affairs. This clashed squarely with the long-standing organizational principle, "the party assuming responsibility for cadres' affairs (*dang guan ganbu*)," which also applied to state-owned enterprises (SOEs). Parallel to this was the debate over ownership reforms, in which it was argued that privatization was necessary to increase efficiency.

Against this background the conservatives in the Central Organization Department insisted that more importance should be attached to virtue than ability. According to the Director of the Organization Department Zhang Quanjing, "to be more revolutionary" should be given top priority among the "four mores" in the training and appointment of young leaders. The struggle over organizational principles intensified before the 15th Party Congress in 1997. The Central Organization Department succeeded in issuing the Party Central Fourth Document in 1997 on Strengthening Party Construction in the SOEs, which emphasized the central role of party committees in SOE management. At the Party Congress, however, Zhang Quanjing failed in the election to become a member of the central committee.

The debate over ownership reforms was won by those who argued for de facto privatization. At the fourth Plenum of the 15th Party Central Committee in 1999, the CCP decided to stop talking about the quantitative majority of state-owned assets as a condition for maintaining a public ownership system. It meant that except for key sectors of the national economy such as infrastructure, finance, and the defense industry, private capital could occupy the majority of assets in other sectors. This revolutionary shift in ownership policy was followed by an extraordinary admission of private enterprise owners into the Party in 2001. At the 16th Party Congress held the following year, the party charter was amended and the CCP identified itself as the vanguard of both the Chinese working class and of the Chinese people and the Chinese nation. This metamorphosis was justified ideologically by the Important Thought of "Three Represents": CCP must represent the requirements for developing China's advanced productive forces, the orientation of China's advanced culture, and the fundamental interests of the overwhelming majority of the Chinese people, which included private enterprise owners.

Against the expectation of the Central Organization Department, however, private enterprise owners did not join the party in a big way. Some joined expecting that they would have quicker access to information. But others apparently found party membership burdensome, since there were various disciplinary requirements that came with it. In addition, investigation in the admission process was stricter for the owners of private enterprises than in other cases, since "the situation of private enterprise owners is rather complicated, and their qualities could not but be uneven" (Ben Shu Bianxie Zu 2003: 181–182). It was said that the following points needed attention: (1) we cannot substitute the productive forces standard for the party member standard. We cannot increase their admission into the party because they are good at making money and have contributed in a big way to the local economy; (2) in developing party membership among private enterprise owners, we must proceed prudently. We cannot rush headlong into mass action, and must uphold the standards and must not be content with the second best; (3) we must conduct a long-term test and an all-round examination. This indicates that, naturally, there was repulsion within the party against the admission of capitalists.

Since 1992, the CCP has promoted marketization in a big way. As a result, the socialist socio-political system changed substantially, aggravating the contradiction between socialist principles and CCP policy. The CCP has dealt with this issue by adapting its ideology to reality, but that could not but strain the relationship among the party members.

Finally, it is worth noting that the Tentative Regulations on Appraising Party and Government Leading Cadres were issued by the Central Organization Department after the approval of the Party Center in May 1998. This is because they specifically stipulated the content of the appraisal, especially that of the achievements of the leading group (*lingdao banzi*) of the party and government of and above county level. The achievements to be appraised included the following: completion of indicated targets in economic work, speed, efficiency, and delayed effect of economic development, and the rate of growth in fiscal revenue and the degree of increase in people's living standards; developments in education, science and technology, culture, sanitation, and sports activities, and the conditions in environmental and ecological protection, population and family planning, and safety and security; results in party work including ideology, organization, style of work, and institution building (Zhongyang Bangong Ting Fagui Shi 2001: 218). Although economic indices were placed at the top of the list, these items reflected the idea that an all-round development was necessary for China. This precisely was the thinking that was to be developed by the next party leader, Hu Jintao.

Developments under Hu Jintao's leadership

Towards the end of Jiang Zemin's reign, in March 2000, Jiang appointed his closest aide, Zeng Qinghong, to lead the Central Organization Department. Most likely Jiang's important aim was to realize a personnel arrangement in his favor at the 16th Party Congress in 2002. However, Zeng's immediate boss at the post was Hu Jintao, the member of the Standing Committee of the Politburo in charge of party organizational affairs. In fact, the working relationship between Hu and Zeng was not so bad. Three months after Zeng's appointment, the Central Organization Department issued the 2001–2010 Outline of Deepening the Reform of the Cadre and Personnel Systems (Zhongyang Bangong Ting Fagui Shi 2001: 261–271).

The focal point of the outline was to deepen the reform of the selection and appointment system, about which several points were listed: (1) improve the democratic recommendation and evaluation system; (2) promote the public announcement of leading cadres of and below prefectural (bureau) level prior to their selection and appointment; (3) promote the open selection of leading cadres; (4) improve the election system of leading cadres; (5) implement the tenure system (*renqi zhi*) of leading cadres (note that they included the party as well as the government leading cadres); (6) implement the trial period system of leading cadres; (7) implement the resignation system of leading cadres; (8) further improve the system to remove the cadres unfit for their posts; (9) establish and improve the systems related to the cultivation and selection of female, minority, and non-CCP cadres; (10) revise the Temporary Regulations on Selecting and Appointing Leading Cadres in Party and Government and draw up related laws and regulations. In fact, this Outline was based on experiments conducted by the Central Organization Department after the introduction of the Temporary Regulations in 1995.

The Regulations on Selecting and Appointing Leading Cadres in Party and Government were adopted accordingly in 2002 (Falü Chubanshe Fagui Zhongxin 2005: 38–53). There was a small but important change from the Temporary Regulations adopted seven years before. The Temporary Regulations had stated that the principles of selection and appointment were: (1) the party assuming responsibility for cadres' affairs; (2) being equipped with both virtue and talent, appointing people on merit; (3) being approved by the masses, paying attention to achievements; (4) open, equal, competitive, and selecting the better; (5) democratic centralism; (6) conducting affairs according to the regulations. In the 2002 Regulations, all the principles were the same, except item (2). That is, the order of the two criteria listed in item (2) was switched and the new principle was: (2) appointing people on merit, being equipped with both virtue and talent. Change in the order of words is important in CCP's documents, as it signifies a shift in policy priority. The Central Organization Department had found that a major problem in the implementation of the Temporary Regulations remained to be the practice of favoritism and nepotism. Pursuing fairness through the introduction of competition was regarded as most important in developing the meritocratic cadre system at the time.

The structure of the selection process was the same as the Temporary Regulations. That is, it begins with democratic recommendation, followed by preliminary discussion, investigation, and discussion and decision. However, this time the procedure was stipulated in more detail. For example, the democratic recommendation process, including a recommendation meeting, will be presided over by the organization department of the upper level party committee. Before deciding who would proceed to investigation, there will be a process of preliminary discussion by a working committee chaired by the party secretary and consultation between the standing committee of the party committee and the upper level organization department. It will be the party committee, or its standing committee if the party committee is not in session, that makes the final decision. It was newly stipulated that the result of democratic recommendation constituted one of the important bases in deciding who will go through to investigation. In the investigation, candidates were to be investigated comprehensively on virtue, ability, diligence, achievement, and also incorruptibility, which was newly added. As was the case with the Temporary Regulations, attention was to be paid to work achievements.

What was completely new in the 2002 Regulations was the introduction of open selection (*gongkai xuanba*) and competition for internal promotion (*jingzheng shanggang*) as ways of selection and appointment. These methods were to be applied mainly to the selection and appointment of local party committees and government departments. Their procedures were as follows: (1) announce the post, qualifications for application, basic procedures and methods, etc.; (2) receive applications and check the qualifications; (3) unified examination (democratic assessment is compulsory in the case of competition for internal promotion); (4) organizational investigation, submission of candidate; (5) discussion and decision by the party committee (or the party small group).

Accordingly, many kinds of experiments were conducted at the localities and departments. The experimented systems could be categorized roughly into three types: first, systems in which examination and investigation constituted the main part; second, systems in which recommendation and election constituted the main part; and third, systems in which competition constituted the main part (Wang and Li 2016).

A typical system of the first type was "public recommendation and public election" (*gongtui gongxuan*). An exemplar case of selecting a head of a county in Jiangsu Province had the following procedure consisting of six parts: (1) application and qualification check, through which 70 people passed; (2) two rounds of democratic recommendation by cadres above certain levels, which reduced the number to 12, and then to 6; (3) the 6 preliminary candidates went down to the basic level and took part in discussions, and then wrote study reports in eight hours' time; (4) the candidates gave speeches and answered questions, an evaluation committee marked them and a public opinion evaluation group filled in the evaluation sheet; then the assessments of the study report, speech and Q&A, and public evaluation were aggregated with the weight of 30 percent, 30 percent, and 40 percent, respectively, resulting in an ordered list of names; (5) the organization department of the provincial party committee inspected and presented a proposal to the prefectural party committee; (6) all the members of the prefectural party committee voted and elected the final candidate. The elected person must go through an election again at the county people's congress formally to become the head of the county (Zhang 2014: 36).

A typical system of the second type of experiments was "public recommendation and direct election" (*gongtui zhixuan*), which was mainly used in selecting village and township party secretaries. Under this system, the public would recommend a candidate from among the party members, or cast a vote of confidence in the candidates presented by the party organization. Those candidates that received relatively low votes would be sifted out. There could be qualification investigation and/or a written examination also. Then, there would be speeches by the remaining candidates and Q&A, followed by direct voting by all the party members, irrespective of rank (Zhang 2014: 36). And in the third type of experiments, competitive written examinations and interviews were conducted, together with speeches followed by direct election by all the party members, or evaluation by an evaluation committee (Wang and Li 2016).

In fact, there were a lot of varieties among the experiments at localities, and the above are only typical examples. But the basic idea was common to all. That is, there should be more transparency, competition, and strict implementation of the procedures. Another element was democratization, in contrast to the widespread practice of "one person, namely, the secretary of the party committee, alone has the say." Whether these targets were met or not will be discussed in a later section, but Hu Jintao and Li Yuanchao, who succeeded He Guoqiang as Director of the Central Organization Department in 2007, tried to design their cadre selection and appointment policies in a way that would contribute to achieving their goal of building a harmonious society. Even before the appointment of Li, "Tentative Regulations on the Term of Office of Party and Government Cadres" was issued by the General Office of the CCP Central Committee in the summer of 2006. The Regulations stipulated that the tenure of both party and government posts was five years, and that after serving in the same post for two terms leading cadres of departments in both party and government would not be recommended, nominated, or appointed again (Xinhua Net 2006).[2]

Another important measure introduced in a similar spirit was "democratic recommendation" for the next Politburo members that took place several months before the party congresses in 2007 and 2012. Over four hundred top level party cadres, mostly full and alternate members of the central committee, were gathered at the Central Party School and distributed a voting sheet, on which around two hundred people were listed. They consisted mainly of cadres of chief ministerial level and commander/political commissar level of military regions, of and under the age of 63. The voting results were taken into account in preparing the final list of names for the top positions.[3] Although organizational investigation followed and behind-the-scenes discussions that involved retired party elders developed and finalized the list, introduction of the voting system seemed to be an important step forward in institutionalizing the transfer of power.

The idea to build a harmonious society was also reflected in Hu Jintao's 2008 declaration that in selecting cadres, they should uphold the principle of "be equipped with both virtue and talent, but virtue comes first" (*de cai jianbei, yi de weixian*). Li Yuanchao provided the following reasons why they had to heighten the level of cadres' virtue and present a stricter demand for it: (1) under the influence of western values and concepts, conviction about socialism with Chinese characteristics has been shaken among a small number of cadres; (2) that year saw the eruption of large scale mass disturbances in some localities, grave accidents in production and food safety, and in many cases they were related to the existence of cadres who lacked the sense of serving the people and the sense of responsibility; (3) being in power for a long period, combined with the development of a market economy, has caused corruption and degeneration among some party cadres; (4) when the masses hold objection against the cadres, it is usually about their "virtue," and not about their "talent." Thus, Li argued that they should clarify the standards and improve the mechanism for evaluating cadres' virtue in a comprehensive way. He also stated that in selecting cadres, the selection could not be based simply on the number of votes, age, educational background, or speeches (Li Yuanchao 2008).

In order to avoid corruption and favoritism and build a harmonious society, Hu Jintao and Li Yuanchao attempted to institutionalize the selection and appointment process and introduced the element of competition. However, the effect of their endeavor was far from ideal. This problem was to become a focus of party rectification under the leadership of the next leader, Xi Jinping.

Developments under Xi Jinping's leadership

What took place after Xi Jinping assumed the position of general secretary was a general denial of democratic recommendation and competition. In June 2013, at the National Organization Work Conference, Xi Jinping presented his "five standards of good cadres": having firm conviction; serving the people; diligent and pragmatic; eager in taking challenges; and clean and honest. These "standards" were rather abstract, and Xi did not advocate for the competitive selection of cadres. This was in stark contrast to the report of the 17th CCP Central Committee to the 18th Party Congress the previous year, in which Hu Jintao had emphasized that the party would perfect the competitive system of selecting cadres.

In November 2013, the "Decision of the CCP Central Committee on Some Major Issues Concerning Comprehensively Deepening Reforms," passed at the Third Plenary Meeting of the 18th CCP Central Committee, included deepening reforms of the cadre and personnel system. It emphasized strengthening the weight of the party committee, the leading cadre in charge, and the organization department in selecting and appointing cadres. The "Decision" also stressed that the phenomenon of selecting people just by votes or by exam points had to be resolutely corrected (Ben Shu Bianxie Zu 2015: 89). As a result, the party center stopped openly encouraging public examinations and public elections with a view to strengthening party leadership over cadre and personnel work, and the practice of public elections came to an end. This meant that the selection and appointment of cadres were internalized with little competition, and that the top leader of the party organization possessed the decision-making power over personnel affairs (Wang and Li 2016).

In the revised Regulations on Selecting and Appointing Leading Cadres in Party and Government, promulgated in January 2014, there still was a chapter devoted to open selection and competition for internal promotion. However, they were restricted to special cases only. Again, although it was still stated that democratic recommendation was compulsory in selecting and appointing cadres, such recommendation only constituted an "important reference." This was a marked change from the 2002 version of the Regulations, which indicated that democratic recommendation would form "one of the important bases" in deciding who will go through to "investigation," the next stage of cadre selection.

The factors that brought about this policy shift included the following (Zhang 2014: 38; Wang and Li 2016). First, the new leadership was not happy about the fact that open competition and election reduced the control of the party organization over the selection of cadres. The party's organization departments originally had the right to recommend and nominate the candidates, but that right was shared with a larger scope of cadres or with the masses. The person that was considered by the organization department as the best choice for nomination did not necessarily succeed in the selection process. Those who were elected would consider themselves to have a stronger democratic legitimacy than those at the upper level, and contradictions could occur between upper and lower level party committees or governments.

Second, there were other problems in open competitions and elections. One was the high cost that they involved, because of the complex and lengthy procedures. Another was the phenomenon that those who did well in exams and elections were not necessarily capable of getting things done once they were in their positions. This was partly caused by the low degree of openness, or unscientific exam questions, or discrimination against the selected cadres who came from other districts or provinces. It was also feared that elections would prompt some cadres to spend much time and energy in currying favor with other cadres, leading to the formation of factions.

There were other questions about the meritocratic system that had been pursued under Hu Jintao's leadership. For example, research found that the link between economic performance (GDP and revenue growth) and promotion was strong for lower level governments, but insignificant for provincial cadres (Landry *et al.* 2016). In addition, the anti-corruption drive by Xi Jinping revealed the astronomical scale of corruption prevalent among party cadres, including the selling and purchasing of official positions. Although the reforms made under Hu Jintao's leadership were supposed to prevent this, they clearly failed to achieve their purpose.

The new policies are giving the impression that Xi Jinping is using the selection and appointment system to promote his political interests. In the new version of Some Guiding Principles for Inner-Party Political Life under New Circumstances, passed at the Sixth Plenum of the CCP Central Committee in October 2016, there was a section on the selection and appointment of cadres. It emphasized that the erroneous tendency of selecting people just by votes, exam points, GDP, or age, had to be resolutely corrected (Xinhua Net 2016). Adding the element of age was interpreted by some as the precursor to the reappointment of Wang Qishan, the entrusted leader and implementer of the anti-corruption drive, who would have exceeded the widely acknowledged retirement age of 68 for Central Committee members at the time of the 19th Party Congress. In fact, the General Office of the Central Committee, headed by Xi Jinping's trusted confidant Li Zhanshu, had already issued in July 2015 Some Trial Regulations on Advancing the Promotion and Demotion of Leading Cadres (Zhongyang Zhengfu Menhu Wangzhan 2015). These regulations indicated that the cadres who reached the age limit had to resign or retire according to fixed procedures. However, it was also stipulated that, if the cadre was really needed for the work, the party committee (or party group) should look into it and submit its views to the upper level party committee for approval.

In addition, the vagueness of the "five standards of good cadres" seems to have opened the way for Xi Jinping to aggressively promote his former subordinates in Fujian or Zhejiang with rather modest credentials. A similar phenomenon of favoritism has happened before with previous top leaders as well. Jiang Zemin's Shanghai Faction (*Shanghai bang*) and Hu Jintao's Communist Youth League clique (*tuan pai*) thrived during the reign of their bosses. However, since Xi was elevated to the party center at a relatively late stage of his career, unlike his predecessors he does not have a large pool of trusted subordinates among the party and government bureaucracies in Beijing. Such concern of factional politics could have been a factor in his negation of institutionalizing the cadre selection and appointment process, and in strongly demanding the party members to be loyal to the "core" of the central party leadership, the position to which he was promoted at the Sixth Plenum of the 18th Central Committee of the CCP in October 2016.

Conclusion

In sum, we can identify three major factors in the post-Cultural Revolution development of the system for the selection and appointment of cadres. First, there is the modernization drive that promotes institutionalization and openness for the sake of efficiency, predictability, fairness, and incorruptibility. This drive was identified at all times except for the reign of Xi Jinping. However, it was also visible that regulations for institutionalization and openness were easier to introduce than to implement. In spite of the reforms, favoritism and nepotism, and purchasing and selling of official positions, remain rampant.

Second, there is the conservative drive that aims at maintaining and strengthening party leadership and integrity, thus tightening party control over the selection and appointment of cadres. This stems partly from ideology and the vested interests of the party and especially its organization department in maintaining the principle of *dang guan ganbu*, i.e., the party assuming responsibility for cadres' affairs. Another factor perhaps is the increasing need to tighten discipline. As the CCP adjusted its ideology to the reality of marketization, party discipline withered. Thus, the Hu Jintao administration felt it had to pay more attention to virtue than to talent, while at the same time keenly promoting institutionalization and openness in the cadre selection and appointment system.

Finally, cadre system reforms are inseparable from the power struggle within the leadership. Xi Jinping has reversed the trend for institutionalization and openness, and increased the weight of party control. It seems likely that he will attempt at more reforms in the cadre system that would contribute to consolidating his power base even further, which may allow him to serve three terms as the top leader of the CCP until 2027.

Notes

1 *People's Daily*, December 10, 1991.

2 The Regulations applied to: the heads of departments and organizations of the Party Central Committee, the Standing Committee of the National People's Congress, the State Council and the National Committee of the Chinese People's Political Consultative Conference (CPPCC); leading members of the local party committees and governments, party discipline and inspection committees, people's courts and people's procuratorates, of and above the county level; the heads of departments and organizations of the party committees, standing committees of the people's congresses, governments, CPPCCs, of the provincial and prefectural level localities.

3 *People's Daily*, October 24, 2007; *People's Daily*, November 16, 2012.

References

Ben Shu Bianxie Zu (Compiling Group of This Book) (2003) *Xin Shiji Dang de Jiceng Zuzhi Gongzuo Shiwu Shouce (Practical Handbook of Party Grassroots-level Organization Work in the New Century)*, Shanghai: Shanghai People's Publishers.

Ben Shu Bianxie Zu (Compiling Group of This Book) (2015) *Zhongguo Gongchandang Dangnei Fagui Xuanbian (2015 Xiuding Ban) (Selected CCP Intra-party Regulations 2015 Revised Version)*, Beijing: China Fangzheng Publishers.

Falü Chubanshe Fagui Zhongxin (Center for Law and Regulation, Law Press) (2005) *Zhongguo Gongchandang Dangnei Fagui Xinbian (CCP Intra-party Regulations New Edit)*, Beijing: Law Press.

Hsu Szu-chien (2006) "Reforming the Party and the State under Hu Jintao," in John Wong and Lai Hongyi (eds.), *China into the Hu-Wen Era: Policy Initiatives and Challenges*, Singapore: World Scientific Publishing Co., pp. 153–190.

Huangfu Ping (1991) "Reform and Opening Requires Many Cadres with Both Virtue and Talent," *Liberation Daily*, April 12.

Landry, Pierre, Xiaobo Lü, and Haiyan Duan (2016) "Does Performance Matter? Evaluating Political Selection along the Chinese Administrative Ladder," paper presented at the APSA 2014 Annual Meetings, introduced in Yang Yao, "An Anatomy of the Chinese Selectoracy," China Center for Economic Research Working Paper Series No. E20160002, February, p. 17.

Li Yuanchao (2008) "Jianchi De Cai Jianbei Yi De Weixian Yongren Biaozhun" (Uphold the Standard of Being Equipped with Both Virtue and Talent but Virtue Comes First in Choosing People), originally appeared in *Qiushi* (*Seek Truth*) magazine, carried by the Xinhua Newsagency, October 16 (www.ce.cn/xwzx/gnsz/gdxw/200810/16/t20081016_17083088.shtml).

Liao Gailong *et al.* (eds.) (1991) *Dangdai Zhongguo Zhengzhi Da Shidian (The Encyclopedia of Contemporary Chinese Politics)*, Jilin: Jilin Wenshi Chubanshe (Jilin Literature and History Publishers).

Wang Bingquan and Li Haiyang (2016) "Zhongguo Zhengzhi Jingying Xina Moshi de Lishi Yanjin yu Zhuanhuan Luoji" (The Historical Development and Transformational Logic of the Model of Co-opting Political Elite in China), *Xueshu Yanjiu (Academic Research)*, No. 12, December 31.

Xinhua Net (2006) "Shouquan Fabu: Dang Zheng Lingdao Ganbu Zhiwu Renqi Zanxing Guiding" (Releasing upon Authorization: Tentative Regulations on the Term of Office of Party and Government Cadres), August 6 (http://news.xinhuanet.com/lianzheng/2006-08/06/content_4927344.htm).

Xinhua Net (2016) "Guanyu Xin Xingshi xia Dang Nei Zhengzhi Shenghuo de Ruogan Zhunze" (On Some Guiding Principles for Inner-Party Political Life under New Circumstances), November 2 (http://news.xinhuanet.com/politics/2016-11/02c_1119838382.htm).

Zhang Yongle (2014) "Zhongguo de Xianneng Zhengzhi ji Qi Minzhu Zhengdang Xing" (China's Wise Men's Politics and Its Democratic Legitimacy), *Sungkyun China Observer*, No. 3 (#7), Sungkyun Institute of China Studies, Academy of East Asian Studies, Sungkyunkwan University.

Zhonggong Zhongyang Wenxian Yanjiushi (CCPCC Document Research Office) (ed.) (1991) *Shisan Da Yilai Zhongyao Wenxian Xuanbian Zhong (Since the 13th Party Congress: Selected Important Documents Vol. 2)*, Beijing: People's Publishers.

Zhonggong Zhongyang Zuzhi Bu Ganbu Diaopei Ju (CCPCC Organization Department Cadre Allocation Bureau) (ed.) (1995) *Ganbu Guanli Gongzuo Wenjian Xuanbian (Selected Documents on Cadre Management Work)*, Beijing: Party Construction Readings Publishers.

Zhongyang Bangong Ting Fagui Shi (Legal Office of the General Office of the CCP Central Committee) *et al.* (2001) *Zhongguo Gongchandang Dangnei Fagui Xuanbian 1996–2000 (Selected Intra-party Regulations of the CCP, 1996–2000)*, Beijing: Law Press.

Zhongyang Zhengfu Menhu Wangzhan (Central Government Gateway Net) (2015) "Zhonggong Zhongyang Bangong Ting Yinfa 'Tuijin Lingdao Ganbu Neng Shang Neng Xia Ruogan Guiding (Shixing)'" (The General Office of the CCP Central Committee Prints and Distributes "Some Trial Regulations on Advancing the Promotion and Demotion of Leading Cadres"), July 28 (www.gov.cn/zhengce/2015-07/28/content_2904339.htm).

11
"THE NEW (OLD) NORMAL"
The CCP propaganda system under Jiang, Hu, and Xi

Anne-Marie Brady

Introduction

Ever since Xi Jinping became General Secretary of the Chinese Communist Party (CCP) in 2012, the CCP government has tightened social, political, and economic controls in China and put renewed emphasis on CCP ideology. This chapter discusses the continuity between Xi's policies and those established by his predecessors Jiang Zemin (1989–2002) and Hu Jintao (2002–2012), the extent to which Xi's initiatives are a new direction, and what they tell us about the CCP's current hold on power.

In December 2012, Xi set his policy on ideology and propaganda in motion in a secret speech to Party members. Xi highlighted the continued importance of ideology as a tool of political control in China and raised the specter of the fate of the Soviet Union. He said the Soviet Union had collapsed because of a belief crisis: the Soviet people lost faith with the Communist Party. In a speech in January 2013 Xi Jinping stated that "beliefs and faith" are the "calcium" of Party members, without them they will "develop rickets" (Wang 2013). In 2015 Chinese journalism specialist Professor Zhan Jiang described the political situation in China under Xi as "the worst time for media and internet freedom since the start of the new century" (Grigg 2015). But to what extent are Xi's measures a continuance of policies established by his predecessors Jiang Zemin (1989–2002) and Hu Jintao (2002–2012)? What is the agenda behind the changes under Xi and what do they tell us about the CCP's hold on power? Do they reflect a new direction for CCP propaganda and information management or is it more of the same?

This chapter will answer these questions by examining the changes in media control under Xi Jinping in the context of the CCP's longstanding media policies and efforts to strengthen governance of the public sphere. In China, all forms of both traditional and new media are controlled within the CCP's propaganda and ideology *xitong* (宣教系统, *xuanjiao xitong*), a vast policy grouping covering advertising, art, culture, education, health, political education, sport, traditional and non-traditional media, and all forms of mass communication. The CCP regards propaganda and thought work as one of its core tasks. Hence any significant change to the way the media is managed in China is always indicative of significant changes going on in the wider political environment in China and the state of social and political control there.

The CCP's system of media control

The General Secretary of the CCP is the key figure within the Chinese political system who sets the ideological line and propaganda policies. Another senior leader on the Politburo is usually put in charge of actually leading the propaganda and ideology *xitong*. This figure heads the CCP Central Leading Group for Propaganda and Ideological Work, which consists of a handful of senior managers in the Party-State media, culture, education, and other relevant sectors. This Central Leading Group guides the policy direction of the propaganda and thought work *xitong*, ensuring CCP policies are implemented within the vast range of State and private entities whose activities fall within the ambit of the propaganda system.

The core CCP organization for managing the Chinese news media is the CCP Central Propaganda Department (中宣部, *zhongxuanbu*). The Central Propaganda Department had a very important role in China in the 1950s and 1960s. It was closed down at the start of the Cultural Revolution and its duties taken over by other agencies. Mao Zedong accused it of being "the Palace of the King of Hell" because it was under the control of Mao's factional rivals. The Central Propaganda Department was not reestablished until 1977. Its activities were marginalized under the leadership of CCP General Secretaries Hu Yaobang (1980–1987) and Zhao Ziyang (1987–1989), both of whom downplayed ideology, prioritized economic development, and were tolerant of media liberalization.

In the post-Mao era, the Central Propaganda Department has been responsible for all matters related to ideological work and public opinion management in China. It issues regular guidance on how the news media should cover topical news stories. It is also in charge of managing the *nomenklatura* system for appointing media, culture, and education leaders. State agencies deal with any infringements of the Central Propaganda Department's censorship instructions. For the news media the relevant organizations are the State Administration of Press, Publication, Radio, Film, and Television (SAPPRFT); the Ministry of Culture; and the State Administration of Industry and Commerce, which polices advertising. All government and Party organizations also have a censorship role over the Chinese media if a sensitive issue touching on their activities goes into the public domain. All web managers operating websites registered in China are also required by law to monitor content on their sites to keep them in line with the latest Central Propaganda Department censorship instructions. SAPPRFT's duties were previously split between two separate agencies; but in 2013 these two bodies were merged. This was an acknowledgment of the multi-platform nature of the modern Chinese media market which incorporates traditional and non-traditional media. All Chinese journalists must be registered with SAPPRFT in order to work as a journalist and each registration lasts for five years. This system has been in place since 1996; it was updated in 2003, then again in 2015 (Brady 2008, 2012).

The Central Propaganda Department's sister organization, the Office of Foreign Propaganda (外宣办, *waixuanban*) more commonly known by its other nameplate the State Council Information Office, is the Party organization in charge of monitoring China's international media management and the Internet. Having one office with two nameplates is a common practice of CCP governance, enabling the Party to disguise its guiding hand within the political system. Another important agency for public opinion guidance is the Office for Spiritual Civilization (文明办, *wenmingban*), set up in 1997. This office is nominally separate from the Central Propaganda Department but operates from the same building. It has overlapping management and even the same website. The Office for Spiritual Education supervises the soft political education of non-Party members of the Chinese population.

Methods of control

Softening control mechanisms

Since the mid 1990s the CCP has tended to avoid using the word "control" (控制, *kongzhi*) when discussing the Chinese media and other aspects of the propaganda system, preferring instead terms such as "manage" (管理, *guanli*), "*mould*" (塑造, *suzao*), and "guide" (指导/引导, *yindao/zhidao*). This approach relies more on norm-setting than punitive action, establishing publicly acceptable terms of debate and using persuasion to influence public opinion. Moreover, instead of the Party-State's previous policies of micro-controlling any forms of resistance or subversion, the government now prefers a strategy of macro management, with the exception of times of crisis (Xuexi chubanshe 1994: 358–361).

Nomenklatura

The *nomenklatura* system is an essential means to maintain the CCP's influence over the Chinese media. *Nomenklatura* are Party-appointed senior management positions within state and society. As the word reveals, this approach was copied from the Soviet Union, but unlike Russian language, there is no specific word in Chinese for this social class. The closest equivalent is the phrase "organization work" (组织工作, *zuzhi gongzuo*), which describes the activity of designating these leadership roles. The *nomenklatura* are the gatekeepers within the Chinese media, they are charged with controlling the flow of information, establishing the norms within their own work unit, as well as making personnel decisions about lower level staff. Senior managers of China's media conglomerates are responsible for controlling the content of their subsidiary newspapers, magazines, radio or TV stations and must take the blame if anything goes wrong. "Organization work" is one of the most politically important tasks of the Central Propaganda Department and its local equivalents.

Agenda-setting

One of the most important means by which information is controlled in China is through establishing the news agenda and the correct political terminology for what can and cannot be said in the public arena. In Chinese this is called the "*tifa*" (提法), the politically correct way of referring to something. The Central Propaganda Department and its local equivalents issue regular detailed materials which set the *tifa* for public discourse in China, and in some cases, even internationally. These guidelines restrict the range of information available to the public, establish the correct phraseology to be used, and set the tone of debate.

Economic measures

Economic measures have become an important means of control in the last 20 years. The central and provincial Party propaganda departments have the power to allocate or take away lucrative contracts or permission to engage in business to State and commercial media organizations. Since 1994 profit-making enterprises within the propaganda system have been measured for their "social efficiency" (社会效益, *shehui xiaoyi*, whether or not they follow the Party line) and "economic efficiency" (经济效益, *jingji xiaoyi*, whether or not they make a profit). Economic reasons have frequently been used as an excuse to close down publications that push the censorship boundaries too far (Brady 2008).

Laws

Historically China's propaganda system was controlled by means of periodic proclamations issued by the Central Propaganda Department. But from 1992, "rule by law" was introduced into China's information management as a new tool of control. This has led to the creation of a vast new body of laws, which are backed up by a complex set of local and national regulations.

Guiding Chinese Netizens (网民, wangmin) on censorship boundaries

In the pre-Internet, pre-social media era, information on China's censorship guidelines and ideological campaigns could only be found in classified publications aimed at senior to mid level foreign affairs officials, propaganda cadres, and media professionals. However from 2002, the Central Propaganda Department's "suggestions" (意见, *yijian*) on online protocol for discussing sensitive topics such as the status of Taiwan or Hong Kong politics were made widely available. Increasingly other such "suggestions" have appeared online (Brady 2015). The Internet and social media make it possible for every citizen to be a contributor to the public sphere. The change of censorship tactics is an official recognition of the power of new media to subvert the CCP's propaganda tropes and to operate outside the Party's traditional means of control over mass communication. The CCP has embraced the Internet as a propaganda tool and driver of the modern knowledge economy, while constantly working to manage its negative aspects through laws, norm-setting, and technological controls.

Censorship

Censorship is a vital component of any successful propaganda system, as is a clear message. The Central Propaganda Department tends to look at censorship issues from a macro level, and is concerned with overall trends in society. It has responsibility for censoring and monitoring national level media, such as CCTV and *People's Daily*, as well as monitoring high-profile scholarly and popular publications and cultural output. Provincial and local level propaganda departments are in charge of censoring and monitoring all non-classified sources of information in their region, including advertising. In recent years as social media has become an important source of public information in China, multiple Party and State agencies within the propaganda system have sought various means to censor social media including closing down some prominent individuals' social media accounts and using armies of online paid and unpaid censors (the so-called "50-cent Party," 5毛党, *wumao dang*) to delete sensitive posts, and to post pro-government comments (King *et al.* 2016).

"Stress politics": media control under Jiang Zemin

Jiang Zemin was appointed General Secretary of the CCP after the crackdown on the student protest movement in June 1989, which also resulted in the house arrest of the previous General Secretary Zhao Ziyang (1987–1989). Jiang was initially regarded as being a very weak leader as he did not have strong military links and was not connected to a major CCP faction. The Chinese media and China-based foreign journalists were strictly controlled during the first three years of Jiang's rule. Li Ruihuan led the CCP Central Leading Group for Propaganda and Ideological Work from 1989 to 1992 during this time. However, in February 1992, senior leader

Deng Xiaoping gave a series of speeches aimed at restarting economic reform, and this also had a profound impact on Chinese media liberalization. These changes were cemented at the 14th Party Congress in 1992 when China formally designated itself as a market economy. Market economics were immediately applied to the propaganda system, which had previously been subsidized by the government. CCP leaders believed that the modernization of management processes and the application of market principles to the propaganda system would lead to both greater profitability and greater receptivity to the Party message, thereby strengthening CCP rule. A protégé of Deng Xiaoping, Ding Guan'gen, was made both head of the Central Propaganda Department and the Central Leading Group for Propaganda and Ideological Work at the 14th Party Congress. He stayed in this role until 2002. Jiang Zemin took over the role of PRC President at the National Party Congress in March 1993. It was the first time this role had been held by the CCP General Secretary.

Soon after the 14th Party Congress, a 3 percent "propaganda industry tax" (宣传事业费, *xuanchuan shiye fei*) was introduced to help fund the costs of expanding and upgrading the CCP propaganda system (Zhonggong zhongyang xuanchuanbu, zhengce fagui yanjiushi 1998). A substantial new investment was required to modernize the CCP's new approach to information management. The new fee taxed the profits of all enterprises managed within the CCP propaganda system. However, it quickly became a lucrative fund for local and senior level propaganda officials to amass vast sums for personal use, as did the propaganda departments' new powers to allocate commercial rights to media enterprises and other commercial entities within the propaganda system.

From 1992 on the CCP also began to create a more modern, systematic, standardized system of media control (Zhonggong zhongyang xuanchuanbu, zhengce fagui yanjiushi 1998). Jiang Zemin announced that the Central Propaganda Department was now an "extremely important department" and granted it increased powers (Han 1997: 238). In 1994, in a break with past precedence, the whole Politburo Standing Committee attended the national annual meeting of propaganda and thought work. Jiang Zemin's speech at the meeting stressed the vital role of CCP propaganda and thought work in this new era (Xuexi chubanshe 1994). Jiang warned of the dangers China faced from hostile foreign forces, noting: "The international community is steadfastly opposed to China becoming strong and powerful and will never give up its plot to 'Westernize' and break up China" (Jiang 1997: 10). Jiang urged the need for greater controls in the propaganda sphere in order to make it clear what could and could not be published (p. 22). From mid-1994 a large scale retraining program of CCP leading cadres was instituted to indoctrinate them in Deng Xiaoping Thought. In 1995 Jiang told Party members to "stress politics" and this became the slogan for an ideological rectification campaign of Party members in 1998, aimed at rooting out corruption. The political education of CCP leaders had been neglected in the 1980s, but from 1994 on, CCP rank and file and non-Party senior State employees underwent intensive political study sessions every few years.

In January 1999 Jiang Zemin told the annual meeting of senior propaganda leaders that they must strive to "unite all forces that can be united" (*Renmin Ribao* 1999). On April 25, 1999 the lack of national unity at the most senior levels of power and a major potential threat to the regime's hold on power was revealed when 10,000 members of Falungong staged a sit-in outside the Zhongnanhai – during a Politburo meeting that was supposed to have been secret. On July 22, 1999, the Ministry of Civil Affairs categorized Falungong as an illegal organization. Falungong adherents were forced to break with their faith – or face arrest. The crackdown on Falungong sparked a retightening of controls on Chinese civil society. An internal publication warned that social groups existing outside of CCP controls were "thought work blind spots" (Quanguo xuanchuan ganbu peixun cankao ziliao 1999: 133).

In February 2000 during a visit to Guangdong Province, Jiang Zemin announced his own new ideological line: the Three Represents. Promoting the "Three Represents" was the "primary task" of the Chinese media that year as well as the one after (China.org 2002). In the same period a further crackdown on dissent began and there was increased surveillance of newspapers, publishers, and websites (Chan 2000). In August 2000 a six-month-long ideological training program for county level party secretaries began at the Central Party School (Stratfor 2000). In September 2000, 400 local newspapers were closed down (Ma 2000). In February 2001 the Chinese news media was reminded to focus on "positive news" and negative reports were banned. Chinese journalists were explicitly forbidden from reporting on sensitive topics that touched on domestic politics, national unity, and social stability (*Hong Kong Mail* 2001).

In 2002, texting was formally incorporated into the propaganda system (Brady 2008), a response to the growing influence of new media and multiple new platforms of communication offered by information communication technology. From the late 1990s the CCP took on the Internet as a new platform for the CCP message, meanwhile managing the risk factors of this new medium by multiple laws and technology such as the Great Firewall of China. Western-based web engines and social media such as Google, Facebook, Twitter, Wikipedia, and YouTube were either blocked outright from China or forced to follow China's censorship rules. Chinese companies were allowed to set up their own equivalents – Baidu, Youku, QQ, Sina weibo, Wechat are the most well-known – as long as they followed CCP censorship guidelines.

"Harmonize": media control under Hu Jintao

In November 2002, at the 16th Congress of the CCP, Hu Jintao was appointed as the new General Secretary of the CCP and at the National People's Congress three months later he was also made PRC President. Five close associates of Jiang Zemin were appointed to the Standing Committee of the Politburo: Li Changchun (who took over the role of heading the Central Leading Group for Propaganda and Ideological Work), Jia Qinglin, Wu Bangguo, Huang Ju, and Wu Guanzheng. Luo Gan and Wen Jiabao comprised the other members of the Standing Committee of the Politburo; meanwhile another Jiang associate, Liu Yunshan, was made head of the Central Propaganda Department.

Given the top-heavy number of Jiang associates in the propaganda system leadership, it is interesting to note that the 16th Party Congress marked the beginning of a marked de-emphasis on overt political education for the masses. The main message of the 16th Party Congress was that the CCP would aim to create a prosperous society for all (小康社会, *xiaokang shehui*) and strive for "political civilization" (政治文明, *zhengzhi wenming*), a reference to political and legal administrative reform. In December 2002 the State Press and Publication Authority announced its five-year plan to vet and license all of China's 400,000 journalists (*The Age* 2002). In early 2003 the Central Propaganda Department organized political study sessions for managing editors of newspapers, radio, and television stations (*Neibu tongxin* 2003: 19).

In January 2003 Li Changchun called on the Chinese media to "monitor some problems and issues in society" (Brady 2008: 53), a statement meant to affirm the traditional media's watchdog-on-a-leash role in China. In March 2003 Hu Jintao gave instructions to the Chinese media that it should be, "Closer to reality, closer to the masses, and closer to life." In the same month the Central Propaganda Department announced new restrictions on how Party history could be reported. Journalists were expressly forbidden from promoting "wrong thinking" on the Mao era, such as discussing the conflicts and mistakes of the period (*Neibu tongxin* 2003: 13). In August 2003 the Central Propaganda Department told party organizations, research institutes, and universities that they were not permitted to hold any conferences or conduct research on the topic of political reform, revisions to the constitution, or the protests of 1989 (Congressional Executive Commission on China 2003).

In May 2004 Peking University journalism professor Jiao Guobiao's diatribe against the illegitimate power of the Central Propaganda Department (Jiao 2004) was widely circulated via emails and blogs in China, stirring up a storm of controversy. Jiao was forced out of his teaching position at Peking University after these comments were made public. In September 2004, Jiang Zemin finally resigned as head of the CCP and State Central Military Commissions, the last of his official roles. Hu Jintao took over both these positions. Hu Jintao then immediately strengthened controls over the propaganda sphere. In December 2004 the Central Propaganda Department publicly criticized the term "public intellectual" and rejected this as a legitimate role in Chinese society (Brady 2008).

In February 2005 Hu Jintao set his own ideological line, calling for China to build a "harmonious society" (和谐社会, *hexie shehui*). The following month Hu also announced a new moral code for CCP officials to follow: "the eight honors and eight shames" (八容八耻, *barong bachi*). In the same month a new campaign was launched to strengthen ideological control over culture, education, and the media. From 2004 to 2006 the CCP conducted the "Party Progressiveness Movement" (先进性教育活动, *xianjinxing jiaoyu huodong*), the longest political campaign the CCP has run since the Cultural Revolution. The goal was to revitalize CCP membership at the local level, which had been seriously affected by the major transformations in the Chinese economy. In the late 1970s 79 percent of China's urban workforce worked in the State sector (Sabin 1994) while 75 percent lived in the countryside. But by the 2000s more than 70 percent of Chinese workers were employed in the private sector (*China Daily* 2010) and China had close to 60 percent of its population living in urban areas. Since 1949 CCP membership had been managed through the work unit (单位, *danwei*). The rapid change in employment and residential patterns from the early 1980s on, accelerated in the 1990s, meant that the CCP lost direct contact with much of its membership in a relatively short time as the majority of workers were no longer employed in government *danwei* (Brady 2012). During the Hu era, *weibo* (微博, the Chinese equivalent of Twitter) became a vibrant alternative news source to China's traditional media and spawned a whole new generation of public opinion shapers in China – outside the CCP's usual means of control on thought leaders. In this era the CCP began utilizing new media as one of the primary new means used to communicate with China's increasingly mobile population.

In May 2006 yet another crackdown on media and culture was announced. Li Changchun stated the propaganda system was no longer able to properly control significant areas in the public sphere and that the CCP would now take action to regain control (BBC 2006). In August 2006 the News Department of the Central Propaganda Department issued instructions to the Chinese media that for the next two years they should focus on promoting the Beijing Olympics (*Neibu tongxin* 2006: 15 and 16). During the Beijing Olympics there were more than 20,000 foreign journalists registered to report in China, when usually there are only 600–700 foreign journalists based there. Beijing Olympics media managers were told to make efforts to win the foreign media over and get them to give positive coverage of China (*Neibu tongxin* 2007: 15).

Foreign journalists continued to benefit from the relaxation of controls on the foreign media in China throughout the final four years of the Hu era. The Chinese media was also increasingly given more leeway in reporting negative stories, as the Central Propaganda Department had come to recognize the value of negative propaganda as a pressure valve during crisis situations (Brady 2008). An anachronism in this era which attracted a lot of international interest was the "red culture campaign" (2008–2012) of Chongqing Mayor Bo Xilai, who used ultra-orthodox propaganda campaigns in Chongqing to lobby for a place on the Politburo Standing Committee. Bo's campaign was not endorsed by the central leadership and eventually contributed to his spectacular fall from power in 2012.

The Hu government, as its predecessors had, reverted to micro control methods to deal with the media during crisis situations. This was the case following multiple demonstrations in Tibetan areas of China in March 2008; after violent inter-racial attacks in Xinjiang in July 2009; and from 2009 when Tibetan dissidents began using self-immolation as a form of protest (Brady 2013). After the violent events in Xinjiang in July 2009 the CCP permanently blocked access to Twitter, YouTube, and Facebook in China. Incredibly, for ten months, residents in Xinjiang Uyghur Autonomous Region – whether ethnic Han or Uyghur – were also denied access to the Internet, international phone calls, and even international post. Although these restrictions were eventually lifted, the media environment in Xinjiang and reporting on any matters to do with Uyghurs or Islam in China was strictly managed for the rest of the Hu years and this situation continues up to the present day. Similarly, the Tibetan Autonomous Region and Tibetan areas within other provinces of China also experienced extreme censorship measures beginning in early 2008 that continue on up to the present. China currently has 44 journalists in prison, more than any other country. Most were arrested during the Hu era. The CCP has ruthlessly repressed any hint of dissent among the Tibetan and Uyghur populations in the last seven years. Twenty-one out of the 44 Chinese journalists in prison are ethnically Tibetan or Uyghur (Committee to Protect Journalists 2014).

In the Hu era the CCP used the most draconian measures ever seen in modern times to try and bring the information environment under control on Tibetan and Uyghur affairs and to ensure only the government's perspective got out to domestic and foreign audiences. The Hu administration also initiated a preemptive tightening of media controls on the rest of China after the Jasmine Revolutions in the Middle East and North Africa in 2011. So to claim, as many have, that Xi's regime is more repressive than what preceded it is to ignore the reality of the experience of a politically significant section of the Chinese population living in territories that amount to more than one third of the Chinese land mass and the vulnerable defenders of China's political and civil rights, human rights lawyers, and activists.

"The new (old) normal": media control under Xi Jinping

In November 2012 at the 18th Party Congress, Xi Jinping was appointed General Secretary of the CCP, head of the Central Military Commission, and of the CCP Foreign Affairs *xitong*. In March 2013 Xi was also made President of the People's Republic of China and head of the Central Leading Group for Finance and Economics. Xi's main rival for power, Bo Xilai, was brought down by a murder investigation earlier that year, and Hu Jintao (unlike Jiang Zemin before him) had resigned all his political roles on stepping down from the General Secretary position. However, like his predecessors Jiang and Hu, Xi still had to deal with a Politburo Standing Committee stacked with factional foes. Factions and leadership rivalry have always been a feature of CCP politics, but the development of a market economy has accentuated differences between inner-Party power blocs as they now compete for both power and financial advantages. For a senior leader, stacking the bureaucracy with your faction's supporters is one way to maintain influence and privileges, even after retirement.

Xi inherited a CCP *nomenklatura* that was divided between the Shanghai faction (Jiang Zemin), the China Youth League faction (Hu Jintao), and the Princelings (family members of Mao era leaders). There are some overlaps between factions and loyalties are not absolute.

Looking at Xi's Politburo Standing Committee from a factional point of view: Li Keqiang is associated with Hu Jintao as is Liu Yunshan – although the latter also has links to Jiang Zemin; while Wang Qishan, Yu Zhengsheng, Zhang Dejiang, and Zhang Gaoli have been closely associated with Jiang Zemin, although Wang Qishan, Zhang Dejiang, and Yu Zhengsheng are also Princelings (CNN 2012). Xi himself had risen to power with the support of Jiang, but during the two years he has been leader, he too has steadily begun to develop his own power base: the Xi faction. Meanwhile, Wang Qishan has become Xi's most reliable comrade-in-arms in this new political grouping.

A noticeable feature of the new leadership team after the 18th Party Congress was the strong presence of Jiang associates all throughout the senior levels of the propaganda system. Liu Yunshan, head of the Central Propaganda Department from 2002 to 2012, was appointed as CCP Politburo Standing Committee leader in charge of propaganda and ideology at the 18th Party Congress. Liu also took on the roles of Secretary of the CCP Secretariat, Chairman of the Commission for Building Spiritual Civilization, leader of the Propaganda and Ideology Group, and President of the Central Party School.

As Xi has moved to strengthen his authority over the Chinese political system, like both Jiang Zemin and Mao Zedong before him, he has had to prioritize tightening his faction's control of the propaganda system. Xi, like Mao, has not attacked his factional rivals directly. Instead he has used a series of strategic tactics identical to those Mao Zedong employed in the 1960s to eradicate both Party moderates represented by Liu Shaoqi and later the Ultra-Left Lin Biao faction within the PLA (Mao 2013). The first tactic Xi has used is called "throwing stones" (甩石头, *shuai shitou*) meaning to ruin the careers of members of a rival faction through political accusations. In the Mao era this took the form of a political movement; the penultimate one was the disastrous Cultural Revolution. Under Xi Jinping "throwing stones" has taken the form of a massive anti-corruption campaign which began in 2013 and has no end in sight – part of what Xi calls China's "new normal" (新常态, *xin changtai*). Xi's anti-corruption campaign has targeted a noticeably high number of officials in central and provincial level propaganda departments, the education and cultural sectors, and the media.

The second tactic Xi has used is called "mixing in sand" (掺沙子, *can shazi*). Mao used this strategy to great effect, placing officials loyal to him within Party and State bureaucracies that he sought to bring under his control. As officials from his factional foes are removed from key positions on corruption allegations, Xi has steadily replaced them with new leaders who will be loyal to him – the Xi faction.

The third Maoist tactic Xi is using is called "undermining" (挖墙脚, *wa qiangjiao*). This means to take power away from existing bodies by creating new organizations or giving additional powers to existing entities under the control of the senior leader. As Jiang did in the early 1990s, Xi has accumulated all the official roles he possibly could. And as Deng Xiaoping did in the 1980s and Mao Zedong did in the 1960s, Xi has created a number of new power groupings under his leadership that have overshadowed the influence of the organizations controlled by his factional foes.

Finally, when it comes to both domestic foes and international threats, under Xi's leadership, the Chinese traditional and social media is adopting a further tried and true Mao-era tactic: the "tongue war" (舌战, *shezhan*), using verbal attacks to bring down an opponent. Virulent attacks against Australia during the 2016 Olympics and against President Tsai Ing-wen of the Republic of China in the same year are recent example of this tactic when it comes to China's foreign relations. Senior Chinese leaders charged with corruption, human rights lawyers, and activists brought before the courts have also had to undergo a "tongue war" via public shaming in the traditional and new media in addition to the charges brought against them.

When he first came to power in 2012, Xi was an unknown quality. Many commentators were critical of what they perceived as the "wasted years" of the Hu era as much-needed economic and political reforms were put off. Xi, it was hoped, would be bold and take action (Minnick 2014). On December 4, 2012, Xi Jinping gave a speech commemorating the thirtieth anniversary of the current Chinese Constitution and spoke of the need to "rule the country according to the Constitution" (依宪治国, *yixian zhiguo*). Xi's speech attracted considerable positive attention within China and internationally, with many speculating that China might be moving toward constitutional governance (宪政, *xianzheng*). But responding to those debates, in April 2013 the CCP General Office of the CCP Central Committee – led by a member of the Xi faction, Li Zhanshu – issued an internal report Document No. 9, "Briefing on the current situation in the ideological field." Document No. 9 was leaked to dissident Chinese media sources outside China and percolated back into the Chinese Mainland via social media (Branigan 2015).

Document No. 9 condemns the promotion in China of the ideas of Western constitutional democracy, universal values, civil society, neoliberalism, Western concepts of journalism, revisionist historical accounts of CCP history, and questioning of the Reform and Opening Up Era and of the socialist nature of socialism with Chinese characteristics. The document states that the antidote to these threats is to strengthen CCP leadership over ideology, provide guidance to help CCP members to distinguish between true and false theories, maintain unwavering adherence to the principle of the CCP's control of media, and further strengthen censorship measures (Document No. 9 2013).

For those who had been following CCP internal discussions since 1989 there was little new in Document No. 9. They were simply the same old tropes that have been a perennial feature of internal CCP threat analysis. Under the longstanding policy of "being internally strict and outwardly relaxed" (内紧外松, *neijin waisong*), the Chinese government does not advertise these perspectives to the wider public in China and certainly not to foreign audiences (Brady 2003). The leaking of Document No. 9 provoked a predictably negative response in Chinese social media and an outpouring of leftist writings in Party papers in defense. In early May the State Council Information Office ordered all materials related to Document No. 9 removed from the Internet as well as any "hate speech" attacking it (Zhong ban fa 2013). At the August 2013 national conference on propaganda, President Xi had a more positive message. Echoing Jiang and Hu, Xi told the Chinese media they should focus on positive news stories that uphold unity and stability, and are encouraging. His comments were the CCP's equivalent of a stuck record message: accentuate the positive, minimize the negative. (See Chapter 22, "Changing Patterns of Chinese Civil Society: Comparing the Hu-Wen and Xi Jinping Eras.")

In November 2013 the Politburo announced it was tightening the registration process for Chinese journalists (Xinhua 2013a). To get a press card, journalists must now pass an exam on socialism with Chinese characteristics, Marxist journalism theory, journalism ethics, regulations on journalism, news reporting norms, and preventing rumours (Wen 2013). Yet despite these efforts, many journalists and editors working for Chinese media organizations still operate outside the new controls. The reason is primarily economic: stringers are more economical and disposable than permanent staff. The Chinese traditional media is under the same economic pressures of the news media elsewhere in the world, as advertising revenue has dried up due to the impact of information communication technology. This means that despite endless CCP "instructions" to the contrary, Chinese media conglomerates will do whatever they can get away with in order to survive financially.

In September 2013 the CCP's Office for Foreign Propaganda's Fifth Department (otherwise known by its other nameplate the State Council Internet Information Office) launched a crackdown on *weibo* and other forms of social media (*Renmin Ribao* 2013). The deputy-director of the Office for Foreign Propaganda and head of the Fifth Department is Lu Wei, a Xi Jinping supporter who was appointed to the role in April 2013. The previous leader in this post, a Jiang loyalist, Gao Jianjun, was brought down on corruption allegations (*Renmin Ribao* 2014). China currently has 700 million citizens online – more than half the total population. In September 2013 China's Supreme People's Court issued a legal interpretation on how the Chinese courts should prosecute Internet-speech related crimes (Supreme People's Court 2013). According to this interpretation, bloggers could be detained if a "rumor" they post is forwarded more than 500 times or is viewed more than 5,000 times. Scores of high-profile bloggers have been detained since this interpretation was issued. In January 2015 the Xi government strengthened China's "Internet sovereignty" by reining in virtual private networks (VPNs) that had been widely used by Chinese Netizens to get around the Great Firewall and access services such as Google, Facebook, and Twitter. Since the crackdown began, the once dominant *weibo* ceased to be the main medium for social media in China and Netizens switched to less public channels such as Wechat. Wechat is the perfect tool for a State that wants to keep close watch on its citizens, its multiple functions encourage users to utilize it for everything from banking to instant messaging, making it far simpler to create big data on an individual user's associations (Kessel and Mozur 2016).

In early October 2013 the PLA-funded documentary *Silent Contest* (较量无声, *jiaoliang wusheng*), an internal political education resource, was leaked to the Chinese public via the Chinese Internet. It was soon removed by censors. The film accuses the USA of undermining China by means of political, cultural, ideological, organizational, and political infiltration (Silent Contest 2013). The film's arguments echoed sentiments frequently aired in internal Party publications, from the Mao era to the present, which are never intended to be seen by foreign eyes (Brady 2008, 2015). Many foreign commentators speculated that the film was indicative of a left turn in Chinese politics. Yet the removal of the film from Chinese websites indicates that its perspectives were not ones the Xi government – along with all previous post-Mao CCP governments – wished to promote to the wider public in China or to foreigners.

In June 2014 the Central Propaganda Department published *A Reader of General Secretary Xi Jinping's Important Speeches* which summarized Xi's contribution to CCP ideology. The volume is a comprehensive introduction to Xi's thinking on a broad range of issues. Notably, it did not include Xi's controversial speech commemorating the 30th anniversary of the Chinese Constitution (Zhongxuanbu 2014). Many outside observers interpreted the Central Propaganda Department's omission of the speech as political sabotage (Qian 2014). In 1967, during a meeting with a delegation from Albania, Mao Zedong labeled this type of subtle undermining as "using the Red Flag to attack the Red Flag" (打着红旗反红旗, *dazhe hongqi fan hongqi*) (Mao 1967).

On October 1, 2014 (Chinese National Day), a new book of Xi's collected speeches was published and this volume *did* include the speech. *Xi Jinping: The Governance of China* was edited by the State Council Information Office of China, the CCP Party Literature Research Office, and China International Publishing Group. This book was published by the Foreign Languages Press in Chinese, English, French, Russian, Arabic, Spanish, Portuguese, German, and Japanese and distributed worldwide as well as within China (CCP Party Literature Research Office and China International Publishing Group 2014). The Foreign Languages Press, China International Publishing Group, and the Office for Foreign Propaganda are all part of the foreign affairs *xitong*, controlled by Xi Jinping – though they are also part of the Propaganda and Thought Work *xitong* led by Liu Yunshan. The CCP Party Literature Research Office is directly under the CCP Politburo, in other words under Xi's leadership.

After the disastrous last ten years of the Mao era when power was concentrated in the hands of one individual, the CCP assiduously divided powerful roles among senior leaders, but Xi has now broken this pattern. In November 2013 at the Third Plenum of the 18th Party Congress, Xi took on the leadership of a new policy grouping, the Central Leading Group for Comprehensively Deepening Reforms. This new supra-agency is in charge of a massive portfolio, focusing on economic, political, cultural, social, and ideological matters (Xinhua 2013b). Then in January 2014 Xi made himself leader of the new CCP Central National Security Commission, which took over control of the police, intelligence, and judiciary sectors, grouped as the politics and law *xitong*. In February 2014 Xi Jinping made himself leader of yet another new policy grouping, the CCP Central Leading Group for Internet Security and Informatization (also known as Central Leading Group for Cyberspace Affairs) (Xinhua 2014). Given the dominance of the Internet in modern mass communication, this means that Xi has now succeeded in setting up his own means of control over the public sphere, thus undermining the Central Propaganda Department and the authority of Liu Yunshan over the Propaganda and Thought Work *xitong*.

Xi Jinping is now widely believed to be the most powerful political leader in China for decades – some even liken his power to Mao. But in the last two years his government has dealt with massive internal and external challenges, including the acute gap between rich and poor, the slowing economy, a series of breath-taking stock market crashes in 2015–2016, the ongoing threat of violent terrorism spreading to China, as well as the debilitating activities of inner-Party factional struggle. In March 2015, at the first meeting of China's Central National Security Commission, Xi stated that while China is stronger than ever before, the nation faces three great threats: namely invasion, subversion, and division. Xi also emphasized the risk that China's economic development and stability will be threatened and that the political system will be challenged (*Liaowang dongfang zhoukan* 2015). This speech is one of many indicators that Xi is running China in crisis mode. Thus the Chinese nation as a whole, no longer just the Tibetan and Uyghur population, are now experiencing micro control of the public sphere as well as many other restrictions. This means only positive messages and resolved problems can be aired in the traditional media, as well as in new media if a posting attracts a readership beyond 5,000 views. (See Chapter 23, "Can the Internet and Social Media Change the Party?")

In June 2015 a new national security law was passed which had the broadest possible notion of national security and will further curb public debate. In January 2016 a new cyber law came into effect that authorizes the government to close down Internet access in China during "major emergencies" (*Shanghai Daily* 2015). In 2009 the Central Propaganda Department took similar action in Xinjiang without referring to Chinese law; it did so under the authority of the Chinese Constitution which guarantees the CCP's leadership role over the whole of Chinese society. However, the liberalization of Chinese media since the 1990s has opened up the Pandora's Box of public opinion. The CCP can no longer rely on moral authority to implement its policies. Creating new laws strengthens its powers and, in the context of Xi's bid to strengthen control over the propaganda system, shifts the regulatory mechanism over to the legal system, which since 2014 has been under his direct leadership.

In December 2014, a close Xi ally, Huang Kunming, was appointed as an Executive-Deputy Director of the Central Propaganda Department and Head of the Office of Spiritual Civilization (*Renmin Ribao* 2015). In July 2015 another Xi ally, Jing Junhai, was appointed as Deputy Director of the Central Propaganda Department (Sina 2015). Xi is steadily moving his own people into place in the propaganda system as in other agencies. Liu Yunshan and all the other members of the Politburo Standing Committee except Li Keqiang are likely to retire at the 19th Party Congress in 2017. The 19th Party Congress will mark the date when Xi – like Mao at the 1969 9th Party Congress – will be able to ensure a significant majority of his own supporters are voted in to the Politburo. In 2015 rumours surfaced on the Chinese Internet that Xi may try to extend his rule beyond the two five-year terms that had been the norm for his predecessors (Lam 2015).

The Xi administration is attempting to achieve what his recent predecessors tried but failed in: to restore popular faith in the CCP, to reset the boundaries of public expression in China, to clean up government, and to stabilize the political system. To do so, as Jiang and Hu were well aware, but unable to achieve, requires concentrated power. Hence Xi is trying to slay his political foes one by one, as well as to silence any potential popular sources of criticism. Xi has clearly taken note of the cautionary lesson of the Cultural Revolution by refraining from unleashing the power of the masses against those who oppose his initiatives within the political system. In March 2015 the Central Propaganda Department banned the independently made Chinese environmental film *Under the Dome* (穹顶之下, *qiongding zhixia*) which urged Chinese citizens to seize the initiative to stop pollution and economic waste in China. The documentary was downloaded 300 million times in China before it was taken down. But the fact that this independent documentary could be made and received the endorsement of the Ministry of Environment Protection – since January 2015 led by a Xi ally Chen Jining – shows that Xi like his predecessors is not trying to completely suppress public opinion, but rather is trying to keep it within boundaries that do not harm the Party's core interests. Like Jiang Zemin and Hu Jintao before him, Xi's media management model is careful to neither veer too far left or too far right, but respond to challenges as they appear.

Conclusion

As Deng Liqun, Susan Shirk, and Rick Baum long ago identified, oscillating cycles of relaxation and contraction (放/收, *fang/shou*) have been the norm in the CCP's approach to political and social control for nearly 40 years (Baum 1994). The CCP set China on the path of reform and opening up in 1978, yet fears the impact of economic, social, and political change for their hold on political power. For over 20 years the CCP has embraced the knowledge economy and the information revolution, understanding that it is an essential component of the modern economy. Yet modern information communication technology offers endless possibilities for the Chinese public and foreign interests to subvert the CCP's efforts to manage the public sphere, which results in perennial government crackdowns aimed at pushing back public discourse to acceptable limits. Intertwined within this dynamic are the inner-Party power struggles of each leadership group that have historically played out through the sectors of society managed within the CCP propaganda system more broadly, and especially the Chinese media, which have frequently given license to brief periods of openness in the public sphere such as 1988–1989, 1997–1998, and 2003–2004.

Jiang Zemin began his leadership in a relatively weak position and had to deal with the influence of Deng Xiaoping and other semi-retired leaders behind the scenes, as well as rivals for power such as Li Ruihuan and Qiao Shi. Jiang gradually concentrated his power by accumulating political roles, forcing his rivals to retire early, while taking a close interest in propaganda and ideological matters to bring public opinion on his side. When Hu Jintao took over as General Secretary of the CCP in 2002, the Politburo Standing Committee was stacked with Jiang supporters, including the leader in charge of the propaganda system, Li Changchun. During the Hu era (2002–2012) the CCP strengthened its controls over the Internet and finessed the methods and means of control over the traditional and non-traditional media. Xi inherited all these unresolved power struggles as well as the new challenges to traditional media management brought by the ever-expanding Internet. The media marketization launched under Jiang Zemin's leadership in the 1990s and continued under Hu Jintao greatly sustained authoritarian rule in China. But it also created the circumstance for political forces both within and outside the CCP to continually undermine the authority of the central leadership.

Xi's "new normal" aims to stabilize Chinese society but in so doing, has swept away many of the pressure valves in Chinese society introduced by his predecessors. Xi's administration has systematically cracked down on corrupt Party and military officials, public intellectuals, human rights lawyers, university teachers, students, NGOs, the traditional and non-traditional media, trade unionists, the Tibetan Autonomous Region, the Xinjiang Autonomous Region, and other restive ethnically diverse areas of China. Xi's administration is running China in crisis mode, so the nation is going through yet another "收" (*shou*, contraction) cycle of political and social control. In times of crisis the Chinese media's "freedom of criticism" is viewed by CCP leaders as undermining and unacceptable.

In modern Chinese political discourse the phrase "上面有政策，下面有对策" (*shangmian you zhengce, xiamian you duice*, those above set policies, while those below resist) is commonly used to describe the endless power struggle between the authorities and those they rule. Both control and resistance exist within the Chinese political system like an endlessly transforming 阴阳 (yin/yang) ☯ symbol. Thus we can expect that unless Xi eventually makes an adjustment in governance – handing more power to society to administer itself through laws and regulatory bodies as advocated in *Under the Dome* and allowing greater freedom of speech – the likely outcome will be increased resistance to CCP rule, not less. The extent to which Xi and his allies within the CCP feel they can afford to permit further administrative reform and greater media openness will reflect the level of confidence in their ability to deal with China's three great threats: invasion, subversion, and division.

A secure state is a tolerant state. Since the crisis of 1989, CCP leaders have understood that they must maintain the one-Party state with public support (Brady 2008). Managing a balance between allowing for the expression of public opinion and maintaining the limits of public expression has been the ongoing task of each Chinese government since 1989 and Xi's government is no different. Xi's "new normal" in the propaganda system follows a pattern that is well-established in CCP politics; where he differs is his ability to enforce it.

References

Baum, R. (1994) *Burying Mao: Chinese Politics in the Age of Deng Xiaoping*, Princeton: Princeton University Press.

BBC (2006) "China: Central Propaganda chief admits losing control over media," BBC Monitoring Media, May 8, original source *Cheng Ming*, May 1.

Brady, A-M. (2003) *Making the Foreign Serve China: Managing Foreigners in the People's Republic*, Lanham, MD: Rowman & Littlefield.

Brady, A-M. (2008) *Marketing Dictatorship: Propaganda and Thought Work in Contemporary China*, Lanham, MD: Rowman & Littlefield.

Brady, A-M. (2012) "Velvet fist in the velvet glove," in Brady, Anne-Marie, ed. *China's Thought Management*, Abingdon: Routledge.

Brady, A-M. (2013) "'We are all part of the same family': China's ethnic propaganda," *Journal of Current Chinese Affairs*, Vol. 41, No. 4: 159–181.

Brady, A-M. (2015) "Unifying the ancestral land: The CCP's 'Taiwan' frames," *The China Quarterly*, Vol. 223 (September): 786–806.

Branigan, T. (2015) "US and EU criticise Chinese journalist's jailing for 'leaking state secrets'," *The Guardian*, April 17. Available from www.theguardian.com/world/2015/apr/17/gao-yu-and-document-no-9-china-jails-journalist-for-leaking-state-secrets.

CCP Party Literature Research Office and China International Publishing Group, eds. (2014) *Xi Jinping: The Governance of China*, Beijing: Foreign Languages Press.

Chan, V.P-K. (2000) "Journalist persecuted in purge on liberalism," SCMP.com, July 5.

China Daily (2010) "China vows equal treatment for private sector talents," June 9. Available from www.chinadaily.com.cn/china/2010-06/09/content_9953634.htm.

China.org (2002) "Ideological work fruitful over past 13 years." Available from www1.china.org/english/features/45918.htm.

CNN (2012) "China's new leaders," November. Available from http://edition.cnn.com/interactive/2012/11/world/china-new-leadership.
Committee to Protect Journalists (2014) "2014 prison census: 221 journalists jailed worldwide," December 1. Available from https://cpj.org/imprisoned/2014.php.
Congressional Executive Commission on China (2003) "China Roundtable." Available from www.cecc.gov/pages/roundtables/092203/huchen.php?mode=print.
Document No. 9 (2013) ChinaFile, November 8. Available from www.chinafile.com/document-9-chinafile-translation.
Grigg, A. (2015) "How China stopped its bloggers," *Australia Financial Review*, July 4. Available from www.afr.com/technology/social-media/how-china-stopped-its-bloggers-20150703-gi34za.
Han, L.C. (1997) "Luoshi de guanjian zaiyu chuangzaoxing de gongzuo" [Innovative work is the key to implementation], January 26, Zhonggong zhongyang xuanchuanbu zhengce fagui yanjiushi, ed. *Shisida yilai xuanchuan sixiang gongzuo de lilun yu shixian* [Theories and Practice of Propaganda Thought Work since the 14th Party Conference], Beijing: Xuexi chubanshe.
Hong Kong Mail (2001) "Tougher rules for media," February 19.
Jiang, Z.M. (1997) "Zai quanguo xuanchuan sixiang gongzuo huiyishang de jianghua" [Talk at the National Conference on Propaganda and Thought Work], January 24, Zhonggong zhongyang xuanchuanbu zhengce fagui yanjiushi, ed. *Shisida yilai xuanchuan sixiang gongzuo de lilun yu shijian* [Theories and Practice of Propaganda Thought Work since the 14th Party Conference], Beijing: Xuexi chubanshe.
Jiao, G.B. (2004). "Declaration of the Campaign against the Central Propaganda Department." Available from www.zonaeuropa.com/20040505_2.htm.
Kessel, J.M. and Mozur, P. (2016) "How China is changing your internet," *New York Times*, August 19. Available from www.nytimes.com/video/technology/100000004574648/china-internet-wechat.html.
King, G., Pan, J., and Roberts, M.E. (2016) "How the Chinese government fabricates social media posts for strategic distraction, not engaged argument," Working Paper. Available from http://gking.harvard.edu/50c.
Lam, W. (2015) "Xi Jinping forever," *Foreign Policy*, April 1. Available from http://foreignpolicy.com/2015/04/01/xi-jinping-forever-china-president-term-limits/.
Liaowang dongfang zhoukan (2015) "Jiefangjun fu zongzhang sunjianguo shang jiang: Zhongguo you bei qinlüe weixian [PLA Deputy Chief Sun Jianguo: China at risk of invasion]," *Liaowang dongfang zhoukan*, March 4. Available from http://news.sina.com.cn/c/2015-03-04/101031565883.shtml.
Ma, J. (2000) "State publications face revamp, axe," *South China Morning Post*, September 6.
Mao, Z.D. (1967) "He A'erbaniya junshi daibiao tuan de tanhua [Talk with Albanian military delegation]," May. Available from www.mzdbl.cn/maoxuan/huibian/aerbaniyajunshidaibaotuan.html.
Mao, Z.D. (2013) "Mao Zedong Nanfang juece [Mao Zedong's Southern decisions]," Chapter 9, October 29. Available from http://dangshi.people.com.cn/n/2013/1029/c85037-23365010.html.
Minnick, J. (2014) "The end of consensus politics in China," *China Spectator*, August 6. Available from www.china-consult.com.au/2014/08/06/the-end-of-consensus-politics/.
Neibu tongxin (a classified publication of the Central Propaganda Department) (2001–2007).
Qian, G. (2014) "The missing speech," September 4. Available from http://cmp.hku.hk/2014/09/04/35905/.
Quanguo xuanchuan ganbu peixun cankao ziliao, ed. (1999) *Xuanchuan ganbu peixun cankao ziliao* [Propaganda Cadre Training Reference Materials], 4 vols. (no publisher or place of publication identified), Vol. 1, 133.
Renmin Ribao (1999) "Tuanjie yiqie keyi tuanjie [Unite all that can be united]," January 1, p. 1.
Renmin Ribao (2013) "Lu Wei: Ba wangshang yulun gongzuo zuowei xuanchuan gongzuo zhong zhong zhi zhong [The online media should be a top priority of propaganda work]," September 17. Available from http://news.sina.com.cn/m/2013-09-17/033728232935.shtml.
Renmin Ribao (2014) "Yuan zhongyang wai xuan ban fu ju ji ganbu gaojianyun bei kaichu dangji he gongzhi [Former Deputy Director of the CCP Central Foreign Propaganda Department Gao Jianjun expelled from the CCP and public office]," September 26. Available from http://politics.people.com.cn/n/2014/0926/c1001-25742539.html.
Renmin Ribao (2015) "Huang Kunming renzhongxuan bu changwu fu buzhang, zhongyang wenming ban zhuren [Huang Kunming appointed as Vice Minister of the Central Propaganda Department, Director of the Office for Spiritual Civilization]," January 4. Available from http://renshi.people.com.cn/n/2015/0104/c139617-26317375.html.

Sabin, L. (1994) "New bosses in the workers' state: The growth of non-State sector employment in China," *The China Quarterly*, Vol. 140: 944–970.
Shanghai Daily (2015) "China voice: Cyber security high on China's agenda," July 9. Available from www.shanghaidaily.com/article/article_xinhua.aspx?id=291666.
Silent Contest (2013) http://chinascope.org/main/content/view/6168/92/. The film is available on YouTube, www.youtube.com/watch?t=85&v=M_8lSjcoSW8.
Sina (2015) "Jing Junhai ren Zhonggong zhongyang xuanchuan bu fu buzhang [Jing Junhai becomes Deputy Director of the Central Propaganda Department]," Sina, July 13. Available from http://news.sina.com.cn/c/2015-07-13/213032103429.shtml [accessed July 14, 2015].
Stratfor (2000) "Beijing's anxiety." Available from www.stratfor.com/SERVICES/giu2000/080800.ASP [accessed August 8, 2000].
Supreme People's Court (2013) Legal Interpretation no. 21 (2013). Available from http://chinalawtranslate.com/spc-and-spp-interpretation-on-internet-speech-crimes/?lang=en.
The Age (2002) "China licences journalists, issues propaganda tests," December 10.
Wang, X.K. (2013) "Lixiang xinnian shi gongchandang ren jingshen shang de 'gai' [Ideals and faith are the 'calcium' of Party members]," December 5. Available from http://theory.people.com.cn/n/2013/1205/c40537-23757123.html.
Wen, Y. (2013) "Learning the news," *Global Times*, December 17. Available from www.globaltimes.cn/content/832671.shtml#.UrE5HvQW1HV.
Xinhua (2013a) "Shouquan fabu: Zhonggong zhongyang guanyu quanmian shenhua gaige ruogan zhongda wenti de jueding [Authorized Release: The CPC Central Committee's decision to deepen overall reform]," November 15. Available from http://news.xinhuanet.com/politics/2013-11/15/c_118164235.htm.
Xinhua (2013b) "Xi Jinping ren zhongyang quanmian shenhua gaige lingdao xiaozu zu zhang [Xi Jinping to chair the Central Leading Group for the Comprehensive Deepening of Reform]," December 30.
Xinhua (2014) "Zhongyang wangluo anquan he xinxi hua lingdao xiaozu chengli: Cong wangluo daguo mai xiang wangluo qiangguo [Establishment of Central Internet Security and Informatization Leading Group: From Internet medium power to Internet great power]," February 27. Available from http://news.xinhuanet.com/politics/2014-02/27/c_119538719.htm.
Xuexi chubanshe (1994) *Quan guo xuanchuan sixiang gongzuo huiyi wenjian hui bian* [Collected Articles from the National Conference on Propaganda and Thought Work], Beijing: Xuexi chubanshe, pp. 358–361.
Zhong ban fa (2013) "9 hao wenzhang [CCP General Office Document 9]." Available from http://bit.ly/1KutyPL.
Zhonggong zhongyang xuanchuanbu, zhengce fagui yanjiushi, ed. (1998) *Xuanchuan wenhua zhengce fagui xuanbian 1996–1997* [Selected Policies and Regulations on Propaganda and Culture 1996–1997], Beijing: Xuexi chubanshe, p. 28.
Zhongxuanbu, ed. (2014) *Xi Jinping zong shuji xilie zhongyao jianghua duben* [A Reader of Xi Jinping's Important Speeches], Beijing: Xuexi chubanshe.

PART IV

Major policy arenas

12

HOW THE PARTY-STATE RUNS THE ECONOMY

A model of elite decision-making in the financial market

Victor Shih

Introduction: a "market" view of financial policy-making

How are financial and economic policies made in China? What motivates policy-makers? This chapter presents a quasi-market model for financial decision-making in which multiple agencies headed by power-maximizing ministers propose a range of policy options on multiple issues to spark the interest of power-maximizing elite policy consumers. If a senior leader or an elite decision body sponsors a policy, then the lead agency that proposes that policy would enjoy elite attention and heightened formal power. A market analysis of financial policy-making suggests an impetus for persistent policy innovations, a strong preference for rapid fixes, a tendency to disregard long-term consequences of policies, and prolonged jurisdictional competition between agencies involved in the financial sector.

The policy-making process in China at times seems like a black box from which one surprise after another springs forth. For example, foreign investors and, indeed, Chinese academics were generally surprised by the sudden devaluation of the RMB in August 2015. This confusion stems partly from the assumptions we make about the Chinese policy process. In democracies, we have an easier time observing the driving forces of policy formulation. Politicians who seek offices or reelections must formulate policies that maximize their electoral prospect, either by appeasing voters or powerful lobbies (Downs 1957; Mayhew 1974). In the absence of democratic pressure, it remains unclear what the driving forces of policy-making are, in China and elsewhere. The naïve assumption that Chinese policy-makers create policies "for the good of the country" is simply unsustainable because it can only explain policy successes. Policy failures and stagnation are then attributed to mistakes, incomplete information, or external shocks. In fact, myriad studies of policy-making have shown leaders in a wide variety of settings are perfectly capable of initiating bad policies on their own (Bates 1981; Rosenbluth 1989; Alesina and Drazen 1995). This chapter attempts to demystify policy-making in China by making some simple assumptions about the incentives of Chinese leaders and bureaucrats.

For the purpose of this analysis, all government organizations involved in the financial arena are divided into "consumers" and "producers." The consumers are elite policy-makers or policy-making groups that make executive decisions about major financial policies. Producers are ministerial-level organizations that can both implement policies and provide policy alternatives to senior policy-makers. Both consumers and producers are presumed to be power-maximizing, meaning that they wish to rise as high in the Chinese Communist Party (CCP) hierarchy as possible. Consumers are Politburo Standing Committee members and other high-level officials in elite organs such as the Central Leading Group for Comprehensively Deepening Reforms (CLGCDR) who wish to retain their positions and to expand their influence in the highest reaches of the party. Producers are ministerial-level officials in the financial bureaucracy who aim to enter the Politburo. This assumption is different from the typical assumption of the budget-maximizing bureaucracy (Niskanen 1971; Weingast and Banks 1992). Unlike the prototypical Weberian bureaucracy, there is no clear distinction between bureaucrats and politicians in China, since they are all eligible to enter the Politburo Standing Committee (PBSC) and the central leading groups, which are the ultimate loci of power in China (Shih 2007).

In this market for financial policy-making, high-level consumers are monopsonists, for whom producers – the various ministries – must compete with one other for "contracts." Thus, this market is imperfect in the sense the elite consumers can artificially suppress the "price" that they pay. This is especially the case since President Xi Jinping consolidated decision-making power in his own hands through the formation of myriad leading groups led by him. If we believe that the main currency in the government is power and prestige, then senior leaders are high net-worth individuals who reward producers with fame and promotion for their policies. Power and prestige, however, are suboptimal metrics for conveying price signals as they do not express themselves in easily observable or continuous units.

Moreover, the market suffers from fundamental information asymmetry and contract enforcement difficulties. For one, the complexity of elite politics does not always allow consumers to pay producers the expected reward for services. Knowing that, the producers do not exert their utmost effort to find the right solutions, especially ones that undermine the producer's own immediate interests. The contract enforcement problem is partially alleviated by the realization of exchange between consumers and producers. That is, the producer automatically gains prestige and a bolstered resume when an elite consumer adopts the policy proposal put forth by a particular producer. This positive incentive motivates policy innovations by the various producer agencies on issues which are high priorities for the consumers.

The "contract" between the consumer and producer, however, also suffers from information asymmetry. That is, producers can exploit the elite's ignorance of policy minutiae to propose apparent solutions, which in reality do not solve the targeted problems in the medium term. Worse, producers may tailor policies to the consumer's own erroneous views of the world, knowing that any opposition to those views will be punished as disloyalty anyway. This is especially likely when the power of the consumers is concentrated in a single leader, whose views are not checked by other political elite.

In the analysis below, I will first describe the makeup, incentives, and organization of both groups of actors (i.e., producers and consumers). I will then describe how these groups of actors fit into the overall policy process in China. The chapter will evaluate the accuracy of this framework through the case of China's "solution" to the problem of local debt. Finally, the chapter concludes with a discussion on policy and theoretical implications of the framework presented, especially in light of the increasing concentration of power in the hands of President Xi Jinping.

Consumers

Because China remains a one-party authoritarian regime, the ultimate consumers of policy are not the citizenry, but rather the top leaders of the CCP. As senior leaders, they have a collective interest in maintaining power and individual incentive to maximize their own prestige and standing. Therefore, these CCP leaders have a stake in promoting financial policy innovation and ensuring the success of some of these policies, although the imperative of maintaining stability is ever present. To this end, senior leaders seek policies they believe would produce the most desirable political and economic outcomes. However, as in any consumer market, this does not preclude producers from shaping consumer preferences through aggressive marketing campaigns. Factional politics further complicate the picture (e.g., one has an incentive to promote bad policies in an area controlled by political rivals), but for the sake of focus this chapter will not address this aspect of policy-making.

Previous to the Xi Administration, the ultimate consumer of policies in China had been the PBSC composed of the top seven or so senior leaders who voted on all major decisions in China. Since Xi took power, power to make key decisions on the economy has migrated toward party organs such as the CLGCDR and the Central Leading Group for Finance and Economics (CLGFE) (discussed below). Thus, when the People's Bank of China (PBOC), for example, announced currency devaluation, it was not announcing a decision made by the PBOC, but rather one made by the PBSC or the CLGFE. Again, previous to the Xi Administration, PBSC members who also served as the premier or the vice-premier in the State Council (SC) had been in charge of economic portfolios, which included state-owned enterprises (SOEs), transportation, energy, finance, agriculture, fiscal affairs, and fixed-asset investment, among others (Lieberthal 2004). Although the member of the PBSC or the Politburo who controlled the finance portfolio (currently Vice-Premier Ma Kai) had considerable agenda-setting power in PBSC discussions on financial issues, he could not unilaterally make decisions on major policies and needed PBSC votes to approve them. With the formation of the leading groups, the decision-making power of vice-premiers in charge of finance likely diminished further.

The incentive of PBSC members is extremely complicated, but if we abstract away from factional struggle, it becomes somewhat manageable. Collectively, PBSC members have an interest to see that growth continues at a healthy pace in China because they know that a large part of the CCP's legitimacy rests on growth. Thus, without considering vested interests and factional conflicts, they are in general open to financial innovations that can promote growth. Still, this concern with growth likely has a short-time horizon, as any sudden drop in growth rates likely will increase political risks to the entire regime. Individually, each PBSC member would like to make his or her own portfolio as successful as possible to increase individual standing in the PBSC and to establish a policy legacy. Failure in a policy area results in the humiliating prospect of being deprived of a particular portfolio, although PBSC members are rarely removed from power for policy failure alone. For example, former Premier Zhu Rongji underwent the humiliating experience of being removed from the SOE portfolio for the perceived failure to galvanize local SOEs (Zong 2002). PBSC members' individual desire to operate successful portfolios thus introduces considerable complication to financial policy. Because money affects every policy area, a financial policy that prevents a PBSC member from maximizing the success of his portfolio would likely generate opposition to the policy. In mid-2016, for example, the SC advocated looser monetary policy despite opposition from the CLGCDR, likely due to the imperative to fulfill growth targets set forth at the National's People's Congress (*Wall Street Journal* 2016).

Soon after Xi took power, a new set of consumer institutions – the leading groups – emerged, which fundamentally altered the policy-making landscape in China. Announced at the Third Plenum in late 2013, the leading groups formally came into being in January 2014, when the umbrella organization, the CLGCDR (中央全面深化改革领导小组), held its first meeting, which was chaired by Xi Jinping (Wang Zhu 2014; Johnson and Kennedy 2015). The leading group has six subgroups ranging from the economy, ecology, judiciary, culture, to social structure, party institutions, and discipline and inspection institutions, which afford the new organs extensive jurisdiction over virtually every policy area in China (Wang Zhu 2014). Also, Xi Jinping personally heads nearly every subgroup, except for the one for culture, headed by Liu Yunshan. Since its formation, CLGCDR has approved decrees ranging from household registration reform to insurance rules, to food safety decrees. Most noticeably, CLGCDR approved the draft of the 13th Five-Year Plan, which previously would have required PBSC and State Council approval (Yao 2015). By routing approval of such important documents to an organization headed by himself, Xi circumvented potential vetoes by his PBSC colleagues and installed himself as the most important policy consumer in the regime.

Unlike previous leading groups, the CLGCDR and its subgroups are filled with some of the most senior officials in various policy areas, including national defense and internal security (Table 12.1). Thus, it can make final decisions on a wide range of issues and still take advantage of the expertise of officials with deep knowledge in these policy areas. A by-product, perhaps intentional, of the leading group structure is that two PBSC members, Yu Zhengsheng and Zhang Dejiang, are effectively shut out of much of the policy process because they are not on the leading group. In their stead, more junior members of the China People's Political Consultative Conference and the National People's Congress, headed by Yu and Zhang respectively, are represented in the leading group.

Besides the PBSC and the CLGCDR, enormous power is vested in the Central Leading Group for Finance and Economics (CLGFE), which was reconstituted in the early 1980s to preside over economic affairs. The CLGFE is typically chaired by the Premier of China, while its members typically include vice-premiers in the State Council with economic portfolios, as well as ministers of essential agencies, including the People's Bank of China, the National Development and Reform Commission (formerly State Planning Commission), the Ministry of Finance, and the Central Securities Regulatory Commission. Xi Jinping, however, has asserted direct control over the CLGFE and has made it the same organization as the economic reform subgroup of the CLGCDR, headed by Xi's high school friend Liu He (Johnson and Kennedy 2015). Liu is also the Director of the CLGFE General Office.

As an elite decision body, the CLGFE serves three important functions in the policy process. First, in the economic arena, the CLGFE sits just below the PBSC and the CLGCDR and can unilaterally make decisions on important issues that do not pertain to the entire economy. For example, the CLGFE routinely allocated fiscal and financial subsidies to various sectors and localities by issuing orders to the ministries (State Planning Commission *et al.* 1986). Second, CLGFE has since its formation been an important forum for senior leaders to debate major economic policies before moving them to the PBSC or the CLGCDR for final approval. For example, both the 1988 price reform and the 1994 tax centralization were debated vigorously in the CLGFE among senior party leaders specializing in economic affairs (Wu 1997; Yang 1997). Thus, in some ways, the CLGFE constituted a more powerful organ for financial and economic policies than the PBSC because a consensus was often reached in the CLGFE before the PBSC voted on it, as was the case for the 1994 fiscal centralization (Zhu 1993b). In the current policy environment, the CLGFE likely collects policy proposals from experts and the ministries before final approval by the CLGCDR. Furthermore, the CLGFE has its own research apparatus that advises senior leaders on various policy options. It also has the authority to "sub-contract" research to various other government agencies. Finally, although CLGFE does not command its own policy implementation capabilities, it often coordinates policy implementation to ensure squabbling ministries and recalcitrant local governments carry out policies with the proper zeal (Lieberthal and Oksenberg 1988). The policy coordination role of the CLGFE has been strengthened since the de facto merger with the economic subgroup of the CLGCDR, which is nominally headed by Xi Jinping himself.

Despite the recent rise of the party in the policy process, the State Council, China's cabinet, remains an important policy consumer in China. The SC is headed by the Premier and holds regular meetings attended by vice-premiers and ministers. Members of the SC overlap with PBSC members, CLGFE members, and now CLGCDR members to a considerable extent (see Table 12.1). Since the ascension of Xi Jinping, a larger number of policies has circumvented SC approval, requiring only CLGCDR approval. However, there was a period in the 1980s when the CLGFE was controlled by Premier Zhao Ziyang, while the SC was mainly controlled by planning stalwarts such as Yao Yilin and Chen Yun (Fewsmith 1994). Under this situation, SC considered different policy alternatives than the CLGFE and at times countermanded the decisions of the CLGFE (Chen 1995). Although this dichotomy is unlikely to arise again under Xi, we cannot rule out the possibility. Also, unlike the CLGFE and the CLGCDR, the State Council still has enormous research and policy implementation capacities that party organs lack, rendering it indispensable in the policy proposal and implementation stages of the policy process.

Beyond these permanent elite bodies, temporary leading groups are often formed to tackle specific problems in the financial arena. When former Premier Zhu wanted to suppress money supply and to centralize monetary policy in 1993, for example, he formed the Central Leading Group on Financial Reform (Zhu 1993a). Zhu also formed the Central Finance Work Committee to oversee the centralization of the banking system in 1998, but it was abolished after centralization was accomplished (Heilmann 2005). After Wen Jiabao took office in 2003, he revitalized momentum to reform state-owned banks by forming the Central Leading Group on State Bank Share-Holding Reform (CLGSBSR). Under Xi, however, such temporary leading groups have been sidelined by the formation of the semi-permanent CLGCDR, which again has extensive jurisdiction across a number of policy areas.

Producers

The main producers of policies in China include the major SC ministries and directly administered units, all of which are at the ministerial level. These agencies tend to be large entities with policy implementation capabilities, provincial and local branches, and a substantial administrative and research staff. Therefore, all producers also serve a consultative role in the policy process, even in the current party-centric policy process. As ministers, the heads of producer organizations can all be seen as ambitious politicians hoping to rise higher in the hierarchy, with the ultimate aim of entering the PBSC and becoming the premier of China. To achieve these aims, senior officials in these producer ministries mobilize their organizations to compete with each other for major policy "contracts," which bolster their administrative accomplishments and increase their promotion prospects. This competition is exacerbated by the ambiguous jurisdiction between these agencies, which gives considerable room for producers to encroach upon the jurisdiction of rival agencies. Thus, despite the centralization of the policy process under the CLGCDR in the Xi Administration, such inter-agency competition still leads to information distortion and competing policy proposals from the various agencies.

Producer agencies in the financial sector can be divided into two groups: more powerful full-service providers and less powerful regulators. Full-service providers have both enormous regulatory capacities, as well as control over a significant source of funding. The latter resource is important because it allows full-service providers to supply comprehensive policy solutions to policy consumers. The People's Bank of China (PBOC), the Ministry of Finance (MOF), and the National Development and Reform Commission (NDRC) all command a wide range of powers and resources. Their importance is reflected by the fact that their ministers are all full

Table 12.1 Main consumers of financial policies[1]

Organization	*Members*	*Authorities*
Politburo Standing Committee (PBSC)	*Xi Jinping* (President, Party General Secretary) *Zhang Dejiang* (Chairman of the National People's Congress) *Li Keqiang* (Premier) *Yu Zhengsheng* (Chairman of Chinese People's Political Consultative Conference) *Zhang Gaoli* (Executive Vice-Premier) *Wang Qishan* (Chairman of the Central Commission for Discipline Inspection) *Liu Yunshan* (Chairman of the Central Leading Group for Spiritual Civilization Construction)	Ultimate authority over all issues of national significance
Central Leading Group for Finance and Economics (CLGFE)[2]	Chairman: *Xi Jinping* Vice-Chairman: *Li Keqiang* Members: *Liu Yunshan* (PBSC member) *Zhang Gaoli* (Executive Vice-Premier, PBSC member) *Liu Yandong* (Vice-Premier) *Wang Yang* (Vice-Premier) *Ma Kai* (Vice-Premier) *Wang Huning* (Head of Central Policy Research) *Li Zhanshu* (Head of CCP Central Committee General Office) *Yang Jiechi* (State Councilor) *Yang Jing* (State Councilor) *Fang Fenghui* (PLA Chief of Staff) *Ding Xuedong* (Executive Vice-Secretary-General of the State Council) *He Lifeng* (Minister, National Development and Reform Commission) *Xiao Jie* (Minister of Finance) *Zhou Xiaochuan* (Governor of PBOC) *Xiao Yaqing* (Chairman of the State Assets Supervision Administration Commission) *Miao Wei* (Minister of Industry and Information Technology) *Jiang Daming* (Minister of Land and Resources) *Jiang Weixin* (Minister of Housing) *Chen Lei* (Minister of Water Resources) *Liu He* (Head of the General Office of CLGFE, Vice-Minister of NDRC) *Wang Yi* (Minister of Foreign Affairs) *Wang Zhigang* (Vice-Minister of Technology) *Chen Jining* (Minister of Environmental Protection) *Li Xiaopeng* (Minister of Transportation) *Nur Bekri* (Chair, National Energy Administration)	Sets agenda for PBSC votes and hosts debates on economic issues Makes final decisions on minor economic issues Makes decisions on the distribution of fiscal and monetary subsidies

Table 12.1 Continued

Organization	*Members*	*Authorities*
The State Council (SC)	The Premier Li Keqiang and all of the vice-premiers are also members of the CLGFE	Similar to CLGFE authorities
Central Leading Group for Comprehensively Deepening Reforms (CLGCDR)	Chairman: *Xi Jinping* Vice-Chairmen: *Li Keqiang* (Premier, PBSC member) *Liu Yunshan* (PBSC member) *Zhang Gaoli* (Executive Vice-Premier, PBSC member) Head of the Office: *Wang Huning* Members: *Ma Kai* (Vice-Premier) *Liu Yandong* (Vice-Premier) *Xu Qiliang* (Vice Chairman, Central Military Commission) *Wang Yang* (Vice-Premier) *Zhao Leji* (Head of Central Organization Department) *Du Qinglin* (Secretary of the Secretariat of the Central Committee) *Wang Chen* (Secretary General of the National People's Congress) *Zhou Qiang* (President, Supreme People's Court) *Zhang Qingli* (Vice-Chairman, CPPCC) *Wang Zhengwei* (Chairman, State Ethnic Affairs Commission) *Liu Qibao* (Head of the Central Propaganda Department) *Li Jianguo* (Chairman, All China Federation of Trade Unions) *Meng Jianzhu* (Chairman, Central Politics and Law Commission) *Li Zhanshu* (Head of CCP Central Committee General Office) *Zhao Hongzhu* (Vice-Chair of the Central Commission for Discipline Inspection) *Guo Shengkun* (Minister of Public Security) *Cao Jianming* (Procurator-General of the Supreme People's Procuratorate) *Zhou Xiaochuan* (PBOC Governor)	Extensive decision-making power over a wide range of policy areas, including the economy, ecology, social structure, culture, judiciary, party institutions, and anti-corruption. This especially pertains to long-term policy planning.

Notes

1 Sources: the *People's Daily* website (www.people.com.cn/), Li (2003).

2 Wang Kai (2014).

members of the CCP Central Committee, an elite body composed of 200 or so of the most powerful officials in China. Furthermore, they all sit on the CLGFE and the CLGCDR. In contrast, regulatory agencies, including the China Banking Regulatory Commission (CBRC), China Securities Regulatory Commission (CSRC), and the China Insurance Regulatory Commission (CIRC), can only provide regulatory services. Politically, the current ministers of these regulatory agencies are only alternate members of the Central Committee, half a step below full Central Committee members in the party hierarchy. These chief regulators are also not represented in the CLGFE (Sina.com 2016). Thus, despite the appearance of gradual movement toward an institutionalized financial regulatory framework, these regulators have found their authorities constantly challenged and diminished by the full-service providers.

In the financial arena, the most powerful and influential agency is PBOC, which has enormous agenda-setting and executive authorities in monetary policy, financial regulation, and increasingly in personnel control. The PBOC's giant presence in the financial sector is a relatively new phenomenon. For much of the 1980s, the State Planning Commission (today's NDRC) served as the main executor of monetary policy through the implementation of the pervasive plan. Money supply, most of which came either from the state investment plan or the cash plan, was subsumed as part of the national or local production plan (Fei 1995). Beginning in 1992, when Zhu Rongji took over as vice-premier in charge of finance, the PBOC began to take a much more active role in formulating monetary policies. Nonetheless, the PBOC's dominance in monetary policy is by no means complete today. For example, the monetary policy committee, an advisory body that makes recommendations to the SC and CLGFE, is composed of PBOC, MOF, CSRC, and NDRC officials (PBOC Monetary Policy Committee 2000). Also, the final arbiter of major shifts in monetary policy is most likely the CLGFE or the CLGCDR, where agencies such as the NDRC and the MOF are represented.

Nonetheless, the PBOC in recent years has consolidated control over monetary policy as the number of monetary instruments it administers rose. As state-directed fixed asset investment became a declining share of the money supply and as the PBOC developed a growing arsenal of monetary instruments, its voice and day-to-day influence in the monetary policy process increased. In the past decade, the PBOC developed a host of monetary instruments, including reverse repo, pledged supplement lending, short-term lending operations, reserve requirements, asset-liability management, and PBOC bonds, all of them exerting important influence in the highly liquid interbank market in China (People's Bank of China 2015). Although elite consumers make ultimate decisions on monetary policy, the PBOC's command of these instruments provides the agency with enormous leverage over the exact implementation of monetary policy.

In the early 2000s, the PBOC's role in financial regulation temporarily declined with the formation of the CSRC, CIRC, and CBRC. In 2003, for example, Premier Wen shifted all banking regulation duties to the CBRC, which resulted in the transfer of many PBOC departments to the CBRC. Even after the CBRC split off from the PBOC, the central bank maintained policing power over money laundering and counterfeiting. This is significant because the anti-laundering portfolio afforded the PBOC and the State Administration of Foreign Exchange great latitude with which to examine the books of all financial institutions, not just those of the banks (State Administration of Foreign Exchange 2004). In addition, as the guardian of "overall financial stability," the PBOC continued to audit the books of every kind of financial institutions.[1] This authority has been strengthened in recent years with the establishment of an interagency meeting system headed by the PBOC, in which regulatory agencies were obligated to share financial data with the central bank. More recently, with the rise of shadow banking, the PBOC began macro-prudential monitoring of major banks and their counter-parties in the other segments of the financial industry, thus giving the PBOC de facto regulatory power over a wide range of financial institutions (People's Bank of China 2015).

The most contested arena in the financial sector, one that the PBOC has fought pitch-battles with rival agencies to command, is political control. The core of political control is the authority over personnel appointment. Before 1998, the PBOC shared appointment power in the financial sector with the local party committee and the Central Organization Department (COD). Under Zhu Rongji, most appointment power in the financial sector was centralized to the party's Central Finance Work Committee (CFWC) (Heilmann 2005). In this period (1998–2003), the PBOC retained considerable influence over the appointment of bankers since several senior members of the PBOC also served in the CFWC. With the formation of the CBRC, however, the PBOC found itself deprived of most of its appointment power. With the formation of the CBRC, PBOC only retained the authority to appoint regional governors of the PBOC itself, while the COD and the CBRC took over appointment of senior bankers (Heilmann 2005).

In 2004, however, the PBOC won back a substantial amount of appointment authority by injecting massive funds into the China Construction Bank (CCB), Bank of China (BOC), Industry and Commerce Bank of China (ICBC), and Bank of Communication (BOCO), thereby gaining "ownership" of these banks through a subsidiary, the Central Huijin Company. Through the Huijin Company, the PBOC further injected funds from the foreign exchange reserve and from central bank loans into scores of banks and even brokerages. In the spring and summer of 2005, for example, the PBOC successively announced that Central Huijin Company would recapitalize Galaxy Securities (Yinhe Zhengquan), Southern Securities (Nanfang Zhengquan), Huaxia Securities, Shenyin Wanguo Securities, and Guotai Jun'an Securities, all of which were illiquid state-owned brokers (Liu 2005). These injections made Huijin, and indirectly the PBOC, the majority shareholders of these companies, which bestowed it appointment power.

Following the PBOC, the Ministry of Finance currently constitutes the most influential full-service provider in the financial sector. Its influence stems from the MOF's traditional role as the "investor" (*chuziren*) of major financial institutions in China. Although its "investor" status has been eroded in recent years, it continues to control a large slice of the financial sector. Furthermore, as the issuer of treasury bonds and the agency in charge of the National Social Security Fund, the MOF carries a loud voice in any debate on the national economy. More recently, its control over the enormous muni-bond program has further consolidated its role as a premier full-service provider for the top leadership.

Since the formation of the Big Four state banks in the 1980s, the MOF has served as the "investor" in these banks, giving the agency primary claimant status over the profits of these banks. Granted, this nominal status did not afford the agency power to make unilateral decisions on major issues relevant to the banking system. Final decisions were still left to the elite consumer. Nonetheless, as the chief investor, the MOF made regulations that determined how much capital the Big Four banks could use to write off bad debt (Bank of China 1995). In 1998, the MOF scored another major "contract" in becoming the "investor" in the four asset management companies (AMCs) set up to digest the Big Four state banks' non-performing loans (NPLs). By injecting 40 billion RMB in start-up capital to the four AMCs, MOF obtained "investor" status over these entities and gained regulatory oversight over the AMCs' NPL recovery ratios and their annual budgets (Ministry of Finance 2001).

Even after the PBOC began to inject funds into China's major banks, the MOF's presence remained formidable. MOF continues as one of the top shareholders in all of China's major banks. Moreover, the MOF is well represented on the board of the Huijin Company, although its influence suffered after the arrest of senior MOF official and Huijin board member Xu Fangming for suspected corruption (Hu 2005). MOF also retains a sizable influence over the stock and bond markets through the 1.9 trillion RMB National Social Security Fund (NSSF) (National Social Security Fund 2016). Finally, the MOF determines all accounting rules and taxation policies, both of which have enormous influence on the profitability of financial institutions.

Beyond these two agencies, the NDRC, the offspring of the once-omnipotent State Planning Commission, constitutes the third full-service provider in the financial sector. Despite its retreating influence in recent years, the NDRC has fought fierce rear-guard battles to maintain its formidable, if narrow, power in the financial sector. The NDRC today continues to enjoy enormous distributive and regulatory authority over financial resources.

Since the First Five-Year Plan in the early 1950s, the Planning Commission has played a dominant role in distributing investment and bank funding to various sectors and localities. Although its investment approval authorities have steadily declined as enterprises and banks gained increasing autonomy from the plan, the NDRC continues to formulate five-year and ten-year guidance plans, which still play a significant role in sectoral development in heavy industrial sectors dominated by SOEs and in the construction of major public work projects. The continual existence of the plan gives the NDRC a significant voice in the formulation of national economic policies. Its minister sits on the CLGFE, and it is represented in the monetary policy committee.

Because the NDRC still controls approval power for large-scale fixed-asset and technical innovation investment projects, the NDRC is the lead agency in charge of coordinating regional development policies, chief among them are the One Belt One Road Plan and the Northeast Revitalization Plan (National Development and Reform Commission 2016). These plans involve the expenditure of an enormous amount of state investment financed mainly by policy bank loans, and the NDRC plays the politically salient role of directing these funds. Government investment projects greatly affect the banking sector because both policy and commercial banks lend generously to finance these investment projects. Therefore, NDRC decisions affect the usage of a significant slice of bank deposits. The Go West campaign, for example, used up some 600 billion RMB in new loans between 2000 and 2003, compared with the 300 billion in new loans made in western provinces between 1997 and 2000 (Shih 2004). Banks willingly lent to these state investment projects because these loans were guaranteed by the government.

Besides the considerable authority of distributing fiscal and monetary resources, the NDRC's traditional power in price control accords it surprising clout in various aspects of the financial industry. For example, the NDRC, rather than the CBRC, makes regulations limiting the prices that asset management companies can pay subcontractors performing auditing and legal work (State Planning Commission 2001). Its traditional power further bestows the NDRC the authority to regulate service fees charged by banks (China Banking Regulatory Commission and National Development and Reform Commission 2003). The NDRC even formulates regulations limiting the regulatory and penalty fees charged by other regulatory agencies such as the CSRC and the CIRC (State Planning Commission and Ministry of Finance 2003).

Finally, because the NDRC traditionally coordinated the entire economy, it retains the authority to determine the overall scale of stock issuance and enterprise bond issuance in conjunction with the CSRC (Walter and Howie 2011). It also has the authority to approve the issuance of enterprise bonds denominated in both RMB and in foreign currencies (Walter and Howie 2011). Despite its much diminished influence, the NDRC's traditional claims over economic management and its continual authority to put a stamp of state approval on trillions of RMB in investment have given the agency a strong foundation on which to maintain a substantial foothold in the financial sector.

Among the three regulatory agencies, the CBRC probably has the most bureaucratic clout as it regulates the enormous banking sector. It was first formed in 2003 out of the former

CFWC and parts of the PBOC. Since its formation, the leadership of the agency has jealously guarded the CBRC's main mission of monitoring bank performance in China. In particular, the CBRC enforces liquidity, capital adequacy, and non-performing loan targets on all depository institutions in China, including state banks, joint-stock banks, foreign banks, credit cooperatives, and investment companies. With the rise of shadow banking, especially wealth management products issued by banks and trust companies, the CBRC's regulatory jurisdiction continues to expand as more departments and personnel are needed to regulate these rapidly rising financial instruments (Wang Peicheng 2014).

Taking over the regulatory departments of the PBOC, the CBRC commands a vast local network of offices that regularly audit local branches and national headquarters of all depository institutions. It is also the main agency in charge of formulating specific policies that ensure China's compliance with the WTO in the financial sector. For example, it determines the specific operation requirements for foreign banks in China and approves the expansion of foreign bank branches (Luo 2007).

Besides routine monitoring of financial institutions, the CBRC also prevents, investigates, and stops financial corruption and fraud. Here, the CBRC's authorities are more diluted. Although the CBRC has the data and expertise with which to uncover financial fraud, many cases of fraud are uncovered by audits conducted by the local or national auditing office. The uncovering of these cases is greatly embarrassing to the CBRC because it calls into question the agency's ability to effectively monitor banks. At the beginning of 2005, for example, the National Audit Office discovered that AMCs regularly reported more staff than they had in order to receive higher subsidies from the MOF (Ding and Wu 2005). This revelation doubtless discombobulated the CBRC leadership because the CBRC conducted two audits on the AMCs every year. In addition, because senior bankers are party officials with vice-ministerial rank, the Central Commission for Discipline Inspection (CCDI), the party's anti-corruption watchdog, often takes control over corruption cases involving senior bankers. For example, the CCDI took charge of the investigations of Wang Xuebing and Zhang Enzhao, both former Presidents of the China Construction Bank (Xinhua News Agency 2002).

The CBRC's regulatory authority is further diluted by the existence of disciplinary committees and supervision committees in all major financial institutions. Because major financial institutions in China are either wholly or partially state-owned, they all have party committees with propaganda, organization, and discipline and inspection (anti-corruption) subcommittees. In addition to reporting to the party secretary of the institution, who often serves concurrently as the chairman of the board, the departmental committee on discipline and inspection (CDI) also reports to the CDI at a higher level and ultimately to the CCDI. Due to the traditional weakness of the courts in China, many important tip-offs and allegations continue to flow through the CCDI network rather than through the judiciary system or through the CBRC. Because of the pervasiveness of corruption in China's financial institutions, the SC and the CFWC in 2000 further ordered the formation of 15 independent boards of supervision in the 15 largest financial institutions in China (Xinhua News Agency 2000). Even after the disbanding of the CFWC, these boards of supervisions remained in place in the major financial institutions to supervise their work. In the recent anti-corruption sweep, roving inspection teams from the CCDI, as well as the boards of supervision, played the pivotal role in investigating financial sector malfeasance, leaving little for the CBRC to do (Central Commission for Discipline Inspection 2016). Because of the existence of a wide array of monitoring institutions, the CBRC merely controls the most technical and in many ways the least important aspects of financial supervision.

Nomenklature power, or the authority to appoint and remove officials, is perhaps the most sought-after authority in any authoritarian country. In the banking system, the turf war over appointment has been extremely fierce. Although the CFWC temporarily put a stop to the dispute by consolidating appointment power, its demise in 2003 renewed the inter-agency scuffle over it (Heilmann 2005). In 2003, the COD acquired the authority to appoint all senior-level bankers at the ten largest financial institutions, while the CBRC obtained appointment power over the CEOs of the four asset management companies, the China Merchant Bank, and the Minsheng Bank (Heilmann 2005). In addition, the CBRC conducts professional qualification evaluations on all candidates for bank presidents and vice-presidents, including candidates for senior positions in foreign institutions operating in China.[2] Despite this formal division of power, the PBOC soon gained significant de facto appointment authorities through Huijin's shareholder control over the restructured banks. With the combination of both party and shareholder power, Zhou's office obtained the authority to approve candidates for all senior positions in banks that plan to list on the stock market.[3] Even after listing, senior management in majority state-owned banks, including the ICBC, BOC, and the CCB, continued to operate under the purview of the Central Huijin Company.

Besides the CBRC, two agencies, the CSRC and the CIRC regulate the activities of the securities and insurance industries respectively. Although these agencies nominally possess great latitude over the securities and insurance industries, their authorities are in reality constrained by rival agencies, especially the PBOC and the NDRC (China Banking Regulatory Commission *et al.* 2004). In the securities industry, the CSRC has grown from a weak advisory body with little real power to a plenipotentiary agency in the industry. Nominally, it now has the authority to regulate the stock exchanges, all securities companies, and mutual funds. It also approves the appointment of senior management in the exchanges and in all of the major brokerages and mutual funds. Finally, it regulates all transactions related to securities (Green 2004). Yet, this power is constrained by the NDRC's continual control over the overall scale of stock and enterprise bond issuance, the PBOC's ownership of several important securities companies through Huijin, and the COD's appointment power over senior CSRC and state-owned brokerage officials.

With the mid-2015 stock market crash and subsequent rescue orchestrated by the PBOC, the CSRC's status was further diminished because both top policy-makers and market participants realized that, in the midst of a stock market crash, only the central bank had the wherewithal to prevent a financial crisis. The only contribution of the CSRC had been to introduce measures which prevented large shareholders from selling shares, a policy that grossly distorted market functioning (Cao and Xie 2015). Unlike the PBOC, the CSRC did not have access to a substantial supply of funds, which would have allowed it to "rescue" the market.

The CIRC is in many ways the weakest policy producer discussed in this chapter. Formed only in 1998 as a vice-ministerial organization, it did not become a ministerial-level agency until 2003 (Guoji Jinrongbao 2003). Before its formation, the Chinese insurance industry was under the supervision of the PBOC and the MOF. After its formation, the CIRC acquired enormous discretion over market entry, allowable investment strategies, and pricing and benefit structure of policies in the insurance industry. Like the CBRC and CSRC, the CIRC also has approval power over senior management in the entire industry, including foreign firms operating in China. Nonetheless, like the CSRC and CBRC, it shares appointment of senior CIRC officials and top management in major state-owned insurance companies with the COD (Guoji Jinrongbao 2003). Moreover, because of its junior status, CIRC defers to more established agencies on a number of other issues. For example, the MOF continues to regulate accounting and auditing standards of insurance companies, and MOF tax policies on the insurance industry have a large impact on the bottom line of insurance companies. The PBOC, although it supposedly handed the bulk of the regulatory authorities to the CIRC in 1998, continues to require insurance

Table 12.2 Producer agencies

Agencies	*Leader (concurrent positions)*	*Major authorities*
People's Bank of China (PBOC)	*Zhou Xiaochuan* Member, CLGCDR Member, CLGFE Vice-chairman, CPPCC	• Formulate monetary policies • Recapitalize and rescue distressed financial institutions (FIs) with PBOC loans or foreign exchange reserve • Participate in appointment of FI management as "investor" • Monitor and regulate all banks and most major financial institutions through "macro-prudential regulation"
Ministry of Finance (MOF)	*Xiao Jie* Member, CLGFE Member, CCP Central Committee	• Monitor FIs as "investor" • Recapitalize FIs with bond issuance • Determine accounting and tax policies for FIs • Control the multi-trillion RMB muni-bond program
National Development and Reform Commission (NDRC)	*Xu Shaoshi* Member, CLGFE Member, CCP Central Committee	• Formulate investment plans and industrial policies to channel bank loans • Determine the overall amount of stock and enterprise bond issuance • Regulate the fees charged by financial regulators and banks
China Banking Regulatory Commission (CBRC)	*Shang Fulin* Alternate Member, CCP Central Committee	• Monitor liquidity, capital adequacy, and NPL ratios of depository institutions • Appoint senior management of FIs (AMCs) • Approve appointment of senior bankers • Prevent fraud and corruption in the banking sector • Approve the commencement and expansion of foreign bank operation in China
China Securities Regulatory Commission (CSRC)	*Liu Shiyu*	• Regulate the stock exchanges, all securities companies, and mutual funds • Approve the appointment of senior management in the exchanges, major brokerages, and mutual funds • Regulate all transactions related to securities • Approve qualified foreign institutional investors (QFIIs) and qualified domestic institutional investors (QDIIs)
China Insurance Regulatory Commission (CIRC)	*Chen Wenhui* (acting)	• Regulate market entry, allowable investment strategies, and pricing and benefit structure of policies • Directly appoint senior management in state-owned insurance firms • Approve appointment of senior management in the entire industry, including foreign firms operating in China • Approve entry and expansion of foreign and joint-venture insurance firms

Source: author's database.

companies to make regular reports under the guise of maintaining financial stability (People's Bank of China 1998).

Although the agencies discussed above by no means exhaust government entities that are involved in the financial sector, these agencies all devote a substantial part of their energy in the financial sector. The discussion above briefly touched on other agencies peripherally involved in the financial sector, including the National Audit Office, the State Asset Supervision and Administration Commission, and the National Social Security Fund. In examining the PBOC, MOF, NDRC, and the three regulatory agencies, a clear pattern emerges. Those agencies with secured access to a large pool of funds, including the PBOC, the MOF, and to a lesser extent the NDRC, can much more aggressively bid for "contracts" from policy consumers. The prime example of aggressive bidding is the PBOC's proposal to recapitalize banks overnight using the burgeoning foreign exchange reserve. Because of the attractiveness of this option for policy consumers, the PBOC was able to implement its preferred policy, which bestowed enormous shareholder power on the agency.

The policy process

Under the market framework, the policy process has four distinctive steps (Figure 12.1). Competing agencies' bids to dominate a particular policy mainly enter into the input and decision stages of the policy process. In the policy proposal or input stage, a plethora of producer agencies and government think-tanks propose policy choices in response to an economic crisis, to a salient issue raised by a consumer, or to a long-term problem in the financial sector. At this stage, there is considerable room for the producers, who are often specialists in the economy or in the financial sector, to influence the preference of the consumer, who are not financial experts. For financial policies, an important audience for producers' marketing campaigns at the initial stage is the vice-premier (VP) in charge of finance, currently Ma Kai. Because finance is the main responsibility of this VP, he or she has a stake in maximizing the success, or at least the apparent success, of this portfolio. With the emergence of the CLGCDR, it has also become a key "shopper" of policies in the initial stage. The head of the General Office of the CLGFE, Liu He, took six inspection trips in the Yangtze River Delta in 2015 and 2016 in order to obtain new ideas on how to carry out "supply side reform," a key policy thrust of the Xi Administration (Yao 2016).

Once a particular proposal is formally adopted by a leading group or by the PBSC, the lead agency, often in conjunction with experts from a group of government think-tanks, would

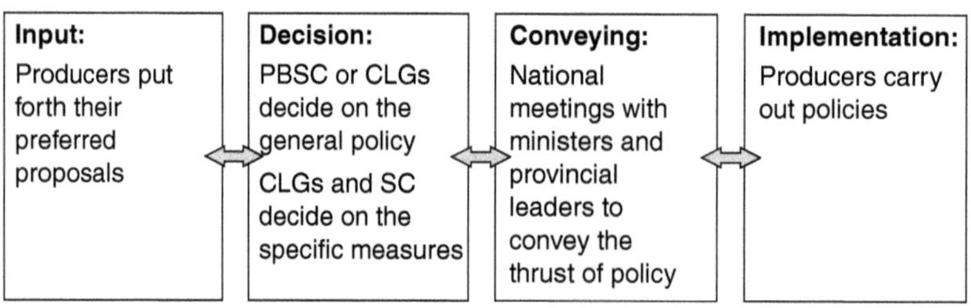

Figure 12.1 Financial policy process.

Source: author's database.

Note
CLGs = central leading groups.

convene to hammer out a concrete proposal. Some policies, such as the formation of the CBRC or a major expansion in government debt, require formal approval by the National People's Congress (NPC), although the NPC seldom rejects major financial policy changes proposed by the SC. Other policies, such as the revaluation of the RMB, require only formal announcements by the PBOC or other implementing agencies.

After a policy is adopted, there is a unique step in the Chinese policy process, which can be labeled as "conveying." Conveying comprises a series of rituals to ensure that relevant agencies understand the new policy and feel compelled to carry it out. Usually, a major policy is announced at either a special meeting (if urgent) or at an annual economic or financial work meeting. Provincial leaders and ministers are all required to attend these meetings. The Party Secretary General and the Premier take turns exhorting the attending officials about the importance of the new policy. The reason for these meetings is that thousands of new regulations cascade down to both central agencies and local governments every year, and central and local officials find it difficult to recognize the top policy priorities of the leadership. If the Secretary General and the Premier both emphasized the importance of a policy, lower-level officials would know that failure to carry out this policy might bring about administrative sanction. For minor policies, the lead agency or the leading group usually sends the new policy to the SC or to the Central Committee so that these powerful organizations can issue these decrees as their own decrees. This step increases the authoritativeness of the decrees.

In the final step of the policy process, the lead agency singly or in conjunction with other agencies carries out the new policy. Changes to the status quo often create both winners and losers in the bureaucracy, as well as give rise to new conflicts of interests. These conflicts often cannot be resolved by rivaling agencies or competing local governments themselves. Many of these conflicts find their way upward to the leading groups, the CLGFE, or even to the PBSC for adjudication (Lieberthal and Oksenberg 1988). A set of policies that fail to affect any meaningful changes or result in disastrous outcomes leads to the disgrace of the lead agency, as well as the elite sponsor of the policy. Policy failure also leads to another around of policy bidding by various agencies.

The policy "shopping" process produces both positive and negative consequences. On the positive side, the incentive to maximize portfolio success provides a constant impetus to financial policy innovation at the elite level. Reform policies abandoned by one administration will be taken up by elite consumers of the next administration. On the negative side, however, elite consumers often care little about the actual long-term impact of a set of policy innovations. Their main objective is to maximize the apparent, short-term success of financial policies. Knowing this consumer preference, producers, who are similarly motivated, provide proposals that maximize short-term results, even if they come at the expense of long-term functioning of the economy. As we see in the case of local debt, the producer which provided the most expedient and politically palatable solution became the selected "provider."

The policy market in action: "resolving" China's local debt burden

The 2008–2009 stimulus China carried out to counteract the global economic slowdown was in reality far greater than the official 4 trillion RMB. In addition to the trillions of expenditure from the government budget, local governments around China also set up thousands of local government financing vehicles (LGFVs), corporate entities wholly owned by local authorities, to borrow money from banks to finance infrastructure investment (Shih 2010). This leveraging initially was not considered by the Chinese government as governmental debt. As international and domestic experts sounded increasingly dire warnings about this issue, China's political leadership was forced to grapple with this growing problem. Initially, policy consumers entrusted technocrats in the CBRC to slow the growth of leveraging. However, such a move proved impossible while fulfilling a host of other policy objectives, including growth and financial stability. Also, as a regulatory agency, the CBRC could not provide funds with which to alleviate the problem. In 2015, a full service producer, the Ministry of Finance, came up with an ingenious plan which essentially deferred the problem at lower costs for the government. Although the local debt problem was not solved, top-level consumers gained a few years of reprieve from a financial crisis while the underlying problem continued to fester.

Through executing a massive stimulus program, China averted sharply slower growth in 2008–2009. Yet, the price of the stimulus became increasingly obvious in subsequent years. Even in 2010, outside analysts estimated that China's stimulus was in fact already over 10 trillion RMB, and once all the stimulus projects were completed, the amount of debt accrued would have exceeded 20 trillion RMB (Shih 2010). This figure in local debt was equivalent to 50 percent of China's nominal GDP in 2010. The combined liabilities of the Chinese government would have exceeded the international warning line of 60 percent of GDP. By the 2011 NPC meeting, many experts had warned the government about the growing local debt problem. Yet, the outgoing premier Wen Jiabao was in no mood to tackle the problem, and thus called on the SC bureaucracy to conduct a comprehensive audit on the issue (Xi 2011).

After taking power in late 2012, the Xi Jinping and Li Keqiang leadership ordered a comprehensive audit of local debt, which saw dozens of auditing teams from the central and provincial governments descending on provincial, prefecture, county, and even township level governments to account for the borrowing of LGFVs in thousands of jurisdictions. After the audit, the initial approach was to force local governments to drastically slow the pace of borrowing. Soon, however, policy-makers realized that the problem was so enormous that any attempt to even slow the pace of increase in local debt would have started a financial crisis. The CBRC, the lead agency initially, was marginalized after a couple of years of failed effort to control local debt.

The 2013 audit uncovered a modest 10 trillion RMB in local government debt. The leadership entrusted the CBRC with the important task of determining which LGFV debt was "commercial oriented" (*shangye xingzhi*) and thus was not government debt, and which was "public oriented" (*gonggong xingzhi*) and thus governmental debt (*21st Century Business Herald* 2013). In addition, the CBRC distributed quotas for new increases in local debt to localities and enforced them. Around the same time, the MOF, PBOC, and CBRC jointly issued a new decree forbidding public oriented LGFVs from borrowing money from non-bank financial institutions such as trust companies (Yi *et al.* 2013). When loans from the initial round of borrowing began to mature in 2010–2011, LGFVs, which had invested in wasteful and unprofitable projects, needed ways to roll over their loans. They began to work with trust companies, which absorbed money from high net worth customers of banks to invest in trust products, which were essentially high interest loans to LGFVs. Instead of the banks bearing the risks of lending to commercially unviable LGFVs, individual investors now held the risks. The SC wanted to put a stop to this practice. Similar to the new quota system for local debt, the CBRC took control of the enforcement of the decree against trust loans to "public oriented" LGFVs because the agency already had a department which monitored trust companies (Yi *et al.* 2013). Through much of 2013 and 2014, the CBRC was the lead agency in charge of managing the local debt issue.

Over time, however, the CBRC discovered that it was entrusted with an impossible task. On the one hand, it had to constrain the pace of local debt growth and prevent it from spreading into the high yielding shadow banking sector. On the other hand, the political leadership continued to demand local governments to invest more so as to maintain economic growth. In 2014, for example, Premier Li Keqiang still called for a growth target of 7.5 percent because "development remains the key to solving all our country's problems" (Li 2014). In order to reach the growth target, local governments needed to increase the scale of investment, much of it wasteful and financed by banks.

The CBRC was for a time able to stop the growth of direct borrowing by local governments through trust products (China Trustee Association 2014). However, banks and local governments soon found new ways of circumventing CBRC regulations. For one, the joint decree only forbade "public oriented" LGFVs from issuing trust products. In response, local governments restructured LGFVs by moving some cash generating assets into LGFVs, making them "commercial oriented" and eligible to issue trust products. Also, instead of forming a trust product with a trust company, LGFVs borrowed money directly from wealth management products, which were high yielding products packaged by banks and sold to their wealthy customers (Li 2013). The overall amount of trust assets grew by 4 trillion RMB in 2014 anyway with a large portion ultimately ending up in LGFVs (China Trustee Association 2014). With such a stupendous credit bubble, any serious attempt to deflate it risked rapid deleveraging and recession, outcomes that the political leadership was clear about avoiding. Even in official audits, local government debt had grown by 5 trillion RMB in just one year from 10 trillion in 2013 to 15 trillion by the end of 2014, and the 2014 audit also uncovered an additional 8.6 trillion in contingent liabilities (Li 2015).

As the local debt problem grew in 2011–2013, experts in the Ministry of Finance began to explore the approach of "open the front door, close the back door," which entailed "enlarging the scale of local municipal debt issuance to exchange and substitute for hidden debt of the local government financing vehicles" (Jia 2013). In other words, local governments could issue municipal debt on a large scale, the proceeds of which would be used to repay high interest bank and trust loans. This would not reduce the overall size of local government debt, but may drastically reduce interest payments and cash flow pressure on the local governments because municipal debt had explicit government guarantees and thus would have much lower interest rates. To be sure, because the substitution of high yielding loans by these bonds reduced banks' profitability, banks were far from pleased by the development. However, the Ministry of Finance's "innovation" was to *force* banks to buy these bonds through "designated sales" of these securities (Li 2015). The SC apparently liked this plan and soon issued a decree compelling banks to participate in the debt substitution program, with which banks had no choice but to comply (State Council 2014). Another innovation was that the municipal bonds would be officially issued by the localities, instead of by the central government. Thus, China's official sovereign debt level would not rise (Wen 2015). Although the global financial market increasingly recognized local debt as quasi-sovereign debt, China still could claim a relatively low sovereign debt level.

The political leadership apparently saw this as the perfect solution. In July 2015, an excited Li Keqiang announced to a group of economists that "we must increase the scale of (the debt exchange program)" (Cheng 2015). Over the course of 2015, the SC authorized the MOF to oversee the issuance of 3.2 trillion RMB in local municipal debt (Cheng 2015). In 2016, municipal debt outstanding grew by an additional 5.8 trillion RMB. Then Minister of Finance Lou Jiwei victoriously announced in December 2015 that local governments which had undergone debt exchange saw the average interest rate of their debt fall from 10 percent to 3.5 percent, drastically reducing the cash flow pressure on these localities (Cheng 2015).

The MOF and its leadership reaped enormous benefits from this successful policy "product" for consumers. First of all, the SC entrusted the MOF with the authority to allocate quotas for the debt exchange to various provinces. The MOF had the authority to determine which pool of debt was "public oriented" and thus was eligible for the debt exchange (Xing 2015). Most important of all, the MOF dictated monetary policy to the PBOC because the central bank had to ensure sufficient liquidity in the interbank bond market while these bonds were issued, else their interest rates would have been higher than desirable (Li 2013). Meanwhile, although Minister of Finance Lou Jiwei did not receive a promotion, he served in his office well past the mandatory age of retirement for a ministerial-level official. Furthermore, in January 2016, Lou was appointed the chairman of the board of overseer for the Asian Infrastructure Investment Bank, which ensured his policy influence for years to come (Chuan 2016).

Despite the short-term effectiveness of the debt swap program, the underlying problem was not solved. According to Tsinghua University economist Bai Chong'en and co-authors, local government debt, whether recognized by the government or not, had grown to 45 trillion RMB by the end of 2015, or 67 percent of China's nominal GDP (Bai *et al.* 2016). In combination with China's official debt of 10 trillion RMB, China's governmental debt to GDP ratio reached 82 percent, well above the international warning line of 60 percent. The alarming debt level will create problems for future ministers of finance, who have to think of ways to service this debt. Furthermore, the debt exchange program had meant to "close the back door" of LGFV borrowing. However, disclosures from the bond market showed that LGFVs continued to issue their own debt to the tune of tens of billions of RMB per month, sometimes exceeding even 100 billion per month. Even with China's top-down decision-making and a large, highly knowledgeable bureaucracy, it still could not tackle a problem such as high debt. In fact, the technocrats had an incentive to deliver solutions which did not cause immediate problems such as slow growth or financial panics to the leadership, even if it meant not doing anything about the underlying issue.

Conclusion

The assumption of power-maximizing elite consumers and producers of financial policies has important implications for policy outcomes in China. First, power-maximizing policy consumers prefer policies that enhance the success of their individual portfolios to the fullest extent possible. Their time horizons, however, are short and medium term rather than long term. In response to these preferences, policy producers are likely to offer policies that make big splashes in the short run, but might produce trivial or harmful consequences in the long run. Relatedly, ministers in charge of producer agencies do not necessarily have the interest of their respective agencies in mind, since they are power-maximizing. They are perfectly capable of supporting policies that confer to them a high degree of elite appreciation in the short run, but create enormous problems for their agencies in the long run. Moreover, because it pays to be the main producer of financial policies, agencies have strong incentives to engage in fierce competitions to control important areas of financial policies. Granted, there are bounds for such competition, as each producer has its comparative advantage. Furthermore, because full-service providers, including the PBOC, the MOF, and the NDRC, each have control over a major source of funding and formidable regulatory capacities, they are expected to encroach upon the jurisdiction of weaker regulatory agencies, including the CBRC, the CSRC, and the CIRC. Indeed, we have seen the PBOC and MOF encroach on the jurisdiction of the CBRC, CSRC, and the CIRC in recent years.

Theoretically, the market model of policy-making provides an alternative explanation of the policy cycles in the Chinese financial sector. That is, the government is expected to implement a bundle of new policies at the beginning of a new administration and to slow down policy innovation toward the end of the ten-year term. This phenomenon is often seen as a "demand-side" issue in that elite policy consumers prefer to initiate policy innovations at the beginning of their tenures. This model, however, suggests a "supply-side" reason for the policy cycle. In essence, the "worth" of a contract at the beginning of the consumer's tenure is higher than at the end because the worth of elite attention and the prospect of promotion for a producer are much higher at the beginning of the consumer's tenure. Producers know that if they implement a policy to the satisfaction of consumers at the beginning of their tenure, the consumer still has time to reward them with expanded jurisdiction, elite attention, and promotions. At the end of the consumer's tenure, however, ministers know that new policy initiatives would not necessarily help their promotion prospects in the next administration under new leaders, thus giving them fewer incentives to propose new policies.

The market view of policy-making in China by no means provides a comprehensive, or even an accurate, view of policy-making in China. For one, the market view cannot account for inter-elite bargaining over financial policies. The heterogeneity of elite preferences for financial policies likely introduces intractable complexity to the analysis of decision-making in the PBSC and in the central leading groups. In essence, actors in these executive organs bargain with each other and "trade" on issues both across time and across issue areas. An added layer of complication is introduced if we consider the existence of rival factions in the PBSC and in the central leading groups. In addition to the goals of regime survival and success in one's portfolio, members of the PBSC must also consider the impact of a given policy on the relative distribution of power between rivaling factions. Factionalism also affects whether elite consumers would favor the proposals offered by a particular producer if the producer agency is headed by someone in his faction. It remains unclear how elite policy-makers balance all three of these considerations in deciding financial policies. In the end, policy-making everywhere is complex, and no single framework can account for every aspect of policy-making. We can only develop different frameworks that compete with each other to explain policy outcomes.

Notes

1 Author's interviews with PBOC officials.
2 Author's interview.
3 Author's interview.

References

21st Century Business Herald (2013) "五部委地方债联席会曝光 银监会拟设举债规模上限 (The five-ministries joint meeting on local debt is revealed; the CBRC may set a ceiling on local debt)," October 12.

Alesina, Alberto and Allan Drazen (1995) "Why are stabilizations delayed?" in T. Persson and G. Tabellini eds., *Monetary and Fiscal Policy: Volume 2, Politics*, Cambridge, MA: MIT Press.

Bai, Chong'en, Chang-tai Hsieh, and Zheng Song (2016) "The long shadow of a fiscal expansion," *Brookings Papers on Economic Activity*, Washington, DC: Brookings Institution.

Bank of China (1995) "Guanyu zhuanfa caizhengbu 'guanyu tiaozheng yinhang daikuan daizhang hexiao shenpi quanxian wenti de tongzhi' de tongzhi (The Bank of China's notice concerning distributing the Ministry of Finance's 'Notice concerning adjusting the banks' authority to evaluate and write-off bad debt')," in The Office of the Bank of China, The Office of the People's Bank of China, The Office of the Agricultural Bank of China, The Office of the Industrial and Commercial Bank of China, and The Office of the People's Insurance Company eds., *1994 nian Jinrong Guizhang zhidu xuanbian (Financial Regulations and Systems for 1994)*, Beijing: Finance Publisher.

Bates, Robert H. (1981) *Markets and States in Tropical Africa: The Political Basis of Agricultural Policies*, Berkeley: University of California Press.

Cao, Belinda and Xie Ye (2015) "China bans stock sales by major shareholders for six months," *Bloomberg*, July 8.

Central Commission for Discipline Inspection (2016) "中央第三巡视组向中国银行党委反馈专项巡视情况 (The report on the repeated inspection of the Bank of China party committee by the third central inspection team)," CDIC, February 4.

Chen, Xiaonong (1995) "Decision and miscarriage: radical price reform in the summer of 1988," in C.L. Hamrin and S. Zhao eds., *Decision Making in Deng's China: Perspectives from Insiders*, Armonk, NY: M.E. Sharpe.
Cheng, Jun (2015) "李克强赞同加大地方债置换力度 消息称第三批正在酝酿 (Li Keqiang supports increasing the local debt swap; sources say a third batch is in the works)," *Hua'erjie Jianwen*, July 14.
China Banking Regulatory Commission, China Securities Regulatory Commission, and China Insurance Regulatory Commission (2004) "Zai jinrong jianguan fangmian fengong hezuo de beimanglu (A memorandum of understanding concerning the division of labor and cooperation in financial regulation)," Chinalawinfo, Beijing: www.chinalawinfo.com.
China Banking Regulatory Commission and National Development and Reform Commission (2003) "Shangye yinang fuwu jiage guanli zhanxing banfa (Temporary method of regulating service fees in commercial banks)," Chinalawinfo, Beijing: www.chinalawinfo.com.
China Trustee Association (2014) "2014 年4季度末信托公司主要业务数据 (Business data for trust companies at the end of 4th quarter 2014)," Beijing: China Trustee Association.
Chuan, Jiang (2016) "亚投行正式开业 公布理事会主席和首任行长 (The AIIB opens for business and announces the CEO and chairman of the board)," *BBC Chinese*, January 16.
Ding, Qingxin and Wei Wu (2005) "Shenjizhe zaici quanmian shenji, sida zichan guanli gongsi midi daiqie (The auditors conduct another comprehensive audit; the puzzle of the four asset management companies awaits uncovering)," *21 Shiji Jingji Baodao (21st Century Economic Report)*, April 13.
Downs, Anthony (1957) *An Economic Theory of Democracy*, New York: Harper.
Fei, Chuanzhi (1995) "A comparison of the lending and monetary adjustments during several major economic adjustment periods since the founding of the country" (Jianguo yilai jida jingji tiaozheng shiqi huobi xindai tiaokong de bijiao), *Financial Reference (Jinrong Cankao)*, No. 5: 33–40.
Fewsmith, Joseph (1994) *Dilemmas of Reform in China: Political Conflict and Economic Debate*, Armonk, NY: M.E. Sharpe.
Green, Stephen (2004) "Equity politics and market institutions: the development of stock exchange governance in China, 1984–2003," in Royal Institute of International Affairs ed., *Working Papers*, London: RIIA.
Guoji Jinrongbao (2003) "Baojianhui shengwei zhengbuji zhongguo baoxianye jianguan shengji (CIRC is elevated to ministerial level; the regulation of Chinese insurance industry is elevated)," *Guoji Jinrongbao (International Finance Journal)*, March 26.
Heilmann, Sebastian (2005) "Regulatory innovation by Leninist means: Communist Party supervision in China's financial industry," *The China Quarterly*, Vol. 181: 1–21.
Hu, Haiyan (2005) "Zhongyang huijin gongsi jinrong bantu qiemi (Unveiling the secret design of the Central Huijing Company)," *Zhongguo Qiyejia (Chinese Entrepreneur)*, July 7.
Jia, Kang (2013) "贾康: 当前地方债务最大的风险在于不透明 (Jia Kang: the greatest risk of local government debt is the lack of transparency)," *People's Daily*, November 25.
Johnson, C.K. and Scott Kennedy (2015) "China's un-separation of power," *Foreign Affairs*, July 24.
Li, Keqiang (2014) "Report on the work of the government," N. P. s. Congress ed., Beijing: NPC.
Li, Yumin (2013) "财政存款为筹码 地方政府加码博弈银行平台贷 (Using fiscal deposits as leverage, local governments increase effort to obtain loans for LGFVs)," *21st Century Business Herald*, October 1.
Li, Yumin (2015) "地方债置换后成本降至 3.5% 2016 年到期 2.8 万亿 (The swapping of local debt lowered costs to 3.5%; 2.8 trillion yuan will mature in 2016)," *21st Century Economic Herald*, December 23.
Li, Zhenhua (2003) "Huang Ju, Zhou Xiaochuan zuozhen gugai lingdao xiaozu (Huang Ju and Zhou Xiaochuan take charge of shareholding reform leading group)," *21 Shiji Jingji Baodao (21st Century Economic Report)*, November 18.
Lieberthal, Kenneth (2004) *Governing China: From Revolution through Reform*, 2nd edn, New York: W.W. Norton.
Lieberthal, Kenneth and Michel Oksenberg (1988) *Policy Making in China: Leaders, Structures, and Processes*, Princeton, NJ: Princeton University Press.
Liu, Ming (2005) "Chongzheng quanshang, Huijin Jianyin zai xingdong (Huijin and Construction Investment are acting to restructure brokerages)," *Jingji Ribao (Economics Daily)*, August 11.
Luo, Jun (2007) "Profit growth triples for foreign banks in China," Bloomberg, July 4.
Mayhew, David R. (1974) *Congress: The Electoral Connection*. New Haven, CT: Yale University Press.
Ministry of Finance (2001) "Jinrong zichan guanli gongsi buliang zichan chuzhi kaohe banfa (Method of evaluating recovery ratios of asset management companies)," www.law-lib.com.

National Development and Reform Commission (2016) "'一带一路'建设取得良好开局 ('One Belt, One Road' enjoys a good beginning)," NDRC, February 15 [cited February 3, 2017]. Available from www.sdpc.gov.cn/xwzx/xwfb/201602/t20160215_774656.html.

National Social Security Fund (2016) "2015 全国社会保障基金理事会基金年度报告 (2015 Annual Report of the Directors of the National Social Security Foundation)," Beijing: NSSF.

Niskanen, William (1971) *Bureaucracy and Representative Government*, Chicago: Aldine Press.

PBOC Monetary Policy Committee (2000) "Zhongguo renmin yinhang huobi zhengce weiyuanhui diqici huiyi jiyao (A summary of the seventh meeting of the PBOC monetary policy committee)," in P.M.P. Committee ed., *Zhongguo Renmin Yinhang Huobi Zhengce Weiyuanhui Huiyi Jiyao (A Summary of Meetings of the PBOC Monetary Policy Committee)*, Beijing: China Finance Publisher.

People's Bank of China (1998) "Baoxianye jianguan zhibiao (Targets for monitoring the insurance industry)," Chinalawinfo, Beijing: www.chinalawinfo.com.

People's Bank of China (2015) "Report on monetary policy in the first half of 2015," in PBOC ed., *PBOC Monetary Policy Report*, Beijing: PBOC.

Rosenbluth, Frances McCall (1989) *Financial Politics in Contemporary Japan*, Ithaca, NY: Cornell University Press.

Shih, Victor (2004) "Development, the second time around: the political logic of developing western China," *Journal of East Asian Studies*, Vol. 4, No. 3: 427–451.

Shih, Victor (2007) "Partial reform equilibrium, Chinese style: political incentives and reform stagnation in Chinese financial policies," *Comparative Political Studies*, Vol. 40 (Oct): 1238–1262.

Shih, Victor (2010) "Local government debt: big rock candy mountain," *China Economic Quarterly*, Vol. 14, No. 2: 26–32.

Sina.com (2016) "中央经济决策最核心部门悄然发生人事变动 (The most crucial economic decision making body in the central government quietly changes personnel)," *Sina Caijing*, June 15.

State Administration of Foreign Exchange (2004) "Jinrong jigou da'e he keyi waihui zijin jiaoyi baogao guanli banfa shishi xice (The fine points of implementing the reporting system for large or suspicious foreign exchange transactions in financial institutions)," Beijing: State Administration of Foreign Exchange.

State Council (2014) "国务院关于加强地方政府性债务管理的意见 (Opinions on strengthening the management of local government debt)," Beijing: State Council.

State Planning Commission (2001) "Guanyu guifan jinrong zichan guanli gongsi shougou yu chuji buliang zichan guochengzhong zhongjie fuwu shoufei youguan wenti de tongzhi (Notice concerning fees paid by asset management companies to intermediary service providers in the course of buying or selling non-performing assets)," www.lawstar.com, Beijing: www.lawstar.com.

State Planning Commission and Ministry of Finance (2003) "Guanyu chongxin heding zhengquan shichang jianguanfei shoufei biaozhun ji youguan wenti the tongzhi jijiege (Notice concerning reassessing the regulatory fees schedule for the equities market)," *Zhengquan Shibao (Securities Times)*, February 14.

State Planning Commission, Ministry of Finance, Industrial and Commercial Bank of China, People's Construction Bank of China, and Adjusting State Council's Planning Office for Constructing and Reforming the Third Front (1986) "Guanyu fuchi sanxian qishiye tiaozheng jige youdai zhengce wenti de tongzhi (Notice on question on adjusting preferential policies to support Third Front industries)," in The Office of the Bank of China, The Office of the People's Bank of China, The Office of the Agricultural Bank of China, The Office of the Industrial and Commercial Bank of China, and The Office of the People's Insurance Company ed., *1986 nian Jinrong Guizhang Zhidu Xuanbian (A Selection of Financial Rules and Regulations in 1986)*, Beijing: Finance Publisher.

Wall Street Journal (2016) "A battle over money in Beijing," *Wall Street Journal*, August 17.

Walter, Carl and Fraser Howie (2011) *Red Capitalism*, New York: John Wiley & Sons.

Wang, Kai (2014) "中央财经领导小组的'领导范'人事更替一般不对外公告" (Personnel changes in the Central Leading Group on Finance and Economics are generally not publicized), *People's Daily Online (Renmin Ribao Wanyeban)*, August 25.

Wang, Peicheng (2014) "央行银监会分歧由来已久 国务院出手治理影子银行" (The differences between the PBOC and the China Banking Regulatory Commission have a long history; the State Council acts to cure the problem of shadow banks), *Caijing*, January 20.

Wang, Zhu (2014) "习近平等23名领导人出席深化改革小组首次会议 (23 leaders including Xi Jinping take part in the first meeting of the Central Leading Group on Comprehensively Deepening Reforms)," *Xinjing Bao*, January 23.

Weingast, Barry and Jeffrey Banks (1992) "The political control of bureaucracies under asymmetric information," *American Journal of Political Science*, Vol. 36, No. 2: 509–524.

Wen, Zi'er (2015) "万亿地方债置换背后 (Behind the trillion yuan local debt swap)," *Zhongguo Jingying-wang*, May 13.

Wu, Guoguang (1997) *Political Reform Under Zhao Ziyang (Zhao Ziyang yu Zhengzhi Gaige)*, Hong Kong: Pacific Century Institute.

Xi, Si (2011) "地方成中央预算支出单位 专家激辩地方债 (Local administrations have become expenditure units in the central budget: experts vigorously debate local-level debt)," *Economic Observer*, March 26.

Xing, Jun (2015) "躲过初一难逃十五 地方债自查待解 (Hard not to get caught; the local government audit awaits solution)," *Caixin*, February 19.

Xinhua News Agency (2000) "State appointed board of supervisors placed in 16 financial institutions," *Xinhua Domestic Service*, August 21.

Xinhua News Agency (2002) "Zhongjiwei: duiyuan jianhang hangzhang Wang Xuebing wenti de shencha jieguo (CDIC: the investigation results on the former president of the CCB Wang Xuebing)," [cited September 8, 2005]. Available from www.people.com.cn/GB/jinji/34/166/20021106/859961.html.

Yang, Dali L. (1997) *Beyond Beijing: Liberalization and the Regions in China*, London; New York: Routledge.

Yao, Jianli (2016) "刘鹤在上海开经济形势座谈会 去年来已5次调研长三角 (Liu He takes part in seminar on the economic situation in Shanghai; this is the fifth time since last year that he has conducted research on the Yangtze River Delta)," *21st Century Business Herald*, June 29.

Yao, Xi (2015) "习近平主持17次深改组会议 "十三五"将推动改革迈向纵深 (Xi Jinping chairs the 17th meeting of the Central Leading Group for Comprehensively Deepening Reforms; the 13th Five-Year Plan will broaden and deepen reform)," *Renmin Ribao (People's Daily)*, October 27.

Yi, Peng, Zhijin Yang, and Xiaoling Zhang (2013) "远离'影子银行'? 463 号文刹车公益性项目举债 (Avoiding 'shadow banking'? Document 463 stopped publicly oriented projects from further borrowing)," *21st Century Business Herald*, January 4.

Zhu, Rongji (1993a) "Zai quanguo jinrong gongzuo huiyi shang de zongjie jianghua (Summary remarks at the national finance conference)," Xinhuanet.com, Beijing: Xinhuanet.com.

Zhu, Rongji (1993b) "Zhengdun caishui jiexu, yansu caijing jilu, qianghua shuishou zhengguan, jiakuai caishui gaige (Rectify order in the budget, restore strictness in budgetary discipline, strengthen management of taxation, speed up fiscal reform)," in Document Research Center of CCP Central Committee ed., *A Selection of Important Documents for Economic Structural Reform in the New Period (Xinshiqi Jingji Tizhi Gaige Zhongyao Wenxian Xuanbian)*, Beijing: Central Document Publisher.

Zong, Hairen (2002) *Di Sidai (The Fourth Generation)*, Hong Kong: Mirror Books.

13

IMPLEMENTING TAX REFORM AND RURAL RECONSTRUCTION IN CHINA

A case study of the CCP's agrarian policy

Chiew-Siang Bryan Ho

Introduction

The Chinese Communist Party (CCP)'s inability to conceive and implement a comprehensive rational policy for economic development and modernization in the Maoist era was clearly demonstrated in the failure of many revolutionary campaigns such as "building a socialist countryside" (collectivization) and the Great Leap Forward. These campaigns and policies were executed with a "one-knife cut" (*yi dao qie*), often without taking into consideration local conditions and needs.

In contrast to the Maoist strategy of emphasizing uniformity in implementation, there was relatively less social engineering in the post-1978 reforms and policies. In reviewing the transformation of rural China since the late twentieth century, Alpermann (2011: 175) points to the decline of the grand comprehensive designs and revolutionary claims that were characteristic of the earlier periods (from the 1920s to the late 1970s). China since Deng has differed significantly, moving away from authoritarian utopianism with the exception of one initiative, "building a new socialist countryside" (BNSC).

During the Maoist era when ideology and politics were of highest priority, factional and bureaucratic politics from the top down dominated much of the formulation and implementation of policy in China (Lieberthal and Lampton 1992). Many of that era's institutional factors in policy-making persisted into the reform era (Huang 2000). Among these are the persistence of factional, bureaucratic and local politics that influenced many levels of the policy process, the persistence of a one-knife-cut approach in implementing policy across rural China after an initial experimental stage, and the ambiguity of policy that generated serious conflicts at the local level, notwithstanding some pragmatic innovations in response to policy ambiguity.

Richard E. Matland's (1995) conflict ambiguity framework has not been previously used to explain Chinese economics and rural issues, but it is particularly useful here. Using his analysis of the processes of implementation and outcomes, this chapter attempts to review some of the most significant policies in rural China since the reform and the opening up of China in 1978. Principal areas of focus are tax reform, the implementation of rural taxation policy or the rural tax-for-fee reform (RTFR) policy, and the policy of BNSC. Examination of these issues by Matland's criteria will be useful in the assessment of the appropriateness and effectiveness of the CCP policy implementation. Good policy and its implementation should be able to provide a fair deal and a "voice" for the rural population, whose average income has lagged substantially behind that of urban populations (often by a factor as great as three). This is very important considering the Party's historical and ideological roots in rural society.

Many China observers are aware of the fragmented authoritarian nature of the Chinese state, which cannot be all-powerful given the size of the country and the complexity of the political system and the bureaucracy (Lieberthal 2004; Yeh *et al.* 2015b). In spite of the dominant role of the CCP, interests are variegated and the context of policy shifts or changes as policy filters downward. A top-down model of policy implementation is necessarily too limiting in explaining the capacity of the state, given the need to take into account the contexts and actors in the policy process. Therefore, this chapter will first briefly introduce Matland's ambiguity conflict framework. Second, it will cover the decentralization process that took off with the reform era, which not only put a strain on central local relations but also led to the drive to rein in control by the central government. The next section discusses the 1994 tax reform, clearly demonstrating the central government's determination, resources and capacity for such implementation in the framework of Matland's ambiguity conflict model of policy implementation (1995).

The reforms engendered incompatible policy goals that warranted the political implementation of the RTFR policy to alleviate villager (or peasant) burden and rural unrest due to the shortcomings of the earlier tax reform. The RTFR policy was adopted after taking into account some successful local experiments before implementing it nationwide in 2002. While the RTFR policy may have, to a certain extent, alleviated peasant burden, the policy itself provoked greater institutional resistance, and in some cases the extent of resistance resulted in greater ambiguity and conflict (depending on local conditions). The abolition of the RTFR policy in 2004 and the agriculture tax policy in 2006, along with the emergence of the policy of BNSC in 2006, saw the state again resorting to experimental implementation to transform rural society as a way out of the conundrum of state involution in spite of the limits and potential dangers in relying on the outcomes of experimental implementation for policy-making.

The ambiguity-conflict framework of policy implementation

Matland's model of policy implementation is one of the attempts to synthesize the top-down and bottom-up models in the policy implementation literature (Matland 1995; deLeon and deLeon 2002). In Matland's framework, the concepts of ambiguity and conflict are useful in explaining success and failure in implementation outcomes. Ambiguity of policy is necessary for alleviating conflict, but it could also lead to more conflicts that eventually cause outcomes to diverge from intentions. This is particularly so when different institutions viewed a policy from different perspectives, resulting in organizational conflict (Sylvester and Ferrara 2003; Cohen *et al.* 2005). According to Sylvester and Ferrara (2003: 3), such conflicts are not necessarily counterproductive because "the original policy can be improved as the organization undergoes an iterative process of interpretation, conflict, and refinement."

The standard top-down model of policy implementation tends to emphasize complete clarity in the flow of authority, resources and information from top to bottom, culminating in the smooth implementation of policy typical of the traditional models of public administration. Matland (1995) terms this "administrative implementation" where policy outcomes are determined by resources. According to Matland (1995: 160), the low levels of ambiguity and conflict provide "the prerequisite conditions for a rational decision making process." Given the low level of ambiguity in ends and means as well as the low level of conflict, normative compliance mechanisms are generally sufficient to secure actors' compliance. Yet, implementation could still fail because of technical problems due to poor communication and management, limited resources and technology, coupled with ineffective regulation (ibid.: 161). As a result, even for policy of low levels of ambiguity and conflict, "an implementation plan can require substantial efforts" (ibid.: 163). The 1994 tax reform, that filled the Chinese state's coffers by increasing its portion of revenue while reining in the independence of provincial and local governments, is an example of such implementation.

In a variant of top-down implementation, policies with a low level of ambiguity and a high level of conflict are typical of politically driven decision-making. While actors have clearly defined goals, conflict occurs because these goals are incompatible (Matland 1995). In political implementation, the central principle is "that implementation outcomes are decided by power" (ibid.: 163). Hence successful implementation "depends on either having sufficient power to force one's will on the other participants or having sufficient resources to be able to bargain an agreement on means" (ibid.: 164). In such implementation, "[c]oercive or remunerative mechanisms will predominate" (ibid.: 164). As resources are "controlled by skeptical actors outside the implementing organization or by actors actively opposed to the proposed policy," compliance is not automatically forthcoming (ibid.: 164). In contrast to the authoritarian public administration models, more sophisticated top-down models take into account such factors as support from politicians, available resources, support from relevant constituencies, and the commitment of the officials responsible for implementation (ibid.). Securing the compliance of actors with resources is therefore critical to successful policy implementation.

Although the central government managed to secure tax returns from the provincial and the local levels, the emptying of local-level government coffers led to local governments engaging in increased legal and illegal collection of taxes, which increased the peasant burden and led to rural mass protests, and cadre-mass relationships became tense.[1] To alleviate rural discontent, the RTFR policy, which was initially a local initiative, was implemented by the central government in 2002. RTFR policy sought to regulate local governments' behavior on the one hand, while on the other asserting the central government's control over rural society. Despite the rhetoric of increasing service provision and improving local governance, such goals could not materialize when local forces resisted the new policy due to the lack of financial support to alleviate their extremely tight financial circumstances, particularly in poorer areas.

In experimental implementation, ambiguity is high where both the goals and means of policy are unclear and the level of conflict is low. Policy outcomes "will depend largely on which actors are active and most involved" (ibid.: 165). As contextual considerations can dominate the policy process, the decision-making process is more likely one of a "garbage can" process where multiple actors are involved and the outcome is hard to predict in different sites. While the system is relatively closed to outside influence in administrative implementation, the system is open to environmental influences in experimental implementation and the "opportunities are excellent for bureaucratic entrepreneurs to create policies to deal with local needs" (ibid.: 166).

Matland (ibid.: 167) also states that "policies with clear and widely supported goals but with unclear means of implementation take on experimental characteristics." Experimental implementation thus offers an opportunity for policy learning rather than achieving policy outcomes and the "process requires a conscious realization that learning is the goal" (ibid.: 167). The bottom-up models of implementation fit into this category where local-level actors have more opportunities to induce change, taking into account diversity rather than the command, authority and uniformity characteristic of top-down models of implementation. The RTFR policy born of local innovation fitted well into this mode of implementation in the pioneering stage until the reform took center stage (Göbel 2011). The subsequent failure of the RTFR policy "paved the road to a new socialist countryside" as the central government played a prominent role to transform rural society. This occurred when the RTFR policy ended in 2006 and a Rural Comprehensive Reform program (*nongcun zonghe gaige*) or BNSC was introduced by the central government to transform rural society. Although the ambiguity of goals and means to accomplish BNSC are both high, outcomes vary in different areas according to the local conditions (i.e., rich or poor areas) and the differentiated roles played by local actors and their involvement.

In symbolic implementation, the levels of ambiguity and conflict are high. Symbolic policies "play an important role in confirming new goals, in reaffirming a commitment to old goals, or in emphasizing important values and principles" (Olsen 1970 in Matland 1995: 168). The high level of conflict determines implementation strategies, leading to variation of outcomes among sites (ibid.: 168). Outcomes are determined by local coalition strength during the implementation process as local actors control resources essential to the success of policy implementation.

Symbolic implementation may appear similar to political implementation. The two differ in that coalition strength for political implementation lies in the upper level, whereas coalition strength for symbolic implementation resides at the local level. In contrast to experimental implementation, outcomes are "bounded and less differentiated … because opposition coalitions are able to put effective limits on policy even when they cannot determine its content" (ibid.: 169). Hence "[A]ctors are intensely involved, and disagreements are resolved through coercion or bargaining; problem solving or persuasion are used to a limited degree only" (ibid.: 169). The practice of the RTFR policy in some areas where resistance was strong is a prime example of symbolic implementation.

It is also important to note that in Matland's framework (1995), ambiguity and conflict are presented as dichotomous for the sake of clarity. The theoretical constructs are in fact continuous:

> as a policy gradually moves across a dimension, for example from low to high conflict, the implementation process is expected to increasingly to show the characteristics of the paradigm being moved toward and decreasingly to show the characteristics of the paradigm being moved away from.
>
> *(Ibid.: 159)*

Administrative and political implementations: the 1994 tax reform and the centralization of state control

John J. Kennedy (2015: 93) describes financial reform after 1994 as "a story of recentralization and national policies designed to recapture local revenues and create a standardized tax system as well as increased local service provision." Since the opening up of the economy in the 1980s, decentralization of resources at the local level to encourage economic development saw an increase in local revenues while diminishing revenues for the central government (Hershler 1995; Wang *et al.* 1995). To redress such a fiscal imbalance the central government implemented a rule-based tax sharing system with provinces which replaced the differential contract system with individual provinces (Wong 1997). Here one can see the state's capacity in carrying out administrative implementation because an efficient top-down implementation of the tax sharing system saw the state's revenues increased while provincial revenues decreased (Hershler 1995; Wong 1997).

The goal of changing the fiscal relations between central and local government and its technical means was relatively clear. At first glance, the policy exhibited a low level of ambiguity and conflict. Hence, the Chinese state had been able to flex its muscles and accomplished the task of recentralization by redefining central-local relations through the 1994 tax reform. Despite the low ambiguity, various systemic problems of the 1994 tax reform gradually shifted it toward a high level of conflict, and as a result preempted the introduction of the RTFR policy to deal with these problems.

Kennedy (2015) has analyzed the various systemic problems of the 1994 tax reform and found that the most significant factors lurking behind its problems were the uneven economic conditions and regional inequality. This explained the differences in local governments' capacity to sustain the impact of the tax reform policy and to provide services to villagers (who constituted a huge population at the village level) and which fell as a burden on town governments (Tao and Qin 2007). Wealthy counties and towns had enough revenue generated from industries to deal with the demand for service provision (Zhao 2006a, 2006b). The same cannot be said in less wealthy and particularly poorer counties or town governments that had already incurred high level of debts to pay for service provision (Kennedy 2015). This was particularly the case when the outcome of the tax reform showed that expenditure at the provincial level increased faster than revenue growth with the implementation of the 1994 tax reform (see table 2 in Kennedy 2015: 100).

In addition, the endemic problems of administrative malfeasance and corruption throughout every level of the bureaucracy should not be overlooked (Wedeman 2000; Bernstein and Lü 2003). As Gong (2009) points out, corruption was endemic due to the double identities played by cadres and local governments during reform (i.e., as officials *and* entrepreneurs). When the decentralization process was incomplete, there was a lack of accountability and public representation.

The 1994 tax reform had given local governments (i.e., county-level and town governments) the autonomy to retain extra budgetary taxes and to collect taxes and fees for meeting the need of public expenditure and service provision. Notwithstanding the issue of corruption, the increase in the villager or peasant burden in the 1990s and the increase in mass protests during this period was in part an outcome of the 1994 tax reform policy, which had led to a heightening in the tension between rural cadres at the town level and the peasantry or villagers (O'Brien and Li 1999, 2006). In part the cadre management system in which town cadres were expected to meet the harsh performance targets set by county authorities also aggravated the tension between cadres and villagers (Smith 2015). The peasant burden was not necessarily always a case of cadres' rent-seeking behavior (Kennedy 2015).

The 1994 tax reform had shifted cadres' responsibility from service provision to revenue collection in spite of the policy emphasizing the incompatible goal of increasing service provision. It is from this perspective that the 1994 tax reform itself was a form of political implementation in which the center managed to exert enormous pressure on the local governments to comply with the tax sharing system on the one hand, and on the other hand to increase the reach of the state by increasing its capacity to extract resources at the local level. However, in emphasizing the incompatible goal of service provision as underfunded mandates, the autonomy granted to local governments instead led to an increase in conflict at the ground level and a vicious cycle that provoked villagers' resistance to tax collection and an increase in the numbers of personnel required to collect taxes and fees from the villagers (Yep 2004). For Yep, villager burden is a structural bias against the rural population. Tao and Qin suggest that market liberalization, income disparity and a regressive tax system were the key factors for the rise in the villager burden (Tao and Qin 2007). However, as O'Brien and Li (2006) and Li (2012) point out, town governments were blamed for the strategic actions of the central and provincial leadership.

Ultimately, implementation of the 1994 tax reform that was intended to increase service provision failed due to the incompatibility of policy goals. Remittances to the central government to increase state revenue and the need to increase local service provision generated serious misunderstanding on the ground because there were insufficient resources at the disposal of local governments. The situation was worse for those governments at the town level that were already entrapped in a vicious cycle of debt (caused by overspending on projects to boost the local economy in order to gain better performance evaluation or promotion, corruption, lack of industry and poor economic development) (O'Brien and Li 1999, 2006; Li 2012). The incompatibility of goals also led to town governments resorting to the illegal practice of land appropriation and industrial expansion as they took advantage of their position at the periphery of the state structure to generate more extra budgetary earnings, either for providing more services or other corrupt practices (Hsing 2009). However, the rise in conflict is not due solely to town governments as the single cause of increasing the villager burden or malpractice. As Zhao (2006a, 2006b), a leading expert on rural governance at the China Development Research Center, explains, "township leaders face a complex array of challenges and they are not simply unruly rent-seeking officials" (cited in Kennedy 2015: 95).

Implementing the RTFR policy: from experimental to political implementation

The reluctance or inability of the central government to channel funds and resources to the local level implies that the rational top-down implementation of policy – administrative implementation – to meet the goal of increasing service provision may gradually shift to political or symbolic implementation, depending on the escalation of the level of ambiguity and conflict on the ground. Given that the 1994 tax reform granted autonomy to local governments in revenue collection, the policy goal of collecting revenue on the part of local governments has a low level of ambiguity, but a high level of conflict, typical of political implementation. When poor town governments resorted to collecting more and more taxes and fees from the villagers, the ambiguity level of the policy could move from low to high from the perspective of villagers. As the villager burden increased and service provision either stagnated or increased minimally, tensions between cadres and villagers rose, particularly in those poor rural areas (Tao and Qin 2007). When some local governments turned predatory as well as corrupt, the ambiguity of goals and means became even higher and so too was the level of conflict.

Implementation outcomes varied across regions. In some poor areas, the commitment to the policy goal of increased service provision was likely to be superficial at best. In richer areas, potential coercion from the center drove the political implementation of the policy to increase service provision despite the low level of ambiguity and high level of conflicts. In some poor towns, implementation was likely to be symbolic as policy became highly ambiguous and conflicting. Since the center's interest was not really in improving governance or in increasing public service at the local level but to fill the central government's coffers, the policy to improve service provision was unlikely to be implemented on the ground. The center was then still oblivious to the offshoot in peasant burden as one of the most serious unintended outcomes of the 1994 tax reform till early 2000.

In an attempt to alleviate the peasant burden, the state implemented the RTFR policy in 2002, expanding "central fiscal control down to the grassroots level" (Kennedy 2015: 101).

Such a policy was not purely a central government initiative and in fact initially owed much to local innovation (Göbel 2011). According to Li (2006), the RTFR was first and foremost a brainchild of He Kaiyin, an agricultural economist and high-level advisor to the government of Anhui Province. The implementation of He's ideas was stalled in the conservative post-1989 political climate as well as being opposed by local forces that subverted two initial experiments in central China in 1993 and 1994 (Chen and Chun 2004: chapter 9).

In experimental implementation, outcomes vary across different contexts, and depend on the local actors who are involved. Experimentations in Anhui Province were initially met with resistance; successful experiments in Anhui and Hebei led to many provincial leaders' visits to these two provinces to learn about such experiments (ibid.: chapter 10). These experiments where the town government signed a contract known as "tax and fee contracts" (*shuifei chengbao*) with each household made taxation straightforward and transparent, met tax quotas, reduced peasant burden, covered administrative outlays and the costs of social service provision (Zhang 2001). Despite the "tug-of-war" among central-level officials of vice-ministerial rank, these experiments were officially recognized and approved for the first time in 1996 (Zhongfa 1996: No. 13). By 1997, more than 50 counties in 7 provinces conducted (pioneering) experiments with what looked like the RTFR policy promulgated later by the center (He and Sun 2000).

Matland (1995: 167) claims that "policies with clear and widely supported goals but with unclear means of implementation take on experimental characteristics." Although initial local experiments were recognized in 1996, "only two years later did a rural tax for fee reform suddenly and quickly move to the top of the national reform agenda" (Göbel 2011: 161). Then Premier Zhu Rongji spearheaded the reform process immediately with President Jiang Zemin's support after Jiang's September visit to Anhui (Göbel 2011). In early 1999, Zhu's team put forward an RTFR policy proposal based on an evaluation of various reform experiments written by Anhui's Ministry of Finance. As Göbel (ibid.: 162) points out: "[M]any of He Kaiyin's ideas were integrated in the proposal, most notably that of collapsing village- and township-level taxes and fees into an increased agricultural tax." Among the various items in the RTFR policy proposal, Zhu's team "suggested setting the agricultural tax rate at 7 percent of a locality's average harvest between 1993 and 1998" (ibid.: 162). Such an agricultural tax rate, however, could not possibly be applied consistently throughout rural China in view of the uneven development in different localities. This was particularly vexing when the condition for burden reduction was tied to complementary reforms of making local government lean and efficient. These complementary reforms include: (1) reducing the number of territorial entities by merging villages and townships, and bypassing prefecture- and township-level governments; (2) reducing offices and employees in counties, townships and villages; (3) strictly regulating personnel management (such as recruitment, evaluation and promotion) in local governments; (4) outsourcing of government services; (5) separation of government and business; and (6) the creation of a supervisory system (see Table 9.1 in Göbel 2011: 163). In other words, the policy embraced contradictory goals of improving local governance while undercutting local governments' tax collection severely and without making clear any forthcoming policy support for funding or resources.

The goal of reducing the peasant burden was unambiguous, but the means to achieve such a goal were highly ambiguous when it was unclear who was responsible for financing the reform. The policy called forth local support as well as resistance, as Göbel (ibid.: 167) explains:

> [The] role of the pioneers in shaping the RTFR has become apparent especially in the initial stage, when local experiments were turned into national policies. However, resistance played an equally important role in shaping outcomes. This becomes especially

> clear with respect to the question of who was responsible for financing the reform, the issue that lay at the heart of the resistance to the RTFR ... minister of finance Xiang Huaicheng was adamant in keeping subsidies from the center to a minimum, something that local governments clearly did not appreciate. They demanded a more substantial commitment by the central government, reasoning that, as the head of W county's RTFR Small Group retrospectively put it, "it was the center's reform, so the center had to pay for it."

Matland (1995: 167) warns that, "ambiguous policies can breed limited accountability and can lead to creation of mini-fiefdoms with leaders pursuing their own interests. These may have little, if any, connection to the public interest." There are possible pitfalls in experimental implementation. The initial experiments by the pioneers were "policies" that operated "in areas where there is insufficient knowledge to institute programmed implementation or of how elements in the policy environment are causally connected" (ibid.: 167). Hence, the implementation "process should not be forced into an artificially constrained form" because "[p]rograms demanding conformity are likely to meet with superficial compliance efforts from local implementers" (ibid.: 167). Additionally, ambiguity offers an opportunity to learn new goals and new means insofar as adequate comparison and evaluation are made on sites under experiment such that the learning process does not occur in a random pattern (ibid.: 167). Hence it was questionable if initial local experiments constituted sufficient sources and if there was adequate comparison undertaken for effective learning through evaluation and feedback.

In experimental implementation, the system (unlike that in administrative implementation) is open to environmental influence. The "opportunities are excellent for bureaucratic entrepreneurs to create policies to deal with local needs" (ibid.: 166). It is in this sense that experimental implementation offers "an opportunity for policy learning rather than achieving policy outcomes" and the "process requires a conscious realization that learning is the goal" (ibid.: 167). But, such a policy learning process ceased as soon as the reform took center stage. While the RTFR policy goal to reduce the peasant burden was clear, the means to achieve such a goal was contradictory, notwithstanding differing conditions in the local contexts. Göbel (2011: 165) judges that the central government's role in the reform is not a creative one because:

> the course of the reform was chartered mainly at the county and sub-county levels. In contrast to the central government, which fixed the parameters and outlined the directions of the reform, and these local actors, which fine-tuned, implemented, or resisted it, the provincial governments played the role of a switchboard without getting too deeply involved in the reform.

Seen in this light, experimental implementation drifts toward political implementation. Those initial experimentations had a high level of ambiguity in terms of the means but were relatively low in conflict in those areas where local actors or officials as pioneers sought to resolve the problems of the peasant burden based on trials and experiments that took into account local conditions. Research in Anhui showed the RTFR policy, unlike the early experiments, presented the case for a reform policy that was relatively low in ambiguity but eventually led to a high level of conflict when the policy neglected the issue of contextual differences as coercion and conflict were the sources for compliance. As the central and provincial governments played a regulatory role in enforcing compliance, cadres faced the prospects of villagers' defiance as well as demotion and having their party membership revoked for failure to implement policies (ibid.: 166). The center played up against the local by means of a zero-sum game, igniting the tensions and conflicts between cadres and villagers (ibid.). The RTFR implementation fell on the shoulders of local actors, namely those cadres at the county and town levels. However, counties seldom applied those austerity measures to their own administration and towns and villages were made to bear the brunt of the reform as county administration expanded despite having been stable for a decade (ibid.). As a result, the implementation outcomes were uncertain and varied across different locales and sites:

> [W]hile the central government probably sought to combine the positive aspects of hierarchical steering and competition to implement nationwide a sustainable policy sensitive to local contexts, policymakers most likely underestimated the negative aspects of these instruments. The consequence was that some took up the challenge and came up with meaningful reform proposals, while others chose to resist because they either lacked the means to do so or had rejected this policy from the start.
>
> *(Ibid.: 165)*

Yep's research (2004) showed the possibility of the RTFR policy implementation shifting to symbolic implementation where the levels of ambiguity and conflict were high in some areas. Li's research (2009) showed how local government attempted to deal with the RTFR policy sustainably through institutional innovations and the reduction of personnel costs. However, opponents refused to implement these reforms and illegal fee-collection persisted in some areas as local cadres employed violent means to collect taxes (cf. Zhang 2003; cf. Gao 2004; Göbel 2011: 167). While some town governments reduced service provisions, others borrowed money in order to provide vital services due to the severe reduction in revenues (Kennedy 2007; Göbel 2011: 167).

On the surface, China appears to be a monolithic state. The many layers of the state system and the myriad actors that are involved in the policy process are likely causes for fragmentation as power concentrates and disperses in different sites and localities. Based on a Foucaultian perspective, in his research on land and power brokering in China's township, Hsing (2009) showed how the capacity of the center could be undermined by the dispersion and concentration of power at each level of the government (i.e., the province, the county and town) as different institutional responses dealt with and played to the central government's directives.[2] In the case of the RTFR policy implementation, Göbel (2011: 168) finds it astonishing "how much an important and far-reaching policy such as the RTFR was shaped not by careful planning, intergovernmental coordination, and cost-benefit calculations, but by decentralized idealism, personal considerations, and pure chance." Personal considerations refer to Jiang Zemin's backing of Anhui's experimentation as a window of opportunity that the then Premier Zhu Rongji seized upon to restore his tarnished image as a rural reformer (Göbel 2010: 93). Göbel (2011: 168) concurs with Li's (2006) view that the RTFR policy was "a mix of strategies in a multilevel system complicated by unintended consequences, departmental power struggles, and a lack of expertise and interest, especially in the Ministry of Finance."

Building a new socialist countryside: a return to experimental implementation?

The income of rural populations stagnated after the initial decade of the reform era that began in the late 1970s and early 1980s. The impoverished conditions of the countryside and the emergence of protests despite the marketization process forced the Hu Jintao-Wen Jiabao leadership to look for resolutions to the "three rural problems" of farmers, the village and rural agriculture, a term first coined by the Chinese scholar Wen Tiejun (Alpermann 2011: 175). Göbel (2011) rightly asserts that inequality as a result of modernization and the breakneck pace of development was one root cause that prompted the reform of rural taxation and administration. Given the low level of income peasants have had, "income inequality directly fed into the inequality of local government revenues" (ibid.: 157).

As the problems faced by poor counties and towns were repeated throughout China with the implementation of the RTFR policy, which was extended nationwide in 2002, the central government announced the gradual phasing out of the agricultural tax in 2004 (Guofa 2004: No. 21). While pioneers in the RTFR helped the center in fine-tuning and implementing the policy, the opponents forced the center to finally make the financial concessions and abandoned the initial reform design (Göbel 2011: 169). Hence the RTFR officially ceased in 2006 and gave way to the Rural Comprehensive Reform (*nongcun zonghe gaige*) which was part of the BNSC program (ibid.: 168).

Rural tax reform could have reduced the immediate tension between cadres and peasants, but it did not solve the problem of stagnant economic development (Thøgersen 2011: 175). Thøgersen (ibid.: 176) explains the rationale for the BNSC program:

> [T]he abolition of the agricultural tax by 2006 left many rural governments penniless and frustratingly incapable of delivering social services. The need for more penetrating and comprehensive reforms was obvious, and the BNSC framework was presented as an ambitious attempt in this direction.

The hollowing out of the towns recalls not only the state involution in the decades following the end of the Qing dynasty but the rural China in the 1990s as well that was characterized by "intensifying economic crisis, predation by entrepreneurial brokers and weakened central capacity" (Day 2015; Yeh *et al.* 2015b: 5). Contemporary Chinese scholars, China researchers and sinologists related the rural reconstruction program of the 1930s initiated by Liang Shuming and James Yan Yangchu with the current social engineering project targeting Chinese villages as the state finally decided to play a prominent role in financing and leading rural development and construction in view of the problematic outcomes in the implementation of the RTFR policy (Göbel 2011; Perry 2011; Thøgersen 2011; Day 2015; Jacka 2015; Yeh *et al.* 2015a; Yan and Chen 2015).

Contemporary prominent activists and scholars such as He Xuefeng, Wen Tiejun and Yu Keping took as reference points the thinking of Liang Shuming and Yan Yangchu in the current debate concerning rural development and Liang's and Yan's ideas about community building, cultural transformation and local ownership are still influential today (Thøgersen 2011: 174). Perry (2011), however, considered the BNSC a managed campaign which was "unabashedly pragmatic" notwithstanding some vestiges of Maoist revolutionary campaigns. For Thøgersen (2011: 174), the BNSC scheme "diverts from the Maoist strategy when it comes to uniformity in implementation." Promulgated as one of the targets in the 11th Five-Year Plan in 2005, three out of the five slogans of BNSC relate to cultural and political aspects of rural development. These are: enhanced production (*shengchan fazhan*), comfortable living standards (*shenghuo kuanyu*), a civilized rural lifestyle (*xiangfeng wenming*), neat and clean villages (*cunrong zhengjie*) and democratic management (*guanli minzhu*) (ibid.: 176). The plan emphasized continued rural-urban integration (*chengxiang tongchou*) with promises of massive investments in rural production and infrastructure (roads, electricity and water supply) as well as improved social services such as reduced school fees and better rural health care (ibid.: 176). Research in Shanxi and Zhejiang showed that BNSC offered some promise for poorer villages to break free from poverty and find a path to development (Ahlers and Schubert 2009). Previously resources were channeled from the countryside to the cities, but the BNSC scheme departed from history in that now resources from the cities were flown in to improve the infrastructures and services in the countryside (Thøgersen 2011: 176).

The outcomes of the BNSC scheme are difficult to predict across rural China because much of it also depends on local initiatives and those actors who are involved, which is true of experimental implementation. Thøgersen (2011: 182) points to the difficulties in a participatory approach to empower villagers when there is no centrally endorsed blueprint and much is left to local initiatives, thereby making active local support a precondition for success. Introducing a communal element also poses a problem when there are no collective resources for entrepreneurial villagers to initiate collective actions that would promote common economic interests, which are essential for strengthening communal life. This particularly applies to villages with no industries or collective resources for boosting economic development (ibid.: 182). The Maoist tradition of generating change through model villages may perpetuate inequality or unequal development; this is so when funds are channeled to those model villages from well-off regions (ibid.: 182). As a learning process, the BNSC scheme presents both opportunities and dangers. As Thøgersen (ibid.: 183) points out:

> The guidelines for how to Build a New Socialist Countryside are quite vague when it comes to how the words "new" and "socialist" should be interpreted and practically implemented in relation to community building. The model villages show how this vagueness is both a danger and a blessing. It is dangerous because it can lead to the spending of a large sum of money on prestige projects, and to investments in wealthy villages whose examples is hard to follow for other localities with less privileged access to funding. But it can also be a blessing because it leaves the field relatively open to alternative visions for rural development, which may lead to experiments that can empower China's villages.

Conclusion

The chapter has addressed the limits of the Chinese state in implementing tax reforms and developing rural China. The implementation process reflects the dynamic of central-local relations: the local does not simply play to the center and the local could be innovative and highly involved in the policy implementation stage. The 1994 tax reform fed the central government's coffers by increasing the portion of the revenues to the center and reined in control on provincial and local governments, which is typical of administrative implementation. It is worth noting again that implementation could still fail because of "misunderstanding, poor coordination, insufficient resources, insufficient time to use the correct technology, or the lack of an effective monitoring strategy to control and sanction deviant behavior" (Matland 1995: 161). As a result, even for policies with low levels of ambiguity and conflict, "an implementation plan can require substantial efforts" (ibid.: 163). This partly explains why some policies may shift toward political implementation and symbolic implementation on the ground or assume "experimental like" characteristics when implementation outcomes are constrained by those factors limiting administrative implementation.

The implementation of the RTFR policy demonstrated the limits of state capacity and the limits of experimental implementation when the implementation of local experiments was treated as implementation outcomes rather than lessons being learnt. The systemic problems of the earlier tax reform with its contradictory goals shifted administrative implementation toward, first, some local experiments of the "tax-for-fee policy," followed by the political implementation of the RTFR policy as the reform again took center stage, leading in some cases toward symbolic implementation as institutional resistance and conflicts heightened.

Even though the center had had the support of the peasantry in implementing the RTFR policy, such coercive or remunerative mechanisms did not work out well in localities where cadre resistance to central government's policy was strong. As resources are "controlled by skeptical actors outside the implementing organization or by actors actively opposed to the proposed policy," compliance is not automatically forthcoming (ibid.: 164). While coalition strength for political implementation lies in the upper level, coalition strength for experimental and symbolic implementation lies in the local level. In contrast to experimental implementation, in symbolic implementation outcomes are "bounded and less differentiated ... because opposition coalitions are able to put effective limits on policy even when they cannot determine its content" (ibid.: 169). Hence disagreements are resolved through coercion or bargaining rather than problem solving or persuasion (Matland 1995).

In experimental implementation, ambiguity is high where both the goals and means of policy are unclear and the level of conflict is low. Policy outcomes "will depend largely on which actors are active and most involved" (ibid.: 165). Similar to the earlier local "tax-for-fee policy" experiments, contextual conditions dominate the BNSC policy implementation, where the decision-making process is more likely one of a "garbage can" process where diverse multiple actors are involved and the outcome is hard to predict in different locations. The system is open to environmental influence and the "opportunities are excellent for bureaucratic entrepreneurs to create policies to deal with local needs" (ibid.: 166). The BNSC scheme in some cases may fit Matland's point (ibid.: 167) that "policies with clear and widely supported goals but with unclear means of implementation take on experimental characteristics."

Although implementing BNSC may offer opportunities for non-state actors to play a role in helping the CCP develop a community and participatory oriented approach to policy implementation, there are substantial concerns about the dangers embedded in the policy process itself. This is because experimental implementation offers an opportunity for policy learning rather than achieving policy outcomes and the "process requires a conscious realization that learning is the goal" (ibid.: 167). The bottom-up models of implementation fit into this category where local-level actors play a significant role in inducing change. But the success of BNSC is unlikely to come about merely by channeling resources to model or well-to-do villages and depending on local initiatives. Without a rational and systematic approach to help those villages in need of transformation and development, inequality will perpetuate and implementation as a political game may undermine efforts at rural reconstruction. This is particularly so when villagers are still deprived of a voice and clear representation in the polity.

Notes

1 The term "cadre" refers to Chinese officials who are members of the Chinese Communist Party and who hold a leadership position.

2 Hsing (2009: 89) employed the concept of the process of power in Foucault's writing (1982) where "power is not a fixed, cardboard like entity and enclosed regime, but an open, endless strategic game."

References

Ahlers, A.L. and Schubert, G. (2009), Building a new socialist countryside: only a political slogan?, *Journal of Current Chinese Affairs*, Vol. 38, No. 4, 35–62.

Alpermann, B. (2011), *Politics and Markets in Rural China*, London and New York: Routledge.

Bernstein, T.B. and Lü, X. (2003), *Taxation without Representation in Contemporary Rural China*, Cambridge and New York: Cambridge University Press.

Chen, G.D. and Chun, T. (2004), *Zhongguo nongmin diaocha [An Inquiry into the Situation of China's Peasants]*, Beijing: Renmin wenxue chubanshi.

Cohen, A., Timmons, J.C. and Fesko, S.L. (2005), The Workforce Investment Act: how policy conflict and policy ambiguity affect implementation, *Journal of Disability Policy Studies*, Vol. 15, No. 4, 221–230.

Day, A. (2015), A century of rural self-governance reforms: reimagining rural Chinese society in the post-taxation era, in Yeh, E.T., O'Brien, K.J. and Ye, J.Z., eds., *Rural Politics in Contemporary China*, London and New York: Routledge, 15–40.

deLeon, P. and deLeon, L. (2002), Whatever happened to policy implementation? An alternative approach, *Journal of Public Administration Research and Theory*, No. 4, 467–492.

Foucault, M. (1982), The subject and power, in Dreyfus, Hubert and Rainbow, Paul, eds., *Michel Foucault, Beyond Structuralism and Hermeneutics*, Brighton, UK: Harvester, 208–228.

Gao, Xinjun (2004), Nongcun shuifei gaige: redian wenti leng sikao [The rural tax and fee reforms: cool thoughts on a hot problem], in He, Zengke, ed., *Jiceng minzhu he defang zhili chuangxin [Grass-roots Democracy and Innovations in Local Governance]*, Beijing: Zhongguo bianyi chubanshe, 180–194.

Göbel, C. (2010), *The Politics of Rural Reform in China: State Policy and Village Predicament in the Early 2000s*, London: Routledge.

Göbel, C. (2011), Paving the road to a socialist new countryside: China's rural tax and fee reform, in Alpermann, Björn, ed., *Politics and Markets in Rural China*, London and New York: Routledge, 155–171.

Gong, T. (2009), Corruption and governance: the double identities of local governments in market reform, in Li, L.C., ed., *The Chinese State in Transition: Processes and Contests in Local China*, London and New York: Routledge, 74–88.

Guofa (2004), No. 21, Guowuyuan guanyu zuohao 2004 nian shenhua nongcun shuifei gaige shidian zhongzuo de tongzhi [Notice by the State Council regarding doing well the intensification of RTFR pilot work in 2004]. Available at www.gov.cn/gongbao/content/2004/content_62900.htm accessed September 1, 2016.

He, K.Y. and Sun, L., eds. (2000), *Zhongguo nongcun shuifei gaige chutan [An Exploration of the Rural Tax and Fee Reform in China]*, Beijing: Zhongguo zhigong chubanshe.

Hershler, S.B. (1995), The 1994 tax reforms: the center strikes back, *China Economic Review*, Vol. 6, No. 2, 239–245.

Hsing, Y.T. (2009), Land and power brokering in China's townships, in Li, L.C., ed., *The Chinese State in Transition: Processes and Contests in Local China*, London and New York: Routledge, 89–107.

Huang, J. (2000), *Factionalism in Chinese Communist Politics*, Cambridge: Cambridge University Press.

Jacka, T. (2015), Chinese discourses on rurality, gender and development, in Yeh, E.T., O'Brien, K.J. and Ye, J.Z., eds., *Rural Politics in Contemporary China*, London and New York: Routledge, 68–92.

Kennedy, J.J. (2007), From the tax-for-fee-reform to the abolition of agricultural taxes: the impact of township governments in North-west China, *The China Quarterly*, Vol. 189: 43–59.

Kennedy, J.J. (2015), Finance and rural governance: centralization and local challenges, in Yeh, E.T., O'Brien, K. and Ye, J.Z., eds., *Rural Politics in Contemporary China*, London and New York: Routledge, 93–110.

Li, L.C. (2006), Path creation? Processes and networks: how the Chinese rural tax reform began, *Policy and Society*, Vol. 25, No. 1, 61–84.

Li, L.C. (2009), Embedded institutionalization: sustaining rural tax reform, in Li, L. C., ed., *The Chinese State in Transition: Processes and Contests in Local China*, London and New York: Routledge, 55–73.

Li, L.C. (2012), *Rural Tax Reform in China: Policy Processes and Institutional Change*, London and New York: Routledge.

Lieberthal, K. (2004), *Governing China: From Revolution through Reform*, New York: W. W. Norton.

Lieberthal, K. and Lampton, D.M. (1992), *Bureaucracy, Politics, and Decision Making in Post-Mao China*, Berkeley: University of California Press.

Matland, R.E. (1995), Synthesizing the implementation literature: the ambiguity-conflict model of policy implementation, *Journal of Public Administration Research and Theory*, Vol. 5, No. 2, 145–174.

O'Brien, K. and Li, L.J. (1999), Selective policy implementation in rural China, *Comparative Politics*, Vol. 31, No. 2, 167–186.

O'Brien, K. and Li, L.J. (2006), *Rightful Resistance in Rural China*, New York: Cambridge University Press.

Olsen, J.P. (1970), Local budgeting – Decision-making or ritual act? *Scandinavian Political Studies*, Vol. 5, 85–118.
Perry, E.J. (2011), From mass campaigns to managed campaigns: "constructing a new socialist countryside," in Heilmann, Sebastian and Perry, E.J., eds., *Mao's Invisible Hand: The Political Foundations of Adaptive Governance in China*, Cambridge, MA: Harvard University Press, 30–61.
Smith, G. (2015), Measurement, promotions and patterns of behavior in Chinese local government, in Yeh, E.T., O'Brien, K. and Ye, J.Z., eds., *Rural Politics in Contemporary China*, London and New York: Routledge, 111–134.
Sylvester, R.K. and Ferrara, J.A. (2003), Conflict and ambiguity implementing evolutionary acquisition, *Acquisition Review Quarterly*, 3–27.
Tao, R. and Qin, P. (2007), How has rural tax reform affected farmers and local governance in China? *China and World Economy*, Vol. 15, No. 4, 19–32.
Thøgersen, S. (2011), Building a new socialist countryside, in Alpermann, Björn, ed., *Politics and Markets in Rural China*, London and New York: Routledge, 172–186.
Wang, C.P., Heady, C. and Woo, W.T. (1995), *Fiscal Management and Economic Reforms in the People's Republic of China*, New York: Oxford University Press.
Wedeman, A. (2000), Budgets, extra-budgets, and small treasuries: illegal monies and local autonomy in China, *Journal of Contemporary China*, Vol. 9, 489–511.
Wong, C.P. (1997), Rural public finance, in Wong, Christine P.W., ed., *Financing Local Government in the People's Republic of China*, Hong Kong and New York: Oxford University Press, 167–212.
Yan, H.R. and Chen, Y.Y. (2015), Debating the rural cooperative movement in China, the past and the present, in Yeh, E.T., O'Brien, K.J. and Ye, J.Z., eds., *Rural Politics in Contemporary China*, London and New York: Routledge, 41–67.
Yeh, E.T., O'Brien, K.J. and Ye, J.Z., eds. (2015a), *Rural Politics in Contemporary China*, London and New York: Routledge.
Yeh, E.T., O'Brien, K.J. and Ye, J.Z. (2015b), Rural politics in contemporary China, in Yeh, E.T., O'Brien, K.J. and Ye, J.Z., eds., *Rural Politics in Contemporary China*, London and New York: Routledge, 1–14.
Yep, R. (2004), Can "tax-for-fee" reform reduce rural tension in China? The process, progress and limitations, *The China Quarterly*, Vol. 177, 42–70.
Zhang, D.Y. (2003), "Bi shui" hai zai ji xu [Tax enforcement still continues], *Gaige Neican [Reform Internal Reference]*, 31, 20–24.
Zhang, P. (2001), *Anhui nongcun shuifei gaige shijian yu tansuo [Practice and Exploration of Anhui's Rural Tax and Fee Reforms]*, Beijing: Dangdai chubanshe.
Zhao, S.K. (2006a), Hard pressed township finances, *Chinese Sociology and Anthropology*, Vol. 39, No. 2, 45–54.
Zhao, S.K. (2006b), The debt chaos of township governments, *Chinese Sociology and Anthropology*, Vol. 39, No. 2, 36–44.
Zhongfa (1996), No. 13 Zhongguo zhongyang, guowuyuan guanyi qieshi zuo hao jainqing nongmin fudan gongzuo de jueding [Decision by the CCP Central Committee and State Council regarding resolutely carrying out work of reducing the peasants' burden]. Available at http://cpc.people.com.cn/GB/64162/71380/71382/71481/4854241.html accessed September 16, 2016.

14
THE PARTY'S POLICY TOWARD LABOR

Bill Taylor[1]

Introduction

The Chinese Communist Party (CCP, herein sometimes also referred to as the "Party") betrays the hollowness of its socialist claim in the way it maintains a problematic relation with the urban working class. As an elite, the Party has upheld a strong division between itself and mass social categories, such as peasants and especially workers, whilst accommodating powerful groups, such as the military as well as capitalists.[2] The Party now fears the working class, reflecting a schism between its brand identity as a socialist, perhaps now *the* socialist, organ, and its complete betrayal of socialism in practice. Having discarded its Marxist roots in the summer of 1923 (Short 2004: 141), workers were paired up with and then subordinated to peasants, before reemerging under the present quasi-capitalist period as the proletariat in all but name. The Party's paranoia toward workers is founded on past practice. A key aspect of Marx's teachings about historical progression is that workers sometimes do overthrow their masters, and the CCP elite feels the vulnerability of Marxist dialectical materialism more keenly than most.

This chapter will briefly explain the origins of the CCP's relations with urban workers. It will look at the twists and turns of party-labor relations during the Maoist period and the Reform Era, and trace developments through to the twenty-first century. Current structures of control will be outlined, focusing on the official party organ to regulate labor, namely the All-China Federation of Trade Unions (ACFTU). Then we examine workers' response and how these are viewed by the party-state, and relate this to the generational change within the leadership. The chapter will conclude with a brief exploration of possible future directions for the relation between labor and the Party.

Background: Maoism as ambivalent socialism

As often occurred among critical scholars of the time, Mao converted to Marxist Leninism from anarchism and being a man of action more than intellectualism, he set about prophesizing the cause to urban workers. He had limited direct involvement with workers or the various leftist trade unions being formed all over China during the 1920s, but accepted the idea of labor as vanguard of revolution. However, his view of labor soon became complicated. First, his 1927 report on the peasant movement in Hunan (Short 2004: 171–172): Mao was confident that the bulk of peasants would rise against their oppressors. Second, efforts by his party colleagues to organize workers to initiate revolution-like insurrections demonstrated the fragility of Chinese laborers as an agent of change. Failures of workers' movements included the so-called Autumn Harvest Uprising in 1927 (Hsu 1983: 554) which was organized in opposition to the suppression of workers' movements in Canton (Hsu 1983: 554); and, rather more thoroughly and brutally, in Shanghai when the Kuomintang (KMT) arranged for the Green Gang to murder trade union organizers in the city, many of whom were communists (Fairbank 1987: 215–216). The contrast between workers' and peasants' willingness to support revolution seems to have confirmed Mao's belief that in predominantly feudalist and agrarian China, the Party had to rely on organized peasants, not members of Marxist proletariats, to achieve revolutionary success.

Mao's ambivalence toward workers led to rejection of his leadership by the Bolsheviks, and Stalin nurtured alternative labor leaders right up to 1949 in preference to Mao. For his part, Mao tried unsuccessfully to appeal to US president Franklin Roosevelt to reduce his dependence on Russia in 1949 (Hsu 1983: 675), further demonstrating his apparent reluctance to follow the Soviet line (Schram 1986: 817).

Mao was later to develop his "peasants as vanguard" to claim an alternative route toward revolution, and a new stage of Marxism that was distinct from that of the Soviets. What became known as Maoism sought to demonstrate a roadmap to communist society based on a combination of the peasants (Mao) and workers (Marx) under the leadership of the Party (Lenin), which was especially applicable to postcolonial revolutions.

Nevertheless, post-1949 China was structured along Soviet lines. The CCP claims to be a faithful practitioner of Marxist-Leninism conjoined with Maoism but the ideological and administrative structures were mostly Soviet. And even after its break with the USSR in the late 1950s, China maintained Soviet structures and Maoist intellectual ideas remained couched in Marxist terms. This was evident in Zhou's eulogy to Mao in 1949 (Zhou 1981: 377):

> As far as the Communist Party is concerned, we represent the proletariat. Numerically, the Chinese proletariat consists of only several million people, less than one percent of the population. How did the Communist Party, which represents this class, win victory in the Chinese Revolution? Chairman Mao makes it his central objective to apply the proletarian Marxist ideology to Chinese reality, win over the overwhelming majority of the people, and rally them around the proletariat to bring the revolution to victory.

The vanguard status of workers also appears in the drafting of the first constitution in 1954 in which the working class are the only group given special status, with rights to strike, guaranteed pay and rest periods, none of which were granted to peasants or soldiers (Diamant and Feng 2015). Although it is not clear why Mao copied the Soviet administrative model so closely, there appear three likely explanations. First, having failed in his overtures to the US, China, being a weak state, needed a protector and help in its development, and Russia became an obvious choice. Second, having relied on the peasants Mao lacked sufficient technical and managerially trained cadres to administer the vast country, and those with any training were mostly educated in Japan and especially Russia. Third, and related to the first two, Mao had ambitions for a strong country and set about setting quotas and targets for industrial growth, which depended on the import of advanced machinery, and foreign trained engineers to run them. So, although Mao thought he had developed a new path to revolution, he still sought a Soviet model of utopia.

Against the revolutionary dogma of "working class as vanguard," actual practice appeared to place workers in a much more marginalized position. The most obvious examples came in the mass drives that accompanied the Great Leap Forward and the later stage of the Cultural Revolution. The Great Leap Forward was not just an anti-intellectual movement – that workers and peasants can boost production in contrast to the Soviet emphasis on experts – it was a disastrous experiment in demonstrating that peasants could not produce industrial goods. However, the idea that industrial work was specialized and required years of learned skills never really held much sway, despite it being central to understanding Marx's writing. As Mao emptied the schools and some factories into the countryside to learn from peasants during the Cultural Revolution the lesson could not be clearer as to the low status in which workers were held in the mindset of the CCP leadership.

There is a subtler position of workers, demonstrated in sharing the national flag with other classes, represented in stars for intellectuals, entrepreneurs and peasants. From the 1920s, Russia had forced the CCP to follow KMT or Nationalist leadership, with Mao, among many others, joining the KMT at one point. The Chinese Communists accepted the KMT sense of nationalism, and this developed into an acceptance of "red capitalists," or entrepreneurs who were Nationalist – and allowed them to function well into the 1950s. In the spirit of "nation building," workers in factories owned by the "red capitalists" were expected to obey their employers. Along with limited land reform – which allowed former landlords to retain enough land to toil – the phenomenon of patriotic employers marked a strong ideological contrast to the Soviet history, where such "leeches" were seen in stark class enemy terms. This resulted in an ironic Chinese model of socialism, with the state-appointed "union" imploring workers not to overthrow their employers but to help them make profits.

Chen (2013) shows how these workers agitated for change: they blamed the Party for their poor conditions rather than employers. Conflict continued as the state nationalized such firms, forcing the state to adopt stabilized employment conditions (what became known as the three irons – guaranteed employment, wages and welfare). Another example is the transfer of 70,000 rural county-level party officials to run factories and "unions" in urban areas during 1953 (Ladany 1992: 194–195). This was despite the fact that almost all such officials were semi-literate and technologically ignorant rural folk. Drafting peasant cadres to the cities reflected problems in recruiting reliable party loyalists among urban workers, but the antipathy that these peasant cadres harboured toward urbanites reflects a heighted contrast between countryside and cities.

During the early reform period of the 1980s, mixed messages as to the status of the "vanguard of socialism" recurred. Reforms toward marketization occurred first in the countryside, before the reform of industrial employment. "Chief Architect of Reform" Deng Xiaoping's brief experiment with pluralism again showed intellectuals, the Party's own ranks and workers that the CCP leadership could not be trusted. Urban workers lost their constitutional securities and the so-called "iron rice bowl" was shattered in the 1980s (Leung 1988). When extensive destruction of the state sector began in earnest in the early 1990s, a mixture of appeasement to the traditional working classes occurred, interspersed with violent repression. Appeasement came from pouring money into under-employment and unemployment payments to laid-off workers in the northern heavy industrial cities, which were paid for by new revenues from the growing use of rural labor in the new industrial zones in the south and along the coast. The material or actual position of urban workers, since the end of the post-planned period, has seen a return to the 1920s levels of being privileged at the expense of peasants, whilst holding the status of *mere* proletariat under capitalism.

There is no question that the Party made life austere for both peasants and workers but workers – and urban areas in general – fared better. The peasants won the revolution for the Party but were after 1949 relegated to second-class citizen status. During the collectivization movement, Mao reneged upon his pledge to divide up the land and allow households to own individual plots. The *hukou* system (promulgated in 1958) prevented peasants from moving to the cities and Mao's industrial policy favored the urban areas (Nolan 2004: 50). Despite the fact that workers also suffered various deprivations, they, as urbanites, have at least enjoyed subsidized education and a system of basic living guarantees (Sbd2012 2015) as well as higher average and minimum incomes.

Structures of control

Returning to how the Party seeks to maintain control over the working class and how these control mechanisms highlight its fear of workers, there are several organizations which handle the relationship between the Party and workers, both directly and indirectly. The party structure itself, together with several party managed "mass organizations" such as the Communist Youth League and All China Federation of Women, constituted the formal interface between the CCP and citizens. The Youth League in particular played an important role as liaison between the Party and workers during the planned period, with many urban youth joining the organization and continuing membership into the workplace. Moreover, the tripartite management of work units, with party, plant and labor leaders meant that party affairs permeated factories through all three channels, particularly in the state-owned enterprises (and some cooperatives). In the wake of Deng Xiaoping's industrial reforms, formal channels of liaison between party organs and workers became much attenuated, something the Central Party Committee has become very worried about since the mid-1990s.

The only other direct influence on workers is if they chose to become CCP members. According to internal figures for 2012: 31 percent of membership came from peasants, 9 percent from workers, 8 percent from party and government cadres, 18 percent from retirees, 3 percent were students; the second largest group – managers, technical and professionals – took up 23 percent (Meng 2012).[3] As China moved from a peasant-based workforce to industrial and urban employment it is logical that the Party's composition should also change. However, it is clear that even by the CCP's own data, it has radically shifted to being an elitist party and away from workers and peasants. It has done this through an active recruitment drive and admitting entrepreneurs to join, resulting in 86.7 million members in 2012, up from 78 million in 2009.

Some commentators thought the reform would undermine the party discipline and pluralism within the Party, which would in turn produce fissures or factions which would eventually lead to the collapse or splintering of the CCP (Li 2012; Mirsky 2014). These developments precipitated fear among the leadership over the reduced relevance of the CCP to the working class; they also prompted top cadres to do more to demonstrate the Party's relevance to a society whose material experience is capitalism (Lam 2015). With the rise of autonomy in state-owned enterprise (SOE) management, especially since 1988 (Taylor *et al.* 2003: 54), and the complete free rein in the private sector, for a time, in the 1990s it appeared as if the CCP was struggling for relevance. The fact that the CCP seemed to have become a party of businesses has ensured a subordinate role for labor could not hide its declining direct hold over productive activity. In response, the Party has given up any pretense to liberalist ideals after the Tiananmen Square crackdown; it has consolidated an extremely conservative role of the authorities in developing a form of capitalism. The Party has taken on a neo-fascist rather than a corporatist persona (Clark 1998: 81–84). The capitalists, who enjoy cozy ties with senior cadres, thrive in the new system. They have access to privileged business information and resources – and can even exert influence on policies (Kennedy 2008). Thanks to extensive capital controls and other policies that favor their cronies, the CCP leadership's stranglehold over wealth is assured (Piketty 2014: 463–464).

The government bureaucracy, as the executive of the party, manages the context in which citizens live. Workers are particularly influenced by these "Big Brother" administrative arms: the Ministry of Human Resources and Social Security; the political-judicial system, particularly the Police; and above all the All-China Federation of Trade Unions (ACFTU). The ACFTU was tasked by the Party to be the primary channel of communication with workers and so this government organization is key to understanding working class relations with the Party.

Under instructions from early Soviet advisors, the ACFTU was formed in 1925 (Taylor and Li 2009: 33) to organize local unions to counter the KMT's successes in establishing unions. Its growth was hampered by both the KMT strategy of forcing workers into enterprise-based unions (unions based on the single workplace) and current employment practices. A tradition of "gang labor" run by secret societies and guilds in the north and labor contracting through supervisors in the south (Frazier 2002: 23–26) created strong dependency relations and diffused lines of authority, making organizing difficult. The KMT's practice of organizing through employers increased numbers because all workers were deemed to be members automatically once an employer had agreed to the union, although few were aware of their membership. Without a base on the shop floor, however, such "paper" unions were weak and allowed the communists to organize workers secretly in the vacuum, one gang at a time. Many embryonic unions were crushed by violent employer reprisals once they were discovered but others grew popular and strong through mass worker support, forcing employers to negotiate. Ironically in the past decade the ACFTU has engaged in the same KMT practice and formed supposed unions by approaching employers without consulting workers. There are even cases where employers are unaware they agreed to recognize a union, the local ACFTU branch having gained some local employer groups such as chambers of commerce to create paper unions among members.

Whilst the ACFTU acted as an administrative office in the public sector, responsible for providing welfare and organizing campaigns to boost production, it became an important agent in the 1950s to project party influence within the private sector. Workers were instructed to obey their capitalist bosses for the greater good of the country and only when they began to agitate with mass strikes and other mass acts of defiance did the party-state's departments come to nationalize these enterprises. As they joined the public sector, the unions melted into welfare departments for workers, whose officers reported through the ACFTU structure. Having been identified as part of management, many suffered during the Cultural Revolution and the ACFTU itself ceased to function until the end of the 1970s.

In April 1978, the ACFTU held a national meeting and laid out plans to rejuvenate shop floor structures though education, encouraging worker participation in management and participation in the new economic reforms. Deng Xiaoping went further, arguing that the ACFTU must make workers feel the union genuinely represents their interests (Taylor and Li 2009: 40). As enterprise reform began with increased autonomy to general managers, relatively liberal cadres in the CCP thought the ACFTU would become an independent voice for workers. This all changed when the ACFTU's loyalty to the party leadership was called into question during the student movement of 1989: academics and students (union cadres) of its own premier training college (now the China Institute of Industrial Relations) in Beijing marched behind the ACFTU banner into Tiananmen Square in support of the student movement. In December 1989, a circular was issued requiring the CCP to take firmer control over the ACFTU, the All-China Federation of Women and the Communist Youth League. By 1992, the ACFTU was required to become directly involved in government decision-making at each level; and on issues relating to workers, it should publish joint statements with the relevant government department when necessary (Taylor and Li 2009: 45). From being a representative of workers, the ACFTU morphed to become a useful check on unpopular and potentially destabilizing policies of local governments so as to ensure the long-time sustainability of the party line. The decade of pluralist ideas was crushed, and although Deng's exact ideas for the role of the ACFTU were unclear, the ACFTU has after 1989 become a passive element within the Party, rather conservative except for its training colleges.

Reviewing a pep-talk given by Xi Jinping in 2013 in the course of the appointment of a new chief of the ACFTU, the head of its political branch, Chen Hao, stated that "we must always adhere to the leadership of the Chinese Communist Party and the socialist system, and without ambiguity or doubt, firmly grasp the correct political direction, at any time [and] under any circumstances" (ACFTU 2013). Whilst most academics are critical of the role of the ACFTU as being a hindrance to promoting labor interests (Taylor and Li 2007), its main positive role for the leadership is that it remains a very effective weapon of the CCP to deny any space for the emergence of an alternative political force. It is almost impossible to build a stable and viable alternative political force at the national level without strong alternative mass organizations having sprung up locally (Goldman 2005; Perry and Goldman 2007; Xie 2010; Leung and Pratap 2011: 160). As the watchdog Human Rights in China (HRiC 2011) argues, the lack of alternative foci "makes the Chinese state a comparatively more stable state than other capitalist states in the world despite China's bad human rights record."

This stability needs to be constantly groomed as the KMT experience shows it is fragile. Wei Jianxing, the former Chairman of the ACFTU and a member of the Politburo Standing Committee, stated in a late 2000 speech at a conference on organizing trade unions in new enterprises (Wei 2000):

> The fact has fully proved that, if there was no trade union in an enterprise, there would not be a perfect and effective mechanism of adjusting labour relations. Once the labour dispute occurred, even a small one, it could not be settled at the grass-roots level without this mechanism. Therefore, the conflict between both parties could not be resolved in its embryonic stage and finally led to a serious collective action. If the current tide could not be reversed in time, it would be extremely disadvantageous to the overall situation of economic reform and social stability, and also, would give way to foreign hostile elements to divide the Chinese working class. Now, the foreign hostile forces are seizing the masses from us [CCP] and the trade union is one of the areas they want to occupy. Their goal is to set up an independent trade union beyond the ACFTU and try to "Westernize" and "split" the Chinese working class. They want to overthrow the leadership of CCP and subvert the socialist system.

Despite the anti-foreign rhetoric, which is a common tone used to conjure images of crisis and thus urgency of his words, Wei is referring to the democratizing tendencies of workers' movements (which are meant to be the foundation of socialist revolutions). More directly, a deputy chairperson of Guangdong Federation of Trade Unions explains (Zhang 2001):

> Now, the non-public enterprises are developing so fast and recruiting so many workers and the international and domestic situations are so complex. The Western hostile organizations and domestic "Falungong" [Buddhist sect] are continuously in contact with our working masses. If we don't organize them, some other organizations will organize them; also, they will organize by themselves. This can threaten the leadership status of the party. Therefore, we must organize them [workers] on our own initiative, we must play the role of "getting the workers massed together and occupying the position [which will otherwise be filled by the other groups]."

Both quotes emphasize that the CCP believes establishing trade unions is required to ensure social stability. Thus, the ACFTU set about a campaign to establish branches in the burgeoning private sector by approaching employers. However, these employers were generally reluctant to allow the ACFTU in. For example, on November 1, 2004 a senior manager of Kodak Corporation replied to the ACFTU's request to establish unions thus (Xin 2004):

> Whether or not to set up trade unions should not be determined by the company, but by employees themselves; according to the Trade Unions Law, the trade union should be voluntarily organized by workers and staff, should represent the interests of workers and staff; therefore, Kodak Corporation, a company which represents the interests of shareholders would not be qualified to set up an organization which represents the interests of workers and staff; if this is the case, the Kodak Corporation would violate the principles of "voluntary organization" and "representing interests of workers and staff," both are the base of setting up trade union.

For the same reasons quoted above, Wal-Mart indicated it did recognize the ACFTU, because it was not a real union federation (WikiLeaks 2006). There has been a recent trend to argue that the ACFTU is attempting to become something more akin to a genuine trade union federation. Friedman (2014) argues that the ACFTU's struggles to reform are hampered because it refuses to democratize while Liu (2008) contends that the ACFTU is more pluralistic than it is given credit for. In both cases, they cite instances of shop floor organizing, regional and local efforts to deal with labor disputes and, especially, progressive labor legislation enacted in 2007.

In line with pressure from the Party on the ACFTU to suppress worker activism, a large-scale and ongoing drive to establish "grassroots" unions in all workplaces started from the 1990s. These are not unions but shams, usually through the appointment of a party cadre or manager (or better, both!) who takes the title as the worksite Union Chair. The Guangdong Federation of Trade Unions (the provincial branch of the ACFTU) became synonymous with progressive unionism. For example, in order to promote recognition and resolve the problem of "who is the organizer of grass-roots unions," the Standing Committee of the Guangdong People's Congress promulgated on September 24, 2004 "the measures for implementing Trade Unions Law of the PRC in Guangdong province." These measures allowed workers themselves to compel any enterprise which employed more than ten workers who already were trade union members (due to prior employment) to recognize a union so long as that previous union was based within the province. Whilst this fundamentally contradicted the ACFTU principle that local-level trade unions must be established by ACFTU units of a higher administrative level, there were still restrictions. First, it required that organizers already be trade union members, thus effectively precluding most non-SOEs in the province, as few workers were unionists (and few workers know whether they are unionists to this day, even though most are). Second, even in those few factories with more than ten union members who are aware of their status, it is still unlikely their membership status falls under the jurisdiction of the Guangdong trade union system, as they may have been union members in other provinces, or from one of the nine industrially organized union federations, neither of which qualified. Nevertheless, the province had a progressive atmosphere, which its proximity to Hong Kong and open discussion of the progressive legislation developed. So, although the Guangdong regulation was progressive in allowing workers to independently establish a union, the conditions were sufficiently restrictive to make this a symbolic rather than transformative regulation. In 2012, the progressive leader of the Guangdong Federation, Chen Weiguang, was replaced by the former head of the provincial police and all progress abruptly stopped. More generally, the period of reform after 1989 meant the ACFTU was compelled to follow the CCP line closely and, consequently, acted against the interests of labor and the working class.

The Constitution gives workers' rights as previously explained, although the right to strike was removed in 1982. A body of laws specifying a fairly comprehensive set of substantive rights for workers, along with some very weak procedural rights developed over many years prior to the 2007 legislation. Substantive rights are those items which give a worker direct benefits, such as limiting hours of work, or period of notice before dismissal, minimum wages and so on. Procedural legal rights specify the methods through which workers negotiate benefits with employers, or deal with claims, such as recovering unpaid wages through a legal system. The CCP responded by drafting three laws: on training and development, on procedures to speed up legal resolution of disputes which had become gridlocked and a substantive law. The ACFTU was given the role of championing the substantive law, to be called the Labour Contract Law[4] (LCL). The law sets limits to short term contracts (no more than two contracts), specifies monthly overtime working limits (36 hours) and details minimum overtime working pay rates, among a host of items. In theory, the provisions amount to one of the highest minimum employment standards in the world. Innovatively, the CCP and the ACFTU asked for public comments on early drafts and this created an international media interest. The law which came into force in 2008 pretty much repeated provisions already in existing laws. The main development was not the content so much as the consultations and a roadshow by top party officials, with the ACFTU chairman warning employers not to ignore the law this time.

The government argues there is a movement toward a rules-based and substantive improvement in workers' situation as a result of the 2007 legislation. In June 2008, Yin Weimin, Minister of Human Resources and Social Security, claimed that workers have enjoyed better social welfare since the introduction of the LCL. He also stated that, among 26 provinces and regions, between 90 percent and 96 percent of employees had signed labor contracts. The payment into the various social security funds (pensions, unemployment, medical, work injury and maternity insurance) amounted to RMB 610.5 billion from January to June 2008, up 31 percent on the previous year. These "facts show that the Labour Contract Law is effective in protecting the rights and interests of ordinary workers," Yin said (Zhu 2008). In Shandong Province Li and Wang (2008) studied 138 small and medium-size enterprises, and found that among 48,316 employees, 47,253 had signed contracts (a 98 percent signing rate) and 95 percent participated in social insurance payments.

In December 2008, a review of the law's effectiveness by the National People's Congress (NPC) led to heated discussion (Liu 2009). Chen Yongjie, director of research at All-China Federation of Industry and Commerce, thought that given the average size of almost 5,600,000 small and medium-sized enterprises is 12 people, it was hard to get such employers to sign employment contracts and obey the wage regulations. However, Guo Jun, Head of the Democracy Administration Department at the ACFTU, accused some local governments of protecting enterprises during the on-going economic downturn (FIDH 2013). The flexible view in applying the law may best be illustrated by a Supreme Court edict in July 2009 differentiating two types of employers in breach of labor legislation (Supreme Court 2009; Ye 2009): those who could pay but refused to pay their debts should be punished, but those with genuine economic difficulties should not be forced into bankruptcy.

The party institutions have not been designed to act as the traditional transition belts as envisaged in Soviet states, as mechanisms to communicate between workers and state. As China becomes quasi-capitalist, the Party required the ACFTU to encourage the workers to follow the new line but when this failed, it was expected to keep a lid on the ensuing conflict.

Conflict and class

The reaction of workers has been mostly to acquiesce and do their jobs, in common with the working class throughout much of world history. Chinese workers, as with peasants before them, have a long history of revolting against their masters, with major strike waves during the KMT period, again in the 1950s as mentioned, and since the 1980s, an ever growing national strike wave. The present period has two related characteristics: it is the longest period of continuous unrest with over 30 years, and the trend is toward more strikes and higher participation rates with the escalation year on year creating a situation where there are major strikes going on in almost all cities constantly. In addition to strikes, workers engage in public demonstrations and occasionally acts of violence, with some kidnapping of managers, beating of supervisors and, more frequently, suicide. In some respects, the conflict pattern which creates the most persistent disruption to the capitalist system is the high rates of labor turnover, which is detrimental to both productivity and profitability.

Strikes carry the most emotive concern for the CCP because the collapse of communism started with the Gdansk strike in Poland in 1980. For this reason, statistics on strikes have become a national secret. Various academics have tried to estimate strike patterns (Elfstrom and Kuruvilla 2014). The Hong Kong-based NGO China Labor Bulletin remains the only reliable source of data (CLB 2017), with almost daily updates since 2011, though the collection of data has become more difficult since July 2016 (Lin 2016).

There are periodic public displays of distress over the rising level of conflicts, such as when Yang Zhiming, the deputy-minister of MOHRSS, argued that many enterprises were closed down due to the 2008 global financial crisis. This led to a rapid increase of labor disputes, by 90 percent in a year, to involve 1.2 million workers by the end of 2008 (Peng and Wu 2009). Provinces with the greatest increases included Guangdong, Jiangsu and Zhejiang, where labor disputes recorded in the first quarter of 2009 rose respectively by 41.63 percent, 50.32 percent and 159.61 percent. In 2015, the strike peak which normally tapers off after Chinese New Year remained high (Lockett 2016), and when it grew still further in 2016 (Hernandez 2016), the government arrested labor activists and NGOs (see Chapter 22, "Changing Patterns of Chinese Civil Society: Comparing the Hu-Wen and Xi Jinping Eras").

The working class has undergone several changes during the past century in both composition and outlook. At the start of the twentieth century, the workers in industrial and service labor formed two distinct groups – the skilled and trained workforce, tied to guilds, gang bosses and occasional unions were supported by a vast, seething underclass of itinerant labor, most of which was recently recruited from rural areas. Language, ethnic and gender divisions meant this group was a vulnerable underclass. The restriction of movement which developed in the early 1950s stopped the problem by formalizing the divide, apart from gender, which became for a period much more equal. The reversion to capitalism did not initially turn the clock back (except for women who suffered badly in the workplace and labor markets) but instead, created two parallel though linked changes. First, the urban workers lost livelihood guarantees and pay stagnated in the reforms of the state sector, and they resisted en masse. They faced unemployment but retained a strong solidarity with their workplace identities and the socialist idea, even if local party officials were poor role models (Wong 2008; Fan 2011). Ultimately, the state bought out the older generation and beat up and imprisoned the vocal dissenters among them. In recent years, a younger generation of urbanites, especially if male, have found opportunities in those SOEs that remain and in some of the prestigious SOEs that have privatized.

The central story of the development of the working class has been the return of rural migrants to the cities (Murphy 2002), but it is not a repeat of the past. Initially the migrants were much divided by gender and occupation, with men building the new cities and industrial fabric and women working in the new export-oriented factories. The new workers replaced the old urban workers as the engine of economic growth, as if capitalism was now based on the migrant underclass. However, the first wave of migrants job hopped, stayed only a few years and were mostly illiterate. A second generation, consisting of the children of those women migrant workers, has become a vital component of the urban work scene – and they are changing everything. First, they can read and write, having been educated in collective schools within the cities and they grew up as urbanites. As industrialization and service sectors have globalized and matured, they compete with urban workers and work alongside them. Their bilingualism means they cannot be discriminated so easily based on their native tongue (what is it anyway – their parents or where they grew up?). Leung and Pratap (2011: 193) described research they conducted in which:

> The new generation workers in the Shenzhen SEZ are better educated. More than 67 percent of them have completed high school and above, while only 49 percent of former generation workers had such a qualification. The majority of the new generation workers use internet and are more exposed to the world. About 60 percent of the new generation migrant workers (in the age group of 20–30) are unmarried; while more than 90 percent of older generation workers in this age group were married. Generally, in Third World countries, young unmarried women are usually considered to be unstable workforce, since the majority stop working or move to another location after marriage. But this is not the case with young Chinese women workers. They were emphatic in their decision to continue working even after marriage.

Perhaps because they are unable to return to make a living on their ancestors' farms, or because their identities have changed, these are only migrants in name (Zwj 2016). They are an articulate, self-conscious and confident new class of urban young workers and they use the law, social media and anything else to fight for their perceived rights. If it were not for the continued faltering of China's current economic growth, the impact of these workers might have been greater in forcing improvements. As it is, they are often behind (or more accurately, leading) the escalating levels of conflict reported throughout China's industrial areas. In contrast to almost all past conflicts where workers sought retribution or restitution once they have left their employer (whether fired or resigned) members of the new generation engage in conflicts with the full intention of retaining their employment relations. The Party must deal with them and it is without a mechanism to do so.

Conclusion

The CCP's credentials come from its Leninist status as the vanguard of the proletariat. Deng's justification for economic reform set the clock back to claim the CCP needed to guide China through a quasi-capitalist stage (the so-called "primary" stage of socialism) to reach socialism. This argument is hopelessly contradictory, because Lenin's articulation of the vanguard party was that it was a workers' organ. Disingenuous as it may have been, the Soviets rejected Mao because of his repudiation of a worker-centered vanguard, and it remains valid today: the idea that workers would actively embrace capitalism under any band name is delusionary, and assigning managers the status of Model Workers (Dickson 2008: 44) appears the best illustration of this self-deception. Giving a narrow and peripheral role to the ACFTU has ensured that workers and the reforming working class remain outside the CCP. Despite escalating conflicts, there is no evidence that workers have become fully conscious of their collective class interests. Even so, a new generation of better educated, rights-conscious laborers is fighting for better working conditions as well as welfare and pension benefits. Although the CCP has always been vigilant to squash working class identities, as the CCP moves from representing the peasant-military alliance toward representing the capitalist-military interests, it may underestimate the power of collective labor in future, at its cost.

Looking to the future, much of the story will depend on the pattern of economic growth. The policy of shifting from an export orientated to a domestic demand economy seems to provide hope to workers, who have seen increased wages forced on employers through higher minimum wages. However, there is no evidence this is subduing workers' demands as strikes are unabated and so in the short term, rising worker expectations will offset wage increases. This will help the Party to develop a more domestically orientated economy but only for a short time. As wages rise, employers are already moving production overseas and, as the reserve army of migrant labor dries up (as they become farmers or urbanites) this will accelerate. At present, many large capitalists have good reasons to stay well connected to the Party, but if such relations threaten profits, they will relocate. There is no reason to think the normal rules of capitalism will not apply, that capital is mobile and transient and workers are immobile and trapped. The Party will be forced to kowtow to the capitalists, if it has not already become a Party of Capitalists.

It is likely, thus, that workers will be squeezed between fragile job security and a rollback in legal protections. The population is too large to expect some sort of transition to an information economy in the way the UK and Switzerland managed. Rather, like the UK and the US, it is possible to see pockets of large cities with vibrant economies surrounded by vast areas of relative poverty. The Party's obsession with social stability will remain both pertinent and pervasive. Much therefore rests on whether workers can establish their own trade unions in defiance of the Party and its mouthpiece, the ACFTU. Comparing to overseas, there is a strong argument to make that such unions will not form or be very effective, and that the age of labor solidarity is now past globally. It is equally possible, however, that Chinese workers will generate a renaissance in the labor movement, acting in ways which challenge capitalism's mobility, by using technology creatively and relying on their collective strength.

Notes

1 My gratitude to Willy Lam, whose thorough editing work transformed this chapter. Alas, the errors and omissions remain my responsibility, whether through neglect or stubbornness.

2 It is popular to refer to China's form of capitalism with the prefix quasi-state or crony-capitalism, but this implies there is some pure form, devoid of state manipulation. Such a liberalist utopia (Nozick 1974) has no empirical foundation and applying caveats such as Friedman's control of money supply (1992) or Keynesian economic management (1936) merely serves to demonstrate the contradictions inherent in liberalism. Coffey and Thornley (2009) explain the development of the notion of varieties of capitalism to account for national differences, but the notion of the "capitalist state" in early Marxist writing (Marx and Engels 1998) is just as apt for present day China as it was for industrializing nineteenth century Britain. The state has aligned its interests with that of capital albeit ambiguously, and capitalists have variously worked with and against state actors as they endeavor to turn a profit.

3 Zheng (2007) has different figures, with peasants and workers combined making up 29 percent of party membership in 2005, down from 83 percent in 1956. Even within these figures, it is likely the "designations" hide the actual standing of members, with many managers and even entrepreneurs being designated workers. Nevertheless, the decline of the status of workers is significant.

4 Labour Contract Law of the People's Republic of China (2007). www.npc.gov.cn/englishnpc/Law/2009-02/20/content_1471106.htm.

References

ACFTU (2013) "Xi Jinping speech on the occasion of the appointment of the new ACFTU General Secretary: Adhere to the correct direction the courage to take responsibility," All China Federation of Trade Unions, November 9, www.acftu.org/template/10041/file.jsp?cid=986&aid=88540.

Chen Fung (2013) "Against the state: Labour protests in China in the 1950s," *Modern China* XX (X): 1–31.

Clark, B. (1998) *Political Economy: Comparative Approach* (second edition), US: Praeger Publishers.

CLB (2017) "CLB strike map," China Labour Bulletin, http://maps.clb.org.hk/strikes/en.

Coffey, D. and Thornley, C. (2009) *Globalization and Varieties of Capitalism: New Labor, Economic Policy and the Abject State*, Basingstoke: Palgrave Macmillan.

Diamant, Neil J. and Feng, Xiaocai (2015) "The PRC's first national critique: The 1954 campaign to 'discuss the draft constitution'," *The China Journal* 73.

Dickson, Bruce (2008) *Wealth into Power: The Communist Party's Embrace of China's Private Sector*, New York: Cambridge University Press.

Elfstrom, M. and Kuruvilla, S. (2014) "The changing nature of labor unrest in China" [Electronic version], *Industrial & Labor Relations Review* 67 (2): 453–480. Cornell University, ILR School site: http://digital commons.ilr.cornell.edu/articles/1001.

Fairbank, John (1987) *The Great Chinese Revolution: 1800–1985*, New York: Harper & Row Publishers.

Fan, Wen-dong (2011) *My 20 Years with a State Enterprise*, Hong Kong: Globalisation Monitor.

FIDH (2013) "China's workers are calling for change, what role should brands play?" International Federation for Human Rights, http://tbinternet.ohchr.org/Treaties/CESCR/Shared%20Documents/CHN/INT_CESCR_CSS_CHN_16961_E.pdf.

Frazier, Mark (2002) *The Making of the Chinese Industrial Workplace: State Revolution and Labour Management*, New York: Cambridge University Press.

Friedman, Eli (2014) *Insurgency Trap: Labor Politics in Postsocialist China*, Ithaca, NY: Cornell University Press.

Friedman, Milton (1992) *A Program for Monetary Stability*, New York: Fordham University Press.

Goldman, M. (2005) *From Comrade to Citizen*, Cambridge, MA: Harvard University Press.

Hernandez, Javier (2016) "Labour protests in China multiply as economy slows, worrying leaders," *New York Times*, March 14, www.nytimes.com/2016/03/15/world/asia/china-labor-strike-protest.html.

HRiC (2011) "The Chinese working class, the ACTFU and engagement," *Human Rights in China*, January 18, www.hrichina.org/en/content/4806.

Hsu, Immanuel (1983) *The Rise of Modern China* (third edition), Hong Kong: Oxford University Press.

Kennedy, S. (2008) *The Business of Lobbying in China*, Cambridge, MA: Harvard University Press.

Keynes, John Maynard (1936) *The General Theory of Employment, Interest, and Money*, New York: Harcourt, Brace & World.

Ladany, Laszlo (1992) *The Communist Party of China and Marxism 1921–1985: A Self-Portrait*, Hong Kong: Hong Kong University Press.

Lam, W. (2015) *Chinese Politics in the Era of Xi Jinping*, London: Routledge.

Leung, Apo (1988) *Smashing the Iron Rice Pot: Workers and Unions in China's Market Socialism*, Hong Kong: Asia Monitor Resource Centre.

Leung, Apo and Pratap, Surendra (2011) "China's capitalist development and its implications for labour with special reference to the Shenzhen SEZ," Hong Kong: Asia Monitor Resource Centre, www.amrc.org.hk/sites/default/files/SEZ%20and%20China's%20Capitalist%20Development.pdf.

Li, Cheng (2012) "The end of the CCP's resilient authoritarianism? A tripartite assessment of shifting power in China," *The China Quarterly* 211: 595–623.

Li, G. and Wang, R. (2008) "The effects on small-medium size enterprises from the implementation of labour contract law," *Shandong Labour and Social Security* 10: 24–27.

Lin, Gene (2016) "Chinese authorities issue arrest notice for founder of protest-tracking blog," Hong Kong Free Press, July 22, www.hongkongfp.com/2016/07/22/chinese-authorities-issue-arrest-notice-for-founder-of-protest-tracking-blog/.

Liu, C. (2009) "The impact of Labour Contract Law on Chinese enterprises' firing costs and employment behaviour," *Economic Management* 30 (21–22): 143–150.

Liu, Mingwei (2008) "Union organizing in China: Still a monolithic labour movement?" *Industrial and Labour Relations Review* 64 (1).

Lockett, Hudson (2016) "China: Strikes and protest numbers jump 20%," *Financial Times*, July 14, www.ft.com/content/56afb47c-23fd-3bcd-a19f-bddab6a27883.

Marx, Karl and Engels, Fredrick (1998) *The Communist Manifesto*, London: Verso.
Meng, J. (2012) *Occupational Structure of CCP Members*, China Development Gateway, http://en.chinagate.cn/archives/18da/2012-11/06/content_27015429.htm.
Mirsky, J. (2014) "Tiananmen: How wrong we were," *The New York Review of Books*, May 20, www.nybooks.com/blogs/nyrblog/2014/may/20/tiananmen-how-wrong-we-were/.
Murphy, Rachel (2002) *How Migrant Labour Is Changing Rural China*, New York: Cambridge University Press.
Nolan, Peter (2004) *Transforming China: Globalization, Transition and Development*, London: Anthem Press.
Nozick, Robert (1974) *Anarchy, State, and Utopia*, Oxford: Blackwell.
Peng Yong and Wu Jun (2009) "Qunian laodong zhengyi anjian shangsheng (The labor disputes increased last year)," www.gov.cn/jrzg/2009-05/08/content_1309121.htm.
Perry, E. and Goldman, M. (Eds.) (2007) *Grassroots Political Reform in Contemporary China*, Cambridge, MA: Harvard University Press.
Piketty, T. (2014) *Capital in the Twenty First Century*, US: Belknap Press.
Sbd2012 (2015) "Minimum living allowance," http://baike.baidu.com/view/168505.htm.
Schram, Stuart (1986) "Mao Tse-tung's thought to 1949," in John Fairbank and Albert Feuerwerker (Eds.) *The Cambridge History of China, Vol. 13: Republican China 1912 – 1949*, Cambridge: Cambridge University Press, pp. 789–869.
Short, Philip (2004) *Mao: A Life*, London: John Murray.
Supreme Court (2009) "Supreme Court's guidelines on how to deal well with labour dispute cases in the period of financial crisis," www.chinacourt.org/flwk/show.php?file_id=136928.
Taylor, Bill and Li Qi (2007) "Is the ACFTU a trade union and does it matter?" *Journal of Industrial Relations* 49 (5): 701–715.
Taylor, Bill and Li Qi (2009) "The ACFTU's role in China's tumultuous social development," in C. Phelan (Ed.), *Trade Unions since 1945: Towards a Global History: Volume 2*, Oxford: Peter Lang, pp. 31–60.
Taylor, Bill, Chang Kai and Li Qi (2003) *Industrial Relations in China*, Cheltenham: Edward Elgar.
Wei, Jianxing (2000) Speech at the National Working Conference on Union Organising in New Enterprises (*zai quanguo xinjian qiye gonghui zujian gongzuo huiyi shang de jianghua*), November 12, China Post Trade Unions website, www.cptu.org.cn/zlhb/ldjh/qzldjh/wjxzqgxjqyghzjgzhysdjh.htm.
WikiLeaks (2006) "Wal-Mart accepts Chinese labor unions," https://wikileaks.org/plusd/cables/06BEIJING17771_a.html.
Wong, May (2008) *Voices from Below*, Hong Kong: Asia Monitor Resource Centre.
Ye, D. (2009) "Rising rate of labor disputes in China," *Caijing* online, July 13, http://english.caijing.com.cn/2009-07-13/110196987.html.
Xie, Y. (2010) *Protest Politics*, Shanghai: Shanghai Education Publishing House.
Xin, M. (2004) "Waiqi qiye jujian gonghui jiang bei qisu [The enterprises rejecting setting up trade unions will be sued by ACFTU]," *Xinkuaibao*, October 29.
Zhang, Wen (2001) "Shock wave from unionization (*xinjian gonghui chongjibo*)." *Nanfengchuang* 4: 51–53.
Zheng, Y. (2007) "Is Communist Party rule sustainable in China," Discussion Paper 22, University of Nottingham: China Policy Institute, www.nottingham.ac.uk/cpi/documents/discussion-papers/discussion-paper-22-ccp-sustainability.pdf.
Zhou, Enlai (1981) *Selected Works: Volume 1*, Beijing: Foreign Language Press.
Zhu, Z. (2008) "Contract law boost for social security," *China Daily*, September 20, www.chinadaily.com.cn/bizchina/2008-09/20/content_7044097.htm.
Zwj (2016) *Survey Report of the New Generation Migrant Workers*, October 10, http://bg.yjbys.com/diaochabaogao/12517.html.

15

REFORM, REPRESSION, CO-OPTATION

The CCP's policy toward intellectuals

Jean-Philippe Béja

Introduction: rationale behind the "transformation" of intellectuals

Communist Parties have always attached a great importance to ideology, which is the main source of their legitimacy: they justify their rule by the fact that they represent the vanguard of the proletariat, and therefore the march forward of history. Keeping the monopoly on ideology, and preventing the rise of competitive ideas, is an essential task of their leaders. Therefore, since the victory of the Russian Revolution, communist leaders have displayed an amazing concern for intellectuals, the social group that has a natural right on the elaboration of ideology.

Whereas in the first year of his rule, Lenin had allowed ideological debate among the Bolshevik party intellectuals, the purge of the worker opposition (led by Alexandra Kollontai) and the advent of Stalin to the general secretariat have gradually suppressed all sorts of debate. Ideas which differed from those of the Vojd (the "Guide") were considered "counter-revolutionary" and their exponents were, in the best cases, expelled from the Party and reduced to silence. Despite his numerous disagreements with Stalin, Mao Zedong has inherited his views on the necessity to prohibit the formation of factions in the Chinese Communist Party (CCP). But, as he regarded himself as a philosopher and a poet, he has always considered the monopoly of political correctness and of the interpretation of Marxist philosophy as the main task of the Leader. Whereas Stalin used ideology to consolidate his power and to industrialize the USSR, Mao was convinced that changing the thought of human beings or "creating the new man" was the prerequisite to the transformation of the country.

Since Mao took over the leadership and even after his death, the Party has adopted a dual approach toward the intelligentsia. In periods of radicalization of the revolution, the emphasis was put on the transformation of intellectuals and the repression of their creativity. In other periods, when the Party needed to test new policies or to renew its legitimacy, it tried to enlist their support by acknowledging the specificity of their contribution to the cause. In Party language it is stated as, in the first case, "intellectuals are bourgeois, and they must be reeducated by the workers and peasants," and in the second case, "intellectuals are part of the working class." The CCP policy has been fluctuating between these two positions since the days of the revolutionary base of Yan'an in the 1930s.

When he became the supreme leader in Yan'an, one of Mao's most pressing tasks was to discipline intellectuals and to "convert them to Maoist thought." Thought Reform (*sixiang gaizao*) was the order of the day. The "rectification movement" which targeted intellectuals was instrumental to the consolidation of his power in 1942. After the Party took power over the whole of China, the Great Helmsman also resorted to mass movements targeting intellectuals to consolidate its rule. Although after Chairman Mao's death, ideology was put on the back burner, and policy toward intellectuals became secondary, the ascendancy of President Xi Jinping in 2012 has spelt a return of Mao's ultraconservative ideals. In a 2014 talk on literature and the arts which was reminiscent of Mao's famous Talks at the Yan'an Forum of Literature and Art in 1942, Xi gave explicit guidance to artists and intellectuals on the nature of the creative process, and more importantly, how they should serve the Party and the masses (Xi 2014). In this chapter, we shall concentrate on the Party's stance toward the intelligentsia and the latter's response during the Reform era. We shall also give an account of the historical background of these policies.

The Yan'an rectification movement: a pattern of the policy toward the intelligentsia

Whereas most communist parties (and the Chinese one is no exception) were founded by urban intellectuals, the vicissitudes of history have led to a transformation of the CCP that was different from that of the Soviet party. The failure of a series of workers' uprisings after the 1927 (Isaacs 2009) Kuomintang (KMT) coup d'etat forced the Party to flee to rural areas. During the 1930s it recruited mostly cadres and members of peasant origin. Although the leadership was still composed of intellectuals, the rural roots of much of the Party leadership had a big influence on the behavior of cadres. Mao Zedong tended to consider the cities as hotbeds of bourgeois ideology and urban residents as potentially hostile to the Party. This is one of the reasons why he was eager to establish his control over ideology, and over its proponents, the intellectuals. He viewed their opposition to the KMT and their patriotism as suspect, and regarded them as people who might challenge his position as the Party's greatest thinker. He therefore devised ways to impose his control. We shall study the pattern that emerged during the 1942 Yan'an rectification movement, a pattern which was to be used time and again after the CCP took over power in 1949.

After the Kuomintang's anti-CCP coup, many young progressive intellectuals denounced one-party dictatorship. At the outbreak of the Sino-Japanese war, a considerable number of them joined the Communist Party and many fled to Yan'an to escape repression. Used to life in the big cities, especially Shanghai, they protested against "bourgeois moralism," practiced free love and had very lively discussions on the numerous interpretations of Marxism. They were convinced that in Yan'an, the Revolutionary Mecca, they would at last be allowed to practice their free lifestyles, and to play a leading role in the revolution. Writers, poets, actors were eager to develop the revolutionary literature and arts for which they had been persecuted in the cities ruled by the KMT. However, they were soon disappointed when they found out that the revolutionary bases were not the freedom havens they had dreamt of. Stalinist morals imposed by the Party were worse than the "Confucian ethics" that reigned in the "white areas"; political discussions were organized by mostly ignorant peasant Party cadres who didn't understand the subtleties of the young intellectuals' interpretations of Marxism, and the equality they had been longing for was far from widespread on the loess plateaux.

Mao Zedong, whose goal was to extend his monopoly over the ideological field, was worried by the absence of discipline, by the "anarchism" of these young urban residents. But he devised a very subtle strategy to oppose them. Instead of confronting them straightforwardly, in March 1942, he launched a rectification movement against the "sectarianism" of the International faction headed by Wang Ming. This was the first of the mass campaigns that were to become characteristic of his rule.

In a first move, he decided to relax the CCP Propaganda Department's grip on expression, and allowed the airing of critical views either under the form of *dazibao* ("big-character posters") or journal articles or op-eds in the literary supplement of *Liberation Daily* (*Jiefang Ribao*). Responding to his call for Party rectification, writers published short stories and essays critical of the situation in Yan'an. For example, in *Wild Lilies* (Wang 1942a) Wang Shiwei, a young writer from Shanghai who had come to Yan'an out of idealism, denounced the hostile attitude of Party cadres toward the young intellectuals coming from the cities. He also castigated the ranking system that reigned in Yan'an and the privileges of ignorant Party cadres who enjoyed better food and clothing than ordinary workers. Moreover, the poorly educated cadres were arrogant and intolerant of freedom of expression. In *Politicians and Artists* (Wang 1942b), he criticized the attitude of the Party cadres and leaders, and praised the idealism of writers and artists. These stories attracted a vast public in a few weeks, as did his criticism of Party leader Li Weihan's literary theories. Wang became a star in Yan'an (Wang 2003).

In "Feelings on the Women's 8 March Festival" (Ding 1942) writer Ding Ling, who had become famous in the early 1930s in Shanghai for her defense of free love, criticized Party leaders' male chauvinism. In a nutshell, young intellectuals, who had not feared to denounce KMT repression at the risk of their freedom, continued to exercise their critical spirit when they got to Yan'an. They were shocked by both the absence of freedom of expression, the puritanism and the inequalities between cadres and the masses. They were convinced that their criticisms were designed to improve the situation and to render Yan'an more conducive to the ideal of communism.

But the Party leadership didn't share these convictions. Deeply influenced by Stalinism, and convinced that the Party's task was to eliminate all "petty bourgeois thoughts" that characterized these intellectuals, Mao Zedong decided to teach them a lesson, especially the writers and artists who had seized the opportunity of the freedom he had granted them to criticize his regime. On May 23, 1942, he delivered his famous speech on literature and art, where he laid down the requirements of the Party (Mao 1942). Writers and artists were supposed to fight petty bourgeois ideology, go to the grassroots to observe the life of "workers and peasants" and to study the official interpretation of Marxism-Leninism. He declared that literature and arts should serve politics, meaning that writers and artists were supposed to become soldiers in the war against the reactionary forces of the KMT and the Japanese invaders, and to obey the orders of the Central Committee which, alone, was allowed to define the Party line. A "cadre screening" campaign ensued. Those who had vented severe criticism of life in Yan'an were sent to the countryside to be "re-educated by workers and peasants." This was the case of female author Ding Ling. Mao accused Wang Shiwei of being a Trotskyite and of having organized an "anti-Party" clique. Later, he declared:

> The Party needs to unify its thinking if it is to go forward, otherwise there will be divergences of opinion. With Wang Shiwei lording over others, there could be no progress. In 1942, Wang Shiwei ... wrote *dazibao* and brought people from all places outside South Gate to look at them. He was the commander-in-chief. We lost the battle. We admitted that we had lost the battle, and so we carried out a thorough rectification.
>
> (*Wang 2003*)

Wang was put under terrible pressure and broken (Wang 2003; Wei 2016). He was jailed and finally executed in 1947, when the Party evacuated Yan'an.

The Yan'an rectification movement inaugurated a pattern of Mao's policy toward intellectuals. Whereas his talk at the Yan'an forum has become the essence of the Party line toward creative intellectuals after 1949 and was celebrated every year from 1949 to his death, the rectification campaign was reproduced recurrently after the founding of the People's Republic. The pattern is always the same. First, Mao denounces "dogmatism" and "sectarianism" in an "important speech" and encourages both Party members and non-Party intellectuals to criticize these shortcomings. After a while, many vent their anger at the absence of democracy and at the oppression by ignorant cadres. A few months later, Mao delivers another speech in which he accuses "rightists" or "traitors" or "KMT agents" of having infiltrated the ranks of the Party to oppose its leadership. Those who had dared express their opinions are either sent to the countryside, to jail, or are submitted to criticism sessions. Finally, all dissenting voices are silenced. This pattern was repeated in 1957.

The hundred flowers campaign and the anti-rightist movement

In February 1957, Mao Zedong delivered his famous speech "On the Correct Handling of Contradictions among the People" (Mao 1957) in which he declared that contradictions among the vast majority of the people who supported socialism should be solved by democratic discussion, and that that dictatorship would only be used to deal with the "handful of enemies." "Let a hundred flowers bloom, let a hundred schools contend!" In a move that recalled his speeches of 1943, Mao criticized sectarianism, dogmatism and bureaucratism, and asked Party members and non-Party members to vent their criticism at the erroneous behavior of Party cadres. This call was addressed especially to intellectuals who had been shocked by the campaign to suppress counter-revolutionaries which had followed the sentencing of dissident writer Hu Feng (Chinese History Net 2009). At the beginning, they were not enthusiastic. Cadres encouraged everyone to speak out, insisting that words could not be considered as criminal (*yanzhe wuzui*), that, on the contrary, criticizing the leaders was the best way to help the Party correct its mistakes.

After this call, a great number of intellectuals who had supported the new regime but were becoming increasingly disappointed with the high pressure under which they worked, started to vent their criticisms. They targeted mainly the absence of freedom of thought, of expression, of publication. They also denounced the omnipotence of incompetent Party secretaries (*waihang lingdao neihang*). Some people denounced the excesses of the various mass movements and requested the rehabilitation of the so-called "counter-revolutionaries." The Soviet Union was not spared in their criticisms. For three months a real freedom of expression reigned over China, without the Party or the Great Helmsman saying anything against it. Critical speeches were reproduced in the official press, unofficial journals were published in some universities. In vehement *dazibao*, students requested the respect of human rights and equality before the law (Niu and Deng 1998, Vol 1), while writers and artists criticized the ceaseless interference by propaganda cadres and asked for freedom of creation. In their works, writers showed how bureaucrats stifled the initiative of the workers, writers and students (Liu 1956; Wang 1956).

In a way, these criticisms were reminiscent of the ones that had been aired in Yan'an in 1942. And the result was similar. In June 1957, Mao Zedong wrote an editorial in the *People's Daily* in which he accused a "handful of counter-revolutionary rightists" (*People's Daily* 1957) of having used the freedoms granted by the Party to launch vicious attacks on socialism. A huge campaign to uncover rightists was launched in the whole country, especially in universities and cultural work units, which resulted in the labeling of more than 550,000 persons as "rightists." As in 1942, those who had dared answer the Great Helmsman's call were labeled counter-revolutionary rightists, were subject to criticism sessions in their work units and denounced in the official press. Others were sent to labor camps, to jail, or to the countryside to be "re-educated by the poor and lower poor peasants." Their children were also discriminated against for two decades; they were barred from entering universities or from good jobs in the cities. Their ordeal was to last for 22 years, until the verdicts were "corrected" in 1979.

This campaign contributed to silence intellectuals' criticisms and opened the way to the triumph of Mao's thought and the catastrophe of the Great Leap Forward. Once again after the Yan'an rectification movement, a campaign whose targets had first been "sectarianism, bureaucratism, dogmatism," or, in Chinese Marxist terms, "leftism," turned into a movement against liberalism, in official terms, "rightism."

Ordinary repression

The CCP, before and after Mao's death, also resorted to more classical forms of control and repression of the intellectuals. These campaigns still had a distinctive Maoist flavor. The movement for the elimination of counter-revolutionaries is a case in point. In 1954, Hu Feng, a literary critic who had been a close associate of Lu Xun, wrote a long letter to Mao Zedong to criticize the intervention by Party leaders in literature and the arts (Hu 1954; Li 2003). In this letter, also known as the "300,000-word Opinion," he demanded freedom of creation. His open letter was published in the supplement of the *Literary Gazette* (Wenyi bao), the organ of the Chinese Association of Writers. In 1955, it was strongly criticized by a *People's Daily* editorial written by Mao Zedong himself (Yuan 1955). Hu was accused of organizing an "anti-Party clique" and all those who had been associated with him in the 1930s, or who had supported his views in 1954, were labeled counter-revolutionaries. Private letters were published, and poets, writers and artists who had dared demand freedom of expression were repressed. The movement touched publishing houses, literary journals and universities. Hu Feng was sentenced to a long jail term in 1955 to be released (in a very sorry state) only in 1979.

In this instance, Mao Zedong didn't call for intellectuals to struggle against sectarianism, but circulated Hu Feng's letter in a small circle, then published his criticism in an official journal before he launched his campaign. This movement was directed essentially against the progressive intellectuals who had become famous in the 1930s and 1940s for their struggle against the KMT. Their shortcoming, in the eyes of Mao, was that, despite their formal adhesion to the New Regime, they hadn't accepted his ideas on the role of literature and art. In fact, after his speech in 1942 was made public, Hu Feng had criticized his conception of art as an instrument of Party policies (Li 2003). And *his* "300,000-word Opinion" was actually a refutation of the talks at the Yan'an forum. After the campaign to "reform the thoughts" of intellectuals in universities which had started in 1953 and which targeted professors who had been educated abroad, Mao castigated the independent progressive writers and artists who had been active in the "white areas" before "Liberation." The campaign to eliminate counter-revolutionaries was circumscribed to "cultural units." The accused were dragged from one criticism meeting to the other, where all their colleagues had to express their anger at their reactionary ideas. Many among these poets and writers couldn't stand the humiliation, and refused at first to "admit their guilt." But pressure eventually succeeded, and Hu Feng wrote a thorough self-criticism where he refuted his "bourgeois conceptions." Mao Zedong, who knew very thoroughly the situation in literary circles in the 1930s, used the antagonism between Hu Feng and the Vice-Director of the Central Committee Propaganda Department, Zhou Yang, to achieve his goal. In a letter to Zhou Yang, Mao refused to accept Hu's first self-criticism (Li 2003) and gave him the go ahead to launch the campaign against counter-revolutionaries.

Reforming the "stinking ninth"

Another instance of repression of intellectuals' freedom of expression through mass criticism (albeit on a much larger scale) is the Cultural Revolution. The movement's latent objective, which was to get rid of Mao's rival Liu Shaoqi and his allies, was in appearance directed against bourgeois intellectuals. It started with the critique of a play that indirectly criticized Mao's firing of General Peng Dehuai at the Lushan plenum in the midst of the Great Leap Forward (Wu 1961). Also targeted were three writers (journalist Deng Tuo, playwright Wu Han and writer Liao Mosha) who denounced the excesses of the Great Helmsman in the early 1960s in an article in the *Beijing Evening News* (Beijing wanbao). The movement was quickly extended to most professors, educators, teachers and writers, who were accused of refusing to reform their thoughts and of sticking to a bourgeois world outlook. As the Party apparatus did not support these denunciations, Mao called for university and high school students to organize themselves into Red Guards and to launch a movement of criticism of their teachers, school administrators and other "intellectuals." Until 1966, the Party had targeted specific categories of intellectuals: first those who had been educated abroad or in the KMT dominated cities, then the progressive intellectuals from the white areas, and finally Party and non-Party intellectuals who had criticized the regime. The Cultural Revolution was directed against all intellectuals, who were viewed as a threat to the hegemony of Mao Zedong's power. Experts were denounced as "white." Objective knowledge not based on Mao Zedong Thought, including science, physics, engineering, was considered reactionary. Agronomists who denounced the universal application of terrace fields, as required by the movement to study Dazhai (Mao's model farm), were sent to reeducation through labor. This was the lot of all serious specialists. In 1966, universities were closed. They were partially reopened in 1972 when students were selected not on the basis of their scholarly results, but on their degree of knowledge of the ruling ideology. Engineers were supposed to work under the leadership of workers' representatives, agronomists under the supervision of revolutionary cadres, etc. Only eight operas were allowed and artistic and literary production dropped to an all-time low in the history of China. The intelligentsia trained before and since "Liberation" became a "black category," the "stinking ninth."

Mao intended to create a new type of "proletarian intellectuals," who, instead of studying books and taking the *gaokao* (the entrance examination to universities), were sent to the countryside after high school graduation to till the land with the peasants, or to work in factories for a few years before being "selected" by the masses (in fact by Party cadres or military officers) to be sent to universities. While at universities, students typically spent two or three semesters working in the fields and factories and practicing military exercises in army barracks. This was called *kaimen banxue* or "education in open-door schools." The rest of the time was spent in ideological studies and the new graduates were more competent in the study of *People's Daily* editorials than in their specialty. "Better red than expert" was the slogan of the day.

On the "literary and artistic front," writers and artists had to submit to the "literary theory" imposed by the leadership, namely that arts and literature were meant to "serve the people." Bourgeois, "feudal" and revisionist works were banned. These included the works of communist and progressive authors written before the Cultural Revolution. Topics such as love and family relationships became taboo. Chinese painting and classical music were banned. Literature was supposed to describe revolutionary farmers and workers fighting landlords, bourgeois elements and traditional intellectuals. When Mao died, China was a cultural desert, all publications having been completely controlled by the Party.

Of course, despite the immense pressure, the reality was quite different. Many ordinary citizens, especially rusticated youths, or apparently compliant intellectuals, had reservations about the new line. In the villages, sent-down youths were reading nineteenth century European literature and twentieth century Chinese novels. Some of them were themselves writing and circulating novels, poems and short stories (Dai 2000). The intelligentsia did not disappear, but it went underground for almost a decade. The result was a disaster for China. Without intellectuals, engineers or technicians, the country's modernization came to a standstill as everybody was singing the praise of Mao's thought while innovation even in apolitical fields such as technology and science stopped.

Enlisting the intelligentsia when the Party needs to renew its legitimacy

If the call to intellectuals' denunciations of cadres' "sectarianism" followed by all-out repression and the annihilation of freedom of expression has been a characteristic of Mao's rule, the CCP is also a past-master in enlisting the support of intellectuals and experts when the Party-state apparatus is engulfed in a legitimacy crisis. We shall present two instances of this behavior: the aftermath of Mao's demise (1978–81), and the period that followed the June Fourth Massacre (1992–98). Then, finally, we will analyze Xi Jinping's policy toward the intelligentsia, which owes more to Mao and the first decades of communist rule, than to Deng Xiaoping.

In communist states, ideology plays an essential part in the regime, especially during the Great Leader's rule. Therefore, the demise of the latter often causes a crisis of legitimacy. When Stalin, the great ideologue, died, his successors had to rekindle Party legitimacy by promising to restore a minimal degree of "normalcy" (the so-called "return to Leninism" promised by Khrushchev). One of Khrushchev's first actions was to allow writers to express their criticism of the previous period in their works. This episode was known as "the thaw" and was behind the emergence of writers such as Ilya Ehrenburg and Nastassia Ginsburg. Then the excesses of the personality cult were denounced at the 20th Congress of the Communist Party of the Soviet Union (CPSU) in 1954.

The aftermath of the Great Helmsman's demise

In China, where ideology played an even greater role than in the USSR, and where persecution of intellectuals had become a main feature of Mao's rule, one of the first decisions by Deng Xiaoping, the strong man who took over a couple of years after the Red Sun's demise, was to extend a friendly hand to the intellectuals and thinkers who had been the main targets of the Cultural Revolution. After two decades of revolutionary discourse which put the creation of the "new man" (totally obedient to the leadership) at the center of the Party's project, Deng chose to revive the Party and country with a clarion call to attain the old dream of *fuguo qiangbing* ("a strong and prosperous country"). This program to restore the party's legitimacy – and relevance – could not have been achieved without the full cooperation of the intelligentsia. Therefore, Deng stated that "intellectuals [were] part of the working class" (Sidane 1979). He then proceeded to rehabilitate those who had been criticized during the recurrent mass movements of the late Great Helmsman's rule, and to allow a margin of freedom of creation as expressed at the 4th Congress of the Federation of Writers and Artists.[1] The campaign for "practice as the sole criterion of the truth" was equivalent to a rehabilitation of objective knowledge, as opposed to ideological conformity. Intellectuals, who were just returning to the cities to be reinstated in responsible positions, supported it wholeheartedly, as they were eager to contribute to the modernization of the motherland. Anxious to obtain their support, the Party, represented by Hu Yaobang, agreed to release its grip on the public sphere. Deng and Hu invited Marxist thinkers who had been purged during the Cultural Revolution to take part in a conference organized by the leadership. During this "conference on theoretical work" (*lilun wuxuhui*) which took place during the first quarter of 1979, intellectuals proposed new ideas which supported the pragmatic interpretation of Marxism (Goldman 2007).

However, the experience of the previous 20 years had convinced many members of the intelligentsia that they could not put themselves completely in the hands of the Party. They therefore tried to create a space of autonomy where they could develop their reflections on the system, and from where they could supervise the Party's actions. Former rightists who founded literary journals such as *October* (*Shiyue*) and *The Harvest* (*Shouhuo*) published many short stories about intellectuals' sufferings during the last 20 years of Mao's rule. Rehabilitated former rightist journalist Qin Benli launched the *World Economic Herald*, which, in the second half of the 1980s, published many articles on Gorbachev's *glasnost* policy. The bold journal went so far as running articles denouncing one-party dictatorship and demanding a multiparty system for China (Zhang 1986).

During the 1980s, the rightist generation, and the Cultural Revolution intellectuals who had graduated in the wake of Mao's demise, succeeded in extending their sphere of intervention. Through their publications, they delegitimized the Maoist interpretation of Marxism, and introduced many Western political concepts. One of the best examples of this all-out offensive was the book series titled *Zou xiang weilai* ("Towards the Future"), which introduced the works of heterodox Western Marxist thinkers, and all sorts of new Western social sciences theories. This collection, put out by the Sichuan People's Publishing House, was headed by two Party members – Chinese Academy of Social Sciences historian Bao Zunxin and Cybernetics specialist Jin Guantao.

The leadership periodically reacted to these endeavors by launching campaigns against "bourgeois liberalization" which aimed at preventing criticism of the one-party rule. But all in all, intellectuals succeeded in influencing the way the Party ruled. Many rusticated youths who had been admitted to universities after the entrance examinations (*gaokao*) were reinstated in 1977, and they staffed the centers for economic and political reforms that emerged in the late 1980s. They therefore were instrumental in the elaboration of the reform policies.[2] Others were putting pressure on the authorities from "outside the system" through the discussions that they launched in universities' salons. A kind of virtuous cycle of collaboration between the Party and the newly rehabilitated intelligentsia developed during that decade (Béja 2004). It culminated in the 1989 pro-democracy movement, when part of the intelligentsia supported the students, and obtained the sympathy of the enlightened forces inside the Party (Zhao 2009). However, the June Fourth Massacre put an end to this collaboration and led the Party to adopt a suspicious attitude toward the intellectuals.

The Party's new strategy: co-opting willing intellectuals and crushing dissent

The two years that elapsed after June Fourth saw a witch hunt during which intellectuals who had supported the pro-democracy movement were jailed, expelled from universities or forced into exile. The salons and outspoken journals that had been the symbol of the new relationship between the Party and the intelligentsia were closed down. Intellectuals were, once again, considered enemies of the regime (Béja *et al.* 1991).

However, the fall of the socialist states of Central and Eastern Europe and the toppling of communist power in the USSR convinced Deng Xiaoping that a return to the old socialist canons would not win the "hearts and minds" of the people who had been shocked by the repression of the pro-democracy movement. Convinced that only economic development and a rise in ordinary people's standard of living could restore the Party's legitimacy, he decided to launch an all-out struggle for economic development. But in order to achieve this goal, the Party's new patriarch needed the collaboration of a demoralized intelligentsia. The new social contract he devised during his "Tour of the South" in early 1992 was aimed at enlisting the support of intellectuals and experts. In the first phase of the reforms (during the 1980s), only the symbolic position of intellectuals was restored, not their economic situation.[3] In the new phase of development, Deng decided to let them share the fruit of the development that they would help engineer (Béja 2004).

Despite the huge shock represented by the June Fourth Massacre, a great part of the intelligentsia accepted the new social contract: it was possible to get rich if one refrained from questioning the legitimacy of the Party's right to rule. Those who signed in had a theoretical justification: they estimated that one of the reasons for the failure of the pro-democracy movement was that the emerging civil society (salons, editorial boards, critical intellectuals) that had developed in the 1980s lacked economic independence. Whether they were writers, professors or artists, intellectuals got their income from the state. Under these circumstances, they did not have the economic wherewithal to question its legitimacy. According to their logic, the only possibility to create a really autonomous civil society consisted in developing an independent market economy that would provide its economic basis. Therefore, it was both progressive and advantageous to "jump into the sea of commerce" (*xiahai*). And sure enough, during the 1990s, a number of professors and other pro-democracy intellectuals created import-export firms, high technology incubators and all sorts of consultancy firms. Some of them became millionaires in real estate, and many of these successful new entrepreneurs became less critical of the Party.

At the same time, the Party made huge investments in education, especially tertiary education. Professors' wages were considerably raised, especially in first-tier universities that had been hotbeds of the pro-democracy movement; scholars were allowed to travel abroad either to participate in international conferences or for long research sojourns. Chinese specialists were allowed to join the international scientific community, in social sciences as well as in hard sciences. Of course, they were asked to refrain from publicly criticizing the government.

This policy enabled the Party to co-opt a sizeable part of the intelligentsia. The latter were eager to take part in the construction of a prosperous and strong China, and they were satisfied with the improved material conditions brought about by economic reform. For the first time since the foundation of the regime, the majority of intellectuals supported the Party, and the best and brightest students were eager to become Party members. The trend, initiated under Jiang Zemin in the late 1990s, has continued into the first decade of the twenty-first century and has not stopped under Xi Jinping.

While the majority of intellectuals accepted Deng's contract, albeit with some reservations, a minority of intellectuals continued to criticize the regime. In universities liberal professors did not refrain from teaching "Western values" to their students, in the process running afoul of propaganda authorities.

The challenge of dissidents

In the early 1990s, some of the thinkers who had been active during the 1989 pro-democracy movement and had stayed in the country, continued to denounce the one-party dictatorship and to speak in favor of the voiceless. Admirers of Vaclav Havel, they decided to refuse to compromise with the authorities and to "live in truth" (Béja 2012). Of course, this choice led them to be banned from publishing their works on the mainland, and resulted in their isolation from the public. Writers such as Liu Xiaobo, Bao Zunxin and Dai Qing continued to reflect over the nature of the regime and to denounce the excesses of the cadres. Their books and articles were, at the time, published by Hong Kong journals or by Taiwanese publishing houses. One of the dividing lines between these dissidents and their liberal counterparts who were becoming increasingly numerous inside the system, was their public attitude toward the June Fourth Massacre. The dissidents supported the "Tiananmen mothers," who demanded that the CCP recognize that it had killed their children in 1989. Every year, they wrote petitions to ask the Party to change its verdict on the massacre. This stance excluded them from publishing in mainland media. Of course, many mainstream intellectuals shared their judgment on the 1989 pro-democracy movement, but they agreed to refrain from publically demanding its reevaluation. These moderate intellectuals thought that the cost of "living in truth" was too high, and that they could push for democratization more efficiently if they acquiesced to the Party's requirements.

The dissidents also tried to express their opinions on important political problems. All throughout the 1990s, and much more frequently after the Internet appeared in the early twenty-first century, they organized petitions to defend prisoners of conscience. For example, they requested the release of Shi Tao, who had been sentenced to ten years in jail for having "revealed state secrets" (Liu 2005), and of Liu Di, whose pen name was the "stainless steel rat," who had made fun of Jiang Zemin's slogans. These radical intellectuals also denounced the exploitation of underage workers in brick factories (Liu 2007). The Internet provided party critics with a much larger audience than before.

However, as the restrictions on travel abroad started to ease after the mid-1990s, their works had already been widely read by "mainstream intellectuals" and they nourished the debates that continued to take place in private among them. The dissidents interacted with the most liberal of the "establishment intellectuals" who were trying to push the envelope inside the system. These contacts, which developed dramatically after the emergence of the Rights Defence Movement (*weiquan yundong*) in 2003, created a new situation until 2012.

A new category, "public intellectuals," appeared during the first decade of the twenty-first century. Philosophers published books discussing liberalism after Hayek's works had been translated into Chinese. They also started debates about the concept of the civil society, and on constitutionalism when Hu Jintao announced in 2003 that the Party would implement the "rule of law." As distinguished from dissidents, public intellectuals did not openly tackle political subjects; they restricted their discussions to concepts, occasionally criticizing authoritarianism. Most of the time, they were able to avoid crossing the red line, but, of course, there were cases when they became themselves the censors' targets.

The Party followed these debates with a great interest and sometimes the *People's Daily* or another official organ denounced some of the most foolhardy professors. But, in a development that was different from the 1980s, when the atmosphere was more open than the later decades, the Party leadership didn't launch campaigns against "bourgeois liberalization." The guilty professors were silently expelled from their universities and sometimes sent to faraway work units (*danwei*).[4] Others lost their jobs such as the case of Peking University journalism professor Jiao Guobiao, who criticized the Department of Propaganda for its stultifying censorship rules. But none of these were jailed (Béja 2007). For a while, the targeted public intellectuals would refrain from writing acute denunciations of the Party power, but then they would start again, using the semi-commercial media to express their thoughts. When criticisms were too harsh, the Propaganda Department would fire the media editors and punish those who had crossed the line.[5] This cat and mouse game went on at least until the end of Hu Jintao's rule, and it actually allowed the Party to continue to enjoy the support of the majority of the intelligentsia. The most enlightened of its members were wary of directly criticizing the government and, if they did, they cited the Constitution to back their opinions.

Of course, the situation was different with "dissidents." Those who tried to launch new political parties, such as the Chinese Democracy Party, were sentenced to long jail terms, and those who organized petitions were often harassed by the political police (*guobao*) and eventually ended up in prison (Béja 2004). They were harrassed, expelled from their jobs when they had one, chased from their apartment as the police put pressure on their landlords, but, at least until 2008, rarely jailed. For example, dissidents like Yu Jie, who had been refused a job after his graduation because of his outspokenness, could publish incisive *zawen* ("critical essays") which indirectly slammed the Party's authoritarianism (Yu 1998). Others such as Liu Xiaobo wrote scathing analyses of the regime on overseas websites and organized collective letters to protest against human rights violations. These intellectuals somehow escaped jail despite their refusal to compromise with the authorities on issues involving freedom of expression and other civil rights. This could be explained by the fact that they were relatively isolated from the rest of society. The government prevented them from publicly commemorating the June Fourth Massacre, but did not interfere when they published articles overseas.

The emergence of the Rights Defense Movement, which started in 2003 and climaxed after 2006, changed the situation. The lawyers, journalists and civil society activists who launched the rights crusade not only presented themselves as inside the system but also pretended that they were implementing the Party's agenda. In 2004, amendments to the Constitution provided for the "protection of human rights" and recognized "property rights." Comforted by this change in the official discourse, a group of young legal scholars and lawyers who had started to help ordinary citizens contest officials' abuse of power in court expanded their crusade to different provinces. Sympathetic journalists gave echo to these cases and, after a few years, the Rights Defense Movement developed under the protection of the Constitution. What was worrying to the Party was the fact that ordinary citizens were joining hands with lawyers, journalists and intellectuals to try to defend their rights.

Ever since it came to power, the Party has been eager to prevent intellectuals from working with the "proletariats." In 1989, it used all means possible to prevent students from joining hands with workers and helping the latter express their grievances. The CCP became very paranoid when, during the first decade of the twenty-first century, dissident intellectuals were working hand in glove with other civil-society components as well as social groups in pushing the Rights Defense Movement.

In 2008 dissidents were joined by liberal establishment intellectuals and activists associated with the Rights Defense Movement to launch Charter 08 – a petition inspired by the Czechoslovak Charter 77[6] – which demanded that the Party renounce its monopoly on power. The CCP reacted by arresting Liu Xiaobo, then the most famous dissident in China. Although he had played only a marginal role in drafting the Charter, he was detained in December 2008 and sentenced to 11 years in jail for "inciting the subversion of state power" (Béja *et al.* 2012). The harsh treatment of Liu prompted more than 10,000 citizens from all walks of life to sign the Charter, which was rapidly taken off the Internet. All the signatories were summoned by the state security organs for "tea drinking sessions," when they were questioned by the police about the existence of a conspiratorial organization and on the way it was financed (Xu and Hua 2013). Liu Xiaobo's sentence showed that the Party was not ready to let intellectuals, especially dissidents, join hands with civil-society activists and lawyers.

Xi Jinping: intellectuals should help achieve the "Chinese dream"

When he succeeded Hu Jintao at the 18th Party Congress in November 2012, Xi Jinping enjoyed support among liberal intellectuals who were convinced that his experience as the son of a purged leader – the liberal ex-vice-premier Xi Zhongxun – and as a rusticated youth in the 1970s made him more open minded than his predecessors. However, far from reversing the trend that had developed since 2008, Xi focused on boosting his own authority in the Party in addition to clamping down on expressions of dissent from intellectuals.

As soon as he took over from Hu, Xi Jinping emphasized the importance of ideology. The new leader gave a speech on the fall of the Soviet Union, which he attributed to the decline of ideological work as well as the absence of a strong man (*nanzihan*) capable of rising to defend socialism. In order to prevent the CCP from following in the footsteps of its predecessor, Xi decided to cleanse its ranks. As soon as he came to power, he launched a campaign against corruption – including senior cadres, who are called "big tigers" – which is still on-going. He has also taken steps to reestablish an efficient Party monopoly in the social and intellectual fields.

Whereas since 1992 Deng Xiaoping had put ideology on the back burner (there needed not be controversy on which measures were socialist and which ones capitalist) to concentrate on economic development[7] Xi has emphasized the importance of ideology in order to achieve the Chinese dream. For example, in August 2013 he declared that "the economy is a central task of the Party whereas ideological work is an extremely important task." Unlike his predecessors who had concentrated on economic development and the enforcement of the "rule by law" – and avoided entanglements in ideological controversies – Xi has made numerous speeches about the imperative that intellectuals must cleave close to the "socialist path." In August 2013, Central Committee Document No. 9 was circulated in the Party. It prohibited college professors from discussing concepts such as constitutional democracy, universal values, civil society, Western conception of the press and neo-liberalism. Also banned were articles that questioned the Party's mistakes or the reform and open door policy (*Mingjing Yuekan* 2013). It was the first time in many years that such a restrictive framework was officially imposed. University professors have of course tried to resist these orders, and, unlike what had happened in the 1950s, they have continued to teach as before. However, pressure from students and from the universities' administrations have made them more cautious: they often have to resort to covert language to convey their ideas.

Xi Jinping has also reinforced control over the press and the new media. Xi created in early 2014 the Central Leading Group for Cyberspace Affairs – and appointed himself head of the top censorship unit on the information superhighways. Laws were passed to sentence those who "circulate rumors or false information." In September 2014, Xi went even further as he organized a gathering of "literature and art workers" where, like Mao Zedong in Yan'an, he set the guidelines for literature and the arts in the twenty-first century. After having listened to speeches delivered by selected "representative" writers, he proceeded to elaborate on what "good" literature and art should be:

> The reason excellent works are "excellent" lies in their ideological profundity, artistic exquisiteness and product superiority ... Literature and art must reflect well the people's wishes; they must persist in the fundamental orientation of serving the people and serving Socialism ... If literature and art workers want to achieve success, they must consciously breathe together with the people, share their fate, link their hearts with the people's hearts, feel joy for the joy of the people, suffer for the suffering of the

> people, and be servants of the people … The vast masses of literature and art workers must carry forward the banner of socialist core values.
>
> *(Xi 2014)*

These guidelines were directly inspired by Mao Zedong's Yan'an talks. But the dangers to which practitioners in the literary and artistic fields are exposed have changed since 1942. Xi therefore reminded writers and artists that they must fully observe the same set of norms and restrictions spelled out for other intellectuals. "We must make patriotism into the main melody of literary and artistic creation, and guide the people to establish and uphold correct views of history, views of the nation, views of the country and views of culture," Xi said. "We must strengthen their fortitude and resolve to be Chinese." To achieve this goal, "Literature and art cannot become slaves of the market, and must not be stained with the stink of money" (Xi 2014). And the best way to ensure that writers and artists toe the line is to have an efficient Party administration to manage their activities:

> Party Committees at all levels must bring literature and art work onto the agenda of important matters, implement the Party's literature and art principles and policies well, and grasp the correct orientation of literary and artistic development. We must choose good leadership for strong literature and art work units, put cadres who have both ability and integrity … in leading positions in literature and art work.
>
> *(Xi 2014)*

It was the first time since Mao's Yan'an talks that a "supreme leader" had given a talk to an audience of selected writers and artists and told them explicitly how and what to write. Deng Xiaoping and Hu Jintao had made speeches at the opening or the closure of the congresses of the China Federation of Literary and Art Circles, but these were mostly formalistic affairs. After Xi's talk, the Chinese Writers' Association attempted to arrange for writers to "learn from the masses" by spending time in farms and factories. However, times have changed since Mao's era: only a few took part, and no substantive work has come out of it. Despite the General Secretary's exhortations, writers have been writing on all sorts of subjects and the influence of his "talk" is hard to find in today's literary production. But this speech as well as other similar attempts at controlling the intellectual field by imposing pure-upon-pure socialist values appeared to be obsolete. And possibilities exist that Xi Dada's determined reinstatement of the ideological imperative among Party members and intellectuals could backfire by engendering cynicism and even sabotage beneath the surface.

Conclusion

The history of the People's Republic shows that the Party has always regarded policy toward intellectuals as an essential element of its rule. It was a regime where ideology played an important role; the political activities of the educated class had to be kept under control. Mao, who particularly distrusted the intelligentsia, repeatedly tricked them into expressing their ideas so as to better get rid of them afterwards. He equated intellectuals' aspirations for freedom of expression and their support of universal civil rights as a conspiracy to "change the color" of the party. During the Cultural Revolution, which was essentially Mao's war against cadres and intellectuals who were accused of harboring "revisionist" views, he used scorched-earth tactics to impose the proverbial "one-voice chamber" on the nation.

When the CCP was faced with a legitimacy crisis after Mao's demise, the Party led by Deng used the intelligentsia to renew the ideological foundation of the regime and co-opted its members in the Party apparatus, making sure that they did not question its leadership. But Deng and his successors considered the policy toward intellectuals as a specific component of a general policy toward society: Party authorities relaxed their control over the social and cultural field, but were cautious to prevent any organized force from emerging in the new space. When intellectuals seized the opportunity of the relaxation of controls to question the nature of the regime, the Party resorted to repression.

Things have changed with the advent of Xi Jinping who has unquestionably reinforced Party control on the intelligentsia. He has emphasized the importance of ideology and has defined more clearly the limitations imposed on freedom of expression. He has resorted to the "classical" methods of repression used under Deng. However, like Mao, the Fifth-Generation leader has tried to appear as a norm-setter in the intellectual field by trying to impose his conception of the role of literature and art on writers and artists. He has also reinforced control on the public sphere through the various "central leading groups" that he chairs.

The reinforcement of ideological control has led many intellectuals to worry about the possibility of a return to Maoism. Of course, this does not mean that iron-fisted control had ever disappeared since the Great Helmsman's demise. Even during the relatively liberal 1980s, Deng launched recurrent campaigns against "bourgeois liberalization," which climaxed with the June Fourth Massacre. Later, Jiang Zemin and Hu Jintao often delivered speeches targeting intellectuals who questioned the Party leadership; they did not hesitate about inflicting long jail sentences on dissidents. But all in all, since 1976, the Party has never allowed ideological controversies to distract its attention from economic development.

After the June Fourth Massacre, the leadership has agreed on the necessity to prevent the emergence of autonomous organizations (civil society) that could challenge its monopoly on the political field. In order to achieve this goal, the Party-state apparatus has pulled out all the stops to prevent intellectuals from forging an alliance with other social groups. Intellectuals who merely discussed political or philosophical theories were often let alone. The moment that they were seen as organizing disenfranchised citizens or publicly demanding a change in the political system, they faced harsh repressive measures including imprisonment.

The situation has become more serious since Xi Jinping took over power in late 2012. Many members of the intelligentsia are worried that he is trying to engineer a "return to the cultural revolution." It is undeniable that the new leader has shown a much stronger concern for ideological issues than his predecessors. Whereas, under Hu Jintao and Wen Jiabao, references to Mao Zedong had become rather rare, and critical reflexions on contemporary history could be published, things have changed since 2012. The attacks on "historical nihilism" that had started under the Hu-Wen leadership, have become much more serious: *Yanhuang Chunqiu*, a journal on contemporary history founded by liberal Party elders which had published innumerable critical essays on Party history, was closed down in 2016 (Zhao 2016). Despite the year 2016 being the 50th anniversary of the start of the Cultural Revolution, no reflexions on this traumatic event have been published on the mainland.

It would perhaps be an exaggeration to say that Xi is orchestrating a return to Maoism. Yet his obsession with control of the campuses and the public sphere – as well as his emphasis on Party guidance of literature and the arts – is reminiscent of the Great Helmsman's insistence on thought control. The putative "leadership core" is determined to reinforce party leadership in all fields, and, as Mao before him, he is convinced that this task starts with the subjugation of the intelligentsia.

However, Chinese society has changed a lot since the Mao era; it has become much more sophisticated than the 1950s: since parts of the economy are no longer under state control, ordinary citizens can eke out a living outside of state-owned enterprises. The reality is so different from the official ideology that ordinary people – not to mention intellectuals – no longer subscribe to it. Even though a sizable portion of the intelligentsia, which has benefited from economic progress brought about by the Era of Reform, may feel challenged about casting aspersions on the return to Maoism, few members of the educated classes would embrace "core socialist values" defined by Xi Dada. In the last four years, public intellectuals – a great number of whom had initially had great expectations of the new leadership – have been very quiet, all the more so as many media outlets have been closed down, the latest being the very popular intellectual website "Consensus" (*gongshi wang*) (Grundy 2016).

This silence does not mean that they support the new line, or the return of ideology. Most of them do not believe in the official discourse, which does not sit well with intellectuals either from the left (the "neo-Maoists") or from the right (the pro-West exponents of international values). Most members of the intelligentsia resent the limitations put on their freedom of expression and even of movement, as it has become more difficult for professors and men of learning to secure permission to travel abroad. Nowadays, Chinese intellectuals are well informed. They can access international websites (despite the Great Firewall) and have become part of the global academic community. It remains to be seen whether intellectuals will remain in the background so as to wait out the Xi era of conservatism. Or whether they will risk official condemnation and personal safety by frontally challenging the Xi administration's restoration of norms that are reminiscent of Mao's worst excesses.

Notes

1 It took place in the fall of 1979. Liu Binyan, Bai Hua and other just rehabilitated "rightists" gave very bold speeches. Deng gave the opening speech on October 30, 1979, https://dengxiaopingworks.wordpress.com/2013/02/25/speech-greeting-the-fourth-congress-of-chinese-writers-and-artists/.
2 For example, Chen Yize at the Research Center on the Reform of the System (*tigaisuo* 体改所) or Wu Guoguang in the Research Bureau on the Reform of the Political System (*tigaishi* 体改室).
3 During the 1980s it was said that ambitious young women would rather marry an illiterate but self-employed technician or merchant (*getihu*) than a university professor as the former's income was much higher.
4 Such was the case of He Weifang, a professor of law at Peking University who was "exiled" to the remote town of Shihezi in Xinjiang Autonomous Region for two years.
5 It happened many times to the editors of *Nanfang Zhoumo* (*Southern Weekend*), a liberal paper based in Guangzhou, Guangdong Province.
6 A Charter launched by dissident intellectuals such as philosopher Jan Patocka and playwright Vaclav Havel which urged the government to respect human rights as it had pledged in the Helsinki agreement signed by Western and Eastern European countries in 1977.
7 During his "Tour of the South" in 1992, Deng declared that "development is the most important concern [for the party]" (*fazhan shi ying daoli*).

References

Béja, Jean-Philippe (2004) *A la recherche d'une ombre chinoise: Le mouvement pour la démocratie en Chine, 1919–2004* (In Search of a Chinese Shadow: The pro-Democracy Movement in China, 1919–2004), Paris: Editions du Seuil.

Béja, Jean-Philippe (2007) "Hu Jintao's Policy Towards Intellectuals: Enlightenment, Deception, Disappointment," in Cheng, Joseph Y.S., *Challenges and Policy Programmes of China's New Leadership*, Hong Kong: City University Press, pp. 567–596.

Béja, Jean-Philippe (2012) "Is Jail the Only Place where One Can 'Live in Truth'?" in Béja, Jean-Philippe, Fu, Hualing and Pils, Eva (Eds.), *Liu Xiaobo, Charter 08 and the Challenges of Political Reform in China*, Hong Kong: Hong Kong University Press, pp. 15–30.

Béja, Jean-Philippe, Bonnin, Michel and Peyraube, Alain (1991) *Le tremblement de terre de Pékin* (The Beijing Earthquake), Paris: Gallimard.

Béja, Jean-Philippe, Fu, Hualing and Pils, Eva (Eds.) (2012) *Liu Xiaobo, Charter 08 and the Challenges of Political Reform in China*, Hong Kong: Hong Kong University Press.

Chinese History Net (guoshiwang) (2009) "The Criticism against Hu Feng's Thoughts," August 21, www.hprc.org.cn/gsgl/dsnb/zdsj/200908/t20090821_28371.html.

Dai, Sijie (2000) *Balzac et la petite tailleuse chinoise*, Paris: Gallimard.

Ding, Ling (1942) "Feelings on the Women's 8 March Festival" (San ba jie yougan 三八节有感), www.marxists.org/chinese/reference-books/yanan1942/2-02.htm.

Goldman, Merle (2007), *From Comrade to Citizen*, Cambridge, MA: Harvard University Press.

Grundy, Tom (2016) "The End of Consensus: More Trouble for Substantive Discussion in China as Another Website is Shut Down," October 3, www.hongkongfp.com/2016/10/03/the-end-of-consensus-more-trouble-for-substantive-discussion-in-china-as-another-website-is-shut-down/.

Hu, Feng (1954) "Report on the Practice and State of Art and Literature in Recent Years" (关于几年来文艺实践情况的报告 Guanyu jinianlai wenyi shixian qingkuang de baogao) also known as "300 000 characters opinion" (三十万言书 Sanshi wan yanshu). Sent to Mao Zedong on July 22, 1954 with a cover letter dated July 7.

Isaacs, Harold (2009) *The Tragedy of the Chinese Revolution*, London: Haymarket Books.

Li, Hui (2003) Hu Feng jituan yuan'an shimo (胡风集团冤案始末) (*The Wrong Case of the Hu Feng Clique, from Beginning to End*), Wuhan: Hubei Renmin Chubanshe, p. 139.

Liu, Binyan (1956) *Our Newspaper's Confidential News* (本报内部消息 Benbao neibu xiaoxi) in *People's Literature* (renmin wenxue), No. 6.

Liu, Xiaobo (2005) "An Open Letter to Jerry Yang, CEO of Yahoo, about the Shi Tao Case" (就师涛被判重刑致雅虎公司董事长的公开信 Jiu Shi Tao beipan zhongxing zhi Yahu gongsi de gongkaixin), *The Observer* (Guancha 观察), August 10.

Liu, Xiaobo (2007) *Briqueteries*, New York: Human Rights in China.

Mao, Zedong (1942) "Talks at the Yan'an Forum on Literature and Art," www.marxists.org/reference/archive/mao/selected-works/volume-3/mswv3_08.htm.

Mao, Zedong (1957) "On the Correct Handling of Contradictions among the People," www.marxists.org/reference/archive/mao/selected-works/volume-5/mswv5_58.htm.

Mingjing Yuekan (Mirror Magazine) (2013) "Scoop: Complete Text of the CCP's Document No. 9," August 19.

Niu, Han and Deng, Jiuping (Eds.) (1998) 记忆中的反右派运动 (Jiyizhong de fanyoupai yundong, *The Anti Rightist Movement in Memory*), a trilogy, Vol. 1 六月雪 Liu Yue xue (*June Snow*), Vol. 2 荆棘路 Jingjilu (*A Road Filled with Thorns*), Vol. 3 原上草 Yuanshang cao (*Grass on the Plain*), Beijing: Jingji Ribao Chubanshe.

People's Daily (1957) "Why is it so?" (Zhe shi weishenme? 这是为什么？), August 6.

Sidane, Victor (1979) *Le Printemps de Pékin*, Paris: Gallimard, Collection Archives.

Wang, Meng (1956) "The Young Newcomer at the Department of Organisation," *Renmin wenxue*, No. 9.

Wang, Ruoshui (2003) "Work-Style Rectification Overwhelms Enlightenment," *Contemporary Chinese Thought*, Vol. 34, No. 4, Summer.

Wang, Shiwei (1942a) "Wild Lilies" (Ye baihehua 野百合花), *Liberation Daily* (Jiefang Ribao), March 23.

Wang, Shiwei (1942b) Zhengzhijia, yishujia (政治家, 艺术家) *Spring Rain* (Guyu 谷雨), Vol. 1, No. 4.

Wei, Shiyu (2016) 王實味 – 文藝整風與思想改造 (*Wang Shiwei: Artistic Rectfication and Thought Reform*), Hong Kong: City University of Hong Kong Press.

Wu, Han (1961) *Hai Rui Dismissed from Office* (Hai Rui Baguan, 海瑞罢官), Beijing.

Xi, Jinping (2014) "Talk at the Forum on Literature and Art" (在文艺座谈会上的讲话 zai wenyi zuotan-hui shang de jianghua), Xinhua, October 15.

Xu, Youyu and Hua Ze (Eds.) (2013) *Encounters with the Rising Dragon*, New York: St Martin's Press.

Yu, Jie (1998) *Fire and Ice* (huo yu bing, 火与冰), Beijing: Jingji Ribao chubanshe.

Yuan, Shuipai (1955) "Interrogating the Editor of the Literary Gazette" (质问"文艺报"编者), *Renmin Ribao*, October 25. This article was actually written under Mao's guidance. Li Hui, op. cit., p. 158.

Zhang, Xianliang (1986) *Literary Gazette* (Wenyi bao, 文艺报), August 23.

Zhao, Kiki (2016) "Chinese Court Upholds Ruling Against Historian Who Questioned Tale of Wartime Heroes," *New York Times*, August 15, www.nytimes.com/2016/08/16/world/asia/china-hong-zhenkuai-langya.html?_r=0.

Zhao, Ziyang (2009) *Prisoner of the State*, New York, Simon and Schuster.

16
THE PARTY AND THE LAW

Eva Pils

Introduction

In post-Mao China, the recognition of legal rights and other liberal principles of law has been a legitimizing promise to Chinese citizens and the international community. But due to its fundamentally Leninist structure, the Party-State has not been able to keep its promise, even though it has introduced many reforms that have helped curb the arbitrary exercise of power. The resulting tension between promises and practices has had delegitimizing effects. It has led to the coagulation of oppositional groups challenging Party rule around ideals of legal rights and rule of law. In response, the Party has sought to promote more authoritarian and anti-liberal conceptions and practices of law to consolidate Party-State power. While the Party's coercive power remains greater than that of any legal institution, the ideal of law-bounded governance might yet play a decisive role in popular contention of Party power.

In February 2015, the Chinese Communist Party (CCP) General Secretary and President of the People's Republic of China Xi Jinping gave a speech titled "The Question of whether the Party or the Law is Greater is a False Question." He said that individual Party members were subject to law, like anybody else. But, Xi said,

> We must keep in mind that Party leadership is the soul of *Socialist Rule of Law with Chinese Characteristics* (*Zhongguo tese shehui zhuyi fazhi*), and that this is the greatest difference between our rule of law and western capitalist countries' rule of law. … Comprehensively promoting *Ruling the Country in Accordance with Law* (*yi fa zhi guo*) does not mean to blur or weaken or indeed deny the Party's leadership; rather, it means further to consolidate the party's governing status, improve the Party's governance methods, raise the Party's governance capacity, and ensure long-term stability of the Party and State.
>
> *(Xi 2015)*

The purpose of the present chapter is to unpack this claim and to show that in fact, the question of whether the Party is subject to the law is as contentious as it is important in contemporary Chinese society. The Party's presence and power can have devastating effects on human lives, including the lives of its eighty-something million members. At times it appears to claim a status outside and beyond the operation of the laws, for example when it detains and tortures its own members in the name of "discipline and inspection" of their alleged conduct, under a system named *shuanggui*. Other times, it uses legal arguments to justify its exercise of power, for example, when it executes people "in accordance with law" and decrees that the number of executions per year is a state secret, protected by laws criminalizing such secrets' divulgence. Yet other times it moves with vicious force against those who, like China's human rights lawyers, contest the Party-State's abuse of power on legal grounds. Thus the Party's relationship with the law is at best ambiguous.

As the discussion in the following shows, law remains too weak to constrain the Party effectively; and this lack of genuine rule of law is the reason why it is so hard to tackle the systemic human rights violations that continue to occur in China. Yet the argument that it *ought to* respect and in that sense is bound by the law – that through its position, institutional design, and mode of governance, the Party violates principles of rule of law which it professes (sometimes at least) to respect – has been an important factor in the contentious politics of the post-Mao era. It in part explains the tightening of spaces for legal advocacy in the current era, discussed toward the end of the chapter.

The Mao era: from law to ~~law~~

In 2003, in a constitutional law lecture in one of the most famous universities of the capital, the teacher told us about the persecution of Liu Shaoqi, then President of the People's Republic of China. When guards of the Cultural Revolution "struggled" with him, he said, President Liu Shaoqi had held up a copy of the Constitution and told them that they had no power to do this to him, the President. "But at that time, it did not help him."[1] President Liu was later to die in custody in ignominious conditions of apparent neglect (History Gang 2014; Zhang Qianfan 2012: 46).

From a liberal perspective, because of what government power can do to people – silence them, dispossess them, lock them up, kill them – seeking to control government power by subjecting it to legal limitations is an important concern. Our law professor at the time was invoking such a liberal conception, according to which not only President Liu Shaoqi, but also anybody else ought to enjoy protections against arbitrary detention.[2] Much of the rest of his course grappled with the fact that the Party-State of the post-Mao era has signed up to principles that encapsulate precisely this concern, most notably human rights principles in international treaties, the Constitution, and other legally binding documents.[3]

But of course, "law" is a complex and highly contested concept (Gallie 1955–56). In the 1960s under Mao Zedong, the idea that law should serve to protect rights may have seemed remote; and the people who came to take Liu Shaoqi away must have felt powerful and unchallengeable. Publicly advocating such principles as equal rights could at certain times also have been dangerous, because of its connection with the repudiated ideology of capitalism.

Legal ideas and practice in the Mao era were largely sourced in two different but related traditions: Marxism and Leninism. Classical Marxism is skeptical toward law. It criticizes the dominant liberal ideas of its age as a product of false consciousness – accordingly, liberty and equality protected by law are akin to (self-) deceptions we accept in the capitalist system. The institutions of the law – courts, prosecution offices, the legal profession, and so on – have thus no intrinsic value; and at certain times Marx argued that law's institutions would altogether "wither away" in a future socialist (communist) society. They must lose significance because they are inherently tied to the ideas of liberalism that Marx rejected as false (Lo 1997; Sypnowich 2014: section 2; Wolff 2015: section 2.2). Leninism – the doctrines developed in the early history of the Soviet Union – takes a different approach to law; it sees the Party as a vanguard institution leading the State, whose bureaucratic and administrative functions are an acknowledged necessity. They include the running of a legal system with codified laws and procedures and legal institutions such as courts and the *prokuratora* (with prosecution and other responsibilities) (Partlett and Ip 2016). However, this system is not meant to protect bourgeois (liberal) rights. Law, according to this conception, is primarily an expression of the will of the classes the Party claims to represent. It is a way of projecting power.

The Mao-era CCP embraced both these ideas at different times and, one might argue, never came to terms with law. Initially, the Party created legal institutions resembling that of the Soviet Union: it practiced a form of law dominated by class ideas. It was also primarily focused on "punishment in accordance with law." As Clarke and Feinermann have argued, law was associated "with dictatorship, compulsion and the enemy" (Clarke and Feinermann 1995: 135). In "On the Correct Handling of Contradictions Among the People" (1957), Mao postulates that "contradictions between ourselves and the enemy" were "a matter of drawing a clear distinction between ourselves and the enemy" whereas "contradictions among the people" were "a matter of drawing a clear distinction between right and wrong (*shi fei*)" (Mao 1957). Put simply, class enemies, such as major property owners, could be presumed guilty; whereas in cases of contradiction "among the people" distinctions between "right and wrong" must be drawn case by case. The entire legal system was permeated by orthodox Marxist-Maoist theory. For example, private ownership was regarded as the fundamental cause of crime (Cohen 1968: 76).

But embracing legality, even if understood on Marxist, Leninist, and Maoist terms, was dangerous; the system remained torn between pro-law and anti-law attitudes. From the early 1940s onward, supporters of legality fell victim to periodic Party purges in the spirit of continued revolution. As Glenn Tiffert has noted, "for the remainder of the Mao era, the CCP would alternately promote codification, higher judicial standards, and legal institutionalization; only to turn abruptly against those initiatives, and persecute their representatives for allegedly harboring the old law standpoint" (Tiffert 2016). Hostility toward legal principles meant that lawyers and judges were in a precarious position. On the one hand, as integral parts of the legal system, they served crucial functions as enforcers of the laws meant to represent the will of the Party. On the other, judges and (perhaps even more so) lawyers were tainted by their membership of bureaucratic elites as well as by their professional proximity to bourgeois-liberal ideas. At certain periods, they were subjected to vilification and persecution as revisionists and rightists, in particular during the anti-rightist campaign and the Cultural Revolution. During the latter, some of the legal institutions of the Party-State were virtually dismantled. The very idea of law was attacked more fundamentally than at any other period, with official newspapers running articles titled, for example, "In Praise of Lawlessness."[4]

This did not – could not – mean that law and legal institutions disappeared altogether. The anecdote of President Liu Shaoqi seeking protection from the Constitution as the highest law testifies to the enduring power of the idea that the law must protect these rights. Even the just-mentioned article argued that in Mao's China, there was still "law" – but, it was the "law" of Mao Zedong Thought and of the proletarian classes, and thus "lawlessness" in capitalist and revisionist terms was explicitly endorsed (*People's Daily* 1967). The Constitution as revised in 1975 reflected this thinking.[5] It is because of its association with the Cultural Revolution that in later years, the expression for "lawlessness," *wu fa wu tian*, was often used to evoke the disorder and terror many had experienced during this era.

In sum, the development under Mao was one from law to ~~law~~, to use an expression coined by China law scholar Flora Sapio (Sapio 2010); and the chaos and suffering caused by Mao's campaigns, in particular by its violence and power abuses, can be attributed to the institutional weakness of the legal system and to the deliberate destruction of key legal institutions by the

Party. As a result of the Cultural Revolution, "lawlessness" and "chaos" (*luan*) became specters to be avoided, specters invoked by later leaders when convenient.

Deng Xiaoping's legal revival

Deng Xiaoping's post-Mao "Reform and Opening" was an attempt to overcome the destructive tendencies of the Maoist system by recreating order, stability, and prosperity through law. According to a dictionary definition, reform is "improvement or amendment of what is wrong, corrupt, unsatisfactory" (Dictionary.com 2016). "Opening" could be interpreted as a domestic opening to new ideas, principles, and practices, as well as opening toward the outside world, in particular "the west." Together, these two terms signaled a dramatic change of policy and outlook that had profound consequences for legal development. The new belief in progressive reform included not only the belief in law's value as a tool to ensure order, but also the belief that well-enforced laws protecting economic and some other liberties were necessary to promote economic growth (Communiqué 1978).

Under Deng Xiaoping the judiciary, the procuracy, and the police, as well as the Ministry of Justice (which had been completely shut down) were reconstructed; laws were enacted, and training for legal professionals as well as "dissemination of law," or of legal knowledge (*pufa*), among the wider population were introduced. The idea of "ruling the country in accordance with law" (*yi fa zhi guo*) could be understood to promise that that law would bind the government, as well as ordinary citizens (Yang 2002); and reforms such as the Administrative Litigation Law gave effect to this point. The Thirteenth Party Congress announced a clearer separation of Party and Government, a move that would curb power concentration in the hands of Party leaders (Wu Wei 2014). The leadership seemed willing to move from using policies (*zhengce*) to using legal rules (*faze*) (Heath 2014: 34). It, or at least some individuals within it, also saw the possible legitimating function of law's ability to curb power.[6] At its core, the idea was a liberal one: limiting public power, and banning the arbitrary use of power, an idea inherently connected to that of substantive rights (Bingham 2007). Compared to the Mao era, the Marxist-Maoist belief that law was an "instrument of oppression of the antagonistic classes" was weakened and challenged (Lo 1997).

Yet, the system remained that of a Party-State; and the Party remained in de facto control of all the institutions of the legal system, even though its position in the constitutional structure was obscure. The 1982 Constitutional Preamble made references to Party leadership, as in:

> The victory in China's New-Democratic Revolution and the successes in its socialist cause have been achieved by the Chinese people of all nationalities, under the leadership of the Communist Party of China and the guidance of Marxism-Leninism and Mao Zedong Thought, by upholding truth, correcting errors and surmounting numerous difficulties and hardships.
>
> *(1982 Constitution: Preamble)*

But, it accorded no specific institutional role to the Party, which consequently resumed the role of a – compared to the 1975 Constitution – grayer eminence, central (Potter 2013: chapter 1) and everywhere, but nowhere in particular, in the Party-State structure. Its undefined and consequently not clearly limited role in the constitutional framework heightened rather than diminished its power. Chapters 1 and 3 of the 1982 Constitution, mainly dealing with China's legislative structure and other political decision-making structures, endorse the principles of "Democratic Centralism,"[7] People's Democratic Dictatorship,[8] and the democratic "mass line."[9]

Democratic Centralism rules out challenges to political (including legislative) decisions once they have been made; and People's Democratic Dictatorship, as a principle explicitly endorsing dictatorial control of the People's enemies, implicitly assigns the power to identify these enemies to the political leadership. On the basis of its "leading" role and of the aforementioned principles, the Party moreover continued to control the institutions of the "State," including its legal institutions; and it also controlled what state laws and regulations were made. There were only rather faint indications that the National People's Congress, supreme within the "State" structure set out in the PRC Constitution, might become less than a "rubber-stamp" institution; and there was never a full recognition, in practice, of the idea that only the designated authorities of the State had the power to make binding rules.

The Law on Legislation, enacted in 2000, purported to provide an exhaustive list of legislative authorities. Yet Party-issued documents retained de facto authority within the legal-political system (Keller 1994: 754–759; Peerenboom 2002: chapter 6). The challenges presented by this somewhat chaotic (Peerenboom 2002: chapter 6) design were enhanced by the doctrine that the author of a rule had primary authority to interpret and ensure compliance with this rule by lower-ranking norms and authorities, because this meant that courts' ability to assess normative hierarchies independently was severely limited.[10] At the level of substantive law, even in the economic area, the (re)introduction of some principles and mechanisms of a liberal economy such as the institutions of contract and private property rights and private companies (Clarke 2007) was also limited. Laws adopted in the 1980s retained, tacitly assumed, or indeed introduced a high degree of Party-State control in all key areas of society and the economy. For example, the Party-State controls appointments in SOEs (Lin and Milhaupt 2013; Zhang Yihong 2012), academia (Perry 2016: 17ff.), and the official media (Esarey 2006; Xu 2015), with some overlap between these. These controls were at times scarcely visible in the laws that ostentatiously regulated these entities. Through its control of government entities it also remained in control of all the land and other resources; and indeed, its legal control of urban land was strengthened in the post-Mao era, in which it became an important source of government revenue (Lei 2014).[11]

It is the firmly entrenched, yet obscure and inscrutable role of the Party that presented challenges to liberal hopes for law in post-Mao China from the start. The liberal principles articulated in Chapter 2 of the 1982 Constitution (last revised in 2004) sharply contradicted the authoritarian principles mostly contained in Chapters 1 and 3 (Teng 2012). Chapter 2 of the Constitution safeguards the right to equality before the law, the right to vote, freedom of speech, freedom of assembly and association, freedom of religion, freedom and security of the person, freedom from insult, freedom from violation of the home, and the privacy of correspondence, as well as certain socio-economic rights.[12] The Constitution also gestures at a principle of genuine rule of law. Its Article 5 states that

> All state organs, the armed forces, all political parties and public organizations and all enterprises and institutions must abide by the Constitution and the law. All acts in violation of the Constitution and the law must be investigated. No individuals or organizations are above the Constitution or the law.

Further, an amendment in 2004 added the phrase "the State respects and preserves human rights" to Article 33 of the Constitution, reaffirming and reinforcing the fact that as of today, China is a State party to a number of important human rights treaties. It has signed albeit not yet ratified the International Covenant on Civil and Political Rights (ICCPR), and it has signed and ratified the International Covenant on Economic, Social and Cultural Rights (ICESCR), the

Convention on the Elimination of All Forms of Discrimination against Women (CEDAW), the Convention on the Elimination of All Forms of Racial Discrimination (CERD), the Convention against Torture and Other Cruel, Inhuman or Degrading Treatment or Punishment (CAT), the Convention on the Rights of the Child (CRC), and the Convention on the Rights of Persons with Disabilities (CRPD). (It has not acceded to the Convention on the Protection of the Rights of All Migrant Workers and Members of Their Families and the International Convention for the Protection of All Persons from Enforced Disappearance.)

However, none of these constitutional rights guarantees and treaty norms have so far led to the creation of reasonably effective institutional mechanisms for safeguarding the standards and principles these norms articulate. At the international level, China has opted out of all the individual complaints procedures that might allow a person whose rights have been infringed to bring a complaint before UN institutions. At the domestic level, Chinese courts are virtually unable to use international human rights norms in deciding cases, because as Ahl has pointed out, courts have generally applied treaty provisions only "on the basis of statutory reference provisions or judicial interpretations commanding application of an international standard" (Ahl 2009) not available in human rights norms. At the level of domestic constitutional human rights norms, the judiciary has so far been unable to overcome bureaucratic obstacles to giving rights norms effect.[13] As a result, Chapter 2 and the international treaties remain, in a phrase used by Albert Chen, "semantic" in significance: they carry meaning, but their meaning has not so far translated into changes to the Party-State's fundamental power structure (Chen 2011: chapter 4).

Or has it? The picture looks a bit different once we move beyond the institutions created and controlled by the Party-State, and turn to civil society reception of these promising, liberal, human-rights-inspired norms. Throughout the 1980s and 1990s, the Party-State itself actively propagated the idea of defending one's legal rights (*weiquan*) (Benney 2013). From the early 2000s, it got warier and turned to persecuting rights defenders in coordinated, and (one might argue) increasingly systematic fashion; but as discussed in the following section, the success of these repressive efforts remains in some doubt. Even as its institutions continued to be controlled and public discourse limited, it might with hindsight seem unavoidable that the inherent tensions of the constitutional design would lead to real legal dispute between citizens and the State, and that, as they began to disagree on what citizens' rights entailed, such disputes would challenge the boundaries of official toleration. As discussed below, from a Party-State perspective, the decades after Mao were therefore decades of trying and often failing to manage this tension, because the legal mechanisms created were too weak to function well in resolving legal disputes. Some citizens, on the other hand, saw themselves in an era of transition to a different system, one that would ultimately reflect what was discussed as a global constitutional order (Waluchov 2010). These promises, however "semantic" their status, led some to hope that the rule of the Party could – and would – ultimately come to be substituted by the rule of law; and it led some to hope, at least initially, that the Party itself was capable of driving this development toward its own transformation.

Bottom-up challenges to Party rule in the name of the law

The 1980s were in many ways a period of restoration and stabilization through introduction and implementation of legal rules that allowed people to act more freely. But the introduction of legal rules also encouraged people to use these rules, and the more fundamental principles on which they drew, for purposes unaligned with those of the Party-State. The movement leading up to June Fourth, 1989, driven by dissatisfied workers, students, and other dynamic groups in

Chinese society, showed more than any other incident of this era how much liberal ideas had caught on in society. While somewhat lacking in technical and practical familiarity with how a sound legal system operates, some of the demands advanced in the movement were clearly law-based; they called for the realization of liberal legal-political principles such as separation of powers, freedom of speech, and human rights more widely. Apparently acting on orders given by Deng Xiaoping himself (Nathan 2001), the Party, fearing loss of control, decided to crack down in a manner flagrantly violating its international and domestic legal obligations to protect its citizens' rights.

The Party-State tried to "sell" the 1989 massacre to domestic and international audiences primarily as a way of avoiding chaos (Bonnin 2009). It framed the various violations of human rights that had occurred, and many more to occur in subsequent decades, as necessary evils attendant on China's slow, but sure and incremental transition to a more open and liberal political order, as captured in Professor Zhang Weiwei's slogan "economic reforms first, political reforms later" (Zhang 2006). Accordingly, following the 1989 massacre, the idea of reform was toned down; it became less politically charged; and there was a (re-)politicization of the judiciary and law enforcement apparatus (Lam 2009). This way of framing, according to Sondrol, is characteristic of authoritarian systems which in contrast to totalitarian ones use "lesser evil" justifications of their exercise of political control. Rather than claiming superiority toward different systems, they rely on "performance legitimacy" and emphasize economic development, political stability, and the avoidance of chaos (Sondrol 2009).

In line with this message, having prosecuted "perpetrators" of the June Fourth movement such as Liu Xiaobo for counter-revolutionary crimes, the Party-State moved to asserting that China *was* protecting international human rights. It issued the first-ever Government White Book on Human Rights in 1991 – which Andrew Nathan has characterized as a paradoxical implication of June Fourth – even though it argued that human rights in a Chinese context primarily meant boosting social welfare and economic prosperity (Nathan 2009). It encouraged expectations to shift toward further top-down, incremental "rule of law reform" – allowing different groups to associate these hopes with different political aspirations – and some form of controlled "civil society" growth. The parameters of civil society development, and hence of "bottom-up" legal challenges to the Party, were set by these conditions. Civil society groups in China have worked on issues ranging from social services (in areas such as education, healthcare, poverty alleviation) to legal advocacy (e.g., representing migrant workers or pollution victims in labor lawsuits). Some have operated as officially registered groups with varying degrees of proximity to the government (called GONGOs), and others have operated without official recognition. Some have drawn primarily on domestic support whereas others were supported by transnational civil society organizations.

Independent and public-minded legal advocates and non-governmental groups from the 1990s onward focused on case-by-case advocacy that could – as they sometimes put it – "teach" the authorities to respect the law. For some of them, working on legal cases was not only a way of strengthening the State's capacity to respect its own rules – for example, rules protecting the rights of suspects and defendants in criminal cases. It also meant connecting to a client base of people who, through their own cases, saw the advantages of having legal rules constraining power, and the importance of legal advocates helping them to challenge the government. Mechanisms to do so were increased, for example through introduction of the 1990 Administrative Litigation Law. The legal (and wider academic) mainstream in the 1990s and early 2000s was liberal. It drew inspiration from liberal critics of communism such as Hayek (Liu 2000). A book published in 1999 by Xia Yong captured this hope: it was titled *Toward a Time of Rights* (Xia 1999).

That perspective was well illustrated by one of China's human rights movement's most widely known incidents. Following the death of Sun Zhigang, a young migrant accused of violating rules that would have required him to register with local authorities[14] in police custody, some scholars challenged the constitutionality of the detention system he had been held under. They succeeded, up to a point: while the National People's Congress, the institution with authority to make such a declaration, never pronounced the regulation in question unconstitutional, the State Council, which had issued it, repealed it in a manner compliant with the procedure contained in the 2000 Legislation Law; and the media reported widely and relatively freely on the "Sun Zhigang Incident" (named after the deceased young man) (Hand 2006).

The incident was one that highlighted important features of the post-Mao legal system and legal practice: first, it showed the great complexity of the legal rules that had been produced in over two decades of legislative reforms. One of the difficulties with tackling the specific detention system in which the young man, Sun Zhigang, had been held, was that a multitude of different agencies of the Party-State had produced rules supposedly governing this system; and to make it worse, the Party, despite having no clear legal status (see above), also produced "documents" expected to be taken into account. These rules were internally inconsistent and violated liberal constitutional principles (in Sun Zhigang's case, the right to liberty of the person). Second, a decisive factor in bringing about a relatively benign result (repeal of the unconstitutional regulation) was public opinion, expressed though an increasingly independent and vocal news printing press, which was partly guided by commercial interest to produce newsworthy and engaging investigative journalism (Bandurski 2015; Svensson 2013, 2014), and whose role in fostering the rise of civil society cannot be underestimated. The role of law in these developments is complex: despite persistent and pervasive media censorship, key liberal media outlets then were protected in a limited sort of way as a commercial enterprise; and the fact that they were so protected was due to the Reform and Opening policies.

At least from the perspective of some liberal observers and participants of civil society's establishment in the 1990s and 2000s, some of the civil society groups in China might come to serve a role roughly analogous to that which Michnik attributed to civil society in the "totalitarian order" of Poland in the 1980s: "we want everybody to enjoy the same rights as [then Polish First Party Secretary] Jaruzelski, secured by the rule of law" (Michnik 1998). Service-oriented civil society groups were crucial in establishing autonomous entities working to address issues in the public interest; in doing so, they exercised relatively new, albeit highly restricted, liberties of association, and often worked with – yet not as part of – the government. Advocacy groups more directly challenged the authorities; yet as their operation was at least in some respects tolerated (Chan and Wu 2012), they were unlike the groups that had driven the June Fourth democracy movement (and earlier movements). At least from the perspective of those who drove these initiatives, they were under the protection of the law, whose Reform and Opening Era promise was that legal rights would be protected.

Teng Biao comments on this by drawing on a conversation with a friend of the 1989 democracy movement who had "spent half of the 1990s in prison."

> When he saw what rights defense lawyers were doing, he burst out with a sudden revelation: "Ah! Why didn't we think of this method of rights defence? What they are seeking is a way to tie intellectuals' concepts of freedom and democracy to issues directly affecting ordinary people, and rights defence provides such a channel…" I replied to him, "It's not that you never thought of it, *it's just that this kind of rights defense couldn't be carried out in the political and social environment back then.* A group of dynamic lawyers have used the legal process, the courts, the traditional media and

the Internet to intervene in individual cases – that was not possible in the 1980s and 1990s, and hard even to imagine at that time. Open letters, street protests, democracy movements on campuses, lectures and salons – those were the forms the democracy movement took back then."

(Teng 2009: 133; emphasis added)

Thus, for a time at least, law was what gave the Party and the people a platform for relatively safe, rational and at times constructive and successful interaction with one another. It also allowed those with liberal leanings – including officials of the legal system, liberal legal academics, lawyers, journalists, and others interested in legal-political change – to cultivate the hope of top-down legal reforms gradually accommodating civil society initiatives, opening up and becoming less repressive. For example, when in 2001, a judicial interpretation issued by the Supreme People's Court directly relied on the constitutional right to education, SPC Vice President Huang Songyou wrote an enthusiastic comment piece announcing that this decision might turn out to be "China's *Marbury vs Madison*" (Kellogg 2009). Like this famous US decision, he thought, the *Qi Yuling* decision might herald a more powerful and independent judiciary able to protect constitutional rights against public power. And out of direct experience with protecting constitutional rights, such as in the Sun Zhigang Incident, grew initiatives that became informal civil society organizations. For example, the organization *Gongmeng* or Open Constitution Initiative was founded by the three young scholars, including Teng Biao, who had initiated legal action in the Sun Zhigang Incident, and went on to become one of the most prominent organizations working to protect the basic rights of Chinese citizens in a number of areas of legal and social concern.

On the other hand, throughout the 2000s, there continued to be repression of those legal activists and advocates who were willing to take on cases and causes the Party-State did not want them to take on. Observers in and outside China were easily led to regard certain challenges to the government as too radical. The repression of such efforts, conversely, was dismissed as merely incidental, hence systemically insignificant departures from the (unquestioned) reform path; and the specter of "chaos" remained powerful, with advocates pointing to the possible chaos that might ensure if advocacy "went too far" (Pils 2007). As a result, as Spires has argued, the Chinese Party-State has in many ways succeeded in controlling much civil society activity through what he characterizes as "contingent symbiosis" (Spires 2011).

If individuals and groups that specialized in promoting public interest (and human rights) advocacy in China were in a precarious situation, their situation in some ways mirrored that of the legal establishment as a whole during the Mao era. Under Mao, being involved with *any* kind of law had posed risks. A fundamental tension playing out in waves of repression was between limited support for law based in ideas of socialist legality (Partlett and Ip 2016) and (at times) Mao-supported more radical rejections of law based on some of Marx's ideas. By contrast, in the post-Mao era, the basic tension identified by scholars and other actors in the legal field was between liberal, tolerant and repressive, authoritarian conceptions and practices of law. Only those legal actors who worked on *particular* kinds of cases (the ones deemed "sensitive") and upheld particularly outspoken liberal conceptions of law and rights took risks of serious persecution. From the majority of judges and other officials of the legal system, as well as the vast majority of lawyers, the Party had secured some (albeit possibly reluctant) compliance and cooperation, while also conceding a somewhat more secure role and status to them. But as rule of law principles were asserted more frequently and insistently, the precariousness of the relationship between the Party and the Law became once more apparent.

Back to ~~law~~ under Xi?

Xi Jinping took over as General Secretary of the Party in late 2012 and as President in 2013. He quickly moved to concentrate power in ways that accelerated and strengthened earlier efforts to do so in the Hu-Wen era.[15] These moves have called the previous achievements toward power control by law of the post-Mao era into question. These moves were largely inside-out: they started from disrupting structures and networks at the centers of power and then, supported by a combination of rhetoric, rules, and crackdowns, brought wider circles of potential resistance to central power under control. They have also been accompanied by efforts to construct and propagate new norms of Party-State governance. The full significance of these changes is still unfolding as of this writing.

A few key developments, briefly mentioned in the following, are underpinned by this new anti-liberal and in some respects anti-rationalist outlook. It was shown above that the main intellectual inspiration for the legal professionals and scholars of the post-Mao era, into the first years of the current century, had come from liberal political thinkers such as Hayek and Rawls (Liu 2000). Law's attraction was its capacity to limit arbitrary power, to provide order and peace; it was the idea of constitutional governance explored earlier on. In contrast, the now more attractive legal scholars are anti-liberal. They include notably the twentieth-century philosopher Carl Schmitt. Legal-political scholars such as Chen Duanhong, Hu Angang, Jiang Shigong, Liu Xiaofeng, Wang Shaoguang, and Zhang Xundong have absorbed Carl Schmitt's work into mainstream legal academia in China (Mittelstaedt 2016; Sapio 2015; Zheng 2013). Schmitt's theory is useful to the Chinese Party-State under Xi, as it provides some basis for a strong emphasis on Party leadership *supported by law* – it can be used as a blueprint for the identification of Party leadership and law (or in Xi's terms, "socialist rule of law with Chinese characteristics"). It also sits comfortably with the idea, clearly important to Xi, that even as law's importance is recognized, Party leadership must never be challenged on democratic or rule of law grounds.[16]

Schmitt's conception of law supported a recasting of the role of the judicial decision as an exercise of "healthy popular feeling," rather than an exercise in reasoning through legal rules and principles (Bielefeldt 1996: 387). It was also defensive of arbitrary uses of power, because "no legal norm, in Schmitt's view, can govern an extreme case of emergency or an absolute state of exception" (Vinx 2014). It thus allowed governments to "switch law on and off" as required (Vinx 2014). Most importantly, according to Schmitt, "the political" defines and determines all aspects of a legal-political order through its fundamental conception of the enemy (Schmitt 1992/2005: 5), identified not by reference to Marxist notions of class. The notion that there must be enemies – that the identity of a polity rests upon its identification of enemies and that having enemies in this political sense entails a right to kill[17] – is central to the definition of "the political"[18] also amongst Chinese scholars. For example, "the primary problem in politics is to distinguish clearly between friend and enemy. Between enemies and friends, there is no question of liberties; there are only violence and conquest" (Jiang 2004).[19]

Because this account of law, as a concept subordinate to that of "the political," needs "enemies" to define the political, it relies on the fear such enemies instill, and sees the power of the sovereign to protect against enemies as central (Schmitt 1932/2007: 52):[20] it is because the sovereign protects against enemies that it can impose obligations. Law, according to this sort of view, is justified by the existence of enemies of the political order, not by banning the arbitrary exercise of power. Since law is subject to the political, and since the arbitrary exercise of power is not banned, moreover, having law is perfectly compatible with unconstrained power to rule. Under a system of this kind, it makes sense for government to create and use fear as a tool, just as it also relies on fear-based justifications of sovereign power. To the extent that it relies on fear, it embraces an anti-rationalist principle of mere assertion of power, in preference to rational argument.

Some central campaigns, policies, and practices, as well as some of the rhetoric adopted by the leadership under Xi, reflect a Schmittian outlook. Most strikingly, the new leadership has greatly emphasized the existence of its – and by implication, the People's – internal and external enemies. It has conducted crackdowns, introduced legislation and Party rules, and used propaganda that center in the idea of enemies, complemented by the notion that enemies are "others" – others who threaten "us," or the People, as a category constructed and defined by the existence of these enemies. It is important to this sort of account that anyone is potentially an enemy, and that everybody has to submit to measures that will protect them from falling into an "enemy" category. This is briefly illustrated by examples.

There was, first, a crackdown on "corruption" that has led to the heightening of the role of the Party's Central Commission for Discipline Inspection (CCDI) in controlling officials, including those of the legal system. The CCDI and its local branches assert power to detain and question individuals without legal authority (*shuanggui*) before they are handed over to the criminal justice process. None of the procedural protections available in the criminal process kick in. This makes the *shuanggui* process a frightening part of the system, infamous for its use of torture (Human Rights Watch 2016; Pu 2014). A revision of Party-internal norms of discipline and surveillance in October 2016 has further consolidated the basis on which Party members are subjected to "education" and discipline. Suggestively, the new rules stipulate, *inter alia*, that Party internal supervision must include "frequent criticism-and-self-criticism through conversations and letters so as to make 'red and sweaty faces' the norm" (CCP 2016: s. 7). A new institution, the National Supervision Commission, might help consolidate this process even if transferring power from the CCDI. Especially if set up as an entity that represents both Party and State, and given a constitutional basis, it could become an embodiment of the now-strengthened principle of the unity of the Party-State (Ning 2016).

Second, under Xi Jinping, efforts to bring civil society advocacy under control have intensified and become more assertive. Crackdowns have prominently also affected rights lawyers, for example in the so-called 7–09 crackdown, which began on the night of July 9, 2015 and affected hundreds of lawyers and legal assistants, some 20 of whom were detained. In contrast to the pre-Xi era, when dissidents, activists, and advocates would be tried but not publicly pilloried, the "7–09" crackdown was turned into a highly visible Party-State media spectacle. Several lawyers and legal assistants were produced on national television on the occasion of their trials for subversion or their release into informal house-arrest. Victims of months of detention without access to counsel, they were shown renouncing their former activism, denouncing their colleagues, thanking and praising the authorities, and admitting to having been goaded into advocacy by "hostile foreign forces" (Buckley 2016). Concurrently, the authorities led a wider campaign to signal new boundaries of acceptable lawyer conduct, and instill the idea that constant education was required to ensure that lawyers remained supportive of the Party. Acceptance of Party leadership also required further weakening of adjudicative dispute resolution mechanisms (Minzner 2011). It required the co-optation of licensed professional lawyers as helpers of the authorities, required to "volunteer" their services to help the Party-State address mass grievances. If successful, co-optation would gradually assimilate lawyers, turning them into functionaries of the Party-State (Wang 2016).

An even more ambitious control system is the Party-State's announced plans, as of 2016, to create what is described as a system of Social Credit Governance, functioning rather like a credit score check writ large, to assess all citizens' trustworthiness or "social credit" (China Copyright and Media 2016). On the basis of their social credit score, the individual citizen might be eligible for being issued with a passport or not; they might or might not have a high enough score to get a loan, or to place their child in a good school, for example (Denyer 2016). "Social Credit Governance" is one of the measures that, if successful, would erode the basis for civil society advocacy.

These changes have been accompanied by changes in rhetoric and legislative rules equally indicating a desire to stop the discussion of "so-called 'universal values'" in places of learning (Mirrorbooks 2013), repress civil society and reorganize society on corporatist principles (Schell 2016), and assert and strengthen total Party control over the legal institutions. For example, a new National Security Law in its Article 2 defines national security in very broad terms as

> the relative absence of international or domestic threats to the state's power to govern, sovereignty, unity and territorial integrity, the welfare of the people, sustainable economic and social development, and other major national interests, and the ability to ensure a continued state of security,

and mentions "People's democratic dictatorship" as a guiding principle. The Law empowers officials as well as others "assisting" officials to take measures to protect national security on these broad terms. A new law on foreign NGOs subjects them to control and supervision by the police and numerous restrictions on their activities, their personnel decisions, and collaboration with domestic entities (Allen-Ebrahimian 2015; Huntonprivacy Blog 2015; Lynch, 2015). The institutions of the legal system have not only come under pressure through the institutionalization of Party-centered anti-corruption supervision. The courts in particular are expected to declare their own subjection to the Party in ever-stronger terms. Thus, in January 2017, Supreme People's Court President Justice Zhou Qiang said in a speech that the judiciary should "resolutely resist erroneous influence from the West: 'constitutional democracy,' 'separation of powers' and 'independence of the judiciary,' [and] make clear our stand and dare to show the sword" (Forsythe 2017).

In sum, in the Xi era, the Party-State has continued to rely on the operation of the legal system with all its paraphernalia of legislators producing new laws and regulations, courts adjudicating cases, and the police and other entities "enforcing the law." But it is trying to recast the intellectual premises on which the legal system is built. The legal order to be perfected under Xi Jinping reflects an attempt to establish an order of identity of state and society, an order on corporatist terms. The reach of the state under this theory is enormous, as – theoretically at least – it attributes no value to the protection of diverse views and interests or groups and individuals in society. It reflects a Carl Schmitt-like idea of "the political" that defines and determines all other aspects of a legal-political order through its fundamental conception of the enemy. This type of order has been critically portrayed in Ernst Frankel's "dual state": a state of norms, and a (prerogative) state of measures, interacting and affecting each other, and a system that neither strives to achieve nor ever could achieve genuine rule of law (Fraenkel 1941). Thus, we must conclude that even though the Party has not reverted to the Maoist tendency to deny the legitimacy of law altogether, it has, perhaps even more troublingly, adopted a conception of law which, if successfully implemented, would allow it to deprive the concept of law of its liberal force, and to perpetuate and further entrench its domination of the legal institutions.

Conclusion

This chapter began by surveying the rejection of the very idea of law as a Marxist-Maoist doctrine, and the extremely precarious position of laws, legal institutions, and individuals working in the legal system in the Mao era, which oscillated between accepting law and legal institutions, and destroying them, and which culminated in the destructions of the "Great Cultural Revolution." It then developed an argument addressing primarily the post-Mao era and the current post-post-Mao era under Xi Jinping. First, since the introduction of Deng Xiaoping's Reform and Opening policies, a liberal conception of rule of law has "caught on" in China along with the wider realization of its potential to protect legal rights, including human rights. The attractiveness of this idea has inspired unprecedented legal advocacy and rights advocacy, and been central to the emergence of a "civil society" presenting bottom-up challenges to the authoritarian Party-State.

Second, more recent changes in the Chinese Party-State, especially under Xi Jinping's leadership, represent a turn toward a legally positivistic, morally relativistic, and anti-liberal conception of law, asserting the very nature of law to be its subordination to political power. Changes discussed here indicate that rather than being *en route* to establishing a more open society of citizens with rights, China's leadership now intends to establish a legal-political order in which the Party-State is all-encompassing and all-powerful in its role as custodian of both the law and the People. In doing so it situates itself within a trend of increasing willingness to embrace models of "illiberal democracy," or of "smart authoritarianism," as alternative to "western liberal democratic capitalism" (Garton Ash 2015).

The discussion here has also shown, however, that actors in the legal system, perhaps most importantly lawyers, show signs of some remarkable resilience against this new trend. Attempts to reassert control have met with significant resistance from liberal communities within Chinese society, who – even though they are embattled – communicate and connect in many State-independent ways, within China and beyond its borders. Legal advocacy and resistance thus continue to present important challenges to the power of the Party-State.

Notes

1 See for an account of this anecdote History Gang (2014); also, with an emphasis on the constitutional rights protections then in place, Zhang Qianfan (2012: 46).

2 This position is also attributed to Liu Shaoqi (Zhang Qianfan 2012: 47).

3 This is discussed in the next section.

4 This article asserted that "proletarian rebels armed with Mao Zedong Thought" were "both lawless and law-abiding" – that while conventional state laws should be disregarded, they received guidance from revolutionary ideas (*People's Daily* 1967).

5 According to Zhang Qianfan it drastically reduced the list of constitutionally protected rights, for example, and effectively merged Party and State functions (Zhang Qianfan 2012: 46f.).

6 Pitman Potter argues this with regard to Peng Zhen (Potter 2002: chapter 2).

7 Democratic Centralism (民主集中制) – the principle that Party members may debate and make suggestions, but, once a decision has been reached, it must be followed: individual members must obey the organization (the Party), the minority must obey the majority decision, and subordinates must obey their superiors. Discussed by Stephen C. Angle (Angle 2005).

8 People's Democratic Dictatorship (人民民主专政) – the principle that the Party-State represents and acts on behalf of the people, but may use dictatorial powers against reactionary forces. The word used for "dictatorship" (专政) does not have clearly negative connotations, unlike dictator 独裁 (者) or hegemon (霸王).

9 Heath (2013); also Xu (2003: 309).

10 PRC Constitution, Articles 63 and 67 clarify this for the NPC and its Standing Committee, for example (1982 Constitution). See also Wang (2004: 372) (谁制定谁审查).

11 By contrast the Party's control of the military is in some ways more visible according to the Constitution.

12 The Constitution also lists duties of citizens and stipulates in its Article 51 that the exercise of constitutional rights may not "infringe upon the interests of the state, of society or of the collective, or upon the lawful freedoms and rights of other citizens."

13 This is discussed in the following section.
14 Under the household registration or *hukou* system which is still in place.
15 For example, by the later toppled head of the Political Legal Committee Zhou Yongkang (Lam 2009).
16 For example, Xi (2014): Phrases such as "there is no legal governance that could escape political governance" draw on scholarship in the Schmittian spirit. The same phrase, translated from Loughlin (1992), is cited in Jiang (2011). Also: Loughlin (2000), at p. 12.
17 According to Schmitt, enmity as a political concept is the essence of the political; and it is connected to a "right to kill" – *ius vitae ac necis* (Schmitt 1932/2007).
18 Mittelstaedt rightly gives prominence to this distinction (Mittelstaedt 2016: 4). The friend-enemy distinction is especially strong in Chen Duanhong's account.
19 See also Zhang (2005).
20 Discussed in McCormick (1994: 622).

References

Articles, books, and book chapters

Ahl, Björn (2009). Chinese law and international treaties. *Hong Kong Law Journal* 39(751). Available at www.cesl.edu.cn/eng/upload/201106214048086.pdf.

Allen-Ebrahimian, Bethany (2015). The chilling effect of China's new cybersecurity regime. *Foreign Policy*. Available at http://foreignpolicy.com/2015/07/10/china-new-cybersecurity-law-internet-security/.

Angle, Stephen C. (2005). Decent democratic centralism. *Political Theory* 33(4).

Bandurski, David (November 25, 2015). News ethics, media controls, and investigative journalism. *China Digital Times*. Available at http://chinadigitaltimes.net/2015/11/news-ethics-media-controls-and-investigative-journalism/.

Bayefsky. The United Nations Human Rights Treaties – China. Available at www.bayefsky.com/bycategory.php/state/36 (last accessed January 20, 2017).

Benney, Jonathan (2013). *Defending Rights in Contemporary China*. Abingdon, Routledge.

Bielefeldt, Heiner (1996). Deconstructing the rule of law. *Archives for Philosophy of Law and Social Philosophy* 82(3): 379–396. Available at www.jstor.org/stable/23680188?seq=1#page_scan_tab_contents.

Bingham, Tom (2007). The rule of law. *Cambridge Law Journal* 66(67).

Bonnin, Michel (2009). The Chinese Communist Party and 4 June 1989: or how to get out of it and get away with it. In Jean-Philippe Béja (ed.), *The Impact of China's 1989 Tiananmen Massacre*. Abingdon, Routledge.

Buckley, Chris (August 5, 2016). Week of TV trials in China signals new phase in attack on rights. *New York Times*. Available at www.nytimes.com/2016/08/06/world/asia/china-trial-activists-lawyers.html.

Chan, Kin-man and Wu Fengshi (2012). Graduated control and beyond: the evolving government-NGO relations. *China Perspectives* 3.

Chen, Albert (2011). *An Introduction to the Legal System of the PRC* (4th edition). Hong Kong, Lexisnexis.

Clarke, Donald C. (2007). Legislating for a market economy in China. *The China Quarterly* 191: 13–31.

Clarke, Donald and James V. Feinerman (1995). Antagonistic contradictions: criminal law and human rights in China. *The China Quarterly* 141: 135.

Cohen, Jerome A. (1968). *The Criminal Process in the People's Republic of China, 1949–1963: An Introduction*. Harvard, Harvard University Press.

Denyer, Simon (October 22, 2016). China wants to give all of its citizens a score – and their rating could affect every area of their lives. *The Independent*. Available at www.independent.co.uk/news/world/asia/china-surveillance-big-data-score-censorship-a7375221.html.

Dictionary.com (2016). Entry under "reform" at www.dictionary.com/browse/reform?s=t.

Esarey, Ashley (2006). Speak no evil: mass media control in contemporary China. *Freedom House*. Available at https://freedomhouse.org/sites/default/files/inline_images/Speak%20No%20Evil-%20Mass%20Media%20Control%20in%20Contemporary%20China.pdf.

Forsythe, Michael (January 18, 2017). China's Chief Justice rejects an independent judiciary, and reformers wince. *New York Times*. Available at www.nytimes.com/2017/01/18/world/asia/china-chief-justice-courts-zhou-qiang.html?_r=0.

Fraenkel, Ernst (1941). *The Dual State: A Contribution to the Theory of Dictatorship*, translated by E.A. Shils. New York, Edith Lowenstein.

Gallie, W.B. (1955–56). Essentially contested concepts. *Proceedings of the Aristotelian Society* 86.

Garton Ash, Timothy (June 1, 2015). Xi Jinping's China is the greatest political experiment on Earth. *The Guardian*. Available at www.theguardian.com/commentisfree/2015/jun/01/war-peace-depend-china-domestic-success.

Hand, Keith (2006). Using law for a righteous purpose: the Sun Zhigang Incident and evolving forms of citizen action in the People's Republic of China. *The Columbia Journal of Transnational Law* 45: 138.

Heath, Timothy (2013). Xi's mass line campaign: realigning party politics to new realities. *China Brief* 13(16). Available at https://jamestown.org/program/xis-mass-line-campaign-realigning-party-politics-to-new-realities/.

Heath, Timothy R. (2014). *China's New Governing Party Paradigm: Political Renewal and the Politics of National Rejuvenation*. Farnham (UK) and Burlington (USA), Ashgate.

History Gang (历史帮, a pseudonym, November 24, 2014). 鲜为人知的刘少奇之死内幕 [Newly discovered inside story of the death of Liu Shaoqi]. Available at www.360doc.com/content/15/0318/10/3595491_456112457.shtml.

Human Rights Watch (December 6, 2016). Special measures: detention and torture in the Chinese Communist Party's Shuanggui system. Available at www.hrw.org/report/2016/12/06/special-measures/detention-and-torture-chinese-communist-partys-shuanggui-system.

Huntonprivacy blog (July 15, 2015). Draft cybersecurity law published for comment in China. Available at www.huntonprivacyblog.com/2015/07/15/draft-cybersecurity-law-published-comment-china/.

Jiang, Ming'an (姜明安, 2011). 法治与发展对策研究的进路与方法 [The way forward and methodology regarding research on rule by law and development]. Available at www.cncasky.com/get/lltt/fxlw/20110715215222210_2.html.

Jiang, Shigong (强世功, 2004). 乌克兰宪政危机与政治决断, 21世纪经济报道 [The constitutional crisis and political decisions in Ukraine]. 21世纪经济报道 [21st Century Business Herald]. Available at http:// club.kdnet.net/dispbbs.asp?id=140825&boardid=24.

Keller, Perry (1994). Sources of order in the Chinese legal system. *The American Journal of Comparative Law* 42(4): 711–759.

Kellogg, Thomas E. (2009). The death of constitutional litigation in China? *China Brief* 9(7). Available at www.jamestown.org/uploads/media/cb_009_7_02.pdf.

Lam, Willy Wo-Lap (2009). The politicisation of China's law-enforcement and judicial apparatus. *China Perspectives* 2: 24–51.

Lei, Chen (2014). Legal and institutional analysis of expropriations in China. In Fu Hualing and John Gillespie (eds.), *Resolving Land Disputes in East Asia*. Cambridge, Cambridge University Press.

Lin, Li-wen and Curtis Milhaupt (2013). We are the (national) champions: understanding the mechanism of state capitalism in China. *Stanford Law Review* 65: 697. Available at www.stanfordlawreview.org/print/article/we-are-national-champions.

Liu, Junning (2000). Classical liberalism catches on in China. *Journal of Democracy* 11: 48.

Lo, Carlos (1997). Socialist legal theory in Deng Xiao-ping's China. *Columbia Journal of Asian Law* 11: 469.

Loughlin, Martin (1992). *Public Law and Political Theory*. Oxford, Clarendon Press.

Loughlin, Martin (2000). *Sword and Scales: The Relationship between Politics and Law*. Oxford, Hart Publishing.

Lynch, Elizabeth (May 10, 2015). A slow death? China's draft foreign NGO management law. China Law and Policy Blog. Available at http://chinalawandpolicy.com/2015/05/10/a-slow-death-chinas-draft-foreign-ngo-management-law/.

Mao, Zedong (1949). On people's democratic dictatorship. Available in translation at www.marxists.org/reference/archive/mao/selected-works/volume-4/mswv4_65.htm.

Mao, Zedong (1957). On the correct handling of contradictions among the people. Posted at www.etext.org. In Mao Tse-Tung, *Four Essays on Philosophy*. Peking, 1968.

McCormick, John P. (1994). Fear, technology, and the state: Carl Schmitt, Leo Strauss, and the revival of Hobbes in Weimar and National Socialist Germany. *Political Theory* 22(4): 619–652.

Michnik, Adam (1998). Toward a civil society. In Adam Michnik and Irena Grudzinska Gross (eds.), *Letters from Freedom: Post-Cold War Realities and Perspectives*. Berkeley, University of California Press.

Minzner, Carl F. (2011). China's turn against law. *American Journal of Comparative Law* 59: 935.

Mittelstaedt, Jean-Christopher (2016). Understanding China's two constitutions: re-assessing the role of the Chinese Communist Party. Available at https://papers.ssrn.com/sol3/papers.cfm?abstract_id=2682609.

Nathan, Andrew (2001). The Tiananmen Papers. Inside China's Politburo. *Foreign Affairs*, January/February. Available at www.foreignaffairs.com/articles/56670/andrew-j-nathan/the-tiananmen-papers.

Nathan, Andrew (2009). China and international human rights – Tiananmen's paradoxical impact. In Jean-Philippe Béja (ed.), *The Impact of China's 1989 Tiananmen Massacre*. Abingdon, Routledge, pp. 207–220.

Ning, Xin (宁馨, presenter, December 9, 2016). 焦点对话: 突设监察委, 为政改还是为王岐山留任, *Voice of America (Chinese Desk)*. Available at www.voachinese.com/a/VOAWeishi-20161209-Pro-and-Con-2/3629772.html.

Partlett, William and Eric C. Ip (2016). Is socialist law really dead? *New York University Journal of International Law and Politics* 48: 463.

Peerenboom, Randall (2002). *China's Long March Toward Rule of Law*, Cambridge, Cambridge University Press.

People's Daily (1967). 无法无天赞 [In praise of lawlessness], January 13.

Perry, Elizabeth (2016). Higher education and authoritarian resilience: the case of China, past and present. *Harvard-Yenching Institute Working Paper Series*. Available at www.harvard-yenching.org/sites/harvard-yenching.org/files/featurefiles/Elizabeth%20Perry_Higher%20Education%20and%20Authoritarian%20Resilience.pdf.

Pils, Eva (2007). Asking the tiger for his skin: rights activism in China. *Fordham International Law Journal* 30: 1209–1287.

Potter, Pitman (2002). *From Leninist Discipline to Socialist Legalism: Peng Zhen on Law and Political Authority in the PRC*. Stanford, Stanford University Press.

Potter, Pitman B. (2013). *China's Legal System*. Cambridge and Malden, MA, Polity Press.

Sapio, Flora (2010). *Sovereign Power and the ~~Law~~ in China*. Leiden, Brill.

Sapio, Flora (October 7, 2015). Carl Schmitt in China. *The China Story* blog. Available at www.thechinastory.org/2015/10/carl-schmitt-in-china/.

Schell, Orville (April 6, 2016). Crackdown in China: worse and worse. *New York Review of Books*/China File. Available at www.chinafile.com/nyrb-china-archive/crackdown-china-worse-and-worse.

Schmitt, Carl (1922/2005). *Political Theology: Four Chapters on the Concept of Sovereignty*. George Schwab (translation). Chicago, University of Chicago.

Schmitt, Carl (1932/2007). *The Concept of the Political. Expanded Edition*. Translated by G. Schwab. Chicago, University of Chicago Press.

Sondrol, P.C. (2009). Totalitarian and authoritarian dictators: a comparison of Fidel Castro and Alfredo Stroessner. *Journal of Latin American Studies* 23(3): 599.

Spires, Anthony (2011). Contingent symbiosis and civil society in an authoritarian state: understanding the survival of China's grassroots NGOs. *American Journal of Sociology* 117: 1–45.

Svensson, Marina (2013) Reporting law and injustices: investigative journalists and the legal system. In Elin Saether, Marina Svensson, and Zhang Zhi'an (eds.), *Chinese Investigative Journalists' Dreams: Agency, Autonomy, Voice*. Lanham, MD, Rowman & Littlefield, pp. 157–177.

Svensson, Marina (2014). Rule of law and public accountability: can investigative journalism promote social justice and human rights? Available at http://lup.lub.lu.se/luur/download?func=downloadFile&recordOId=3346487&fileOId=3346490.

Sypnowich, Christine (2014). Ideology and law. Entry in *Stanford Encyclopaedia of Philosophy*.

Teng, Biao (2009). What is rights defence. In Patrick Poon and Stacy Mosher (eds.), *China's Human Rights Lawyers*. Hong Kong, China Human Rights Lawyers Concern Group.

Teng, Biao (2012). Rights defence, microblogs, and the surrounding gaze: the rights defence movement online and offline. *Locating Civil Society: Communities Defending Basic Liberties*, Special Issue of *China Perspectives 2012/no. 3*.

Tiffert, Glenn (2016). Socialist rule of law with Chinese characteristics: a new genealogy. Draft quoted with author's permission.

Vinx, Lars (2014). Carl Schmitt. Entry in *Stanford Encyclopaedia of Philosophy*. Available at http://plato.stanford.edu/entries/schmitt.

Waluchov, Will (2010). Constitutionalism. Entry in *Stanford Encyclopedia of Philosophy*. Available at http://plato.stanford.edu/entries/constitutionalism/#ConLawVerConCon.

Wang, Xuejun (王学钧, 2016). 监察革新 [Innovation of supervision]. Available at http://news.sina.com.cn/o/2016-11-13/doc-ifxxsfip4607494.shtml.

Wang, Zhenmin (王振民, 2004). 中国违宪审查制度 [*Constitutional Review in China*]. Beijing, Chinese University of Politics and Law Press.
Wolff, Jonathan (2015). Marx. Entry in *Stanford Encyclopaedia of Philosophy*. Available at https://plato.stanford.edu/entries/marx/.
Wu, Wei (吴伟, September 30, 2014). 十三大后的党政分开改革 [The reform to separate the Party and the Government following the Thirteenth Party Congress]. *New York Times*. Available at http://cn.nytimes.com/china/20140930/cc30wuwei31/.
Xia Yong (夏勇, 1999). 走向权利的时代: 中国公民全力发展研究 [*Toward a Time of Rights: A Perspective of the Civil Rights Development in China*]. Beijing, China University of Politics and Science Press.
Xu, Beina (April 7, 2015). Media censorship in China: a backgrounder. *Council on Foreign Relations*. Available at www.cfr.org/china/media-censorship-china/p11515.
Xu Chongde (徐崇德, 2003). 中华人民共和国宪法史 [*A Constitutional History of the People's Republic of China*]. Fuzhou, Fujian People's Press.
Yang Deshan (杨德山, September 6, 2002). 依法治国, 以德治国 [Ruling the country in accordance with law, ruling the country in accordance with virtue]. Available at http://news.xinhuanet.com/newscenter/2002-09/06/content_552721.htm.
Zhang, Qianfan (张千帆, 2012). *The Constitution of China: A Contextual Analysis*. Oregon, Hart Publishing.
Zhang, Weiwei (November 2, 2006). The allure of the Chinese model. *International Herald Tribune*. Available at www.sinoptic.ch/textes/articles/2006/20061102_zhang.weiwei_chinese.model-en.pdf.
Zhang, Xundong (张旭东, 2005). 施米特的挑战 – 读《议会民主制的危机》. [The challenge of Carl Schmitt: on reading *The Crisis of the System of Parliamentary Democracy*]. Available at www.aisix iang.com/data/6350.html.
Zhang, Yihong (2012). The party's long shadow: the party's control and influence over the corporate governance of Chinese listed companies. *International Company and Commercial Law Review* 23: 323.
Zheng, Qi (2013). Carl Schmitt, Leo Strauss, and the issue of political legitimacy in China. *American Foreign Policy Interests: The Journal of the National Committee on American Foreign Policy* 35(5): 254–264.

Audio-visual material

Pu, Zhiqiang (February 2014). Ningyuan Shuanggui. Translated by HKU Media Project and China Change. Available at https://vimeo.com/104070378 [original with Chinese subtitles: 双规噩梦–-湖南永州宁远双规访谈实录, available at www.youtube.com/watch?v=ovpCJR8Ciho].

Speeches, lectures

Partlett, William (July 15, 2016). The supervisory role in socialist law and its legacy. Public seminar presentation at King's College London.
Xi Jinping (习近平, January 7, 2014). 在中央政法工作会议上的讲话 [Excerpt from speech given at Party Central Meeting]. Available at http://cpc.people.com.cn/xuexi/n/2015/0511/c385475-26978527.html.
Xi Jinping (习近平, April 15, 2015). 党大还是法大是伪命题 [Excerpts from Xi Jinping on comprehensively ruling the country in accordance with law]. Speech available at http://opinion.haiwainet.cn/n/2015/0430/c456318-28688962.html.

Treaties, laws and regulations, official documents

Convention on the Elimination of All Forms of Racial Discrimination (adopted December 21, 1965, entered into force January 4, 1969) 660 UNTS 195 (CERD).
International Covenant on Economic, Social and Cultural Rights (adopted December 16, 1966, entered into force January 3, 1976) 993 UNTS 3 (ICSECR).
International Covenant on Civil and Political Rights (adopted December 16, 1966, entered into force March 23, 1976) 999 UNTS 171 (ICCPR).
Convention on the Elimination of All Forms of Discrimination against Women (adopted December 18, 1979, entered into force September 3, 1981) 1249 UNTS 13 (CEDAW).

Convention against Torture and Other Cruel, Inhuman or Degrading Treatment or Punishment (1984) 1465 UNTS 85.

Convention on the Rights of the Child (adopted November 20, 1989, entered into force September 2, 1990), 1577 UNTS 3 (CRC).

Convention on the Protection of the Rights of All Migrant Workers and Members of Their Families (adopted December 18, 1990, entered into force July 1, 2003) 2220 UNTS 3 (CPRM).

International Convention for the Protection of All Persons from Enforced Disappearance (adopted December 20, 2006, entered into force December 23, 2010) 2716 UNTS 3.

Convention on the Rights of Persons with Disabilities (adopted March 30, 2007, entered into force May 3, 2008, CRPD).

中华人民共和国宪法 [PRC Constitution], passed on December 4, 1982, promulgated and effective as of December 4, 1982, last revised on March 14, 2004.

中华人民共和国立法法 [PRC Law on Legislation], promulgated March 15, 2000, effective July 1, 2000.

中华人民共和国行政诉讼法 [PRC Administrative Procedure Law], adopted and promulgated on April 4, 1989 and effective as of October 1, 1990.

中华人民共和国国家安全法 [National Security Law of the People's Republic of China], passed on July 1, 2015 at the 15th meeting of the Standing Committee of the 12th National People's Congress.

Communiqué of the Third Plenary Session of the 11th Central Committee of the Communist Party of China (1978), available at www.bjreview.com.cn/special/third_plenum_17thcpc/txt/2008-10/10/content_156226.htm.

中国共产党党内监督条例 [CCP Intra-Party Supervision Regulation], issued October 27, 2016, http://news.xinhuanet.com/politics/2016-11/02/c_1119838242.htm.

Mirrorbooks (明镜), 《明镜月刊》 独家全文刊发中共9号文件 ["Mirrorbooks Monthly" exclusive, full text of CCP Document No. 9], (August 20, 2013), available at www.molihua.org/2013/08/9_7925.html translated by ChinaFile, "Document No. 9," available at www.chinafile.com/document-9-chinafile-translation.

China Copyright and Media, "State Council Guiding Opinions concerning Establishing and Perfecting Incentives for Promise-keeping and Joint Punishment Systems for Trust-Breaking, and Accelerating the Construction of Social Sincerity" (updated October 18, 2016), translated by Rogier Creemers, available at https://chinacopyrightandmedia.wordpress.com/2016/05/30/state-council-guiding-opinions-concerning-establishing-and-perfecting-incentives-for-promise-keeping-and-joint-punishment-systems-for-trust-breaking-and-accelerating-the-construction-of-social-sincer/.

17
TWO STEPS FORWARD, ONE BACKWARD
The CCP's policy toward women

Marina Thorborg

Introduction: different levels of emancipation

Partly inspired by the Soviet Union, the Chinese Communist Party (CCP) has had a clear-cut definition of what it considers women's interests since its inception in the 1920s. This has been characterized on the one hand by an ideology promising full emancipation for women on equal terms with men, and on the other hand by accommodations to pressing realities and changing priorities. Since 1949, the CCP's policies toward women have constituted one aspect of the overall attempt to transform the whole country. Every change in the party-state apparatus' general developmental strategies has engendered a concomitant change in the policy on women (Thorborg 1978: 536–538).

The CCP stance on women has generally worked on three different levels. The first level is the lofty, ideological level with pure theory inspired by anarchistic, democratic, and socialist ideas that are derived from the Western women's movement as well as the laws of the early Soviet Union. These laws were often in their turn copied from the U.S., which were regarded at that time as the leading anti-colonial country (Salaff and Merkle 1970; Thorborg 2003). This level has manifested itself in party programs, laws, and constitutions.

The intermediate or propaganda level has been used to carry out different campaigns. This is the level of social engineering geared toward changing traditional values, and accordingly, behavior. On this level, social and economic conditions in the country have to be taken into account. The third level, that of the grassroots, has consisted of adjusting daily practice to whatever is going to be accomplished in relation to the party's current policy on women by different agents of the party-state bureaucracy (Thorborg 1980a: 205–207).

In an ideal world all three levels would be in harmony sending out the same message. However, more often than not this has not been the case. The highest ideological level is always there supposedly unchanged, but the two other levels have to adjust to socio-economic changes as well as other CCP policies of the day. This interplay between three levels explains much of the zigzags and contradictions in the party's policy toward women. The goal seems to be clear but the road to reach it keeps meandering.

Early CCP policy on women

After the end of the Chinese empire in 1911 a tumultuous decade followed crystallizing into two main movements for modernizing China: the Guomindang (GMD), which was also known as the Kuomintang (the "Nationalists") from 1912; and the Chinese Communist Party from 1921. During its two alliances with the GMD, the CCP was sometimes forced to adjust its policies; it was also exposed to internal fighting between a more totalitarian, Bolshevist orientation and a more anarchistic one. Many Communist leaders had begun as anarchists; they stressed social and cultural revolution and the establishment of an anarchist society. Others were known as May Fourth Feminists. Influenced by the May Fourth Movement – sometimes called China's Renaissance – they demanded a complete modernization of Chinese society, including the full emancipation of women (Dirlik 1989: 74–94 and 217–220; Thorborg 2014: 71–75).

During the CCP's formative – and underground – period, its "women's work" was subordinated to the policies of the Women's World Alliance in Shanghai. Founded in 1919 as an independent, radical organization, this alliance conferred legitimacy to and supplied the CCP with resources and contacts. Chen Duxiu, founder of the CCP and its first national leader, demanded in a 1921 directive that all Communist cells should develop their "women's programs" by following the programs of the Women's World Alliance. The Alliance's first female organizers, Gao Junman and Wang Huiwu, were married to the male leaders of the CCP (Thorborg 1980b).

In the economic realm, the CCP's major policies toward women involved issues of land and marriage reform. New marriage regulations and laws stressed equality of the sexes, free and individual choice in selecting a spouse; they banned child betrothal, bigamy, interfering with the remarriage of widows, and exaction of money or gifts in connection with marriage (Thorborg 2014: 94–95) In 1932, Mao Zedong, who was supposed to be the man in the CCP leadership most engaged in gender equality issues, set up a committee dedicated to "reforming the lives of women" (China News Service 2013).

In October 1934, the CCP's armed forces broke out of GMD encirclement. While they were severely decimated, Mao and his comrades arrived at the Yan'an base in 1935 and gained precious breathing space. In this backward, desolated place in Northern China, the party's policy regarding women turned more conservative – and invited criticism by outspoken female members. Theory and practice were two different things. Ding Ling, a famous author and CCP member, published in 1942 an article called "Thoughts on March Eighth." Ding's denigration of the practice of elderly party men giving up their illiterate country wives for young, urban, educated women was not well received by the male leadership. Her criticism of the daily discrimination of married women with children was also disparaged by the party leadership. Ding and other advocates of feminist rights were sent away for "thought reform" (Ding 1942; Thorborg 2014: 74–75 and 100–101).

Women's political status post-1949

In March 1949 the CCP convened the First All-China Congress of Women and one month later the All-China Democratic Women's Foundation (ACDWF) was set up to act as a transmission belt for party policies. (The ACDWF changed its name to All-China Women's Federation or ACWF in 1957.) Women's organizations across the political spectrum were all subsumed under the ACWF, which frowned upon any non-party affiliated feminist movements. Moreover, no provision was made for participation by individual feminists. This meant that a male dominated leadership defined the official ideology on women's emancipation. Women under this system became even more vulnerable than before, as leading men who were building up a totalitarian state gained absolute power over women – and they could hide their sexual predation in a politically correct language. For example, women of "bad" class background as well as innocent young women could be sexually abused by men in power since the victims had nowhere to turn. This was what I encountered time and again when interviewing Chinese women from 1973 onwards (Xinran 2003; Thorborg 2014: 249–250 and 320–321).

The fact that women leaders of the ACWF were also cadres in party-and-state organs ensured the party's control over the women's movement. Most senior women officials were married to political and military leaders. Some women were originally politicians in their own right such as Deng Yingchao, who was strongly influenced by May Fourth feminism. A CCP member since the mid-1920s, Deng was the vice president of ACWF; she was better known, however, as the wife of Premier Zhou Enlai and a senior official in the National People's Congress. Cai Chang, the first president of ACWF, was one of the few female members of the ruling CCP Central Committee. Luo Qiong was an early CCP member and she was put in charge of propaganda and education of the ACWF. Kang Keqing, one of the relatively few women who excelled in her military career, was the wife of Zhu De, commander of the Red Army and later a vice-chairman of the CCP. Kang focused on the child welfare section within the ACWF (All-China Women's Democratic Federation 1953; Thorborg 2014: 71–96).

Not a single woman has made it to the highest level of real power in China, the Standing Committee of the Politburo. Three wives of prominent party leaders – Jiang Qing, wife of Mao Zedong, Deng Yingchao, wife of Deng Xiaoping, and Ye Qun, wife of Marshal Lin Biao – were inducted to the Politburo during the 1949–1976 period. During the Cultural Revolution, Wu Guxian, a "model worker" and protégée of Jiang Qing, became an alternate Politburo member. But she disappeared from politics after the demise of the Gang of Four. Chen Muhua, a financial expert and cadre with real power, was an alternate Politburo member from 1977 to 1987 (Rosen 1995).

Wu Yi, a skilled trade negotiator, served in the Politburo as an alternate member from 1997 to 2002, and as full member from 2002 to 2007. She was vice-premier when she retired in 2008. With substantial power over economic portfolios, she was interchangeably called Iron Lady and Goddess of Transparency. In the new millennium, State Councilor in charge of education Liu Yandong has served in the Politburo since 2007. Her father was Liu Ruilong, former vice-minister of agriculture with close ties to former president Jiang Zemin. She earlier worked as a deputy for ex-president Hu Jintao in the Communist Youth League. Sun Chunlan, the only other female member of the current Politburo, rose from a humble background to become the first woman to have headed a directly administered city, the Tianjin metropolis, from 2012 to 2014. She is currently the director of the CCP's United Front Department (Coonan 2012; Bo 2015).

On the next lower level, the CCP Central Committee, female membership has hovered around 4–10 percent. During the first half-century of CCP leadership, the great majority of women cadres who rose to top-level jobs were given portfolios related to "women's work" or family planning. This was despite the fact that they might have excelled in their earlier careers in other types of party or government work (Rosen 1995).

CCP policies toward women during the rehabilitation period

In areas it conquered the CCP had carried out land reform giving all adults, regardless of sex, a piece of land. This was spelled out in *The Outline for a Land Law* in October 1947. Land and marriage reform were two big issues laid out by the new regime in 1949. The CCP had up to

1949 worked in three ways to promote emancipation of women; (1) to organize women; (2) to change the marriage system; (3) to get women to take part in production. The second measure was seen as a precondition for the others and given the highest priority. To carry through changes in the marriage system women's organizations were mobilized. The CCP usually adopted a dual and contradictory approach to women's liberation: first, oppression will naturally cease when the CCP victory is assured; and second, women have to organize themselves and they must fight for their own liberation. The first approach stressed class oppression and the other one sex oppression. Women were always told to fight class oppression. However, they were sometimes encouraged to fight sex oppression but other times discouraged from this very action (Central Committee of the Chinese Communist Party 1948). The total membership of the ACDWF was estimated at 22.6 million in March 1949, while the CCP counted roughly 4.15 million members and women made up less than a tenth of total party membership. In contrast to the ACDWF, membership of the CCP was personal and exclusive and not collective and inclusive. This meant that women were collectively drafted into the ACDWF and professional women were automatically affiliated through their places of work (Deng 1949; Shishi Shouce 1951).

After 1949 China tried to accomplish a number of goals simultaneously, some of which were contradictory. While policy toward women was not deemed a major policy by the leadership, it manifested the contradictions that were associated with dictator Mao's proclivities. During the leadership of Mao Zedong the party and the state were intertwined. An increasingly totalitarian state was taking over (Thorborg 2014). The remnants of the old society were supposed to be wiped out through the "five-anti" and "three-anti" campaigns. A great number of small and private firms were closed down, resulting in increased urban unemployment. The service sector shrank rapidly and low-paid, unskilled jobs that used to enable destitute women to make ends meet disappeared. Despite high-sounding ideology and propaganda, the economy was floundering and many urban women lost their economic independence (Thorborg 2014: 137–141).

The main reforms in 1950 were the Marriage Law of May 1 – the first official law of the People's Republic of China – and the Land Reform Law of June 30 the same year. The Marriage Law amalgamated the main points of seven different marriage laws and regulations earlier promulgated under CCP control. Building upon earlier additions to previous marriage laws the 1950 statute stressed the ban on concubines, the granting of divorce after mutual consent, and the right to free choice of occupation (V.ifeng.com 2010).

CCP policies in rural areas during the first five-year-plan period 1952–1957

The marriage and land reform laws were connected. In the marriage law women could be granted divorce, while the CCP land reform program stipulated that poor peasants regardless of sex were entitled to a piece of land taken from the landlords. In theory a divorced woman could then survive on her new piece of land. This also meant that a male peasant who had married in accordance with traditional norms would after a divorce in effect lose half of "his" land, as well as the gifts he gave for the marriage, which were often equivalent to more than one year's income. While many CCP cadres encouraged couples who had been married under feudalistic conditions to seek a divorce, newly divorced men felt they had been subjected to unfair dispossession. Great social unrest ensued. When filing for divorce many women were murdered, tortured to death, buried alive, or forced to commit suicide. According to a September 1951 *Directive on the Investigations of the Conditions arising out of the Operation of the Marriage Law* issued in the name of premier Zhou Enlai on behalf of the central government, 10,000 women in the

Central South Area were murdered, forced to kill themselves, or committed suicide in the past year. The figure for all of China was given at 70–80,000 women, most of whom were under 25 years of age (Xin Zhongguo Yuebao 1951).

After investigations and rectifications a new CCP Campaign for Harmonious Marriages started on Women's Day in 1953. The recommendations were to employ a "soft approach" – and feminism was not to be encouraged. A party document called *Important Documents on the Movement for a Marriage Law*, indicated that "We cannot adopt a hasty slip-slop attitude nor methods used in class struggles." "It is absolutely not allowed to extend the [existing] problems to the relations between men and women in general so as not to confuse the movement," it added. "You must not one-sidedly protect the interests of women and let this influence you in your favourable consideration of the members of the Revolutionary Army" (Zhongyang guanche hunyinfa yundong weiyuanhui 1953).

However, CCP policy on women in rural areas was more consistent over time than in urban areas. Rural women were encouraged in different CCP campaigns to achieve emancipation through work in agriculture. For the sake of prioritizing production, even those women who were very unhappy about their marriage were asked to postpone divorce for the time being. Instead so-called "speak bitterness" meetings between daughters-in-law and mothers-in-law were to be employed as remedies. The CCP's transformation of agriculture meant institutional changes after the 1950s: from Mutual Help Teams in 1952 to Lower Producers Cooperatives in 1954, and Higher ones in 1956 and the People's Communes in 1958. The collectivization of agriculture in 1956 was closely connected with vigorous campaigns by the CCP to induce women to participate in farming. An editorial in the *People's Daily* stated, "Participation in agricultural production is the inherent right and duty of rural women" (*Renmin Ribao* 1956a).

Overzealous male cadres from higher levels of the newly established collectives were pushing women to ever more working hours with little concern for their health or other tasks. The Chinese press was overflowing with examples of overwork by women (Thorborg 1978: 557–562). The relentless CCP campaigns imposed an excessively heavy workload on women which resulted in miscarriages, injuries, and death. During the summer season in 1956, a *People's Daily* correspondent summed up reports on miscarriages due to excessive farm work in an article entitled "We can't again give in when unusual things in the villages happen and women and children are injured and killed" (*Renmin Ribao* 1956b).

As reporter Li Jiang revealed in the *Liaoning Daily*: "According to incomplete statistics from Liaoning province, there were 689 miscarriages in 46 counties, 594 women went down with uninterrupted menorrhagia during their monthly periods in 41 counties, and 117 women vomited blood in 38 counties." The daily also reported that 25 women died because of hard labor in 14 counties. It added that the cadres involved did not care for the welfare of women (*Liaoning Ribao* 1956). After more reports appeared about women being overworked to the point of death the production campaign was toned down. As the *People's Daily* put it after an ACDWF conference, "The idea of simply mobilizing women into production is not correct" (*Renmin Ribao* 1956c). The ACDWF was itself criticized for passivity. "The Federation concerns itself too much with small things," a 1957 Xinhua News Agency commentary said. "For example, at the height of the agricultural collectivisation drive cases of death and injury of women were reported because women were forced to work too long hours." The commentary also said the Federation only sent a report to the higher levels but did not talk publicly about the problems (New China News Agency 1957a).

The demand that women work extra hours so as to attain "emancipation" reflected the clash between propaganda and grassroots-level policy on the one hand, and high-level theory on the other. Moreover, this also demonstrated that the ACDWF lacked independent power. The CCP's intense production campaign in 1956 led to 100 million more women working in agriculture. Simultaneously problems of urban unemployment were coming to the surface. Some 2 million urban school graduates and 800,000 urban cadres were being "sent down" (*xiafang*) to rural areas in 1957 (Bernstein 1977; Thorborg 1978: 567–585). Moreover, owing to the fact that a third of all agricultural labor was underutilized, no more women were needed in farming. Under the direction of the party leadership, the ACDWF made a discreet ideological U-turn. ACDWF vice-chairwoman Zhang Yun had this to say during its Third National Congress of Women: "Henceforward, management of the household with industry and thrift must be seen as an important part of the country's construction." It seemed that doing household chores – and building "socialist families" – would be the best means for women to help the country in socialist construction (*Renmin Ribao* 1957a).

Owing to the fact that no more women were needed in agriculture, their time-consuming traditional household duties were stressed. Since working in the fields was no more seen as a sine qua non for emancipation, the party propaganda machinery began to give higher priority to sideline production as well as household work. To make the best of the situation the CCP started a campaign on taking care of women's and children's health. In the words of an editorial in *People's Daily*: "Not enough attention has been paid to women's labour power and this has resulted in casualties. We must provide education to men and women about safe production and women's health ... Women should be given enough time to rest" (*Renmin Ribao* 1957b).

In the "Decision on the Development of Agricultural Producers' Cooperatives of 1953" issued by the central government, the principle of equal pay for equal work was explicitly stated. In order to induce more women to work in farming the CCP and ACDWF ran campaigns in the early 1950s to promote equal remuneration regardless of sex. These campaigns were repeated in the early 1960s and early 1970s. In times of great political mobilization such as the 1958–1959 and 1966–1969 periods when ideological fervor and self-sacrifice were the order of the day, income was downplayed. However, equal pay equal work campaigns returned several times. The fact that the same campaigns had to be revived over and over again showed the persistence of traditions belittling women (Thorborg 1978: 540–555).

Developments in urban areas during the first five-year plan, 1952–1957

From 1949 to 1952, the CCP pushed a policy in the urban areas of encouraging women to participate in production. Being "only" a housewife was considered backward as social productive work was generally regarded as a precondition for emancipation. In the early 1950s at least three million people were jobless in urban areas (*Renmin Ribao* 1952a). Unemployment, considered a temporary problem in 1949, was increasingly regarded as more serious than anticipated. The Soviet-inspired Preobrazjensky policy, stressing heavy industry, led to the shutting down of much of light industry where women traditionally worked. Thus more urban women than men lost their jobs despite CCP propaganda telling women to seek emancipation through productive work. Here ideology and propaganda were in harmony but clashed with reality at the grassroots level. An official employment conference concluded in 1952 that the time was not yet ripe for inducing women to work full-time in production given the precarious employment situation (Thorborg 1978: 67–85). Influential cadres in the ACWF argued that at this stage of China's economic development, "we must also guard against the idea of looking down upon household work" (*Renmin Ribao* 1952b).

However, there were voices of opposition against upgrading household work. For example, Vice-Chairwoman Zhang Yun stressed that women "should be mobilised to take part in production and social and economic activities. They are our greatest sort of reserve labour in the country" (Zhang 1952). She conveniently forgot that CCP propaganda usually accused capitalism of using women as a reserve labor army.

ACWF told women that for the time being the important thing for them was to upgrade their skills. What was seen as a temporary measure became over time more of a goal in itself. One way to be useful to society was participating in the CCP's "Five Good Campaign" which started in 1954. Women were told that while directly engaging in production was good, they would make an equally salutary contribution to the economy through "managing the household with industry and thrift" and through looking after their husbands better. These two types of "domestic work" would make valuable indirect contributions to production. It was thus that the CCP could buttress the egalitarian aspect of its ideology through backing up the appropriateness of house work for women.

The party ran a number of movements directed at housewives who were now referred to as workers' dependents. A campaign to alleviate population pressures in the cities also unfolded. Here CCP ideology ran into a logical dilemma wriggling with two contradictory views at the same time. In the "Five Good Campaign" women were seen as useful members of society even if they were "only" working in the home, while in the next one they were seen as only passive consumers of social resources (Thorborg 2014: 183–187).

A good autumn harvest in 1955 gave more resources to light industry and more work for women. The "Five Good Campaign" was toned down. However, a bad spring harvest in 1956 combined with the collectivization drive in agriculture saw 20 million peasants fleeing to the cities. Another poor harvest resulted in an economic contraction in 1956. According to ACWF propaganda, household work was further upgraded and a campaign to dismiss female cadres began in 1957. This movement consisted of forcing female cadres into early retirement. Citing their husbands' approving and supportive attitude, the authorities ruled that no pensions needed to be given to female retirees. A concomitant drive concentrated on sending women and children to the countryside. A typical headline in the newspapers said: "Do not stay in the cities and eat free meals; go back to the countryside to be farmers" (*Guangming Ribao* 1957). Another headline went this way: "Urban population of consumers in Taiyuan have returned to rural areas!" (New China News Agency 1957b).

The Great Leap Forward of 1958

In 1958 China had an unusually good harvest and the leadership decided to break with the Soviet Model. This was the origin of the Great Leap Forward, which led to the formation of the People's Communes. From 1959 to 1962, the CCP started a frenzied production drive which finally resulted in the greatest man-made famine in the world. At least 45 million died due to starvation and related causes (Becker 1998; Dikotter 2010; Yang 2012). By substituting manpower for capital China would modernize implying not only a sharp turn in economic policy but as well a changed role assigned to women. Ideology made another U-turn with theoretical and propaganda levels more in harmony. The CCP again told women that participation in production was considered an ideologically necessary precondition for women's liberation (*Renmin Ribao* 1958).

The CCP and especially the ACWF delighted in telling women how much closer they were to liberation by participating in production. But the preconditions for it were the "socialization" of housework (Xin Zhongguo Funu 1959). In theory, all housework in rural areas was to be socialized with women of working age drafted into full-time work while communal canteens, laundry teams, and childcare stations would be run by elderly women, and those women not fit for full-time work in the fields.

Though this was a radical period men who misbehaved were punished by having to work with women in the canteens! In reality resources were insufficient. In many places social services eventually stopped working. The CCP propaganda exhorted everybody to participate in primitive steel-making. Women were forced to do double work because at times most able-bodied men were away on construction projects or making steel (Thorborg 1978: 575–587; Thorborg 2014: 213–242).

Street industries for housewives and old men were being established in urban areas in the autumn of 1958. When I interviewed women activists in China in early 1973 about this supposedly spontaneous movement, they always began with "The Party told me to ..." As long as motivation and not income was prioritized these street industries continued working (Thorborg 1992: 176 and 186). The CCP started campaigns to transfer men from government, administration, and services to heavy industry, while housewives and those reaching working age were to replace men or devote themselves to street industries (*Da Gong Bao* 1958).

In the spring of 1959 famine broke out in China. The most widespread starvation occurred in counties that most closely had followed the collectivist line and abolished the private plots. China censored all news about the famine and imported wheat from abroad which only reached coastal, urban areas. The government even exported grain in 1960 that could have saved four million lives (Thorborg 2014: 230–234). While soldiers guarded granaries that were reserved for the local political elite and for export peasants starved to death. Traditionally grandparents were first served food, then men and lastly women; but very often, the women allowed the kids to eat up a good part of their meager portions. Hence more young girls and women died. Rural party members and cadres survived. In Anhui province hardly any girls below 10 could be found in 1962. The census in 1964 showed that 4.7 million more girls aged 5–14 died than boys. The starvation occurred in inland areas and was worsened by the CCP hindering people leaving starvation areas. The famine could have stopped earlier in 1959 if Chairman Mao had listened to his critics. Instead it lasted until 1962. According to latest research the number of fatalities from this man-made famine ranged from 45 million to 60 million (Becker 1998; Dikotter 2010; Yang 2012).

The party as well as the ACWF began to change their emphasis and tone after the worst of the famine was over (*Da Gong Bao* 1962). In a directive issued on Women's Day 1962, the ACWF stressed that "under no circumstances should production be disturbed." "Everything must be done to make sure that propaganda activities do not add to the fatigue of the masses," the directive said (New China News Agency 1962).

In order to first save its grip on power and second prevent more loss of lives, the CCP resorted to emergency policies. Tenancy agriculture was once again allowed in individual regions, which resulted in a quick recovery in production since the link between work and reward was reestablished. Eventually enough resources had accumulated for marriages – which had not been possible during the famine period – to take place again. When resources went to weddings the young couple, particularly the bride, became more bound to the family and old traditions resurfaced. Because of relaxed controls local cadres often abused their positions. In 1963, Mao started a Socialist Education Campaign to stop the misrule by local cadres and prevent the return of old customs. According to new party directives, rural resources should be used for needed infrastructure and not for weddings. This was despite the fact that peasants saw marriages – and the birth of sons – as a long-term investment in their own survival because manpower was in short supply and there was no social security for old age (Thorborg 2014: 254–256).

The legitimacy of the CCP hit a low point after the devastating famine. The ACWF used the occasion to change its emphasis, this time targeting persistent attitudes among both women and men about women's perceived inferiority. The focus of the ACWF until the mid-1970s was to promote changes in ideologies and attitudes. In 1963 the ACWF magazine *Women of China* began a series called "What do women live for?" Implied was the question of whether the revolution – or the husband – should be the priority choice of women. In 1964 this debate moved on to something like "Which criteria should I use for choosing a husband?" Not surprisingly this CCP mouthpiece stressed class consciousness and revolutionary ideals. Women who wrote letters to the magazine saying they preferred tender men who love fun and food – but who did not have revolutionary fervor – were condemned by the authorities for displaying feelings of the petit bourgeoisie. Soon the army paper *Red Flag* accused the editor of *Women of China*, Dong Bian, of forgetting class struggle. She was dismissed for "bourgeois deviation." This was a forewarning of the Cultural Revolution when class struggle reigned supreme at the expense of everything else (Thorborg 2014: 250–253; Zeng 2015).

The Cultural Revolution 1966–1976

The Cultural Revolution started in 1966. In radical CCP propaganda at this violent time, women were seen having above all common class interests and no separate interests. There was no need for a special party-government unit handling the women's portfolio. Party organizations such as its federation of women, youth, and the trade unions ceased to function. During political struggles at the top, Mao often criticized his opponents for having neglected the "class viewpoint" by stressing women's special problems. China's president Liu Shaoqi was blamed by the Maoists for "advocating mothers' rights," and for emphasizing "the special needs and interests of women" in such a way that women should be kept within homes. "The gangster element" Dong Bian was slandered for promoting special welfare for women (Thorborg 2014: 250–253).

Women were told to study "Mao Zedong Thoughts" as a solution to their "problems" such as double-work and lack of social service. Housewives were increasingly referred to as "idle laborers" in party propaganda. The CCP proclaimed women to be the equal of men – and women were held to the same standard as men in terms of industrial or agricultural production. Propaganda based on new ideological interpretations about women's full ability to do men's work led to attempts at grassroots levels to oblige women to do heavy manual work that had previously only been assigned to men. Teams of strong, young, unmarried women called Iron Girls were depicted performing back-breaking labor. Being hailed as labor heroines they performed dangerous work, usually reserved for men, such as being members of high-tension electric wire brigades. Later it turned out 15 percent of the Iron Girls were injured and many became sterile. Lack of female leaders was blamed for these mishaps (Thorborg 2014: 257–262).

The CCP started a new movement in 1972 to groom more women to become party-and-government cadres. This was partly to fill in the vacuum after the forced retirement of women cadres in 1957. Women cadres were regarded as vital liaison between the CCP and female citizens in transmitting party directives to women. In 1973 the party called upon women to challenge the teachings of Confucius. For good measure, Lin Biao, minister of national defense, was branded as a disciple of Confucius after his alleged flight attempt and death in 1971. Both were seen as ideologically responsible for sex discrimination in Chinese society, Confucius for having sanctioned it and Lin Biao for not having stopped it (An 2009).

Resurrected by the CCP in 1973 the ACWF started a feminist campaign against "The Five Olds" – and in favor of "The Four News" attitudes toward women. This was against slighting women, regarding them only as mothers, spouses, laborers, and not as individuals. Women should bear half the responsibilities, deserve equivalent employment positions, and be seen as a revolutionary force. Men could "help with" household work. Earlier many had perceived the CCP policy on women as excessively reductionist emphasizing the economic aspect to the detriment of everything else. Economic development would lead to gender equality, stressing class struggle at the expense of gender. In these campaigns theory and propaganda levels were in harmony while contradictions arose at the grassroots level. Just as was the case in 1974, Deng fell into disgrace in 1976. Together with former state president Liu Shaoqi and former minister of defense Lin Biao, Deng was made a scapegoat for all failures in CCP's policy on women (Thorborg 2014: 245–259).

After Mao's death in 1976 and the subsequent imprisonment of his wife, Jiang Qing, the feminist terminology used in her campaigns was characterized as "poisonous weeds" by the ACWF. Rumor had it that the old leadership of the ACWF disapproved of Jiang Qing becoming its head. Jiang and her three accomplices, called the Gang of Four after their arrest, became scapegoats for the mistakes committed during the Cultural Revolution. In addition to her ultra-leftist political errors, Jiang also bore responsibility for the party's faulty policy on women. Everything not accomplished in the CCP's policy on women during the 1970s was because of her blocking it (Thorborg 2014: 257–262).

On Women's Day in 1976, Jiang Qing wrote an article in the *People's Daily* criticizing the lack of women in positions of real power. "The situation in the Party Politburo is unreasonable," she wrote. "There is serious male domination … This situation should be changed" (*China Reconstructs* 1977). The Politburo consisted of 28 men as ordinary members and 1 woman, Chen Muhua, as an alternate member. After she lost power, Jiang's criticism of male chauvinism was used against her. In a "struggle session" against Jiang, the Beijing Women's Federation claimed that Jiang was using "women's liberation" as an excuse for "egging women on to struggle against men, seizing power from men and exercising dictatorship over men" (*Renmin Junyi* 1977; Thorborg 2014: 271–274).

The renewed emphasis on training more women party members and cadres seemed to confirm Jiang Qing's observation of a male dominated leadership. At the Fourth Women's Congress in 1978, chairperson Kang Keqing accused Jiang Qing of attempting to make the ACWF an organization outside the purview of the CCP. Therefore it was especially urgent for the CCP to strengthen its absolute leadership over the ACWF. In December 1978 at the Third Plenum of the 11th CCP Central Committee, the development policy of the Maoist era was repudiated. In 1976 at least one out of five in the population – about 200 million people – was suffering from chronic malnutrition. In 1977 the per capita production of grain was lower than that in 1955–1958, showing the failure of collective agriculture (Thorborg 2014: 274; Dikotter 2016: 266). With a change in general policy followed a concomitant change in CCP policy on women.

The new era of reform

"If you want to promote the initiative of peasants you should give them the power to earn money," new patriarch Deng Xiaoping told the *New York Times* in 1985. The informal tenancy system of the early 1960s showed what peasants could accomplish if they were allowed to see a connection between work and reward. In 1978 this system was revived called the Household Responsibility System. After its rapid success in the countryside equivalent measures to link profits with personal endeavors were eventually applied to urban areas (Du 2006; Thorborg 2014: 277).

An agriculture stagnating for decades with food production not keeping up with population growth led to a drastic one-child-family campaign in 1979. The cadres of the ACWF were made responsible for enforcing this new policy. Party propaganda in rural areas had a hard time telling rural women that one child was enough, particularly if it was a girl. Given the lack of mechanization of farming, manpower was needed as hiring of labor was prohibited. Sons were also seen as guarantees for old age when the social security net of the people's communes had crumbled. Subsequently in 1986 a son was allowed if the first child was a daughter. Tensions developed between ACWF cadres forcing abortions until the last trimester for over-the-plan children and the population eliminating female foetuses with whatever means possible until a son was secured (Thorborg 2005; Thorborg 2014: 283–286). At the same time, the Four Modernizations in agriculture, industry, science, and defense were announced in 1978; participation of women in different types of work was seen as crucial to the achievement of this goal (*Hong Qi* 1978).

Deng's new economic policies included privatization of state enterprises, globalization, and development of collective Town and Village Enterprises (TVEs). Special Economic Zones (SEZs) were set up in Guangdong and Fujian provinces to attract foreign investment. Until 1980 roughly 80 percent of the population was rural. The CCP's main issues on women had been related to marriage, land reform, and production campaigns with the highly unpopular one-child-family campaign added in 1979. To document earlier achievements and to keep up with the times, the ACWF decided to establish research centers and archives in urban and rural basic units. Moreover, the first national conference on research on women was held in 1984 (Thorborg 2014: 276–280).

During the movement to implement the new marriage law of 1980 the ACWF attempted to promote marriage for "elderly" women, meaning those over 30 years of age. The latter were labeled *chulipin*, or low-priced products, by the urban population. Being part of 17 million urban youth sent down during the Cultural Revolution to "learn from the peasants," many urban women stayed unmarried in order to have a chance to make it back to the cities. Upon their return to urban areas, they found to their horror that they were seen as beyond marriage age. However, ACWF propaganda attempted to portray *chulipin* as "singles with a modern outlook" who were economically independent women – and even socialist models for late marriages! (Thorborg 2014: 337–339).

As soon as administrative prices stopped and industries were allowed to retain some of their profits, efficiency campaigns had begun in state industry, which was characterized by high inefficiency, great waste, and slack worker discipline. During my visit to factories in this period, nobody seemed to bother if a worker was curious, shut the machine, and followed me for half a day! The CCP authorities decided to loosen its permanent employment system in the early 1980s. The ACWF had in cooperation with the official trade unions tried to interfere when efficiency movements in the mid-1980s resulted in mainly married women with children losing their jobs and being forced into early retirement. In response to this negative phenomenon, the official *Women of China* magazine conducted a year-long discussion on "ways out for women." One recommendation was to encourage women to become entrepreneurs (Thorborg 2014: 306–313). The ACWF also started a campaign to "protect the legal rights of women and children" when numerous reports surfaced about the increase of violence against women and baby girls, as well as the kidnapping and trafficking of women (Thorborg 2014: 293 and 313).

When the ACWF tried in the mid-1980s to speak for all women with old CCP slogans, it met with strong opposition particularly from the urban young, who refused to stomach a totalitarian approach. These young women had been roaming the country under the Cultural Revolution and declined to accept what they perceived as simplistic slogans from an earlier period (Barlow 2004: chapter 6). Here theory and propaganda worked to change daily practice revealing a growing discrimination of women. The old ACWF leaders, who were deeply enmeshed with the CCP, felt unfairly accused, while its critics maintained that the organization did not represent women but was an instrument of a totally male dominated party.

In juxtaposition to the "old revolutionaries" in the women's movement, new feminist theorists and critics emerged such as Chang Ying, Xiao Li, Li Meige, Chen Ping, and Li Xiaojiang. These young feminists dominated the scene in the 1980s as part of the resurgence of a movement for educated women. Li Xiaojiang together with Tan Shen established an independent association for women's studies in 1985. Two years later in cooperation with the German researcher Maria Jaschok and the Ford Foundation, they opened The Women's Study Centre at Zhengzhou University (Maher 2016). In the 1980s Li developed the discipline of women's studies, organized conferences with international support and participants, and published widely both in popular and academic fora. Being a former rusticated, educated youth Li discussed the state's crimes against women in a new debate about culture, Marxist humanism, and how Maoism made women into "Superman." A crucial question they asked was whether there was some DNA in Chinese culture that could have created and sanctioned the excesses and crimes of Maoism (Barlow 2004: chapter 6; Thorborg 2014: 14–15). However, this debate in the 1980s was as much urban, metropolitan, and among overseas Chinese as it was international and Western therefore hardly filtering down to ordinary women, three quarters of them still living in the countryside.

However, when the ACWF reorganized in 1988 it still considered itself the sole representative of Chinese women. Criticism against the ACWF during the 1980s implied that earlier mobilization drives had obliterated natural sexual differences by combining traditional demands on women for modesty in dress and behavior with new socialist ones for simple and plain lifestyles. It was easy to forget that in a society with strong sex segregation, as in China, playing down sexual differences in outlook made it easier at that time for women to enter a men's world (Thorborg 2014: 294–308).

The Beijing massacre in 1989 of unarmed students calling for a more just and participatory society led to an international boycott of China. In 1992, patriarch Deng Xiaoping managed to jump-start the economy after his "Southern Tour," which reoriented the Chinese economy back toward market reforms. In this setting the ACWF with some backing from the CCP and women scholars were trying to promote a "Marxist Theory on women" asking the CCP not to abandon its theoretical goal of gender equality (Barlow 2004: chapter 7). This was out of fear that the development of the market-oriented economy would result in the "commercialization" of women.

Chen Muhua, a CCP member since 1938, was vice-premier in the state council in 1982 and director of the Bank of China from 1985 to 1988. Half a year later she was, to her own surprise, asked to lead the ACWF. In addition to providing educational training for 10 million and vocational training for 90 million rural women, her main contribution was laying down laws protecting women and children. In 1992, the National People's Congress promulgated the "Law on the Protection of Rights and Interests of Women and Children." As with most Chinese laws at that time it was criticized for lack of "teeth," but the statute brought together an array of different rules and regulations in relation to women (NPC.gov.cn 2007; Thorborg 2014: 287–291).

In 1993 the state-assigned employment for all urban graduates stopped. The result was that male school graduates found it much easier to find jobs compared to female counterparts. The ACWF urged the party leadership to organize campaigns against discrimination of women practiced both by state and private industry. Women's causes received a shot in the arm when

Beijing was chosen as the site for the UN Fourth World Congress on Women of 1995 (United Nations 1995). Chen Muhua became the chairwoman for this world congress representing the host country, China. As preparation for this conference I became in 2004 a member of an international group working with Chinese authorities to train 100 would-be organizers on gender issues from all over the country. In a survey we conducted with these 100 experts on what Chinese women want most, sufficient and stable food – not gender equality – was deemed their highest concern. The contribution to this congress by the Swedish Development Authority was *Chinese Women, An Annotated Bibliography* which I edited (Thorborg 1995).

The ACWF was then turned into a GONGO, Government Owned NGO, with its employees still being paid by the state. After this GONGO's international profile was raised, interactions with Western organizations dealing with women's rights flourished. In preparation for the UN Women's World Congress the party-state was increasingly promoting itself as a guarantee for women's rights in a changing society with increasing abuses against women, and the sexualization of the public space as expressed in advertisements with scantily clad women. Resources were poured into showing China as a model for the world's women (Thorborg 2014: 306–309 and 322–342). The main gains for Chinese women out of the Women's World Congress was the introduction of NGOs into China and official acceptance of increased international cooperation particularly with welfare-oriented foreign NGOs (Zhang 2004).

To keep China-based foreign NGOs under control, the CCP decided that all such organizations required a domestic-Chinese "sponsor." While the ACWF was at first reluctant to act as sponsors, its attitude changed owing to the fact that it could get registration fees and other incomes through hosting successful projects in conjunction with foreign NGOs. For example, the ACWF cooperated with Hong Kong NGOs in launching the "Spring Buds" programs, which provided education to illiterate rural teenage girls (Thorborg 2014: 337–339).

Between 1988 and 2008, Deng's economic policies helped the middle income groups of urban and rural China experience a rise in their real per capita income by respectively 3 and 2.2 times (Milanovic 2016: 11–17). But while the standard of living had gone up, women suffered a higher degree of inequality compared to men. The proportion of urban, employed women in the 20–59 age group sank from 77 percent in 1990 to 61 percent in 2010. At the same time, the average income of this group as a percentage of that of men dropped from 78 percent in 1990 to 67 percent in 2010. Urban unemployment was 50 percent higher for women in 2010. While rural women's income was a mere 79 percent of that of men in 1995, the comparable statistic sank to 56 percent in 2010 (Attané 2012).

Thanks to enhanced interaction with the Western world, the Chinese women's movement in the 1990s picked up inspiration from French feminism, philosophy, and psychoanalysis, which was evident in a genre now identified as *ecriture feminine chinoise*. Two early twentieth century novelists, He-Yin Zhen and Xiao Hong, were rediscovered by a younger generation of readers who were impressed by how they had foreshadowed values explored by French and European feminism. He-Yin Zhen, who wrote in the 1910s, saw nationalism as a trap for women; she argued that women always had to sacrifice their own interests for the so-called higher ones of the nation. The *ecriture feminine* tried to invent new ways to speak and write about women, which included challenging patriarchal and nationalistic norms. He-Yin Zhen also attempted to develop characters and tell stories using female psychology and feminine literary expressions (Liu *et al.* 2013; Thorborg 2014: 69–70). Through these new movements the writer Xiao Hong was also resurrected. Xiao's novel *Field of Life and Death*, first published in the 1930s, was seen as an early exponent of the themes associated with *ecriture feminine chinoise*. She described a brutal male world in which women felt out of place. Peking University literature professor Dai

Jinhua became a keen exponent of this new *ecriture*, particularly in the media and in her reworking of poststructuralist, Marxist feminism (Barlow 2004: chapter 7).

In 1999 the book *Shanghai Baby* by Wen Hui started a veritable sexual revolution in China. By banning it the party promoted its success. Wen Hui told the story about Coco, a rebellious young waitress who befriended members of Shanghai's "decadent groups." She had relationships with anarchistic artists, drug addicts, homosexuals, and transvestites. Readers were particularly struck by the contrast of her two lovers: a poetic but drug-addicted and impotent artist versus a married, virile, and rich German businessman. Did the contrast between the impotent Chinese artist and the virile Western big boss upset the party? Or were the frequent comments on Shanghai's superiority to the West interpreted as an inferiority complex among young Chinese? Coco's careless, individualistic, hedonistic, and exploratory lifestyle was contrasted to the mores of her straight-laced parents, who practiced abstinence most of their lives. Coco, a child of the new age, was questioning the sacrifices of the older generation. Maybe this was too subversive a thinking for the CCP? (Davis 2005: 47; Thorborg 2014: 335–337).

Conclusion: in the new millennium

In 2001 homosexuality was no longer defined as a mental illness. The first anthology on different sexual orientations, *As Normal as Possible: Negotiating Sexuality and Gender in Mainland China and Hong Kong*, was published in 2010. This work documented the experiences of people with non-heterosexual life-styles which was emerging in metropolitan areas and how they faced difficulties when confronting parental expectations and the homophobic attitudes of the party and society. China of the early millennium was increasingly opening up to more international communication and developing toward more pluralism, particularly in the economy. In 2001 the CCP had made another ideological U-turn by admitting "capitalists" – deemed "advanced elements" of new social classes – into the party. This meant that both rich businessmen and the children of the political elite, the "red aristocracy," could join the CCP. Hence talk of class struggle was conveniently forgotten in a China growing at break-neck speed. This was despite the fact that social inequality was growing so fast that the National Bureau of Statistics stopped publishing statistics on the subject for a decade (*The Telegraph* 2013).

According to a World Bank report in 2001, 58 percent of China's population was in 1995 living on less than two U.S. dollars a day, the international definition of poverty. In order to help poor women and to minimize female suicides in the countryside, the ACWF helped rural left-behind women to develop a "court-yard economy" and vigorously promoted unskilled service-jobs for female migrants to urban areas (Thorborg 2014: 338–342).

Since Xi Jinping became supreme leader in 2012, the CCP has again followed a zig-zag course in relation to women. While the Xi administration promulgated China's first law on domestic violence in March 2016, it has vigorously clamped down on NGOs and civil society, including those associated with the advocacy of women's rights (Tatlow 2016). In anticipation of Women's Day in 2015 the CCP arrested five female activists who had planned to hold protests against sexual harassment on buses and the metro in Beijing. This led to an international outcry putting the five activists, Wang Man, Wu Rongrong, Zheng Churan, Wei Tingting, and Li Tingting and their NGOs in the international limelight. After five weeks behind bars the activists were released. However, their NGO was closed in the wake of massive government harassment and confiscation of resources. Xiao Meili, a well-known feminist activist, saw the arrests as a mixed blessing. On the one hand, they highlighted for the whole world the CCP's obsession with control over civil society, and the still widespread discrimination against women.

On the other hand, this episode demonstrated increased public awareness of feminist struggles in the country (*The Economist* 2016).

In which direction will China develop? According to UN projections, Chinese in the critical age group of 20–30 will decrease from 295 million in 1995 to 159 million in 2025. This represents a one-third reduction of the population cohort that is best educated, most technically advanced, most dynamic, and most open to new ideas. This graying of society will most likely turn it more conservative, unless something totally unforeseen happens.

While CCP propaganda still advocates women's emancipation, an increasingly overwhelming demand for social control seems to be winning the upper hand. The party is anxious to keep in check new forms of expressions of feminism by sometimes ad hoc advocacy groups who are using platforms ranging from street performances to Internet campaigns. Gender equality is hard to impose from above. At the same time, feminist ideals cannot develop totally on their own, as this is about giving more influence and voice to those who are having less of it. The unfettered blooming of market forces often works against women's rights. It is important to notice that the principles which underpinned the transition of a planned economy to a market-driven economy are the same principles setting in motion the movement for gender equality. What are required are genuine political participation and representation, freedom of expressions of diversity, and the widening of choices in different socio-economic sectors. Largely because of the work of the CCP, women gained basic rights and secured education opportunities. A paradox has developed. Increasingly urban women want to realize themselves, protest against sexual discrimination, and define their emancipation on their own terms – not those of the party. Yet the CCP still thinks it has earned the right to make decisions affecting women's emancipation. This is where China stands today.

References

All-China Women's Democratic Federation (1953) Zhongguo funu yundong de zhongyao wenjian [Important documents on the Chinese women's movement], Beijing: Renmin chubanshe.

An, J. (2009) Mao Zedong yu "pilin pikong" ruogan wenti ("Certain questions regarding Mao Zedong's Campaign against Lin Biao and Confucius"), China.com.cn, September 9, www.china.com.cn/aboutchina/txt/2009-09/09/content_18495512.htm.

Attané, I. (2012) "Being a woman in China today," *China Perspectives*, No. 4: 5–15.

Barlow, T. (2004) *The Question of Women in Chinese Feminism*, Durham, NC: Duke University Press.

Becker, J. (1998) *Hungry Ghosts: Mao's Secret Famine*, New York: Henry Holt and Company.

Bernstein, T.P. (1977) *Up to the Mountains and Down to the Villages: The Transfer of Youth from Urban to Rural China*, New Haven, CT: Yale University Press.

Bo, Z. (2015) "What one new CCP appointment tells us about Chinese politics," http://thediplomat.com/tag/sun-chunlan/.

Central Committee of the Chinese Communist Party (1948) *Zhongguo gungchandang zhongyangweiyuanhui guanyu muqian xianfangqu nongcun funu gongzou de jueding* [Decision of the CCP central Committee on the present village women's work in the liberated areas], December 20.

China News Service (2013) Mao Zedong guli funu dapo fengjian zuquan ("Mao Zedong encourages women to break up feudalism and clannish domination"), June 1, www.chinanews.com/cul/2013/06-01/4882252.shtml.

China Reconstructs (1977) "Chinese women on Chiang Ching: The enemy of women's liberation," June 5.

Coonan, C. (2012) "China's most powerful woman – but how far can Sun Chunlan go?" *The Independent*, November 22, www.independent.co.uk/news/world/asia/chinas-most-powerful-woman-but-how-far-can-sun-chunlan-go-8340893.html.

Da Gong Bao (1958) "Women replace men to assist construction," November 9.

Da Gong Bao (1962) "Be concerned about women workers' thought and life," March 8.

Davis, E.L. (2005) *Encyclopaedia of Contemporary Chinese Culture*, Abingdon, Oxon: Routledge.

Deng, Y. (1949) Guanyu zhongguo funu yundong dangqian renwu de jueyi (Decision on the current tasks of the Chinese women's movement), All China Women's Federation, April 1, http://acwf.people.com.cn/GB/99061/136280/136281/8206630.html.

Dikotter, F. (2010) *Mao's Great Famine: The History of China's Most Devastating Catastrophe, 1958–62*, London; New York: Bloomsbury.

Dikotter F. (2016) *The Cultural Revolution: A People's History*, London: Bloomsbury.

Ding, L. (1942) Sanba jie yougan ("Thoughts on March Eighth"), *Liberation Daily* (Yan'an), March 9, www.douban.com/group/topic/34813403/.

Dirlik, A. (1989) *The Origins of Chinese Communism*, New York; Hong Kong: Oxford University Press, 74–94 and 217–220.

Du, R. (2006) Gaige kaifang chuqi nongcun baochan daohe de jingguo ("The process of the introduction of the household responsibility system in the villages at the early stage of the reform and open-door era"), *Guangming Ribao*, June 1, www.gmw.cn/02sz/2006-06/01/content_457857.htm.

Guangming Ribao (1957), "Do not stay in the cities and eat free meals, but go back to the countryside to be a farmer," November 25.

Hong Qi (1978) "Fully develop the great use of women in achieving the four modernizations," No. 3, 89ff.

Liaoning Ribao (1956) "Talk of figures," October 3.

Liu, L., Karl, R.E., and Ko, D. (2013) *The Birth of Chinese Feminism: Essential Texts in Transnational Theory*, New York: Columbia University Press, 179–186.

Maher, V. (2016) "Contemporary Chinese Studies: Gender, voice and change conversation with Maria Jaschok, August 2014," www.wcaanet.org/downloads/dejalu/feb2016/Anuac.pdf.

Milanovic, B. (2016) *Global Inequality: A New Approach for the Age of Globalization*, Cambridge, MA: The Belknap Press of Harvard University Press.

New China News Agency (1957a) "Non-party leaders in women's work hold forum," June 6.

New China News Agency (1957b) "Urban population of consumers in Taiyuan have returned to rural areas!" December 20.

New China News Agency (1962) "All-China Women's Federation issues notification about the commemoration of 'March 8th' 1962, International Working Women's Day," February 16.

NPC.gov.cn (2007) "Law of the People's Republic of China on the Protection of Rights and Interests of Women," December 12, www.npc.gov.cn/englishnpc/Law/2007-12/12/content_1383859.htm.

Renmin Junyi (1977) *Pipang Jiang Qing zai funu jiefang wenti shang de fandong miulun* ("Criticizing Jiang Qing reactionary fallacies on the question of women's liberation"), Vol. 3, 16–19.

Renmin Ribao (1952a) "Carry through step by step in a planned way total employment," and "Employment Decisions of the Administrative Council of the Central People's Government," August 4.

Renmin Ribao (1952b) "Announcement to the Women's Federation at all levels, ACDWF in cooperation and carrying through the Employment Decisions of the Administrative Council of the Central People's Government," August 10.

Renmin Ribao (1956a) "Protect the health of rural women and children," May 16.

Renmin Ribao (1956b) "We can't again give in when unusual things in the villages happen and women and children are injured and killed," August 12.

Renmin Ribao (1956c) "Demands by the ACDWF on a discussion meeting on village women's work for cooperation of agricultural cooperatives in using women's labour," December 28.

Renmin Ribao (1957a) "With industry and thrift build the country and manage the household and fight to build socialism," September 10 and 11.

Renmin Ribao (1957b) "Reasonably use and arrange village women's labor power," March 26.

Renmin Ribao (1958) "A further step to liberate women's labour for the sake of serving more better and quicker the construction of socialism," June 2.

Rosen, S. (1995) "Women and political participation in China," *Pacific Affairs*, Vol. 68, No. 3 (October): 315–341.

Salaff, J. and Merkle, J. (1970) "Women and revolution: The lessons of the Soviet Union and China," *Berkeley Journal of Sociology*, Vol. 15 (January): 166–191.

Shishi Shouce (1951) "Post 1945 growth of the Communist Party in China," June 5.

Tatlow, D.K. (2016) "Year after detention Chinese feminists mark setbacks and progress," *New York Times*, March 7.

The Economist (2016) "Daring to think, daring to act," July 9, www.economist.com/news/special-report/21701654-civic-engagement-all-sorts-becoming-much-more-widespread-daring-think-daring.

The Telegraph (2013) "China breaks long silence on inequality statistic," January 18, www.telegraph.co.uk/finance/economics/9810436/China-breaks-long-silence-on-inequality-statistic.html.

Thorborg, M. (1978) "Chinese employment policy in 1949–78 with special emphasis on women in rural production," in *Chinese Economy Post-Mao*, Vol. 1, Washington, D.C.: Government Printing Office, 535–604.

Thorborg, M. (1980a) *Women in Non-Agricultural Production in Post-Revolutionary China*, Dissertation, Uppsala University.

Thorborg, M. (1980b) "Women's economic position in Republican China 1911–1949," in Lanciotto, L. (ed.) *La Donna Nella Cina Imperiale e Nella Cina Repubblicana* [Women in Imperial and Republican China], Vol. 36, 123–146.

Thorborg, M. (1992) "Women under Maoism: The struggle to end discrimination Against and to introduce welfare for women workers," in Ying, C., Gransow, B., and Leutner, M. (eds.) *Frauenstudien*, München: K.G. Saur Verlag.

Thorborg, M. (ed.) (1995) *Chinese Women, An Annotated Bibliography*, Stockholm: Swedish International Development Authority, 1–129.

Thorborg, M. (2003) "Gendered notes on economic development and transition with special reference to the East of the Baltic Sea," in Knopf, K., Putensen, D., and Schneikart, M. (eds.) *Frauen im Ostseeraum* [Women around the Baltic Sea], Herbolzheim: Centaurus, 151–170.

Thorborg, M. (2004) Mänskliga rättigheter i Kina, tal vid Hearing i Sveriges Riksdag [Human rights in China speech at hearing in Swedish Parliament], May 12. Swedish Parliament, arranged by MP Göran Lindblad *et al.*, 23–28.

Thorborg, M. (2005) "Where have all the young girls gone? Fatal discrimination of daughters – a regional comparison," *China Perspectives*, No. 57 (January–February): 2–11.

Thorborg, M. (2014) *Kvinnor i Kina: pirater, järnflickor och finanslejon* [Women in China: Pirates, Iron-girls, and Financial Wizards], Stockholm: Bokförlaget Atlantis.

United Nations (1995) "Fourth World Conference on Women," September, www.un.org/womenwatch/daw/beijing/fwcwn.html.

V.ifeng.com (2010) 1950 nian jishi: Xinzhongguo diyibu "hunyinfa" ("Major events of 1950: New China's first Marriage Law"), August 31, http://v.ifeng.com/documentary/history/201008/31cbab39-6420-43c2-a6c5-4932a7aaf458.shtm.

Xin Zhongguo Funu (1959) "Talking about the new stage of the women's movement," May 19.

Xin Zhongguo Yuebao (1951) *Zhongyang renming zhengfu zhengwuyuan guanyu jiancha hunyinfa zhixing qingkuang di zhizhi* [Directive on the Investigations of the Conditions arising out of the Operation of the Marriage Law], No. 23, September 21, 1244.

Xinran (2003) *The Good Women of China: Hidden Voices*, London: Vintage Publishing, Chapter 8.

Yang, J. (2012) *Tombstone: The Great Chinese Famine 1958–1962*, New York: Farrar, Strauss and Giroux.

Zeng, Z. (2015) Wode muqin Deng Bian ("My mother Dong Bian"), Zhongguo Lunwen Net, August 10, www.xzbu.com/5/view-6888606.htm.

Zhang, C. (2004) "A study of contemporary NGOs on Chinese women," *Journal of Beijing City University*, 2: 101–103.

Zhang, Y. (1952) Guanyu dangqian funu gongzuo wenti de baogao ("A report on the issue of women's work at this moment") in *Zhang Yun Wenji* (*Selected Works of Zhang Yun*), Beijing: Zhongguo Funu Chubanshe.

Zhongyang guanche hunyinfa yundong weiyuanhui (1953) *Ganche hunyinfa yundong de zhongyao wenjian* [Important documents on the movement for a marriage law], Beijing: Renmin chubanshe, 54.

18

PUBLIC POLICY AND LGBT PEOPLE AND ACTIVISM IN MAINLAND CHINA

Elaine Jeffreys

Introduction

This chapter looks at the lack of explicit public policies relating to lesbian, gay, bisexual and transgender (LGBT) people in the People's Republic of China (PRC), and recent events and activist efforts that highlight or challenge that omission. Although the term LGBT does not specify the full range of sexual and Gender non-conforming people, it is used in this chapter as a short-hand to represent all sexual and gender minorities, in part because other possible terms such as "queer" also reference western academic theories, and do not have the same significance in China. The term "PRC" is used to refer to post-1949 mainland China. The chapter does not examine the evolution of LGBT-related policies in Hong Kong and Macau, which have different histories of social organization and LGBT activism (Engebretsen *et al.* 2015; Kam 2013; Kong 2010; Yau 2010).

While the movement for equality for LGBT people in western liberal-democratic societies has been pronounced "one of the most successful in recent history," the state of LGBT rights in China is described as "lousy" with grim prospects for LGBT people and organizations (Hong 2015). Such pessimism is associated with the authoritarian nature of the Chinese Communist Party (CCP)-state apparatus and its historical failure to acknowledge individual and sexual rights, as demonstrated by the absence of national legislation to empower LGBT people. In December 2013, however, the CCP administration accepted recommendations at the Human Rights Council of the United Nations (UN) that it establish anti-discrimination legislation to ensure that LGBT people enjoy equal treatment, and prohibit workplace discrimination based on sexual orientation and gender identity (United Nations General Assembly 2013). This has encouraged various LGBT individuals to file a series of landmark legal cases with the Chinese courts against different government departments to oppose discrimination and demand affirmative legislation. Many of these cases are managed by a loose affiliation of volunteers known as the "Rainbow Lawyers" – the rainbow is an international symbol of gay pride (Fan 2016). These efforts simultaneously highlight the emergence of an LGBT movement in China and provide a basis for domestic critique of government inaction, especially given President Xi Jinping's oft-expressed commitment to enhancing rule by law (Liebman 2014: 97).

The chapter contextualizes the emergence of LGBT activism in mainland China by first defining some key terms and explaining the CCP administration's historical lack of attention to

LGBT issues. It then explains how the development of LGBT communities, and advocacy groups, have been and are constrained by Party-state censorship of media and controls over civil sector organizations, even though homosexuality is not criminalized in Chinese law. Finally, the chapter highlights some key areas of LGBT activism in China and the associated challenges.

Background and key terms

In most western societies, it is unlawful to discriminate against or treat another person less favorably on the basis of their sexual orientation or gender identity than someone without that attribute would be treated in the same or similar circumstances (Australian Human Rights Commission 2013). Sexual orientation means a person's sexual orientation toward persons of the same sex, a different sex, or the same sex and a different sex. Common terms that are used to describe a person's sexual orientation include heterosexual/straight, homosexual, lesbian, gay and bisexual. Gender identity means the gender-related identity, appearance or mannerisms or other gender-related characteristics of a person, including how a person presents their gender which may be an identity that is neither male nor female (ibid.). Terms used to describe a person's gender identity include transgender, trans and gender diverse. Despite policy advances, inequality and prejudice persist in relation to LGBT people and there are lawful exceptions to anti-discrimination laws. Same-sex marriage is not legal in all western countries, although same-sex partnerships usually have legal protections, and the Catholic Church is permitted to employ men only as priests.

In China, there are no protective national laws and there is no national political discourse on LGBT matters; moreover, no specific Ministry or government department has responsibility for issues relating to sexual orientation and gender identity (UNDP, USAID 2014: 11). This situation, in conjunction with political controls on civil sector organizations and media censorship of sex-related content, has limited the development of LGBT culture and expression, and public discussion and advocacy on LGBT matters.

The absence of LGBT policies in mainland China reflects the historical "invisibility" of LGBT people, organizations and advocacy until recently. One way of highlighting the newness of the term "LGBT" more generally is to note that it was only included in the online Oxford English Dictionary in 2006, although the draft entry for the term indicates that it was used in a gay magazine in the early 1990s. LGBT communities and organizations have developed a strong public profile in western societies since the first major gay liberation march was held in New York in 1970. However, there is little documentation about or evidence of gay and lesbian communities in the PRC until the 1990s.

Following the founding of the PRC under the leadership of the CCP in 1949, state control of industry and allocation of resources removed the space for public discussions and expressions of sex and sexuality until after the introduction of market-based economic reforms in December 1978 (Jeffreys 2012: 2–3). During the Mao era (1949–1976), most urban Chinese spent their entire lives in the closed community of a socialist work-unit and rural agricultural producers became tied to their place of birth because the state allocated jobs, housing and social services, and therefore needed to know the identity and location of its workers. Everyday life was organized around work and collectivist political movements, and public venues were highly restricted in number until the opening-up of the country's hospitality and service industries in the late 1980s. This situation, combined with both the importance placed in Chinese culture on marriage for procreation and the establishment of a state-controlled media, literally eliminated the space for public discussions of sexual orientation and identity.

LGBT people are now a visible feature of life in the PRC, as demonstrated by the publicized release of a letter from over 190 organizations across China condemning violence based on sexual orientation, after a gunman killed 49 people in a gay nightclub in the USA in 2016 (Bai 2016). The letter added that LGBT people in China experience unacceptable violence and discrimination, as evidenced by the existence of "gay conversion therapy" and school-yard bullying of LGBT youth. As this action suggests, LGBT people are marginalized in the PRC, but they are no longer invisible or voiceless.

The growth of LGBT-friendly websites and social media since the 2000s has provided expanded means of communication and socialization for gays and lesbians, and to a lesser extent for bisexual and transgender people (UNDP, USAID 2014: 12). Large and medium-sized cities now have bars and cafés that are frequented by young urban gays and lesbians, and low- and high-end bathhouses that are patronized by older men who have sex with men but who may not self-identify as homosexual (Jeffreys and Yu 2015: 75–76). LGBT organizations can also be found in numerous cities, with organizations such as the Chinese Lala [Lesbian] Alliance holding networking, capacity building and advocacy training camps in different cities since 2007 (UNDP, USAID 2014: 50).

In 2015, Jin Xing, once China's best male dancer while performing with the People's Liberation Army troupe, and now an internationally acclaimed dancer and the married mother of three adopted children, started hosting her own television talk show, after a popular stint as a "hard" judge on China's *So You Think You Can Dance* (*Jin Xing tuokou xiu* 2015). Widespread public interest in Jin's life story has opened the space for discussions of transgender people. However, her life is typically presented in the media in terms of gender conformity – the struggle of a woman trapped in a man's body to become her true self and realize her dreams – rather than challenging the male/female gender binary (Davies and Davies 2010). Her parents' acceptance of her decision to have sex reassignment surgery and her public, rich and glamorous lifestyle also stand in marked contrast to the lives of most transgender people in China who cannot afford costly hormone replacement therapy and surgery, which are difficult to access through the state-funded health care system (UNDP, USAID 2014: 7).

Along with their growing visibility, new terms have emerged to describe LGBT people in China. The most common words used to describe same-sex attracted people are: "*tongxinglian*" (same-sex love), a term that is now primarily used by older married men who have sex with men; "*tongzhi*" (comrade), an appropriation of Chinese revolutionary modes of address that entered mainland China in the 1990s from Hong Kong-based homosexual activist groups and is now used in ways that are comparable with the English word LGBT; and the English term "gay," which gestures toward identification with global "gayness" (Jeffreys and Yu 2015: 76–77). Same-sex attracted women are often referred to as "*lala*" or "*lesi*" (both transliterations of "les/lesbian") or "lily" (*baihe*, borrowed from Japanese anime and games). The Chinese term "*ku'er*" is a homophone for "queer," which similarly refers to a range of non-heteronormative sexualities and subjectivities, but translates as "cool." It has been adopted as a marker of social distinction by alternative artists, film-makers and academics (ibid.: 78). The Chinese term for bisexual (*shuangxinglianzhe*) is a transliteration from English that is unfamiliar to most mainland Chinese (Chou 2000: 42). A 2014 UN-affiliated report on being LGBT in Asia notes that public perceptions of transgender phenomenon in the PRC refer to persons who have undergone a sex change (*bianxingren*), rather than persons who transgress gender boundaries (*kuaxingbie*), which is a term that is mainly used only by activists (UNDP, USAID 2014: 28, n35).

The PRC now also has LGBT festivals, which are designed to celebrate LGBT people and raise public awareness of LGBT issues. In 2016, the winner of the first Mr Gay China competition, a franchise from the international pageant Mr Gay World, described the event as "a great platform to raise awareness of the LGBT community" (Roxburgh 2016). A 2009 article in the *China Daily*, a state-run English-language newspaper, similarly praised the PRC's first mass

LGBT event – ShanghaiPride – for showcasing the country's social progress and raising public awareness of China's gay community ("Pride of tolerance" 2009: 8).

But people who wish to live openly as LGBT still face considerable obstacles. ShanghaiPride is typically run as a film and art festival, rather than as a street march, to avoid difficulties associated with obtaining a license for a march from police. Media censors have banned certain films from being screened at ShanghaiPride, and queer film festivals organized in Beijing since 2001 have been variously stopped by police or held in "secret" locations (Hamer 2014). Although LGBT organizations have run gay culture festivals in northeastern China since 2011, the organizer of a gay march in Hunan Province in 2013 was detained for failing to obtain permission to hold the event ("Changsha" 2013; UNDP, USAID 2014: 48). There is limited information on LGBT activities in rural and western regions of China, and a survey of some of the 27 million users on a Chinese gay dating application suggests that fewer than 5 percent of the respondents were "out" (Roxburgh 2016; UNDP, USAID 2014: 12).

The term LGBT therefore applies to people of diverse ages and socio-economic, cultural, religious and ethnic backgrounds who may experience being homosexual, gay, lesbian, bisexual and transgender, in different ways in different parts of China, with access to LGBT support networks and levels of public acceptance generally diminishing with the size of the city.

Law, science, society and censorship

In western societies, the three main goals of the push to obtain legal rights for LGBT people have been decriminalization, anti-discrimination legislation and legal recognition for same-sex partnerships respectively (UNDP, USAID 2014: 23). In the UK, for example, consensual and private homosexual acts between two men aged over 21 years were decriminalized in England and Wales in 1967 and in Scotland and Northern Ireland in the early 1980s (Bedell 2007). Homosexual sex was previously treated as an act of gross indecency, resulting in the arbitrary arrest of many homosexual men. The first gay march in the UK took place in London in 1971. The age of consent for consensual homosexual sex was lowered from 21 years to 18 years in 1994 and to 16 years in 2001 (16 is the age of consent for heterosexual sex in the UK). The British government lifted bans on lesbians and gays in the armed forces in 2000 and the first civil partnerships between homosexuals took place in 2005 (ibid.).

The Criminal Law of the PRC (1997), which was first issued in 1979 and revised in 1997, does not directly criminalize homosexuality. It prohibits violent and non-consensual sex acts, such as rape, sexual assault, forced prostitution and sex with minors (Articles 237–238 and 358). The age of consent for sexual activity is 14 years, with no restrictions on gender or sexual orientation. An amendment to Article 237 in 2015 stipulates a maximum of five years' imprisonment for indecent assault on others (male or female), whereas it previously only referred to the sexual assault of women ("Zhonghua renmin gongheguo xingfa xiuzhengan (9)" 2015: Item 13). But the Law criminalizes some acts as harmful that may limit freedom of sexual expression, such as the third-party organization of prostitution and orgies, and the manufacture and distribution of pornography (Sections 8–9 and Article 301).

Prior to 1997, homosexual men were sometimes detained by police for engaging in acts of "hooliganism" (*liumangzui*) or "other hooligan activities" (*qita liumang huodong*) based on a 1984 ruling by the Supreme People's Court (Zuigaorenminfayuan, zuigaorenminjianchayuan 1984). The ruling defined "hooliganism" in terms of fighting, looting, sexually harassing women and causing public disturbance. "Other hooligan activities" referred to group sex, the dissemination of pornography, the not-for-profit luring or sheltering of women in prostitution, the seducing of male adolescents and foreigners, the sodomy of children, the forced sodomy of juveniles and violent or non-consensual anal sex involving adults. While referring in theory to non-consensual sex acts, the police often used the category of "hooliganism" as an umbrella term for acts they deemed to be causing public disturbance or offense until it was deleted from the Criminal Law in 1997. To the extent that police targeted homosexuals, they tended to police public spaces that men who have sex with men were known to frequent to find sexual partners and engage in sex acts, such as public toilet blocks and parks (Li 2009: 86–87). Lesbianism remained a more hidden, as in non-public, practice.

The establishment of support organizations for homosexuals was also restricted by Party-state authorities. In late 1992, Wan Yanhai (2001: 60), now a renowned LGBT activist, organized a salon called "Men's World," a health promotion group for same-sex attracted men, which held a Valentine's Day celebration in 1993. While encouraging similar gatherings in other cities, the salon was promptly closed down. The Ministry of Public Security issued a document about this titled Notice on the Closure of the "Men's World" Homosexual Culture Salon (Gonganbu 1993). The Notice stated that the salon had been closed down at the request of the Ministry of Health because of public complaints. It rejected Wan Yanhai's contention that homosexuality was normal, stating instead that homosexuality was a perverse form of human behavior that violated public morality, corrupted social values, destroyed family harmony, encouraged criminality, endangered public security and contributed to the spread of AIDS. While noting that such gatherings did not comprise a form of hooliganism, the Notice concluded that similar homosexual gatherings could be investigated and closed down as "unlawful assemblies" (ibid.).

In addition to negative policing approaches, homosexuality was defined medically in terms of sexual dysfunction and mental disorder until 2001. Scholars contend that the pathologization of homosexuality in terms of deviancy, perversion and psychosexual disorder entered China from western sexology in the early- to mid-twentieth century. While medical understandings of homosexuality changed dramatically in western societies from the late 1970s onwards, they remained largely unquestioned in the more closed society of China until the 1990s (Chou 2000: 110–113).

Homosexuality was defined as a psychosexual disorder in a text published by the Chinese Society of Psychiatry in 1981, which was used as a clinical guide for the diagnosis of mental disorders. That text was retrospectively titled the first Chinese Classification of Mental Disorders (CCMD-1) in 1989, when it was replaced by the official "second" Chinese Classification of Mental Disorders (CCMD-2). The description of homosexuality in terms of mental disorder was not removed from the Chinese Classification of Mental Disorders until it was revised again in 2001 (CCMD-3) (Chinese Society of Psychiatry 2001). It is worth noting that the World Health Organization (1992) only removed homosexuality from its classification of mental and behavior disorders at the Forty-Third World Health Assembly in May 1990, with a new International Classification of Diseases coming into effect in member states in 1994. Hence, the PRC's scientific redefinition of homosexuality followed from the eventual adoption of international standards.

Despite a history of policing and medical controls, public expressions of LGBT identities in the PRC were and are constrained mainly by social expectations. Wah-Shan Chou (2000: 27) argues that, strictly speaking, there were no "homosexuals" or "bisexuals" or even "heterosexuals" in China until recently. Although some people engaged in same-sex sexual practices, Chinese society was not divided according to a homo-hetero binary as in modern western societies, and same-sex eroticism was not associated with a particular form of personality or identity. Instead, Chinese society was organized around class hierarchies and different levels of responsibilities to family and kinship networks. This meant that same-sex eroticism was tolerated to the extent that it did not interfere with the familial obligation to marry and have male children to continue the family line, and hence was publicly "invisible."

Some same-sex attracted people claim that the major problem faced by people in China who wish to live openly as LGBT is "not state oppression, religious fundamentalism, or job discrimination," but rather their relatives and peers (Chou 2001: 34). People of marrying age are pressured to get married by family, friends and work colleagues, with data from the PRC's 2010 Population Census demonstrating that fewer than 2 percent of men and women aged 40 years and over had never married (Jeffreys and Yu 2015: 15). An estimated 2 percent of LGBT people avoid heterosexual marriage by coming out to their parents (Fullerton 2015). Some avoid or delay social pressures to marry by "going out" (*chuzou*), literally moving away from their place of birth and family home, and practicing a classical Chinese aesthetic of "don't ask, don't tell" with their families and colleagues (Jeffreys and Yu 2015: 89). However, many gays and lesbians view entering a heterosexual marriage as "the right thing to do" despite their sexual orientation, and others enter marriages of convenience in order to pass as "straight" to family and work colleagues (see below).

The PRC's now defunct one-child-per-couple policy has variously eased and enhanced pressure on young LGBT people to enter a heterosexual marriage. It has ensured that some parents and grandparents are prepared to accept the non-traditional sexual and lifestyle choices of their only child/grandchild in order to retain a relationship with them (ibid.: 94). But other parents place even more pressure on an only child to marry, reproduce and otherwise lead a successful, "normal" life. This situation has trapped an estimated 16 million homosexual men and heterosexual women in marriages; comparative estimates are not available for lesbians (ibid.: 39). In the words of one self-identified Chinese gay man who says he would consider marrying a woman to please his parents: "I am not ashamed of being gay at all. I only care about my family" (Lau 2010, see Wuhan – Robin's story).

Although the PRC has legislation that includes general anti-discrimination provisions, the body of Chinese law contains no specific reference to sexual orientation and gender identity. Article 33 of the Constitution of the PRC (1982) stipulates that all citizens are equal before the law and Article 48 states that women enjoy equal rights with men in all spheres of life, and are entitled to equal pay for equal work and equal access to opportunities for work. However, the focus is on gender discrimination against women understood as a disadvantaged group by virtue of biological sex. The Labor Law of the PRC (1995) similarly prescribes that there should be no employment and workplace discrimination based on the factors of ethnicity, gender (read biological sex) and religious affiliation, and makes no reference to sexual orientation or gender identities.

Yet reports exist of bullying and discrimination against LGBT individuals in education and work situations, and of people choosing not to reveal their sexual orientation or gender identity in these contexts (UNDP, USAID 2014: 9). Such discrimination is largely hidden and unaddressed. This is because public discourse on LGBT issues has been stymied by the historical invisibility of LGBT people, and by state controls over the media and civil sector.

State controls over the PRC's media and civil sector mean that there are limited venues for positive self-presentations of LGBT issues or for organized advocacy designed to report and end discrimination against LGBT people. Mainstream media coverage of LGBT issues is often inadequate or based on stigmatizing stereotypes that associate homosexuality with deviancy and disease (ibid.: 12). Regulations issued by the State Administration of Press, Publication, Radio, Film and Television in 2006 banned the inclusion of content relating to pornography, licentiousness, rape, commercial sex, sexual perversion and sex organs ("Guojia guangbo dianying dianshi zongju ling" 2006: Article 14, Item 3). A 2008 Notice on "film and television censorship standards" added homosexual sex and masturbation to the list of banned sexual content (Zhonghua renmin gongheguo guojia xinwen chuban guangdian zongju 2008: Article 3). Although the 2008 Notice was replaced by new regulations in 2010 that make no explicit mention of homosexuality, the potential for government censorship encourages self-censorship on the part of individuals and organizations both to avoid regulatory repercussions and maintain commercial viability. This means that the majority of LGBT-themed media products and publications are independently produced and not widely circulated outside of LGBT circles (Jeffreys and Yu 2015: 82–84; UNDP, USAID 2014: 44–45).

The potential for government censorship encourages the circulation of specific types of LGBT-themed information. LGBT-related publications are usually associated with AIDS education; the few available studies of sexual and gender minorities are often published in Hong Kong or Taiwan because they are declined by publishers on the mainland (UNDP, USAID 2014: 44–45). Although the number of LGBT community websites and social networks is increasing, education- and advocacy-orientated sites practice self-censorship to avoid the risk of being shut down. Other sites are commercialized rather than advocacy-orientated in order to avoid censors and attract traffic and money from advertising (Jeffreys and Yu 2015: 82–83).

Government regulations also indirectly restrict the number and types of LGBT organizations by requiring civil sector organizations to be legally registered and comply with national policy goals, directing resources toward issues such as AIDS and excluding others. Chinese NGOs in most social issue areas have emerged and flourished "only insofar as their activities complement government interests" (Hildebrandt 2012: 853). In the case of LGBT organizations, the lion's share of international and domestic funding has gone to groups working on HIV prevention, with such groups being "loud about AIDS but quiet about other issues in order to enjoy the most political space" (ibid.). Fewer organizations focus on the lived experiences of LGBT people and encourage capacity building for new groups across the country, including in poorer regions (UNDP, USAID 2014: 19).

Bisexual and transgender organizing is chiefly conducted through online chat groups rather than offline, and groups working with transgender communities typically work with male-to-female transgender sex workers on HIV prevention (Asia Catalyst 2015). Research and organizing on intersexuality – people who have physical, hormonal or genetic features that are neither wholly female nor wholly male or a combination of female and male or neither female nor male – is even less available than it is for other LGBT groups (UNDP, USAID 2014: 28). Small LGBT organizations are often unregistered and staffed by volunteers, which enables them to pursue agendas other than those endorsed by government but also potentially weakens their sustainability (ibid.: 50). International NGOs fear that the enforcement of the Law on the Management of Overseas NGOs' Activities in Mainland China, effective January 1, 2017, will enhance existing controls and constraints.

Last, but not least, LGBT communities and organizations are recent phenomena in China; as such, they do not comprise a unified or coherent social movement. Conflicts and tensions between groups are common "due to lack of communication, mutual discrimination and the unbalanced distribution of resources" (UNDP, USAID 2014: 47; see also Hildebrandt 2012: 857). But domestic activism by and on behalf of LGBT people is taking place, as the next section explains.

Anti-discrimination and same-sex marriage

In recent years, LGBT activists have staged a series of coordinated events designed to raise public and government awareness of LGBT issues in the PRC via media publicity of landmark legal cases and innovative public advocacy. Some of these activities are detailed below. They include legal suits filed against diverse government departments for failing to restrict homophobic representations and attitudes, preventing positive self-presentations of LGBT people and denying the civil rights of same-sex couples.

In August 2015, a female university student named Chen Qiyan filed a case of administrative inaction against the Guangdong Education Department with the Beijing Second Intermediate People's Court, after a letter of complaint about a homophobic textbook that she had written to the department in March 2015 was ignored. Regulations stipulate that government departments should reply to complaints within 15 days (Xu 2015). The *Los Angeles Times* endorsed the courts' acceptance of the case as an "important step" forward for gay rights in China, while noting that a university counselor had telephoned Chen's parents about the case and informed them of her sexuality without her consent (Kaiman 2015). Chen withdrew the case later that year, telling reporters that her goal of drawing public attention to the negative impact of homophobia had been achieved (Xu 2016).

This case comprised a formal extension of earlier activism associated with International Day against Homophobia and Transphobia. Founded on May 17, 2005 to commemorate the removal of homosexuality from the WHO's International Classification of Diseases, this annual event aims to raise awareness of LGBT rights' violations worldwide (http://dayagainsthomophobia.org/). China's largest gay website, Danlan.org, launched a campaign called Expose the Homophobic Teaching Materials Around You in 2012 ("Danlan 5.17 xilie huodong" 2013). Danlan's popularity is demonstrated by its location-based flirting app, Blued, which had 27 million members in 2017 (www.blued.com/en/). Thirteen textbooks were exposed at a May 2013 press conference for including claims that homosexuality undermines social order and spreads AIDS (Yang 2013: 16–17).

In December 2015, the Beijing Number One Intermediate People's Court ruled on a landmark case filed by independent filmmaker, Fan Popo, asking the State Administration of Press, Publication, Radio, Film and Television (SAPPRFT) why trailers for his LGBT-themed documentary, *Mama Rainbow*, had been removed from video-streaming websites (Zhang Weibin 2015). *Mama Rainbow* documents the love of six Chinese mothers for their homosexual children (Fan 2012). The court determined that SAPPRFT had not issued any notice asking for the trailer to be removed. Fan hailed this ruling as a victory against government censorship and associated corporate self-censorship, because it implied that his documentary was not banned and therefore could be shown on the Internet (Zhang Weibin 2015).

In another history-making case, a labor arbitration panel in Guizhou Province ruled against China's first case of transgender job discrimination in May 2016 (Piao 2016). A man named "Mr. C" filed a suit against his employer, a health center, for wrongful dismissal at the end of a brief probation period. Mr. C argued that he was born a woman and had been denied ongoing employment for wearing male clothing to work. The court accepted instead the employers' claim that Mr. C's employment had been terminated for documented reasons of incompetency.

In yet another landmark case, a man named Sun Wenlin filed a case against the Furong Civil Affairs Bureau in Changsha City for refusing to register a marriage between him and his male partner. The court's acceptance of the case in January 2016 attracted international publicity in the wake of the June 2015 US Supreme Court ruling, which ruled that individual states in the USA could not ban same-sex marriage without abrogating constitutional guarantees of due process and equal protection under the law. President Obama described the ruling as a milestone in American justice and the White House was lit in rainbow colors to mark the administration's support of the court's decision. The ruling generated widespread interest on Chinese social media, resulting in companies such as Taobao, an online shopping platform, placing the rainbow flag on its homepages (Hewitt 2015).

In April 2016, the Changsha court rejected Sun's claim that the PRC's Marriage Law is non-gender specific and affirmed that marriage can only take place between a man and a woman according to extant law. However, the court's acceptance of the case is viewed as a milestone in terms of LGBT affirmative action on civil rights. It highlights the potential to alter regulations related to the legal registration of a marriage in China, which are administrative rather than celebratory or religious in nature (Jeffreys and Wang 2013: 349–354).

Previously, same-sex marriage had been debated in China chiefly in relation to the negative effects of family and social pressure for LGBT people to enter heterosexual relationships, rather than as a regulatory reform issue. Social pressure on men to marry for the purposes of continuing the family line has reportedly resulted in 16 million Chinese women being married to homosexual or bisexual men, with most women being unaware of their spouse's sexual orientation, at least initially (Jeffreys and Yu 2015: 39). As married women in the PRC typically use intra-uterine devices for contraception, condom use is not normally practiced in the context of marital sex with an associated potential for the spread of sexually transmissible infection. Studies of the sexual behaviors of Chinese men who have sex with men, including male-male sex workers, indicate that approximately 30 percent of such men have concurrent female partners, and nearly 77 percent have unprotected sex with primary female partners (Wang *et al.* 2015: 126–127).

Some LGBT people have responded to heteronormative social demands by entering a "cooperative marriage," that is, a marriage between two homosexuals of the opposite gender who present themselves to family and work circles as a heterosexual couple, while maintaining separate gay and lesbian sex lives. There is no detailed information available about the practical and psychological complications of performing heterosexual love in front of families and colleagues for prolonged periods, or the legal complications regarding finances and child custody should the "marriage" fail (Kam 2013: 101). But there are now websites that help individuals to find cooperative-marriage partners, and provide pre- and post-marriage advice and support. ChinaGayLes.com claimed to have had more than 400,000 registered users and assisted nearly 49,000 such marriages by 2017 (www.chinagayles.com/).

Anecdotal evidence suggests that LGBT people experience cooperative marriages in mixed ways. In a media interview, one participant described his wife as a "sister" and spoke of his love for their son, who his wife had conceived by using a plastic syringe to insert his sperm (Jeffreys and Yu 2015: 40). Conversely, cooperative marriage is described as a "nightmare" by a lesbian who experienced difficulties dealing with her partner as a "wife" and dealing with his "husband," and as "torture" by a gay man who described his "wife" as unreasonable and was pressured to have a child by both his parents and his "wife's" parents (ibid.: 92). Although cooperative marriages underscore the strong social pressure to marry, they also point to the growth of LGBT communities, a development which may limit the number of such marriages in the future.

Activists Li Yinhe and Lin Xianzhi have advocated instead for legal protections for same-sex couples during the annual meetings of the National People's Congress (NPC) and the Chinese People's Political Consultative Conference (CPPCC), the PRC's legislature and a political advisory body respectively. Li Yinhe is a famous sociologist and sexual rights' activist; her Sina.com blog alone had received nearly 100 million visitors by 2017 ("Li Yinhe de boke" 2017). Li unsuccessfully lobbied delegates at the CPPCC to consider a proposal on legalizing same-sex marriage on at least seven occasions between 2003 and 2016. Her proposal states that legalizing same-sex marriage will reduce the spread of HIV, revive China's traditional cultural acceptance of same-sex eroticism, and build the PRC's international reputation as a promoter rather than violator of human rights (Jeffreys and Yu 2015: 165). While failing to obtain formal political traction, Li's lobbying has attracted publicity and debate, being praised for demonstrating China's social progress and criticized for encouraging "abnormal" behaviors (ibid.: 165).

Li Yinhe also attracted publicity in 2014–2015 when she announced on China's Twitter-like *Weibo* that her longstanding partner is a transman (a person categorized as female at birth whose gender identity is that of a man). The *People's Daily* – the official mouthpiece of the Communist Party – responded to her revelations with support on its *Weibo*. The Editor stated that homosexuality and transsexuality are increasingly accepted in mainstream Chinese society, and that respecting one's personal views also means respecting "the choices of the Li Yinhe's among us" (Renmingwang weiping 2014).

Lin Xianzhi, a retired government official and member of PFLAG China, petitioned representatives at the NPC in 2015 to give young gay couples legal protections, while capitalizing on his son's temporary fame as a finalist in the 2015 Valentine's Day "Rainbow Love" contest hosted by Taobao (Doland 2015). Founded in 2008, PFLAG China has subgroups across the PRC (pflag.org.cn) and is an independent version of PFLAG (an acronym for Parents and Friends of Lesbians and Gays, an organization founded in the USA in the 1970s that now supports families and friends of LGBT and queer people). Taobao hosted the contest, which featured as a rotating advertisement on the Taobao homepage, through partnerships with the global marketing company China Luxury Advisors and Danlan, PFLAG China and the Beijing LGBT Center. The competition offered ten same-sex Chinese couples an all-expenses paid trip to California to get married during a group wedding there, with funding from a Chinese bedding company. Taobao users voted on the finalists based on short videos of the couples telling their stories about how they met and fell in love, and why they want to get married. Over 400 couples competed, one million people viewed the event page and more than 75,000 people voted.

Lin's actions highlight an interesting convergence of activist, parental and commercial concerns to promote LGBT rights in the formal political context of the NPC. The couples who entered the Taobao-hosted competition were recruited through LGBT networks, and had the support of families, friends and work colleagues to compete, or else were unconcerned about the social consequences of having their images and love stories presented on social and broadcast media. Lin's son entered the competition as an "out" gay with a father who openly supports his son's right to live without discrimination as a member of PFLAG China. Lin petitioned the NPC as a parent speaking for the parents of all children who worry about the future security of their child and their child's partner, and especially when their child's sexual orientation or gender identity affords them no legal protections in relation to medical care, property purchase and inheritance (Zhang Y. 2015). Here, Lin used conservative (Confucian) conceptions of family obligations to argue for improved legal protections for people in non-heterosexual relationships.

Taobao's use of advertising featuring same-sex couples demonstrates commercial interest in the Chinese "pink market" potential. Taobao representatives did not emphasize this point, saying instead that the "Rainbow Love" contest aimed to increase "respect and understanding for homosexuality, and support the realization of dreams" (Doland 2015). The company reiterated this claim by featuring the rainbow flag on its homepage following the US Supreme Court ruling. However, given the limited media and political spaces for positive self-portrayals of LGBT people in China, business interest in the pink market has the potential to open the space for public discussion of LGBT issues.

As in other parts of the world, Chinese LGBT struggles for sexual citizenship may soon become entangled with commercial interests and consumer activities. This could expand the availability of LGBT-themed venues, products and events, especially for members of younger generations. It could also generate alternative funding for LGBT events and activism via niche and cause-related marketing, and through the gradual expansion in China of corporate- and celebrity-endorsed philanthropy.

Conclusion

The preceding discussion suggests that some LGBT people in the PRC are moving away from a "don't ask, don't tell" mentality, but that the development of a more enabling environment for LGBT individuals and groups requires recognition and support from the government and private sector. In the words of one gay man: "The current situation is more and more people are becoming open-minded. But the government does not say anything good or bad about it. They just keep silent" (Lau 2010, see Wuhan – Robin's story).

Somewhat paradoxically, in a country where struggles for sexual rights are usually couched as demands for diminished Party-state intervention in the "private" domain of sexuality, this is in part a call for enhanced government intervention to realize legal and social reform. Homosexuality is neither criminalized nor a focus of religious proscriptions in contemporary China. However, government inaction on LGBT issues to date has been ensured by economic and political priorities, and conservative family and sexual mores. To the extent that government in general views changes in community public perception as a signal for regulatory change, this approach may alter in the near future. Such a shift is also indicated by the CCP administration's acceptance of UN recommendations that it establish anti-discrimination legislation to ensure that LGBT people enjoy equal treatment (United Nations General Assembly 2013).

What kind of support is required? There is a need to introduce and enforce anti-discriminatory and affirmative legislation. This would include: (1) banning stigmatizing and discriminatory practices in the media, the workplace and in schools; (2) promoting positive representations of LGBT people; (3) making same-sex couples equal to married heterosexual couples by protecting partner rights, such as joint property, hospital visits, adoption and inheritance; and (4) extending healthcare services to include the needs of homosexual, transgender and intersex people. That means training Party officials, government employees, police officers, lawyers, media professionals, healthcare providers and educators, and creating a relevant government department to oversee the introduction and implementation of such policies (UNDP, USAID 2014: 13–16).

There is also a need for the reform of regulations relating to media censorship and the registration of LGBT community and HIV prevention groups. These restrictions directly or indirectly limit the development of LGBT culture and expression, and subsequently public awareness and acceptance of LGBT people. They also limit the potential for commercial and philanthropic funding to support research that can inform community actions and policymaking, and to establish support groups for LGBT youth, transgenders, bisexuals and people living in undeveloped parts of China.

In short, overcoming the lousy state of LGBT rights in China will not happen overnight for three reasons. First, it requires the political will and funding necessary for a significant restructuring of sectors of government. Second, it demands the development of a coordinated LGBT movement with influential organizations and spokespersons, and capacity-building professionals that can both support LGBT people *and* generate community support for LGBT issues. Finally, it means developing a domestic consumer and philanthropic culture that promotes sexual diversity by providing private services and sources of funding for LGBT people, organizations and events.

References

Asia Catalyst (2015) *"My Life Is too Dark to See the Light": A Survey of the Living Conditions of Transgender Female Sex Workers in Beijing and Shanghai*, New York: Asia Catalyst.

Australian Human Rights Commission (2013) "New protection," August 1. Available at: www.humanrights.gov.au/our-work/sexual-orientation-sex-gender-identity/projects/new-protection (accessed January 22, 2017).

Bai, T. (2016) "190 Chinese LGBT groups condemn Orlando club shooting," *Global Times*, June 14. Available at: www.globaltimes.cn/content/988160.shtml (accessed January 22, 2017).

Bedell, G. (2007) "Coming out of the dark ages," *The Guardian*, June 24. Available at: www.theguardian.com/society/2007/jun/24/communities.gayrights (accessed January 22, 2017).

"Changsha – yi nanzi wei jing xuke zuzhi fandui tongxinglian qishi youxing bei juliu" [Changsha – a man is detained by police for holding a parade to protest discrimination against homosexuality without permission] (2013) *Xinhua*, May 21. Available at: http://news.china.com/domestic/945/20130521/17844850.html (accessed January 22, 2017).

Chinese Society of Psychiatry (2001) *Zhongguo jingshenzhang'ai fenlei yu zhenduan biaozhun disanban* [Chinese Classification for Mental Disorders Version 3 (CCMD-3)], Jinan: Shandong Kexuejishu Chubanshe.

Chou, W.-S. (2000) *Tongzhi: Politics of Same-sex Eroticism in Chinese Societies*, Binghamton, NY: The Haworth Press.

Chou, W.-S. (2001) "Homosexuality and the cultural politics of *tongzhi* in Chinese societies," *Journal of Homosexuality*, 40, 3–4: 27–46.

Constitution of the People's Republic of China (1982) Adopted December 4, 1982. Available at: http://en.people.cn/constitution/constitution.html (accessed January 22, 2017).

Criminal Law of the People's Republic of China (1997) Adopted by the Second Session of the Fifth National People's Congress on July 1, 1979 and amended by the Fifth Session of the Eighth National People's Congress on March 14, 1997. Available at: www.fmprc.gov.cn/ce/cgvienna/eng/dbtyw/jdwt/crimelaw/t209043.htm (accessed January 22, 2017).

"Danlan 5.17 xilie huodong: jielu ni shenbian de kongtong jiaocai" [Danlan May 17 activities: exposes the homophobic teaching materials around you] (2013) *Danlan.org*, May 25. Available at: www.danlan.org/disparticle_43578.htm (accessed January 22, 2017).

Davies, G. and Davies, M.E. (2010) "Jin Xing: China's transexual star of dance," in L. Edwards and E. Jeffreys (eds.) *Celebrity in China*, Hong Kong: Hong Kong University Press, pp. 169–191.

Doland, A. (2015) "For Valentine's Day, Alibaba helps gay Chinese couples get married in the U.S.," *AdvertisingAge*, February 12. Available at: http://adage.com/article/global-news/alibaba-helps-chinese-gay-couples-married-u-s/297108/ (accessed January 22, 2017).

Engebretsen, E., Schroeder, W. and Bao, H. (eds.) (2015) *Queer/Tongzhi China: New Perspectives on Research, Activism and Media Cultures*, Nordic Institute of Asian Studies Gendering Asia.

Fan, Popo (2012) *Mama Rainbow* – trailer, *YouTube*, May 12. Available at: www.youtube.com/watch?v=hFTVOnaixKM (accessed January 22, 2017).

Fan, Y. (2016) "Meet the lawyers fighting for LGBT rights," *Sixth Tone*, April 8. Available at: www.sixthtone.com/news/meet-lawyers-fighting-lgbt-rights (accessed August 26, 2016).

Fullerton, J. (2015) "China's attitude toward homosexuality is beginning to shift, with parents leading the way," *Vice News*, April 10. Available at: https://news.vice.com/article/chinas-attitude-toward-homosexuality-is-beginning-to-shift-with-parents-leading-the-way (accessed January 22, 2017).

Gonganbu (1993) "Guanyu qudi tongxinglian wenhua shalong 'nanren de shijie' de qingkuang tongbao" [Notice on the closure of the "Men's World" homosexual culture salon], Gong tong zi [1993] 62 hao. Available at: www.chinaacc.com/new/63%2F71%2F2006%2F3%2Fxu6735315913360023029-0.htm (accessed January 22, 2017).

Guojia guangbo dianying dianshi zongju ling: di 52 hao' [Order No. 52 of the State Administration of Radio, Film and Television] (2006) "Dianying juben (genggai) bei'an, dianying pian guanli guiding" [Regulations for the administration of the records of screenplay (outline) and films], issued April 3, 2006, effective June 22, 2006. Available at: www.sarft.gov.cn/art/2006/6/22/art_1583_26305.html (accessed January 22, 2017).

Hamer, D. (2014) "Hiding in plain sight: the Beijing queer film festival," *Filmmaker*, January 7. Available at: http://filmmakermagazine.com/88879-hiding-in-plain-sight-the-beijing-queer-film-festival/#.Vl-RsM7otjo (accessed August 11, 2016).

Hewitt, D. (2015) "US Supreme Court ruling on gay marriage prompts 'unprecedented' debate in China, gives hope to gay activists," *IBT*, June 29. Available at: www.ibtimes.com/us-supreme-court-ruling-gay-marriage-prompts-unprecedented-debate-china-gives-hope-1987592 (accessed January 22, 2017).

Hildebrandt, T. (2012) "Development and division: the effect of transnational linkages and local politics on LGBT activism in China," *Journal of Contemporary China*, 21, 77: 845–862.

Hong, B. (2015) "China has one amazing transsexual celeb – but lousy LGBT rights," *The Daily Beast*, March 28. Available at: www.thedailybeast.com/articles/2015/03/28/china-has-one-amazing-transsexual-celeb-but-lousy-lgbt-rights.html (accessed August 11, 2016).

Jeffreys, E. (2012) *Prostitution Scandals in China: Policing, Media and Society*, Abingdon: Routledge.

Jeffreys, E. and Wang, P. (2013) "The rise of Chinese-foreign marriage in mainland China (1979–2010)," *China Information*, 27, 3: 347–369.

Jeffreys, E. and Yu, H-Q. (2015) *Sex in China*, Cambridge: Polity.

Jin Xing tuokou xiu [The Jin Xing Show] (2015) *Sohu*. Available at: http://tv.sohu.com/s2014/jxtkx/ (accessed January 22, 2017).

Kaiman, J. (2015) "'An important step' for gay rights in China," *Los Angeles Times*, November 24. Available at: www.latimes.com/world/asia/la-fg-gay-rights-china-20151124-story.html (accessed January 22, 2017).

Kam, L.Y.L. (2013) *Shanghai Lalas: Female Tongzhi Communities and Politics in Urban China*, Hong Kong: Hong Kong University Press.

Kong, T.S.K. (2010) *Chinese Male Homosexualities: Memba, Tongzhi and Golden Boy*, Abingdon: Routledge.

Labor Law of the People's Republic of China (1995) January 1. Available at: www.china.org.cn/living_in_china/abc/2009-07/15/content_18140508.htm (accessed January 22, 2017).

Lau, S. (2010) "Homosexuality in China," *US-China Today*, March 10. Available at: www.uschina.usc.edu/w_usct/showarticle.aspx?articleID=14740&AspxAutoDetectCookieSupport=1 (accessed January 22, 2017).

Li, Y. (2009 [2006]) "Regulating male same-sex relationships in the People's Republic of China," in E. Jeffreys (ed.) *Sex and Sexuality in China*, Abingdon: Routledge, pp. 82–101.

"Li Yinhe de boke" [Li Yinhe's blog] (2017) *Sina.com*. Available at: http://blog.sina.com.cn/liyinhe (accessed January 22, 2017).

Liebman, B. (2014) "Legal reform: China's law-stability paradox," *Daedalus*, 143, 2: 96–109.

Piao, V. (2016) "Chinese panel rules against plaintiff in transgender job discrimination case," *New York Times*, May 10. Available at: www.nytimes.com/2016/05/11/world/asia/china-transgender-job-discrimination.html?_r=0 (accessed January 22, 2017).

"Pride of tolerance" (2009) *China Daily*, June 10, p. 8.

Renmingwang weiping [People's commentary] (2014) *People.cn*, December 19. Available at: http://weibo.com/2286908003/BBAf1EJ7W?type=comment#_rnd1464314720702 (accessed May 27, 2016).

Roxburgh, H. (2016) "Risqué business: first Mr Gay China shows new, more public face of LGBT," *The Guardian*, August 6.

UNDP, USAID (2014) *Being LGBT in Asia: China Country Report*, Bangkok.

United Nations General Assembly (2013) Human Rights Council Twenty-fifth Session Agenda Item 6: Universal Periodic Review, Report of the Working Group on the Universal Periodic Review, China (including Hong Kong, China and Macao, China), December 4.

Wan, Y-H. (2001) "Becoming a gay activist in contemporary China," *Journal of Homosexuality*, 40, 3: 47–64.

Wang, S., Song, D., Huang, W., He, H., Wang, M., Manning, D., Zaller, N., Zhang, H. and Operario, D. (2015) "Heterosexual partnerships and the need for HIV prevention and testing for men who have sex with men and women in China: a qualitative study," *AIDS Education and Prevention*, 27, 2: 126–138.

World Health Organization (1992) *The ICD-10 Classification of Mental and Behavioural Disorders – Clinical Descriptions and Diagnostic Guidelines*, Geneva: World Health Organization.

Xu, Jing (2015) "Yi wumie tongxinglian xuesheng jubao jiaocai" [Students reported textbooks for slandering homosexuals], *Guangzhou Ribao*, March 20, A16.

Xu, Xiaoyang (2016) "Yin jiaocai 'kongtong' qisu jiaoyubu zhongda nüsheng chesu: jiben suqiu yijing dadao" [The female Chinese university student who filed a case against the Ministry of Education on 'homophobic' textbooks withdrew her case because the appeal had already achieved her objectives], *Pengpai Xinwen*. Available at: www.thepaper.cn/newsDetail_forward_1421090 (accessed January 22, 2017).

Yang, J. (2013) "Activists battle to eliminate discrimination taught in schools," *Global Times*, May 24, pp. 16–17.
Yau, C. (ed.) (2010) *As Normal as Possible: Negotiating Sexuality and Gender in Mainland China and Hong Kong*, Hong Kong: Hong Kong University Press.
Zhang, Weibin (2015) "Fan Popo shengsu, fayuan de panjueshu youdian aimei" [The court ruling in favor of Fan Popo is ambiguous], *163.com*, December 6. Available at: http://news.163.com/15/1226/08/BBOH2GA100014AEE.html (accessed January 22, 2017).
Zhang, Y. (2015) "Gay marriage advocates ask legislators to present their proposals at the two sessions," *Global Times*, March 16. Available at: www.globaltimes.cn/content/912260.shtml (accessed January 22, 2017).
Zhonghua renmin gongheguo guojia xinwen chuban guangdian zongju (2008) "Guangdian zongju guanyu chongshen dianying shencha biaozhun de tongzhi" [The State Administration of Radio, Film and Television Notice on Reiterating Film Censorship Standards], March 7. Available at: www.sarft.gov.cn/art/2008/3/7/art_106_4477.html (accessed January 22, 2017).
"Zhonghua renmin gongheguo xingfa xiuzhengan (9)" [Criminal Law of the People's Republic of China Amendment (9)] (2015) Adopted by the Fifth Session of the Eighth National People's Congress on March 14, 1997 and amended by the Sixteenth Session of the Twelfth National People's Congress on August 29, 2015. Available at: http://epaper.legaldaily.com.cn/fzrb/content/20150905/Articel02002GN.htm (accessed January 22, 2017).
Zuigaorenminfayuan, zuigaorenminjianchayuan (1984) "Zuigaorenminfayuan, zuigaorenminjianchayuan guanyu dangqian banli liumang anjianzhong juti yingyong falü de ruogan wenti de jieda" [Supreme People's Court and Supreme People's Procuratorate: answers on questions about the current handling of cases of hooliganism according to law], November 2. Available at: www.chinalawedu.com/news/1200/21994/22009/2006/3/li79920231013600214-0.htm (accessed January 22, 2017).

19

THE CCP'S TIBET POLICY

Stability through coercion and development

Tsering Topgyal

Introduction

Two weeks after taking over as Party Secretary of Tibet Autonomous Region on January 12, 1989, Hu Jintao told a Beijing newspaper *Zhongguo Xinwen She* that the key priorities of his new job were to "*safeguard the unification of the motherland*, adopt a clear-cut stand to *oppose separatism, and stabilize the situation in Tibet* … [and] to continue to carry out *economic construction*, make redoubled efforts to develop the commodity economy." This came to be known as Hu's strategy of "grasping with both hands": subjugating Tibet through forceful application of security and economic instruments. During a Politburo meeting on October 19, 1989, Hu's game plan was formally unveiled (Rabgey and Sharlho 2004: 15). The new policy emphasized greater integration of Tibet to China, including bringing the monasteries and other traditional institutions under Beijing's regulation, and focused on undercutting Tibet's separate identity. This shift reflected Beijing's loss of faith in the relatively liberal policies of Hu Yaobang and Wu Jinghua, Hu's predecessor as TAR Party Secretary, which were viewed as aggravating Tibetan nationalism rather than winning their loyalty. It also signaled waning confidence in the Dalai Lama to be helpful in realizing the CCP's goals in Tibet. Hu Jintao has moved on from becoming China's president and has since retired, but the broad parameters of the policy framework that he outlined have remained constant throughout the tenure of five TAR Party Secretaries who succeeded him. Indeed, China's Tibet policy since then has closely adhered to the broad parameters of coercive stabilization and economic development. Barring a radical political break, it will remain so beyond the leadership of the current Party Secretary, Wu Yingjie. Therefore, the core argument of this chapter is that the security interests of the Chinese Party-state have been the fundamental driver of its policy in Tibet. This chapter puts "grasping with both hands" into the context of the broader policy landscape of the National Regional Autonomy system, charts the historical backdrop from which it came into being, and assesses how the strategy has been implemented in the last three decades.

Policy goals and instruments

The CCP's primary policy goal in Tibet includes securing its sovereignty, territory and strategic benefits as well as ideational values such as national identity or national unity (*minzu tuanjie*), national image, legitimacy and soft power (Carlson 2004; Topgyal 2016a: 53–88). The declaration of Tibet as a "core national interest" since 2006 confirms the importance that Beijing attaches to protecting its rule over Tibet (*Shenzhen Daily* 2012; Swaine 2010).

A range of policy instruments have been deployed in the pursuit of these objectives. The threat and use of coercive force have been enduring and well-documented features of Chinese rule. Yet, a range of subtler instruments has also been used to varying degrees of success to meet the Party-state's security objectives. Introduced at various historical junctures since the incorporation of the Tibetan regions into the PRC, most of these instruments pre-date the policy shift in 1989. The prominence of some instruments may have waned over time in the overall repertoire, but the CCP continues to draw upon them. The Nationality Identification Program is illustrative. Although the main work of identifying nationalities was done in the 1950s by "ethnographers" using Stalin's definition of nationhood, Chinese authorities continue to exploit the project to buttress China's case. For instance, in the wake of the Tibetan protests in 2008, Zhu Xiaoming, deputy director of the Beijing-based China Tibetology Research Center and former official in the United Front Department, criticized the Tibetan demands for administrative unification with this argument: "Besides, the Qinghai–Tibet Plateau is actually a multi-ethnic region. Apart from Tibetans, there have been more than ten ethnic groups living on the plateau for generations, such as Han, Hui, Mongolian, Tu, Monba and Lhoba" (Xinhua News Agency 2008). This confirms Zhao's argument that Beijing's aim behind the Nationality Identification Project was to "obfuscate" and negate the aspirations of the non-Chinese minorities (Zhao 2004: 180). Similarly, the affirmative action policies that were introduced during the National Frontier Defense Work Conference in 1979 persist prominently in both official and popular Chinese discourses on Tibet and the Tibetans (Sautman 1998). Chinese officials and people frequently remind the Tibetans of the preferential treatment they receive and accuse them of being ungrateful; they advertise these points when confronted by criticism from third parties. Maoist-style political campaigns of mass mobilization and ideological indoctrination have remained a constant feature right up to the time of completing this chapter (Smith 2008: 165–197). However, the instruments that have most defined Beijing's Tibet policy since 1989 have been the coercive forces (People's Liberation Army, People's Armed Police, Public Security Bureau and police and the wider surveillance apparatus), economic development and political campaigns. The United Front strategy has also been used against exiled Tibetans and the Dalai Lama, but it is beyond the remit of this chapter. However, these instruments are being deployed within the broader legal and political context of the National Regional Autonomy system. Different sections of this chapter will demonstrate the widened gap between the legal provisions of autonomy and the reality of its practice in Tibet in the functional areas of administration and political representation, culture (religion and language), education and economy. All these areas fell under the axe of the hard-line shift in policies.

National Regional Autonomy system in Tibet

National Regional Autonomy (NRA) has been the most prominent and enduring element of China's nationality policy. NRA derives its legal strength from the Regional National Autonomy Law (Autonomy Law) as per Article Four of the PRC Constitution. Article Four provides:

> Regional autonomy is practised in areas where people of minority nationalities live in compact communities; in these areas organs of self-government are established for the

exercise of the right of autonomy. All the national autonomous areas are inalienable parts of the People's Republic of China. The people of all nationalities have the freedom to use and develop their own spoken and written languages, and to preserve or reform their own ways and customs.

Despite being contiguous to each other, Tibetan areas have been divided into one Tibet Autonomous Region (TAR), ten Tibetan Autonomous Prefectures (TAP) and two Tibetan Autonomous Counties (TAC). The Tibetan areas of Kham and Amdo were organized into TAPs and TACs in Qinghai, Gansu, Sichuan and Yunnan provinces by 1956 (Sorensen and Phillips 2004: 9). TAR, corresponding to the areas under the rule of the Dalai Lama before 1950 (Central and Western Tibet), was formally established on September 1, 1965. The Party-state's security is the raison d'être of the NRA system. A White Paper on autonomy in TAR claims: "To institute regional ethnic autonomy in Tibet is the natural requirement for safeguarding national unification and national solidarity, and for the equal development and common prosperity of the Tibetan people and people of other ethnic groups in China" (State Council 2004). We now turn briefly to discuss the written and practical realities of autonomy as experienced by the Tibetans in the areas of administration and representation.

Administrative autonomy and political representation

The Constitution and the Autonomy Law specify that the People's Congresses and Governments are the organs of autonomy with the power to enact autonomy regulations and specific regulations consonant with the local political, economic and cultural characteristics of the nationality or nationalities in that jurisdiction. Since TAR was established in 1965, the number of Tibetan cadres has steadily increased, as Table 19.1 shows.

The number of Tibetans in the Party increased from 7 in June 1956, to 3,000 in 1963, to 40,000 in 1988, to 57,000 in 1991 (He 2005: 76). Government employment is certainly remunerative for the individual cadres and their families, but increases in their numbers do not translate into greater self-rule for the Tibetans as a group. Although Beijing brandishes these figures as proof that Tibetans enjoy genuine autonomy, they are problematic for a number of reasons.

Table 19.1 Tibetan cadres in TAR

Year	*No. of Tibetan cadres*	*Percentage*
1965	7,508	32.9
1978	20,023	44.5
1981	29,406	54.4
1994	37,000	66.6
2005	49,752	73.88
2014	110,000	70.00

Source: The State Council Information Office of the People's Republic of China, "Successful Practice of Regional Ethnic Autonomy in Tibet," Beijing, September 2015.

Note
The figures for 2005 and 2014 include non-Tibetan minority cadres.

First, even Chinese scholars agree that

> most high-ranking Tibetan cadres wield only titular power. Candidates for the chairpersons of the TAR are chosen by Central leaders, while TAR Party Secretaries are appointed by central Party leaders and are non-Tibetans. ... Only regional government leaders are Tibetans...
>
> *(Dodin 2008: 195–197; He 2005: 76)*

Second, the Tibetans are better represented in cultural and religious institutions with less political power, and less well represented in the most powerful Party and state institutions, such as the Tibetan Party Committee, People's Congress and government (He 2005: 77). Third, the centrality of security, with emphasis on open-ended themes like stability and anti-separatism and the disproportionate influence of the PLA and internal security agencies, are curtailing Tibetan autonomy. Tibetan officials complain that even demanding Tibetan language education and its use in public life invites accusations of separatism. In his letters to Hu Jintao, Phunwang (2007: 78), the veteran Tibetan revolutionary, denounced this obsession with stability and anti-separatism as "residual leftist opportunism." Consequently, anti-separatism and anti-Dalai Lamaism has become a " 'money-earning tree' for some departments to keep on asking for funds from the Central Government." On the other hand, Tibetan cadres cannot articulate Tibetan interests publicly for fear of being branded "separatists" or associated with the "Dalai clique."

The quantity of laws and regulations passed in the local People's Congresses are as misleading as the number of Tibetan cadres. The 2015 White Paper on "Regional Ethnic Autonomy System" claims that as of 2014, 300 local laws and regulations have been enacted by TAR (123 local regulations; 148 "resolutions and decisions that have the same legal standing as regulations"; 29 "regulations, resolutions and decisions it ratified were repealed by the National People's Congress"). These laws and regulations are only formalistic repetitions of national or provincial laws, not separate legislations by the local autonomous organs. In fact, not a single piece of separate autonomous legislation has been passed successfully in any of the five autonomous regions of China. This is perhaps because of the requirement of approval by higher executive and legislative bodies, which are dominated and controlled by Han Chinese, of local legislations to become laws, and the asymmetric state-versus-nationality conflicts of interest built into the NRA system (Heberer 1989: 52). When the TAR Regional People's Congress in Lhasa legislated a basic law for TAR in the 1980s, as the Constitution and Autonomy Law provide for, 15 draft versions were rejected by the National People's Congress (NPC) Standing Committee in Beijing before it was abandoned (Davis 2007: 161). The unitary self-image of the Party-state and its unilateral practices frequently trump Tibetan autonomy.

Perhaps the most symbolically telling statistic is that a Tibetan has never been appointed TAR Party Secretary, the most powerful regional position. Tibetans have been appointed as heads of the regional government, but they play second fiddle to the Party Secretary who supervises all "political and administrative work" in Tibet and is accountable only to Beijing. All but one TAR Party Secretary have been Han Chinese with a reputation for hostility toward the Tibetans' separate identity and interests. As one analyst puts it, this renders autonomy "only theoretical" (Dodin 2008: 195). Wu Jinghua (1985–88), an ethnic Yi official, was exceptional in winning Tibetan approval for his relatively liberal attitude and respect for Tibetan culture (Panchen Lama 1987). In minority regions, the ethnicity of the Party Secretary makes both perceptual and practical differences.

The institutional context of making Tibet policy, over and above the regional government and its "autonomous" organs, clearly reveals the salience of security as the key driver of policy.

In the post-Mao era, the United Front Department has been the nominal manager of China's policy toward the Dalai Lama and Tibetan exiles. However, decision-making has been much more crowded with the involvement of the PLA, Public Security Bureau, Ministry of National Security, Foreign Ministry and the State Council. Above the United Front, a Central Leading Group (also known as "Leading Small Group") has been instituted to give overall direction and coordination to Tibet policy-making at the highest level. Headed by the chairperson of the Chinese People's Political Consultative Conference (CPPCC), the Central Leading Group includes the head of the United Front Department, Minister of Public Security and the Foreign Minister (Rabgey and Sharlho 2004: 33). The perpetual involvement of the PLA and the internal security apparatus in Tibet is an impediment to the exercise of autonomy in Tibet. Possibly, it contributes to the hard-line positions in the dialogue process as the military has increasingly taken tougher stances on key issues than the government (Wu 1998: 139). Above the Central Leading Group, the general policy direction is set during Tibet Work Forums, through which the Party General Secretary, President and Prime Minister exercise overall control. In short, these institutional hurdles, concentration of power in the Party and Beijing, the obsession with unitary statehood, and the political climate of fear and suspicion turn Tibetan autonomy into an Orwellian exercise. Chinese security fears perpetuate this condition. The patriarch Deng Xiaoping emphasized the overriding primacy of stability, i.e., security over ethnic interests, leading one Chinese scholar to argue that the Dengist model of autonomy "may override the need to protect some rights of autonomy." This observation extends to all functional areas of autonomy in most Tibetan regions, including Tibetan Buddhism, language and education, where the disconnect between legal provisions and practical realities is gaping. The following passage from a missive that Chen Kuiyuan – who succeeded Hu Jintao as TAR Party Secretary in March 1992 – sent to Beijing is representative of the Chinese attitude toward Tibetan Buddhism in particular and toward Tibetan culture generally:

> The continuous expansion of temples and Buddhist monks and nuns should be contained. We shall not allow religion to be used by the Dalai clique as a tool for their splittist activities. This is an outstanding and key issue concerning party construction in Tibet. Under the precondition that we shall rely on education, we shall also take some forceful measures to stop this perverse trend.
>
> *(Chen 1994)*

The escape of high reincarnate lamas such as the Karmapa and Arjia Rinpoche, the on-going (second) crackdown on the sprawling Larung Gar and Yachen Gar Buddhist institutes, unending anti-Dalai Lama campaigns, the spate of self-immolations by monks and nuns (initially, but later joined by lay Tibetans), the regulations governing the selection and education of reincarnate lamas, and the securitization of monastic life in general are all manifestations or consequences of the policies that express such attitudes (for detail on these, see Topgyal 2016a, 2016b). The policies instituting Mandarin Chinese as the language of education and demoting Tibetan language in all Tibetan regions and the consequent student protests are no less illustrative of this. Indeed, in all functional areas, Tibet has far less autonomy than any of the Chinese regions.

Implementing "grasping with both hands"

The application of the dual strategy of enforcing economic development and stability has been reasonably successful insofar as Tibet has not spiraled completely out of control, despite the persistence of grave problems in the region. This section fleshes out the implementation of the policy in the post-1989 period.

Stabilizing Tibet and stemming the frequent Tibetan protests and riots in Lhasa preoccupied Hu Jintao well into the early 1990s. A number of coercive steps were taken, ranging from a massive show of PLA force, arrests and incarceration, introduction of an identity card system (*shengfenzheng*), a widespread drive to identify anti-Chinese elements in the Party and government, a political campaign of "screening and investigation" [གཙང་བཤེར་དང་ཞིབ་བཤེར་] and the expulsion of monks and nuns from their monasteries and nunneries and foreigners from Tibet (Barnett 2003: 229–230; Schwartz 1994: 168–182; Shakya 1999: 431–433). Under martial law, Major General Zhang Shaosong, Political Commissar of the Tibet Military District, was in charge of stabilizing Tibet. The PLA presence in Lhasa was beefed up with reinforcement from other parts of Tibet and China under the Chengdu Military Region, who subjected the Tibetans to frequent demonstrations of threatening military power. Although martial law was lifted on May 2, 1990, the threat and use of state violence has been ever present. Military intimidation was accompanied by the trial and sentencing of participants in the protests and riots for a range of violent and non-violent political offenses, with the rioters receiving stiffer sentences. Between 1987 and 1991, over 3,000 Tibetans were held under detention without trial and 179 Tibetans received prison sentences (Barnett 2003: 319). Chinese court documents attested to the incarceration of state employees and Party members who participated in the protests (Schwartz 1994: 169–170).

Simultaneously, there was a vigorous two-stage campaign of "screening and investigation" involving work units, government departments and neighborhood committees to ferret out "those who plan behind the scenes to cause disturbances," "those who command the organizations," the ringleaders and principal members of "secret counter-revolutionary organizations" and "instigators of evil counter-revolutionary propaganda" – in short, anti-Chinese protesters and sympathizers within the state and Party hierarchy and beyond ("Work Plans of the Regional Party and the Regional People's Governments for Resolutely Striking Splittists and Other Serious Criminals through Screening and Investigation"; see Schwartz 1994: 235–243 for translation). The monasteries and nunneries in and around Lhasa, besieged by armed PLA soldiers since the imposition of martial law, were also subjected to "screening and investigation." By April 1990, 200 monks and nuns were expelled from their religious institutions and prohibited from performing religious duties outside their homes, forcing many of them to escape to Nepal and India (Human Rights Committee of LAWASIA and TIN 1991: 18–19). Perceiving that the presence of foreign tourists and journalists emboldened the Tibetans, and in order to prevent information about the crackdown from getting out, they were expelled, some of them at gunpoint, and prohibited from reentering Tibet. These measures constituted what the Chinese authorities of the time referred to as a move from "passive" or reactive policing to "active" or preemptive policing. By the time Chen Kuiyuan became TAR Party Secretary in March 1992, these measures successfully ended major protests in Tibet. As altitude sickness forced him to spend about five months each year in Beijing, Hu Jintao "left no lasting impact on Tibet" (Nathan and Gilley 2002: 69). Chen inherited the policy of "grasping with both hands," which he implemented with notorious harshness toward Tibetan identity and aspirations. This shows that while policies were formulated in Beijing, Party Secretaries have scope for personalizing the implementation with either positive or negative implications for the Tibetans.

Chen Kuiyuan, Third Tibet Work Forum and economic development

Economic development has always been part of the policy mix since the reform era began. The Second Tibet Work Forum in 1984 made economic development the cornerstone of Beijing's

Tibet policy – "to get rich as soon as possible" was the slogan. Hu Jintao had also arrived with a program of investment and commodity market expansion in Tibet. Under the more stable conditions, Chen Kuiyuan could focus attention on economic development, buoyed by Deng's famous Southern Tour to promote economic reforms in early 1992 and the availability of growing economic resources to spend in Tibet. However, what was different about the push for economic development this time was its explicit linkage with security: "raising the standard of living ... as a way to dilute Tibetan nationalism" (Barnett 2003: 231; Goldstein 1997: 95). This was no doubt influenced by the Marxist economic-determinism which held that ethno-national identity and religious belief, features of a premodern stage of socio-economic development, will wither away in the course of modernization. Chen proved to be a staunch believer in economics as the panacea against Tibetan nationalism (BBC SWB 1994a). Economic backwardness, he added, made the Tibetans succumb to their "religious illusion" and strengthened their "splittist" ideas. Chen's ideas were entirely in sync with the prevailing attitude in Beijing.

The Party's Central Committee organized the Third Work Forum in Beijing in July 1994 to formulate the work program in Tibet for the next five years. It was presided over by Premier Li Peng and attended by General Secretary Jiang Zemin, CPPCC Chairman Li Ruihuan, then Vice-President Hu Jintao and Chen Kuiyuan, among other national and regional officials. The Forum set out two main goals for the next five years (BBC SWB 1994b). First on the cards was rapid economic development, to achieve 10 percent economic growth per year and double Tibet's GDP by 2000. A program of 62 developmental projects worth 2.38 billion Renminbi (RMB) (US$270 million) was unveiled. The first stock exchange in Lhasa was opened to expand TAR's market economy. There was also a visible shift in emphasis from agricultural development to energy and light industry and infrastructure. The second element of the Third Work Forum was the strict enforcement of stability, which called for a wide-ranging effort against Tibetan nationalism. This included "resolute opposition" against separatists, the purging of cadres in the state and Party hierarchy who had shown the slightest signs of "local nationalism," and a renewed campaign against the Dalai Lama's spiritual and political authority. Recognizing the central role of culture in Tibetan nationalism, there was also a vigorous effort to chip away at the distinctiveness of Tibetan identity. Jiang Zemin exhorted in his address, "[I]t is also necessary [for the Tibetans] to absorb the fine cultures of other nationalities in order to integrate the fine traditional cultures with the fruits of modern culture" (BBC SWB 1994b). Here, it is important to remind ourselves of the security instrumentality of economic development in China's Tibet policy. The issue of Chinese migration into Tibetan areas, which has been an integral element of the economic development strategy, is illustrative in this regard.

The decision to open Tibet for business and economic activities by Han and Hui Chinese was taken deliberately during the Second Tibet Work Forum in 1984, despite opposition from Tibetan officials. Since then, Beijing has consistently refused to regulate and restrict, let alone terminate, the flow of non-Tibetans into Tibet. Consequently, a large number of legal and illegal Han and Hui migrants have since flooded and dominated economic life in the major urban centers of Tibet. The Qinghai–Tibet railway line, inaugurated in 2006, has only stacked the demographic odds further against the Tibetans. The policy of deliberate settlement to encourage or enable migration is consistent with the security and nation-building rationale of packing in as many nationalities, and ideally Han Chinese, as possible in any one autonomous entity. Chinese migrants, legal or illegal, will be a more formidable pro-Chinese constituency, which would be useful in obfuscating Tibetan aspirations and supplement the coercive role of the security forces. These migrants are also expected to have a "modernizing" influence upon the Tibetans, so that the latter will be less enamored by monks and lamas (Goldstein 1997: 96). This is consistent with the frequent call by Chinese leaders for the Tibetans to "absorb the fine cultures of other nationalities" or to engage in "cultural exchanges" with the mainland. At the same time, Chinese migration curtails the Tibetans' ability to practice regional autonomy in the economic field. Better-educated, better-skilled and better-connected Chinese dominate economic and political power in Tibet.

Security was also the central rationale behind the Western Development Campaign (*xibu dakaifa*), the flagship project of Beijing's economic development strategy in Western China, which was officially launched in 2000. The Western Development Campaign (WDC) is an extension of the existing economic development strategy with higher levels of urgency, investment and a wider participation base, including other Chinese provinces. As Fischer and others have shown, WDC has a programmatic bias toward "hard" or physical infrastructure building, at the expense of developing human resources or soft infrastructure (Fischer 2005: 33–58). Chinese officials and scholars have openly confirmed that security considerations were central to the inception and implementation of WDC in Tibet (Shan and Clarke 2011; Wang and Bai 1991).

The policy of "grasping with two hands" was extended during the Fourth Tibet Work Forum held in Beijing over June 25–27, 2001 (Xinhua News Agency 2001). Jiang Zemin identified "two major issues" to be "resolved" in his speech: "The first issue is to accelerate development, and the tasks relating to economic and social development remain arduous. The second issue is to promote stability." He was clear about the security rationale: "[T]he development, stability and safety of Tibet is related to the strategic implementation of great western expansion, to national unity and social stability, to the unification and security of the motherland, and to our national image and international struggle." Development, stability and security were also the central themes in the Fifth and Sixth Tibet Work Forums held in 2010 and 2015.

It is clear that economic development has been a centerpiece of China's Tibet policy throughout the post-Mao period and, unsurprisingly, Beijing invokes it as the main legitimizing factor in its rule over Tibet. In statistical terms, rapid progress has been made and the living standards of the Tibetans have been visibly raised. TAR's GDP increased from 91.18 million RMB in 1998 to 138.73 million RMB in 2001, with an annual growth rate of 17.4 percent (Chinese Statistical Yearbook (CSY) 2002: tables 3–1 and 3–9; and CSY 2001, 2000 and 1999). After posting negative growth until 1995, the annual percentage change in real per capita GDP grew 8.7 percent in 1996 and registered double-digit growth ever since, with 16.3 percent in 2001 (Fischer 2005: 23). In 2007 TAR's GDP was 34.22 billion RMB, with a growth rate of 14 percent over the previous year (Statistics Bureau of Tibet Autonomous Region and Tibet Survey Organization of the National Bureau of Statistics 2008). The official GDP figure for 2016 was 114.8 billion RMB, representing a growth rate of 11.5 percent (Xinhua News Agency 2017).

As admirable as these statistics sound, they mask some unsavory realities. TAR's economy is so heavily and increasingly dependent upon subsidies from Beijing that some Chinese economists have dubbed it a "blood-transfusion economy" (Wang and Bai 1991). By the mid-1990s the rate of subsidization was around 45 percent of TAR's GDP, rising to 71 percent in 2001 and almost 75 percent in 2003 (Fischer 2005: 59). Hence, the main source of the scintillating GDP growth in TAR is direct central subsidies and government spending. Government officials and Chinese nationalists make much of these subsidies, but such high levels perpetuate inefficiencies and distortions with grave implications for long-term growth prospects. More government spending in TAR goes toward capital construction and government administration, including a large portion for the internal security apparatus, and less toward education, health and agriculture, relative to national spending on these sectors. In 2001, 33.3 percent of government expenditure in TAR went toward infrastructure-building, such as the Qinghai–Tibet railway, 14 percent to government administration and only 8.5 percent to education, compared to the national figures of 12.5 percent, 9 percent and 15.5 percent respectively (Fischer 2005: 63–65). At the least, these spending priorities foster the perception that Beijing is more interested in controlling Tibet than improving the condition of the Tibetans. Furthermore, because most of the subsidy and government spending go into capital construction and administration, the investment makes its way back to China in the form of contracts for Chinese-owned or state-owned construction companies or as wages for laborers from China, leading Fischer to label Beijing's economic support to Tibet as "Boomerang Aid." Furthermore, most of the development is concentrated in the urban centers of Tibet where most of the Chinese migrants reside, and away from the rural areas where 85 percent of the Tibetans live. As Yeh (2013) argues, development in Tibet imposed by the Chinese is "both present and poison." For these reasons, economic development has become a part of the problem rather than the panacea that the CCP takes it for.

Political campaigns

As mentioned in the previous section, Tibetan culture, especially as it relates to Tibetan Buddhism, is seen as the basis of Tibetan nationalism and a security threat to the CCP administration. The Dalai Lama and what the Chinese call the "Dalai clique" abroad and "separatists" in Tibet were singled out for particular hostility. As Chen Kuiyuan said in a speech to important non-Party personalities in Tibet:

> Outside the region, there are the Dalai clique and its Western supporters; within the region, there are splittists and their behind-the-scenes sympathizers. They will seize every opportunity to make trouble. It is obvious to all that class struggle is far from being over in Tibet.
>
> *(BBC SWB 1997)*

To combat these domestic and exile enemies, the Tibetans were subjected to a number of political campaigns particularly after the mid-1990s.

Mass political campaigns have been recurrent features of Chinese politics since 1949. These campaigns invariably assume ethnic dimensions in minority regions. Patriotic Education campaigns, Strike Hard campaigns, Spiritual Civilization campaigns and anti-Dalai Lama campaigns have been conducted continuously since the mid-1990s in Tibet. Without exception, they evolve into campaigns against the Dalai Lama and elements of Tibetan identity under the cloak of anti-separatism. The case of the Patriotic Education campaign (PEC) in Tibet is instructive. As Smith writes, "In Tibet, the purpose of the campaign was to transform Tibetan national identity into Chinese identity, to eradicate Tibetans' loyalty to the Dalai Lama, and to cultivate Tibetan loyalty to China instead" (Smith 2008: 170). PEC was initially conducted all over China after the Tiananmen Square Massacre. It "represented a state-led effort to rebuild the legitimacy of the [CCP] … on the basis of non-Communist ideology rather than Marxism or anti-traditional iconoclasm…" (Zhao 1998: 296). Two dominant themes of the campaign were (Han) Chinese tradition and history (especially of the CCP and its achievements) and national unity and territorial integrity (BBC SWB 1994a). In Tibet, when the campaign was first launched in 1996, monks and nuns were special targets because of the centrality of religion to Tibetan national identity. The main goals of PEC in Tibet have been to undermine the influence of the Dalai Lama, to teach the Chinese version of Tibet's history to the Tibetans, and to promote atheism and materialist values (TAR Leading Committee for Patriotic Education in Monasteries 2002a, 2002b). Tibetan students, officials and others were subjected to PEC as were Party officials in TAR. Cadres and students have been prohibited from visiting monasteries or demonstrating religious faith, such as taking religious objects to work and taking part in religious festivals. In 1998 and 2000, Tibetan cadres were told to withdraw their children from exile schools or lose their jobs and pension, so that they would not be corrupted with separatist thoughts. Although PEC was declared officially over in China itself in 2000, it is still being actively conducted in the Tibetan regions, sometimes with disastrous consequences such as self-immolations.

To complement PEC, the Spiritual Civilization campaign was launched in the mid-1990s to promote socialist spiritual civilization and to eradicate "feudal thinking, superstition and outdated conventions and bad habits": euphemisms for Tibetan traditions (BBC SWB 1996). The Strike Hard campaigns targeted "separatists and serious criminals" (Dillon 2001: 19). The anti-Dalai Lama campaign was launched in January 1995 and continues to this day, during which the Dalai Lama is subjected to demonization unprecedented since the Cultural Revolution (Rabgey and Sharlho 2004: 17).

"Grasping with both hands" after 2008

In March 2008, Tibetans rose up in an unprecedentedly widespread uprising against Chinese rule. From March 10–14, Tibetan monks and nuns in Lhasa carried out peaceful marches to commemorate the anniversary of the March 10, 1959 uprising. Invariably, the security forces broke up the peaceful rallies with brutality, but on March 14, the Tibetans turned violent and attacked Chinese migrants and their businesses and government properties. The Chinese government claimed that 18 civilians and one policeman died and 382 civilians were injured on March 14, 2008 (*People's Daily* 2008, 2009). The Tibetan Government-in-Exile (TGIE) and rights groups claimed that 220 Tibetans were killed, 5,600 arrested, 1,294 injured, 290 sentenced and over 1,000 disappeared in the ensuing crackdown (Central Tibetan Administration 2009; Voice of America 2009). The Tibetans attributed the protests to the "deep-rooted resentment of the Tibetan people" against the "flawed and repressive policies" (Private Office of His Holiness the Dalai Lama 2008). The Chinese authorities claimed to have "plenty of evidence" proving that the uprising was "organized, premeditated, masterminded and incited by the Dalai Lama clique" (*China Daily* 2008). Then Party Secretary of Tibet Zhang Qingli went so far as to call the Dalai Lama "a wolf in monk's robes, a devil with a human face but the heart of a beast." *Tibet Daily* quoted Zhang as saying that "we are now engaged in a fierce blood-and-fire battle with the Dalai clique, a life-and-death battle between us and the enemy" (Associated Press 2008). To date, the Chinese authorities have not produced credible evidence to back up that claim. Be that as it may, the Chinese authorities stepped up the strategy of buying Tibetan acquiescence with wealth and tightening the security noose even further (Smith 2010; Topgyal 2011).

Effectively, martial law was imposed in Lhasa and overwhelming military and paramilitary force was used in other Tibetan regions (Chang 2008; Miles 2008) to quell the rebellion. Using CCTV clips, images from other surveillance devices, and intelligence gathered through a network of human spies, paramilitary forces conducted multiple raids across Tibet to arrest those who were believed to have participated in the protests and riots. A considerable number of intellectual, literary, cultural, artistic and business personalities, including a number of state employees and Party members, were also detained, interrogated and incarcerated. A full-scale information blackout, tourism block-out and media censorship was imposed in Tibet, while the Chinese State media went into full gear with its domestic and international propaganda. Monasteries and nunneries were blockaded and PEC and anti-Dalai Lama campaigns were intensified all over Tibet, further aggravating Tibetan resentment. The suffocating restrictions on religious and cultural practices provoked various forms of Tibetan resistance ranging from the celebration of identity to the spate of self-immolations (Topgyal 2016b; Woeser 2016). Between February 2009 and 2016, at least 146 Tibetans self-immolated in Tibet.

At the same time, the reliance on economic development as the second plank of Tibet policy remained. The Fifth Tibet Work Forum was held in Beijing in January 2010 when development and stability were the overriding themes (Congressional-Executive Committee on China 2010). Calling Tibet a "special contradiction" with implications for national unity, social stability, national security and foreign relations, Hu Jintao told the gathering that the focus of Tibet work must be to promote "development by leaps and bounds and long-term stability." Chen Quanguo, who succeeded Zhang Qingli as TAR party boss, began his term in September 2011 by vowing to pursue development and stability (Associated Press 2011).

Chen set about immediately to harden the policy of enforcing security and throwing money at the Tibet problem. Chen's first inspiration appears to be a classified speech given by then President Hu Jintao on the so-called "four stabilities" in Tibet – internet control in towns and in the rural areas; strengthening the management of news media; striking hard against the crime of creating and spreading rumors through the internet and text messaging; and stricter regulation of foreign visitors (*Tibet Daily* 2012a, 2012b). Tibetans from eastern Tibet also faced stricter travel restrictions to Lhasa and other TAR regions from March 2012. These measures gave rise to the slogan that "stability overrides all" (*wending yadao yiqie*). China has effectively declared all-out war on Tibetan freedom of expression and information with special focus on what Chen Quanguo referred to as ensuring "the absolute security of Tibet's ideological and cultural realm" (Human Rights Watch 2012). This strategy was designed to cut off the access of Tibetans to information and content over which the CCP and the Chinese government do not have control, particularly from the Dalai Lama and other external sources. It called for intensified surveillance and censorship over the Tibetan use of the internet, texting, phone ownership, music publishing and photocopying. At the same time, the authorities intensified the broadcasting of state propaganda via new TV channels, village education sessions, film screenings, books and satellite television receivers programmed to receive only government channels (for details, see Human Rights Watch 2012). As Chen told *Tibet Daily* on November 18, 2011, these steps were meant to "enable the voice of the Party and government to cover the whole of this vast [TAR] ..." and "to effectively purify the public opinion environment ... and strike hard at separatist elements entering Tibet to carry out reactionary propaganda." He exhorted officials in June 2012 to "make sure that the Central Party's voices and images can be heard" and that "no voices and images of enemy forces and Dalai clique can be heard and seen." In a demonstrably ingenious career move, Chen once again latched onto a speech that the newly installed President Xi Jinping made by writing an essay titled "Ensuring the Security of Tibet's Ideological Realm with the Spirit of Daring to Show The Sword – Conscientiously Studying and Implementing the Important Essence of the Speech Made by the General Secretary Xi Jinping at the National Propaganda and Ideology Work Conference" in the Party's theoretical journal *Qiushi* ("Seeking Truth") (see the translation by *High Peaks, Pure Earth* in Chen 2013). Tibet, he claimed, "is at the forefront of the anti-separatist struggle" and in the "teeth of the storm in the struggle of [*sic*] the ideological realm" between the Party and "hostile forces" colluding with the "clique of the fourteenth Dalai Lama." In this ideological war-effort, Chen called for a number of steps. Referring to the traditional and online media as the "two battle-fields," he ordered the replication of the so-called "inter-locking directorate" in the virtual reality by inserting "CCP branches (Party groups) ... at all websites." He insisted that the monopoly over and control of the state media and public opinion should be strengthened, boosting the training and deployment of propaganda and ideological cadres, and saturating the local media and websites with positive stories about the CCP and the Chinese government, while keeping out or refuting the separatist activities and voice of the Dalai Lama clique and exposing and criticizing their advocacy of the "Middle Way," "Greater Tibet" and "genuine autonomy." Chen did not stop at attempting to neutralize the internet, airwaves and print media.

As part of an elaborate program known as "Stability Maintenance," three highly intrusive systems have been implemented since 2011. First, over 20,000 officials were dispatched to the Tibetan villages to conduct surveillance, political reeducation and security operations. Second, while conspicuous security presence has receded into the shadows, an enhanced form of surveillance, known as the "grid" (དྲ་བ་) management, was introduced to spy upon and monitor the thinking and activities of individuals deemed to be politically suspect (Human Rights Watch 2016). This has been accompanied by the building of hundreds of so-called "convenience police-posts," which are equipped with high-tech surveillance gadgets, and mobilization of volunteer groups known as "Red Armband Patrols" (དཔུང་རྟགས་དམར་པོ།). Third, on January 4, 2012, Chen Quanguo announced the unprecedented decision to place the management of all monasteries permanently in the hands of government or Party officials, some of whom would be ranked at the level of a deputy director of a provincial-level government department. This is consistent with Chen's guidance to the Tibetan clergy that Tibetan Buddhism should conform to socialist principles; the Party boss also mandated that all monasteries and nunneries should display portraits of Chinese leaders from Mao Zedong to Xi Jinping, fly the Chinese flag and serve as centers of official propaganda (Cao 2015). It is for these reasons that Freedom House judged Tibet to be the least-free among 50 "countries and territories" in 2017 ranked after Syria (Freedom House 2017). Chen is also credited with the attempt to socially remake Tibet by giving official incentives for inter-ethnic marriages between Tibetans and Han Chinese (Wan and Xu 2014). Indeed, Chen was proactive and skilled in pandering to the top leader in Zhongnanhai, for which he was awarded with a transfer in mid-2016 as Xinjiang Party Secretary, a post which usually confers the office-bearer the status of Politburo member. Chen is now busy replicating his Tibet policies in Xinjiang (Richardson 2017).

All these measures confirm the continued relevance of the "grasping with both hands" approach. Security and development remained the predominant themes of the most recent and Sixth Tibet Forum held in Beijing on August 24–25, 2015. China Tibet Online (2015) answered its own question, "Why the Sixth Forum on Tibet is held now?":

> Under these circumstances [unfulfilled work and official significance given to the realization of stability and development by top-level officials], the Sixth Forum on the Work of Tibet focusing on the research and deployment of the work for the *economic and social development and long-term stability* of Tibet was held.

As early as March 2013, Xi Jinping told the Tibetan delegation to the 12th National People's Congress that the regional officials should implement Central directives to achieve "the leapfrog development and long-term stability of Tibet." On Tibet, Xi is in sync with Hu's "grasping with both hands" strategy.

Conclusion

This chapter outlined the policies pursued by the Chinese Communist Party in Tibet since the tumultuous events of 1989. It reviewed how the strategy known as "grasping with both hands" initiated by Hu Jintao in 1989, was implemented in the 1990s – and how it will continue to dominate policy under the new TAR Party Secretary Wu Yingjie. Putting this strategy of employing ruthless coercion and imposing economic development into the broader context of National Regional Autonomy, the chapter assessed the legal provisions and actual reality of the Tibetan experience of autonomy. The chapter reflected the centrality of the Party-state's security concerns as the driver of its policy as demonstrated by the application of the security and economic instruments as well as the implementation of political campaigns in Tibet. Although there is optimism in some quarters that after the 19th Party Congress in Autumn 2017, when Xi Jinping will have consolidated his powers, he might pursue some reformist policies, this author expects that "grasping with both hands" will not fundamentally change in the Xi Jinping era.

References

Associated Press (2008) "Dalai Lama 'Wolf in Monk's Robes': China," March 19.

Associated Press (2011) "China's New Tibet Boss Makes No Mention of Struggle with Dalai Lama in First Public Comments," September 2.

Barnett, Robert W. (2003) "Chen Kuiyuan and the Marketisation of Policy," in Alex McKay ed., *Tibet and her Neighbours: A History*, London: Hansjörg Mayer.

BBC Summary of World Broadcast (SWB) (1994a) "A Program for Education in Patriotism," September 8.

BBC SWB (1994b) "Jiang Zemin: Forum Is 'a New Starting Point for the Work in Tibet," July 28.

BBC SWB (1996) "Tibet Party Leader Chen Kuiyuan Discusses Spiritual Civilisation," September 16.

BBC SWB (1997) "Study the Spirit of the 15th National Party Congress, Reinforce the Patriotic Front and Strive for Tibet's Stability, Reform, and Development," November 17; translated from Tibet News program, Tibet People's Broadcasting Station, Lhasa, November 9.

Cao Siqi (2015) "All Tibet Temples Required to Fly National Flag," *Global Times*, April 9.

Carlson, Allen (2004) *Beijing's Tibet Policy: Securing Sovereignty and Legitimacy*, Washington, DC: East–West Center.

Central Tibetan Administration (2009) "Fact Sheet: Tibetan Deaths under China's Crackdown since March 2008," March 20. Available from www.tibet.net/en/index.php?id=760&articletype=flash&rmenuid=morenews&tab=1#TabbedPanels1.

Chang, Andrei (2008) "Analysis: Controlling Tibet Part 1," July 2. Available from www.upi.com/Security_Industry/2008/07/02/Analysis-Controlling-Tibet-Part-1/UPI-88751215000000/2/.

Chen, Kuiyuan (1994) "The Situation of Tibet and the Problems We Request the Central Authorities to Solve," *Xizang de Jiaobu (Tibet Steps)*, February: 134–136.

Chen, Quanguo (2013) "Ensuring the Security of Tibet's Ideological Realm with the Spirit of Daring to Show the Sword – Conscientiously Studying and Implementing the Important Essence of the Speech Made by the General Secretary Xi Jinping at the National Propaganda and Ideology Work Conference," *Qiushi ("Seeking Truth")*, No. 21; Translated by *High Peaks, Pure Earth*, November 11. Available from http://highpeakspureearth.com/2013/tar-party-secretary-chen-quanguo-on-new-propaganda-and-control-of-social-media-strategy/.

China Daily (2008) "Dalai-Backed Violence Scars Lhasa," March 15.

China Tibet Online (2015) "Why the Sixth Forum on Tibet Is Held Now?" August 28. Available from http://english.chinatibetnews.com/tt/201508/t20150828_777340.html.

Chinese Statistical Yearbook (CSY) (1999) China Statistics Press. Available from www.stats.gov.cn/english/statisticaldata/yearlydata/YB1999e/index1.htm.

Chinese Statistical Yearbook (CSY) (2000) China Statistics Press. Available from www.stats.gov.cn/english/statisticaldata/yearlydata/YB2000e/index1.htm.

Chinese Statistical Yearbook (CSY) (2001) China Statistics Press. Available from www.stats.gov.cn/english/statisticaldata/yearlydata/YB2001e/ml/indexE.htm.

Chinese Statistical Yearbook (CSY) (2002) China Statistics Press. Available from www.stats.gov.cn/english/statisticaldata/yearlydata/YB2002e/ml/indexE.htm.

Congressional-Executive Committee on China (2010) "Communist Party Leadership Outlines 2010–2020 'Tibet Work' Priorities at 'Fifth Forum'," March 9. Available from www.cecc.gov/pages/virtualAcad/newsletterListing.phpd?mode=print&NLdate=20100316&show=TIBET&PHPSESSID=287043d1e3723e3c9624436aef1ec36a.

Davis, Michael C. (2007) "The Quest for Self-Rule in Tibet," *Journal of Democracy*, Vol. 18, No. 4: 157–171.

Dillon, Michael (2001) *Religious Minorities and China*, London: Minority Rights Group International.

Dodin, Thierry (2008) "What Policies Has the Chinese Government Adopted in Regard to Minority Nationalities?" in Anne-Marie Blondeau and Katia Buffetrille eds., *Authenticating Tibet: Answers to China's 100 Questions*, Oakland, CA; London: University of California Press, pp. 191–197.

Fischer, Andrew Martin (2005) *State Growth and Social Exclusion in Tibet: Challenges of Recent Growth*, Copenhagen: Nordic Institute of Asian Studies Press.

Freedom House (2017) *Freedom in the World 2017: Populists and Autocrats: The Dual Threat to Global Democracy*, Washington, DC.

Goldstein, Melvyn C. (1997) *The Snow Lion and the Dragon: China, Tibet and the Dalai Lama*, Oakland, CA: University of California Press.

He, Baogang (2005) "The Dalai Lama's Autonomy Proposal: A One-Sided Wish," in Barry Sautman and June Teufel Dreyer eds., *Contemporary Tibet: Politics, Development, and Society in a Disputed Region*, Armonk, NY; London: M.E. Sharpe, pp. 67–84.

Heberer, Thomas (1989) *China and its National Minorities: Autonomy or Assimilation?*, Armonk, NY; London: M.E. Sharpe.

Human Rights Committee of LAWASIA (Law Association for Asia and the Pacific) and TIN (Tibet Information Network) (1991) "Defying the Dragon: China and Human Rights in Tibet: A Report Issued Jointly by the Human Rights Committee of LAWASIA and TIN," Manila and London.

Human Rights Watch (2012) "Attempts to Seal Off Tibet from Outside Information: Escalating Restrictions on Media and Travel in Tibetan Areas," July 13.

Human Rights Watch (2016) "Relentless: Detention and Prosecution of Tibetans under China's 'Stability Maintenance' Campaign," May 22.

Miles, James (2008) "Transcript: James Miles Interview on Tibet," *Cable News Network (CNN)*, March 20.

Nathan, Andrew J. and Gilley, Bruce (2002) *China's New Rulers: The Secret Files*, New York: New York Review of Books.

Panchen Lama (1987) "Speech by the Panchen Lama to the TAR Standing Committee Meeting of the National People's Congress in Beijing," March 28.

People's Daily (2008) "18 Civilians, 1 Police Officer Killed by Lhasa Rioters," March 22.

People's Daily (2009) "Appalling March 14 Riot in Lhasa," March 26.

Phunwang (Wangyal, Baba Phuntsok) (2007) *Witness to Tibet's History*, New Delhi: Paljor Publications.

Private Office of His Holiness the Dalai Lama (2008) "Press Release from the Office of His Holiness the Dalai Lama," March 14.

Rabgey, Tashi and Sharlho, Tseten Wangchuk (2004) "Sino-Tibetan Dialogue in the Post-Mao Era: Lessons and Prospects," Policy Studies 12, Washington, DC: East–West Center.

Richardson, Sophie (2017) "China Poised to Repeat Tibet Mistakes," January 20.

Sautman, Barry (1998) "Affirmative Action, Ethnic Minorities and China's Universities," *Pacific Rim Law and Policy Journal*, Vol. 7, No. 1: 77–116.

Schwartz, Ronald D. (1994) *Circle of Protest: Political Ritual in the Tibetan Uprising*, New York: Columbia University Press.

Shakya, Tsering W. (1999) *Dragon in the Land of Snows: A History of Modern Tibet since 1947*, New York: Columbia University Press.

Shan, Wei and Clarke, Ryan (2011) "China's Western Development Strategy in Tibet and Xinjiang," EAI Background Brief No. 639, National University of Singapore, July 1. Available from www.eai.nus.edu.sg/publications/files/BB639.pdf.

Shenzhen Daily (2012) "Taiwan, Tibet Issues China's Core Interest," March 7.

Smith, Warren (2008) *China's Tibet? Autonomy or Assimilation*, Lanham, MD: Rowman & Littlefield.

Smith, Warren (2010) *Tibet's Last Stand? The Tibetan Uprising of 2008 and China's Response*, Lanham, MD: Rowman & Littlefield.

Sorensen, Theodore C. and Phillips, David L. (September 2004) *Legal Standards and Autonomy Options for Minorities in China: The Tibetan Case*, Cambridge, MA: BCSIA, Harvard University.

State Council Information Office of the People's Republic of China (2004) "White Paper on Tibetan Autonomy," Beijing, May.

State Council Information Office of the People's Republic of China (2015) "Successful Practice of Regional Ethnic Autonomy in Tibet," Beijing, September 6.

Statistics Bureau of Tibet Autonomous Region and Tibet Survey Organization of the National Bureau of Statistics (2008) "Statistical Communiqué of the Tibet Autonomous Region of the People's Republic of China on the 2007 Regional Economic and Social Development," *Beijing Review*, March 27. Available from www.bjreview.com.cn/special/tibet/txt/2008-06/11/content_130496_4.htm.

Swaine, Michael D. (2010) "China's Assertive Behavior Part One: On 'Core Interests'," *China Leadership Monitor*, No. 34.

TAR Leading Committee for Patriotic Education in Monasteries (2002a) "TAR Patriotic Education for Monasteries Propaganda Book No. 2: Handbook for Education in Anti-Splittism," May.

TAR Leading Committee for Patriotic Education in Monasteries (2002b) "TAR Patriotic Education for Monasteries Propaganda Book No. 4: Handbook for Education in Policy on Religion," May.

Tibet Daily (2012a) "提拔重用维稳表现优秀干部" ("Promote Superior Cadres Who Excel in Upholding Stability"), March 18.

Tibet Daily (2012b) "继续着力维护社会和谐稳定" ("Continue to Pay Attention to Maintaining Social Harmony and Stability"), March 19.

Topgyal, Tsering (2011) "Insecurity Dilemma and the Tibetan Uprising in 2008," *Journal of Contemporary China*, Vol. 20, No. 69: 183–204.

Topgyal, Tsering (2016a) *China and Tibet: The Perils of Insecurity*, London: Hurst & Company.

Topgyal, Tsering (2016b) "The Tibetan Self-Immolations as Counter-Securitization: Towards an Inter-Unit Theory of Securitization," *Asian Security*, Vol. 12, Issue 3: 166–187.

Voice of America (2009) "Dharamsala Condemns Chinese Court's Death Sentence for Riots," April 9.

Wan, William and Xu Yangjingjing (2014) "China Promotes Mixed Marriages in Tibet as Way to Achieve 'Unity'," *Washington Post*, August 16.

Wang, Xiaoqiang and Bai, Nanfeng; Knox, Angela trans. (1991) *The Poverty of Plenty*, New York: St. Martin's Press.

Woeser, Tsering; Carrico, K. trans. (2016) *Tibet on Fire: Self-Immolations Against Chinese Rule*, London; New York: Verso.

Wu, Xinbo (1998) "Security Practice of a Modernizing and Ascending Power," in Muthiah Alagappa ed., *Asian Security Practice: Material and Ideational Influences*, Stanford: Stanford University Press, pp. 115–156.

Xinhua News Agency (2001) "Chinese President, Premier Address Tibet Work Meeting in Beijing," June 29.

Xinhua News Agency (2008) "Expert: Dalai Clique Never Gives up 'Tibet Independence' Behind 'Middle Way'," March 31.

Xinhua News Agency (2017) "Tibet Reports Robust Growth in 2016," January 1.

Yeh, Emily (2013). *Taming Tibet: Landscape Transformation and the Gift of Chinese Development*, Ithaca, NY; London: Cornell University Press.

Zhao, Suisheng (1998) "A State-Led Nationalism: The Patriotic Education Campaign in Post-Tiananmen China," *Communist and Post-Communist Studies*, Vol. 31, No. 3: 287–302.

Zhao, Suisheng (2004) *A Nation-State by Construction: Dynamics of Modern Chinese Nationalism*, Stanford, CA: Stanford University Press.

20

THE PARTY-STATE'S NATIONALIST STRATEGY TO CONTROL THE UYGHUR

Silenced voices

Dru C. Gladney

Introduction

Governing the Uyghur in China has often pushed in two quite distinct directions, secularism or separatism. The Chinese Communist Party (CCP) has regularly suggested that Uyghur militants have killed and are threatening to kill other Chinese citizens in the name of radical Islam, drawing direct parallels to violent events in the Middle East and Europe. Since the end of the nineteenth century, China has been engaged in an unremitting project of nationalization and secularization that includes, among other things, emancipation from its imperial past, engagement with Western political institutions, and establishment of its sovereignty over its bounded territory. One recent challenge to this nationalist project, with roots in the early twentieth century, is that of a widespread separatism movement among one Muslim group known as the Uyghur. That the largest Muslim group in China, known as the Hui, have not participated in, nor been sympathetic to, such a movement speaks volumes regarding the diversity of Islamic identity and practice in China over the last century in response to state projects of nationalization and secularization.

Most scholars agree that the post-Cultural Revolution period in the Xinjiang Uyghur Autonomous Region was welcomed by most Xinjiang residents due to the harsh treatment of minorities and religious practitioners between 1966 and 1976. Indeed, many Muslims point to the 20 years of discrimination against religious practice since the initiation of the Religious System Reform Campaign in 1958, which led throughout the country to the further consolidation and restriction of religious practice. In the wake of the market liberalization policies of Deng Xiaoping, cultural and religious practice also flourished, leading to widespread mosque-building and the revival of religious education in the region. It was during this period that most of the mosques in the region were built or reopened, Islamic training of young Imams permitted, and pilgrimages to Mecca resumed. Indeed, there are many residents of Xinjiang, Uyghurs included, who continue to strongly support the Deng Xiaoping reforms as they have been continued under Jiang Zemin, Hu Juntao, and now Xi Jinping. As loyal citizens, they see the dramatic progress made since the end of the Cultural Revolution and generally share in the government's vision of a modernized, developed Xinjiang region. Working not only in the state sector as cadres, teachers, production corps farmers, and factory workers, but also in the growing private sector in private and semi-private small businesses, these supporters of the state's development program are generally quite unwilling to listen to any criticism of state policies, especially from outsiders or disgruntled minorities.

Given the lack of public polling or uncensored media in the region, it is difficult to ascertain if these supporters are a silent majority or a tiny minority, speaking out in support of state policies because it serves their interest. Nevertheless, the Deng reform era in general can be characterized as a period of heightened loyalty to the state and new-found optimism after the previous 20 years of internal chaos and repression, similar in many respects to the period of relative loyalty when Xinjiang was first brought into the PRC and established as an Autonomous Region.

Growing Uyghur resentment from the late 1980s and mid-1990s

However, in the late 1980s and mid-1990s, this period of loyalty gave way to increasing expressions of dissent, not only among Uyghur but also among a wide cross-section of local residents that felt the northwest was not keeping pace with the rapid development of the rest of the country. Many Uyghurs were particularly disappointed that the independence of the former Soviet Central Asian Republics in 1991 did not lead to independence or at least increased autonomy in their own Autonomous Region. Throughout the early and mid-1990s, increasing expressions of "voice" demonstrated these concerns from university protests to greater ethnic and civil unrest. Whether there were smaller, unreported incidents in the past, the mid-1990s witnessed a number of public expressions of dissent and dissatisfaction with state policies in the region.

The 1990s period of voiced opposition began with the report of a major uprising in Akto County (near Kashgar) in April 1990, that official reports stated involved an "armed counter-revolutionary rebellion" suppressed by the People's Liberation Army that led to 22 deaths.[1] In 1995, Chinese People's Police reported finding a large weapons cache, and in May 1996, a Xinjiang People's Political Consultative Conference official was assassinated, all later attributed to "East Turkestan" terrorists (McNeal 2001).

In the spring of 1996, the *Xinjiang Daily* reported five serious social eruptions in the region since February 1996, with a crackdown that rounded up 2,773 terrorist suspects, 6,000 lbs of explosives, and 31,000 rounds of ammunition. Overseas Uyghur groups claimed that over 10,000 were arrested in the round-up, with over 1,000 killed.[2] The largest protest from February 2 to 8, 1996, was sparked by a Chinese raid on an evening *Mashrap* cultural meeting, where young Uyghur men and women gather for prayer, singing of religious and folk songs, and feasting.[3] Protests against the arrests made during the meeting led to 120 deaths and over 2,500 arrests. Immediately following the uprising and crackdown in Yining, on February 25, the day of Deng Xiaoping's memorial speech, in a well-coordinated operation, three bombs exploded simultaneously on three buses in downtown Urumqi leading to 20 civilian deaths and scores of injured (including some Uyghurs), with the subsequent execution of eight Uyghurs allegedly responsible for the bombings (McNeal 2001).

Later that spring, the violence came to Beijing when on March 7 and then again on March 8, two separate bombs exploded on public buses. The first bomb in Xidan claimed three lives with ten injured, while the second bomb killed two. The bombs were timed to take place during the Chinese National People's Congress and were widely attributed to Uyghur separatists, though this has never been independently verified and no group has ever claimed responsibility.[4] On May 29, 1996 the pro-government *mullah* of Kashgar's Idgah mosque, Arunkhanji, and his son were stabbed by knife-wielding Uyghur militants, on May 27 there was another attack on a senior government official, and in September of the same year six Uyghur government officials were killed by other Uyghurs in Yecheng.

The Yining uprising on February 7, 1997, and the subsequent bombings in Urumqi and Beijing, were heavily covered by the world's media (*The Economist* 1997b). This distinguishes the late 1990s events from on-going problems in the region in the mid-1980s that met with little media coverage. In the late 1990s, the government responded with a host of arrests and new policy announcements. In Spring 1998, the National People's Congress passed a New Criminal Law that redefined "counter-revolutionary" crimes to be "crimes against the state," liable to severe prison terms and even execution. Included in "crimes against the state" were any actions considered to involve "ethnic discrimination" or "stirring up anti-ethnic sentiment" (Amnesty International 1999). Many human rights activists have argued that this is a thinly veiled attempt to criminalize "political" actions and to make them appear as illegal as traffic violations, supporting China's claims that it holds "no political prisoners." Since any minority activity could be regarded as stirring "anti-ethnic feeling," many ethnic activists have suggested that the New Criminal Law was easily turned against them.

The "Strike Hard Campaign," launched in Beijing in April 1997, was originally intended to clamp down on crime and corruption, and included severe restrictions on religious practice.[5] These campaigns, according to an April 1999 Amnesty International report, have led to 210 capital sentences and 190 executions of Uyghurs since 1997 (Amnesty International 1999).

Until 2009, the 1997 riot in Xining described above marked the apex of rioting and civil unrest among the Uyghur. Indeed, after 1997 there was a marked decline in Xinjiang civil unrest and so-called separatist events, perhaps because of the government's harsh crackdown and arrest of prominent Uyghur activists. On August 11, 1999, Rebiya Kadeer – a well-known Uyghur businesswoman and a delegate to the 1995 UN Fourth World Conference for Women in Beijing, who was scheduled to meet with a United States Congressional Research Service delegation to the region – was arrested for "revealing state secrets" (Ian 1999). Human rights activists claim that she was merely handing over Xinjiang news items previously published in the official news media to be taken back to her husband, Sidiq Rouzi, who was living in exile in Washington, D.C., and working for the U.S. government funded radio stations, Radio Free Asia and Voice of America. After reviewing her case, Amnesty International concluded that there was not enough evidence to detain her and launched an international campaign in the spring of 2002, that eventuated in her release in March 2005 (Amnesty International 2000). Although Beijing hoped her arrest and exile would silence her voice, she has been active among the nearly million-strong Uyghur diaspora in helping to organize international fora including the World Uyghur Congress, which has elected her twice as its President.[6] Another voice for the Uyghur that the Chinese state has sought to silence through arrest and detention is the China Minzu University economist, Ilham Tohti. After being accused of "separatism" for his class lectures and having hosted a blocked website in 2006, Uyghur Online (www.uighurbiz.net), Tohti was sentenced to life imprisonment and his assets seized in September 2016.[7]

Despite on-going tensions and frequent reports of isolated terrorist acts, there has been no evidence that any of these actions have been aimed at disrupting the economic development of the region. Most confirmed incidents have been directed against Han Chinese security forces, recent Han Chinese émigrés to the region, and even Uyghur Muslims perceived to be too closely collaborating with the Chinese government.[8] Most analysts agree that China is not vulnerable to the same ethnic separatism that split the former Soviet Union. But few doubt that should China fall apart, it would divide, like the USSR, along centuries old ethnic, linguistic, regional, and cultural fault lines (Gladney 1995: 1–8). If China did fall apart, Xinjiang would split in a way that, according to Anwar Yusuf, President of the Eastern Turkistan National Freedom Center in Washington, D.C., "would make Kosovo look like a birthday party."[9] Uyghur organizations have sought to pressure various U.S. government administrations to support the Uyghur cause, with varying degrees of success, arguably more so with the Bush administration than with Obama's, given the successful release of Rebiya Kadeer. Many Uyghurs with whom this author has spoken hope that the Trump administration, with its tougher talk on China and seemingly public support for Taiwan, might be more supportive of Uyghur efforts to press China on human rights and greater freedom. Yet many fear that with the U.S. and China cooperating on a war on terrorism, there is little real hope for U.S. support of Uyghur human rights' issues. The Obama administration showed less interest in the Uyghur cause than the Bush administration, refusing to meet with any Uyghur representatives, and keeping the Dalai Lama at a polite, but safe distance.

Since the high point of the late 1990s expressions of voice and ethnic violence, there has been a gradual decline in the scale and number of incidents. Documented separatist and violent incidents in Xinjiang have dropped off dramatically since the late 1990s. Philip Pan reported in a July 14, 2002 *Washington Post* interview that local Xinjiang security officials were only able to cite three relatively small occurrences (Pan 2002). Interestingly, despite increasing violence in the Xi Jinping era, few have noted that despite many incidents of ethnic and civil unrest in the region, not one significant terrorist attack against any strategic infrastructural target (oil refinery, pipeline, railroad, dam, or bridge) has ever been documented, nor have any local or international incidents been positively identified to have been orchestrated by any international Uyghur or Islamic organization. Uyghur acts of violence seem to be increasingly inspired by Jihadist Islam, but not coordinated by any single group or organization. In addition, visitors to the region have increasingly reported a sense of disillusionment and disappointment among activists. One acquaintance mentioned to this author as early as August 2001, "We've given up on independence, we just want to emigrate." Since then, many frustrated Uyghur, especially young men, have tried to leave through Pakistan, India, and Burma, with various rates of success. A key issue influencing Uyghur loyalty and voice has been the rise of Chinese nationalism, particularly in the later reform period under Xi Jinping. The following discussion will address some of the complexities of Chinese nationalism affecting the expression of Uyghur voices today and many of their reasons to seek outlets for resistance to Chinese rule.[10]

Chinese nationalisms

In the broad body of literature on nationalism, there are two main schools of thought. The modernist school of thought focuses on actions undertaken by individuals, mostly intellectuals, with the specific purpose of engendering sentiments of nationalism within a specific group of people (Cole 2002: 453). Michael Hechter (2000: 312) has described this as "rational nationalism," in that it often entails individuals acting even violently for the instrumentalist goals for the greater good of the "nation."[11] In other words, the modernist view is that nationalism is in a sense *man-made*, and born out of the structural conditions of modern society. The primordialist school of thought focuses on the natural tendency of humans to organize into distinct groupings based on an affinity of birth (Llobera 1999: 3). The primordialist view is that nationalism is *inherent* in human beings, and is a natural phenomenon. It is generic to humanity, and not constructed by history or human-inspired political movements.

The study of the origin of nationalism tends to lend itself to the modernist point of view, because of the artificiality of national identity (Guo 2004). In China, this is consistent with the fact that the concept of nationality only developed in the late Qing dynasty. Chow *et al.* state, "Chinese intellectuals looked to language, custom, history, and religion for the common bond of a nation. They found none" (Chow *et al.* 2001). Nationalism, like Western ideas of "democracy," "science," and even "religion," were introduced to China during its late nineteenth-century period of opening to the West. As this author has suggested elsewhere (Gladney 1996: 5), "nationalism" with Chinese characteristics can be seen to be, in Partha Chatterjee's (1986) terms, a "derivative discourse" introduced to China, and much of Asia, as a result of and response to Western imperialist expansion. China has had to negotiate its response to Western nationalism, creating several kinds of uniquely Chinese nationalisms, not unlike China's own brand of "socialism" and "communism," which were, like nationalism, Western exports to China. Consequently, the concept of *hanzu*, or "people of Han lineage," was artificially created by anti-Manchu scholars to attack the Qing dynasty (Chow *et al.* 2001: 75). Influenced by the Western concept of "race," these revolutionary scholars began to search for new identities for the Chinese nation "in order to articulate a distinction between the Manchus and themselves" (Gladney 1996: 180). Since its creation, the concept of *hanzu* has been utilized for a number of political purposes, including resistance to the Japanese during the Kuomintang's rule. Thus, most authors view nationalism from the early 1900s to the end of the Mao era in the 1970s as inspired and promoted by the state (Dittmer and Kim 1993; Chow *et al.* 2001). (See Chapter 4, "The CCP's Use and Abuse of Nationalism.")

However, although national identity in China is inherently a modern construct, the dynamics of nationalism have evolved over time. For example, bottom-up nationalism, which is popularly based, supports the idea that national identity can originate from the people, as posited by primordialist theory (Gries 2004). As described by Clifford Geertz, this theory posits that people are born with certain proclivities toward language, religion, and even political activism.[12]

In fact, Peter Gries argues that the emergence of this popular nationalism has become a threat to the government, resulting in the formation of "pragmatic nationalism" in recent years (Gries 2004: 116). Guo also notes that cultural nationalism, though primordialist in nature, is often an extension of state nationalism in China (Guo 2004: 53). Thus, the lines between primordialist and modernist thought are blurred in the analysis of contemporary Chinese nationalism, requiring one to gain a more nuanced understanding of whether nationalism is a top-down or bottom-up phenomenon.

The following four categories of nationalism are selected for examination: top-down or state nationalism, Han nationalism, bottom-up or popular nationalism, and utilitarian nationalism. The analysis of nationalism among the Uyghur in China requires examining these topics in depth, because each category sheds light on a unique aspect of Chinese national identity (which includes both Han and minorities). Furthermore, although the four categories are distinct and seemingly unrelated, they should be viewed as a whole in order to understand the various mechanisms through which nationalism is constructed.

Top-down nationalism

One way of analyzing state nationalism is to examine the state's cultural policies and their effects on national identity that come from the top and move downward toward the people. The Uyghur scholar Enze Han presents an interesting analysis of state nationalism by distinguishing between three periods of "nation-building": (1) The tolerant and pluralistic policies of the early years, (2) The cultural destruction and political repression of the Cultural Revolution, and (3) The return to a more pluralistic approach, but with significant limitations in today's society.

During the first stage, the CCP's policies toward ethnic minorities were relatively inclusive (Han 2013: 50). Although the CCP did not include a clause allowing ethnic minorities to pursue self-determination in its constitution, minority languages were promoted and protected. For example, Article 53 of the Common Program, the provisional constitution for the PRC passed in 1949, "guaranteed ethnic minorities the right to develop and use their native languages and scripts … and promised government assistance in those efforts" (Han 2013: 52). In addition, the 1952 General Program for the Implementation of Regional Autonomy, the 1953 Election Law, and the PRC Constitution of 1954 all mandated proportional minority membership in legislative bodies, pledged that ethnic minorities would have the same rights as the Han majority, and banned discrimination based on ethnicity (Guo and Guo 2008: 140).

During the Cultural Revolution, many of these policies were reversed. The UC Berkeley Political Scientist, Lowell Dittmer (Dittmer and Kim 1993: 89), noted, "During the Cultural Revolution, radical factions of the CCP grew impatient with the slow pace in national integration." Bilingual education for ethnic minorities was either stopped entirely or drastically curtailed, ethnic minority organizations were disbanded, and passages dealing with minority autonomy in the Constitution were eliminated. Many autonomous units were dissolved and ethnic minority leaders deposed. Most importantly, the suffering caused by these policies created irreparable damage to the relations between the Han and ethnic minorities, and "many of the wounds from this period would take a long time to heal, if ever" (Han 2013: 112).

The return to more tolerant and pluralistic policies began after the death of Mao in 1976 (Han 2013: 130). Members of the old minority elites were restored to their previous positions in government, legal reforms provided more institutionalized autonomy and rights for various ethnic minority groups, and bilingualism was once again permitted and promoted (Han 2013: 132). In addition, affirmation action for minority students applying to university, exceptions to the one-child policy, and quotas for representation in the government were all instituted to ensure equality between ethnic minorities and the Han (Lee *et al.* 2012: 89). In recent years, it appears as though the government not only accepts minorities, but intends to highlight China's diversity on the international level through supporting initiatives such as creating films on ethnic minorities and developing ethnic tourism (Montefiore 2013).

However, despite the many policies favoring minorities, many authors agree that these policies are only superficial attempts at promoting equality, and in effect, minorities continue to be marginalized in society (Guo and Guo 2008; Lee *et al.* 2012; Han 2013). Some authors even criticize the Chinese government's lack of proactive and effective policy as a deliberate neglect, because it is obvious that the laws governing ethnic-minority cultural rights and political autonomy are becoming increasingly inadequate in the context of the rapid economic and social change in China (Wasserstrom 2010: 77). For example, although preferential university admission for minority students is still in place, the system through which the government would automatically assign jobs to university graduates is not (Wasserstrom 2010: 80). Thus, ethnic minority students often find themselves at a disadvantage when competing with Han Chinese students for jobs that require substantial proficiency in Mandarin Chinese (Wasserstrom 2010: 81). In addition, with economic development focused in the urban centers where Han Chinese are the majority, more and more ethnic minorities, who are disproportionately male, have chosen to leave their villages for economic opportunities (Zheng 1999). This has ultimately threatened the survival of ethnic minority culture, because many of these men do not return to village life and instead choose to assimilate into the Han culture and their way of living (Zheng 1999).

Han nationalism

As discussed previously, the concept of *hanzu*, or the "Han identity," is undoubtedly artificial and highly politicized. The CCP, like the Kuomintang (KMT) and the revolutionaries before them, has utilized the Han identity to create a sense of pride among people who supposedly share Han cultural values, and to gain support for their political agenda of unification (Gladney 1996: 188). Thus, the boundaries between cultural nationalism and state nationalism are undoubtedly blurred because the two categories are closely related (Gladney 1996: 180). However, whereas state nationalism focuses on policies directed at ethnic minorities, cultural nationalism focuses on the indirect subjugation of ethnic minorities – for example, through the portrayal of the Han as superior, and the indirect pressures on ethnic minorities to assimilate. From a broader perspective, the CCP has effectively combined cultural and state nationalism to create a new type of nationalism – Han nationalism (Zheng 1999: 214). Essentially, this type of nationalism is more Han-centric than intentionally discriminatory.

From the beginning of the People's Republic, the Han people have been celebrated by the Communist Party as the "vanguard of the people's revolution" (Gladney 1990). A cable issued by the Central Party Propaganda Office of the New China News Agency in 1949 states,

> The Han occupy the majority population of the country; moreover, the Han today are the major force in China's revolution. Under the leadership of the Chinese Communist Party, the victory of China's people's democratic revolution mainly relied on the industry of the Han people.
>
> *(Gladney 1996: 182)*

In the effort to recognize ethnic minorities in the Ethnic Identification Project, the Chinese government classified minority groups according to what historical development stage it considered them to be at, and the Han majority group was classified as the one that had progressed furthest into the feudal stage, while other groups were labeled "primitive," "slave," or "feudal" (Chow *et al.* 2001: 156). Though today there are laws prohibiting the explicit discrimination of ethnic minorities, Han superiority is still asserted in implicit ways.

In a subtler way, the policies of the CCP today assert the superiority of the Han by pressuring ethnic minorities to adopt the Han language and customs. Many authors refer to the assimilation of ethnic minorities as "Sinification," or *hanhua* (Gladney 1995; Han 2013). The Uyghur scholar Enze Han notes,

> Today, it is very hard for younger-generation ethnic-minority people to grow up in a monolingual environment. Mass media, modern communication channels, pop culture, and all the conveniences and excitements offered by contemporary Chinese society all require one, especially a young person, to conform, acculturate, or assimilate into the majority Han language and culture.
>
> *(Han 2013: 122)*

Recent nation-building policies such as the prohibition of under-18-year-olds from praying at mosques and the banning of civil servants and students from fasting during the month of Ramadan are examples of even stronger measures taken to accelerate Sinification (Rauhala 2014).

Additionally, the dynamics of the Han identity under the CCP reflect the purposes of Han nationalism. As this author has argued, "the identification of certain groups within China as 'minorities' and the recognition of the Han as a 'unified' majority played a fundamental role in forging a unified Chinese nation, because minorities were induced to follow the Han example" (Gladney 1996: 185). Similarly, Chow notes,

> This myth [of a *hanzu*] also sustains a belief that there is a majority ethnic group that is running the government, therefore justifying domination over "minority ethnic groups" such as the Tibetans and the Uyghurs, who are "less civilized and advanced."
>
> *(Chow et al. 2001: 160)*

However, Chow also points out that the Han identity "has allowed political leaders to hide conflicts and tensions between ethnic groups within the *hanzu*" (Chow *et al.* 2001: 160). Therefore, Han identity is simultaneously inclusive and exclusive – reflecting the CCP's desire to consolidate power in the "Han majority" and weaken the autonomy of ethnic minorities.

Bottom-up nationalism

Whereas state nationalism and Han nationalism focus on the dynamics of ethnic identity, bottom-up or popular nationalism and utilitarian nationalism focus on allegiance to the state. In some ways, these differences can be demarcated as internal and external nationalism – where internal nationalism refers to how one ethnic group within a country perceives themselves in comparison to other ethnic groups, and external nationalism is how citizens of a country perceive themselves in relation to other countries.

Although many Western scholars insist that Chinese nationalism has always been a top-down phenomenon, it is clear that popular nationalism has been prevalent throughout modern Chinese history, and in fact, has defined much of its course. The Boxer Rebellion in 1900, for example, was an uprising in northern China against the spread of Western and Japanese influence led by the Society of the Righteous and Harmonious Fists, a secret vigilante group (Wei and Liu 2001). In the 1890s, China had given territorial and commercial concessions in this area to several European nations, and the Boxers blamed their poor standard of living on foreigners who were colonizing their country. This rebellion, as one of the first instances in modern Chinese history where the masses united to protest against foreign imperialism, set the precedent for popular nationalism through the end of the twentieth century and provided inspiration for other anti-imperialist protests, such as the May Fourth Movement in 1919, where students protested the Chinese government's weak response to the Treaty of Versailles (Wei and Liu 2001: 129). In other words, the Boxer Rebellion and May Fourth Movement gave rise to the "victim narrative" that united the Chinese people with the idea that China needed to be strong in order to avoid being continually victimized by foreign powers.

Since its creation, the CCP has relied upon popular nationalism to gain and maintain support. In line with Marxist thought, much of its success in the Chinese Civil War came from its ability to appeal to the masses – indeed, the CCP positioned itself as the "party of the people" with the goal to "liberate" the masses from oppression by the KMT and imperialist forces (Zheng 1999: 115). Thus, from a pro-CCP perspective, the Chinese Civil War is often portrayed as a nationalist revolution from the masses.

The lines between popular and state nationalism became even less defined after the 1949 "liberation" by the CCP. The cult of personality achieved by Mao Zedong, combined with the lasting fervor of revolution, led to popular nationalism defined by fanaticism and xenophobia (Ouyang 2005: 151–175). When allegiance to the state became threatened, Mao began the

Cultural Revolution in an attempt to revive nationalism through purging remnants of capitalist and traditional elements from Chinese society (Wu 2008). Although initiated by Mao, the Cultural Revolution can be viewed as a combination of popular and state nationalism. For example, the Red Guards, one of the primary agents of the Cultural Revolution, were independently formed by students at Tsinghua Middle School in Beijing (Wu 2008: 472).

Utilitarian nationalism

Popular nationalism, however, is not always beneficial for the state. Just as the masses can rally behind anger toward the actions of foreign countries, they can also unite to express their dissatisfaction toward the state. Both the Boxer Rebellion and May Fourth Movement, for example, expressed anger toward the Chinese government in addition to foreign countries. In a more contemporary example, although the protests against Japan's claims over the Diaoyu or Senkaku islands were inherently anti-Japanese, protesters were also largely unsatisfied by the Chinese government's response. In fact, in the 1996 national bestseller *China Can Say No*, the authors maintain that "China has been too warm and accommodating towards Japan" and implicitly condemn the government for suppressing popular anti-Japanese protests (Gries 2004).

Popular nationalism also appears to be undermining the state's agency. Gries states, "In China today, popular networks are challenging the state's hegemony over nationalism, threatening to rupture the Chinese nation-state" (Gries 2004: 134). For example, in the midst of popular protests about the 1999 Belgrade bombing, 2001 spy plane collision, and more recent island disputes, Chinese leaders had no choice but to condemn foreign nations and adopt a hard-line approach to discerning who was "right" and who was "wrong" (Gries 2004: 135). As a result, the CCP recognized that utilitarian nationalism could be a double-edged sword and began approaching nationalism in a more careful way, leading to what scholars such as Peter Gries and Suisheng Zhao call "pragmatic nationalism" (Gries 2004; Zhao 2004).

Utilitarian nationalism is, in essence, pragmatic in nature. It does not have a fixed, objectified, or defined content, and is not driven by any ideology, religious beliefs, or other abstract ideas (Gries 2004: 140). Instead, it is a tool of the communist state to bolster the faith of Chinese people and hold the country together during the period of rapid and turbulent transformation from a communist to a post-communist society (Zhao 2004: 130). For example, in response to popular nationalist calls for the government to take a tough position against the United States and Japan, CCP leaders have mainly adopted a two-pronged strategy (Zhao 2004: 154). On the one hand, they have tolerated and even encouraged the expression of liberal nationalism to make their own policy positions more credible to the U.S. and Japan on issues involving China's vital interests such as the Taiwan issue (Zhao 2004: 155). On the other hand, the state has been very cautious to prevent the nationalist sentiment of Chinese people from getting out of hand and cause backlash in both domestic and foreign affairs (Gries 2004: 140). To make sure that the government's policy is not dictated by emotional nationalist rhetoric on the streets, they have described nationalism as a force that must be "channeled" in its expressions, including restraining or even banning popular anti-American and anti-Japanese demonstrations (Zhao 2004: 158).

China's response to the EP-3 spy plane incident in April 2000 is a good example of this. On the one hand, Beijing's public stance was particularly uncompromising on the demand that the spy plane crew would only be released after a formal apology by the U.S. government (Zhao 2004: 160). However, Secretary Powell did not apologize, only mentioning that "we regret that the Chinese plane did not get down safely, and we regret the loss of the life of that Chinese pilot," and instead only emphasized expediting the resolution of the situation (Best *et al.* 2001). In the end, the CCP, careful to avoid a repeat of the anti-U.S. demonstrations after the 1999 embassy bombing in Belgrade, finally accepted the "very sorry" in Ambassador Prueher's letter as close as an equivalent to an apology that they would get, even though the translation of "very sorry" in Chinese (*baoqian*) is significantly less severe than "daoqian," the Chinese expression of "apology" that Beijing demanded initially (Best *et al.* 2001: 5). This author, while serving as the inaugural Dean of the Asia-Pacific Center for Security Studies, personally appointed by Admiral Prueher (who later served as the U.S. Ambassador to China, 1999–2001), was surprised to learn from the Admiral that he held the highest respect for Chinese restraint during that unfortunate incident. Later, in 1999, at an informal dinner at Admiral Prueher's home in Honolulu in honor of a visit by the late Mayor of Shanghai, Wang Daohan, Admiral Prueher once again expressed his regret for the unfortunate incident and his great admiration for the Chinese people.

These examples are testimonies to the CCP's utilitarian flexibility. The two-pronged strategy of appearing tough but acting in a calculated manner has allowed the state to contain popular nationalism (Gries 2004: 150). As a result, the rise of nationalism has not made Chinese foreign policy particularly aggressive or irrational. As the middle class grows, Chinese leaders will be increasingly constrained by the rise of popular nationalist sentiments, making utilitarian nationalism even more important (Zhao 2004: 172).

Uyghur resistance to Chinese rule

In the summer of 2002, both the United States and the United Nations supported China's claim that an organization known as the East Turkistan Islamic Movement (ETIM) should be recognized as an international terrorist organization (Eckholm 2002: 1). It is important to note, however, that China makes little distinction between separatists, terrorists, and civil rights activists – whether they are Uyghurs, Tibetans, Taiwanese, or Falun Gong Buddhists. One person's terrorist may be another's freedom fighter. Are the restive Uyghurs of Xinjiang terrorists, separatists, or freedom fighters? How can the incidents of recent years be seen in the context of the Chinese efforts to integrate the region in the course of two decades of the post-Deng reforms?

After denying the problem for decades and stressing instead China's "national unity," official reports and the state-run media began in early 2001 to detail terrorist activities in the regions officially known as the Xinjiang Uyghur Autonomous Region (*People's Daily* 2001).[13] Prior to the release of a 2009 White Paper by the State Council, and the subsequent media reports, the term "Eastern Turkestan" was rarely allowed to be used in the official media, and anyone found using the term or referring to Xinjiang as Eastern Turkestan could be arrested, even though this is the term most often used outside China to refer to the region by Uyghurs and other Turkic-speaking people. In the northwestern Uyghur Autonomous Region of Xinjiang, China's State Council and the official media have continued to report on an on-going series of incidents of terrorism and separatism since the large riot in the Xinjiang town of Yining of February 1997, with multiple crackdowns and arrests that have rounded up thousands of terrorist suspects, large weapons caches, and printed documents allegedly outlining future public acts of violence (Brahimi 1999). Amnesty International has claimed that these round-ups have led to hurried public trials and immediate, summary executions of possibly thousands of locals. One estimate suggested that in a country known for its frequent executions, Xinjiang had the highest number, averaging 1.8 per week, most of them Uyghur (Amnesty International 1999: 24). Troop movements to the area, related to the nationwide campaign against crime known as "Strike Hard" launched in 1998 that includes the call to erect a "great wall of steel" against separatists in Xinjiang, were reportedly the largest since the suppression of the large Akto insurrection in April

1990 (the first major uprising that initiated a series of unrelated and sporadic protests) (Hutzler 2001a). Alleged incursions of Taliban fighters through the Wakhan corridor into China where Xinjiang shares a narrow border with Afghanistan have led to the area being swamped with Chinese security forces and large military exercises, beginning at least one month prior to the September 11 attack.

International campaigns for Uyghur rights and possible independence have become increasingly vocal and well organized, especially on the internet. International organizations are increasingly including Uyghur indigenous voices from the expatriate Uyghur community. Notably, as early as 1995 the elected chair of the Unrepresented Nations and People's Organization (UNPO) based in the Hague was a Uyghur, Erkin Alptekin, son of the Uyghur nationalist leader, Isa Yusuf Alptekin, who is buried in Istanbul where there is a park dedicated to his memory.[14] Supporting primarily an audience of mostly expatriate Uyghurs, there are at least 25 international organizations and websites working for the independence of "Eastern Turkestan," and based in Amsterdam, Munich, Istanbul, Melbourne, Washington, D.C., and New York. Following September 11, 2001, the vast majority of these organizations disclaimed any support for violence or terrorism, pressing for a peaceful resolution of on-going conflicts in the region. Nevertheless, the growing influence of "cyber-separatism" is of increasing concern to Chinese authorities seeking to convince the world that the Uyghurs do pose a real domestic and international terrorist threat.

The real question is, what changes in the region have the events of September 11 wrought in terms of local response to Chinese rule? It is clear that the so-called separatist activities are not new and that China is taking advantage of the international war on terrorism to attempt to eradicate a domestic problem. The Istanbul-based groups have existed since the 1950s, the Central Asian Uyghurs under Soviet rule received tremendous support in their anti-China rhetoric regarding policies in Xinjiang, and the Uyghurs have been increasingly vocal since the independence of the Central Asian Republics in 1991 led many to hope for an independent Uyghuristan would have followed on the heels of the other newly independent -stans. Separatist actions have taken place on a small but regular basis since the expansion of market and trade policies in China, and with the opening of six overland gateways to Xinjiang in addition to the trans-Eurasian railway, and China's Western development campaign, there seems to be no chance of closing up shop. The Chinese government itself in a landmark 1999 white paper, admitted serious economic shortfalls in the region despite 50 years of state investment in the development of the region: "The Chinese government is well aware of the fact that … central and western China where most minority people live, lags far behind the eastern coastal areas in development."[15]

In previous years, China denied any serious social or political problems in the region and followed the old Soviet "divide-and-rule" strategy which sought to limit all references to Turkestan or even Turkology that might link the Uyghurs, Kazakhhs, and other Turkic-speaking minorities to broader pan-Turkic movements. Nevertheless, CCP administration continues to pressure nearby countries to repatriate Uyghurs and their sympathizers. In June 2002, under U.S. and Chinese pressure, Pakistan returned one Uyghur activist to China, apprehending among hundreds of Taliban detainees, which follows a pattern of repatriations of suspected Uyghur separatists in Kazakhstan, Kyrgyzstan, and Uzbekistan. This detainee was supposedly one of several hundred Uyghurs arrested fighting with the Taliban, with up to six Uyghurs placed in the Guantánamo Bay detention facility (Eckholm and Smith 2001; Pun 2001; *Reuters* 2001), that later expanded to a total of 22 Uyghur detainees (all released to third countries by 2013) (Savage 2013). Clearly, domestic responses to Chinese rule have changed dramatically in the last 30 years for there to be large groups of Uyghur militant Muslims fighting abroad, and for the Chinese government to publicize separatist actions inside and outside the region, launching large-scale suppressions of potential terrorists. Yet, despite China's increasing crackdowns, fewer reports of civil unrest or terrorist acts have been reported since the late 1990s. The dramatic increase of Uyghur violence in Xinjiang, as well as the rest of China, since the early 2000s, suggests that Chinese policies have done little to stem the tide of Uyghur unrest. It is clear that globalization and the rise of Jihadist Islam through the internet and personal Uyghur activists radicalized abroad, have dramatically changed the scene of Uyghur resistance to Chinese rule, that began with the "cyber-separatism" of the mid-1990s.

Cyber-separatism: giving voice to the Uyghur opposition

Though silenced within China, Uyghur voices can still be heard virtually, on the internet. Perhaps due to Chinese restrictions on public protest and a state-controlled media, or the deleterious effect of a war on domestic terrorism that this chapter has documented began in the late 1990s, very few Uyghur voices can be heard today in the region critical of Chinese policies, at least not public ones. International campaigns for Uyghur rights and possible independence have become increasingly vocal and well organized, especially on the internet. Supporting primarily an audience of approximately over 500,000 to 1 million expatriate Uyghurs (yet few Uyghurs in Central Asia and China have access to these internet sites) there are at least 50 international organizations and websites working for the independence of "Eastern Turkestan," and based in Amsterdam, Munich, Istanbul, Melbourne, Washington, D.C., and New York.[16]

Although the United Nations and the United States government have agreed with China that at least one international organization, ETIM, is a Uyghur-sponsored terrorist organization, the vast majority of the Eastern Turkestan independence and information organizations disclaim violence. Supported largely by Uyghur émigrés who left China prior to the communist takeover in 1949, these organizations maintain a plethora of websites and activities that take a primarily negative view of Chinese policies in the region. Although not all organizations advocate independence or separatism, the vast majority of them do press for radical change in the region, detailing not only human rights violations, but environmental degradation, economic imbalances, and alternative histories of the region. In general, these websites can be divided roughly into those that are mainly information-based and others that are politically active advocacy sites. Nevertheless, whether informational or advocacy, nearly all of them are critical of Chinese policies in Xinjiang.

It is difficult to assess who the audience is for these websites, as they are all blocked in China, and mostly inaccessible in Central Asia due to either inadequate internet access or the high costs of getting on the net. Many Uyghurs I have talked with in China and in Central Asia have never heard of most of these sites. Interestingly, government officials in Xinjiang interested in the information provided on these sites also have said they do not have access. It is clear that Uyghurs in the Western diaspora, particularly in Europe, Turkey, the United States, Canada, and Australia, are frequent readers and contributors to these sites. In addition, events in the region since September 11 have led an increasing number of journalists and interested observers of the region to begin visiting the sites more regularly. In terms of content, it is interesting to note that a cursory monitoring of these sites reveals very little that can be associated with militant or radical Islam, and almost no calls for an Islamic "Jihad" against the Chinese state.[17] Most of the issues as noted above involve documenting the plight and history of the Uyghurs under Chinese rule in Xinjiang as opposed to their glorious, independent past and long history in the region. It is also important to note that few Chinese inside or outside of China have visited these sites so that they are quite unaware of these alternative histories. Although there are several sites available in Turkish and Uyghur, there is not one in Chinese. As such, like all internet groups, it is a self-selected audience and rarely reaches beyond those who already support and are interested in the agenda supported by the site. Financial support for these organizations and websites comes mostly from private individuals, foundations, and subscriptions (though these are rare). While it has been reported that wealthy Uyghur patrons in Saudi Arabia and Turkey, who became successful running businesses after migrating to these countries in the 1940s, have strongly supported these organizations financially in the past, there is no publicly available information on these sources.

Although most of these websites have limited funding and circulation, they should not be dismissed as forming only a "virtual" community without any substantial impact on events within Xinjiang. Not only have these websites served as an important source of information not available in the official Chinese media, but some scholars have begun to argue that internet sites often help to sway public opinion by virtue of their widespread availability and alternative reporting of important events.[18] While analysts are divided about the potency of the internet for swaying public opinion or influencing domestic events, there is an emerging consensus that it has clearly altered the way information is circulated and opinions are formed. Perhaps more importantly, scholars have concluded that the "virtual communities" formed by internet websites establish links and connections that can lead to broad social interactions and coalitions which have impacted political and socio-economic events. For example, it has been shown that social movements in Syria, Iraq, East Timor, Aceh, Chechnya, and Bosnia have been given strong support through these internet communities, providing not only increased information but large financial transfers as well.[19] The facility with which ISIS and its affiliates have used the internet to mobilize disgruntled young Muslims around the globe illustrates the potency of social media to garner a wide and disparate audience. While "cyber-separatism" would never be able on its own to unseat a local government, it is clear that it does link like-minded individuals and raise consciousness about issues that were often inaccessible to the general public. For an isolated region such as Xinjiang, and the widely dispersed Uyghur diaspora, the internet has dramatically altered the way the world sees the region and the CCP administration must respond to issues within it. To date, the Chinese party-state apparatus has been woefully incapable of utilizing the internet and social media to present an alternate message than radical Islam to disgruntled Uyghur youth.

It is clear that there are more than just internet organizations involved in separatist activities in and around Xinjiang. As noted above, the ETIM was recognized by the United Nations in October 2002 as an international terrorist organization responsible for domestic and international terrorist acts, which China claimed included a bombing of the Chinese consulate in Istanbul, assassinations of Chinese officials in Bishkek, and Uyghur officials in Kashgar thought to collaborate with Chinese officialdom.[20] This designation, however, created a controversy in that China and the U.S. presented little public evidence to positively link the ETIM organization with the specific incidents described (*People's Daily* 2001; Eckholm 2002; Hutzler 2002). In 2001, the U.S. State Department released a report that documented several separatist and terrorist groups operating inside the region and abroad, militating for an independent Xinjiang (McNeal 2001; Fogden 2002). The list included "The United Revolutionary Front of Eastern Turkestan" whose leader Yusupbek (Modan) Mukhlisi claimed to have 30 armed units with "20 million" Uyghurs primed for an uprising; the "Home of East Turkistan Youth," said to be linked to Hamas with a reported 2,000 members; the "Free Turkistan Movement" whose leader Abdul Kasim is said to have led the 1990 Baren uprising discussed above; the "Organization for the Liberation of Uyghuristan" whose leader Ashir Vakhidi is said to be committed to fighting Chinese "occupation" of the "Uyghur homeland"; and the so-called "Wolves of Lop Nor" who have claimed responsibility for various bombings and uprisings. The State Department report claims that all of these groups have tenuous links with al Qaeda, the Taliban, the Hizb-ut-Tahrir ("Islamic Revival"), and the Tableeghi Jamaat. Many of these groups were listed in the Chinese report that came out in early 2002, but failed to mention ETIM. It came as some surprise, therefore, when at the conclusion of his August 2001 visit to Beijing, Deputy Secretary of State Richard Armitage identified ETIM as the leading Uyghur group to be targeted as an international terrorist group.[21] The main issue for those critical of this designation, with so many identified groups, was why ETIM itself was singled out, unless it was for the political purpose of strengthening U.S.-China relations. The real issue for this chapter, however, is that despite the designation of ETIM, there are active Uyghur-related terrorist groups which can be said to be supportive of terrorism, as well as Uyghurs said to be sympathetic to and indeed fighting alongside of ISIS, but have never been proved to be directly implicated in any specific incident. Nevertheless, the Chinese party-state still tends to focus on ETIM or its avatar, TIP (The Islamic Party of Eastern Turkestan), as the main culprit behind all Uyghur related violent incidents.

Chinese authorities are clearly concerned that increasing international attention to the treatment of its minority and dissident peoples has put pressure on the region, with the U.S. and many Western governments continuing to criticize China for not adhering to its commitments to signed international agreements and human rights. As noted above, China ratified the International Covenant on Economic, Social, and Cultural Rights. Article 1 of the covenant says: "All peoples have the right of self-determination. By virtue of that right they freely determine their political status and freely pursue their economic, social and cultural development." Article 2 reads:

> All peoples may, for their own ends, freely dispose of their natural wealth and resources without prejudice to any obligations arising out of international economic co-operation, based upon the principle of mutual benefit, and international law. In no case may a people be deprived of its own means of subsistence.

Although China continues to quibble with the definition of "people," it is clear that the agreements are pressuring China to answer criticisms by Mary Robinson and other human rights advocates about its treatment of minority peoples. Clearly, with Xinjiang representing the last Muslim region under communism, large trade contracts with Middle Eastern Muslim nations, and five Muslim nations on its western borders, Chinese authorities have more to be concerned about than just international support for human rights. Xi Jinping's "One Belt, One Road" program depends on the peaceful resolution of China's "Xinjiang Problem." But on-going violent incidents suggest that an equitable solution is a long way off.

China's Uyghur separatists are small in number, poorly equipped, loosely linked, and vastly out-gunned by the People's Liberation Army and People's Armed Police. And note that though sometimes disgruntled about other rights' and mistreatment issues, China's nine other official Muslim minorities do not in general support Uyghur separatism. Few Hui support an independent Xinjiang, and the one million Kazakhs in Xinjiang would have very little say in an independent "Uyghuristan." Local support for separatist activities, particularly in Xinjiang and other border regions, is ambivalent and ambiguous at best, given the economic disparity between these regions and their foreign neighbors, including Tadjikistan, Kygyzstan, Pakistan, and especially Afghanistan. Memories in the region are strong of mass starvation and widespread destruction during the Sino-Japanese and civil war in the first half of this century, including intra-Muslim and Muslim-Chinese bloody conflicts, not to mention the chaotic horrors of the Cultural Revolution. Many local activists are calling not for complete separatism or real independence, but generally express concerns over environmental degradation, anti-nuclear testing, religious freedom, over-taxation, and recently imposed limits on childbearing. Many ethnic leaders are simply calling for "real" autonomy according to Chinese law for the five Autonomous Regions that are each led by First Party Secretaries who are all Han Chinese controlled by Beijing. Freedom of religion, protected by China's constitution, does not seem to be a key issue, as mosques are full in the region and pilgrimages to Mecca are often allowed for Uyghur and other Muslims (though recent visitors to the region report an increase in restrictions against mosque attendance by youth, students, and government officials) (Rotar and Homemann 2016). In addition, Islamic extremism does not as yet appear to have widespread appeal, especially among urban, educated Uyghur, yet it is only a matter of time until disgruntled young Uyghur males, like homegrown terrorists in Brussels, Paris, and San Bernardino, Los Angeles are drawn to the radical message of Jihadi Islam. However, the government has consistently rounded up any Uyghur suspected of being "too" religious, especially those identified as Sufis or the so-called Wahabbis (a euphemism in the region for strict Muslim, not an organized Islamic school). The admitted problem of Uyghur terrorism and dissent, even in the diaspora, is thus problematic for a government that wants to encourage integration and development in a region where the majority population are not only ethnically different, but also devoutly Muslim. How does a government integrate a strongly religious minority (be it Muslim, Tibetan, Christian, or Buddhist) into a Marxist-Capitalist system?

Conclusion

To an extent never seen before, the continued incorporation of Xinjiang into China has become inexorable, and perhaps irreversible. The need for the oil and mineral resources of the region since China became an oil importing nation in 1993 means that Chinese influence will only grow.[22] To be sure, the Uyghur are still oriented culturally and historically toward Central Asia in terms of religion, language, and ethnic custom, and interaction has increased in recent years due to the opening of the roads to Pakistan and Almaty. Certainly, pan-Turkism was appealing to some, but not all, Uyghurs during the early part of this century. Historical ties to Central Asia are strong. Yet separatist notions, given the current political incorporation of Xinjiang into China, while perhaps present, are not practicable. As noted above, this is predicated on the assumption that China as a nation holds together. If China should fail at the center, the peripheries will certainly destabilize, with Xinjiang and Tibet having the strongest prospects for separation given the history of dissent and organized separatist activities in the region. It is important to note here that other border regions with large minority populations, such as Yunnan, Guizhou, Guangxi (with 16 million Zhuang), Hainan, and even the Ningxia Hui Autonomous Region, have not had any reported separatist or terrorist activities. Clearly, by its own admission, the problems in Xinjiang and the oppositional voices of mostly Uyghur groups must be addressed by the state.

The problems facing Xinjiang, however, are much greater than those of Tibet if it were to become independent. Not only is it more integrated into the rest of China, but the Uyghur part of the population is less than half of the total and primarily located in the south, where there is less industry and fewer natural resources. As noted above, however, unless significant investment is found, Tarim oil and energy resources will never be a viable source of independent wealth. Poor past relations between the three main Muslim groups, Uyghur, Kazakh, and Hui, suggest that conflicts among Muslims would be as great as those between Muslims and Han Chinese. Most local residents believe that independence would lead to significant conflicts between these groups, along ethnic, religious, urban-rural, and territorial lines. Given the harsh climate and poor resources in the region, those caught in the middle would have few places to flee. Xinjiang Han would naturally seek to return to the interior of China, since Russia and Mongolia would be in no position to receive them. Yet given the premise that only a complete collapse of the state could precipitate a viable independence movement and internal civil war in Xinjiang, there would be few places the Han would be able to go. Certainly, the bordering provinces of Gansu and Qinghai would be just as disrupted, and Tibet would not be an option. Uyghur refugees would most likely seek to move south, since the north would be dominated by the Han and the western routes would be closed off by Kazakhstan and Kyrgyzstan. That leaves only the southern routes, and with the exception of Pakistan, no nation in the region would probably be equipped to receive them. Certainly, they would not be better off in present-day Tajikistan and Afghanistan. Given the on-going conflicts in Kashmir, even Pakistan, the most likely recipient of Uyghur refugees, would probably not wish further destabilization of the region. Note also that the main southern route to India and Pakistan, along the Karakhorum highway through the Torghurat pass, is generally passable less than six months out of the year. India, despite its poor relations with China, would certainly not want to add to its Muslim population. During many conversations in Xinjiang with local residents, Muslim and Han alike, it became clear that this fact is well known. Most think that in such a worst-case scenario, there would be nothing to do but stay and fight.

Clearly, China needs a new approach to resolve tensions in Xinjiang; purely Marxist and top-down developmentalist Keynesian economic strategies are not enough. The "Develop the West" campaign has slowed considerably since September 11, 2001 and international tourism has slowed dramatically in the region. Xi Jinping's "One Belt, One Road" strategy may actually be geared to merely leap-frog the region, not unlike the Soviet-inspired trans-Siberian railroad, which did little to bolster Inner Mongolian and even Mongolian economies, in favor of Beijing–Moscow bilateral trade links. The state's economic investment plan has proven not to be a panacea for resolving on-going ethnic problems in the region, that are based on more than just poverty. In a July–August 2002 *Foreign Affairs* article, Chien-Peng Chung, then with the Singaporean Institute of Defense and Strategic Studies, called for immediate political changes in the region to avoid further deterioration in ethnic relations (Chung 2002).

China is a sovereign state, and like all modern nations in the era of globalization faces tremendous challenges from migration, economic imbalance, ethnic unrest, and cyber-separatism. Clearly, the Xinjiang model must be as unique to the region as the region is to China itself. Not unlike Hong Kong (which under the "one country, two systems" formula continues to fly its own flag), and many proposals for Taiwan integration, the unique situation in Xinjiang, and possibly Tibet, calls for dramatic and creative solutions to local opposition in the region documented in this chapter. The future of this vastly important region, which Owen Lattimore once called the "pivot of Asia," depends upon it.

In the past 20 years, the opening of China to the outside world has meant much for the Uyghur who, despite many restrictions, have managed to travel beyond China's borders through Pakistan along the Karakhoram highway, through the Ili valley into Kazakhstan, or through Burma to Thailand and Malaysia, or by several CAAC flights to Istanbul from Urumqi. The number of Uyghur pilgrims traveling on the *Hajj* to Mecca has increased by 300 percent. These contacts have allowed the Uyghur to see themselves as participants in the broader Islamic *Umma*, while at the same time being Muslim citizens of the Chinese nation-state. As they return from the *Hajj*, many Uyghurs who generally travel together as a group have told me that they gained a greater sense of affinity with their own as one people than with the other multi-ethnic members of the international Islamic community. State-promoted tourism of foreign Muslims and tourists to Muslim areas in China in hopes of stimulating economic investment is also an important trend related to this opening of Xinjiang and its borders. Urumqi, a largely Han city constructed in the last 100 years, is undergoing an Islamic facelift with the official endorsement of Central Asian and Islamic architecture which serves to impress many visiting foreign Muslim dignitaries. Most foreigners come to see the colorful minorities and the traditional dances and costumes by which their ethnicity is portrayed in Chinese and foreign travel brochures. The re-creation of Uyghur ethnicity has come full circle: the Chinese party-state has identified a people who have in the last 40 years taken on that assigned identity as their own, and in the process, those who have accepted that identity have sought to define it and exploit it on their own terms. The Uyghur believe they have a 6,000-year cultural and physical history in the region. They are not likely to let it go. Unless new models are explored, patterns of Uyghur resistance may coalesce to increasingly resist Chinese nationalism, both pragmatic and popular, that have only served to inspire a stronger, and increasingly conservative Islamic Uyghur identity. As of today, among the nearly 10 million Uyghurs in China, and the nearly 1 million outside of China, there are an increasing number of voices struggling to be heard regarding the deteriorating situation in the Xinjiang Uyghur Autonomous Region.

Notes

1 See discussions of this event which had only sketchy reports by Michael (1995: 26) and Mackerras (2001: 38).

2 *Xinjiang Daily*, April 9, 1997, cited in *People's Republic of China: Gross Violation of Human Rights in the Xinjiang Uyghur Autonomous Region* (Amnesty International 1999); and *Xinjiang Daily*, July 21, 1997, cited in *Reuters*, Beijing, June 26, 1997.

3 See Ildiko Beller-Hann (2001: 9–23); Nathan Light's dissertation (1998), as well as his very informative webpage on Uyghur and Turkic culture and art, www.utoledo.edu/~nlight/mainpage.htm.

4 See Tyler (1996: 3); *The Economist* (1997a). Note that many Uyghurs in the diaspora believe that the bombs were set by Chinese authorities in order to justify a crackdown on Uyghurs in Xinjiang.

5 *Xinjiang Daily*, July 21, 1997, cited in *Reuters*, Beijing, June 26, 1997; see Becquelin (2000).

6 See her autobiography, Kadeer (2009), and the documentary film by Daniels (2009); see also a YouTube video interview with Ms. Kadeer conducted by Al Jazeera (2010).

7 See Carlson (2014). Tohti's daughter, a student at Indiana University, now living in exile, has published a book (Ilham 2015) about her efforts to win her father's release.

8 Two exceptions include a reported derailment of a Xinjiang train due to a bombing on February 12, 1997, and an attack on a power station in Hejing on July 10, 1999 (unpublished Rand Report).

9 Anwar Yusuf, President of the Eastern Turkistan National Freedom Center, Washington, D.C. Personal interview, April 14, 1999.

10 An excellent photo essay from Southern Xinjiang on *Sixth Tone* has been circulated on the web detailing recent struggles of the Uyghur. See Sun (2017).

11 In the Chinese context, see Ivan Rasmussen's (2015) interesting dissertation on Chinese "rational nationalism."

12 See Geertz (1973: 255–310). Note, the author was inspired by his 1988–89 year with Clifford Geertz at the Institute for Advanced Study in Princeton to examine Uyghur nationalism from a primordialist perspective. Prof. Geertz once told the author that he wished he had never written the article cited above, since many later associated Geertz with supporting primordialist-inspired nationalism, which he wholeheartedly rejected.

13 PRC State Council White Paper, *Development and Progress in Xinjiang*, September 21, 2009. www.chinaconsulatechicago.org/eng/zt/wp/t585843.htm (accessed February 22, 2017).

14 See writings by Isa Yusuf Alptekin's son, Erkin Alptekin (1978), which also present alternative histories of the Uyghur from that of the Chinese state; see also an article in *South China Morning Post* (Hong Kong) (2002). For Alptekin's involvement with the Unrecognized Nations and People's Organization in The Hague, see its website: www.unpo.org/member/eturk.html.

15 See Information Office of the State Council of the People's Republic of China (1999: 50). See also the Law of the People's Republic of China on Regional National Autonomy (1984), with full text of White Paper on Minority Policies, September 28, 1999, at www.China.org.cn. For poverty in the region specifically among the Uyghur, see Gilley (2001).

16 Estimates differ widely on the number of Uyghurs living outside of China in the diaspora. Uyghurs in Central Asia are not always well represented in the state censuses, particularly since 1991. Shichor (2002) estimates approximately 500,000 living abroad, about 5–6 percent of the total world Uyghur population. Shichor notes that as in many statistical matters, Uyghur websites differ dramatically on the official Uyghur population numbers, from up to 25 million Uyghur inside Xinjiang, to up to 10 million in the diaspora; see, for example, www.Uyghur.org, the site supported by Anwar Yusuf, President of the Eastern Turkistan National Freedom Center in Washington, D.C. Uyghurs in Turkey boast there are over 100,000 Uyghur there, but Turkey does not count any Turkic sub-ethnic group in its state censuses, only *non*-Turkish groups (Armenians, Jews, Arabs, etc.). Thus, an estimate of 1 million Uyghur outside of China is not overly inflated since it is well known that the largest Uyghur populations outside of China are in Central Asia, South Asia, and Turkey, where population statistics are especially unreliable.

17 There is an increasing number of examples of websites calling for jihad among the Uyghur against China, but it is impossible to gauge how influential these sites are and how widely they are viewed by the Uyghur. See Page and Levin (2014).

18 For studies of the influence of the internet in influencing wider public opinion in Asia, see a recent collection of essays in the *Asian Journal of Social Science* edited by Zaheer Baber (2002).

19 See Foster (1997); Jones (1997); Jordan (1999); Rushkoff (1994); Smith and Kollock (1999).

20 The East Turkestan Islamic Movement (ETIM) is known only as a shadowy group known only to be previously active in Afghanistan and founded in the mid-1990s by Hassan Mahsum. Mahsum had served three years in a labor camp in Xinjiang and had recruited other Uyghurs, including his number three leader Rashid who was captured with the Taliban and returned to China in Spring 2001. See Hutzler (2001b).

21 Conclusion of China Visit Press Conference, Deputy Secretary of State Richard L. Armitage, Beijing, China, U.S. Department of State, August 26, 2002.

22 One active list-serv and website documenting China's growing exchange with the Middle East is moderated by the Turkish scholar, Tugrul Keskin (Keskin 2017).

References

Al Jazeera (2010) One on One – Rebiya Kadeer, YouTube video. Available from: www.youtube.com/watch?v=n0JtQTb-YxE [accessed: January 5, 2017].

Alptekin, E. (1978) *Uygur Türkleri* [The Uygur Turks], Istanbul: Boğaziçi Yayınları.

Amnesty International (1999) *People's Republic of China: Gross Violation of Human Rights in the Xinjiang Uyghur Autonomous Region*, April 21.

Amnesty International (2000) "Arbitrary Detention of Rebiya Kadeer – a Women's Human Rights Defender and Prisoner of Conscience," February 2. Available from: www.amnesty.org/en/documents/asa17/004/2000/en/.

Baber, Z. (2002) "The Internet and Social Change in Asia and Beyond," *Asian Journal of Social Science*, Vol. 30, No 2: 195–198.

Becquelin, N. (2000) "Xinjiang in the Nineties," *The China Journal*, No. 44: 65–90.

Beller-Hann, I. (2001) "Making the Oil Fragrant: Dealings with the Supernatural Among the Uyghurs in Xinjiang," *Asian Ethnicity*, Vol. 2, No. 1: 9–23.

Best, R., Bolkcom, C., Chapman, R., Cronin, R., Dumbaugh, K., Goldman, S., Manyin, M., Morrison, W., and O'Rourke, R. (2001) "China-US Aircraft Collision Incident of April 2001: Assessments and Policy Implications," Congressional Research Service [Library of Congress].

Brahimi, R. (1999) "Russia, China, and Central Asian Leaders Pledge to Fight Terrorism, Drug Smuggling," CNN News Service, August 25.

Carlson, K. (2014) "Ilham Tohti, Online Voice of China's Uyghurs, Sentenced to Life in Prison," *Electronic Frontier Foundation*, September 25. Available from: www.eff.org/deeplinks/2014/09/ilham-tohti-sentenced-life-prison [accessed: January 7, 2017].

Chatterjee, P. (1986) *Nationalist Thought and the Colonial World: A Derivative Discourse*, London: Zed Books.

Chow, K.W., Doak, K.M., and Fu, P.S. eds. (2001) *Constructing Nationhood in Modern East Asia*, Ann Arbor: University of Michigan Press.

Chung, C.P. (2002) "China's 'War on Terror': September 11 and Uighur Separatism," *Foreign Affairs*, July/August.

Cole, S. (2002) "Nationalism and Modernism," *MFS Modern Fiction Studies*, Vol. 48, No. 2: 453–460.
Daniels, J. (2009) *The 10 Conditions of Love*. Documentary Film. www.imdb.com/name/nm1809246/.
Dittmer, L. and Kim, S.S. eds. (1993) *China's Quest for National Identity*, Ithaca, NY: Cornell University Press.
Eckholm, E. (2002) "U.S. Labeling of Group in China as Terrorist is Criticized," *New York Times*, September 13.
Eckholm, E. and Smith, C.S. (2001) "Fearing Unrest, China Pressures Muslim Group," *New York Times*, October 5.
Fogden, S. (2002) *Writing Insecurity: The PRC's Push to Modernize China and the Politics of Uighur Identity*. Thesis (M.Sc.), University of Wales, Aberystwyth.
Foster, D. (1997) "Community and Identity in the Electronic Village," in David Porter, ed., *Internet Culture*, New York: Routledge, pp. 23–38.
Geertz, C. (1973) "The Integrative Revolution: Primordial Sentiments and Civil Politics in the New States," in *The Interpretation of Cultures*, New York: Basic Books.
Gilley, B. (2001) "'Uyghurs Need Not Apply'," *Far Eastern Economic Review*, August 28.
Gladney, D.C. (1990) "The Peoples of the People's Republic: Finally in the Vanguard?" *The Fletcher Forum of World Affairs*, Vol. 12, No. 1: 62–76.
Gladney, D.C. (1995) "China's Ethnic Reawakening," *Asia-Pacific Issues*, No. 18: 1–8.
Gladney, D.C. (1996) *Muslim Chinese: Ethnic Nationalism in the People's Republic*, Cambridge, MA: Harvard University Press.
Gries, P.H. (2004) *China's New Nationalism: Pride, Politics, and Diplomacy*, Berkeley: University of California Press.
Guo, Y.J. (2004) *Cultural Nationalism in Contemporary China: The Search for National Identity Under Reform*, London: Routledge.
Guo, S.J. and Guo, B.G. (2008). *China in Search of a Harmonious Society (Challenges Facing Chinese Political Development)*, Lanham, MD: Lexington Books.
Han, E. (2013) *Contestation and Adaptation: The Politics of National Identity in China*, New York: Oxford University Press.
Hechter, M. (2000) "Nationalism and Rationality," *Journal of World-systems Research*, Vol. 6, No. 2: 308–329.
Hutzler, C. (2001a) "Trade Is China's Carrot to Muslim Separatists," *Wall Street Journal*, September 21.
Hutzler, C. (2001b) "China-Iraq Policy Is Risky for U.S.," *Asian Wall Street Journal*, September 10.
Hutzler, C. (2002) "U.S. Gesture to China Raises Crackdown Fears," *Wall Street Journal*, September 13.
Ian, J. (1999) "China Arrests Noted Businesswoman in Crackdown in Muslim Region," *Wall Street Journal*, August 18.
Ilham, J. (2015) *Jewher Ilham: A Uyghur's Fight to Free Her Father*, New Orleans: University of New Orleans Press.
Information Office of the State Council of the People's Republic of China (1999) "National Minority Policies and Its Practice in China," p. 50.
Jones, S.G. (1997) "The Internet and Its Social Landscape," in Steven G. Jones, ed., *Virtual Culture: Identity and Community in Cybersociety*, London; New Delhi: Sage.
Jordan, T. (1999) *Cyberpower: The Culture and Politics of Cyberspace and the Internet*, London; New York: Routledge.
Kadeer, R. (2009) *Dragon Fighter: One Woman's Epic Struggle for Peace with China*, Carlsbad, CA: Kales Press.
Keskin T. (2017) "China, Islam, and the Middle East," http://chinaandthemiddleeast.blogspot.com.tr/2017/01/note-to-abbas-wake-up-china-is.html [accessed: January 5, 2017].
Lee, J.T.H., Nedilsky, L.V., and Cheung, S.K. eds. (2012) *China's Rise to Power: Conceptions of State Governance*, New York: Palgrave Macmillan, p. 89.
Light, N. (1998) *Slippery Paths: The Performance and Canonization of Turkic Literature and Uyghur Muqam Song in Islam and Modernity*. Thesis (Ph.D.), Indiana University.
Llobera, J.R. (1999) "Recent Theories of Nationalism," Working Papers, Universitat Autònoma de Barcelona. Available from: https://pdfs.semanticscholar.org/f6d0/6f5434d794c3fc8a5d9c69821064e598e7f4.pdf.
Mackerras, C. (2001) *The New Cambridge Handbook of Contemporary China*, Cambridge, U.K.; New York: Cambridge University Press.
McNeal, D.L. (2001) "China's Relations with Central Asian States and Problems with Terrorism," U.S. Department of State, Congressional Research Service Report. Available from: http://fpc.state.gov/documents/organization/7945.pdf.

Michael, D. (1995) *Xinjiang: Ethnicity, Separatism and Control in Chinese Central Asia*, Durham, NC: University of Durham, Department of East Asian Studies.

Montefiore, C.S. (2013) "How China Distorts its Minorities Through Propaganda," BBC Culture. Available from: www.bbc.com/culture/story/20131215-how-china-portrays-its-minorities.

Ouyang, L.B. (2005) "Music, Memory, and Nostalgia: Collective Memories of Cultural Revolution Songs in Contemporary China," *China Review*, Vol. 5, No. 2: 151–175.

Page, P. and Levin, N. (2014) "Web Preaches Jihad to China's Muslim Uyghurs: China Says Internet, Social Media Incite Terrorism Among Uyghur Minority," *The Wall Street Journal*, June 24. Available from: www.wsj.com/articles/web-preaches-jihad-to-chinas-muslim-uighurs-1403663568 [accessed: January 10, 2017].

Pan, P. (2002) "In China's West, Ethnic Strife Becomes 'Terrorism'," *Washington Post*, July 14.

People's Daily (2001) "China Also Harmed by Separatist-Minded Eastern Turkistan Terrorists," October 10.

Pun, P. (2001) "Separatists Trained in Afghanistan, Says Official," *The Standard*, October 22.

Rasmussen, I.W. (2015) *Rational Nationalism on the Rise: Chinese Public Opinion and Foreign Relations*, Unpublished Ph.D. dissertation, The Fletcher School of Law and Diplomacy, Tufts University.

Rauhala, E. (2014) "The Politics of Pop in China's Xinjiang Region," *Time*, October 24.

Reuters (2001) "Uyghur Separatist Sentenced to Death," October 18.

Rotar, I. and Homemann, M. (2016) "CHINA: Xinjiang – What You Can't Do in a Mosque," *Forum 18*, September 28. Available from: www.forum18.org/archive.php?article_id=421 [accessed: January 11, 2017].

Rushkoff, D. (1994) *Cyberia: Life in the Trenches of Hyperspace*, New York: Harper Collins.

Savage, C. (2013) "U.S. Frees Last of the Chinese Uighur Detainees from Guantánamo Bay," *New York Times*, December 31.

Shichor, Y. (2002) "Virtual Transnationalism: Uygur Communities in Europe and the Quest for Eastern Turkestan Independence," unpublished paper.

Smith, M.A. and Kollock, P. eds. (1999) *Communities in Cyberspace*, London; New York: Routledge.

South China Morning Post (Hong Kong) (2002) "Xinjiang a Time Bomb Waiting to Explode," May 29.

Sun, J.B. (2017) "The Quiet Undercurrents of South Xinjiang," *Sixth Tone*, February 3. Available from: www.sixthtone.com/news/quiet-undercurrents-south-xinjiang [accessed: February 6, 2017].

The Economist (1997a) "A Bomb in Beijing," March 13.

The Economist (1997b) "China Fears for its Wild West," November 13.

Tyler, P.E. (1996) "Chinese Muslims Recount Their Days of Terror," *New York Times*, November 10.

Wasserstrom, J.N. (2010) *China in the 21st Century: What Everyone Needs to Know*, New York: Oxford University Press.

Wei, C.X.G. and Liu, X.Y. eds. (2001) *Chinese Nationalism in Perspective: Historical and Recent Cases*, Westport, CN: Greenwood Press.

Wu, G.G. (2008) "From Post-imperial to Late Communist Nationalism: Historical Change in Chinese Nationalism from May Fourth to the 1990s," *Third World Quarterly*, Vol. 29, Issue 3: 467–482.

Zhao, S.S. (2004) *A Nation-State by Construction: Dynamics of Modern Chinese Nationalism*, Stanford, CA: Stanford University Press.

Zheng, Y.N. (1999) *Discovering Chinese Nationalism in China: Modernization, Identity, and International Relations*, Cambridge; New York: Cambridge University Press.

PART V

The CCP in the twenty-first century

21
THE FUTURE OF THE CHINESE COMMUNIST PARTY

Kerry Brown and Konstantinos Tsimonis

Introduction

The future of the Chinese Communist Party (CCP) is important because of the relative uniqueness of the political model that the People's Republic of China (PRC) still has in the twenty-first century. There are five countries remaining in which a Marxist Leninist Communist Party still has a monopoly on power – Vietnam, the Democratic People's Republic of Korea (DPRK), Laos, Cuba and the PRC. Of these, the PRC is self-evidently the most important. It is the world's most populous nation, its third largest in terms of physical size and the second in terms of economic ranking. It is likely to overtake the US sometime in the next two decades as the world's largest single economy. That it stands alone in the world's top ten economies in its adherence to communism (the rest are all multiparty democracies) makes it even more of an anomaly.

The continuing survival, and even prospering, of the Chinese governance system poses questions about the assumed universality of democratic systems as the most superior by many western scholars and politicians. It has also raised questions about just how necessary democratic processes are for capitalist growth. As Alexander Pantsov and Stephen Levine (2015) argue in their study of Deng Xiaoping, China's paramount leader after 1978 who inspired the Reform and Opening Up process, Deng showed that Chinese style communism was viable, and that it could exist side by side with capitalism. Subsequently, others have unpacked the idiosyncratic manner in which China has developed its economy in ways compatible with capitalism, but maintained its socialism with Chinese characteristics political model.[1]

The CCP has never seemed to look more integral and necessary to Chinese future growth trajectory. After the crisis of faith during the Tiananmen Square Massacre period in 1989, it has sought new sources of legitimacy, looking in ways which have never been explored before at nationalism, traditional Chinese culture and deeper integration into the outside world through entry to global governance institutions[2] like the World Trade Organization in 2001. This has resulted in a hybrid, but pragmatic model. At heart, the Party has maintained its core priority – a fierce hold on power. But the tools and strategies that it has used to achieve this objective have changed dramatically and now include both traditional authoritarian repression and the fear of coercion, as well as public diplomacy, mechanisms for societal feedback, consultation and responsiveness. Despite the stresses and contradictions such an arrangement entails, it has enabled the CCP to resist the so-called "end of history" model proposed by some in the 1990s predicting the universal victory of liberal democracy. While the Communist Party of the Soviet Union and many of its satellites have been swept away since 1990, China continues on its course.

Even so, its experiment is still a young one. Chinese leaders in the era of Xi Jinping are as fond of talking about crisis and not becoming complacent about power as those in the past. Speaking to Party officials in 2014 and into 2015, Xi has berated them for treating power as some market commodity, a thing to monetarize, with the phenomenon of "buying and selling officials." The idea of the Party being in a distinct place above society and guiding it has been sullied by this other narrative of it being a money making machine, pumping out material growth and wealth, and allowing its elites to live off the good results of this. Such a phenomenon, to Xi at least, is a violation of the Party's historic mission, and, more importantly, a sure way for it to take its eyes off the key political goal – the creation of a rich, strong country restored to its position in premodern times as the center of the world. The CCP after all has to worry about just how short lived communist parties on its model have proved. The longest serving of them, the Soviet Union, clocked up 74 years. The CCP will reach this mark in 2023, if it stays in power. Then it will be moving into the unknown. The question nagging in the background is, if communism eventually failed in its birthplace, then why will the PRC be different?

Wrecked futures

One of the issues immediately involved in thinking about the future of the CCP is the terrible record that experts and others have in predicting its future. After the massacre in 1989, the consensus was that the Party's days were numbered, and that it would go the way of other similar regimes. Throughout the 1990s, there was a desire particularly by some constituencies in the US, to see "regime change" through a process of a more or less "peaceful [democratic] evolution" of the Chinese polity, driven by the same market forces it itself had unleashed. Events like the entry into the WTO and the 2008 Beijing Olympics were interpreted as being moments leading toward domestic change within the PRC. It was just a matter of time before the third wave of democratization reached Beijing, and the system succumbed to the universally sustainable model of multiparty, rules based modern democratic governance.

As the years have gone on, and history so far seems to be resisting this route, then the speculation has been simply that the Party in some ways is cheating destiny, and living on borrowed time. Gordon Chang (2001, 2011) is perhaps the best known and most insistent on the collapse of the current system, on its unsustainability and intrinsic instability. Throughout the decade after 2000, he has declared that the country is about to collapse, even being brave enough to give dates. These dates have come and gone. But the CCP has continued moving forward.

In one overview of predictions in economic, political and social areas, Australian scholar Roger Irvine (2015) draws together the various expert commentary on China's future. The record is not a particularly impressive one. Not a single western economist foresaw the reforms that started in 1978. Only figures like former diplomat Stephen Fitzgerald were prescient enough before 1978 to suspect that the Party was about to fundamentally change its policies and its governance philosophy. Over the ensuing four decades, in the economic realm in particular, predictions have proved remarkably wide of the mark. Perhaps because expert communities have become more careful, political scientists now hedge their language about where the Party might be heading and how durable it is. While not as parlous as the record of economists in trying to tell what the future holds for the PRC, political and social scientists have failed to see events like the ability of the Party to allow entrepreneurs to enter its ranks (2001), the ultimately relatively smooth succession between the leadership of Hu Jintao and Xi Jinping (2012 to 2014) and since that year a whole series of surprising events (the charging and imprisonment of former Politburo Standing Committee member Zhou Yongkang in 2015, and the rising autocratic nature of Xi's leadership) seem to buck the assumed laws of Chinese domestic politics.

Over 2015 and into 2016, however, noted Sinologists such as David Shambaugh (2015) and Minxin Pei (Forsythe 2016) have become harder in their assertion that the CCP is in perpetual crisis, that the hardening of its political stance from 2013 is a sign of weakness rather than strength, and that it is facing the moment of its ultimate demise. They see signs within the Party of a crisis of legitimacy, and an inner lack of certainty that it will, in the end, make it through the next half a decade or so. Shambaugh and Pei are right to question Chinese exceptionalism, the view that China will escape the pressures of modernity for an open political system. Shambaugh, in a recent (2016) defense of his "Coming Chinese Crackup" argument, asks "why should China be immune to the processes that afflicted other late-stage Leninist regimes?" and goes one step further by suggesting that modernization theory may explain not only some of the systemic pressures to the CCP but also its "likely future evolution." The end of history for China may be delayed but is certainly coming. Alas, like Beckett's characters in *Waiting for Godot*, we are perpetually doomed to simply need to wait a bit longer, with the final day of judgment never truly arriving.

Of course, such assertions have not gone unchallenged. Stein Ringen (2016) is highly critical of liberal views that interpret political, social and economic developments in China as steps in a path leading to an inevitable democratic future. He develops a well-rounded analysis of the Chinese party-state, its coercive apparatus, public service, state finances, economic model and relations with society and concludes that scenarios of regime demise and democratization are highly improbable. Instead, he argues that resilience and continuity of the CCP's dictatorial rule (what he refers to as "controlocracy") is a more convincing scenario, even within the context of Xi's more ideological and repressive style of governance. In two other recent studies, Wenfang Tang (2016) and Bruce Dickson (2016) examine opinion surveys from China and conclude that despite mounting governance challenges the CCP still enjoys high levels of public support. Tang attributes pro-CCP political attitudes to China's "populist authoritarian" political culture, which is the product of socialization of the Party's ideology, mobilization patterns and organization systems since the founding years of the People's Republic (Tang 2016: 152–164). At the heart of China's populist authoritarianism is a hyper-responsive government that attempts to compensate for the lack of democracy and its weak political institutions by addressing the demands of at least some sectors of Chinese society (ibid.: 156–159). Following a different line of argument, Dickson explains that current high levels of public support for the Party are the result of a strategy that combines repression, legitimation (through normative appeals and material incentives) and co-optation of new elites. Responding to recent speculation on the effects of an economic slowdown, Dickson provides evidence suggesting that GDP growth rates are not a threat to the Party's legitimacy as long as personal income is increasing (2016: 223–233). Although both authors are careful to acknowledge that public opinion is far from static, they appear confident about the ability of their findings to reflect future trends.

There is always a question about futurology. Being about something that, by definition, doesn't yet exist means that it is prone to the urges of specific desires, imaginations and agendas. The future is a field for subjectivity – it is impossible to be objective about it. And in speaking about the CCP's future, it is often the case that individuals betray their own feelings about the Party now and project into the future some wish for either its prosperous development, or its demise.

Internal views

One way of trying to mitigate this issue of thinking about the future involving projecting one's own aspirations and desires rather than being particularly objective, is to look hard at what individuals in the system say about the future. How do Chinese elite CCP leaders within the system speak about the future? In many ways, the future is a huge political asset for them. As a developing country, China's chances of seeing more prosperity, more growth, more development in the future are high. Regressing would be disastrous. Staying with the status quo and maintaining current development levels would also be hugely disappointing. Chinese people on the whole look forward to a future which will be better than today. In this sense, their attitude would be different to publics in western developed systems where the idea of simply preserving the good things of today into the future would be acceptable.

Speaking to the sense of optimism about the future is something Xi Jinping has been keen to do, with his reference to "the China Dream" from 2013. He and other leaders have also created a framework with which to structure the future – the idea of centennial goals. Anniversaries have always mattered to Chinese leaders. Marking the creation of the PRC, or specific historic events, offers a moment to showcase their achievements and promote their narrative of historic development. Of course, ideologically they are married to a belief in dialectic development, and a teleology in which things will continue to improve. This was the idea behind scientific development promoted by Xi's predecessor Hu Jintao. Not only will the future be better; under this mentality, it *has to* be better. Ironically, in their fundamental utopianism and idealism, Chinese leaders from 1949 have been at one. As Deng said, "I am a Communist, and consequently an optimist" (Pantsov and Levine 2015: 95).

The Centennial goals, which started to appear in leader's speeches from 2014, were linked to the history of the Party, and reinforced the sense that the Party and state are so tightly hitched together that there cannot be one without the other. For China, therefore, 2021 will matter for two reasons, in this reckoning. The first is that it will mark the moment when the country will achieve middle income status, with a per capita GDP of $13,000. This in itself is an important moment for any society. It is one in which other economies like that of South Korea, Japan and Singapore did face challenges in their domestic situation – from the problem of how to balance rising living standards, and satisfy not just the material but the political and cultural demands of a rising middle class to the problem of middle income trap – shifting from one model where manufacturing and export led growth with low wages moves to one involving more services and consumption, but where a country is too expensive for the first model, and not yet ready to wholly rely on growth from the second.

Linked to this moment of achieving middle income status is the accompanying hugely symbolic event – the hundredth anniversary of the foundation of the CCP in 1921. The second centennial goal is set for 2049 and marks the delivery of full Chinese style modernity, but also the centenary of a hundred years of the PRC being in existence. In fact, this goal has existed in the imaginations of Chinese leaders since the time of Deng, when he referred to its importance. Beyond this, however, the Party elite's language about the future is highly abstract. For a system in which it is often claimed that the Chinese are able to plan and invest in the long term future in ways which are more defined than democracies where the key aim is to respond to short term objectives tied to elections, the fact that the longest term that Chinese leaders really focus on is the five years for their macro-economic national development plans, the latest of which, the thirteenth, was issued in 2016, seems to contradict this.

What one can say is that the CCP leadership has outlined, in a very abstract sense, what the future aim of its society should be, even while it has avoided being bogged down in specifics.

The Party mission in the last four decades has been linked to the broad achievement of modernity. This in some senses provides the link between the pre and post 1978 era, despite their very clear ideological and political differences. Under Mao Zedong, China was diplomatically isolated, 99 percent of the economy was in state hands, and the core ideology was promoting class struggle through 16 mass campaigns from 1951 onwards culminating in what Chinese writer Ba Jin called the "spiritual holocaust of the Cultural Revolution" from 1966. After 1978, China reversed position in many issues, linking up with the outside world and developing so much that by 2016 it was the chief trading partner of over 130 countries, its ideology was based on economic development success and delivering national greatness, and less than 50 percent of the economy was in state hands. Despite this, Xi Jinping is adamant that there is a link between before and after 1978 – both were focused on achieving modernity in China. Without the Mao period, China's chance to be where it is now would not have existed. That is the link. Both were guided by the commitment to a Chinese style of modernity.

The CCP's role in delivering this modernity is an instrumental one. Once it has achieved whatever full modernity turns out to be, however, there is a question about what its future role will be. Once society is generally prosperous, the cities sustainable and clean, society stable and balanced, rural China well governed and well developed, and a vibrant middle class large and politically mobilized, what then? The Party in achieving modernity performs a facilitating role. The principal role is not about preserving it and its role in society for its own sake, but to achieve the goals of modernity outlined above. Once those are achieved, where does the Party stand? Surely, to paraphrase Marx, it should wither away.

The fear factor

While the future for Chinese leaders is a zone of opportunity and optimism as stated above, it is also through uncertainty regarding the CCP's relations with Chinese society and its internal cohesion, a source of fear. This fear enters into their political messaging. While Chinese leaders talk of a bright future, they also refer at the same time to the complex situation in the outside world meaning that there is the paramount need to maintain stability and to fight against enemies within society who challenge delivery of this great possible future. As with the vision of modernity referred to in the section above, this offers a second bridge with the Maoist era, because that period too was rich in the sense of enemies within, saboteurs and wreckers who had to be constantly guarded against. In Xi's China, the enemies are those who worship inappropriate political models from the outside world, who try to destabilize society to return it to the nightmare of disunity and victimized weakness from the past. These people in being opposed to the Party mission are also enemies of the state and the nation it is trying to create for its people.

This fear about the future can only be combated by creating at least some places for certainty. The Chinese leadership portrays a future where the great prize is the full achievement of Chinese style modernity and great nation status. But it also makes clear that this dream will not be achieved without the Party leading the people. The Party with its hold on power creates at least some level of certainty and stability. Removing it from the equation means contemplating a future with far higher levels of risk. This is not to deny that a China with a different political model can also achieve national greatness. What it does show is that this will happen with higher levels of uncertainty, and therefore greater potential risk. The Party therefore purveys provision of higher levels of certainty as one of its key attractions. Chinese people may no longer be attracted by its ideology. Its history might be problematic. But its function as a tool to provide at least some strategic clarity and stability is regarded as worth supporting.

Addressing the fear factor within the Party has proved complex. China's leaders understand that the CCP in claiming it provides more certainty has to somehow deliver on this. For this reason, they have developed norms and institutions to manage levels of uncertainty. As Andrew Nathan (2003) and others have observed, one of the key ingredients for the CCP's success in the last two decades has been the institutionalization of checks and balances at the center and consultative channels at the periphery. At the very top, regular and consensual procedures aim at identifying competent leaders, securing stable terms, avoiding uncontrolled elite infighting and minimizing systemic weakness during power transitions. At the periphery, the official opening of Party membership to China's entrepreneurs as well as the establishment of new processes and institutions such as forums for consultation and deliberation with key social groups, village elections and feedback mechanisms are meant to provide pressure relief valves for the regime, co-opt new social forces and direct the dynamism of an increasingly sophisticated society to the Party's developmental vision. Public participation in these institutions demonstrates the importance of "consultative Leninism" (Tsang 2009) in dealing with the future.[3] Overall, the rationale for institutionalization has been to protect the regime from itself and the many degenerative tendencies historically present in Leninist parties: personalistic rule, ideology-driven economic policies, introverted Party life that breeds factionalism and opportunism, bureaucratic lethargy and policy-making stasis. Chinese politicians have repeatedly attributed the Soviet Union's collapse to these factors.

Still, Xi Jinping has been among those that were apprehensive about the way the CCP's future was shaping up in the last decade. China's leaders took a conservative turn in the period 2008–2009 when the country faced a series of domestic challenges (tensions with minorities, dissidents, struggles with civil society actors) and the unknown consequences of a global economic downturn that exacerbated the problems of China's developmental model. Since he assumed power in 2012, year after year, Xi has appeared increasingly autocratic. Why? Optimists see political centralization as tactically the preparatory stage before the launch of a new round of economic reforms that will be extensive and comprehensive even when compared to those by Zhao Ziyang in the 1980s and Zhu Rongji in the 1990s, and which therefore could create uncertainty and unforeseen outcomes. In this context, the CCP has to get its own house in order and be very stolid and disciplined in itself, before unleashing change on the rest of society. However, very few of the economic and social reforms announced in 2013 have been carried out, and those implemented, such as the free trade zones in Pudong, Guangdong, Fujian and Tianjin, have produced limited results. Similarly, SOE reform, a key aspect of the economic agenda of the 18th Party Congress, has yet to materialize.

Skeptics view Xi as a leader who has succumbed to the great temptation of authoritarian politics: reliance on Weberian style charismatic leadership. But this is not just a matter of leadership style preference. Legal scholar Carl Minzner (2015) explains that in the face of mounting structural failures in China's socioeconomic model, Xi Jinping has opted for unwinding the new institutions and internal Party norms of his predecessors in an attempt to clear the regime's pervasive weaknesses as well as respond to the various policy dead-ends of the last decade. At the top, collective leadership norms that maintained the General Secretary as "first among equals" have been replaced by calls for obedience to the "core leader" and a personality cult. In the CCP, Party organs and organizations rise and fall as a result of Xi's attempt to centralize power. The powerful Central Commission for Discipline Inspection in charge of the anti-corruption "struggle," in this framework, operates as Xi's own purging mechanism for opponents without institutional or, even, political checks and balances.[4] The Communist Youth League, on the other hand, an assumed bastion of support for Li Keqiang and Hu Jintao, has suffered a significant blow with its budget halved and many of its officials demoted. But perhaps more worrying for

China's future is that at a time when better technocratic management of the economy and the state is needed, the trend for separation between Party and government initiated by General Secretary Zhao Ziyang from 1987 to 1989 and supported by Deng Xiaoping appears to have been reversed.[5]

Centralization is therefore Xi Jinping's "only path to a breakthrough" according to Minzner, his way to prevent a version of the future that is full of uncertainty and instability. If this view is correct, Xi Jinping's centralization of power can be compared to Yuan Shikai's attempt to install himself as emperor in 1915 in the Republican era when facing economic uncertainty and political challenges to his authority. But as with Yuan's fateful decision, Xi's centralization appears to cause concern and negative reactions within some of China's political establishment. Only in 2016, criticism and even a call for Xi's resignation appeared in the least expected places and forms: an essay titled "A Thousand Yes-Men Cannot Equal One Honest Advisor" published on the website of the Central Commission for Discipline Inspection expressed apprehension about Xi's style of leadership (CCDI 2016); and a call for Xi's resignation surfaced at a news website with links to the provincial government of Xinjiang (Wu Jie News 2016). These incidents follow rumors circulating since 2014 on mounting dissatisfaction against Xi even among the top echelons of the Party and the Army. Although the extent of dissatisfaction in the CCP is difficult to measure precisely, so far, Xi's attempt to deal with the fear factor within his Party is highly circumscribed. It is an ongoing project, with no end-point clearly in sight yet.

China 2030

There is much more policy detail about the future trajectory the country might take as it aims toward the ultimate goal of achieving by 2049 democracy with Chinese characteristics under the leadership of the CCP in a report issued by the World Bank and the Development Research Council under the State Council in 2012. In this long study, 2030 is posited as a year in which China will achieve what it calls in its title "A Modern, Harmonious, High Income Society." To realize this goal, it focuses on six areas:

1. Implement structural reform to strengthen the foundations of a market economy
2. Accelerate the pace of innovation and create an open innovation system
3. Seize the opportunity to go green
4. Promote social security
5. Strengthen the fiscal system
6. Seek mutually beneficial relations with the world.

(World Bank and DRC, State Council, PRC 2013: xv)

There are some ways in which parts of this list of objectives have already been enshrined in official state and Party policy. Making the market "necessary for reform" rather than preferential was the key ideological change of the Third Plenum in 2013. Strengthening the fiscal system has centered on the creation of an international finance center and its Free Trade Zone in Shanghai. Going green has appeared in the important accords signed with the US in late 2014, and through China's 13th Five-Year Plan from 2016, along with greater enforcement for state and non-state enterprises.

These are core areas in which the Party has to deliver. Its success is posited on achieving things in these specific sectors. So its future is contingent. It does not have a divine right to rule, even though there are some elite leaders who might believe this. Its legitimacy, internal cohesion and, ultimately, its longevity are dependent on delivery. So if we want to think about the Party future, we have to think about how easy it might be to achieve these six goals.

Market reform: In the Third Plenum of the 18th Central Committee held in November 2013, the Communist Party stated that the market is "necessary" for reform, not preferential (*Decision* 2014). They have since discussed allowing marketization of, for instance, utility pricing, exposing state owned enterprises to greater competition in order to increase their productivity and efficiency. Non-state partial ownership of state companies was even contemplated the following year. Despite this, there is clearly a division in the current leadership between those like Zhou Xiaochuan, head of the People's Bank of China, who believes in more complete marketization, and more conservative thinkers who want the state to maintain control of major industries in order to intervene when necessary. The Shanghai Stock Exchange in 2015 and early 2016 illustrated this story. It showed that despite commitment to markets, the authorities will, and do, intervene to preserve stability. Similarly, at the SOE front, the necessity for reform appears to resonate with Xi less than the ability to maintain control over the economy does. Despite frequent calls for imminent reform of major state-controlled industries, there is doubt regarding Xi's actual willingness to break up SOEs and quasi private enterprises with close ties to the state and to powerful political families and "princelings." In addition, as these reforms will include mass layoffs of workers, there is understandable concern regarding the ability of an economy experiencing a slowdown to absorb them. These dilemmas regarding the future of market reform are no more than an indication that, ideologically, the Party is in a highly ambiguous position. It maintains strong support for the role of the state in the economy, but also wants to see market forces challenge this in order to drive growth. So far, the Party has taken an ad hoc and sometimes capricious position. The question is, in the hunt for more efficiency and greater competitiveness in the economy, which are prerequisites for China's transition to a more developed model, will the Party be able to occupy this inconsistent position – sometimes intervening against market principles, sometimes desisting in order to strengthen those rules? Is this sort of tactic and positioning sustainable? Is it coherent and philosophically credible to be committed to markets when convenient, and then not when it suits the Party?

Innovation: Xi and his predecessor Hu have been mellifluous in their words on innovation. A national 15-year innovation plan running from 2006 privileged product creativity over process innovation. But China's hunt for innovation has been vexed, with patents internationally consistently underselling competitors like the US and the UK. Chinese universities have received generous funding, and yet as one study made clear, Chinese tertiary level education produces students who "are good at solving existing problems in predictable ways, but not at coming up with radical new solutions or inventing new problems to solve" (Zhao 2014: 133). China's aspirations to be innovative are clear; but can the Party truly "demand" or "enforce" creativity in some areas, while clearly resisting it in others? Can it impose a huge firewall between scientific and technological creativity and socio-political innovation? And under Xi Jinping, can the clear element of fearfulness and calculation of risk really enable strongly individual, innovative figures? The Chinese worship of Apple founder Steve Jobs is a case in point. China has yet to produce a figure in the business realm of similar iconic status. Is this partly because of its authoritarian, centralized and monopolized political system? And can China, under such a system, create a unique, tailored model for innovation, undercutting some of the assumptions of the outside world that creativity only really thrives in liberal, open atmospheres?

Going green: The costs of the last four decades since 1978 of rapid industrialization on the environment in China have been staggering (Economy 2010; Shapiro 2012). Several studies have shown just how serious China's challenges are in this space. Since 2013, Chinese cities have been blighted by thick smogs, physically running against the government rhetoric of doing more to clean up the air. The all important middle class citizens only need to look out of the windows to see failure of government policy. Despite stricter enforcement of green legislation from 2014, and greater commitment to international accords through bilateral deals with the US at APEC in November 2014 and the Paris Conference of Parties on Climate Change in December 2015, China is still trying to climb an immense mountain to clean up. Committed to its carbon emissions capping by 2030, this laudable aim is running against the brute fact that at the moment, and long into the future, China is still dependent for 66 percent of its energy on fossil fuels. In 2015 alone, China was building one coal fired plant every 7 to 10 days (Institute for Energy Research 2015). Sourcing from renewable and nuclear energy has increased lately, but is not remotely likely to become a replacement for coal. The Party's authoritarian and prescriptive role in policy making and implementation does mean that at least in accelerating green strategies it has an advantage. It can do things quickly and forcefully. The problem is that without some radical new technology, it is unlikely China will be able to cure its environment problems. Deteriorating environment hurts the most important constituency for the Party – the emerging middle class, on whom future service and consumer based growth is dependent. In this realm, it is possible that the Party is hostage to a problem it cannot control the outcomes of. In 1980s Taiwan, the Guomindang faced a bourgeoning environmental movement that questioned the regime's developmental priorities and, ultimately, its authoritarian rule (Tang and Tang 1997). In fact, there are plenty of examples of environmental movements challenging single party systems. In China, the Party is committed to economic results as the basis of its legitimacy; and these results are currently dependent on a polluting model. Can the Party seek legitimacy in other spaces where its exposure is less extreme? Perhaps, but that would imply some kind of political development, diversification and reform, all things it has so far opposed.

Promoting social security and strengthening the fiscal system: Welfare, pension and healthcare costs are all complicated in China. Pensions alone place considerable stress on central and local government budgets. China's pension reforms in the last decade have not been able to achieve universality nor address regional disparities. The pension system's medium to long term sustainability is also in question, especially due to an aging population (Lou and Wang 2008; Liu and Sun 2015). Healthcare in 2015 is only 5 percent of GDP, despite several reforms to create a national system, way below the 11 percent of the UK and 16 percent for the US. Chinese disease profiles are changing, from infection to chronic diseases arising from lifestyle – heart disease from obesity, and cancer from smoking (Brown *et al.* 2015). To make things worse, environmental degradation poses a direct threat to public health. A 2015 report by Greenpeace (Dong 2015) warned that 80 percent of 367 Chinese cities under air pollution monitoring failed to meet even the relatively lax national safety standards. Not surprisingly, respiratory diseases and lung cancer are on the rise among the urban population. Establishing a proper national healthcare system would be dependent on funding. And that would involve a major fiscal reform, something also promised, in the abstract, in the 2013 Plenum. China's current fiscal system is centralized. Seventy percent of government revenue is to Beijing. The tax base is dependent on profits from state enterprises. Personal taxation as a percentage of this national figure is very low – around 10 percent. In this light, can China seek to fund welfare, as in developed countries, by raising personal tax revenue? In an era of rising wages, this would seem logical, and yet, tax reform in China would involve complex political issues. As the statement goes, "no taxation without representation." As China seeks to fund better social welfare, something expected by its more demanding population, can it do this through raising levels of personal tax, and not involve greater enfranchisement of people, their participation in decision making, and in particular, in the key area of deciding where and how budgets are spent? Again, if China did succeed in maintaining a one party system, but creating a modernized tax base, funding modernized welfare, it would have succeeded where no one else has.

Seeking mutually beneficial relations with the outside world: Since 1978, China has enjoyed peaceful relations with the world. After the military clash with Vietnam in 1979, China embraced links with the outside world, underpinned by the approach that as long as it was clear sighted about what it wanted (technology, access to overseas markets and capital) then it would be able to control these links and not fall into the trap of exploitative, asymmetrical relations with the wider world which had existed before 1949. In the twenty-first century, China is a global power, and it is now the largest trading partner of over 130 countries. Its economic importance gives it an unprecedented international status. And yet, China's image outside the borders of the country is complex. Its soft power assets are circumscribed by the largely negative attitude the world has to its political model. People in surveys show they like Chinese culture, cuisine and the Chinese people they meet. But the Chinese regime is a different matter, dealt with in foreign media with consistent negativity, with its human rights record in particular creating antipathy. Especially under Xi, China has demonstrated a new willingness to pursue its goals according to the Thucydidean dictum "the strong do what they can." Chinese state security agents persecute critics, dissidents and political opponents abroad. For instance, China has received much criticism for the abductions of Hong Kong publishers and booksellers, including the Swedish citizen Gui Minhai and the British citizen Lee Bo. In addition, its increasingly assertive stance in the East and South China Sea disputes reinforces the perception of it being an aspiring regional hegemon among its Asian neighbors and beyond. Its defiance of the 2016 ruling by the Permanent Court of Arbitration against Chinese claims in the South China Sea fuels criticism of China's disregard for international law. Under its current political model, China is always placed as a unique actor, part of the international community and yet somehow set apart from it. Can China under this model, which sets it apart, be a truly global, trusted leader? Can it reclaim what Yan Xuetong (2011) from Tsinghua University called its "moral mandate," offering a genuine alternative to the so called Washington consensus?

Chinese exceptionalism in the political realm

All these areas are clearly critical ones for the CCP administration to address. They are all integral parts of the mission to deliver a middle income, bourgeois Chinese society which is sustainable in the next decade and a half – the Chinese Dream, as it were, which Xi referred to from 2013. The core question is in which ways delivery of these will be helped or impeded by the political model that China currently has? One party rule is arguably a model that might work in earlier stages of development. But faced with the complex social and economic issues the country now is coping with, can it resolve these without similar reforms in the political realm? Can it really, for instance, build social welfare and a modern tax base without also addressing participation in decision making, with the Party ceding a greater voice to the public? Can it build a viable, modern finance sector without rule of law, truly independent courts which are not answerable to the Party, and without a free press?

Some, like Australian political scientist John Keane, have argued that the Party can rewrite the rules of politics by creating a "phantom democracy" – a system that looks like it contains choice and public input but in fact remains highly organized by the Party, with only the superficial appearance of choice. Chinese thinkers like Yu Keping (2009) for instance have talked about democracy within a one party system. The Party itself says that in 2049 there will be in China a "democracy with Chinese characteristics." But what does this mean? That the Party within itself has divisions which are meaningful and involve meaningful choices between different groups? This idea was tried with the intra-Party democracy rubric under Hu Jintao, though it appears to have been abandoned under Xi as the Party emphasizes obedience to the "core" leadership and does not tolerate criticism.[6] Phantom democracy might be a good description of the village election process since the 1980s, where there was at village level a choice of candidates, and secret ballots, although the choice is between only CCP candidates or those with no party affiliation rather than representatives of any other political party. Critics have made it clear that village elections in China have led to underwhelming results in terms of improving rural governance and have no prospect of "trickling up" to higher levels of government.[7] There are also concerns that they have become more restrictive under Xi,[8] thereby reducing their effectiveness further. It could be argued that were the Party able to convince people in China that one party rule did involve meaningful choice, then it would have achieved one of the greatest confidence tricks of all time. At a lower stage of development, Chinese people might be willing to accept few formal routes to have input into decision making over policy and the allocation of resources. But would this be feasible when they are property owning, higher wage earning, tax paying members of the middle class?

Many have pointed to Singapore as being precisely such a model. Parallels between the Singapore model of development and that of China have been drawn by, amongst others, Daniel A. Bell (2015). The issue however is that while Singapore has managed to maintain to all intents and purposes a one party system, in recent years even that has been increasingly challenged, with the People's Action Party having 70 percent of the vote in 2015, after just 60 percent in 2012. In addition, a city state of 7 million people is so different from a vast nation state of 1.4 billion people that it is hard to see how the model of the former can truly be extrapolated and applied to the other. Elements of the Singaporean experience have been studied closely by Chinese officials, for sure. But the idea of China taking what Singapore does wholesale and applying it to itself is hard to imagine.

If China is able to address the set of problems listed above and yet maintain a Communist Party with a monopoly on power, it would have achieved something unique and unprecedented. Many within the Communist Party would argue that this is no more than what it has done for the last 40 years – doing things in a way and with a structure that has never been achieved elsewhere. They might argue that the CCP is a pragmatic entity, and one that is the only true entity that bounds the whole country together. Because of its role as a stabilizer, therefore, it does have a unique function, and a role long into the future. But the simple proposition has to be accepted: according to most precedents, China's current political model is increasingly likely to become a hindrance rather than a help in solving many of its core problems. Recognizing this does not mean endorsing the teleology of modernization theory. Structure matters but so does the agency of the actor. The CCP has indeed defied structural pressures in the past and relied more on the power of its agency. Looking ahead, in what ways can the CCP argue that it must maintain its current role with such strong agency and offer benefits which counterbalance the negative effects of its model? This is the core calculation running into the coming decades. There might come a point when the consensus will be that all the other changes in the economic and social realm must involve a profound change in the political realm, one where end of one party rule becomes not only something to be contemplated, but actually preferential. The issue at this point is whether the Party works within this reform, or opposes and fights it. In the latter case, the outcomes could be very catastrophic.

Paths into the future

Lacking a dependable crystal ball with which to peer into the future, the best option now might be to look at five broad possibilities about the Party's future, from benign to doomsday. It has been said that the best option when talking about the future is to predict disaster, because if the prediction is right then you were vindicated making it, and if it proves wrong, that was because of your wise and timely advice helping to avert it. It is likely that China's political future is going to be complex. So a scenario in the middle of the spectrum given below is more likely.

Option one: fair weather: the current CCP China dream: The best option for the Party, according to the current CCP leaders, would be to maintain its one party position and its privileged unique role in society. Bearing in mind that China's current leaders are in the best position to influence the future of the country they lead, then this option does have the most evidentiary support. The question is whether, in view of all the challenges listed above, it can truly be achieved. If Chinese growth continues to be steady, if its environmental and other problems prove in some ways either partially or wholly soluble, if it achieves 70 percent urban population levels, a good tax base, good public health and welfare, and enjoys a benign and stable international situation in the coming two decades, then by 2035, the CCP will have achieved something unique. Under this model, its legitimacy will be clearly demonstrated by it achieving this transition while maintaining stable governance. The Party will be able to argue at the end of this phase that it is integral to China's modernity mission, not ultimately inimical to it. The CCP under this model will be able to argue that it embraces all public views within itself, that it is inclusive, reflects the views of the population, and in that sense has achieved democracy with Chinese characteristics. It will preside over an innovative, high income, service sector orientated and predominantly bourgeois society. It might also argue that it has removed the uncertainty of democratic systems through its one party model.

Option two: the Western China dream: Under this scenario, the CCP makes a pragmatic decision after a decade of successful growth and the creation of a strong diamond shaped middle class to significantly strengthen rule of law, to allow courts to challenge the Party, to enfranchise civil society, and to embark on a controlled but committed process of allowing alternative political actors to operate. This model might be called the Taiwan model, emulating the process from martial law to democracy that the island pursued from the 1980s onwards. There would be no bloodshed, the Communist Party, like the Guomindang, would tolerate organized political opposition, and then eventually even allow free, open elections. A China under this model has strong sustainable growth, a highly urban population, strong innovation, global companies and benign relations with its neighbors.

Option three would be more rocky, and might best be paralleled to what happened to the USSR after the collapse of the Party there after 1991. The Party in its reform process will need to cede some political space to other forces, but still remain dominant. This might take the form of allowing an orderly competition among factions (as has the Liberal Democratic Party in Japan) or even contestation for leading political posts (as in the Vietnamese Communist Party). China will have less impressive growth, significant environmental and sustainable problems, but will have largely managed these. Its relations with the outside world, rather like that of Russia in 2016, will be tetchy and defensive. A China under this model is likely to be governed by a Communist Party which is more contested, and which is willing to deploy a more shrill nationalism, which will cause tensions with the world around it. Within, it will have an economy and domestic politics which are more divided, between successful and less successful provinces, with a federal model which is much less capable of producing unity than the one that exists in 2016. A China under this model will be stable, but disruptive. It would politically be dominated by groups similar to the oligarchs of the USSR, vested interest and corruption would be high, and the Party would be the puppet of these forces, rather than their master.

Option four would be partial failure, with growth stagnant, the environment problems in some parts of the country destructive and insoluble, and relations with some of its neighbors bellicose and unstable. The Party under this model would not have a monopoly on power, but would have ceded considerable space to opponents. It would be highly decentralized, with some provinces on the coast almost able to pursue their own agendas and only very loosely answerable to Beijing. Middle provinces and western provinces will contain some which resemble failed states, with moribund economies. The CCP will be divided, and other highly fractious political forces would have arisen. Militarism would be more prevalent, in a model which resembles the state failure of the DPRK, and a country coming into existence.

Option five would be fragmentation, economic collapse, environmental implosion and the complete eradication of the Communist Party from the country. In this model China would have a massive negative effect on the world around it, no longer functioning as a cohesive state by descending into internecine conflict. There might be civil war; there will definitely be the rise of local actors and a wholly decentralized entity. Such an outcome would mark the end of the current state.

Conclusion: the Western paradox of China choice

Casting an eye over these options, it is clear that the best option would be the second, the most likely is either the first or the third, and the least desirable would be the fourth and the fifth. The fifth, in fact, would mark a moment of global crisis, because a collapsed China would have a knock on effect on supply chains, the global environment, migration and other issues that would prove unmanageable.

Option two, smooth democratic change, is idealistic. Joseph Wong and Dan Slater have suggested that China may follow the example of authoritarian parties that opted to embrace democratization rather than resist it (Slater and Wong 2013). They argue that authoritarian leaderships have in the past opted for democracy as a way to stay in power. In the case of Taiwan, the ruling Kuomintang (Guomindang) conceded democratization at a point when its strength gave confidence to its leadership that they would win a fair election. Still, after KMT victories in both legislative and presidential elections in the 1990s, Taiwan eventually experienced the cycle of alternation of parties in power that is commonplace in parliamentary systems. There is no evidence to suggest that the CCP will accept the prospect of power sharing in the foreseeable future. Taiwan does offer a viable model of transition which can be used to support such a view. But the whole discourse of the current leadership in Beijing is antagonistic to this model. Under Xi, the opposition to bicameral parliamentary systems and judicial independence as well as the insistence on "perennial one-party rule" are entrenched – and there are few signs of possible changes. The Communist Party has been so closely tied to Chinese national identity, and to the mission to create a strong, unified state that there is almost visceral elite opposition to contemplating any other options. The logic is brutally simple: strong China means strong, unified leadership, and the only body that can supply that is the Party. A new generation of Chinese leaders might think less defensively about political change in their country. There is little sign at the moment that this change in mindsets is on the horizon.

Option one, therefore, is the most realistic, and the one where at least some of China's prime needs and those of the outside world in terms of stability are met. This gives rise to a paradox. Option one, after all, is one that the outside world gains much from, in terms of growth, stability and certainty. But it is, of course, predicated on the Party maintaining its privileged position. Therefore, while what we broadly call the West through its dialogue with China in the last 40 years has consistently urged political reform leading to multiparty systems, pursuing this route will lead to higher levels of uncertainty than the Party maintaining its current function and trying to maintain the status quo. Therefore, while repeatedly saying it wants the Communist

Party to change, in many ways the West is amongst its greatest supporters. It gains from the stability and certainty it brings. A China without this would stand a high risk of greater instability and uncertainty. In the economic, sustainability and global governance realm, and in terms of geopolitics, with the Party in control the West at least has a unified point to refer to and a dependable interlocutor to engage with. A democratic or more loosely governed China would be much messier to work with.

This lends western discourse on the CCP therefore a slightly schizophrenic tone. On the one hand, there are many ways in which one party rule makes life easier for the West. But ideologically, of course, and emotionally, having the world's second largest economy run by a Communist Party with a monopoly of power is regarded as incongruous, anachronistic and, in the words of former President Bill Clinton, "on the wrong side of history" (Clinton 1997).

Is it just hubris that the CCP's continuing existence in its present format attracts so much opprobrium and distaste from Washington, London and other centers? Does the fact that each day it continues as it is, the CCP disproves the end of history thesis and renders the final victory of the western liberal order a real bugbear? An attitude not based on logic but on the western emotional adherence to a position that has no inner necessity? If the CCP does manage to achieve option one, will the West review its attitude to governance, and broaden its views? There are figures like Eric X. Li who do argue that this is the case, and that the West needs to broaden its views and simply accept China's political model (Li 2013, 2014).

The achievement of option one, of course, would entail a recalibration of western views of how necessary pluralistic democracy is to a developed society. It would give huge support to the idea that authoritarian models are more viable than perhaps had been believed. As of 2016, however, the options are finely balanced. The Communist Party under Xi Jinping is undertaking reform while practicing repressive policies. It has rounded up rights lawyers, blocked media, clamped down on discussion of western models in classrooms, and enforced the Party mass line. At the same time as it introduces promises for more rule of law in the Fourth Plenum of 2014,[9] it has also frozen the space for civil society, continued to imprison dissidents and resolutely closed down any kind of public debate about multiparty reform.

Is this a dark moment before the dawn of surprising and revolutionary change in China's domestic politics? Is the strategy of the Xi leadership to develop society materially, and once this has been achieved to then grant accelerated political change, at a time when it was more capable to countenance these changes? As Machiavelli said, "To trust is good, but control is better." The Party at the moment needs to control, because society is not yet ready and it does not have the capacity to enter a period of deep political change. It would cause too much social tension, uncertainty and conflict. Once the time is right, the Party's pragmatic side will cede space to other political actors.

The problem with this benign option is that the Party up to now has decimated every possible viable form of domestic political opposition. The China Democracy Party in 1998 was closed down after gaining only a handful of members, its ringleaders given jail sentences and its infrastructure ripped apart. A decade later, and the Charter 08 demand for more political freedoms was also treated brutally. Attempts under Xi to open up discussions in even the most harmless area, like constitutionalism or legal reform, have been similarly harshly dealt with. When it suits the Party to involve other actors in power sharing in China, there might, under this current framework, not be anyone left standing able to step forward and take up their option. Nor does this strategy imply that the Party has any scenario over the future where such reforms would be desirable. With limited political channels available and the freedom of association restricted, the role of Chinese people in future developments becomes highly uncertain. So far, opting for "voice" and "exit" is contained in both cities and rural areas. Still, violent protests in the countryside or emigration of wealthy citizens[10] to western countries are different reactions to the same problem: poor governance. Despite its success in macro-economic management, the Party has not found ways to control its agents in an effective and routine manner, nor has it demonstrated the willingness to commit the resources needed for improving the environment, public health and welfare provision. Corruption in village land sales, unbreathable air, rising costs in education, poor public services, the unreliability of legal channels, restrictions in the freedom of expression and the unchecked capacity for arbitrary coercion by local state agents are problems that will persist even in the best possible scenario of sustained economic growth. As the formal political space for the articulation and diffusion of bottom-up grievances is small, the possibility of more violent forms of protest will remain on the table.

In many ways, the CCP has been the victim of its own success. The choice of undertaking economic reforms but maintaining one party rule from 1978 proved hugely successful. But its long term political sustainability never properly figured in this process. As long as it produced solid growth (which it did), the questions about the political future could always be deferred to another day. But with growth falling from 2014, the pressure to have a vision by the governing party that works more in the political rather than the solely economic domain has grown. The emergence of a new social contract, where the Party delivers more than just "food and clothing," to use the usual benefits outlined in leadership discourse, is important. Will Chinese people accept a uniquely different social contract to others across the world? Are they so very different that they are willing to continue ceding key decisions about their destinies to ruling elites without any transparent and regular modes of articulating their future and at least attempting to mold it? That is the story of China's political future in the coming two decades, and that of the role of the CCP.

Notes

1 For one powerful critique, see Huang 2008.
2 China is a member or observer in 74 International Organizations and a signatory to an even greater number of Conventions and multilateral agreements.
3 A concept developed by Steve Tsang, "consultative authoritarianism" groups the institutional initiatives by the CCP for "continuous governance reform designed to pre-empt public demands for democratization" and to "enhance the Party's capacity to elicit, respond to and direct changing public opinion" (Tsang 2009: 865).
4 Critics compare the CCDI with "Eastern Depot," the Yongle Emperor's spy agency used to repress real or imaginary enemies (Schell 2016).
5 Xi has appointed himself as head of the Central Leading Group for Finance and Economics and of the Central Leading Group for Comprehensively Deepening Reforms, thereby becoming involved in the country's economic and financial management.
6 Characteristically, in October 2015 Yu Keping resigned from his post as deputy chief of the Central Compilation and Translation Bureau amidst rumors about his dissatisfaction with Xi's administration (Mai 2015).
7 For a discussion on the implementation and future of village elections in China, see O'Brien and Zhao 2013; Brown 2011.
8 Recent events in Wukan reinforce this view (Ramzy 2016).
9 Since 2014 there are more frequent references in state discourse on the rule of law, and an increase of televised confessions of suspects that have become quite popular.
10 Many wealthy Chinese citizens buy property and send their financial assets overseas or travel abroad to give birth so that their offspring can obtain foreign citizenship (Shambaugh 2015).

References

Bell, D.A. (2015) *The China model: Political meritocracy and the limits of democracy*. United States: Princeton University Press.

Brown, K. (2011) *Ballot box China: Grassroots democracy in the final major one-party state*. London: Zed Books.

Brown, K., van Nieuwenhuizen, S. and Knight, J. (2015) *Australia–China healthcare opportunities*. Available at: https://sydney.edu.au/china_studies_centre/images/Business%20Forum/2015/reportchinesehealthcarereportfinal.pdf (accessed: September 13, 2016).

Central Commission for Discipline Inspection (2016) *A thousand yes-men cannot equal one honest advisor*. Available at: https://web.archive.org/web/20160318162236/www.ccdi.gov.cn/xcjy/lsjj/201602/t20160229_75034.html (accessed: April 4, 2016).

Chang, G.G. (2001) *The coming collapse of China*. London: Random House.

Chang, G.W. (2011) "The coming collapse of China: 2012 edition," *Foreign Policy*, December 29.

Clinton, W.J. (1997) *The President's news conference with President Jiang Zemin of China*. Available at: www.presidency.ucsb.edu/ws/?pid=53468 (accessed: April 4, 2016).

Decision of the Central Committee of the Communist Party of China on some major issues concerning comprehensively deepening the reform (2014) Available at: www.china.org.cn/china/third_plenary_session/2014-01/16/content_31212602.htm (accessed: April 4, 2016).

Dickson, B. (2016) *The dictator's dilemma: The Chinese Communist Party's strategy for survival*. United States: Oxford University Press.

Dong, L. (2015) *367 shades of grey: Why China needs a coal cap*. Available at: www.greenpeace.org/eastasia/news/blog/367-shades-of-grey-why-china-needs-a-coal-cap/blog/54429/ (accessed: April 13, 2016).

Economy, E.C. (2010) *The river runs black: The environmental challenge to China's future*. 2nd edn. United States: Cornell University Press.

Forsythe, M. (2016) "Q. and A.: Minxin Pei on the future of Communist rule in China," *New York Times*, February 29.

Huang, Y. (2008) *Capitalism with Chinese characteristics: Entrepreneurship and the state*. Cambridge: Cambridge University Press.

Institute for Energy Research (2015) *As U.S. shutters coal plants, China and Japan are building them*. Available at: http://instituteforenergyresearch.org/analysis/as-u-s-shutters-coal-plants-china-and-japan-are-building-them/ (accessed: April 2, 2016).

Irvine, R. (2015) *Forecasting China's future: Dominance or collapse?* London: Routledge.

Li, E.X. (2013) *A tale of two political systems*. Available at: www.ted.com/talks/eric_x_li_a_tale_of_two_political_systems#t-157303 (accessed: September 13, 2016).

Li, E.X. (2014) "The middle kingdom and the coming world disorder," *New Perspectives Quarterly*, 31(2), pp. 26–30. doi: 10.1111/npqu.11443.

Liu, T. and Sun, L. (2015) "Pension reform in China," *Journal of Aging & Social Policy*, 28(1), pp. 15–28. doi: 10.1080/08959420.2016.1111725.

Lou, J. and Wang, S. (2008) *Public finance in China: Reform and growth for a harmonious society*. Washington, DC: World Bank Publications.

Mai, J. (2015) *Chinese author of "Democracy is a good thing" resigns from Communist Party bureau*. Available at: www.scmp.com/news/china/policies-politics/article/1873493/chinese-author-democracy-good-thing-resigns-communist (accessed: September 1, 2016).

Minzner, C. (2015) "China after the reform era," *Journal of Democracy*, 26(3), pp. 129–143.

Nathan, A. (2003) "Authoritarian resilience," *Journal of Democracy*, 14(1), pp. 6–17.

O'Brien, K.J. and Zhao, S. (eds.) (2013) *Grassroots elections in China*. London: Routledge.

Pantsov, A.V. and Levine, S.I. (2015) *Deng Xiaoping: A revolutionary life*. Oxford: Oxford University Press.

Pei, M. (2006) *China's trapped transition: The limits of developmental autocracy*. Cambridge, MA: Harvard University Press.

Ramzy, A. (2016) *Protests return to Wukan, Chinese village that once expelled its officials*. Available at: www.nytimes.com/2016/06/21/world/asia/china-wukan-protest.html?_r=0http://international.nytimes.com/subscriptions/inyt/lp8W37Q.html?adxc=284004&adxa=414231&page=gateway.nytimes.com&pos=Gateway&campaignId=66XRJ (accessed: September 1, 2016).

Ringen, S. (2016) *The perfect dictatorship: China in the 21st century*. Hong Kong: Hong Kong University Press.

Schell, O. (2016) *Crackdown in China: Worse and worse.* Available at: www.nybooks.com/articles/2016/04/21/crackdown-in-china-worse-and-worse/ (accessed: September 10, 2016).

Shambaugh, D. (2015) *The coming Chinese crackup.* Available at: www.wsj.com/articles/the-coming-chinese-crack-up-1425659198 (accessed: April 2, 2016).

Shambaugh, D. (2016) *China's future.* United Kingdom: Polity Press.

Shapiro, J. (2012) *China's environmental challenges (China today).* Cambridge, UK: John Wiley & Sons.

Slater, D. and Wong, J. (2013) "The strength to concede: Ruling parties and democratization in developmental Asia," *Perspectives on Politics*, 11(03), pp. 717–733. doi: 10.1017/s1537592713002090.

Tang, S.-Y. and Tang, C.-P. (1997) "Democratization and environmental politics in Taiwan," *Asian Survey*, 37(3), pp. 281–294. doi: 10.2307/2645664.

Tang, W. (2016) *Populist authoritarianism: Chinese political culture and regime sustainability.* United States: Oxford University Press.

Tsang, S. (2009) "Consultative Leninism: China's new political framework," *Journal of Contemporary China*, 18(62), pp. 865–880.

World Bank and Development Research Center, State Council, PRC (2013) *China 2030: Building a modern, harmonious and creative society.* Available at: www.worldbank.org/content/dam/Worldbank/document/China-2030-complete.pdf (accessed: September 1, 2016).

Wu Jie News (2016b) *Open letter regarding Xi Jinping's resignation from Party and national leadership positions.* Available at: http://web.archive.org/web/20160304150122/http:/www.watching.cn/show-2-76713-1.html (accessed: April 4, 2016).

Yan, X. (2011) *Ancient Chinese thought, modern Chinese power.* Edited by Daniel A. Bell and Sun Zhe. United States: Princeton University Press.

Yu, Keping (2009) *Democracy is a good thing: Essays on politics, society, and culture in contemporary China.* Washington, DC: Brookings Institution Press.

Zhao, Y. (2014) *Who's afraid of the big bad dragon? Why China has the best (and worst) education system in the world.* United States: John Wiley & Sons.

22

CHANGING PATTERNS OF CHINESE CIVIL SOCIETY

Comparing the Hu-Wen and Xi Jinping eras

Chloé Froissart

Introduction

Until recently, China has offered a striking paradox to observers: that of an authoritarian regime with a vibrant – albeit immature because constrained – civil society. In this chapter, I explain why, although the Chinese state has not granted an institutionalized space for civil society, the use of the term "civil society" was still relevant under the Hu Jintao-Wen Jiabao leadership (2002–2012) and offer an overview of its dynamics at that time. I then expose the Xi Jinping leadership's multi-fold endeavors to reformat the space allotted to social organizations, religious associations, the media, and academics according to the state's goals, underlining a common logic across different sectors. I finally discuss the effectiveness of these efforts and the sustainability of the new model of "People's society," which the leadership attempts to substitute for the previous one. My general take is that, although China has entered an unprecedented era of suppression and restriction, which already has a chilling effect on civil society and is at the same time detrimental to the Chinese Communist Party (CCP), the Xi administration's ability to fully reverse the trend might be limited in the long run.

Change in paradigms: from civil society to People's society

The use of the term "civil society" is contested in an authoritarian regime such as China, which has not elaborated a legal framework granting autonomy to civil society. According to China's corporatist legal framework, all religious sites or groups have to be affiliated to one of the national associations set up by the state to represent the religions it has officially recognized. "The CCP has also endeavored to shape the values and beliefs of religious leaders and adherents within those structures in line with its political agenda" (Vala 2012: 46). Likewise, social organizations, business associations, lawyers' associations, and students' associations are all constrained by a corporatist and very restrictive legal framework. Let's take social organizations[1] as an example. Until the recent publication of the Charity Law, they were required to find a government agency in their realm of work that would be willing to take the non-profit under its wing and take responsibility for supervising it. Once a relevant (generally state or Party-affiliated) "supervisory agency" had agreed, NGOs wishing to register as legal non-profits then had to apply for official registration with the Ministry of Civil Affairs at the local, provincial, or national level. In other words, in order to be officially recognized as an "NGO," social organizations had to be state or Party-affiliated in some way. But given the political suspicion toward these organizations, many of them failed to find a supervisory unit and thus to register, or were registered as businesses. According to official views and regulations, social organizations should act as extensions of the state and auxiliaries of the Party, helping to carry out three major tasks: maintaining social order, reinforcing the political and ideological domination of the Party, and relieving the state of its welfare burdens. These missions were further theorized with the coining of the term "social management with Chinese characteristics" (*Zhongguo tese shehui guanli*), which appeared for the first time in a May 2011 article by Zhou Benshun, then Secretary-General of the Central Politics and Law Commission. This landmark article describes "the structure of social management [as one] whereby Party committees lead, the government bears responsibility, society coordinates, and the masses participate" so as to "giv[e] concrete expression to [the Party's] political and institutional advantage" (*Legal Daily* 2011; Pils 2012: 3–4).

Yet, despite the multiple legal and systemic constraints the CCP has imposed on collective social actors, the actual space for civil society organizations in China had been much larger than the institutional space allowed by formal laws and regulations (Yu 2011). The number of actually existing social organizations greatly exceeds the number of those formally registered with governmental departments, while the number of social organizations and religious associations has greatly increased since the 2000s.[2] Given the many ways for social organizations and religious associations to evade the restrictive legal framework and subsist in a gray area, this increase in number has naturally harbored a diversification of social actors during the Hu-Wen era. The de facto autonomy of some social and religious organizations, the existence of some room for critics and circumscribed acts of resistance that would not challenge the authority of the Communist Party, as well as the possibility for activists to sometimes influence political decisions explain the persistent use of the term "civil society" among social actors and the academia during this time.

The Hu-Wen leadership's fundamentally ambiguous stance reflected this development. President Hu and Premier Wen believed that a certain amount of ideological openness, forms of democracy, and limited respect of the rights stated in the law and the Constitution was beneficial to the Party's legitimation as well as the overall functioning of the regime, and thus to its durability. Some degree of citizens' participation in public affairs as well as citizens' restraint on state power was tolerated as long as they could serve as a governance technique. While emphasizing the building of the rule of law, Hu thus vowed to expand "citizens' participation," especially that of NGOs. In his report to the 17th Congress of the CCP in 2007, the president linked the development of socialist democracy to the "expansion of public participation" and pledged that "citizens' participation in political affairs [would] expand in an orderly way." He also "encourage[d] social organizations to help expand the participation by the public and report on their petitions to improve the self-governance capability of society" (Hu 2007). The leadership also allowed some diversification of civil society provided that social organizations were submitted to "graduated-controls" (*fenlei guanzhi*) according to their profile (Wu and Chan 2012). Wu and Chan use this concept to describe the state's differentiated approach to three kinds of NGOs, namely those involved in service delivery and charity, those involved in service to marginal – and sometimes potentially disruptive – groups as well as in advocacy in favor of these groups, and those involved in political, religious, ethnic, or other sensitive areas. The authors argue that, while NGOs in the second category attracted more attention from authorities, "they were given considerable breathing space and were not subject to constant crackdown as were NGOs in the third category" (Yuen 2015).

The Hu-Wen era thus witnessed the rise of mid-range, moderate, and reformist issue-oriented NGOs. Defending the interests of a particular social group, and shying away from universal demands for all Chinese citizens as well as from broad claims for political reforms, these NGOs were to some extent fitting into the corporatist pattern of interests' representation in the Chinese regime. By emphasizing their role in maintaining social cohesion and social stability and nurturing their relations with party cadres to counterbalance their uncertain status, those grassroots organizations somehow managed to survive in a gray zone and to gain some legitimacy. They also greatly enhanced their advocacy capacity throughout this period of time in a bid to push the state to acknowledge the rights of the people they were defending. They were indeed instrumental in winning new rights for social groups such as migrant workers, women, disabled people, people with HIV-AIDS or hepatitis B, etc. Vala notes the same tolerance toward moderate religious groups, namely churches registered with "weak Protestant (official) associations," which could de facto enjoy a lot of autonomy, but also the unregistered churches that dealt respectfully and conciliatorily with local authorities and could enjoy "tacit approval" from the latter (Vala 2012: 51–52). Overall, President Hu's announcement during the 17th Chinese Communist Party Congress in 2007 that religious believers could play a "positive role in promoting economic and social development" pointed to more opening toward religious groups, namely those able to complement authoritarian rule by fulfilling welfare needs and providing services not offered by the state or to generate revenues by developing touristic activities (Vala 2012: 47).

Regarding the media, although Hu reemphasized their propaganda work and mission in guiding public opinion (*yulun daoxiang*), he did not completely stifle their critical role in exerting "public supervision" (*yulun jiandu*). In an important speech in 2008, President Hu thus acknowledged that the media also had an obligation to reflect the will of the people (*mingyi*) and mentioned the need to "protect the people's right to know, participate, express and supervise" (Bandurski 2008). This fundamental ambiguity over the role of the media still left some room for investigative journalists to remain faithful to the imperative of serving the public and being critical of power, and expose some of the biggest scandals of the decade (such as the Sanlu contaminated milk, the "tofu skin schools," or deadly faulty vaccines), albeit many were prosecuted and had to flee the country. The ambiguity of the leadership toward the media was also reflected in "the state's [continuous] attempt to utilize investigative journalism as a governance technique" (Wang and Lee 2014: 233), as epitomized by the telecast Focus (*Jiaodian fangtan*), whose relatively independent – albeit carefully circumscribed – investigations led to many legal and administrative sanctions targeting local officials (Zhao and Sun 2007).

Technological advances offered new opportunities for the construction of a public sphere and a more systematized resistance to the CCP's political hegemony. New media such as Weibo and other platforms played a key role in building up new and more interactive communities by enhancing solidarity and mobilization capacities (Svensson 2012; Teng 2012). They were also instrumental in shaping breaking news, and enabled the rise of a new engaged digital citizenry. As David Bandurski, a media scholar, put it: "Netizens, activists and journalists spoke hopefully about 'the surrounding gaze' (*weiguan*) and the coalescing of 'micro-forces' as tens of thousands, even millions, became actively involved with social issues online, often impacting the government response" (Bandurski 2016a; see also Xiaomi 2011; Froissart 2015: 134–136).

A good example of how online mobilization could impact political decisions is the 2011 PM2.5 air quality campaign. It was launched by public figures such as Zheng Yuanjie, a well-known writer, and Pan Shiyi, a successful businessman, who asked their numerous followers on Weibo to speak about their feelings about obviously very strong levels of pollution – the American Embassy index was displaying pollution levels at an overwhelming 500 – while official data were merely announcing "light pollution." The campaign was relayed by journalists and environmental NGOs, who played a crucial role in both mobilizing people to measure PM2.5 and in advocating for information disclosure. The obligation to measure and disclose PM2.5 levels was eventually incorporated into the law and local governments were forced to comply. If in this case, the mobilization and its outcome indeed turned out to be as beneficial to the people as to the Party, which now claims to be a strong advocate of the environment, new media could also enable political mobilization clearly challenging the CCP.

Allowing isolated activists to maintain informal networks and to "organize without organization" (Shirky 2008), new media were for example instrumental in organizing the signature campaign of the Charter 08, published in 2008 on the occasion of the 60th anniversary of the Universal Declaration of Human Rights and the 10th anniversary of the signing by the PRC of the UN Convention on Civil and Political Rights. This text, inspired by Charter 77 and promoted by Liu Xiaobo, was signed by 303 intellectuals, ordinary citizens, but also party cadres and people's congress deputies at various levels, and then online by more than 5,000 people. On the basis of the main principles which China undertook to respect, it called for constitutional democracy and a federal republic respecting the right of minorities to self-determination.

The ambiguity of the leadership's discourse (between building the rule of law and reaffirming the leading role of the CCP) and its willingness to leave some room for public participation also presided over the development of the rights defense movement (*weiquan yundong*), which could be considered as one of the main dynamics characterizing the Hu-Wen era. This movement had two components, which could sometimes coalesce. The elitist and scholarly component was embodied in a new breed of highly educated and professional lawyers engaged in cause lawyering, and fighting to promote constitutionalism, public good, and universal rights for Chinese citizens. Although the principle underlying their action, which consisted of taking the law seriously, was intrinsically subversive and albeit they had to frequently resort to media exposure as well as public demonstrations to compensate the lack of independence of the judiciary, Open Constitution Initiative (*Gongmen*), the NGO which was at the heart of the movement, was able to operate for ten years – that is during the whole Hu-Wen era – despite constant harassment.

The popular component of the rights defense movement, encapsulated by the concept of "rightful resistance" (O'Brien and Li 2006), consisted of protesters such as peasants deprived of their land, urbanites expelled from their homes, disgruntled workers and NGOs supporting them, of relying on laws and official discourses as well as media support to mount collective actions spanning the boundaries between official modes of conflict resolution (for example resorting to legal action) and outright protest. As demonstrated by the authors, the core dynamic of such resistance lay in the alliance – either tacit or explicit – between high ranking officials and protesters against local cadres. The rationale behind such ad hoc alliances was that the central government had also an interest in relying on popular mobilization to rein in corruption and abuses of power at the local level, as such mobilizations were usefully compensating for the shortcomings of the authoritarian system while exempting the Party to carry out systemic reforms.

During the Hu-Wen era, civil society was hence performing a functional role in the way the Chinese regime was operating, namely by acting as an ad hoc and flexible counter power integrated into the system exempting the Party from formally implementing institutional reforms. Civil society also forced the Party to adapt and devise public policies better tuned to people's needs and expectations. The game, which consisted of mutual instrumentalization on the part of the CCP and social actors to further their respective goals, was undoubtedly very dangerous as it harbored a risk that social mobilization would eventually overtake the Party. The challenge for the CCP was thus to maintain this critical and combative civil society within certain limits where it could serve the Party's overall objectives instead of threatening it. Hence alternative periods of control (*shou*) and relaxation (*fang*), coupled with the deliberate maintenance of a legal gray zone, could expand the space for bold social innovations while at the same time allowing repression when needed. But the risk that the development of civil society would eventually shape the Party's future was precisely what Xi Jinping feared and the reason why he launched a severe crackdown on civil society while striving to promote – namely by the series of new laws that were recently passed – the consolidation of what could be called a "People's society" subservient to the Party.

The Xi Jinping era clearly displays a paradigm shift in the pattern of Chinese civil society and the way the CCP relates to it, which can be summarized by the following points:

- The abandonment of the alternating pattern of control and relaxation that unleashed China's era of "reform and opening up," as targeted suppression is now being replaced by a more uniform and systematic crackdown on civil society.
- This crackdown aims not only at suppressing anything pertaining to a liberal, combative (so-called "Western-style") definition of civil society but also the mid-range, moderate, and issues-oriented NGOs and activists.
- The forcible promotion of "social management with Chinese characteristics" (*zhongguo tese shehui guanli/zhili*) and charity (*cishan*), refocusing the development of "civil society" on organizations that complement or even strengthen the resilience of the current regime.
- The drastic shrinking of the space for "citizens' participation." Except in scarce and designated areas such as environmental protection, only the Party can lead change and innovation. This is namely illustrated by the replacement of the central state's tacit and ad hoc alliances with social actors in controlling local cadres by the state-led campaign against corruption.

Shaping People's society

In July 2013, well-known new leftist Tsinghua University Professor Hu Angang wrote an op-ed for the *People's Daily* entitled "Why People's society is superior to civil society" (Hu 2013). According to Hu, People's society differs from Western conceptions of civil society centering on the rights and interests of individuals as it emphasizes the collective over the individual, the integration of the government and the masses (*zhengfu yu qunzhong yitihua*) over the opposition between state and society, and the maintenance of harmony over conflicting relations between them. People's society mainly aims at improving people's livelihood and social management under the aegis of the Communist Party; its method of governance is the mass line.

This op-ed echoed Xi Jinping's important speech on the mass line (June 2013), in which the new president distanced himself from his predecessor's emphasis on citizen participation by reaffirming the validity of the organizational and leadership method developed by Mao Zedong. It also mirrored the Document No. 9 which denounced "civil society" as a Western theory used by "some people with ulterior motives within China" to topple the Party and expressed concerns about its advocates becoming "a serious form of political opposition." Retrospectively, this op-ed reads as a program for the measures that were taken since then to remold Chinese civil society to the image of the Party.

Guiding principles

The Xi Jinping era has been characterized by two guiding principles: efforts to immunize Chinese society from any influence from foreign ideas and foreign support and stringent limitation of freedom of speech in order to eradicate any form of criticism. The Party's program for tightening ideological control, which somehow recalls the campaigns against spiritual pollution that took place in the 1980s, has been detailed at length in the Document No. 9, first known during the Spring of 2013 as the "Seven don't Speak" (*Qi bushuo*) as it bans the use of seven locutions denounced as "Western ideas": universal values, freedom of speech, civil society, civil rights, the historical errors of the CCP, official bourgeoisie, judicial independence. This document, which warns that "Western anti-China forces and internal 'dissidents' are still actively trying to infiltrate China's ideological sphere and challenge our mainstream ideology," has been the spearhead to regain control over the media, the Internet, and academic debates, and presided over the enactment of a new legislative framework intended to bring to heel domestic and overseas organizations. (See Chapter 15, "Reform, Repression, Co-Optation: The CCP's Policy Toward Intellectuals.")

The struggle against "Western reporting" – that is investigative or merely critical journalism – was forcefully initiated by the case of the *Southern Weekly* (*Nanfang Zhoumo*) New Year's greeting in January 2013. Originally entitled "China's Dream, the Dream of Constitutionalism," the editorial recalled that this dream had been persistent in China since the end of the nineteenth century and advocated political reforms. The editorial was entirely rewritten overnight by the Guangdong Province Propaganda Department and was eventually published with the headline "We Are Now Closer to Our Dreams Than at Any Time Before," a phrase taken directly from an editorial in the Party's official *People's Daily*. Purged of all references to constitutionalism and words like "justice," "truth," and "citizen" typically used by this newspaper known for its criticism of those in power and its commitment to uphold justice, the final text celebrated China's greatness as well as its cultural exception in politics (Qian 2013).

Since then, Xi has consistently emphasized that the media should be completely subservient to the Party and should focus on "positive reporting" – as opposed to critical reporting – supposed to disseminate a "positive energy" within the people. This "so-called positive energy now denotes patriotism, love for the government, love for the Party. It even bears along with this the sense of opposing Japan, opposing America and opposing the West" (Zhang 2015). Xi's visit to the major state media outlets in February 2016, during which he said all media "must be surnamed Party," and must "love the Party, protect the Party and serve the Party," gave him the opportunity to articulate his full-fledged media policy. The two main features of this new policy are, first, to entirely subvert the distinction between "supervision by public opinion" and propaganda, as the two are now said to be "unified" (Bandurski 2016b) and, second, to replace Hu's strategic and selective control over the media by "a map for all-dimensional control" (*quanfangwei kongzhi*).

The leadership's determination to crack down on reformist thinking and to eradicate "historical nihilism" – meaning any version of history other than the official one, one of the seven taboos listed in the Document No. 9 – was displayed in July 2016 by the reshuffle of the *Yanhuang Chunqiu*, which eventually led its publisher to stop the publication. The journal, which carried out forthright articles that contested official versions of Communist Party history, was based on testimonies and historical information that no other outlets would dare to publish. It fostered public discussion on the Cultural Revolution, the anti-rightist movement, and the Great Famine, in a bid to urge the Party to advance political reforms that were stalled after the crackdown on the 1989 pro-democracy movement (Yu 2016). Founded in 1991 by reform-minded Party veterans, the

Yanhuang Chunqiu was a torchbearer for liberal-minded intellectuals. Its forced disappearance was intended to deal a blow to the entire reformist liberal camp, either inside or outside the Party.

The Xi leadership's will to strictly limit the impact of outspoken media and to break their solidarity with other civil society actors – a solidarity that used to be at the heart of the rights defense movement – was clearly demonstrated in October 2016 by Caixin Online's two-month suspension from the Party's list of news outlets whose content may be freely syndicated and reposted online. The directive came after Caixin Online covered the opposition by a large group of Chinese rights lawyers to a set of new regulations from the Ministry of Justice threatening them with the loss of their jobs if they speak to the media or take protest actions against injustice, including forced confessions or torture of their clients (RFA 2016).

This sanction takes place in a more general trend to curb the role of online media and microblogging in building up a public sphere and enhancing mobilization capacities. As early as August 2013, the Party moved aggressively against influential Weibo users, arresting several "Big Vs," popular microbloggers who have been verified not to be writing under a pseudonym (and so have a V beside their name) on the charge of "creating social disturbance" (*The Economist* 2013). Such opinion leaders, who sometimes boasted millions of followers and used to be instrumental in mounting key mobilizations that had an impact on governmental decisions, have now left the scene of the public sphere. Since Xi Jinping placed himself at the helm of the powerful Central Leading Group for Cyberspace Affairs in November 2013, Weibo has been further controlled, outspoken analysis websites, such as ConsensusNet (Gongshiwang), were shut down, and media regulators banned the country's Internet portals like Tencent and Sina from conducting any independent journalism of their own. (See Chapter 23, "Can the Internet and Social Media Change the Party?")

Academics were also one of the main targets of the Document No. 9, which was followed by a number of political directives banning liberal topics in the classroom and the arrest of a few free thinkers, such as Ilham Tohti. The much respected economist at the Central University for Nationalities in Beijing was known for advocating human rights and equality for Uyghurs, as well as more autonomy for the Xinjiang province. A more formal campaign to fight against foreign ideas and reassess the correct ideology was launched within the universities during the fall semester 2014. Following a controversial report carried out by the *Liaoning Daily*, which accused college instructors of not being sufficiently supportive of China's political system, and of "being scornful of China" (Ramzy 2014), academics were asked to cut criticism and be more "positive" (Bandurski 2014). Officials were required to lecture on Xi Jinping's speeches and socialism in colleges each semester (*Global Times* 2015). University authorities were called to step up the Party's "leadership and guidance" as well as to "strengthen and improve the ideological and political work" (Xinhuanet 2014). In January 2015, a new directive required universities' leaderships to set clear political, legal, and moral limits to teaching content and stressed that no textbooks that espouse Western values should be allowed to enter the classrooms (Xinhuanet 2015). This campaign was dramatically illustrated by Ilham Tohti being sentenced to life imprisonment on a charge of "spreading separatist thought and inciting ethnic hatred" in September 2014.

All these measures attempted to deprive the Chinese population of any space, either online or offline, for public debate and forbade any form of criticism, even the most constructive one, by treating it as an act of dissidence or, so to speak, "an attack on state security." By requiring absolute obedience to the Party, the Xi leadership reintroduced the "friend or foe" logic (Yuen 2015) that characterized the Maoist era.

The crackdown efforts

This friend or foe logic was displayed in the arrest of prominent activists and independent thinkers, which namely decapitated the rights defense movement, but even more obviously in the crackdown on issue-oriented NGOs and activists focused on gender issues, labor rights, or discriminations whose moderate orientation was tolerated thus far.

President Xi expressed his will to eradicate anything pertaining to a liberal, democratic, and combative definition of civil society as early as 2013 with the arrest of several dozens of activists, the most prominent being Xu Zhiyong, a lawyer who founded the legal NGO Open Constitution Initiative in 2003 and the New Citizen movement in 2012. This movement, which was dedicated to the awakening and improvement of Chinese citizens' civil rights awareness, won fame namely by its campaigns for equal rights for education (equal treatment for rural and urban *hukou* bearers) and for the disclosure of the wealth of government officials. Xu's sentencing to four years in prison in January 2014, the arrest of several hundred members of the movement,[3] among them Tang Jinglin, a Guangzhou-based lawyer who was campaigning against graft and land seizure and was charged on "inciting subversion," clearly indicated that the struggle against corruption had to be carried out by the Party alone without the support of civil society actors relying on legal means and public criticism.

The crackdown has since then continuously intensified. Although it is not possible to list here all those who have been silenced by the regime, let's mention the shutdown in July 2013 of the Transition Institute, a moderately positioned think tank engaged in rights advocacy, the detention of a dozen participants of a closed-door seminar held to commemorate the 25th anniversary of June Fourth in May 2014, and the subsequent sentencing and disbarment of one of its participants, the lawyer Pu Zhiqiang, charged with "picking quarrels and inciting ethnic hatred" on the basis of his sarcastic postings on social media. In July 2015, the round-up against the Beijing Fengrui law firm and lawyers supporting one of its employees, Wang Yu, represented the most systematic and coordinated crackdown ever on rights defense lawyers. (See Chapter 16, "The Party and the Law.") Altogether, at least 319 lawyers, law firm staff, human rights activists, and family members have been questioned, summoned, forbidden to leave the country, held under house arrest, residential surveillance, criminally detained or arrested (CHRLCG 2016).

What these people and organizations had in common was that they tried to offer a counterweight to the regime by promoting alternative values and by seeking to restrict state authority over society and individuals. Those who are not currently detained in China's prisons or held under house arrest have now found refuge in the United States.

Moderate reformist NGOs and activists defending the rights of some social groups within the current political system have been targeted through the arrest of ten feminist activists – five of them having been charged with "picking quarrels and provoking trouble" – who were planning to mark International Women's Day in March 2015 with peaceful demonstrations against sexual harassment on public transportation; the subsequent crackdown on Yirenping, an NGO defending the rights of disabled people, people with Hepatitis B and HIV-AIDS; as well as labor NGOs in Guangdong Province. The case of the latter is particularly revealing. The coordinated crackdown on labor groups in the Guangzhou region on December 3, 2015, which led to the formal arrest of five activists and the temporary detention of a dozen others, swept altogether the leader of an organization helping workers suffering from work injuries, an activity considered as not sensitive thus far, and activists helping workers to bargain with employers over salary increase, but mostly to hold employers to their legal rights. Albeit the organizations involved in collective bargaining had enhanced workers' capacities to organize and helped them obtain hundreds billion RMB in wages, lay-off compensation, social insurance contributions, and other benefits, they were helping to mitigate social problems, always seeking collaboration with trade unions and local authorities and asking workers to favor social dialog over strikes and other rights defense means regarded as threatening social order (Froissart 2014). These organizations may have somehow been acknowledged as relieving some burden from the state and as improving the government's level of social management since they have been able to support collective bargaining for five years, despite constant harassment. Yet, four of the arrested activists, who were working in Guangzhou-based Panyu Workers' Center, were criminally charged with "gathering a crowd to disturb social order," including the director of the organization who was targeted by a smear campaign launched by local authorities. In the fall of 2016, three of them got suspended sentences ranging from 3 years to 18 months while the fourth activist was sentenced to a 21-month jail term (CLB 2016). This harsh crackdown recalls that the CCP "persists in opting to maintain its hierarchical and arbitrary power" (Fewsmith 2013: 33), refusing any alliance with civil society and preventing workers' collective action from growing into "anything long-term, programmatic, or institutional" (Gallagher 2014: 91).

These crackdown efforts display a few new worrisome approaches and techniques: they are more systematic (versus specifically targeted) crackdowns; they use televised confessions to shame detained lawyers, journalists, and activists; they rely on smear campaigns aiming at portraying activists dedicated to social justice as venal and morally deprived persons committed to toppling the regime, as well as on systematic deprivation of rights acknowledged by Chinese law, frequently resorting to forced confession, denial of procedural rights, and access to lawyers, persecution of family members, and so forth.

It should be nonetheless mentioned that this sweeping crackdown took place at a time when Chinese civil society, which had long been compartmentalized and vertically structured along the lines of private relations with those in power, started to form horizontal alliances via new solidarities and networks across different sectors. Examples include close cooperation between Yirenping and the feminists, as the organization used to employ three of them; or between the feminists, who usually target middle-class or elite women to which they belong, and female workers in Guangdong (Fincher 2016). At the same time, some segments of civil society had pushed the boundaries further, such as the Feminist Five who not only did not shy away from cross-class solidarity and included the rights of gay people in their advocacy for gender equality, but also subverted traditional forms of advocacy. Instead of just targeting high-ranking officials, the Feminist Five have fostered more colorful forms of public advocacy that rely on happenings and art performances, which were performed without consideration for the Party's political agenda[4] and were widely publicized on social media. Other segments of civil society even started to radicalize, such as the New Citizens' Movement, which did not hide from being a political movement relying on a liberal definition of citizenship, openly opposed to authoritarian rule, and dedicated to the promotion of constitutional governance (Xu 2014).

Since spring 2014, the Xi leadership has also forcefully cracked down on Christians, in a bid to limit the influence of "Western values" and to regain control over underground churches. The suppression-drive notably also targeted official churches – either Catholic or Protestant – in Zhejiang Province, namely the Wenzhou region, a hotbed of Christianity in China. By the end of 2016, dozens of churches were bulldozed, which was in addition to the 64 churches demolished in 2014 and about 1,500 in 2015 (Asianews 2014; *Catholic Herald* 2015); nearly 2,000 crosses have been torn down, church leaders and followers blocking the demolitions have been arrested and imprisoned. A crackdown on underground religious sites followed suit in 2016, while the release of a tougher version of the Regulations on Religious Affairs and other measures stress the necessity to Sinicize religions in China, change believers' thoughts, and bring back religious sites under strict party control. The laws have become much more specific in controlling every aspect of religion, including cult and doctrine, and greatly empower local government bodies all the way down to the communities so that the latitude enjoyed till now by some communities would virtually become impossible (Mansfield 2016).

Erasing the legal gray zone: further constraints on Chinese and foreign NGOs

Following on the heels of the sustained crackdown on domestic civil society and the ratcheting up of pressure on international NGOs, the legal framework in 2016 governing the third sector has shifted dramatically. A series of new laws and regulations was passed to further shape the Chinese People's society. They basically consist of erasing the legal gray zone that enabled the surge of civil society organizations over the past period, reinforcing the Party's direct control over the third sector while forcefully limiting it to service delivery, and drastically curbing foreign NGOs' and foundations' presence and activities in China as well as their linkages with local organizations.

The promulgation in early 2016 of the Charity Law and the Overseas NGO Management Law represents the central government's most powerful statement ever about the role and limits of the third sector in China. Important to note is that the Charity Law introduces a new term, "charitable organization" (*cishan zuzhi*), into the official lexicon. The Overseas NGO Management Law, on the other hand, uses the internationally recognized "non-governmental organization" (*feizhengfu zuzhi*) to describe the target of the law. The implication, building on years of avoidance of the term "non-governmental organization," is that China will have no domestic NGOs, but rather charities. "NGO" is deemed a universe of discourse only for foreigners and foreign conceptions. While the Charity Law is an important step toward building a system of social governmentality (*shehui zhili*) with Chinese characteristics, which will leave little space for social engagement other than philanthropic activities, the Overseas NGO Management Law is reflective of Beijing's growing fear about an "infiltration by hostile Western forces" that could, in its eyes, eventually trigger a color revolution.

The Overseas NGO Management Law, which came into force in January 2017, establishes procedures for foreign-based organizations, but also organizations from Hong Kong, Taiwan, and Macao, to register formally and conduct activities in China. It targets a broad and ill-defined – thus potentially limitless – range of non-governmental and non-profit organizations spanning common NGOs, membership associations, and foundations specialized in public welfare but also any private organization that provides non-profit social services, such as private non-profit hospitals, schools, research institutes, nursing homes, child welfare agencies, various social service agencies, environmental and other public service organizations.

The law symbolically criminalizes overseas organizations as it requires them to register with the Ministry of Public Security (MPS) or its provincial bureaus rather than the Ministry of Civil Affairs as it used to be the case before or like their domestic counterparts. Before doing so, they have to be sponsored by a professional supervisory unit (PSU) authorized by the MPS. Activities with a duration of less than a year require a Chinese partner approved by the MPS that would act as a guarantor and apply for an approval of the competent authority. PSUs are also responsible for overseeing the activities of overseas NGOs and for assisting public security authorities in investigating and punishing illegal activities by overseas NGOs (Article 40).

This dual registration system not only creates overlapping layers of authority, but also extra administrative constraints and burdens. Overall, the law gives much more latitude to the state – actually the police – to screen the "good" and the "bad" organizations (Jia 2016) and will potentially prevent organizations working on sensitive sectors such as advocacy, capacity building, legal aid, labor, ethnic minority or religious affairs, to further their work in China. But the law also places overseas organizations considered as desirable under much greater state scrutiny regarding their program, work plan, budget, sources of funding, and staff recruitment. It gives sweeping power and discretion to the police and the PSU to keep track on and influence overseas organizations' activities, namely by granting the police unrestricted access to organizations' office, staff, computers, and bank accounts. Under such scrutiny, overseas organizations will face higher risk of their registration being revoked and their persons-in-charge being detained, especially under the charges of "endangering state security" or "damaging national unity and national or public interest" (Article 5, 47). Those concepts have been interpreted so broadly by Chinese authorities so far that they can be invoked in any circumstances, especially as violations of the law will be handled by the public security alone and will not require court ruling. Perpetrators can be detained for up to 15 days and face repatriation or deportation.

While this law is expected to greatly reduce the number of overseas organizations in China, it will also hold important implications for domestic civil society actors. The law prohibits any organization or individual inside the Chinese border from accepting funds from, working, or indirectly working with a foreign NGO that has not obtained legal permission to operate in China (Article 46). Conversely, as overseas NGOs and foundations could get into trouble for working with unregistered domestic partners, they are expected to greatly reduce their cooperation with the more grassroots or sensitive ones. Altogether, this law is intended to curb overseas NGOs' funding to local civil society actors and stifle their cooperation and exchanges with domestic partners. This, together with the Charity Law, will further reduce the diversity of Chinese civil society, well beyond the current crackdown.

Enforced since September 1, 2016, the Charity Law is an important move to ease restrictions on the registration, the fundraising, and operational activities of charity groups. The law targets associations, social service organizations, or foundations engaged in activities such as aid to the poor, assistance to the elderly, orphans, the sick, and the disabled; disaster relief and help in public health crises; promotion of projects involving education, science, culture, health, and sports; pollution and public hazard prevention and protection of the environment. Under the new law, those organizations are now formally allowed to register directly with the Ministry of Civil Affairs, thus escaping the dual management system, that is the difficult task of finding a PSU to sponsor them and the obligation to comply with onerous reporting requirements.[5]

But the law also gives the state wide discretion over which organizations are allowed to register, especially in assessing if an organization's activities can be regarded as "represent[ing] the core values of socialism and promot[ing] the traditional morals of the Chinese nation" (Article 5), or as "not endanger[ing] national security or harm[ing] societal public interests" (Article 4). The Charity Law as a whole tends to identify the "public good" to "charity" and thereby prevents any non-charity-oriented organization from being acknowledged as contributing to the public good, or even to subsist. Indeed, organizations that have not been recognized as charities by authorities are not allowed to solicit public donations, which will further marginalize other types of organizations in a context where overseas funding will dry up. This move was further confirmed by the draft registration and management regulations published by the Ministry of Civil Affairs in June 2016, which renamed "civil non-enterprise units" (*minban feiqiye danwei*) as "social service organizations" (*shehui fuwu jigou*), hence implying that all social organizations other than foundations and membership associations should now have a social service mission as defined by the Party. It is obvious that the leadership wants to make sure that there is no avenue for social organizations to do something else than charity.

At the same time, the Charity Law and the revised registration and management regulations for foundations and other social organizations[6] will make it easier for relevant organizations to access domestic social resources because they lower the barriers to public fundraising and provide greater tax incentives for donations. It also intends to enhance public trust toward such organizations, as it includes strict regulations, namely an obligation to information disclosure, to prevent fraud, and imposes tighter supervision on the management of charity groups. However, the top-down approach to managing the groups could come at the price of their independence and make it harder for them to monitor the government. Moreover, several legal provisions mainly favor big well-established organizations – that usually have close ties to the government – to the detriment of small newly established ones.[7]

The determination to further tighten the Party's grip over civil society organizations was confirmed by the Joint Opinion on Reforming the Management System of Social Organizations published by the general offices of the CCP and the State Council in August 2016. The Opinion underlines the CCP's determination to comprehensively cover the third sector in a bid to make sure that social organizations do not have the potential to threaten the position of the CCP as the ruling party. It devotes particular attention to strengthening controls over the founders of social organizations, including pulling them in for political education, and reasserts the obligation to establish party branches in social organizations having three or more party members. While this requirement is not new,[8] it now gains more authority and emphasizes the CCP's anxiousness to establish its leadership over the third sector and guide its development: "the party will have to play … the political role within social organizations … to ensure that [they] are developing on the correct political path" (Zhonggong zhongyang bangongting 2016). Lastly, the Opinion sets 2020 as a date for establishing a universal registration system and rendering more uniform the situation of domestic civil society groups in China.[9]

The two new laws and subsequent (draft) regulations undoubtedly display the Party's will to channelize Chinese civil society toward charity oriented, service activities delivered on behalf of the Party, to the detriment of the development of rights defense, advocacy oriented groups but also of the building of a welfare state. Charity has indeed nothing to do with the guarantee of social rights. Social rights are distinguished from charity in that everyone has a personal right to claim them: they represent a right that the individual holds over the state. On the contrary, as noted by Thomas Humphrey Marshall, charity, whether dispensed by the state or the private sector, represents an alternative to citizenship: it excludes its beneficiaries from being citizens (Marshall 1964). Indeed, charity particularizes and stigmatizes some social groups as "poor and needy" while rights (as citizens' rights) are universal and enhance human dignity. The Charity Law can thus be interpreted as a state's attempt to further curtail the advancement of rights, especially in light of the few efforts made under the Xi Jinping leadership to improve the social security system. However, the law remains ambiguous: "charity" is also taken in its broad sense of "public good" and notably includes environment protection activities, which are obviously beneficial to all Chinese citizens and beyond.

These past few years, environment protection and namely pollution control have been acknowledged as a CCP key commitment by, among others, the passing of the new and much more restrictive Environmental Protection Law, the 2015 Thirteenth Five-Year Plan as well as the signature of Paris Agreements in December 2015 followed by their quick ratification. In this particular sector, the CCP has explicitly called upon public participation to help it fulfill its commitments and environmental NGOs (ENGOs) indeed appear as the last sector of the rights defense-oriented civil society that enjoy some freedom or even empowerment. The new Environmental Protection Law namely formalizes the possibility for ENGOs to mount public interest litigations, hence giving them a key and officially endorsed role in pollution control. In this sector, it seems that the Party wants to not only preserve but also further develop and legalize the public participation that was experienced during the Hu-Wen era. This opening might give rise to innovative and semi-institutionalized forms of public participation, including advocacy.

Is this model sustainable?

No matter how restrictive this new legislative framework is, it is likely that, as they have always done so in the past, civil society actors will devise new strategies to circumvent or even subvert this new framework in order to pursue their own agenda. The most likely effect of these two new laws and subsequent measures might not be to successfully reformat the Chinese third sector according to official state goals but rather to force some social actors to develop even more informal networks and new strategies so as to avoid appearing on the state's radar. According to informal conversations I had with various civil society actors, some social organizations considered as sensitive (such as think tanks or legal groups) are already finding ways to sell their services and expertise so as to reregister as businesses while at the same time continuing their initial activities. Besides, an increasing amount of domestic organizations are presenting themselves as social enterprises, especially in Shanghai. Although this legal status still does not exist in China, those organizations are registering as businesses, which allows them to be financially and administratively independent and articulate their profitable activities with freely chosen social endeavors. Contrary to NGOs that are registered as businesses by default, and whose commercial activities are developed to support social ones, social enterprises claim a chosen and assumed identity, and their profitable and social activities are fully integrated to each other. This might lead to further reconfigurations between the third and commercial sectors, which might free social endeavors from political control but at the same time subject it to the market. Simultaneously, the new legal framework will also clarify the status of many organizations registered as civil non-enterprise units while already having profitable activities.

It is also important to note that, while some NGOs are already choosing circumventing tactics, others opt for the opposite tactic by favoring a more open, daring, and self-confident activism. This is the case for example of a non-registered labor NGO located in Shenzhen, founded at the beginning of the 2000s and which has been actively involved in collective bargaining since 2010 despite constant harassment by the authorities, which resulted in some temporary interruptions of its activities. Neither the December 2015 crackdown on labor NGOs in Guangzhou nor the passing of the new laws deterred the organization from pursuing its commitment to advance collective bargaining in the Shenzhen area. Between December 2015 and December 2016, it has been involved in eight collective bargaining cases, keeping its activities transparent to convince authorities of their righteous nature and that it is not secretly challenging state authority. This tactic proved efficient as the organization managed to involve local unions and authorities in at least two cases during which they constructively supervised the negotiations and helped secure beneficial outcomes to workers. This example shows that, whenever local authorities estimate that it is beneficial to them, they will still maintain ad hoc and circumscribed alliances with social actors, which will continue to be tolerated if not officially recognized. Indeed, even if the central state wants to get rid of moderate issue-oriented NGOs, local authorities cannot completely forgo their help in fostering social dialog and diffusing contradictions. Without their support as precious intermediaries between state and society, the social situation might become explosive. It is thus likely that rights-defense and advocacy-oriented groups will not completely disappear, but will be faced with the same dilemma as before, perhaps receiving informal support but unlikely to obtain formal recognition by the government and the financial and other benefits conferred by a formal legal status.

Indeed, the legal gray zone will likely not be fully eradicated. The sometimes imprecise wording of this new legal framework, which leaves some room for interpretation, as well as its decentralized implementation by local governments, might constitute an obstacle to its smooth implementation, either in favor or against social organizations. The Overseas NGO Management Law adds a tremendous amount of administrative work not only to social organizations but also to PSUs designated among state administration as well as Public Security organs that might not have the capacity and manpower to take up this extra work. This might trigger foot dragging and failure to comply among officials and lead to selective enforcement of the law. Due to their long-lasting chilly relationships with public-interest organizations, local officials might also be reluctant to significantly lower the barriers to the registration of domestic organizations as charities, especially against the backdrop of the anti-corruption campaign and other contradictory signals pointing toward tighter control and suspicion toward social organizations. Likewise, emphasizing that officials are either ignorant or suspicious of their activities, many domestic organizations said that they did not plan to attempt to register despite the encouraging aspects of the Charity Law (Spires 2016).

To some extent, these new laws as well as the efforts to crack down on civil society and to put a gag on criticism might have an unintended contradictory side effect by encouraging the most adamant and boldest actors to join the "hidden sphere" Havel mentions in *The Power of the Powerless* (Havel 1978), nurturing even fiercer resistance and opposition to the regime and further depriving the Party-state of its means to control the most radical elements of civil society. While some organizations may seem to have disappeared, informal networks remain and can reemerge at any time.

In this regard, Protestants deserve a special attention due to their growing number, their organization capacities, and their commitment to preserve the religious sphere's independence from political intrusion. Koesel attributes Protestants' rising number to their extraordinary capacity to organize under the state's radar in a hostile political context, and assesses that they constitute "one of the largest and most sophisticated civil-society networks in China" (Koesel 2013: 587). Although "many empirical studies demonstrate that, in the eyes of the majority of house church members, Christianity is not opposed to the communist party …, rather, it is only a way of 'spiritual life' and 'social life' of the believers" (Hong 2012: 252), paradoxically, those studies at the same time show that most church members also give themselves a broader political, social, and moral mission toward society. Vala finds for example that some urban churches in different cities that hold outdoor worship protests against state domination of religion are engaging in a kind of public activism that "combines religious worship with protest and defends the priority of religion over state domination of society," with their leaders "implicitly seek[ing] to limit state authority over religion and, by extension, over all of society" (Vala 2012: 52). Witnesses already report that "Christianity is growing fastest where the persecution is the most severe" (LifeSiteNews 2016). Koessel stresses for his part that "while church leaders do not see themselves as revolutionaries and are quick to downplay any political aspirations in favor of a spiritual and patriotic mission, this does not mean that they will always do so." "One is reminded of the role civil society played in the collapse of communism in Eastern Europe," he wrote. "Its power came not from a project to end the regime so much as its ability to establish an existence separate from the regime" (Koesel 2013: 587).

Social resistance is already palpable and it mainly targets censorship. Albeit scarce and scattered, resistance is overtly expressed by demonstrations, open letters, petitions, outspoken op-eds and statements, that multiplied during the year 2016 both from within and outside the Party.

The *Southern Weekly* incident in January 2013 triggered a strong response by journalists, who mounted a public demonstration in front of the journal's building, but also academics and students, public intellectuals, and ordinary citizens. An open letter called on Guangdong's party chief to sack the chief of the provincial propaganda department. It was echoed three years later by Ren Zhiqiang's outspoken opposition following Xi's visit to leading state media outlets. The retired businessman expressed the anger of a part of the public, declaring to his 38 million followers on Weibo that the party press organs were financed by the taxpayers and thus had to serve them first, not the Party.

Critics crystalized around the two sessions of the NPC and the CPPCC in March 2016, which opened in great tension with the publication of an open letter calling for Xi Jinping's resignation from all state and Party leadership positions, posted on the state-linked Wujie News website. The letter blamed Xi for an atmosphere of political, diplomatic, economic, ideological, and cultural anxiety currently sweeping China, and accused him of excessively concentrating the power in his own hands. The letter mentioned that the "personal safety" of the president and his family could be in jeopardy if he did not comply (*China Digital Times* 2016). Signed by a group of "loyal Party members," the letter was likely written by personalities both inside and outside the system. The two sessions gave delegates the opportunity to echo social resentment as well as to express themselves as victims of the leadership's increasing intolerance of alternative viewpoints in party dialogue and efforts to limit "improper discussions." Wang Guoqing, the spokesman for the National Committee of the CPPCC, underlined that by dodging questions they find "sensitive," spokespeople may end up stoking confusion and undermining the credibility of the institutions they represent. In that regard, as noted by the Europe edition of the *China Daily*, Zhu Zhengfu, deputy chairman of the All China Lawyers Association and a member of the CPPCC National Committee, "set a laudable example for other CPPCC members and NPC delegates." He brought to the session a number of proposals targeted at some of the most pressing issues concerning judicial justice. Among those was the suggestion to stop criminal suspects confessing on TV, which, he stressed, is against the jurisprudential principle of assumption of innocence that China has adopted (*China Daily* 2016). Another CPPCC delegate, Jiang Hong, said in an article that appeared on Caixin's Chinese-language site on March 3, 2016 that advisors should be free to give Communist Party and government agencies suggestions on economic, political, cultural, and societal issues. Jiang also recalled in the interview that the Communist Party has a tradition of "listening to different opinions" and that the right of people to speak freely was enshrined in the Constitution. The article was censored for "containing illegal content," but Caixin pushed back with an English article – which too was quickly removed from the Internet – denouncing this censorship and Jiang subsequently announced his plan to propose a measure to the NPC on ensuring the legal right to self-expression. Official media expressed their support for this plan, namely the *Global Times*, which reported Jiang's words, quickly followed by an open letter by a Xinhua employee accusing censors of using tactics reminiscent of Maoist times to silence and smear critics, and pointing out that the public's freedom of expression has been violated to an extreme degree (Buckley 2016). Critics continued during the summer 2016 when 78 scientists from the elite Chinese Academy of Sciences and other top scientific and engineering institutes sent a petition to the CCP calling on Xi Jinping to lift censorship of the Internet, which, as stressed by one of the signatories, has already "resulted in severe losses to people engaged in scientific research." Another op-ed published by the *People's Daily*, which warned that "absolutist egomania will bring a nasty demise to top cadres," was construed as indirectly denouncing Xi's grab on power (Lam 2016).

However, despite the fact that several official statements are echoing social resentment, and that this very resentment would not be able to be voiced without the support of Xi's opponents, a crisis scenario similar to 1989 when reformists among the government struck an alliance with social activists seems improbable for now (see Chapter 21, "The Future of the Chinese Communist Party") and Xi was eventually successfully elected Core Leader of the CCP during the Sixth Plenum in October 2016.

Conclusion

Although the Hu-Wen era was not devoid of fierce – yet circumscribed – crackdowns on civil society, the leadership tolerated forms of critical or even combative civil society as long as it served the overall objectives of the Party. Both civil society and governance methods experienced a certain amount of diversification and even pluralization, which bestowed a unique dynamism yet precarious balance to the Chinese authoritarian regime. Conversely, the Xi leadership has restored greater orthodoxy, considerably reduced space for civil society, and set up significant obstacles to China's openness to the outside world, which used to be the main driving force behind reforms.

The Xi administration has enhanced and clarified the legal framework for social organizations but only to foster organizations that complement authoritarian rule by fulfilling needs and providing services not offered by the state and even strengthen the resilience of the current regime. Except maybe in the environmental sector, the new laws make it obvious that the Party wants to guide social life and make it harder – if not impossible – for social organizations to monitor the government and promote social changes. The same drive has affected religious associations. While they enjoyed some degree of de facto autonomy under the previous leadership, they are now either being suppressed or brought under much stringent party control and ordered to serve the state's goals.

President Xi's endeavors to bridge the gap between the Party and society as well as to eradicate enemies of the people, a category that may now include anyone who does not strictly toe the Party's line, revive the totalitarian temptation of the regime. Overall, the CCP plays a very dangerous game for itself. The Party forgoes the constructive proposal strength of civil society and its role in diffusing social contradictions. The leadership's strong grip on criticism has nurtured antagonism and radicalization among the boldest rights activists, as well as among some party members and officials. Xi has potentially created a situation of permanent crisis whose management cost might be extremely high, as no government can secure its power sustainably by only relying on coercion.

However, the leadership's coercion power might not be as strong as expected. While, in the short term, the new constraints have undoubtedly engendered a chilly effect on civil society, social actors might strengthen and diversify their resources to resist pressure in the long term. The crisis may well never explode into the open and be merely diffused by circumvention tactics, foot-dragging, and refusal to comply on the part of both social actors and officials, which in turn may erode Xi Jinping's power.

Notes

1 The Chinese law distinguishes between associations (*shetuan*), civil non-enterprise units (*minban feiqiye danwei*), and foundations (*jijinhui*).

2 According to official statistics, the total number of registered social organizations (including *shetuan* and *minban feiqiye danwei*) grew from 153,322 in 2000 to 606,048 in 2014 (China Statistical Yearbook 2015), while estimates of the number of informal NPOs run from 1 million to 3 million depending on which types of organizations are counted as NPOs (ICNL 2016). But according to the estimates of various scholars, the number of "illegal" organizations could be up to or over ten times the number of

"legal" ones (Jia 2016). Assuming that the rise in the number of Protestants could be taken as an indicator of the growth of religious communities, the members of the official Three-Self Churches should have approximately 20 million while house church members should be between 20 and 60 million (Hong 2012: 258; Koesel 2013: 574).

3 For a detailed list, see CHRD 2013.

4 The demonstration against sexual harassment in public transportation, which led to the arrest of the Feminist Five, was held just days before the annual assemblies of the National People's Congress (NPC) and the Chinese People's Political Consultative Conference (CPPCC), a quite sensitive time in China.

5 The Charity Law thus endorses the experimentations carried out by local authorities, namely the Guangdong Province government, over the last few years to lower the barriers to entry for certain categories of social organizations, especially those involved in social service provision.

6 In June 2016, the Ministry of Civil Affairs issued draft registration and management regulations for public comment for foundations (*jijinhui*) and social service organizations (*shehui fuwu jigou*), followed, on August 1, by draft registration and management regulations for the third type of social organizations: social (membership-based) associations (*shetuan*). These regulations specify which government bodies are responsible for their registration and management, the registration requirements and procedures, the internal governance of the organization, their legal responsibilities, and so on.

7 E.g., organizations recognized as charities should own their own premises and should not use more than 10 percent of the funds they raise to cover administration and payroll costs, meaning that they have to be able to raise substantial amounts of funding to be able to provide competitive salaries to their staff, and thus attract skilled workers and retain employees. Organizations will also have to wait for two years before being allowed to publicly raise funds, which raises questions about the survival of the smaller organizations.

8 Party cells have long been required in social organizations as well as other entities having three or more party members by the Party Charter, Article 29. By the end of 2012, the CCP had established grassroots party branches in over 40,300 social organizations (*shehui tuanti*) and more than 39,500 private non-enterprise units (*minfei*) according to Thornton who traces back the party-building efforts in the third sector to as early as 1997 (Thornton 2013). This requirement was emphasized again in the 2015 CCP Party Branch Work Interim Regulations (*Zhongguo gongchandang dangzu gongzuo tiaoli shixing*) and was also inserted into the draft revisions of the Regulations regarding the three types of social organizations that were put out for comment in 2016.

9 The Opinion also states that industry associations and those involved in science, charity, or urban and rural community services will be able to directly register with civil affairs authorities or local governments. It thus seems to loosen the state's authority and control over social organizations only to reinforce the Party's one.

References

Asianews (2014) "Zhejiang: list and pictures of 64 demolished Christian churches," May 21, www.asianews.it/news-en/Zhejiang:-list-and-pictures-of-64-demolished-Christian-churches-31135.html [accessed November 1, 2016].

Bandurski, D. (2008) "Propaganda leaders scurry off to carry out the 'spirit' of Hu Jintao's 'important' media speech," *China Media Project*, June 25, http://cmp.hku.hk/2008/06/25/1079/ [accessed October 20, 2016].

Bandurski, D. (2014) "College teachers must be more 'positive'," *China Media Project*, November 15, http://cmp.hku.hk/2014/11/15/37149/ [accessed October 21, 2016].

Bandurski, D. (2016a) "Innovation, so the Party can shine," *China Media Project*, September 2, http://cmp.hku.hk/2016/09/02/39893/ [accessed October 20, 2016].

Bandurski, D. (2016b) "Under Xi, the media has turned from a 'mouthpiece of masses' to the Party's parrot," *China Media Project*, June 21, www.hongkongfp.com/2016/06/21/under-xi-the-media-has-turned-from-a-mouthpiece-of-masses-to-the-partys-parrot/ [accessed June 21, 2016].

Buckley, Chris (2016) "China's censor denounced in online attack," *New York Times*, March 11, www.nytimes.com/2016/03/12/world/asia/china-censorship.html?_r=0 [accessed March 11, 2016].

Catholic Herald (2015) "Number of churches demolished in just one Chinese province has reached 1,500," December 30, www.catholicherald.co.uk/news/2015/12/30/number-of-churches-demolished-in-just-one-chinese-province-has-reached-1500/ [accessed November 2, 2016].

China Daily (2016) "Welcome willingness to tackle sensitive issues," March 3, http://europe.chinadaily.com.cn/opinion/2016-03/03/content_23716666.htm [accessed March 4, 2016].

China Digital Times (2016) "Loyal Party members urge Xi's resignation," March 16, http://chinadigitaltimes.net/2016/03/open-letter-devoted-party-members-urge-xis-resignation/ [accessed March 16, 2016].

China Human Rights Defenders (CHRD) (2013) "Individuals detained in crackdown on peaceful assembly, association and expression," July 17, www.nchrd.org/2013/07/individuals-detained-in-crackdown-on-assembly-and-association/ [accessed July 30, 2013].

China Human Rights Lawyers Concern Group (CHRLCG) (2016) "'709 crackdown' latest data and development of cases," September 29, www.chrlawyers.hk/en/content/%E2%80%98709-crackdown%E2%80%99-latest-data-and-development-cases-1800-29-september-2016 [accessed September 30, 2016].

China Labour Bulletin (CLB) (2016) "Labour activist Meng Han sentenced to 21 months," November 4, www.clb.org.hk/content/labour-activist-meng-han-sentenced-21-months [accessed November 4, 2016].

China Statistical Yearbook (2015) "22–35: Statistics on social organizations," www.stats.gov.cn/tjsj/ndsj/2015/indexeh.htm [accessed September 30, 2016].

Fewsmith, Joseph (2013) *The Logic and Limits of Authoritarianism in China.* Cambridge: Cambridge University Press.

Fincher, Leta H. (2016) "China's Feminist Five," *Dissident Magazine*, Fall, www.dissentmagazine.org/article/china-feminist-five [accessed October 22, 2016].

Froissart, Chloé (2014) "The emergence of autonomous collective bargaining in China," *Critique internationale*, 2014/4 (65): 43–63. English translation: www.cairn-int.info/abstract-E_CRII_065_0043-the-emergence-of-autonomous-collective.htm#anchor_citation [accessed October 21, 2016].

Froissart, Chloé (2015) "La démocratie en Chine, une question d'équilibres," in J.M. Bouissou ed., *La démocratie en Asie*, Arles: Picquier, 103–143.

Gallagher, Mary E. (2014) "China's workers' movement and the end of the rapid-growth era," *Daedalus*, 143 (2): 81–95.

Global Times (2015) "Officials required to lecture on Xi Jinping's speeches, socialism in colleges each semester," August 6, www.globaltimes.cn/content/935717.shtml [accessed October 21, 2016].

Havel, Vaclav (1978) *The Power of the Powerless.* Trans. by Paul Wilson. www.vaclavhavel.cz/showtrans.php?cat=eseje&val=2_aj_eseje.html&typ=HTML [accessed April 4, 2017].

Hong, Zhaohui (2012) "Protecting and striving for the rights to religious freedom: Case studies on the protestant house churches in China," *Journal of Third World Studies*, 29 (1): 249–261.

Hu, Angang (2013) "Renmin shehui weihe youyu gongmin shehui" (Why People's society is superior to civil society), *Renmin Ribao* (People's Daily), July 19, http://paper.people.com.cn/rmrbhwb/html/2013-07/19/content_1270853.htm [accessed April 4, 2017].

Hu, Jintao (2007) "Report to the Seventeenth National Congress of the Communist Party of China on Oct. 15, 2007," www.china.org.cn/english/congress/229611.htm#4 [accessed October 13, 2016].

International Center for Not-for-Profit Law (ICNL) (2016) "Civic Freedom Monitor: China," www.icnl.org/research/monitor/china.html [accessed October 15, 2016].

Jia, Xijin (2016) "Legislations for foreign NGOs: How will the second boot land?" *China Development Brief*, April 14, http://chinadevelopmentbrief.cn/articles/legislations-for-foreign-ngos-how-will-the-second-boot-land/ [accessed April 30, 2016].

Koesel, Karrie J. (2013) "The rise of a Chinese house church: The organizational weapon," *The China Quarterly*, 215, September: 572–589.

Lam, Willy (2016) "Intellectuals lobby for more freedom as President Xi faces pushback from party rivals," *China Brief*, 16 (12), August 1, www.jamestown.org/programs/chinabrief/single/?tx_ttnews%5Btt_news%5D=45659&tx_ttnews%5BbackPid%5D=25&cHash=de0c660ce045befe3a7c09dfdcafd709#.V8UnAbVm0zF [accessed September 30, 2016].

Legal Daily (2011) "Zhongguo tese shehui guanli chuangxin conghechu fali" (From where should the innovation of social management with Chinese characteristics get its strength?), May 26, http://news.xinhuanet.com/2011-05/26/c_121459315.htm [accessed October 30, 2016].

LifeSiteNews (2016) "As China plans another crackdown to suppress religion, Christianity continues to grow," September 29, www.lifesitenews.com/news/as-china-plans-another-crackdown-to-suppress-religion-christianity-continue [accessed October 30, 2016].

Mansfield, Katie (2016) "China launches 'religious winter' in bid to destroy Christianity in fierce crackdown," *Express*, September 30, www.express.co.uk/news/world/715834/China-Christians-launches-religious-winter-bid-destroy-Christianity [accessed November 2, 2016].

Marshall, Thomas Humphrey (1964) *Class, Citizenship and Social Development.* Westport, CT: Greenwood Press.
O'Brien, Kevin and Li Lianjiang (2006) *Rightful Resistance in Rural China.* Cambridge: Cambridge University Press.
Pils, Eva (2012) "Discussing 'civil society' and 'liberal communities' in China," *China Perspectives*, (3): 2–7.
Qian Gang (2013) "Why *Southern Weekly*?," *China Media Project*, http://cmp.hku.hk/2013/02/18/31257/ [accessed October 16, 2016].
Radio Free Asia (RFA) (2016) "China slaps website with two-month suspension from media 'whitelist'," October 13, www.rfa.org/english/news/china/caixin-punishment-10132016123546.html [accessed October 21, 2016].
Ramzy, Austin (2014) "Newspaper calls on Chinese academics to cut the criticism," November 17, http://sinosphere.blogs.nytimes.com/2014/11/17/newspaper-calls-on-chinese-academics-to-cut-the-criticism/ [accessed November 17, 2014].
Shirky, Clay (2008) *Here Comes Everybody: The Power of Organising Without Organisations.* London: Penguin.
Spires, Anthony (2016) "Grassroots NGOs' feedback on the draft Charity Law," http://anthonyjspires.weebly.com/charity-law-in-china.html [accessed September 30, 2016].
Svensson, M. (2012) "Media and civil society in China," *China Perspectives*, (3): 19–30.
Teng, B. (2012) "Rights defence (weiquan 维权), Microblogs (weibo 微博), and the Surrounding Gage (weiguan 围观)," *China Perspectives*, (3): 29–41.
The Economist (2013) "Big Vs and bottom lines," August 31, www.economist.com/news/china/21584385-authorities-move-against-some-chinas-most-vocal-microbloggers-big-vs-and-bottom-lines [accessed October 10, 2016].
Thornton, Patricia (2013) "'Civil society' or 'People's society': Where is the Party?," *China Development Brief*, August 27, http://chinadevelopmentbrief.cn/articles/civil-society-or-peoples-society-wheres-the-party/ [accessed August 30, 2013].
Vala, Carsten T. (2012) "Protestant Christianity and civil society in authoritarian China," *China Perspectives*, (3): 43–52.
Wang, Haiyan and Lee Francis L.F. (2014) "Research on Chinese investigative journalism, 1978–2013: A critical review," *The China Review*, 14 (2): 215–251.
Wu, Fengshi and Kinman Chan (2012) "Graduated control and beyond: The evolving government-NGO relations," *China Perspectives*, (3): 9–17.
Xiaomi (2011) "Weibo/weiguan neng fou gaibian Zhongguo?" (Can Weibo/the surrounding gaze change China?), http://yyyyiiii.blogspot.jp/2011/01/no2.html [accessed October 15, 2016].
Xinhuanet (2014) "Xi Jinping: Jianchi lideshuren sixiang yinling, jiaqiang gaijin gaoxiao dangjian gongzuo" (Xi Jinping: Stick to "practice virtue to train competent persons" as a guiding thought to strengthen and improve the Party building in colleges and universities), December 29, http://news.xinhuanet.com/politics/2014-12/29/c_1113818177.htm [accessed October 21, 2016].
Xinhuanet (2015) "Zhonggong zhongyang bangongting, Guowuyuan bangongting yinfa 'Guanyu jinyibu jiaqiang he gaijin xin xingshi xia gaoxiao xuanchuan sixiang gongzuo de yijian'" (Central Committee General Office, State Council General Office, *Opinion concerning Further Strengthening and Improving Propaganda and Ideology Work in Higher Education Under New Circumstances*), January 19, http://news.xinhuanet.com/2015-01/19/c_1114051345.htm [accessed April 4, 2017].
Xu, Zhiyong (2014) "New citizens' movement," *Chinese Law and Government*, 46 (5–6): 148–154.
Yu, Keping (2011) "Civil society in China: Concepts, classification and institutional environment," in Deng Zhenglai ed., *State and Civil Society: The Chinese Perspective*, Singapore: World Scientific, 63–96.
Yu, Verna (2016) "The death of a liberal Chinese magazine," *The Diplomat*, July 19, http://thediplomat.com/2016/07/the-death-of-a-liberal-chinese-magazine/ [accessed July 19, 2016].
Yuen, Samson (2015) "Friend or foe? The diminishing space of China's civil society," *China Perspective*, (3): 51–56.
Zhang Ming (2015) "What is this 'positive energy'," *China Media Project*, December 15, http://cmp.hku.hk/2015/12/15/39476/ [accessed October 16, 2016].
Zhao, Yuezhi and Sun, Wusan (2007) "Public opinion supervision: Possibilities and limits of the media in constraining local officials," in Elizabeth J. Perry and Merle Goldman eds., *Grassroots Political Reform in Contemporary China*, Cambridge, MA: Harvard University Press.

Zhonggong zhongyang bangongting, Guowuyuan bangongting (General offices of the CCP and the State Council) (2016) "Guanyu gaige shehui zuzhi guanli zhidu cujin shehui zuzhi jiankang youxu fazhan de yijian" (Joint Opinion on Reforming the Management System of Social Organizations and Promoting the Healthy and Orderly Development of Social Organizations), August 21, http://news.xinhuanet.com/politics/2016-08/21/c_1119428034.htm [accessed August 30, 2016].

23

CAN THE INTERNET AND SOCIAL MEDIA CHANGE THE PARTY?

David Bandurski

Introduction

In March 2000, speaking about a newly minted agreement for China's entry into the World Trade Organization, US President Bill Clinton asked his audience at Johns Hopkins University to imagine how the elimination of tariffs on information technology products might lead to a more open society in China. "We know how much the Internet has changed America, and we are already an open society," he said. "Imagine how much it could change China" (Clinton 2000: 404). Clinton then introduced an analogy that for years to come would add a note of whimsy to the firmly held belief that the Internet would lead inevitably to political change in the world's most populous country, and that state restrictions were powerless to stem the tide of democratic progress. China's attempts to crack down on the Internet, Clinton said, were "like trying to nail Jell-O to the wall" (Clinton 2000: 404).

The notion of the Internet as an unstoppable force of political liberalization faces serious questioning today, and many now discount this "cyber-utopianism" (Morozov 2012: xii–xiii). These sanguine views of technology-driven change, they argue, have failed to foresee or acknowledge "how masterfully dictators would learn to use [the Internet] for surveillance, and how sophisticated modern systems of Internet censorship would become" (Morozov 2012: xiv). The Chinese Communist Party (CCP), which now operates what is beyond doubt the world's most sophisticated system of Internet censorship, has spent the past two decades gainsaying in practice – through political, technical, legal and regulatory means – the sanguine belief that the Internet is necessarily an agent of change, by which proponents of the idea generally mean *democratic* change. In this chapter, I offer an overview of Internet development and control in China, placing it in the larger context of media development, and argue that while the Internet has in fact changed China a great deal, including offering new tools for personal expression and political discussion, part of this change has brought greater sophistication in how the Party controls communications – a sophistication that has evolved with each successive shock brought on by media development itself. I also discuss the possibility that Xi Jinping's rise to power has corresponded with a dramatic shift in the overall media landscape, in China and right across the world, that in many ways has made it far more feasible for the Party to achieve more sustainable dominance of public opinion at the expense of competing agendas.

Molding the Jell-O: "guidance of public opinion"

The possibility of co-opting the Internet was a foregone conclusion in China, regarded from the outset as a matter of political necessity. Already at the dawning of the Internet era, even as the first pilot network was set up in Beijing in April 1990 with the help of loans from the World Bank (China Education and Research Network 2001), the primary catchphrase in official Party discourse for the business of censorship and propaganda was – as it remains today – the need for "correct guidance of public opinion." This policy dated to the June 4, 1989, crackdown on democracy demonstrators in Beijing and other Chinese cities, and originated from the conviction among Party hardliners that the ousted premier, Zhao Ziyang, had precipitated chaos by urging a more open approach to the media (Qian 2006: 5). In the aftermath of the crackdown, the journal *China Comment*, published by Xinhua News Agency, said Zhao Ziyang's relaxed approach had "rapidly caused the incorrect guidance of public opinion toward support for the student movement and toward chaos" (Banyuetan 1989). The following November, Jiang Zemin formally introduced this new policy of media control, saying that "if public opinion tools are not grasped in the true hands of Marxists, if public opinion guidance is not carried out in accord with the will of the party and the people, this will result in serious harm and immense losses" (Zhu 1989: 1).

Internet sites were expected, like their traditional media parents, to abide by propaganda guidelines enforcing "correct guidance," and to avoid discussion of sensitive issues. In April 2000, just weeks after Clinton's remarks on the Internet in China, the State Council Information Office and its fledgling Internet News Management Office – launched that very month (Zhang 2004: 98), and "making a formal appearance for the first time" – held a conference attended by major state-run news websites. In his opening remarks to the conference, Information Office director Wang Qingcun said certain information on the Internet might "mislead web visitors." Wang underscored the imperative of control with his own analogy, saying that "a highway without regulation is fraught with dangers and, in the same way, an unregulated information superhighway will not benefit mankind" (Ren and Jia 2000: 5). Like consumers of traditional media, Internet users required "correct guidance."

In Wang Qingcun's coupling of infrastructure-enabled communications and hard-wired restrictions, we can glimpse again the CCP's commitment to the marriage of Internet development and political control. Wang Qingcun's position was entirely consistent with the Party's take on development in general, epitomized by Deng Xiaoping's policy of "grasping with both hands" (Deng 2014). This was the insistence that the Party must "grasp opening and reform with one hand, and grasp the campaign against various criminal activities with the other hand" (Deng 2014). Why build a communications infrastructure in the first place if there was the potential for disruption? Because these modern developments were more crucial to shoring up legitimacy than they were likely to undermine it. Internet development was considered "a necessary step in boosting China's national pride and bringing legitimacy to the rule of the Communist Party in the country" (Tai 2006: 94).

By 2000, the early infrastructure for Internet control was already in place. In December 1997, just one year after the first group of Chinese websites was launched (China Education and Research Network 2001), the Ministry of Public Security implemented the country's first comprehensive regulations for the Internet, with explicit prohibitions against forms of expression vaguely labeled subversive, including "making falsehoods or distorting the truth" (Ministry of Public Security 1997). Plans were by this point already in the works for a new technical infrastructure for Internet censorship, beginning with the so-called "Golden Shield Project" launched in 1998 – preventing access inside China to unwanted IP addresses (Guo 2015: 67). On June 27,

2002, China's publishing regulator, the General Administration of Press and Publishing (GAPP), released a new set of provisions governing "Internet publishing" (OpenNet Initiative 2005), further extending to the Internet the controls already in force for print and broadcast.

For the CCP, Internet development, and media development more broadly, could advance hand-in-hand with control, so long as public opinion could be molded in such a way as to bolster the Party's legitimacy and insulate it from destabilizing voices. Understanding China's position toward development and control, we might imagine Party leaders offering the following retort in response to Bill Clinton's remark about desserts that cannot be nailed to the wall: "Yes, Mr. President, but Jell-O can be molded." But maintaining the right balance was never an easy matter, and this fact was made painfully clear to Chinese leaders by 2003, as changes in the media, including but not limited to the rise of the Internet, combined with broader social and economic changes to create an unpredictable environment in which alternate and competing agendas could emerge despite the overriding imperative of control.

Breaking the mold: media development challenges control

In the mid-1990s, several years before the Internet was a visible priority or concern, China underwent a rapid process of media development, with the launch of a new generation of commercial newspapers and magazines that relied on advertising and aimed to satisfy the demands of their readers with more exciting and relevant content (Huang and Zhou 2003: 200). In the more developed media markets of the West, the Internet seemed by the late 1990s to be truly revolutionary, with the popular view that "the Internet changes everything" (Farrand 2014: 87). The revolution in China at the turn of the century, however, had much more to do with the rapid development of traditional media and their reorientation toward reader demand.

In the economic reform push of the 1990s, following Deng Xiaoping's "southern tour," state subsidies for media were reduced and they were pushed toward greater financial autonomy. These changes "forced media outlets to think differently about journalistic form and content as they now had to appeal to readers who could use their purchasing power to pick and choose between different media products" (Svensson *et al.* 2013: 4). While the point of media transformation was to seek economic efficiencies – not least to meet the looming challenge of China's entry into the World Trade Organization (Min 2001a) – while maintaining political control of the media, these newly commercial media often posed a challenge to the Party's goal of maintaining "correct guidance of public opinion." Newspapers like *Southern Weekly* led the way with harder-hitting stories like their 2001 investigation into corruption at the state-run Project Hope charity (Bandurski and Hala 2010: 61–72).

Outside China, champions of the Internet as a force revolutionizing journalism often highlighted its role in decentralizing "traditionally centralized news-gathering and distribution" as a liberating force (Lasica 2003: vi). In China, meanwhile, leaders made sure that the primary manufacture of news remained centralized around the state's own press apparatus, meaning state-run newspapers and periodicals and their authorized commercial spin-offs, as well as state-run news websites such as People's Daily Online. Shortly after the launch of the Internet News Management Office in April 2000, the office issued regulations stating that "commercial websites do not have the right to do news gathering, but only the right to edit the news" (Min 2001b). According to the rule, websites could, after receiving proper authorization, "repost news from traditional media." This meant that commercial Internet portal sites like Sohu, Netease and Sina – all launched between 1996 and 1998 – were restricted to serving as news aggregators. They could repost and repackage, but could not themselves maintain teams of reporters.

Propaganda authorities did not anticipate the important role commercial Internet portals would play in amplifying the impact of stories appearing in the increasingly freewheeling commercial press. As local and regional newspapers sought to distinguish themselves with more relevant coverage, gaps appeared between these commercial ventures and their Party-run counterparts, still seen as the primary standard bearers of "propaganda discipline." Local stories on wide-ranging issues, from environment and health to corruption, often appeared in commercial newspapers before local propaganda authorities could put a stop to them. Quickly reposted by commercial Internet portals with audiences across the country, these stories galvanized national attention. By 2003, the intersection of commercialization, journalistic professionalism and the Internet had opened up a new space for the pushing of agendas outside the Party's restrictive "mainstream," culminating in a number of major stories that put the leadership on the defensive – including the beating to death in Guangzhou of a young migrant named Sun Zhigang, first reported by the brand new investigative division of the *Southern Metropolis Daily* (Zhao 2008: 253–254), pursuing a lead appearing on the Internet (Xiao 2004). The print version of Chen's investigative story reached several million readers in Guangdong province, but when the story appeared on Sina.com, it spread like wildfire across the country, drawing more than 4,000 comments within its first two hours online (Xiao 2004). Once the story had gone national, dominating public opinion, it became far more difficult to stop.

The Internet played a crucial role in galvanizing action in the wake of the Sun Zhigang story. In May 2003, three law students communicated over the Sun Zhigang case via BBS and email to push for the repeal of China's custody and repatriation administrative detention system (Teng 2013). It is important to note, however, that while the Internet was an important part of the changing information picture in China, it was not the primary driver of change, and in fact one of the core considerations to be made by the three law students as they pushed their reform agenda was "how to publicize the open letter and which newspaper(s) to choose" (Teng 2013: 1).

The Sun Zhigang incident and other stories in 2003 brought into sharp focus the CCP's crisis of public opinion guidance. While the circulations of Party-run "mouthpiece" newspapers – which had always sought to please Party superiors rather than readers – had seen a dramatic decline, the new metropolitan newspapers were enjoying a rise not just in commercial success but also a surge of professional prestige (Liu 2009). In retrospect, the Sun Zhigang case would prove to be an isolated success story (Liu 2009; Teng 2013: 3). Nevertheless, the Sun Zhigang story and others in 2003, including Chinese reporting of the outbreak of Severe Acute Respiratory Syndrome, were for leaders worrying demonstrations of the potential for agenda setting outside Party-controlled news and propaganda. Chinese leaders did not wait long to send a strong message to these media. On June 18, 2003, after two months of aggressive reporting by commercial media, the Central Propaganda Department issued a stern criticism of more than ten media, accusing them of "violating news discipline" and committing "errors of public opinion guidance" (*Economic Times* 2003).

The Internet comes of age

The dynamics of media development and control are complex, but we can understand the period after 2003 and through the leadership of President Hu Jintao as a prolonged effort by China's leaders to rein in the trends that had led to the serious disruption of "guidance of public opinion" that year. In 2004, the founder and former editor-in-chief of *Southern Metropolis Daily*, was arrested in Guangzhou on corruption charges, in a case linked clearly to the paper's outspoken coverage (*Ming Pao Daily* 2004). The crusade against more daring journalists would prove unrelenting through the decade, with the temporary shutdown of the *Freezing Point* supplement of the *China Youth Daily* newspaper in January 2006 (Bandurski and Lin 2006) – and the permanent sidelining of its two well-known editors, Li Datong and Lu Yuegang – the firing of a top editor at the *China Economic Times* after the paper exposed a scandal involving tainted vaccines (Branigan 2010a), the eventual forced closure of the same paper's investigative reporting unit (Chin 2011), and so on.

In 2005, central Party leaders finally succumbed to pressure from local leaders over the practice of "cross-regional reporting," in which newspapers from one city or region pursued hard news or investigative reporting in another city or region, thereby avoiding censure by the local government officials immediately responsible for enforcing discipline at their respective organizations (Du 2010: 8). Much to the chagrin of local officials across China, this tactic had been highly effective, resulting in the breaking of major stories like the Henan AIDS epidemic (Bandurski and Hala 2010: 35–60), but a 2005 ban on the practice closed the door for all but a handful of media with sufficient political backing to run the risk (Du 2010). As the Party moved to rein in the commercial media and movement of professional journalism they had fostered, commercial Internet portals proved critical to the advancement of local hard news stories that might otherwise have been quashed by propaganda officials. To cite one of many cases, a serious case of mass lead poisoning in the city of Fengxiang in Shaanxi province became the focus of national attention in 2009 after a commercial newspaper in the city, *Sanqin Metropolitan Daily*, reported complaints by local villagers. The story was picked up by the Internet portal site Netease, prompting other portals, including Sina, QQ and Sohu, to follow suit (Qian 2009). In the case of Fengxiang, even the state-run Xinhua News Agency joined in the critical coverage before the story dissipated with the aid of explicit reporting bans (Qian 2009).

By 2006, the Internet was also showing its strength in coalescing public opinion over breaking stories and ongoing issues like those mentioned above. This owed in part to the emergence of popular blogging platforms, which allowed ordinary Chinese Internet users to express their views in ways that had not previously been possible. The number of bloggers in China increased dramatically from 2002, when there were fewer than 300,000 in the entire country, to 2005, when there were more than 16 million (Liu 2011: 50). But the most decisive factor in 2005, eventually dubbed the "Year of the Blog" by Chinese media (Xinhua News Agency 2005), was the effort by Sina.com to recruit and promote a group of "celebrity bloggers" (Xinmin Evening News 2005), publicly recognized entertainers, business people, lawyers, academics and journalists who could draw more widespread attention. Many of the most popular blogs were those of actors and other celebrities, but intellectuals found large audiences too. Zhao Jing, a journalist writing under the pen name "Anti," kept a blog on media and politics that attracted 7,000 daily visits before access to the blog was blocked in 2005 (Pan 2006).

Blogs were the newest and most exciting aspect of what one commentator in 2006 pointed to as a new "posting culture," the word "posting," or *gentie*, referring here to the short comments Internet users could routinely make to articles they read at online news portals, adding often copious public conversations to breaking news stories (Zhang 2006). This "posting culture," said the commentator, was "a reflection of a kind of cultural democracy, and also a channel for the public to voice its opinions" (Zhang 2006). Moreover, he said, "the strength of this posting culture has the ability to promote the resolution of problems." Blogs were a regular source of scandals by 2006, as when an actress alleged through her Sina blog that a producer at the state-run broadcaster, China Central Television, had demanded sex in exchange for a role on his show (Goldkorn 2006). But political issues were also now fair game as Internet users took up their newfound voices with alacrity. When Chinese media reported in September 2006 that Shanghai's top leader, Chen Liangyu, had been removed in a broadening scandal over the misuse of pension funds, a single article posted to the front page of Sina.com drew close to

15,000 comments in a matter of hours (Bandurski 2006). In amongst the posts praising top leaders for being tough on corruption were *gentie* highly critical of the system, like this one: "Actually, the power of Chinese officials is too great. It's lack of oversight that has created this situation" (Bandurski 2006).

This new comment culture presented a very real challenge to the Party's control of the agenda, and in a 2006 article addressing the challenges facing online editors, the *Beijing Times*, a spin-off of the official *People's Daily*, concluded: "The interactive nature of online news is strong, and there will often be discussion posts enabling real-time attention and discussion. For online editors, how to maintain guidance of public opinion while interacting with web users is a major challenge" (*Beijing Times* 2006). Adding to this challenge, from the Party's standpoint, was the fact that China's most popular Internet news portals were privately owned, a number of them listed on overseas exchanges (Tai 2006: 91), and so were not a part of the traditional press command structure in which Party or government organs at various levels were responsible for enforcing discipline. Starting in 2006, controlling public opinion on the Internet became a core priority for China's leadership, and one important step was to enforce loyalty among major online sites, emphasizing their duty to enforce correct guidance of public opinion. In April 2006, major websites in China, both private and state-run, signed an agreement to promote a "civilized internet," which was in fact about extending traditional propaganda discipline to the Internet (*Beijing Daily* 2006).

Recognizing the immense popularity of commercial Internet portals and the limitations of traditional propaganda, the Party leadership also moved to utilize the Internet to push its own messages more actively. During a "collective study" session of the Party's politburo in January 2007, President Hu Jintao emphasized the important role of the Internet in propaganda and "guidance of public opinion," saying leaders must "develop it well, use it well and manage it well" (China Media Project 2007). As though illustrating how the policy itself would be applied, the announcement of Hu's speech remained as a top news headline on China's major Internet portal sites for an entire week (Bandurski 2006). Hu Jintao's 2007 efforts to "utilize" commercial Internet portals anticipated his 2008 speech during a visit to the *People's Daily*, in which he laid out a full-fledged media policy for the first time since assuming office in 2002.

Several major stories in 2008 had by June underscored the renewed challenges facing "guidance of public opinion" in the era of rapid information sharing across the Internet. In March, violent ethnic clashes in Tibet drew unwanted international attention as China prepared to host its first Olympic Games (Yardley 2008). Internet services overseas, notably the video sharing site YouTube, proved crucial in shaping the international story of Tibetan unrest, despite Chinese leaders' eagerness to contain what they regarded as a strictly domestic matter. Access to YouTube in China was blocked for a time, though service eventually returned after the Olympics, and major news portals as well as traditional media were restricted to the use of official Xinhua copy (Ford 2008).

The next major story unfolded as a massive earthquake struck western China on May 12, 2008. Within the first two hours, the Party's Central Propaganda Department issued an order to the traditional media against sending reporters to the scene. The order, however, was widely disregarded by commercial media (French 2008), and during the first week following the quake, as rescue and relief efforts were underway, unofficial accounts proliferated, turning to such unwelcome issues as the collapse of shoddily constructed schools (BBC News 2008). The Internet was by this time playing a leading role in generating and promoting sensitive stories.

The loss of control over the international agenda on Tibet, and probing coverage of the earthquake, meant the Party had to be more effective not just in restricting coverage of domestic stories, but also in advancing its own information. Hu Jintao's answer, outlined in a June 2008 speech given during a visit to the *People's Daily*, was to employ a combination strategy in which restrictions were applied to breaking news – the traditional "guidance" approach – while trusted state media reported the same stories quickly. If state media could "take the initiative" and dominate stories early on, in the space of several hours, the Party could enforce guidance while avoiding vacuums in which unofficial information could proliferate online (Bandurski 2008). The Party could, in this way, utilize the substantial audiences of commercial media and websites, which Hu Jintao for the first time referred to as "propaganda resources" (Bandurski 2008).

No sooner had Hu Jintao mapped out his vision of more proactive media control and propaganda – encompassed by the phrase "channeling of public opinion" – than the next wave of Internet communication put his formula hopelessly behind the curve. Chinese journalists nicknamed Hu's 2008 media strategy "grabbing the megaphone" (Qian 2009), but the Party had wrested the megaphone from commercial media and Internet news portals only to find within the next year that a new generation of Twitter-like microblogs had in principle put megaphones in the hands of every Internet user. By the end of 2008, the total number of Chinese using their mobile phones to access the Internet had reached more than 192 million, and the stage was set for the next burst of media development (D. Liu 2009: 5).

Microblogs drive the agenda

In 2007, just as Hu Jintao was focused on properly "using" commercial Internet portals, several microblogging platforms launched in China, following on the success of Twitter, which had been launched in the United States the previous year. Like Twitter, these platforms – including Jiwai, Fanfou, Zuosa and Diga – allowed users to send short 140-character messages. None of the services were greatly popular, and by the close of 2008, as Western media remarked on the novelty of Twitter as a tool to report breaking news stories like the November bombings in Mumbai (Beaumont 2008), Chinese tech blogger Gang Lu doubted whether Chinese would ever have enough interest in microblogging to make it an area of consequence: "Microblogging? … I would be surprised if microblogging ever became truly popular in China" (Leung 2008).

From April to June 2009, as events in Moldova and Iran highlighted the power of Twitter and other social media to organize protest movements, Chinese media paid greater attention to the emerging social media trend (Schectman 2009). On June 27, Shanghai's *Liberation Daily* newspaper decried Twitter's impact on the Iranian elections, saying that "information technologies that have brought many conveniences for mankind have this time become tools to interfere in the internal affairs of other countries" (Pan 2009: 4). One week later, the story had shifted to China as violent riots broke out in the northwestern region of Xinjiang, and social networking and image sharing services like Twitter, YouTube and Flickr were used to share images, video and personal accounts from the scene (*Telegraph* 2009). Authorities blocked access to both YouTube and Twitter (MacDonald 2009), and by July 7, all of the country's domestic microblogging sites had been permanently shut down (*Yazhou Zhoukan* 2009: 8).

The eradication of China's first generation of domestic microblog services in fact marked the beginning of the country's microblogging era. In August 2009, right in the wake of the Urumqi riots, Sina Corporation launched its Weibo service – originally called "Sina Weibo" (Blum 2014). This time, the growth of microblogs in China was phenomenal. By April 2010, as other Internet portal site operators, including Tencent and Sohu, were getting competing microblog services off the ground (Zhang 2010: 33), Sina Weibo had an estimated 10 million registered users (Wu 2010: 3). By the end of 2011, the service would report having more than 300 million registered users (China Internet Watch 2012). Here was yet another salient illustration of the conviction within China's leadership that communication technologies could be harnessed, and their destabilizing potential kept at bay. In fact, the launch of this new microblogging platform was as much an opportunity as a risk: it allowed the authorities to hardwire controls into the platform itself, allowing them to track and block unwanted content (Sullivan 2012). In July 2010, Sina Weibo and other microblogging platforms were appended with "Beta" labels, suggesting all were undergoing trial periods as the authorities ensured compliance with government controls (Zhou 2010). Posts on Sina Weibo were censored virtually in real-time using a combination of keyword blocks and human controls, with posts removed from the service labeled "permission denied" in the Application Programming Interface (API) mediating the interaction between user and platform (Fu 2013).

But in 2010, which came to be known in Chinese media as the "Year of the Microblog" (Qian 2010), the pace of development of these new social media platforms posed a serious challenge to control. By July 2010, the total number of monthly posts to Sina Weibo had surpassed 90 million, with more than three million posts each day (Yang 2010). One of Sina's most innovative strategies, mirroring its earlier approach to its blog platform, was to actively develop a group of "verified" accounts for users with a minimum of 100 followers, or "fans" (Publicitas Hong Kong 2011). These "V" account holders, many of whom were visible entertainment stars, sports figures, public intellectuals and journalists, had the ability to cohere large audiences around breaking news stories and hot-button issues (Yuan 2010). This generated activity for the platform, but also created the potential for sensitive news stories to develop rapidly, preempting controls on information. One of the most prominent early examples came in September 2010, as three villagers in Jiangxi province set themselves on fire to protest the forced demolition of their family home (Chan 2010). During the first week following the tragic protest there was no coverage by Chinese media, but video of the incident was shared on the Internet, and a number of journalists, including Deng Fei, a reporter for the Beijing-based *Phoenix Weekly*, posted about the case through Sina Weibo and maintained contact with Zhong Rucui and Zhong Rujiu, the daughters of one of the victims. When the Zhong sisters finally attempted to leave Yihuang and lodge a petition in Beijing, they were pursued by police and forced to hide out in an airport bathroom. For the next three hours, the sisters corresponded with Deng Fei, the *Phoenix Weekly* reporter, who made more than 20 posts about the situation in Yihuang to his Sina Weibo account. The news rapidly took hold on the Internet, with follow-up reporting by Chinese newspapers. Attention to the case in Beijing forced the provincial government to punish the local officials responsible (Ni 2010). The incident even prompted several commentaries in the Party's official *People's Daily* (Fan 2010a, 2010b).

The Yihuang incident was among the first in China to demonstrate the power of social media to drive the agenda by releasing information from the scene in real time. Moreover, microblogs, as a form of "fragmented and decentralized communications" (Chan 2010) were difficult to censor because "the microblogged story is told in fragments as information becomes available" (Chan 2011). The role of mainstream journalists and other professionals, however, was still crucial to driving stories beyond the social media platforms themselves. As one commentator remarked on the Yihuang case: "Journalists remain an unruly and determined lot intent on obtaining and moving information to the people" (Chan 2011).

The role of the professional press was evidenced repeatedly in 2011, as commercial newspapers and magazines pursued stories generated on social media aggressively, much as they had during the first week following the Sichuan earthquake in 2008. The culmination of this powerful intersection of professional reporting and real-time social media crowdsourcing came on July 23, 2011, as two of China's first-generation high-speed trains collided near the city of Wenzhou, killing 40 people and injuring close to 200 (Burkitt 2012). Even as propaganda guidelines instructed Chinese media not to send reporters to the scene, and not to investigate the causes of the crash (Branigan 2011), Chinese social media users watched virtually real-time videos of diggers attempting to bury train cars in the first hours following the tragedy (Bandurski 2011a). Images and video from the scene of the crash, including those of grieving and angry relatives that gave the story a startlingly human dimension, proliferated through social media (Bandurski 2011b). They then made their way into the pages of the newspapers as journalists and editors realized the story, already the focus of national attention and outrage, would be impossible to contain quickly. Weibo users with verified accounts and large followings – known by this time as the "Big V's" – became instrumental in spreading the story, and, quite tellingly, propaganda directives instructed: "No calling into doubt, no development [of further stories beyond the emergency response], no speculation, and no dissemination [of facts] on personal microblogs!" (Bandurski 2011a). *China Transport News*, a paper published by the Ministry of Transport, noted "major and careless mistakes" in the handling of the Wenzhou train collision and added: "Another important factor was that 2011 was a period in which social media in China were rapidly expanding in influence, and there was especially the explosive development of microblogs as a newly emerging media" (*China Transport News* 2014).

The repeated breakdown of the official agenda in 2011 was indeed a wake-up call for Chinese leaders. In September 2011, as the government tightened social media controls under the auspices of a campaign against "rumors" (FlorCruz and Tian 2011), an article in the Party's official *Red Flag* journal said that "while Weibo has lowered the threshold for public expression, it has also bred rumor," and "under the malicious promotion of online pushers, rumors have spread rapidly across Weibo, misled online opinion ... interfered in government decision-making, and even endangering social stability" (Jiang 2011). By "online pushers" *Red Flag* referred to social media account holders with tens of thousands or even millions of followers – the likes of Deng Fei, the *Phoenix Weekly* reporter who had pushed the Yihuang story. The key difference with the previous online generation characterized by the dominance of Internet portals, according to a paper the same month by a pair of Chinese scholars, was that the public had remained "in a relatively passive position relative to the large-scale internet portal sites" and "web users simply read whatever was posted online" (Jing and Wang 2011: 36–38). With the emergence of "Weibo 'opinion leaders,'" the equation was upended: "These 'opinion leaders' issue their own information, or issue their own opinions, from various parts of the Internet, playing a role in triggering or influencing public opinion" (Jing and Wang 2011: 36). They could also potentially inspire collective social action, an issue of growing concern to Chinese leaders. In January 2011, Yu Jianrong, a scholar at the Chinese Academy of Social Sciences, had set up a special Weibo account dedicated to the search for abducted children across the country. The account, which mobilized citizens to search their own communities, quickly gathered more than 200,000 followers (Ji 2011).

Once again, the Party's answer was a combination of control and appropriation. Three months after the Wenzhou crash, President Hu Jintao addressed a plenum on "cultural system reforms" and urged the need to "strengthen the channeling and control of social media and other communications tools" and to preserve "national information security" (Sixth Plenary Session of the 17th Central Committee 2011). The decision from the plenum was affirmed by Wang Chen, the director of the State Internet Information Office, an agency created on May 4, 2011, to "direct, coordinate and supervise online content management" (Xinhua News Agency 2011a). The Party, said Wang, must "strengthen the channeling and control of social media and real-time communication tools" (Bandurski 2011c). In a statement in September 2011, China's Ministry of Public Security said police organs "at all levels" must "fully understand the importance of microblogs for public security," and police were urged to establish microblog accounts in order to more effectively spread official information and "guide public opinion" (Blanchard 2011). Party leaders, it seemed, were once again playing catch up, grappling with the implications of new communications tools. An article posted in 2011 to the website of the State Council's Information Office said that "only by effectively grasping the operational processes of the online public opinion ecosystem can online sentiment be monitored effectively, warnings be made promptly ... and public opinion be channeled correctly" (State Council Information Office of the People's Republic of China 2011).

Xi Jinping and the era of cybersovereignty

A strong case could be made in the latter half of the Hu Jintao era – citing the examples outlined above as well as other cases – for the growing role of the Internet as an agent of social change in China. To some observers it seemed that the rise of "online activism and other contentious forms and issues marks a new stage of popular contention in post-enlightenment Chinese modernity" (Yang 2009). But it was also clear during this period that the Internet was increasingly taking center stage in the Party's efforts to maintain control of public opinion. In a June 2010 white paper on the Internet, the government affirmed that the Internet was "a significant technological invention of the 20th century and a major symbol of contemporary advanced productive forces" (Information Office of the State Council of the People's Republic of China 2010). But the document stressed at the same time that "national economic prosperity and development" relied upon the creation of "a healthy and harmonious Internet environment" – harmony by this point being a term synonymous in China with online censorship (Branigan 2010b). The 2010 white paper, which came just months after Google pulled out of the China market in a high-profile row over censorship (Helft and Barboza 2010), was also one of the first prominent statements on Internet censorship as a matter of national security and sovereignty: "The Internet sovereignty of China," said the white paper, "should be respected and protected."

In 2011, China's government moved to further centralize Internet controls by creating the State Internet Information Office, a State Council department tasked with directly coordinating and supervising online content (Xinhua News Agency 2011b). Wang Chen, the office's director, emphasized the need both to control and utilize social media platforms. "As a social network, anyone can use microblogs," Wang told propaganda leaders, "but they also present new challenges for the work of management" (*Nanfang Daily* 2011). Party and government offices, said Wang, needed to "clear away rumors" and share official information through an expanded presence on microblogs, actively "occupying" the territory of social media. Through 2012, the State Internet Information Office continued to criticize microblog platforms as "rumor mills," and Sina was pressured into implementing a credit system in which user accounts were suspended or even shut down for repeatedly making sensitive posts (Bei 2012).

Since Xi Jinping became general secretary at the CCP's 18th National Congress in November 2012, the Party's efforts to control and co-opt social media have been far more robust, and these have been part of an all-encompassing strategy to reassert Party control over media in all forms – and in particular to limit the capacity of breaking stories to take root in public opinion as they had done despite controls throughout the Internet era. On December 28, 2012, just weeks after Xi Jinping formally assumed power, the Standing Committee of the National People's Congress passed a decision on "strengthening protection of Internet information" (Xinhua News Agency 2012). The decision paid lip service to the rights of Internet users, but it sent worrying signals by requiring users to register with their real names, and service providers to play a far more active role in both content censorship and reporting of violations to the authorities (Bradsher 2012).

Xi Jinping has moved aggressively since the beginning of his administration against key influencers in the traditional media and on the Internet. One key defining moment was the *Southern Weekly* incident in January 2013, in which staff at the celebrated newspaper in Guangzhou staged a walkout to protest worsening censorship that had dramatically narrowed the space for professional journalism (Qian 2013). The social media platforms Weibo and WeChat were in fact instrumental in the organization of the protest, which broadened into online calls to dismantle censorship and uphold the constitutional right to freedom of expression (Zhang 2013). Chinese leaders responded in a propaganda directive to all media that, "Party control of the media is an unwavering basic principle," and demanded that all media personnel "discontinue voicing their support for *Southern Weekly* online" (Henochowicz 2013). The *Southern Weekly* incident revealed the extent to which the commercial media, which had been relatively successful in exploiting gaps and ambiguities in the press control system, had been brought to heel by new prior constraints, including the installation at newspapers and magazines of news readers charged with preapproving story ideas and cutting submitted drafts (Cheng 2012).

Internal calls to strengthen Party control of the traditional media were matched by a broad crackdown on Internet voices, focusing on social media. Among the most influential microbloggers on Sina Weibo was former Google China chief Kai-Fu Lee, and property tycoon Ren Zhiqiang, both with more than 13 million followers – and both influential verified account holders, or "Big Vs," who had openly voiced support for *Southern Weekly* during the January walkout (Zhou 2013). In early 2013, the State Internet Information Office, under the leadership of then Director Lu Wei, who was a former minister of Beijing's propaganda department, singled out "Big V" account holders, saying they "caused unsuspecting web users to follow along" in the spreading of rumors and falsehoods, "damaging the credibility of online media and upsetting the normal order of communications" (Xinhua News Agency 2013). Authorities shut down Kai-Fu Lee's Weibo account in February 2013 (*The Atlantic* 2013). By this time, journalists at traditional media, frustrated by tightening controls, were increasingly turning to Weibo as an outlet for more sensitive reports, including exposes of corruption (Hong 2013). But by May 2013, microbloggers were in full retreat, and many prominent academics, writers, journalists and businesspeople found their accounts deleted (Murong 2013).

A communiqué circulated by the General Office of the Chinese Communist Party in April 2013, known as "Central Document 9," also indicated a clear hardening of ideology under Xi Jinping (ChinaFile 2013). (See Chapter 11, "The New (Old) Normal": The CCP Propaganda System under Jiang, Hu, and Xi.") Central Document 9 also presaged Xi Jinping's formal media policy, which he finally unveiled on February 19, 2016, emphasizing that media operated by the Party and the government "must be surnamed Party," meaning that they must "love the Party, protect the Party and serve the Party" (Xinhua News Agency 2016). But he explicitly extended the mandate of "correct guidance" to all media and content forms:

> Party newspapers and periodicals, and radio and television stations at all levels must follow correct guidance; metropolitan newspapers and magazines, and new media must follow correct guidance; news reports must follow correct guidance, and supplements, special programs and advertisements must follow correct guidance; current affairs news must follow correct guidance, and entertainment and society news must follow correct guidance; domestic news reports must follow correct guidance, and international news reports must follow correct guidance.
>
> *(Xinhua News Agency 2016)*

The renewed effort to control cyberspace and new media has been a crucial aspect of President Xi's vision of all-dimensional control (Bandurski 2016). In February 2014, announcing his intention to build China as a "cyber power," Xi consolidated control over the Internet with the formation of the Central Leading Group for Cyberspace Affairs, also known as the Cyberspace Administration of China (CAC) (Lu 2014) – a central agency for cyberspace policy, oversight and censorship. Reflecting the international dimensions of cyberspace control that Xi Jinping would outline more clearly in 2016, the CAC began in 2014 to promote more actively the idea of cybersovereignty, or Internet sovereignty, essentially the position that Internet governance globally should respect the principle of multilateralism, with each nation having unquestioned sovereignty over its own Internet policies and terrain (Bandurski 2015a). Document 9 had spoken firmly against international criticism of China's policies toward cyberspace, which it said "slander[ed] our country's efforts to improve Internet management by calling them a crack-down on the Internet" (ChinaFile 2013). The push for cyber-sovereignty was essentially about legitimizing China's Internet controls, and gaining tacit approval and cooperation by foreign countries and foreign Internet companies. "The key aspect of this strategy," wrote one analyst, "is to promote the idea of Internet sovereignty through international forums (e.g., the World Economic Forum, NETmundial, ICANN50, etc.) in order to gain de jure international support for China's de facto Internet censorship policies" (Gady 2014).

On April 19, 2016, in his first major policy speech on cyberspace, President Xi said China needed to "strengthen governance of the online space, strengthen online content and strengthen positive propaganda on the Internet" (Caixin Media 2016). The message of control was clear. But so was the message of development. In one particularly revealing portion of his speech, Xi Jinping said:

> [Internet] authorities and companies must build close cooperation and coordination, avoiding the situation that has often emerged in the past, in which "loosening brings chaos, and control bring death"; [We must] take a new path of joint management and positive interaction.

More so even than his predecessors, Xi Jinping has sought to advance media development while maintaining – and even advancing – Party control of information and public opinion. In his April speech, Xi said "security is the precondition of development, and development is the guarantee of security; security and development must advance in stride" (Caixin Media 2016).

Under Supreme Leader Xi, the idea of "innovation" in communication technologies has been promoted aggressively even as controls on speech have tightened to a degree unprecedented in the reform era. Under its "Internet plus" strategy – focusing on the mobile Internet, big data, cloud computing and e-commerce (Wu 2015) – China has pushed not just tech innovation but the extension of technology to all aspects of society, including the creation of "fully wired communities" (Jung 2016). China is now home to four of the world's top-ten Internet technology companies (Wired 2014), an industry prowess it leverages at events like its annual World Internet Conference to press foreign companies to accept Internet restrictions as a condition of market access (Reuters 2016). As Lu Wei, the then head of the CAC, told a panel on the future of the global Internet at the World Economic Forum's 2014 Summer Davos in Tianjin in September 2014: "What we cannot permit is taking advantage of China's market, of profiting from Chinese money, but doing damage to China" (Bandurski 2014). In the same speech, to make the case for stronger global regulation of the Internet, Lu echoed the words of Information Office director Wang Qingcun at the start of China's journey as a networked society. "The Internet is like a car," he said.

> If it has no brakes, it doesn't matter how fast the car is capable of traveling, once it gets on the highway you can imagine what the end result will be. And so, no matter how advanced, all cars must have brakes.

Meanwhile, the repression of online speech and of traditional media has entered the fast lane under Xi Jinping. In 2013, a new law issued by China's highest court ruled that users making social media posts broadly regarded as "libelous" that attracted 5,000 or more visits, or 500 or more shares, could be subject to three-year jail terms (Guilford 2013). In November 2016, China adopted a restrictive cybersecurity law affecting both domestic and international technology firms that included a requirement that they store personal information and other core data in China (*The Economist* 2016).

Harsh Internet rules and enforcement, combined with strict restraints on traditional journalism, have had a clear chilling effect on the development of breaking news stories in China. China's silencing of key influencers, including popular social media users, public intellectuals and professional journalists, has for the time being effectively disrupted the pattern of agenda setting we saw with some regularity in the Jiang and Hu eras, in which professional media and the Internet had the capacity to advance stories outside the Party mandate of "guidance of public opinion." One of the most outstanding examples came in June 2015, as the *Oriental Star*, a cruise ship on the Yangtze River, capsized, killing more than 400 people. Coverage in the traditional media and on the Internet closely followed the official line released by Xinhua News Agency – and in stark contrast to the Wenzhou rail collision four years earlier, newspaper pages across the country were almost uniform in design and treatment (Bandurski 2015b). In the more than four years since Xi Jinping came to power, just a handful of major stories have gained traction, the most notable being the Tianjin explosions in August 2015, a rare case of an incident that was virtually impossible to contain owing to sheer scale and proximity to the major media center of Beijing (Han 2015).

The dominant discourse under Xi Jinping suggests the CCP is increasingly confident that its control methods and infrastructure at home are not just effective, but have applicability and relevance for the entire world, over and against the Clintonesque view of the Internet as a force of inescapable liberalization. Party leaders and official state media now talk about a "path of Internet governance with Chinese characteristics" (*People's Daily* 2016). What the party refers to as "the great project of building socialism with Chinese characteristics" – in other words, maintaining one-party rule over a prosperous nation with a strong military and a globally influential culture – is "inseparable from Internet development and governance," according to the Cyberspace Administration of China (*People's Daily* 2016).

The question of whether or not the Internet will change the Chinese Communist Party has in a sense been resolved. The growth of the Internet in China, one of a number of media-related factors, has indeed ushered in changes to how the Party governs – though this has far more to do with the adaptation of control than with the unleashing of new developments that challenge control or undermine one-party rule. Moreover, in light of China's growing influence over global Internet development, it is probably time to phrase the question in reverse, to ask whether the leaders in China will be able not just to control the Internet but to harness it effectively to ensure the stability of a regime that remains unchanged in fundamental ways. In other words: How might the Chinese Communist Party change the Internet?

References

Bandurski, David (2006), "Web Users Respond to Removal of Top Shanghai Leader in a Flurry of Postings," China Media Project, September 25. http://cmp.hku.hk/2006/09/25/109/.
Bandurski, David (2008), "Propaganda Leaders Scurry Off to Carry Out the 'Spirit' of Hu Jintao's 'Important' Media Speech," China Media Project, June 25. http://cmp.hku.hk/2008/06/25/1079/.
Bandurski, David (2011a), "History of High-Speed Propaganda Tells All," China Media Project, July 25. http://cmp.hku.hk/2011/07/25/14036/.
Bandurski, David (2011b), "Images on Social Media Chronicle Days of Disaster," China Media Project, July 6. http://cmp.hku.hk/2011/07/26/14149/.
Bandurski, David (2011c), "More Signals on Social Media Control," China Media Project, December 6. http://cmp.hku.hk/2011/12/06/17390/.
Bandurski, David (2014), "Lu Wei: the Internet Must Have Brakes," China Media Project, September 11. http://cmp.hku.hk/2014/09/11/36011/.
Bandurski, David (2015a), "Re-Defining Cyberspace," China Media Project, October 8. http://cmp.hku.hk/2015/10/08/39309/.
Bandurski, David (2015b), "Taming the Flood: How China's Leaders 'Guide' Public Opinion," ChinaFile, July 20. www.chinafile.com/reporting-opinion/media/taming-flood.
Bandurski, David (2016), "Mirror, Mirror On the Wall," China Media Project, February 22. http://cmp.hku.hk/2016/02/22/39646/.
Bandurski, David and Hala, Martin, ed. (2010), *Investigative Journalism in China: Eight Cases in Chinese Watchdog Journalism*, Hong Kong: Hong Kong University Press.
Bandurski, David and Lin Hui (2006), "China's Shadow Censor Commissars," *Far Eastern Economic Review*, Vol. 169 (March): 28–30.
Banyuetan (1989), "Da shiji" [Major events], No. 7, under entry for May 6.
BBC News (2008), "China Anger Over 'Shoddy Schools'," May 15. http://news.bbc.co.uk/2/hi/asia-pacific/7400524.stm.
Beaumont, Claudine (2008), "Mumbai Attacks: Twitter and Flickr Used to Break News," *Telegraph*, November 27. www.telegraph.co.uk/news/worldnews/asia/india/3530640/Mumbai-attacks-Twitter-and-Flickr-used-to-break-news-Bombay-India.html.
Bei, Feng (2012), "Microblogs Have Become the Focus of Internet Censorship in China," China Rights Forum, Human Rights in China, November 26. www.hrichina.org/en/crf/article/6406.
Beijing Daily (2006), "Beijing wangluo meiti zilv gongyue" [Beijing online media self-discipline agreement], April 13.
Beijing Times (2006), "Wangluo bianji cong 'She Yun Gong' gan qi" [Online editors begin as 'Bellhops'], April 24.
Blanchard, Ben (2011), "China Urges Police to Use Microblogs to Dispel Rumors," Reuters, September 26. www.reuters.com/article/us-china-police-microblogs-idUSTRE78P3QM20110926.
Blum, Jeremy (2014), "Sina Weibo Removes the 'Sina' From its Name, Now Just 'Weibo'," *South China Morning Post*, March 31. www.scmp.com/news/china-insider/article/1461827/sina-weibo-removes-sina-its-name-now-just-weibo.
Bradsher, Keith (2012), "China Toughens its Restrictions on Use of the Internet," *New York Times*, December 28. www.nytimes.com/2012/12/29/world/asia/china-toughens-restrictions-on-internet-use.html.
Branigan, Tania (2010a), "Wang Keqin and China's Revolution in Investigative Journalism," *The Guardian*, May 23. www.theguardian.com/world/2010/may/23/wang-keqin-china-investigative-journalism.
Branigan, Tania (2010b), "Ai Weiwei Supporters Gather for Party at Condemned Studio," *The Guardian*, November 7. www.theguardian.com/artanddesign/2010/nov/07/china-artist-ai-weiwei-party-studio.
Branigan, Tania (2011), "Chinese Anger Over Alleged Cover-Up of High-Speed Rail Crash," *The Guardian*, July 25. www.theguardian.com/world/2011/jul/25/chinese-rail-crash-cover-up-claims.
Burkitt, Laurie (2012), "A Year After the Wenzhou Train Crash, Burying Continues," China Real Time Report (*Wall Street Journal*), July 20. http://blogs.wsj.com/chinarealtime/2012/07/20/ a-year-after-the-wenzhou-train-crash-burying-continues/.
Caixin Media (2016), "Xi Jinping wangxin gongzuo 4.19 jianghua: Quanwen" [Xi Jinping's April 19 speech on cyberspace affairs work], Caixin Media, April 25. www.caixin.com/2016-04-25/100936452.html.
Chan, Ying (2010), "Microblogs Reshape the News," China Media Project, October 12. http://cmp.hku.hk/2010/10/12/8021/.

Chan, Ying (2011), "Chinese Journalists Circumvent Government's Tight Restrictions," Nieman Reports, April 20. http://niemanreports.org/articles/chinese-journalists-circumvent-governments-tight-restrictions/.
Cheng, Yizhong (2012), "The Virus of Censorship," *New Statesman*, October 17. www.newstatesman.com/politics/politics/2012/10/virus-censorship.
Chin, Josh (2011), "Beijing State Newspaper Closes its Investigative Team," *Wall Street Journal*, July 19. www.wsj.com/articles/SB10001424052702304567604576453723875263218.
China Education and Research Network (2001), "Evolution of Internet in China," January 1. www.edu.cn/introduction_1378/20060323/t20060323_4285.shtml.
ChinaFile (2013), "Document 9: A ChinaFile Translation," November 8. www.chinafile.com/document-9-chinafile-translation.
China Internet Watch (2012), "Sina Weibo Has Over 300 Million Users Now Who Generate Over 100MM Posts Everyday," February 29. www.chinainternetwatch.com/1395/sina-weibo-users-2011/#ixzz4PPHlqjngwww.chinainternetwatch.com/1395/sina-weibo-users-2011/.
China Media Project (2007), "Hu's News That Just Wouldn't Go Away: The Party Delivers its Message Through China's Commercialized Web," January 31. http://cmp.hku.hk/2007/01/31/169/.
China Transport News (2014), "Jiaotong hangye meiti fansi Wenzhou dongche shigu: Eyi chaozuo rang Zhongguo gaotie fuchu daijia" [Transportation industry media reflect on the Wenzhou rail collision: High-speed rail in China pays the price for malicious hype], September 24. Via The Paper. www.thepaper.cn/newsDetail_forward_1268351.
Clinton, William J. (2000), "Remarks at the Paul H. Nitze School of Advanced International Studies," Public Papers of the Presidents of the United States (2000–2001), March 8, Office of the Federal Register.
Deng Xiaoping (2014), "Nanxun jianghua" [Southern tour speech], People's Daily Online (Guangdong Channel), August 11. http://gd.people.com.cn/n/2014/0811/c123932-21952148.html.
Du, Yaoming (2010), "Meiti jiancha shibi de boyi kongjian" [Tactical space for the media in investigating ills], *Twenty-First Century*, Vol. 119, (June): 4–16. www.cuhk.edu.hk/ics/21c/media/articles/c119-200911054.pdf.
Economic Times (2003), "Zhonggong piping meiti, weifan xinwen jilu" [Chinese Communist Party criticizes the media for violations of news discipline], Mainland News Center, June 26.
Fan, Zhengwei (2010a), "'Weidu' wu zhu huajie maodun" ['Containment' does not help resolve conflict], *People's Daily*, September 20.
Fan, Zhengwei (2010b), "Zhide jingsi de 'Qiangchailun'" [The 'View of Forced Demolition' that deserves alarm and consideration], *People's Daily*, October 14.
Farrand, Benjamin (2014), *Networks of Power in Digital Copyright Law and Policy: Political Salience, Expertise and the Legislative Process*, Abingdon, Oxon: Routledge.
FlorCruz, Jaime and Shao Tian (2011), "Social Media to Curb 'Rumors' in China," CNN, September 23. http://edition.cnn.com/2011/09/23/world/asia/china-social-media-rumors/.
Ford, Peter (2008), "China Blocks YouTube, Reporters Over Tibet News," *The Christian Science Monitor*, March 18. www.csmonitor.com/World/Asia-Pacific/2008/0318/p06s02-woap.html.
French, Howard (2008), "Earthquake Opens Gap in Controls on Media," *New York Times*, May 18. www.nytimes.com/2008/05/18/world/asia/18press.html.
Fu, King-wa (2013), "About WeiboScope," WeiboScope, Journalism & Media Studies Centre, The University of Hong Kong. http://weiboscope.jmsc.hku.hk/webpagegrid/aboutushtml.html.
Gady, Franz-Stefan (2014), "The Wuzhen Summit and Chinese Internet Sovereignty," *Huffington Post*, December 9. www.huffingtonpost.com/franzstefan-gady/the-wuzhen-summit-and-chi_b_6287040.html.
Goldkorn, Jeremy (2006), "Actress Accuses CCTV Director on Blog," Danwei.org, September 8. www.danwei.org/danwei_noon_report/actress_accuses_cctv_director.php.
Guilford, Gwynn (2013), "In China, Being Retweeted 500 Times Can Get You Three Years in Prison," Quartz, September 9. http://qz.com/122450/in-china-500-retweets-of-a-libelous-statement-can-get-you-three-years-in-prison/.
Guo, Rongxing (2015), *Cross-Border Management: Theory, Method and Application*, Berlin, Heidelberg: Springer, p. 67.
Han, Xiao (2015), "Chinese Media and the Tianjin Disaster," China Media Project, August 20. http://cmp.hku.hk/2015/08/20/39159/.
Helft, Miguel and Barboza, David (2010), "Google Shuts China Site in Dispute Over Censorship," *New York Times*, March 22. www.nytimes.com/2010/03/23/technology/23google.html?_r=0.

Henochowicz, Anne (2013), "Ministry of Truth: Urgent Notice on *Southern Weekly*," *China Digital Times*, January 7. http://chinadigitaltimes.net/2013/01/ministry-of-truth-urgent-notice-on-southern-weekly/.
Hong, Zhang (2013), "How Chinese Reporters Have Turned to Weibo to Expose Corruption," *South China Morning Post*, July 30. www.scmp.com/news/china/article/1292945/chinese-reporters-try-weibo-expose-corruption-when-print-fails.
Huang, Shengmin and Zhou Yan, ed. (2003), *Zhongguo chuanmei shichang da bianju* [A new century of Chinese media markets], Beijing: CITIC Publishing House, p. 200.
Information Office of the State Council of the People's Republic of China (2010), "The Internet in China," June 8. www.china.org.cn/government/whitepaper/2010-06/08/content_20208007.htm.
Ji, Huihui (2011), "Weibo huyu heyi yinfa xianshi jiti xingdong" [How Weibo calls unleash collective action], *Young Journalist*, April 2011. Available through People's Daily Online. http://media.people.com.cn/GB/22114/42328/227852/15331848.html.
Jiang, Shenghong (2011), "Weibo chuanbo zhong zhide zhuyi de wenti" [Problems in Weibo communications deserving attention], *Red Flag*, September. Available at Seeking Truth Online. www.qstheory.cn/hqwg/2011/201109/201105/t20110510_79977.htm.
Jing, Ming and Wang Rui (2011), "Weibo 'Yijian Lingxiu' zai Weibo yulun jiandu zhong de zuoyong yu wenti" [The problem and role of Weibo "Opinion Leaders" in supervision by public opinion on Weibo], *News and Writing*, Vol. 9 (September): 36–38.
Jung, Edward (2016), "China's Internet Boom," *MIT Technology Review*, June 21. www.technologyreview.com/s/601686/chinas-internet-boom/.
Lasica, J.D., ed. (2003), "We Media: How Audiences Are Shaping the Future of News and Information," The American Press Institute (The Media Center). www.hypergene.net/wemedia/download/we_media.pdf.
Leung, Jenny (2008), "Chats With Gang Lu," *China Digital Times*, December 2. http://chinadigitaltimes.net/2008/12/chats-with-gang-lu/.
Liu, Dong (2009), "China Next Generation Internet Deployment and Green IT," Beijing Internet Institute, July 9. http://cms.comsoc.org/SiteGen/Uploads/Public/Docs_Globecom_2009/3LiuDong BIIG26p.pdf.
Liu, Fengshu (2011), *Urban Youth in China*, New York: Routledge.
Liu, Weiwei (2009), "Zhengzhi, shichang yu dangbao de yingxiangli" [Politics, Market and the Influence of Party Papers], *Twenty-First Century*, Vol. 115 (October): 120–127. www.cuhk.edu.hk/ics/21c/media/articles/c115-200809053.pdf.
Lu, Jinghua (2014), "China's First Step Towards Becoming a Cyber Power," *China-US Focus*, March 13. www.chinausfocus.com/peace-security/chinas-first-step-towards-becoming-a-cyber-power.
MacDonald, Emily (2009), "China's Facebook Status: Blocked," ABC News, July 8. http://blogs.abcnews.com/theworldnewser/2009/07/chinas-facebook-status-blocked.html.
Min, Dahong (2001a), "Meiti chanye zhenghe shi dashi suoqu" [The general trend is toward media integration], *People's Daily* (Overseas Edition), April 6. www.people.com.cn/GB/paper39/3116/413778.html.
Min, Dahong (2001b), "Zhongguo wangluo meiti de fazhan" [The development of China's web media], Eastday.com, February 1. http://news.eastday.com/epublish/gb/special/class000000178/hwz277881.htm.
Ming Pao Daily (2004), "Nanfang dushibao qian zhubian beipu zuiming 'tanwu' lvshi zhiyi fumian baodao rehuo" [Former chief editor of southern metropolis daily detained on charges of "corruption," lawyer suspects negative reporting invited trouble], March 21.
Ministry of Public Security (1997), "Computer Information Network and Internet Security, Protection and Management Regulations (1997)," Approved by the State Council on December 11, promulgated by the Ministry of Public Security on December 30. www.lehmanlaw.com/resource-centre/laws-and-regulations/information-technology/computer-information-network-and-internet-security-protection-and-management-regulations-1997.html.
Morozov, Evgeny (2012), *The Net Delusion: The Dark Side of Internet Freedom*, New York: Public Affairs.
Murong, Xuecun (2013), "Chinese Internet: 'A New Censorship Campaign Has Commenced'," *The Guardian*, May 15. www.theguardian.com/world/2013/may/15/chinese-internet-censorship-campaign.
Nanfang Daily (2011), "Wang Chen tan wenhua qiangguo jianshe, zhichu zhengfu guanyuan yao zhongshi Weibo zuoyong" [Wang Chen talks about building a cultural strong nation, points out government officials must prioritize the use of microblogs], November 2. Via Xinhua Online. http://news.xinhuanet.com/politics/2011-11/02/c_111139540.htm.

Ni, Tao (2010), "Pity Poor Petitioners Forced to Hide in Toilet," *Shanghai Daily*, September 22. www.shanghaidaily.com/opinion/chinese-perspectives/Pity-poor-petitioners-forced-to-hide-in-toilet/shdaily.shtml.

OpenNet Initiative (2005), "Internet Filtering in China in 2004–2005: A Country Study," April 14. https://opennet.net/sites/opennet.net/files/ONI_China_Country_Study.pdf.

Pan, Philip P. (2006), "Bloggers Who Pursue Change Confront Fear and Mistrust," *Washington Post* Foreign Service, February 21. www.washingtonpost.com/wp-dyn/content/article/2006/02/20/AR2006022001304_pf.html.

Pan, Zhi (2009), "Wuxing wangluo bei youxing zhi shou caocong, chengwei ganshe bieguo neizheng gongju: 'TWITTER Geming' bushi bangyang" [The invisible web is manipulated by visible hands, becoming a tool to interfere in the internal affairs of other countries: The "Twitter Revolution" is not a model], *Liberation Daily*, June 27.

People's Daily (2016), "Rang dang de zhuzhang chengwei wangluo kongjian zuiqiangyin" [Letting the positions of the party become the strongest voices in the online space], January 7.

Publicitas Hong Kong (2011), "7 Reasons Why Sina Weibo Beats Twitter for Your China Social Media Campaign," Publicitas Hong Kong, September 29. www.publicitas.com/hongkong/media-solutions/market-insights/further-insights/7-reasons-why-sina-weibo-beats-twitter-for-your-china-social-media-campaign/.

Qian, Gang (2006), "Daoxiang, jiandu, gaige, ziyou: Touguo meiti yuci fenxi kan zhongguo xinwen chuanmei" [Guidance, supervision, reform, freedom: Viewing the Chinese news through analysis of media discourse], *Twenty-First Century*, Vol. 95 (June): 4–16. www.cuhk.edu.hk/ics/21c/media/articles/c095-200411082.pdf.

Qian, Gang (2009), "Central Party Media 'Grab the Megaphone'," *China Media Project*, August 21. http://cmp.hku.hk/2009/08/21/1709/.

Qian, Gang (2013), "Why *Southern Weekly* Said 'No'," China Media Project, January 11. http://cmp.hku.hk/2013/01/11/30623/.

Qian, Yu (2010), "Jinnian Zhongguo Weibo fangwen yonghu yi da 1.25 yi, 2012 nian 'Weibo' cheng dui baofaxing zengzhang" [Weibo users this year surpass 125 million, in 2012 "Weibo" will see explosive growth], *Shanghai Evening Post*, December 29.

Ren, Jianmin and Jia Xiping (2000), "Jing cheng chun ri wangluo chao" [An online wave in the capital city], *People's Daily*, April 21.

Reuters (2016), "China's Xi Urges Cooperation Among Nations in Governance of Global Internet," November 16. www.reuters.com/article/us-china-internet-idUSKBN13B1FF.

Schectman, Joel (2009), "Iran's Twitter Revolution? Maybe Not Yet," Bloomberg, June 18. www.bloomberg.com/news/articles/2009-06-17/irans-twitter-revolution-maybe-not-yet.

Sixth Plenary Session of the 17th Central Committee (2011), "Zhonggong Zhongyang guanyu shenhua wenhu tizhi gaige tuidong shehui zhuyi wenhua da fazhan da fanrong ruogan zhongda wenti de jueding" [China Communist Party decision on the major question of deepening cultural system reforms to promote the great development and prosperity of socialist culture], October 26. http://old.chinacourt.org/html/article/201110/26/467709.shtml.

State Council Information Office of the People's Republic of China (2011), "Cong 'Hudie Xiaoying' tan wangluo yulun redian shengcheng lujing" [Discussing the path of generation of public opinion interest points from the "Butterfly Effect"], March 24. www.scio.gov.cn/wlcb/llyj/Document/879684/879684.htm.

Sullivan, Jonathan (2012), "A Tale of Two Microblogs in China," *Media Culture & Society*, Vol. 34, No. 6 (September): 773–783.

Svensson, Marina, Elin Saether and Zhi'an Zhang, ed. (2013), *Chinese Investigative Journalists' Dreams: Autonomy, Agency, and Voice*, Lanham, MD: Lexington Books.

Tai, Zixue (2006), *The Internet in China: Cyberspace and Civil Society*, New York: Routledge.

Telegraph (2009), "China Riots: Twitter and YouTube Frustrate 'Censorship Attempts'," July 6. www.telegraph.co.uk/news/worldnews/asia/china/5756766/China-riots-Twitter-and-YouTube-frustrate-censorship-attempts.html.

Teng, Biao (2013), "The Sun Zhigang Incident and the Future of Constitutionalism: Does the Chinese Constitution Have a Future?" Chinese University of Hong Kong, CRJ Occasional Paper, December 30. www.law.cuhk.edu.hk/en/research/crj/download/papers/2013-tb-szg-constitutionalism.pdf.

The Atlantic (2013), "How China's Most Influential Micro-Blogger Got Himself Banned From Weibo," February 19. www.theatlantic.com/international/archive/2013/02/how-chinas-most-influential-micro-blogger-got-himself-banned-from-weibo/273280/.

The Economist (2016), "China Adopts a Tough Cyber-Security Law," November 12. www.economist.com/news/china/21710001-foreign-firms-are-worried-china-adopts-tough-cyber-security-law.

Wired (2014), "China's Innovation Has Outstripped its 'Follow-Fast' Reputation," July. www.wired.com/insights/2014/07/chinas-innovation-outstripped-follow-fast-reputation/.

Wu, Nan (2015), "Is China's New 'Internet Plus' Ambition All About New Smartphones?" *South China Morning Post*, April 23. www.scmp.com/tech/enterprises/article/1773737/chinas-new-internet-plus-ambition-it-all-about-more-smartphones.

Wu, Shuai (2010), "Weibo 'Bodong' yingxiao 'Xinxian'" [Weibo "stirs" the "strings" of marketing], *Entrepreneurs' Daily*, May 7.

Xiao, Qiang (2004), "The Rising Tide of Internet Opinion in China," *Nieman Reports*, June 15. http://niemanreports.org/articles/the-rising-tide-of-internet-opinion-in-china/.

Xinhua News Agency (2005), "Fang Xingdong: The Year of the Blog," December 20. http://news.xinhuanet.com/book/2005-12/20/content_3946077.htm.

Xinhua News Agency (2011a), "China Sets Up Office for Internet Information Management," Xinhua News Agency, May 4. http://news.xinhuanet.com/english2010/china/2011-05/04/c_13857911.htm.

Xinhua News Agency (2011b), "China Sets Up State Internet Information Office," May 4. www.chinadaily.com.cn/china/2011-05/04/content_12440782.htm.

Xinhua News Agency (2012), *Standing Committee of the National People's Congress Decision Concerning the Strengthening the Protection of Online Information*. Via Central People's Government of the PRC, December 28. www.gov.cn/jrzg/2012-12/28/content_2301231.htm.

Xinhua News Agency (2013), "Guojia hulianwang xinxi ban bushu daji wangluo zaoyao chaunbo yaoyan xingwei" [State internet information office attacks online fabrication and dissemination of rumours], May 2. www.gov.cn/jrzg/2013-05/02/content_2394679.htm.

Xinhua News Agency (2016), "Xi Jinping: Jianchi zhengque fangxiang chuangxin fangfa shouduan tigao xinwen yulun chuanboli yindaoli" [Xi Jinping: Cleaving to the correct line, innovating methods and techniques, raising the transmission force and guiding force of news and public opinion], February 19. http://politics.people.com.cn/n1/2016/0219/c1024-28136159.html.

Xinmin Evening News (2005), "2005 Niandu 10 da liuxingyu" [10 Popular terms in 2005], December 31.

Yang, Guobin (2009), *The Power of the Internet in China: Citizen Activism Online*, New York: Columbia University Press, Chapter 1.

Yang, Yang (2010), "Xinlang Weibo chi pangxie shou she yingli luxiantu" [Sina Weibo eats crab, eyes first blueprint for profit], *Economic Observer*, September 13. www.eeo.com.cn/2010/0913/180597.shtml.

Yardley, Jim (2008), "Violence in Tibet as Monks Clash With the Police," *New York Times*, March 15. www.nytimes.com/2008/03/15/world/asia/15tibet.html.

Yazhou Zhoukan (2009), "Zhongguo dangju quanian daya weiboke wangzhan: Wangmin fantan duili qingxu yue lai yue qiang" [Chinese authorities launch full-scale assault on microblog sites: Oppositional mindset grows stronger among web users], August 9.

Yuan, Wen (2010), "Qi cheng shoufangzhe guanzhu Weibo" [70 percent of survey respondents follow Weibo], *Financial News*, January 20, 2010.

Zhang, Jun (2010), "Menhu wangzhan zhengxiang 'Zhi' Weibo" [Web portal sites compete to "Weave" microblogs], *Wuhan Morning Post*, April 20.

Zhang, Yanshuang (2013), "The *Southern Weekly* and Censorship in China: a Nation Fights Back," *The Conversation*, January 14. http://theconversation.com/the-southern-weekly-and-censorship-in-china-a-nation-fights-back-11539.

Zhang, Yiwu (2006), "'Gentie Wenhua' de chang duan" [The long and short of "Posting Culture"], Caixin.com, August 6. http://zhangyiwu.blog.caixin.com/archives/31044.

Zhang, Yonghua (2004), *Zhong wai wangluo xinwenye bijiao* [Online journalism: A comparative study], Beijing: Tsinghua University Press.

Zhao, Yuezhi (2008), *Communication in China: Political Economy, Power, and Conflict*, Lanham, MD: Rowman & Littlefield.

Zhou, Kangliang (2010), "The Power of the Chinese Netizen? How Microblogging is Changing Chinese Journalism," Reuters Institute. https://reutersinstitute.politics.ox.ac.uk/sites/default/files/The%20Power%20of%20the%20Chinese%20Netizen%20How%20Microblogging%20is%20Changing%20Chinese%20Journalism.pdf.
Zhou, Laura (2013), "Businesspeople Top Weibo Microbloggers List," *South China Morning Post*, January 16. www.scmp.com/news/china/article/1128952/businesspeople-top-weibo-microbloggers-list.
Zhu, Weixin (1989), "Qinqie huijian shengbao zongbianji xinwen gongzuo yantaoban tongzhi Jiang Zemin chanming xinwen gongzuo jiben fangzhen" [Meeting with comrades from the provincial newspaper editors in chief news work discussion group, Jiang Zemin clarified the basic principles of news work], *People's Daily*, November 30.

24

CHINA AND THE WORLD

From the Chinese Dream to the Chinese World Order

Simon Shen

Introduction

Since Xi Jinping became the supreme leader of the People's Republic of China, the country's foreign policy has shown greater proactivity and confidence, with more emphasis placed on constructive engagement with international institutions. Although the rebalancing strategy adopted by former American president Barack Obama may not have been hugely effective, the Chinese Communist Party (CCP) administration has been threatened by it in a way similar to that posed by the USSR during the late Cold War. Since Donald Trump came to power in early 2017, the CCP's anxiety about what it sees as his China-bashing policies, ranging from reconsidering the "One China policy" to threatening to label China as a currency manipulator, has also prompted Xi to take action in presenting China as a legitimate alternative global leader to the US. Xi's well-crafted speech presented at the Davos World Economic Forum in January 2017 that suggested Communist China was assuming worldwide leadership in globalization and open markets (despite the non-open nature of China's domestic economy) while capitalist America under Trump was becoming increasingly protective and inward looking, was probably one of the most ironic moments in contemporary politics (Xi 2017).

The supposedly aggressive postures of Presidents Obama and Trump thus offer a chance for China to construct a "sense of threats," which enables Beijing to play up the values of patriotism/nationalism so as to consolidate its domestic governance. Since the Asian financial crisis, China's relative capability, at least in terms of GDP (from US$4,601 billion in 2008 to US$11,006 billion in 2015), has continued to increase while the relative growth of the US has gradually diminished. Despite the continuing supremacy of American technology and its dollar remaining unchallenged, the CCP leadership is tempted to forfeit the strategy of "hide one's capacities and bide one's time" as adopted in the Deng Xiaoping era. The new policy orientation also undermines the significance of former president Jiang Zemin's dictum – "to act in accordance with the situation in order to maximize benefits" (*bawojiyu yinshilidao*) – and former president Hu Jintao's "Peaceful Rise/Peaceful Development" (*heping jueqi/heping fazhan*) mantra, both of which call for quietly accepting the status quo and yielding at least for the time being to American global hegemony.

The abandonment of these strategies can be attributed to several factors. The increase in China's national capabilities implies that it is not necessary for China to act strictly in accordance with the existing international situation. Instead, China now possesses the confidence to construct its own favorable international conditions so as to maximize benefits to itself. As a consequence, its foreign policies have undertaken a number of transformations. Today, China has partially acclimated to a Sinicized version of "international democracy" provided that the global rules and norms are partly shaped by China. Meanwhile, authoritarianism has remained a quintessential element of the "Chinese Value Outlook." As such, China has in its unique ways made accommodations regarding the Western discourse, such as human rights, authority, democracy, and liberty by redefining them according to Chinese characteristics such as the insistence that rights and liberties should be enjoyed by Chinese without compromising sovereignty and stability. As a result, in the Xi era, a significant change with regard to the strategy of nationalist propaganda has emerged at an ideological level with the construction of the "Core Socialist Values." This has become an essential template for Xi in his handling of domestic and foreign issues, also enabling him to tacitly challenge the West-defined universal values.

The Xi administration is prepared to take on the "American Dream" with its "Chinese Value Outlook" shored up by the "Chinese Dream." At the same time, it has offered the rest of the world another type of developmental path, namely the "China model." In contrast with the old days when the leadership was adamant that China's "model" would not be exported, the new moves signify a more confident China ready to compete with the United States in the ideological field. While the extent of the internalization and Sinicization of Universal Values within the parameters of the "China model" is certainly debatable, we should not underestimate the assertiveness of the Xi administration in its ideological competition with the United States and the West in general. Before analyzing these changes, it is necessary to have an understanding of the CCP administration's "responsible state" discourse.

The establishment of the "Chinese responsibility outlook"

No changes happen just like that. China as a permanent member of the UN Security Council had always been inclined to use abstaining as a strategy in voting on draft resolutions. However, during the First Iraq War, which followed the Tiananmen incident, the CCP administration began to take a more active role in the international arena; for example, China is prepared to intrude in the domestic affairs of other countries in the name of promoting and effectuating "international democracy." This subtle change became more pronounced after Xi came to power. Iraq, again, offers an example of this. Despite hesitation among certain Western countries to support US air strikes on extremist armed Islamists in ISIS, the Chinese Foreign Ministry extended its immediate "limited support" to the United States, explaining that such a move was to maintain the independence and sovereignty of Iraq. Beijing's rationale was that if Washington had been given authorization by the Iraq government, this was not the same as interfering in another country's domestic affairs. Still, no matter how the Foreign Ministry packaged its endorsement, it was in distinct contradiction with its long-standing "Non-Interference Policy," which was the most salient feature of the Five Principles of Co-existence formulated by late premier Zhou Enlai in the mid-1950s.

Since then, China has more frequently committed itself to being a "responsible stakeholder," or simply a "responsible power," employing Western narratives to talk about "global morals," especially toward Third World countries. This is reminiscent of the Maoist morality in China's diplomacy that was anchored upon Third World solidarity. In recent years, China has sent large contingents of troops and police officers to UN-mandated peace-keeping missions around the world. It has also offered humanitarian support in other crises. When China dispatched medical teams to Liberia and Sierra Leone during the spread of the Ebola virus, the Xinhua News

Agency praised China's assistance to those countries as practicing the "cornerstones" of the Sino-African relationship proposed by Xi, namely "sincerity, practicality, friendship, and candidness" (Xinhuanet 2014a). Unlike China's passive reaction during the SARS crisis, Xi's China shows that it is willing to take the initiative in propagating China's commitments to the world: it is actively expounding on what "being responsible" means so as not to let the West monopolize its conceptualization. Up to now, it has only been through the reports of the official Xinhua News Agency or Chinese Academy of Social Sciences academics that one can see the criticism directed at the United States, such as during the 2011 US debt-ceiling crisis and the 2013 fiscal cliff. Should this development continue, there might be an increase in the frequency with which the senior Chinese cadres lock horns with their US counterpart over the definition of "responsibility."

Of course, China's move under the name of "responsibility" comes not without controversy. For example, Chinese state-owned enterprises (SOEs) have been criticized for corruption and over-focusing on resources exploitation, thus resulting in environmental damage in developing countries in Africa and Southeast Asia. China's large-scale reclamation of South China Sea islands has also aroused serious concerns in neighboring countries and international society, despite China's argument that it is contributing "international public goods" in the area of navigational services to the global shipping community. As China's willingness and ability to participate in international affairs grow, more controversies like these can be expected. But at least one thing has become clear: China no longer worries about taking a leading role in the world when such a role is now justified morally. The next task, however, is more challenging: to present the "Chinese Dream," a term frequently used since Xi's inauguration, as a legitimate, if not better, alternative to the "American Dream," for both domestic and international audiences.

The competition between the "Chinese Dream" and the "American Dream"

The "Chinese Dream," a somewhat Westernized slogan, is complemented by the "Chinese Value Outlook" and "Chinese Responsibility Theory," differentiating it from such previous stereotyped party-state slogans as the "Three Represents Theory" (under Jiang Zemin) and the "Scientific Outlook on Development" (under Hu Jintao). (See Chapter 9: "Evolution of the Party since 1976: Ideological and Functional Adoptions.") It is not entirely original, however: even the Xinhua News Agency acknowledged that Xi's Chinese Dream could be tracked back to Thomas Friedman's article in the *New York Times* (*Xinhua Daily Telegraph* 2012). It is not a coincidence that in comparison with his colleagues, Xi seems to have a better understanding of the "American Dream." He has a firsthand experience of the US from a brief stay with an American family in Iowa in 1985; Xi has often since reminisced about this experience. If one looks at what drives the "Chinese Dream," while "the pursuit of economic liftoff, improvement in livelihood, and social and environmental progress" largely typifies the capitalist dream in the United States, Beijing has played up the distinctiveness of its own "dream" with one notable codicil. The additional yardsticks – "the pursuit of fairness and justice, democracy and the rule of law, civic growth, cultural prosperity, educational progress, and technological innovation" – are said to delineate China's unique pathway despite using the universal rhetoric (*People's Daily* 2013). So the de facto name of the "Chinese Dream" could well be the "Chinese American Dream," but with the ambition of surpassing the pure "American Dream" in terms of its breadth of vision.

Suggesting that the "Chinese Dream" has an edge over the American one, Singaporean Chinese scholar Shi Yuzhi's article "Seven Differences between the 'Chinese Dream' and the 'American Dream'" in *the News of the Communist Party of China* described seven ways in which the "Chinese Dream" outweighs its American counterpart by outlining an over-simplistic dichotomy between the two:

- the "Chinese Dream" is a dream for the collective, while the "American Dream" is a dream for individuals;
- the "Chinese Dream" is to realize the great rejuvenation of the Chinese nation, whereas the "American Dream" is to realize personal success;
- the "Chinese Dream" depends on the Chinese themselves, whereas the "American Dream" requires the resources of other countries;
- the "Chinese Dream" is about the harmonious happiness of the masses, whereas the "American Dream" is about the freedom and enjoyment of each individual;
- the "Chinese Dream" is to carry historical roots, whereas the "American Dream" emphasizes the realistic experience;
- the "Chinese Dream" is to depend on the collective forces, whereas the "American Dream" encourages the presentation of an individual's personality traits;
- the "Chinese Dream" is for national dignity, whereas the "American Dream" is for an individual's success.

(Shi 2013)

While it is clear that Shi's analysis mirrored to some extent official propaganda on the subject, it is evident that emphasis on the collective values of the "Chinese Dream" constitutes the core of the "Chinese Value Outlook." A problem lies only in the third point of difference, namely "the 'Chinese Dream' depends on the Chinese themselves." This restricts the influence of the "Chinese Dream" and may not do justice to Xi's international aspirations. It is no exaggeration to say that instead of insisting as his predecessors did that the "China model" cannot be exported, Xi is ready to provide foreign countries with China's success story as a reference point.

The non-exportable, but learner-friendly "Chinese Dream"

Like the "Chinese Dream" and the "Chinese Value Outlook," the "China model" is by no means an invention of Xi. As early as Jiang's time in office, the "China model" was thrust into the limelight. It is an American concept which can be traced back to *Time Magazine* editor Joshua Cooper Ramo who had contrasted the "Washington Consensus" with the "Beijing Consensus" (Ramo 2004). Chinese scholars and the media gradually developed his thinking into various "China's models," without giving him official recognition (Zhang 2006).

Very simply, the China model is viewed as the opposite of the "Washington Consensus." It advocates a "market economy" to be managed by an authoritarian government, including population and foreign currency manipulation, and political macroscopic readjustment and control. The China model argues that the benefits of market forces can be best harnessed under the watchful eye of a benevolent state: *dingchen shezhi* ("top-level design") is a key to Xi's economic policy. Even though the Chinese government prides itself on its developmental model, Xi's predecessor Hu had repeatedly noted that China was not going to export its model since there is no single pathway for a country to grow, nor can other countries claim the same national conditions. It might thus be paradoxical if China were to underscore its national conditions on the one hand, and to tout its model on the other. Such a move could risk demonstrating that China's national conditions are not so unique after all.

While in the Xi era the "red line" demarcating the "China model" for internal use only is still supposedly in place, China has been active in making gestures about its success through global investment and development aid. Some Third World countries have even taken lessons from the "China model" to straighten out their own internal matters. As a result, a fresh state directive has been released that the "China model" has significant international value not because it can simply be copied by other countries, but because the latter can incorporate the model while taking into account their own conditions (Xu 2013). In 2014, a *People's Daily* report dialectically analyzed the worldwide application of the "China model," saying that neither the "definiteness" (or country-specific requirements) nor "openness" (or universality) of this model are mutually exclusive as the two natures concurrently exist. The article concluded that the "China model" is not available to copycats, but only learners (*People's Daily* 2014). However clumsy the logic, the implication is clear: although other countries have different growth paths when compared with China, some patterns of the China model, such as the emphasis on infrastructure building for triggering economic growth as well as an authoritarian decision-making apparatus, could well be "copied and pasted." Since these features differ significantly from the strings-attached loan model of the World Bank or International Monetary Fund (IMF), the more countries "referencing" the China model, the more bargaining power China could have compared with the US. The CCP administration now also realizes that playing a more active role in exporting and promoting its ideology and development model can more effectively preempt following the final steps of the Soviet Union, whose demise was at least partly owing to the loss of national pride and faith in comparison with their Western counterparts. The development of the "One Belt, One Road" initiative, as will be discussed later, is a direct extension of this concept.

The Beijing Consensus was also seen as serving as a reference point for countries seeking an alternative approach to Western-styled democracy. Many China scholars argue that Western democracy is merely only one form of democracy, much less a universal value, by pointing to the unrest in the post-political reform eras in Thailand, Ukraine, Egypt, as well as Iraq. They further contend that blindly employing the "Western democratic model" and setting aside national conditions would likely result in dire social cleavages (Yang 2014). According to the same logic, the specific social and cultural contexts of these regions have largely affected the extent and quality of democratic institutional building: it is more a process of stable state building rather than just promotion of democracy that civilians of such countries really need. When many recent cases of democratization have failed so dramatically, and the democratic choices available in leading Western democracies – such as the alternative right movement in the US and Brexit in the UK – have magnified social contradictions, China's authoritarian model, which allows very limited democracy but a growing level of freedom and prosperity which are available under the premise that the regime is not challenged, becomes increasingly convincing to many countries.

The "anti-corruption" dream equals the "Chinese Dream"

The Chinese Dream has gained particular momentum in Chinese society not only because of its nationalistic rhetoric and impetus. There is also a materialistic dimension to the discourse which subtly links the Chinese Dream to Xi's anti-corruption campaign. Several well-connected research centers have carried out public opinion surveys that show the "Anti-Corruption Dream" plays a leading role in Xi's "Chinese Dream." As an example, the Guangdong Province survey conducted in June 2013 by the Provincial Situation Survey Research Center of Guangdong led by the provincial propaganda organ and the Social Science Academy of Guangdong, found that 49 percent of respondents were able to appreciate the "correct connotation" of the "Chinese Dream," such as the national power, national rejuvenation, and well-being of people.

But most importantly, 66.14 percent thought the major obstacle to the realization of this dream was "corruption and decadency" (Chinanews.com 2013). This finding can also be applied to other provinces. In Zhejiang's 2014 survey of its young residents, "corruption and decadency" was picked as the biggest stumbling block to the "Chinese Dream," with up to 54.6 percent, followed by "incomplete rule of law" and "social unfairness." Those problems are all domestic ones emanating from China's opening up and reform (Chinanews.com 2014).

Such statistics, of course, fail to offer the most genuine information in that the research centers had to ensure that all the questions were politically correct. Typically, there were no choices for "Constitutional Dream" in the questionnaire and respondents were even "guided" to tick the "Powerful Nation Dream" as the final goal of the "Chinese Dream." However, considering that the grassroots' aversion to corruption has made it possible for Xi to go the distance in his anti-graft campaign, it is believable that such surveys do partly reflect genuine public opinion. For example, in the Zhejiang survey, the choices of "disadvantageous international environment" and "corruption" were given in the question of impediments to the "Chinese Dream" (ibid.). Working on those statistics, one might consider that a large portion of nationalist narratives with regard to the "Chinese Dream" care only about daily life issues such as anti-corruption. If Beijing mobilizes the public effectively by domestic political campaign, and transfers the momentum to its international saga, if properly managed, this could become a very effective formula like what Putin has already achieved in Russia.

"One Belt, One Road" as the Chinese Marshall Plan?

To promote the "Chinese Dream," China has been making shifts at the operational level of foreign affairs since Xi assumed office. One of the earlier signals that Chinese foreign policy was turning proactive can be picked up from Foreign Minister Wang Yi's 2014 article "Peaceful Development and the Chinese Dream of National Rejuvenation" in the journal of the *China Institute of International Studies*; in this article he emphasized that the concepts of the "Chinese Dream" and "Peaceful Development" are consistent with one another (Wang Y. 2014). In fact, however, not only is China no longer "hiding its capabilities and biding its time," it is also reluctant to just accommodate itself to the status quo and stick to the "Peaceful Development" principle. On the contrary, the CCP administration appears confident enough to create a custom-made-for-China global milieu through modifying, if not directly challenging, the status quo – and to capitalize on the changes it has made in the world order. While the idea of building a "community of mutual destiny" among China's regional neighbors is of significance, the question, such as what China is up to, were its interests to run against others, was not mentioned by Wang or his ultimate boss. Tracing China's recent diplomatic moves, however, one might find that when the Xi administration has encountered such problems, it tends actively to make its own rules of the game, changing the vested international interests (with the US as the major stakeholder) by creating international infrastructures and institutions to foster a global environment suitable to China's long-term growth. The flagship of this strategy can be best illustrated by the "One Belt, One Road" (OBOR) initiative.

OBOR refers to the Silk Road Economic Belt and the 21st Century Maritime Silk Road. Both were introduced by Xi in 2013: the former in Kazakhstan and the latter in Indonesia. Despite the enthusiasm demonstrated by China for this grand strategy, the strategic goals of OBOR have received diverse individual interpretations. Recently, international relations scholars like this author have compared OBOR with the US-led Marshall Plan in the post-World War II era, but scholars from China argue that OBOR and the Marshall Plan are not comparable (Wang W.D. 2014). Still, predicting the hidden strategic goals of OBOR is not complicated – they can be inferred by combining Chinese official discourse and strategic arrangements in response to the US rebalancing strategy in the Asia-Pacific region. Those goals can be summarized in the following five points – which are actually quite similar to the strategic aims of the Marshall Plan as summarized by scholars (Leffler 1988).

Boosting exports

By the end of World War II, the United States was a strong manufacturing country equipped with high industrial capacity. However, the saturation of the domestic market and a failure to export excess capacity caused economic growth to stagnate. In order to cope with the post-war economic transformation and the problem of overcapacity, the United States was forced to seek overseas markets for its products. The terms of the Marshall Plan stated that European countries receiving US aid should accept US investment and import US goods. By providing aid to so many different countries, the United States simultaneously underwent an economic transformation.

In a similar way, China has recently found itself needing to export excess capacity, resources, and labor through foreign investment in order to achieve its own economic transformation. As fate would have it, the strength of China's manufacturing industry is in infrastructure building, and Central and Southeast Asia lack investment in this field. China, therefore, oversaw the establishment of the Asian Infrastructure Investment Bank (AIIB) in accordance with the OBOR initiative in order to promote "Made in China" goods and services in Central and Southeast Asia.

Exporting currency

The Marshall Plan allowed the United States to export its currency. The total amount of aid provided was US$13 billion, which is now equivalent to roughly US$100 billion. The US dollar was used for the subsidies, while European countries purchased US goods with their own currencies. Over time, the US dollar has become a tool for stability; the "Money Credit" provided by the plan created a basis for future frequent quantitative easing.

China is also seeking to increase the international use of its currency. The International Monetary Fund recently included China's renminbi (RMB) in its Special Drawing Rights basket of currencies. However, the most effective way to promote cross-border circulation of the RMB is still regional economic cooperation. The RMB is regarded as the strongest currency among the major regions of the OBOR initiative. Though the details of the policy have not been decided, a significant number of Chinese specialists state that the RMB should be used as the settlement currency of large-scale commodity trade in the region. At the same time, the engagement of Chinese capital investment in infrastructure building should be increased and cross-border payments by RMB promoted. This sort of "currency war" theory argues that the internationalization of the RMB through OBOR can allow China to challenge the United States' leading role in the international financial arena, just as the status of the US currency was consolidated through the Marshall Plan.

Countering a rival

The United States hoped to use the Marshall Plan to revive war-torn Western Europe in order to demonstrate the superiority of capitalism over communism and undermine the influence of the Soviet Union. The instability of the European community favored the growth of communism;

the Communist Party in countries such as Italy received strong support. Marshall believed that Europe was the key for an effective balance of power between the Soviet Union and the United States. If the European economy declined, the traditional capitalist world economic structure of the United States, Europe, and Southeast Asia could not be sustained. Therefore, providing long-term and short-term subsidies as well as lowering trade barriers in Western Europe was essential to defend against communism and the Soviet Union.

The Marshall Plan provided a blueprint for undermining the influence of the Soviet Union. Similarly, China's OBOR targets the United States as a potential competitor. The emphasis on interconnection stresses the construction of onshore energy pipelines as well as harbors. By importing energy through dispersed channels, China can lower the strategic risk of energy imports and enhance control over Indian Ocean shipping routes. At the same time, the consolidation of trade relationships among China (with its exports of manufactured goods), the Middle East and Central Asia (energy exports), and Southeast Asia (exports of raw material) can counterbalance the rebalancing strategy of the United States and reduce China's economic dependence on the US.

Fostering strategic divisions

In the post-World War II era, the United States wanted to incorporate all of Germany (not only West Germany) into the capitalist camp. If this could not be accomplished in the short-term, the United States had to ensure a prolonged division in Germany in order to prevent the whole country from entering the Soviet Union's camp. The US emphasis on Germany was rooted in the high geopolitical strategic significance of the country. Germany is home to the Ruhr, a large industrial area that provided the essential natural resources (such as coal) and industrial capacity for the revival of the European economy. Also, Germany is located at the intersection between Eastern and Western Europe; allowing the Soviet Union to control Germany would obstruct the balance of power in Europe. In order to prevent the geopolitical risk of a possible Soviet Union–Germany coalition, the Marshall Plan strengthened political and economic ties between West Germany and Western Europe. The unification of Germany has been viewed as the key to ending the Cold War and bringing down the Iron Curtain.

As stated above, the Marshall Plan can be viewed as a factor that contributed to the division of West and East Germany. Similarly, OBOR may lower the solidarity of Asia-Pacific integration organizations headed by the United States and Japan, such as APEC. By searching out APEC member states which desperately need infrastructure, OBOR allows China to foster bilateral integration with those member states. That, in turn, will undermine the significance of APEC and delay these states' entry in the US-led Trans-Pacific Partnership (whose future is doubtful anyway after Trump's decision to withdraw from it). Though those countries will still keep diplomatic ties with the United States, OBOR limits the chance of forming of coalitions against China, such as the US–India and US–South Korea coalitions in the past, or potentially the US-Vietnamese, US-Philippine, and US-Australian defense alliances.

Siphoning away diplomatic support

The final purpose of the Marshall Plan was to target countries in Eastern Europe with the aim of getting their support. Though Eastern European satellite states were not the primary targets of the Marshall Plan, the United States still provided aid for those countries if they abandoned the communist model. Tito's Yugoslavia was an example of an Eastern European state that benefited by accepting Marshall Plan aid. In other words, the United States hoped to use the economic development of Western Europe as an incentive that could increase US influence in Eastern Europe.

Today, the endpoint of OBOR is located in Europe. It shows that China wishes to intensify relations with traditional US allies in Western Europe, which in turn undermines US influence in the region. Recent frequent interactions between leaders of China and major Western European countries as well as decisions by the UK, France, and Germany to join the AIIB despite the objections of Washington seem to indicate the decline of US influence. If economic and strategic integration are achieved between Asia and Europe, China may become the center of the world, leaving the United States marginalized.

Having said all that, it should also be noted that the scale of the Marshall Plan, in terms of absolute figures proposed, is relatively more modest than OBOR. The Marshall Plan was completed during a period of fast-rising US might in economic and military growth. In terms of cultural affinition, the US and Europe are closer compared to China and Near Eastern countries. Europe, even after WWII-related devastation, seems better endowed than many countries within the OBOR chessboard in terms of economic revival. Another point to note is that in the long run, whether China has a big-enough war chest to finance its deals in OBOR remains uncertain: the entire costs run to US$8 trillion, whereas China's forex exchange holdings have slipped to under US$3 trillion in January 2017. The bulk of Chinese companies active in OBOR projects are giant SOEs, many of which are still operating in their premarket mode. As a result, the outcome of OBOR is likely to be more uncertain than that of the Marshall Plan, to say the least.

Institutional realism: modifying the rules of the game

In order for OBOR as a centralized, state-sponsored macro strategic scheme to be operated effectively, domestic institutional reengineering is essential. The most innovative institution that Xi has made in China's domestic and foreign policy is probably the establishment of the Central National Security Commission of the CCP (CNSC). As early as the US air strike on China's embassy in Belgrade in 1999, China was thinking of having such an organization; this was temporarily suspended due to the improvement of Sino-American relations and the launch of a hotline between them. During Xi's tenure, such thinking has been renewed by the demands of realizing the "Chinese Dream." The CNSC operates independently of the State Council, directly led by the CCP Politburo Standing Committee in order to sidestep excessive checks and balances. To various degrees, China's CNSC resembles the US National Security Council (NSC). Observed from an organizational angle, the CNSC is in fact more similar to the US Department of Homeland Security, integrating internal and external affairs which involve the People's Liberation Army, the Ministry of State Security, the Ministry of Justice, the Ministry of Foreign Affairs, the Ministry of Public Security, the People's Armed Police (PAP), the Publicity Department, even the Hong Kong and Macao Affairs Office of the State Council as well as the Liaison Office of the Central People's Government in Hong Kong. Only with this huge vehicle in place, guided by nationalistic and patriotic rhetoric, could Xi put his words into real diplomatic practice.

If one wishes to summarize the strategic design behind OBOR in a couple of words, from international relations academic terminology, it should be called "institutional realism": a strategy aimed at maximizing national interests through building international institutions, in order to ensure other countries' structural reliance on China and to bolster China's legitimacy in its bid to assume regional, or even global, leadership. Besides the CNSC as an internal vehicle and the OBOR as an external grand strategy, Xi's China has made many other attempts to modify the existing rules of the game in the international arena. Its Air Defense Identification Zone (ADIZ) and AIIB provide two sound examples of different fronts for our further observation of the strategy.

Modifying rules of the sovereignty game: ADIZ, Sansha, and beyond

To protect China's sovereignty, the Xi administration is prepared to be strident in its handling of sovereignty disputes in the East China Sea and the South China Sea over the Diaoyu/Senkaku Islands and the Spratly Islands, respectively. Although its row is with Japan, Vietnam, and the Philippines, China believes these countries to be backed by the United States in its "Pivot to the Asia-Pacific Region" in an attempt to circumvent China. Keeping in mind the strategic setting of these rows, Chinese concerns are no longer confined to bilateral or even multilateral issues in relation to Japan, Vietnam, the Philippines, or ASEAN. What is at stake is direct competition with Washington regarding the US-led international structure, the grand chessboard of Washington's "Pivot to the Asia-Pacific Region" (or its Trump equivalent), as well as the America-led rules of the game in international intercourse.

The most telling instance is China's unilateral establishment of an Air Defense Identification Zone (ADIZ) in the East China Sea on November 23, 2013. As the Chinese pointed out, the world's first such zone was created by the United States when it announced that foreign aircraft have to declare themselves before entering the area around its territorial airspace, despite this not being international law. Whereas the United States claimed that the establishment of their airspace had the advance endorsement of its neighbors (which is still open to question) and thus should be seen as an act by a "status quo defender," China, as a subtle "status quo challenger," considered using its ADIZ to promote unilateralism in the region (Clover 2014). The United States did not recognize China's self-claimed regulation of its ADIZ in the East China Sea, and immediately sent B-52s to challenge its claims. Shortly after, South Korea followed suit by fine-tuning the scope of its ADIZ. Since China lacks the capabilities to make it genuinely effective, Beijing just counted on the zone indicating its preference and capability to amend or even create international rules.

After this, the West was left wondering if China had the intention of establishing an ADIZ in the South China Sea. Prior to Xi's inauguration, China upgraded Sansha to a prefecture-level city and gave it jurisdiction over the Spratly Islands, the Paracel Islands, and the Macclesfield Bank, although its declared administrative scope also included a large number of small islands with abundant natural resources outside China's actual control. This administrative establishment became the basis from which Xi began to pursue more aggressive policies in the South China Sea, most notably reclamation to create man-made islands extending from China-controlled areas and to deploy military facilities and personnel on them. This is seen as a Chinese attempt to learn from nineteenth-century imperialist logic – and to make the first move in the contested area. The move is, however, angrily rebutted in the twenty-first century by other claimants of the area. When the Permanent Court of Arbitration (PCA) in the Hague announced the result of arbitration on the South China Sea dispute case in July 2016 in favor of the Philippines, the Chinese government and the public reacted strongly by fundamentally discrediting the PCA for its lack of credibility and binding power, its judges for being "recipients of Philippine money," and the US for orchestrating the choir at the back. From the observation of Kurt Campbell, then Assistant Secretary of State for East Asian and Pacific Affairs during Obama's first term in office, Chinese diplomacy had now turned active from passive and every single step had been well rehearsed, allowing no errors in the implementation that could detract from China's determination to become a regional power (Campbell 2014).

Modifying rules of the economic game: AIIB, APEC-FTA, and beyond

On top of dealing with territorial disputes, Xi has been establishing new institutions in the fields of global economy and finance. At the China-led BRICS Summit in 2013, the leaders of the five emerging powers agreed on building a bank headquartered in Shanghai. It was formerly established with the Fortaleza Declaration, the five powers sharing equally the start-up funding (China's actual contribution is greater). Chinese investment also accounts for an overwhelming share in the BRICS Contingency Reserved Fund (CRF), totaling US$41 billion, an indicator of China's national power and influence in the group. A more aggressive Chinese creation was the Asian Infrastructure Investment Bank (AIIB), whose official responsibilities are to facilitate Asian regionalization and collectively rise to financial challenges. Seeing the positive response from ASEAN member states, Washington tried to persuade Japan, South Korea, Australia, and Western European allies not to join. Eventually, only Japan complied. The response was regarded as a major Chinese triumph and a major mishandling by Obama.

Key drivers for founding the AIIB and the BRICS Bank are not difficult to identify. They probably include counter-balancing the US-led World Bank and Japan-led Asian Development Bank; narrowing the disparity between South and North countries; offering financial support for the OBOR initiative; making new rules in the Asian economic system after China's rising and even contending with "dollar hegemony." Were those China-steered institutions to blossom, the Bretton Woods System and even the post-war global economic order might find itself thoroughly rivaled. After all, these banks succeeded in detracting from the predominance of US-led global banks – and led to calls for a more transparent and fair international financial infrastructure. At home, their establishment was seen as a response to the heated discussion on the "currency war" and thus is welcomed by Chinese financial circles.

During the APEC Economic Leaders' Meeting in 2014 hosted by China, Xi further promoted China's proactive economic institutional framework building. The request to set up the APEC-Free Trade Area (APEC-FTA) has been interpreted as a contingency plan based on the framework of the China-led Regional Comprehensive Economic Partnership (RCEP) to oppose the US-led Trans-Pacific Partnership (TPP), before Trump's eventual withdrawal. The injection of US$40 billion announced in the meeting to set up the Silk Road Fund is, as expected, aimed to promote the construction of OBOR initiatives.

The OBOR roadmap and these newly developed financial initiatives have facilitated the ambitious planning of a series of aggressive external infrastructure schemes. Some involve official state investment, such as plans to develop a series of strategically located ports in Pakistan, Sri Lanka, Malaysia, and even Greece. Some involve strategic investments by SOEs in remote countries of Africa and Latin America. Some involve official financial commitments to buy over countries with strategic conflicts with China, most notably the Philippines (or, in contrast, imposing economic pressure on defiant neighbors like Singapore). Some involve private companies whose relationship with Beijing remains dubious, such as the Hong Kong Nicaragua Canal Development Group, a Hong Kong-registered company that was commissioned to build the Nicaragua Canal. Some alleged plans are yet to be confirmed, such as those for a Kra Canal in Thailand. All of them suggest an aggressive Chinese grand chessboard by means of which China hopes to make significant improvements in its international strategic, economic, and commercial postures. Like the strategy employed by the United States during the Iraq War, the "doctrine of preemption" is now in Chinese minds, but with the United States the target to be preempted.

Aggression at the expense of soft power?

Whereas the Chinese government has gone the extra mile to broaden the appeal of the "Chinese Dream," the congenital gaps between it and the official limitations in the "Chinese Dream" present difficulties to the realization of this goal. Examples are plenty. For instance, Xi mobilized diplomats and pro-Beijing academics to publish their policy analyses in the Western media. The most typical example is the rhetorical warfare launched by more than 40 Chinese diplomats against Japanese Prime Minister Shinzo Abe, although its reception was poor. During the Hu era, China's Confucius Institutes won favor in publicizing Chinese culture and received many compliments. Xi further invested in the Institutes, but China's image overseas has since become more problematic. Beijing's attitude toward Taiwan's representatives overseas, even civilian ones, has been particularly hostile, much deviating from the original principle of building "united fronts." During a session of the international academic conference sponsored by the Chiang Ching-kuo Foundation (CCKF), for example, Xu Lin, the Director General of the Hanban – the Chinese National Office of the PRC for Teaching Chinese as a Foreign Language that runs all the Confucius Institutes – to the astonishment of the entire audience asked the organizer to tear off the page which introduced the CCKF from the official brochure. It is hard to estimate how much this act has hurt China's long-cultivated publicity.

According to Pew figures, the favorable views held by the US and Japan toward China were 52 percent and 27 percent in 2006, respectively. They had declined to 37 percent and 11 percent, respectively, in 2016 (Pew Research Center 2016). There are, of course, still countries which continue to view China favorably, like Pakistan. Yet, the general trend is rather obvious. It will be of no great surprise if the same trend continues to be evident in the near future if Chinese foreign policies remain the same.

Conclusion: the New Asian security concept as Asia's Monroe Doctrine?

As Sinologist Wu Guoguang has observed, China's contemporary nationalism that has recently guided all its foreign policy initiatives, symbolized by its endorsement of China's developmental model, authoritarianism, and superficial identification of Chinese culture, is nearly at polar opposites with traditional nationalism as defined in the early twentieth century (Wu 2008). Through the initiatives described above, Chinese nationalists today, led by Xi, are attempting to participate in institutional competition in the Asia-Pacific region and beyond. The CCP administration can achieve quite a lot in the short run, as the areas and issues they are targeting are not well addressed by existing institutions: for example the infrastructure investment in Central Asia and Southeast Asia. China's institutional initiatives are thus quite unique and provide a complement to the existing institutional building across the Asia-Pacific. That said, the ambitions of these initiatives have come at a time when China's economic growth is slowing down. Being realistic, it is not sustainable for China alone to provide long-term finance for infrastructure development across the vast region of Asia. It is essential, therefore, for China to take the lead in building the platform and to invite others to cooperate on projects related to regional development. The key question is: Can China become the indisputable, exclusive regional leader of Asia-Pacific, or at least the Western Asia-Pacific, before China's growth completely comes to a halt?

As a potential solution for China in its position of a major power in waiting, constructing regional cooperative platforms with its own guiding principle is of strategic significance. As an example, the New Asian Security Concept was raised by Xi when China hosted the Conference on Interaction and Confidence-Building Measures in Asia (CICA). The concept included "four securities," namely the "Collective," the "Comprehensive," the "Cooperative," as well as the "Sustainable" (Xinhuanet 2014b). As a guide to understanding the concept, "Collective Security" claims to respect and ensure the security and equality of each country, which reflects China's adjustment to the "Non-Intervention Policy" and refusal to accept "universal values." "Comprehensive Security" means to pay attention concurrently to "conventional security" (such as military threat) and "unconventional security" (such as terrorism); this is similar to the Chinese definition of the "Three Evils" (terrorism, separatism, and religious extremism) as contained in the charter of the Shanghai Cooperation Organization (SCO), which places "anti-separatists" on the same footing as "anti-terrorists." "Cooperative Security" involves promoting regional security through collaboration, implying that unconstrained democracy in any country could have negative impacts on regional harmony. Last but not least, "Sustainable Security" refers to taking into account both security and development, hinting that underdeveloped countries do not have to strictly follow the ecological and security requirements set by developed countries.

This meticulous interpretation aims at conveying only one message: the four "Securities" are designed to construct the "Asian Outlook" based on the "Chinese Value Outlook" and the "China model" as discussed earlier in this chapter, and differ considerably from the West's-led security outlooks. For China and its regional audiences, "Collective Security" differs from "universal values" and implies that countries should not interfere in others' internal affairs (to avoid precedents like Iraq); "Comprehensive Security" constrains attempts by separatists to call for independence via referendums (to avoid precedents like Kosovo); "Cooperative Security" emphasizes harmonious society instead of competitive Western-styled democracy (to avoid precedents like Thailand and Ukraine); and "Sustainable Security" dismisses Western attempts to impose environmental yardsticks based on the standard of developed economies. Coining these new concepts, China is, glaringly, taking pains to attract countries at similar stages of development to stand together in opposition to the US-led status quo.

More inspiring, at the CICA Xi concluded with three "Ultimately's," asking that "Asian affairs ultimately rely on Asian people, Asian conundrums ultimately rely on Asian people, and Asian security problems ultimately rely on Asian people" (*People's Daily Online* 2014). The overtones of this rallying cry are to dissuade the US-led forces from interfering in the issues of Asia. This bears comparison to the 1823 Monroe Doctrine when the United States was still on its path to ascendency, cautioning the European powers against colonizing America by declaring that such moves would be treated as a threat to US security. In addition to asserting that "American affairs ultimately rely on American people," the Monroe Doctrine also declared that the United States had no interest in meddling in European affairs. Throughout many decades of reconstruction, inference, and distortion, the Monroe Doctrine has become the dogma of neo-colonialism, a manifesto that "American affairs rely on the United States." When Xi raises the idea that "Asian affairs ultimately rely on Asian people" today, the question of who should represent "Asian people" is seen as the linchpin of the "New Asian Security Concept."

In the eyes of Southeast Asian countries, China's foreign policy in recent years has sent mixed signals: Despite the growing potential of economic cooperation, China's increasing maritime assertiveness, especially in the South China Sea, is perceived as a threat to regional security. Most countries therefore apply "hedging" tactics between China and the US so as to share the economic benefits of Chinese investment on one hand, and eagerly accepting US strategic protection on the other in the hope of maximizing their own interests without leaning to either side completely. If the CCP leadership could show more self-constraint and transparency in its strategic intentions in its maritime claims, and try to find room for compromise and cooperation, other Asian countries would perhaps show more enthusiasm toward China's economic and security initiatives. A number of American academics have thought Xi's contribution might be a parody of the Monroe Doctrine, not the least of which is detailed in the book *Peaceful War* by Patrick Mendis. While most Chinese believe in a grandiose picture of the China century, Mendis hints that even though Xi's "Chinese Dream" is viewed as the equivalent of the "American Dream," the overlap in the respective claimed influential sphere of the two "dreams" may serve as the biggest threat to peace in this century (Mendis 2013). Which version of the two extremes would eventually prevail, we as observers can only apply the most pragmatic attitude: to wait and see. After all, China's Great Leap Outward is serving both international and domestic purposes, that is also central to the CCP's domestic goal of ensuring the perennial ruling status of the Party. If the regime miscalculates its foreign policy, the nationalist public opinions could also bounce back. How to strike a balance between achieving diplomatic greatness and controlling expectation management for the public is essentially part of the greatest challenges for the regime.

References

Campbell, K. (2014) "Trouble at Sea Reveals the New Shape of China's Foreign Policy," *Financial Times*, July 22.

Chinanews.com (2013) "Guangdong jin qicheng jumin renwei tanwu fubai zhangai 'Zhongguomeng' de shixian" [Nearly 70% Guangdong Residents Thought Corruption Was Retarding the "Chinese Dream"], June 18.

Chinanews.com (2014) "Chao banshu Zhejiang qingnian renwei tanwu fubai cheng 'Zhongguomeng' zuida zhangai" [Over Half of the Zhejiang Youth Thought Corruption Was the Biggest Obstacle to the "Chinese Dream"], April 28.

Clover, C. (2014) "John Kerry Warns China against Declaring Second Air Defence Zone," *Financial Times*, February 14.

Krasner, St. (1982) "Structural Causes and Regime Consequences: Regimes as Intervening Variables," *International Organization* 36(2): 185–205.

Leffler, M. (1988) "The United States and the Strategic Dimensions of the Marshall Plan," *Diplomatic History*: 277–306.

Mendis, P. (2013) *Peaceful War: How the Chinese Dream and the American Destiny Create a New Pacific World Order*, United States: University Press of America.

People's Daily (2013) "Zhongguo meng de Dongliyuan" [Driving Forces of the Chinese Dream], February 1.

People's Daily (2014) "'Zhongguo moshi': queding xing yu kaifang xing de bianzheng tongyi" [The "China Model": The Dialectic and Unity Relationship between Definiteness and Openness], May 8.

People's Daily Online (2014) "Xi's Keynote Speech at CICA Summit Receives High Praises," May 23. Available at http://english.people.com.cn/n/2014/0523/c98649-8731334.html.

Pew Research Center (2016) "How Are Global Views on China Trending?" CSIS website, http://chinapower.csis.org/global-views/.

Ramo, J.C. (2004) *The Beijing Consensus*, Occasional Paper, The Foreign Policy Center.

Shi, Y.Z. (2013) "Zhongguomeng qubie yu Meiguomeng de qida tezheng" [Seven Differences between the "Chinese Dream" and the "American Dream"], *Cpcnews.cn*, May 23.

Wang, W.D. (2014) "Zhongguo ban Maxieer jihua fuchu shuimian" [The Appearance of Chinese Version Marshall Plan], *Wallstreetcn*, November 4.

Wang, Y. (2014) "Heping fazhan yu minzu fuxing de Zhongguomeng" [Peaceful Development and the Chinese Dream of National Rejuvenation], *China International Studies*, March 11.

Wu, G.G. (2008) "From Post-Imperial to Late Communist Nationalism: Historical Change in Chinese Nationalism from May Fourth to the 1990s," *Third World Quarterly* 29(3): 467–482.

Xi, J.P. (2017) "President Xi's Speech to Davos in Full," World Economic Forum, 2017, www.weforum.org/agenda/2017/01/full-text-of-xi-jinping-keynote-at-the-world-economic-forum.

Xinhua Daily Telegraph (2012) "'Zhongguomeng' jingju fenjin lijiang" [The "Chinese Dream" Summons Power for Moving Forward], December 7.

Xinhuanet (2014a) "Zhongguo yuanzhu xifei kangji Aibola yiqing xian daguo zeren" [China Helps West Africa Attack Ebola Presenting Major Power's Responsibility], August 12.
Xinhuanet (2014b) "Yazhou xianghu xiezuo yu xinren cuoshi huiyi (Yaxin huiyi)" [The Conference on Interaction and Confidence-building Measures in Asia (CICA)], May 21.
Xu, C.W. (2013) "'Zhongguo moshi' de shijie yiyi" [The "China Model's" Global Significance], *Xinhua Ribao [Xinhua Daily]*, November 4.
Yang, G.B. (2014) "Jige liuxing de minzhuhua mingti de weizheng" [The False Evidence of Several Popular Democratization Topics], *Beijing Ribao [Beijing Daily]*, March 17.
Zhang, W.W. (2006) "The Allure of the Chinese Model," *International Herald Tribune*, November 2.
Zhang, W.W. (2009) "Jujiao Zhongguo moshi" [Focusing on the China Model], *Reminwang [People.com.cn]*, http://theory.people.com.cn/GB/40557/149513/.

INDEX

Page numbers in *italics* denote tables.

abducted children, Weibo account dedicated to the search for 380
abductions, of Hong Kong publishers and booksellers 344
activists: arrests 359; imprisonment 360; political influence 353; smear campaigns 360
Afghanistan, Soviet invasion 114
"Against liberalism" (Mao) 49
agenda-setting, as means of media control 167
agrarian policy 205–16; building a new socialist countryside 213–15; experimental implementation 213–15; Matland's policy implementation framework 206–8; rural tax-for-fee reform policy 205–16; tax reforms of 1994 and centralisation of state control 208–10; universal application of terrace fields 237
Ahl, Bjlnt 253
Air Defense Identification Zone (ADIZ) 400
air quality, PM2.5 internet campaign 354–5
All-China Democratic Women's Foundation (ACDWF), total membership 269
All-China Federation of Trade Unions (ACFTU) 85; and the 1989 student movement 223; changing role 223–4; Deng's argument 223; formation and responsibilities 223
All-China Federation of Women (ACWF) 85, 222–3, 267–8
Alptekin, Erkin 322
Alptekin, Isa Yusuf 322
Amnesty International 314
anti-bourgeois liberalization campaigns 37, 139
anti-corruption campaign, Xi's 13, 76, 87, 116, 149, 162, 173, 243, 258, 340
anti-rightist movement 36, 123, 137, 235–6, 250, 357
anti-spiritual pollution campaign 139
Arab Spring 147, 151
armed forces, control agencies 110
As Normal as Possible: Negotiating Sexuality and Gender in Mainland China and Hong Kong (2010) 279
Asia-Pacific Economic Cooperation (APEC) 3, 343, 398, 401
Asia-Pacific neighbours, Jiang's charm policy 60
Asian Infrastructure Investment Bank (AIIB) 4, 200, 397, 399–401Asian financial crisis 391
asset management companies (AMCs) 193
Autumn Harvest Uprising 220

Ba Jin 339
Bai Chong'en 200
Baidu 170
Bandurski, David 354
banking system, centralization 187
Bao Zunxin 241
Beijing massacre 277; *see also* Tiananmen Square Massacre
Beijing Olympics 171, 336, 377
Belgrade, NATO bombing of the Chinese Embassy in 116, 144–5, 321, 399
Bell, Daniel A. 7, 13, 345
Bismarck, Otto 60–1
blogging, "Year of the Blog" 376
Bo Zhiyue 129
Bo Xilai 11–12, 40–1, 54, 129, 172
bombings, attributed to Uyghur separatists 313–14, 325
Boxer Rebellion 319–20
Brezhnev, Leonid 65
building a new socialist countryside (BNSC) campaign 205–6, 208, 213–16BRICS 4, 20, 401

Bush, George W. 315

cadre, definition 216n*1*
cadre system: administrative innovations 147; appraisal criteria 158; developments under Hu Jintao's leadership 158–61; developments under Jiang Zemin's leadership 156–8; developments under Xi Jinping's leadership 161–2; institutionalization of cadre promotion 154; introduction of the civil service system 156; malpractices 156; modernisation drive 156; post Cultural Revolution developments 153–5; retirement/resignation procedures 162; rural tax reform, impact of 209–10; scale of corruption 162; selection processes 148, 159–61 (*see also* selection and appointment of cadres); and the Tiananmen Square protests of 1989 155; Xi's "five standards of good cadres" 161
cadres: "five insistences" 148; pressure to perform 145
Cai Chang 268
Cai Yingting 131
Caixin Online 358, 366
capitalism, China's application of 60
capitalism within a cage 7
categoric groups, institutional and non-institutional 126
CCP Central Committee, representational perspective 17
CCP Central Committee Departments, and the state 83–4
CCP Central Secretariat, and the state 80
CCP Secretary General, institutional responsibilities 78
CCTV, censorship 168
censorship: journalists' protest against 382; as means of media control 168; social resistance to 365
Central Commission for Disciplinary Inspection (CCDI) 79–80, 87, 97, 149, 193, 258, 340–1; responsibilities 79; Secretariat's coordination with 80
Central Document 9 *see* Document No. 9 (Briefing on the current situation in the ideological field)
Central Leading Group for Comprehensively Deepening Reforms (CLGCDR) 11, 42, 82–3, 176, 184–7, 190, 196
Central Leading Group for Finance and Economics (CLGFE) 39, 78–9, 83; chair and membership 186; functions in the policy process 186; membership 190; research apparatus 186
Central Leading Groups (CLGs): agriculture 81–2; Cybersecurity and Informatization 78, 82; Cyberspace Affairs 42, 82–3, 150, 176, 243, 358, 383; and economic policy decision-making 185; emergence 185; Financial Reform 187; Foreign Affairs 78, 81–2, 86; Hong Kong and Macau 81; maritime security 78; and Party control of the state 80–4; Party Edification and Propaganda 81; PLA leaders' representation 86; Propaganda and Ideological Work 166, 168–70; security 78; State Bank Share-Holding Reform 187; steering and coordination role 78; Taiwan Affairs 81; Xi creates additional 78
Central Military Commission (CMC) 110; establishment 112; structure and role 86; and Xi's military reform 86
Central National Security Commission (CNSC) 78, 80, 82–3, 86, 176, 399
Central Organization Department (COD) 13, 77, 132, 148, 154–60, 191, 194
Central Politics and Law Commission (CPLC) 82–3, 87, 189
Central Propaganda Department (CPD): censorship responsibilities 168; closure and re-establishment 166; Jiang grants increased powers to 169; Jiao Guobiao's diatribe against the illegitimate power of 171; publishes *A Reader of General Secretary Xi Jinping's Important Speeches* 175; rejection of "public intellectuals" 171; Xi's appointments 176
Chang, Gordan 336
Chang, Parris H. 126
Chang Ying 277
charity, social rights vs 363
Charity Law 352, 361–3, 365
Charter 08 242, 355
Chatterjee, Partha 316
Chen, Albert 253
Chen Boda 123
Chen Duanhong 257
Chen Duxiu 267
Chen Fung 221
Chen Kuiyuan 301–2, 305; Third Tibet Work Forum 302–5
Chen Muhua 268, 277–8
Chen Ping 277
Chen Qiyan 290
Chen Quanguo 307–8
Chen Weiguang 225
Chen Xilian 124
Chen Yun 124, 153–4, 187
Chen Zhu 84
Chiang Ching-kuo Foundation (CCKF) 402
Chiang Kai-shek 66
China Banking Regulatory Commission (CBRC): 190–1, 195; corruption and fraud prevention role 193; dilution of regulatory authority 193; evaluation of candidates senior banking positions 194; regulatory jurisdiction 192–3

China Insurance Regulatory Commission (CIRC) 190, 192–5, 200
China model 54–5; the basics 7; the CCP and 7–10; the claim of authoritarian efficiency 8–9; comparison with the Washington Consensus 394; the concept 392, 394–5; meritocratic personnel system 13; overview 7–9; vs the Western model 7; Xi's goal 54–6
China Model, The: Political Meritocracy and the Limits of Democracy (Bell) 7
China Securities Regulatory Commission (CSRC) 190, 192, 195, 200; and the stock market crash 194
"Chinese communism and the 70-year itch" (Diamond) 18
Chinese Communist Party (CCP): and the Beijing consensus model 147–50; change vs no change 18–19; and China's international influence 4; constitution 77; constitutional background to the leading role of 75–6; core priority 335; "core socialist values" 9; and division of labour 78; exploitation of legalism and Confucianism 47–56; factors underlying the Party's omnipotence 75–6; female membership 269; formal interface between citizens and 222; formula for political stability 146–7, 149; future of 335–49; goal 319; ideological and functional adoptions since 1976 135–51; impact of the Tiananmen Incident 141–3, 168; internet and social media impact 372–84; key ingredients for success 340; leadership and control 76–7; lifespan 336; loss of direct contact with membership 171; Marxist-Leninist ideology 220; membership 5, 76–7, 222; membership composition 222; meritocratic cadre system 153–63; mission 76–7; modernization programs of the 1990s 138–41; obsession with power and control 89; organization principles and structure 77; populist authoritarianism and the interests of the people 16–18; post-Deng challenges 143–6; pre-1978 perspective 136–8; primacy of and capability of far-reaching reform 10–12; priorities 5; propaganda system 165–78 (*see also* media control; propaganda system); rectification campaigns 122–3, 146–7, 233–5; state control at local level 86–9; state control at national level 77–80; state control mechanisms 75–89; sub-periods of rule 136; use of new media 171; utilisation of Han identity 318; "Yan'an syndrome" and "three magic weapons" 136
Chinese Dream 16, 67; as the anti-corruption dream 395–6; boosting exports 397; diplomatic support 398–9; exporting currency 397; fostering of strategic divisions 398; the model 394–5; and the Soviet Union 397–8; Xi on the importance of ideology for 243; and Xi's expectations of intellectuals 243–4; Xi's optimism 338
Chinese economy, percentage of total global growth 3
Chinese Embassy, NATO bombing 116, 144–5, 321, 399
Chinese nationalism: anti-Russian narrative 65; CCP's use and abuse of 59–71; context of the rise in 59–60; exacerbation after the 2008 financial crisis 60–1; Han nationalism vs borderland minorities 64–6; Mao's rejection of victim identity discourse 66; national heroes 66; nationalistic roots of Chinese hegemony 68–9; as pillar of regime legitimacy 61–3; and the political future 69–70; switch from Deng's nationalism to Xi's 60; transformation into chauvinistic xenophobia 66–8
Chinese People's Political Consultative Conference (CPPCC): criticisms 85; local 88–9; the Party's control over 84–5; Secretariat's role 80; structure 85
Chinese women's movement 278
Chou Wah-Shan 287
Chow Kai-Wing 319
Christianity 67, 145, 360, 365
Civil Service Law 147
civil service system, introduction of 156
civil society: changing patterns of 352–67; diversification of 353; Document No. 9's denunciation 356; during the Hu-Wen era 353–5; paradigm shift to People's society 352–6; and Protestants' rising number 365; restrictions on and the likely development of informal networks 364–5; role of the media 354; shaping People's society 356–64; "social management with Chinese characteristics" 353; under an authoritarian regime 352; under the Hu-Wen leadership 352–3; Xi administration's constriction 150; Xi's crackdown 258, 356–8; *see also* People's society
civil society advocacy, crackdowns on 258
civil–military relations (CMR) 107–9, 113, 115–16civil-society groups, Xi leadership's policy toward 17
Clarke, Donald 250, 252
climate change 3, 343
Clinton, Bill 372
collapse of the Soviet Union, Xi on the reasons for 165
collective bargaining 359–60, 364
collective leadership norms 340
collectivization 34, 36, 137, 205, 221–2, 270; demonstration of failure 275; impact on rural women 270–1; impact on urban women 272
collectivization campaign 34
"color revolutions" 147–8, 151, 361

commissions for discipline inspection (CDIs) 87, 193
communism: collapse of in Eastern Europe 227, 365; the last Muslim region under 325; and the Marshall Plan 397–8; Marxist perspective 32–3; as a phase of social development 34–5; as Western export to China 316; Xi's Communist ambitions 6
Communist Party of the Soviet Union (CPSU) 5–6, 12, 33, 40, 42, 62, 64, 108, 238; collapse 108, 336
Communist Youth League (CYL) 85, 221, 223, 268, 340
Communist Youth League Faction 14, 126, 129, 162, 172, 222–3
Confidence on Interaction and Confidence-Building Measures in Asia (CICA) 403
Confucian virtues, revival 145
Confucianism: 47; authority recognition model 53; the CCP's exploitation of legalism and 47–56; Confucianist flavor of ethical norms upheld by Hu 148; and the cultural/ideological legitimacy of the CCP 54–6; ideological analysis 47–9; Mao's changing relationship with 48–9; media promotion 50–1; referenced in Mao's works 7; revival of in post-Mao China 49–52; and rule of law with Chinese characteristics 53–4; utopian vision 52; vision and strategy 52–4; weaknesses 48; Xi's revival 49, 50, 51–2, 54; Yi Baisha's critique 48; *zhengjiao heyi* (integration of politics and religion/education) paradigm 52
Confucius, influence on Mao 48
Constitution, role of the Party 251
consultative democracy 88–9
"consultative Leninism" 340
cooperative marriages 291
core socialist values 9, 246, 392
correct guidance mandate 373–4, 377, 382
corruption: as biggest obstacle to the "Chinese dream" 396; cases involving senior bankers 193; Chinese Dream as the anti-corruption dream 395–6; drive against in the PLA 116; endemic nature of 209; party's anti-corruption watchdog 193; pervasiveness in China's financial institutions 193; prevalence among party cadres 162; rampant spread of in the 1980s 140; role of the CCDI deputy secretary 79; Suizheng Zhao's concerns 7; Xi's campaign against 13, 76, 87, 116, 149, 162, 173, 243, 258, 340; Zhou Yongkang imprisoned for 82
coup d'états and attempted coups 113–14, 233
crackdowns: on Christianity 360–1; on civil society 258, 356–8; on Falun Gong 169, 360–1; on investigative journalism 357; on labour groups 359–60; on lawyers 87, 242, 250, 256, 258, 260, 293, 352, 359–60, 376; on the media 357–8; on microblogging 358; on NGOs 359, 361–4; on People's society 359–61; on religion 169, 360–1; on social media 175, 358, 382; use of televised confessions 360
criminal law, appearance of first 138
criminal procedural law, appearance of first 138
Critique of the Gotha Program (Marx) 32
crony-capitalism 229n2
Cuba 335
Cui Jian 31
Cultural Revolution: 50th anniversary 31; Ba Jin's description 339; beginning of the process of reversal 138; Cui's observation 31; Deng's criticisms 36; and division of labour 78; impact on factional politics 128; impact on the people's support for the regime 138; impact on the PLA 113; impact on women 274–5; launch of 112, 137; literary works on 138; Nathan's analysis 128; and the persecution of professionals 154; purpose 320; as repression of intellectuals' freedom of expression 237; reversal of ethnic minority protections 317; and workers' status 221
currency devaluation 183, 185
currency export, Chinese aspirations 397
Cyberspace Administration of China (CAC) 383–4; *see also under* CLGs

Dai Huang 10
Dai Qing 241
Dalai Lama 4, 297, 298, 301, 303, 305–8, 315
Dazhai (Mao's model farm) 237
Decision on Some Major Issues Concerning Comprehensively Deepening Reforms (2013) 15, 53–4, 342
Delury, John 4
democracy and human rights, introduction of Western ideas 139
"Democracy is a good thing" (Yu) 9
democratic dictatorship 92, 111, 140, 154, 259
democratic parties 77, 84–5
Democratic People's Republic of Korea (DPRK) 335
democratic systems, assumed universality and superiority 335
Deng Fei 379–80
Deng Maosheng 13
Deng Xiaoping: 126, 128, 130, 268; attitude towards intellectuals 238–9; becomes Supreme Leader 61, 114; disagreement between Chen Yun and 153–4; dual identity as civilian and military leader 114; economic openness orientation 62; extension of the socialist enterprise 37; Four Cardinal Principles 38, 138, 140; Four Modernisations 114; impact of industrial reforms on liaison channels 222; national reconstruction policy 37;

Deng Xiaoping *continued*
on one-party rule 10; political and institutional reform 38; post-Cultural Revolution developments in the cadre system 153–5; primary state of socialism concept 7; reaction to the Tiananmen Square incident 38; redressing of Mao's mistakes 36–8; resumption of Maoist tactics 38; southern tour 39, 142, 155, 156, 240, 277, 303, 374
Deng Yingchao 268
Deng Zihui 126
Diamond, Larry 18
Dickson, Bruce 337
Ding Ling 234, 267
discipline inspection commissions (DICs) 76, 86
dissent, repression of among Tibetan and Uyghur populations 172
dissidents: imprisonment of 242; travel restrictions 241
Document No. 9 (Briefing on the current situation in the ideological field) 149, 174, 356–8; circulation of 382; contents 243; on international criticism of China's policies toward cyberspace 383; leaking of 174
Domes, Jürgen 124–6
domestic violence, China's first law on 279
Dong Bian 274
Draper, Hal 33

earthquake, in Sichuan (Wenchuan) 86, 377, 379
East China Sea 400
East Turkistan Islamic Movement (ETIM) 321, 323–5
Ebola outbreak, China's assistance 392–3
economic measures, as means of media control 167
economic policy: centralization of the banking system 187; CLGFE's role 186; composition of the monetary policy committee 190; conflicts of interests and policy failure 197; consumer institutions, emergence of 185–6; currency devaluation 183, 185; elite decision-making in the financial market 183–201; and the formation of temporary leading groups 187; local government debt audit 198–9; main consumers of financial policies 188–9; party leadership's role in policy-making 184–7; policy process 196–7; producer agencies in the financial sector 187; producers of 187–96; reformation of state-owned banks 187; regulatory agencies 190; resolving China's local debt burden 197–200
economic reform, uncertain future of 15–16
education, *Qi Yuling* decision 256
elections, management at local level 88
elite emigration 18, 41
embassy bombing, Belgrade 116, 144–5, 321, 399
employment patterns, impact of the rapid change in 171
"end of history" model, CCP's resistance to 336
energy imports, China's strategy 398
Engels, Friedrich 7, 32, 34; referenced in Mao's works 48
entrepreneurs: opening of Party membership to 340; Party recruitment 222
environment, environmental impact of industrialisation 342–3
Environmental Protection Law 363
Enze Han 316
ethnic minorities: language protections 317; marginalisation 317; Xi leadership's policy toward 17–18
executions 11, 313–14, 321; secrecy under law 249
external infrastructure schemes, state investment 401

Facebook 170, 172, 175
factional politics: associations in Xi's Politburo Standing Committee 173; and the cadre selection and appointment process 162; and the cadre selection and appointment process (*see also* selection and appointment of cadres); corporate groups vs factional groups 126; "factionalism" as an analytical tool in studies of CCP politics 124–5; "factionalism" as a political label 122–4; Lin Biao Anti-Revolutionary Faction 123; Mao's rectification campaign 122–3; methodological and practical implications of research 129–31; Nathan's 15 characteristics 127–9; in the party-state apparatus 122–32; power bases of factions 126–7; practical implications 130–1; problems with the model 129–30; Qinghua Clique and Shanghai Gang 127; structural characteristics of factions 125; theoretical debate 124–7; victims of factionalism 123; ways forward for future studies 131–2; Xi Jinping Faction 14, 122, 130, 132, 173
factionalism: first major victim 123; negative connotations of the label 124; spread of 137
Falun Gong 145, 169, 224
famine, impact on women 272–4
Fan Changlong 82, 86
farmers, state exploitation 17
farming, Party requirements 237
"Feelings Festival about the March 8 Women" (Ding) 234
Feinermann, James V. 250
feminist activists, arrested 359
Feminist Five 360
Fenby, Jonathan 19
Ferrara, Joseph A. 206
Fewsmith, Joseph 8

Field of Life and Death (Xiao) 278
financial institutions, independent boards of supervision 193
financial sector, producer agencies 187
Finer, Samuel E. 109, 112, 128
First Five Year Plan 112, 137
First World War 61
Fischer, Andrew M. 304–5
Fitzgerald, Stephen 336
Five Principles of Co-existence 392
Five-Year Plan 214
flawed and repressive policies 306
former Yugoslavia: NATO intervention 116; presidential election 144
Fortaleza Declaration 401
Four Cardinal Principles 38, 138, 140
Four Modernizations, Deng's development blueprint 114
Fourteenth Party Congress 141–3
Free Trade Zone 340
free-trade arrangements 4
freedom of expression, Xi's restriction 149
Friedman, Eli 225
Friedman, Milton 229
Friedman, Thomas 393
"friend or foe" logic, reintroduction of 358–9
Fromm, Erich 10
future scenarios for the CCP 335–49; centennial goals 338; democracy with Chinese characteristics 341–4; exceptionalist perspectives 344–5; and the global financial crisis 340; green initiatives 342–3; innovation 342; internal views 338–9; international relations 344; market reform 342; and populist authoritarianism 337; the possibilities 345–7; and public participation 340; signs of crisis 336–7; and uncertainty regarding Party relations with Chinese society 339–41; welfare and fiscal improvements 343–4; the Western paradox of China choice 347–9; Xi's optimism 338

G20 3
Gang of Four 36, 114, 124, 129, 138, 268, 275
Gao Gang 123–4, 126, 129
Gao Jianjun 175
Gao Junman 267
GDP, comparison of China and USA 391
Geertz, Clifford 100, 316
gender equality, Mao's interest 267
gender identity, meaning of an terminology 284
Georgia, rose revolution 148
Germany: portrayal on Chinese television 61; unification 398
Gladney, Dru C. 316
glasnost 239
global financial crisis 8, 60, 147; China's debt level 200; China's stimulus package 197–8; exacerbation of Chinese nationalism 60–1; rise in labour disputes following 227
Go West campaign 192
Göbel, Christian 211–14
Golden Shield Project 373
Goldman, Merle 224, 238
Gong Ting 209
Google 170, 175; censorship row 381
Gorbachev Mikhail 64, 239
"grasping with both hands" strategy: after 2008 306–8; continued relevance 308; implementation 301–5; and the internet 373; Jiang's extension 304; objectives 297
grass-roots committees, in villages 87
Great Firewall of China 170, 175, 246
Great Leap Forward 37, 41, 112, 123, 136–7, 205, 221, 236–7, 272; failure 137; and women 272–4
Great Leap Outward 4, 404
Green Gang 220
Gries, Peter 316, 320
Guan Zi 12
Guantánamo Bay, detention of Uyghurs 322
guanxi (personal networks) 140, 142
Gui Minhai, kidnapping 4
Gulf War (1991) 116
Guo Yingjie 316
Guo Boxiong 54
Gutian Conference (1929) 110

Han Fei Zi 47–9, 53
hanzu (Han identity) 316
Harbingers of History, The: The Promises Once Made by the CCP (Xiao) 10
harmonious society 50, 146–8, 160–1, 171, 403
Havel, Vaclav 240, 365
Hayek, Friedrich 241
He Xuefeng 214
He-Yin Zhen 278
Henan AIDS epidemic 376
Hirohito 62, 65, 70
"historical nihilism" 6–7, 149, 245, 357
HIV/AIDS 289, 376
Hô Chí Minh 49
Holubnychy, V. 48
homosexuality 279, 284, 287–90, 292–3; legal position in the PRC 286; medical understandings 287
homosexuals, Party restrictions on support organisations 287
Hong Kong: elite emigration to 18; LGBT activism 283
Hsing You-tien 213
Hu Angang 257, 356
Hu Feng 235–6
Hu Jintao 50, 127, 241; appointment as CCP General Secretary 170; awkward transition

Hu Jintao *continued*
between Jiang and 78; cadre system developments under 158–61; handling of the Maoist tradition 38–40; introduces moral code for CCP officials 171; loyalty based personnel movements under 14; media control under 170–2; military spending 116; power transition from Jiang to 129; reinstatement of Maoist values 39; resignation of all political roles 172
Hu Yaobang 37, 64, 114, 238, 297; marginalisation of the Central Propaganda Department 166; purge of 140; relationship with Deng 131
Hu-Wen administration: achievements 147–8; administrative innovations 147; civil society under 353–5; expansion of public participation 353; formula for political stability 146–7, 149; sensitivity to potential unrest 148
Hua Guofeng 114, 124, 126, 138
Huang Ju 170
Huang Kunming 176
Huangfu Ping 155
hukou (household registration system) 40, 222
human rights 9; constitutional amendment 252; implications of legalising same-sex marriage for 291; introduction of Western ideas of 139; treaties signed by China 252–3
human rights lawyers, detention and incarceration of 15
Hundred Flowers Campaign 137, 235–6

ideology, as main source of legitimacy for Communist Parties 232
independent trade unions 17, 142, 224
industrialization, environmental impact of 342–3
intellectual freedom, Xi's restrictions 149
intellectuals: and the aftermath of Mao's death 238–9; CCP's policy towards 232–46; and the challenge of dissidence 240–2; hundred flowers campaign and the anti-rightist movement 235–6; and the June Fourth Massacre 239–40; Mao's hatred 36; Mao's view 233; new social contract, acceptance 240; ordinary repression 236; the Party's dual approach 232; the Party's enlistment of support for legitimacy 238–40; rationale behind the "transformation" of 232–3; rectification movement 233–5; reforming the "stinking ninth" 237–8; reinstatement 240; support for Xi 243; Xi leadership's policy toward 17, 243–4
international boycott, following the Beijing massacre 277
International Covenant on Economic, Social and Cultural Rights (ICESCR) 9
international law, Beijing's violations of 4
International Monetary Fund (IMF) 63, 395, 397
international perspective, "Chinese responsibility outlook" 392–3
international perspectives 391–404; aggression at the expense of soft power 402; the China model 394–5; China's image overseas 402; Chinese Dream vs the American Dream 393–6; external infrastructure schemes 401; institutional realism 399–401; New Asian security concept as Asia's Monroe Doctrine 402–4; OBOR as the Chinese Marshall Plan 396–9
international security environment, the PLA and 113, 116
International Women's Day 359
internet 378–81; as agent of social change in China 381; CCP's embrace of as propaganda tool 168; CCP's use of as communication platform 170; Clinton's Jell-O analogy 373–4; coming-of-age 375–8; comment culture as challenge to Party control 376–7; "correct guidance of public opinion" 373–4; dissidents' use of 241–2; example of political impact of online mobilization 354–5; government white paper 381; and "grasping with both hands" strategy 373; Great Firewall of China 170, 175, 246; impact of censorship on scientific research 366; internet plus strategy 383; Jiang's suggestions 144; major stories broken on 375–7, 379–80; media development and control dynamics 374–5; new legislation 176; new media's mobilization capability 354–5; PM2.5 air quality campaign 354–5; propaganda and guidance role 377; registration requirements 381; social media reporting of rioting in Xinjiang 378; and the Sun Zhigang incident 375; technical infrastructure for censorship 373–4; Tibetan access 307, 308; tightening of control over 150; Uyghurs' cyber-separatism 323–6; *see also* microblogs/microblogging/microbloggers
Internet News Management Office 373–4
investigative journalism: commercial interest and 255; crackdown on 357; under the Hu-Wen administration 354; *see also* journalists
Iraq 392
"iron rice bowl" 221
Irvine, Roger 336
ISIS 324–5, 392
Islam, Uyghurs and the rise of jihadist Islam 315, 323, 326

Japan: China's war with 110; Deng's attitude towards 62; Mao's courting of post-war 70
Jaschok, Maria 277
Ji Dengkui 124
Jia Qinglin 50, 170
Jiang Qing 49, 124, 138, 268, 275
Jiang Shigong 257

Jiang Zemin: appointed General Secretary of the CCP 168; appointment of Zeng Qinghong 158; associates of in the propaganda system leadership 170; assumes role of PRC president 169; cadre system developments under 156–8; charm policy with Asia-Pacific neighbours 60; close associates 173; and the coexistence of reformist and conservative tendencies 144; confirmation as Party Secretary General 78; example of Chinese-style management 8; "grasping with two hands" strategy 304; handling of the Maoist tradition 38–40; installation as first civilian CMC chairman 109; loyalty based personnel movements under 14; media control policy 168–70, 373; military spending 116; and the PLA 115–16; power transition to Hu Jintao 129; reinstatement of party governance 39; resignation 171; "rule by virtue" principle 145; takes over party leadership 38; "Three Represents" theory 13, 39–40, 55, 144–5, 157, 170; on Tibetan nationalism 303; trading policies 62; trend of intellectual party support under 240; weak beginning to leadership 177
Jiang Zemin Faction 130
Jiangxi self-immolation incident 379
Jiao Guobiao 241
jihadist Islam, Uyghurs and the rise of 315, 323, 326
Jin Kai 16
Jin Xing 285
Joint Opinion on Reforming the Management System of Social Organizations 363
journalists: currently imprisoned in China 172; tightening of registration process for 174; *see also* investigative journalism
judiciary, CCP oversight 82
June Fourth Massacre: dissidents' attitudes 241; *see also* pro-democracy movement of 1989, Tiananmen Square Massacre

Kadeer, Rebiya 314–15
Kang Keqing 268
Kang Youwei 48
Kennan, George F. 18–19
Kennedy, John J. 208–9
Kim Dae-jung 10
Kim Il-sung 111
Kissinger, Henry 61
Kodak Corporation 225
Koesel, Karrie J. 365
Korea, Chinese relations with 5
Korean War 111
Kuomintang (KMT) 267; coup d'état 233; enterprise-based unions strategy 223; leader 70; and the murder of trade union organisers 220; overthrow 34–5; role of defected troops in the PLA 110
Kyrgyzstan, tulip (yellow) revolution 148

labour groups, crackdown on 359–60
labour policy 219–29; background 219–22; conflict and class 227–8; enterprise-based unions 223; formal interface between Party and citizens 222; and Mao's ambivalence towards workers 219–22; and Party concerned around strikes 227; structures of control 222–6; trade unions 224–5; vanguard status of workers 220; workers' reactions to 227; workers' rights 226
Lam, Willy Wo-Lap 129, 366
Laos 335
Lardy, Nicholas 16
law: ambiguous nature of the Party's relationship 248–50; attacks on during the Cultural Revolution 250–1; bottom-up challenges to Party rule 253–6; and civil society groups 255; "contradictions among the people" 250; Deng's reform and opening up policy 251–3; human rights perspectives 252–3, 255; and the June 4 massacre (Tiananmen Square) 253–4; Law on Legislation (2000) 252; in the Mao era 249–51; Marxist-Leninist perspective 249–50; as means of media control 168; the Party and the 248–60; Party dominance under Xi 257–9; and the pro-democracy movement 253–6; Schmitt's conception of 257; *shuanggui* (discipline and inspection) system 249, 258; the "Sun Zhigang Incident" 255; Xi's speech on rule of law with Chinese characteristics 248
lawyers, crackdown on 87, 242, 250, 256, 258, 260, 293, 352, 359–60, 376
lead poisoning 376
leading small groups (LSGs) *see* CLGs (central leading groups)
Lee Bo 344
Lee Kai-fu 382
Legalism, ethos 53
Lenin, Vladimir Ilyich 33–4, 232; *see also* Marxism-Leninism
Leung, Apo 228
Levine, Stephen 335
LGBT activism: anti-discrimination 289; main goals 286; "Rainbow Lawyers" 283; on same-sex marriage 290–2
LGBT festivals 285–6
LGBT issues 283–93; anti-discrimination and same-sex marriage 289–93; background and key terms 284–6; censorship 289; government regulations 289; and the internet 289; lack of policies/discourse in mainland China 284; law, science, society and censorship 286–9; in the media 288–9; raising awareness 289–90; raising public awareness 285; transgender people 285

LGBT people: commercial perspectives 292–3; and "cooperative marriages" 291; family pressures 288; implications of Chinese attitudes for spread of sexually transmissible infection 291; and the one-child-policy 288; treatment of in the PRC 284–5
LGBT rights: CCP's acceptance of UNHRC recommendations 283; convergence of activist, parental and commercial concerns to promote 292; legal perspectives 286–8; scientific/medical perspectives 287; social perspectives 287; state of in China 283; UK situation 286
Li Changchun 170–1
Li Cheng 129
Li, Eric X. 348
Li Keqiang 15, 42, 78, 80, 82–3, 86, 173, 176, 198–9
Li Lianjiang 210
Li, Linda Chelan 211
Li Meige 277
Li Peng 155, 303
Li Ruihuan 50, 168, 303
Li Si 49
Li Tingting 279
Li Xiaojiang 277
Li Yinhe 291–2
Li Zhanshu 6, 82, 162, 188–9
Li Zuopeng 123
Liang Shuming 214
liberalism, Mao on 49
Lin Bao 49
Lin Biao 49, 111–12, 137, 173, 268, 274; coup attempt 113; death of 123; demise of 137–8
Lin Biao Affair 129
Lin Xianzhi 291–2
Ling Jihua 20n3, 54, 131
Ling Wancheng 20n3
Liu Mingwei 225
Liu Binyan 141
Liu Bocheng 111
Liu Di 241
Liu He 83, 196
Liu Ruilong 268
Liu Shaoqi 10, 36, 123–4, 128, 131, 137, 173, 237, 249, 274; on one-party rule 10
Liu Xiaobo, prosecution 254
Liu Xiaofeng 257
Liu Yandong 130, 268
Liu Yunshan 79, 81–3, 170, 173, 175–6, 186, 188–9
living standards, proposals for improving 146
local government: four levels of 86–7; levels of 93; management of elections 88; Party control at local level 86–9; structural perspective 87
local government financing vehicles (LGFV) 197–9
Local Party congresses: functions and powers 96–7; political awkwardness and institutional embarrassment 101–3
Lu Wei 175
Lu Xun 236
Luo Gan 170
Luo Qiong 268
Luo Ruiqing 128
Luxemburg, Rosa 33

Ma Kai 196
Macau, LGBT activism 283
malnutrition 275
Mama Rainbow (2015) 290
Man on Horseback, The (Finer) 109
Mao Zedong: ambivalence towards workers 219–22; anarchist roots 219; assassination attempt 123; basic points of Mao Zedong Thought 37; Bolshevik rejection 220; chairmanship of CCP's Central Military Commission 35; China's diplomatic isolation under 339; creation of CLGs 81; criticisms of 36; cult of personality 319; the Cultural Revolution 31–2; death of 61, 66; dictatorship and the uninterrupted revolution 34–6; Hundred Flowers Campaign 137, 235–6; influence of Marx, Engels, Lenin and Stalin 32–4; launch of rectification movement 233; law in the Mao era 249–51; legacy 31–42; "On the Correct Handling of Contradictions among the People" speech 235; opinion on cities 233; rectification campaign against factionalism 122–3; references in the works of 7, 48; rejection of victim identity discourse 66; seizure of military power 110; speech on literature and art 234; support for abolition of one-party dictatorship 10; theory of perpetual revolution 35–7; vision of communism 48–9; Zhou's eulogy 220
Maritime Silk Road 396
market economy, Deng's pragmatic criteria 142
market reform 277, 342; dilemmas regarding the future of 342
marketization, CCP promotion of 158
marriage reform: CCP policies 267–9; impact on rural women 269–70
Marshall, Thomas H. 363
Marshall Plan 396–9; OBOR as the Chinese version 396–9
martial law 115, 302, 306
Marx, Karl: assertion of historical materialism 32; opinion on revolutionary dictatorship 33; referenced in Mao's works 7, 48
Marxism: influence on China's political development 10, 32–4, 37, 48, 146; intellectuals-related policy 232, 238–9; labor, rights of 219–20; legal development 250–1,

257, 259; media policy 174, 372; minorities-related policy 302, 319, 327; reassessment of 139; Sinicization of 54–6; treatment of women 277, 279
Marxism-Leninism 138–9, 142, 146, 220, 335
Matland, Richard E. 205–6, 206–8, 211–12
May, Theresa 4
May Fourth Movement 319–20; influence on women 267–8
Mearsheimer, John J. 69
media: development and control dynamics 374–5; Jiang's control policy 168–70, 373; journalists, actions against 375–6; law as means of media control 168; legal protections 255; role of in civil society under Hu-Wen leadership 354; unveiling of Xi's formal policy 382; Xi leadership's crackdown 357–8; Xi's insistence on subservience to the Party 357
media censorship, draconian measures 16–17
media control: and the Beijing Olympics 171; and the CCP's loss of direct contact with membership 171; CCP's system of 166; and the crackdown on Falun Gong 169; Great Firewall of China 170, 175, 246; harmonization under Hu Jintao 170–2; impact of Deng's economic reform speeches on Chinese media liberalisation 169; imprisonment of Chinese journalists 172; and the internet 168; introduction of "propaganda industry tax" 169; legislative mechanisms 168; methods of 167–8; pre-emptive tightening after the Jasmine Revolutions 172; "stress politics" under Jiang Zemin 168–70; tightening of registration process for Chinese journalists 174; Uyghur and Tibetan areas 172; watchdog role of traditional media 170; Xi's media management model 172–7
Medvedev, Roy 34
Mendis, Patrick 404
meritocratic cadre system 153–63; assessment criteria 13–14; *see also* cadre system
Michnik, Adam 255
microblogs/microblogging/microbloggers: crackdown on 358; deletion of accounts 382; Party "occupation" 381; success of 378–81
military: principle of party leadership over 110; Xi's reform 86; *see also* PLA
Military Administrative Commissions 111
Milosevic, Slobodan 144
Ministry of Finance (MOF): influence 191–2; investment role 191; "open front door, close the back door" approach 199; regulating and auditing role in the insurance industry 194; role in resolving China's local debt burden 198
Ministry of Human Resources and Social Security 223
Minzner, Carl 258, 340–1
mobilization, new media's capacity for 354–5
monetary policy committee, composition 190
Monroe Doctrine 403–4; New Asian Security as Asia's version 402–4
Muslims: discrimination against 312; largest group in China 312

Nanchang Uprising 110
Nathan, Andrew J. 4, 8, 12, 125, 127, 129, 254, 340
National Defense Law (1997) 86
National Development and Reform Commission (NDRC) 187–8, 190, 192, 194–6, 200
national flag, representation of social classes 221
National Party Congress: elections 97; electoral system 99–100; as highest decision-making body 94; institutional inconsistency 96; meeting duration 99; meeting frequency 95; number of delegates 99; overview *98*; political show under institutional manipulation 97–101; terms 95
National People's Congress (NPC): the delegates 84; function 93; the Party's control over 84–5; reactivation 84; role and power 94; structure 85
national security, new legislation 176
National Social Security Fund (NSSF) 192
nationalism: with Chinese characteristics 316; impact of NATO bombing of the Chinese embassy in Belgrade 144–5; as powerful trend in contemporary China 144; *see also* Chinese nationalism
Nationality Identification Project 298
NATO, bombing of the Chinese embassy in Belgrade 116, 144–5, 321, 399
Naughton, Barry 16, 37, 83
New Asian Security, as Asia's Monroe Doctrine 402–4
New Citizens' Movement 359, 360
new media, civil society role 354
New Youth magazine 48
Nomenklatura system 76–7, 88, 166–7, 172, 193
non-governmental organisations (NGOs): CCP policy towards 17, 136, 278–9; crackdowns 359, 361–4; differentiated approach of the state 353–4; expansion of citizens' participation 353; legal restrictions on 259; Overseas NGOs Management Law 289, 361–2, 365; police policies 150; registration requirements 353; scrutiny of 149
Nordlinger, Eric A. 109, 111, 113
Norway, Chinese relations with 5
Nove, Alec 33

Obama, Barack 4, 290, 315, 391
O'Brien, Kevin J. 209–10

Office for Foreign Propaganda 166, 175; *see also* State Council Information Office
Office for Spiritual Civilization 166, 176
Office for Spiritual Education 166
official discourse of the CCP, dissemination mechanisms 76
Ollman, Bertell 32
Olympic Games, Beijing 171, 336, 377
"On the Correct Handling of Contradictions among the People" (Mao) 235, 250
One Belt One Road (OBOR): aim 3; as the Chinese Marshall Plan 396–9; currency implications 397; introduction 396; NDRC's role 192; the strategy 19, 42, 396; and the "Xinjiang Problem" 325
one China policy 391
one-child policy: exceptions for ethnic minorities 317; impact on LGBT people 288; trigger for the campaign 276
Open Constitution Initiative 256, 355, 359
Opium War 63, 66
Oriental Star incident 384
Outline for a Land Law, The (1947) 268
Overseas NGOs Management Law 289, 361–2, 365
ownership reforms 157

Palmer, James 18
Pan, Philip 315
Pan Shiyi 354
Pantsov, Alexander 335
Parents and Friends of Lesbians and Gays (PFLAG) 292
Party congresses: Charter stipulations 96; difference between national and local 101–3; differences between people's congress system and 93–4; essential role of the system 104; features and roles 93; instability of congressionally-elected provincial party leaderships *102*; institutional inconsistency 92–3, 96–7; local level 93, 96, 101–3; national level 97–101; nominal authority vs political impotency 93–7; non-territorial divisions 94; role of 92–105; *see also* Local Party congresses; National Party Congress
Party Progressiveness Movement 171
Patriotic Education campaign (PEC) 305–6
patriotism, of the Chinese people 8; *see also* nationalism
Peaceful War (Mendis) 404
peacekeeping missions, PRC's contribution 3
Pei Minxin 12–13, 337
Peng Chong 126
Peng Dehuai 111, 123
Peng Zhen 128
pension scheme, for rural residents 146
People's Armed Police (PAP) 17, 86, 115
People's Bank of China (PBOC) 185, 342; appointment authority 191, 194; bank recapitalization proposal 196; economic policy role 190–1; injection of funds into state banks 191; and the stock market crash 194
People's Daily: censorship 168; reassessment of Marxism 139
People's Liberation Army (PLA): beginnings 110; commander-in-chief 86; delegation to the National People's Congress 94; and the democracy movement of 1989 115; Deng's modernisation and restructuring plans 114–15; impact of the Cultural Revolution 113; impact of perpetual involvement in Tibet 301; infrastructure construction role 111–12; and the international security environment 113, 116; Jiang-Hu era 115–16; as the lifeline of the Party 108–18; major departments 86; modernization plan 112–14; Party committees 77; political and economic influence 111–12; and the principles of a political army 111; professionalization 112, 114–15; relationship with the Party and the state 86; role in establishing the People's Republic 109–10; Xi Jinping's reforms 116–17; Xi's anti-corruption drive 116
People's Republic of China (PRC): administrative regions 111; budget for maintaining social stability 8; distribution of wealth 12, 146; establishment 110, 136; founding 147; global influence 3–5; PLA's role in establishing 109–10; political model, relative uniqueness of 335; trading relationships 339; Western economists' estimation of social debt 15
People's society: crackdown efforts 359–61; guiding principles 357–8; Hu Angang's conception of 356; NGO constraints 361–4; paradigms shift from civil society to 352–6; shaping 356–64; sustainability of the model 364–7
Perfect Dictatorship, The (Ringen) 7
perpetual revolution, Mao's theory 35–7
Perry, Elizabeth J. 214, 370
phantom democracy 344–5
Phunwang (Phuntsok Wangyal Goranangpa) 300
planned commodity economy, depiction of 143
PM2.5 air quality campaign 354–5
Poland: Gdansk strike 227; role of civil society 255
Politburo: and the state 80; *see also* PBSC
Politburo Standing Committee (PBSC): economic policy-making role 185; factional perspective 173; and the state 78–9; structure 78; as ultimate consumer of policies 185; working body 80
political reform, efforts towards 140
Politicians and Artists (Wang) 234

pollution, internet campaign 354
Populist Authoritarianism (Tang) 16
Power of the Powerless, The (Havel) 365
praetorianism 109
Pratap, Surendra 228
preemption doctrine, China's adoption 401
Premier of the State Council 78–9
primary state of socialism, Deng's concept 7
princelings of the CCP 11–12, 126–7, 130, 155, 172–3
private sector, impact of the emergence 76
pro-democracy movement of 1989: and the ACFTU 223–4; bottom-up challenges to Party rule in the name of the law 253–6; estimated reasons for failure 240; impact of repression on intellectuals 239–40; and the PLA 115; student protests as precursor of 38
Project Hope charity 374
propaganda, role of the internet 377
propaganda system: application of market economics to 169; formal incorporation of texting 170; strong presence of Jiang associates 173; Xi's appointments 176; *see also* Central Propaganda Department; media control
Pu Zhiqiang 359
public intellectual, rejection of the role 171
public opinion 8, 11, 145, 167, 176–8, 255, 307, 324, 337, 372–7, 380–1, 383, 396
public participation: expansion under the Hu-Wen leadership 353; new media's mobilisation capability 354–5
punishment, as primary focus of Mao-era law 250
purges 250
pushijiazhi (universal values) 9
Putin, Vladimir 8, 148
Pye, Lucian W. 130

Qi Biao 40
Qin Benli 239
Qin Ping 209
Qinghai–Tibet railway 303, 304
Qinghua Clique 127, 130
Qiu Huizuo 123
QQ 170

radical Islam 312, 323–4
Rao Shushi 126
Rawls, John 257
rebalancing strategy, Obama administration's 391, 398
rectification campaigns 122–3, 146–7, 233–5
red aristocracy 11–12, 19, 279
Red Army, historical perspective 110
Red Guard, formation 237, 320
reform: capability of CCP for 3–19; CCP retrogression on 12–15; economic and social reforms 340; Reform and Opening Up policy 38, 174, 251, 255, 335, 356; relationship between national strength and 12; and stagnation in political liberalization 12–15; Xi's characterization 15
Regional Comprehensive Economic Partnership (RCEP) 4, 20, 401
regional ethnic autonomy 298–9, 304, 317
relative capability, comparison of China and US in terms of GDP 391
religion: affiliation requirements 352; centrality to Tibetan national identity 305; and civil society networks in China 365; crackdown on 360–1; restrictions on religious practice 314; state tolerance under Hu-Wen leadership 354
Ren Zhiqiang 366, 382
renminbi, inclusion in Special Drawing Rights 397
Republic of China (ROC) 35, 66, 146, 173; ruling regime 34–5
residential patterns, impact of the rapid change in 171
Resolution on certain questions in the history of our party since the founding of the People's Republic of China (Deng) 36–7
resources exploitation, criticisms of China's 393
responsibility outlook, Chinese establishment 392–3
rights, systematic deprivation of 360
rights defence lawyers, crackdown on 359
Rights Defence Movement 241–2, 355, 358–9
Ringen, Stein 7–8, 337
"Rise of Great Powers, The" (TV series) 61
Roosevelt, Franklin 220
Rouzi, Sidiq 314
rule by virtue 47, 52, 54, 145
rule of law: announcement of implementation 241; CCP version 14–15; Chinese conception 143; and the expansion of public participation 353; Xi administration's problematic attitudes to 15
rural migrants, return of and the development of the working-class 227–8
rural tax-for-fee reform (RTFR) policy 206–16 passim
Russian Revolution 232

Śākyamuni 48
same-sex eroticism, China's traditional cultural acceptance 291
same-sex marriage: implications of legalising for human rights 291; legal perspective 284; and the potential to alter regulations in China 291; USA position 290
same-sex partnerships, legal perspective 284
Sapio, Flora 250
Schell, Orville 4
Schmitt, Carl 257

Schurmann, Franz 94
scientific research, impact of internet censorship on 366
Secretary General, strengthened role 79
Selden, Mark 36
selection and appointment of cadres: and factional politics 162; major factors in post-Cultural Revolution development 162–3; principles 158–9; reform of the system 158–9; standards 153–7; Xi's policies 162
self-immolations, of Tibetan dissidents 17, 172, 301, 306–7
separation of Party and government 11, 38, 42, 143, 251; Deng's experiment 38; Deng's introduction 143; reversal of the trend 11, 341; Zhao Ziyang's proposals 140
September 11 attacks 322
"Seven Differences between the 'Chinese Dream' and the 'American Dream'" (Shi) 393–4
"Seven Don't Speak" 357
Severe Acute Respiratory Syndrome (SARS) 375
sexual activity, age of consent 286
sexual harassment: activism against 279; peaceful demonstrations against 359
sexual orientation, meaning of 284
Shambaugh, David 19, 148, 337
Shanghai Baby (Wen) 279
Shanghai Gang 14, 38–9, 127, 130, 132, 162, 172
Shanghai Stock Exchange 342
Shanghai Pride 286
Shi Yuzhi 393–4
Shi Tao 241
Shirk, Susan L. 126
Sichuan earthquake (Wenchuan) 86, 377, 379
Silent Contest (documentary) 175
Silk Road Economic Belt 42, 396
Silk Road Fund 20, 401
Sina Weibo 170; *see also* Weibo
Singapore: development model 345; elite emigration to 18
So You Think You Can Dance 285
social change, the internet as agent of social change in China 381
Social Credit Governance 258–9
social debt: estimations of China's 15; percentage of GDP 149
social enterprises 364
social media: blockage of access to 172; CCP control 170; and reporting on the Sichuan earthquake 379; and reporting on Wenzhou train collision 379–80; as source of public information 168; and the *Southern Weekly* incident 382; tightening of control over 150, 175
social organizations, official statistics 367n*2*
social stability, China's budget for maintaining 8
social welfare, improvements in 226
socialism, reasons for the emergence of 32
Socialism: Utopian and Scientific (Engels) 32
socialist market economy, official recognition of the concept 143
Society of the Righteous and Harmonious Fists 319
Soldiers in Politics: Military Coups and Governments (Nordlinger) 109
South China Sea 4, 68, 116, 344, 393, 400, 403
South China Sea dispute 4; Hague ruling 4
Southern Weekly incident 357, 366, 382
sovereignty disputes 400
Soviet Union, collapse 68, 151, 165, 340
Special Drawing Rights (SDR), inclusion of the renminbi 397
Spires, Anthony 256
spiritual pollution, campaigns against 357
spy plane incident 320
Stalin, Joseph 7, 32, 34–5, 40, 220, 232, 238; referenced in Mao's works 48
State Administration of Press, Publication, Radio, Film, and Television (SAPPRFT) 166, 290
State Council (SC) 11, 39, 78–85, 139, 141, 155, 187
State Council Information Office 81, 166, 174–5, 373
State Council Internet Information Office 174
State Internet Information Office 380–2
State-Owned Assets Supervision and Administration Commission (SASAC) 83, 188
state-owned banks, reformation of 187
state-owned enterprises (SOEs): bureaucracy in charge of 83; communication channels 222; criticisms of 393; increase in management autonomy 222–3; necessity for reform 342; percentage of Chinese industry 16
"stinking ninth", reforming the 237–8
stock market crashes in 2015–2016 16, 176, 194
Strike Hard Campaigns 305–6, 314, 321
strikes, Party concerns 227
student protests: December 1986 38; *see also* pro-democracy movement of 1989; Tiananmen Square Massacre
Sun Chunlan 268
Sun Wenlin 290
Sun Yat-sen 48, 66–7, 70
Sun Zhigang incident 255–6, 375
Sylvester, Richard K. 206

Taiwan: Bureau in charge of 81; model of transition 347
Taiwan Strait Crisis 116
talent, primacy of 154
Talk on Art and Literature in Yan'an (Mao) 36, 235
Tan Shen 277
Tang, Wenfang 16, 337

Tang Jinglin 359
Tao Ran 209
Tao Zhu 128
Taobao: rainbow flag display 291; Valentine's Day "Rainbow Love" contest 292
Teiwes, Frederick C. 136
Ten Years of Chaos 35
Teng, Biao 255–6
terrace fields, universal application of 237
terrorism 176, 313–15, 321–6, 403
texting, formal incorporation into the propaganda system 170
third sector, Party control 361
Third World, China's demonstration of responsible stakeholdership 392
Thøgersen, Stig 214–15
"Thoughts on March Eighth" (Ding) 267
Three Evils, Chinese definition 403
"Three Represents" theory 13, 39–40, 55, 144–5, 157, 170
Tiananmen Square Massacre: and the cadre system 155; and the development of capitalism 222; dissidents' attitudes 241; impact on collaboration between students and intellectuals 239; impact on political reform measures 141–2; international boycott following 277; and internet policy 373; Mao's influence 38; new policies brought about by 155; and the patriotic education campaign 305; policy impact 155; political aftermath 38, 141–3, 168, 335; presentation of by the Party-State 254
Tibet: freedom ranking 308; Russian policy 65; self-immolation incident 379; violent ethnic clashes 377; Xi leadership's policy toward 17
Tibet Autonomous Region (TAR): ethnicity of Party Secretaries 300; formal establishment 299; GDP 304; government spending 304–5; Hu takes over as Party Secretary 297; infrastructure building, percentage of government expenditure 304; local laws and regulations allegedly enacted by 300; Tibetan cadres in 299
Tibet policy: 297–309; administrative autonomy 299–301; and attitudes towards Tibetan culture 301; coercive steps 302; and the Dalai Lama 4, 297, 298, 301, 303, 305–8, 315; economic development 302–5; "four stabilities" 307; fundamental driver 297; "grasping with both hands" strategy 297, 301–5, 306–8 (*see also* "grasping with both hands" strategy); immigration into Tibet 303; incentives for inter-ethnic marriages 308; introduction of identity card system 302; media censorship 306; Nationality Identification Project 298; Patriotic Education campaign 305–6; PLA, perpetual involvement of and its impact 301; policy instruments deployed 297–8; political campaigns 305–6; political representation 299–301; primary goal 297–8; "Red Armband Patrols" 308; regional autonomy system 298–301; security as key driver 300, 304; "Stability Maintenance" program 308; and the Tibetan uprising 306–8; United Front strategy 298
Tibetan Buddhism: Chen Quanguo's directives 308; Chinese attitude towards 301; as security threat 305
Tiffert, Glenn 250
Tohti, Ilham 314, 358
"tongue war", Maoist tactic 173
torture, *shuanggui* system 249, 258
Toward an Age of Rights (Xia) 254
trade unions, importance for social stability 224–5
trading relationships, PRC's development 339
train collision, Wenzhou 379–80
trans-Eurasian railway 322
transgender job discrimination, China's first case 290
Transpacific Pact (TPP) 4, 20, 401
Trump, Donald J. 3–4, 20, 71, 315, 391, 398, 400–1
Tsai Ing-wen 173
Tsou Tang 128
Tucker, Robert C. 33–4
Twitter 170, 172, 175, 378; Chinese equivalent 171

Ukraine, orange revolution 148
UN Convention on Civil and Political Rights, signing of by the PRC 355
UN Security Council, China's membership 65
Under the Dome (2015) 177
universal values, compatibility with Chinese modernisation 9–10
university entrance examinations, reinstatement 239
Ürümqi riots 378
USA, pro-China policies 65
USSR, collapse 68, 151, 165, 340
Uyghurs: arrests 314; Chinese nationalist perspective 315–16; communication restrictions 172; control strategy of the Party-State 312–28; cyber-separatism 323–6; detention in Guantánamo Bay 322; dissent, growth in from the late 1980s and mid-1990s 313–15; executions 321; and Han nationalism 318–19; international support 322–3; marginalization of 65; and popular nationalism 319–20; religious perspective 326; repatriation 322; resistance to Chinese rule 321–3; and the rise of jihadist Islam 315, 323, 326; separatist movement 312; and state nationalism 316–17; US support 315; and utilitarian nationalism 320–1; Xi leadership's policy toward 17

Vakhidi, Ashir 324
Vala, Carsten T. 354, 365
Vietnam 69, 113–14, 335, 344, 400
village elections 340, 345
virtue: as cadre selection criteria 154–5; Chen Yun's argument 154; Deng's understanding 154; vs talent 155, 157

Wal-Mart 225
Wan Li 126
Wan Yanhai 287
Wang, Shiwei 234
Wang Dongxing 124
Wang Gang 84
Wang Guoqing 366
Wang Hongwen 124
Wang Huiwu 267
Wang Huning 188–9
Wang Man 279
Wang Ming 122
Wang Qishan 13, 79–80, 149, 162, 173, 188
Wang Shaoguang 257
Wang Xuebing 193
Wang Yang 81
Wang Yu 359
wealth distribution in the PRC 12, 146
Wechat 170; and the *Southern Weekly* incident 382; and state surveillance 175
Wei Jianxing 224
Wei Tingting 279
Weibo: arrests of users 358; censorship 379; crackdown 175, 358; and the Jiangxi self-immolation incident 379; launch 378; mobilisation role 354; *Red Flag* article 380; and the *Southern Weekly* incident 382; and the spread of Wenzhou train collision story 380
Wen Hui 279
Wen Jiabao 8–9, 129, 170, 187, 190
Wen Tiejun 214
Wenchuan earthquake (Sichuan) 86, 377, 379
Wenzhou train collision 379–80
Western ideas, locutions denounced as 357
Western influences, concerns about 144
Whampao Military Academy 110
"Why People's society is superior to civil society" (Hu) 356
Wikipedia 170
Wild Lilies (Wang) 234
Wolves of Lop Nor 324
women: Chinese women's movement 278; kidnapping and trafficking of 276
women, CCP policies 266–80; in the twenty-first century 279–80; and the ACWF 267–8; and the Cultural Revolution 274–5; and Deng era reform 275, 279; Ding Ling's criticism 267; during rehabilitation period 268–9; early Party policy 267; female Politburo members 268; "Five Good Campaign" 272; and the Great Leap Forward 272–4; Jiang Qing's criticisms 275; land reform 268–9; levels of emancipation 266; marriage reform 267–9; and the May Fourth Movement 267–8; Party definitions of women's interests 266; post-1949 political status 267–8; in rural areas during first five-year plan 269–71; in urban areas during first five-year plan 271–2
Women of China (magazine) 274, 276
Women's World Alliance 267
Woo Jongseok 108
World Trade Organisation (WTO): China's entry 8, 335–6, 372, 374; entry to as symbol of qualitative change 145; foundation of China's application 39; impact of China's entrance 60, 144
workers: failures of workers' movements/uprisings 220, 233; improvements in social welfare 226; substantive and procedural rights of 226; vanguard status of 220
working class: changing composition and outlook 227; loss of constitutional securities 221; marginalization of workers 220–1; the Party's relationship with 219; return of rural migrants and the development of 227–8; rights granted to 220
Wu Bangguo 170
Wu De 124
Wu Faxian 123
Wu Guanzheng 170
Wu Guoguang 402
Wu Guxian 268
Wu Jinghua 297, 300
Wu Rongrong 279
Wu Yi 268
Wu Yingjie 297

Xi Jinping: agenda of 3, 19; anti-corruption campaign 13, 41, 76, 87, 116, 149, 162, 173, 243, 258, 340; assumption of CMC chairmanship 117; becomes leader of the CCP 3; cadre system developments under 161–2; calls for resignation of 341, 366; characterisation of reform 15; Chinese Dream mantra 8, 16, 42; Communist ambitions 6–7; "core leadership" 79, 340, 367; economic power and control 83; efforts against "factionalism" 122; and the emergence of the CLGs 185–6; extent of power 176; father 40; first-hand experience of the US 393; foremost task 5; governing strategy 53–4; guiding principles characterizing the era 357; on the importance of ideology as a tool of political control 165; influence of Maoism on the tenure of 10–11, 40–2; institutional responsibilities 78; internal and external challenges for 176; level of control exercised

by the regime of 149; on literature and art 234, 243–4; local debt audit 198; military reform 86; "mixing in sand" tactic 173; the Party and the Beijing consensus model 147–50; Party dominance of the law under 257–9; policy towards intellectuals 17, 243–4; and the Princelings Faction 130; publication of Speeches 175; retrogressive philosophy 5–6; revision of separation of Party and government 11, 42; revival of Confucianism 49, 50, 51–2, 54; structures created by 82; "throwing stones" tactic 173; use of Maoist authority-strengthening tactics 173; WEF speech 3; Xi Jinping Faction 14, 122, 130, 132, 173
Xi Jinping the Governance of China 175
Xi Zhongxun 243
Xia Yong 254
Xiao Hong 278
Xiao Li 277
Xiao Meili 279
Xiao Shu 10
Xing Beinan 49
Xinjiang: replication of Tibet policies in 308; *see also* XUAR
Xinjiang Uyghur Autonomous Region (XUAR): communication restrictions 172; Deng's reforms 312–13; detailing of terrorist activities 321; establishment 313; ethnic and civil unrest 313–15; impact of September 11th attacks 322; increase of Uyghur violence 323; incursions of Taliban fighters 322; overland gateways to 322; treatment of minorities and religious practitioners during the Cultural Revolution 17, 312; violent riots 378
xitong, definition and examples 78
Xu Caihou 54
Xu Lin 82, 402
Xu Qiliang 83, 86
Xu Zhiyong, imprisonment 359
Xun Zi 49

Yan Xuetong 12, 344
Yan Yangchu 214
Yang Baibing 115, 130, 141
Yang Guangbin 18–19
Yang Lijun 14
Yang Shangkun 114–15, 130, 141
Yang Yang 52
Yang Zhiming 227
Yao Wenyuan 124
Yao Yilin 187
Ye Qun 123, 268
Yeh, Emily 305
Yep, Ray 209, 213
Yi Baisha 48
yifa zhiguo (rule by law with Chinese characteristics) 14, 53
Yihuang self-immolation incident 379
Yirenping 359–60
Youku 170
Youth League Group 130
YouTube 170, 172, 377–8
Yu Keping 9, 150, 214, 344
Yu Jianrong 9, 380
Yu Zhengsheng 173, 186
Yuan Shikai 48, 341

Zeng Qinghong 84, 158
Zhang Chunqiao 124
Zhang Dejiang 79, 81–2, 173, 186
Zhang Enzhao 193
Zhang Gaoli 173
Zhang Guotao 110
Zhang Weiwei 254
Zhang Weiying 19
Zhang Xundong 257
Zhao Jing 376
Zhao Suizheng 7, 298, 320
Zhao Ziyang: belief in neo-authoritarianism 8; civil service proposals 140–1, 156; CLGFE control 187; house arrest 168; imprisonment 38; marginalization of the Central Propaganda Department 166; political reforms 140; relationship with Deng 131; relaxed approach to the media 373; selected as Party General Secretary 114; separation of Party and government 11, 38, 341
Zheng Churan 279
Zheng Yongnian 14
Zheng Yuanjie 354
Zhongnanhai 129, 131, 169, 308
Zhou Enlai 123–4, 137, 268
Zhou Yongkang 54; factions related to 130; imprisonment 82, 337
Zhu Rongji 8, 39, 185, 190–1, 211
Zhu Xiaoming 298
Zunyi Conference (1935) 110

For Product Safety Concerns and Information please contact our EU
representative GPSR@taylorandfrancis.com
Taylor & Francis Verlag GmbH, Kaufingerstraße 24, 80331 München, Germany

www.ingramcontent.com/pod-product-compliance
Ingram Content Group UK Ltd.
Pitfield, Milton Keynes, MK11 3LW, UK
UKHW050053200926
475702UK00019B/2813

* 9 7 8 0 3 6 7 5 8 1 1 6 9 *